The Neolithic Cemetery at Tell el-Kerkh

AL-SHARK 5
University of Tsukuba: Studies for West Asian Archaeology

Excavation Reports of Tell el-Kerkh, Northwestern Syria, vol. 2

Series Editors: Akira Tsuneki and Jamal Hydar

The Neolithic Cemetery at Tell el-Kerkh

edited by

Akira Tsuneki, Naoko Hironaga and Sari Jammo

with contributions by

Sean P. Dougherty, Ken-ichiro Hisada, Yuko Miyauchi, Yuki Tatsumi, Minoru Yoneda and Yu Itahashi

ARCHAEOPRESS ARCHAEOLOGY

ARCHAEOPRESS PUBLISHING LTD
Summertown Pavilion
18-24 Middle Way
Summertown
Oxford OX2 7LG

www.archaeopress.com

ISBN 978-1-80327-026-5
ISBN 978-1-80327-027-2 (e-Pdf)

Front and back cover images: Excavation scenery at Kerkh Neolithic Cemetery

This book is available direct from Archaeopress or from our website www.archaeopress.com

Contents

Chapter 1
Introduction
Akira Tsuneki

Chapter 2
Geological Conditions of Tell el-Kerkh
Ken-ichiro Hisada

Chapter 3
The Tell el-Kerkh Site and Stratigraphy
Akira Tsuneki

Chapter 4
Burial Types and the Transition of Kerkh Cemetery
Sari Jammo

Chapter 5
Burial Catalogue of Kerkh Cemetery
Akira Tsuneki, Naoko Hironaga, Sari Jammo, Yuko Miyauchi and Yuki Tatsumi

Chapter 6
The Human Remains of Tell el-Kerkh
Sean P. Dougherty

Chapter 7
Radiocarbon Dating at Tell el-Kerkh
Yu Itahashi and Minoru Yoneda

Chapter 8 (Discussion 1)
Body Transformation: Skull Retrieval, Manipulation and Circulation of Human Remains at Kerkh Cemetery
Sari Jammo

Chapter 9 (Discussion 2)
The Meaning of Cremation
Naoko Hironaga

Chapter 10 (Discussion 3)
Stable Isotope Analyses of Human and Animal Bones at Tell el-Kerkh
Yu Itahashi and Minoru Yoneda

Chapter 11
Conclusion
Akira Tsuneki

Appendix
Neolithic Burials Outside of the Cemetery
Naoko Hironaga

List of Figures and Tables

Chapter 4

Chapter 5

Chapter 6

Chapter 7

Chapter 8 (Discussion 1)

Chapter 9 (Discussion 2)

Chapter 10 (Discussion 3)

Appendix

Acknowledgements

This book is the second volume of the final excavation reports at Tell el-Kerkh, northwest Syria. Excavations at Tell el-Kerkh began in 1997 and continued until 2010, the year before the outbreak of the conflict in Syria. For the execution of archaeological research at Tell el-Kerkh, we are deeply grateful to the government of the Syrian Arab Republic, especially the Ministry of Culture, and the Directorate General of Antiquities and Museums (DGAM). Dr. Sultan Muhesen, then director of the DGAM, allowed a joint archaeological excavation with the University of Tsukuba to commence work in 1997 at Tell el-Kerkh in the Rouj Basin, Idlib Governorate. For the excavation permit, Dr. Adnan Bounni, then Director of Archaeological Excavations and Studies of DGAM, also provided valuable advice. Subsequently, many staff members of DGAM in Damascus extended the greatest consideration and permissions to enable our work. We cannot mention the names of all the DGAM staff members who took care of us in this regard, but we would like to express our deepest gratitude to the following colleagues in particular: Mr. Mohammad Qador; Mr. Nassib Salibi; Dr. Bassam Jammous; Dr. Michel al-Maqdissi; Dr. Ammar Abdulrahman; Dr. Ali al-Kayem; Dr. Abd al-Razzaq Moaz; Dr. Ahmad Serrieh; Dr. Maamoun Abdulkarim; Mr. Ahmad Taraqji; Dr. Haitham Hassan; Dr. Mahmoud Hamud; Dr. Ahmad Deeb; Dr. Samer Abdel Ghafour; and Mr. Tony Gerroug. We also thank Dr. Antoine Suleyman, Mr. Hamido Hammade, and Dr. Youssef Kanjou of the Aleppo National Museum for their unwavering cooperation with our studies.

We deeply appreciate the enormous help given by the staff at the Department of Antiquities of Idlib, in particular, Mr. Abdo Asfari, Mr. Nicola Kabbad, and Mr. Fajer Haji Mohamad, all of whom supplied the conveniences and bridges necessary for our investigation in the field. In the excavations at Tell el-Kerkh, many people from the Ainata village, where our base camp was situated, as well as neighboring villagers worked for us as excavation workers. It is thanks to them that our investigation went very well. Their consistent hospitality was very encouraging for us. In particular, there are no words of gratitude that will suffice for the work of Mr. Mohammad Subhi Khalifa, who lives in the village of Ainata and serves as a guardian for the site of Tell el-Kerkh.

Last but not least, we express special thanks to Dr. Giro Orita, advisor of ICARDA for his inestimable support to our mission and Ms. Yayoi Yamazaki, an archaeologist who lived in Aleppo for her constant warm support.

Sadly, many of those mentioned above have already passed away. They are Dr. Bounni, Mr. Qador, Mr. Salibi, Dr. Suleyman, Mr. Hammade, and Dr. Orita. One of our important excavation members from the University of Tsukuba, Prof. Takuya Iwasaki, has also passed away. We pray for the souls of those who have passed and apologize for the time it took to complete the excavation reports.

The financial support for Tell el-Kerkh excavations came from grants for excavations provided by DGAM, grants under the Scientific Studies of Japanese Ministry of Education and Science, and grants-in-aid for Scientific Research of the Japan Society for the Promotion of Science. The grants are titled: 'A Study of the Settlement Organization in Neolithic Syria' (08041004), 1996–1998; 'A Study of the Prehistoric Urbanization in the Northern Levant' (13571034), 2001–2003; 'An Archaeological Studies on the Urbanization: Based on the Excavations at Tell el-Kerkh, Northwest Syria (17401025) 2005–2008; 'The Emergence of Cemetery in West Asia: Based on the Results of Archaeology and Natural Sciences' (21320145) 2009–2011, 'Social Complexity and Urbanization in Prehistoric West Asia' (22251009) 2010.

In addition to the above research grants from the Syrian and Japanese governments, we also received scientific research grants from the Suntory, Takanashi, and Mitsubishi Foundations. We are deeply grateful for the many grants from these institutions for the excavation and research at Tell el-Kerkh.

Akira Tsuneki and Jamal Hydar
Co-directors for the Investigations
at Tell el-Kerkh

Contributors

Dougherty, Sean P.
Instructor, Department of Biological Sciences,
Milwaukee Area Technical College, USA

Hironaga, Naoko
Assistant Researcher, Research Center for West Asian
Civilization, University of Tsukuba, Japan

Hisada, Ken-ichiro
Former Professor, Faculty of Life and Environmental
Sciences, University of Tsukuba, Japan

Itahashi, Yu
Assistant Professor, Faculty of Humanities and Social
Sciences, University of Tsukuba, Japan

Jammo, Sari
Researcher, Research Center for West Asian
Civilization, University of Tsukuba, Japan

Miyauchi, Yuko
PhD Candidate, Science and Technology in Cultural
Heritage, The Cyprus Institute, Cyprus

Tatsumi, Yuki
Engineer, Research Department, Archaeological
Institute of Kashihara, Nara Prefecture, Japan

Tsuneki, Akira
Professor Emeritus, Faculty of Humanities and Social
Sciences, University of Tsukuba, Japan

Yoneda, Minoru
Professor, The University Museum, The University of
Tokyo, Japan

Chapter 1

Introduction

Akira Tsuneki

1. Process Leading to the Investigations

Questions such as where did human beings change their way of life from hunter-gathers to farmer-herders and why did human societies become more complex are timeless. As are those considering how and why human beings began to form large settlements and why did they begin to construct large cities. These questions seem to be some of the most challenging and exciting ones in the study of human history. All of these great transitions appeared in West Asia earlier than any other region in the world. Therefore, West Asian archaeology entices and attracts our attention. As such, archaeological investigations in West Asia will provide the basis for answering some of these questions.

The University of Tsukuba executed the first archaeological investigation in the Rouj Basin, Idlib province, northwest Syria, from 1990 to 1992 (Figures 1-1, 1-2). The purpose of these investigations was to pursue the above-mentioned questions, especially the formation of early farming societies and the development of complex societies based on archaeological data retrieved from the field. The Rouj Basin was chosen for exploration, because this small

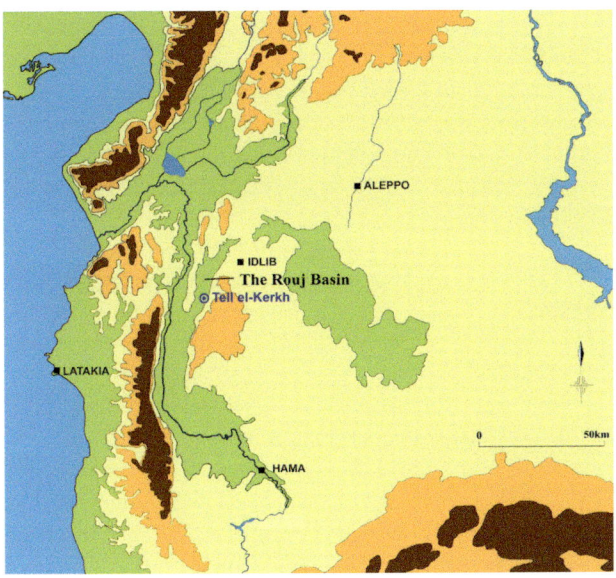

Figure 1-1. Location of the Rouj Basin, northwest Syria.

basin, measuring 37km from north to south and 2-7km from east to west, has extremely rich soil and water for farming fields, and the basin is full of artificial tells. The Rouj Basin was first surveyed archaeologically by a French mission (Courtois 1973) which was mainly concerned with Bronze Age tells. The University of Tsukuba team focused on a more holistic approach, with special emphasis on tracing the transition of settlement patterns. The director of the mission, the Late Professor Takuya Iwasaki, and the current field director, Akira Tsuneki, took part in the excavations as members of the Tell Mastuma (5km south of Idlib city) team led by the Ancient Orient Museum of Tokyo since 1980. Besides the excavations at Tell Mastuma, both of them repeated general survey around Tell Mastuma (Tsuneki 2009). This work revealed that the Rouj Basin was one of the richest areas for studying neolithization and urbanization in northwest Syria. A request was made to the Syrian Directorate General of Antiquities and Museums for approval to undertake investigations in the Rouj Basin. Fortunately, permission was granted to conduct an archaeological investigation for three years from 1990.

Three seasons' investigations in the Rouj Basin reconfirmed how this basin was rich in both prehistoric and historic period remains (Iwasaki, Nishino and Tsuneki 1995; Iwasaki and Tsuneki 2003). We discovered thirty-eight tell-type settlements within the relatively small basin (Figures 1-3, 1-4). In pursuit of our research aim, i.e., the formation and development of farming societies, twenty-two of thirty-eight tell-type settlements produced materials from Neolithic periods (Tsuneki 2012, Tsuneki n.d.). Therefore, there was no doubt that this basin was very prolific area for our study focus. Furthermore, a very large Neolithic tell complex, Tell el-Kerkh, is located in the south of the basin. The size of this tell complex, as a Neolithic settlement, was beyond our imagination, and it was believed that further investigation of Tell el-Kerkh would reveal how ancient people began to form large settlements based on the new farming way of life. It also seemed that the site would provide a hint to understand the background for the formation of complex societies and in turn the emergence of urbanism.

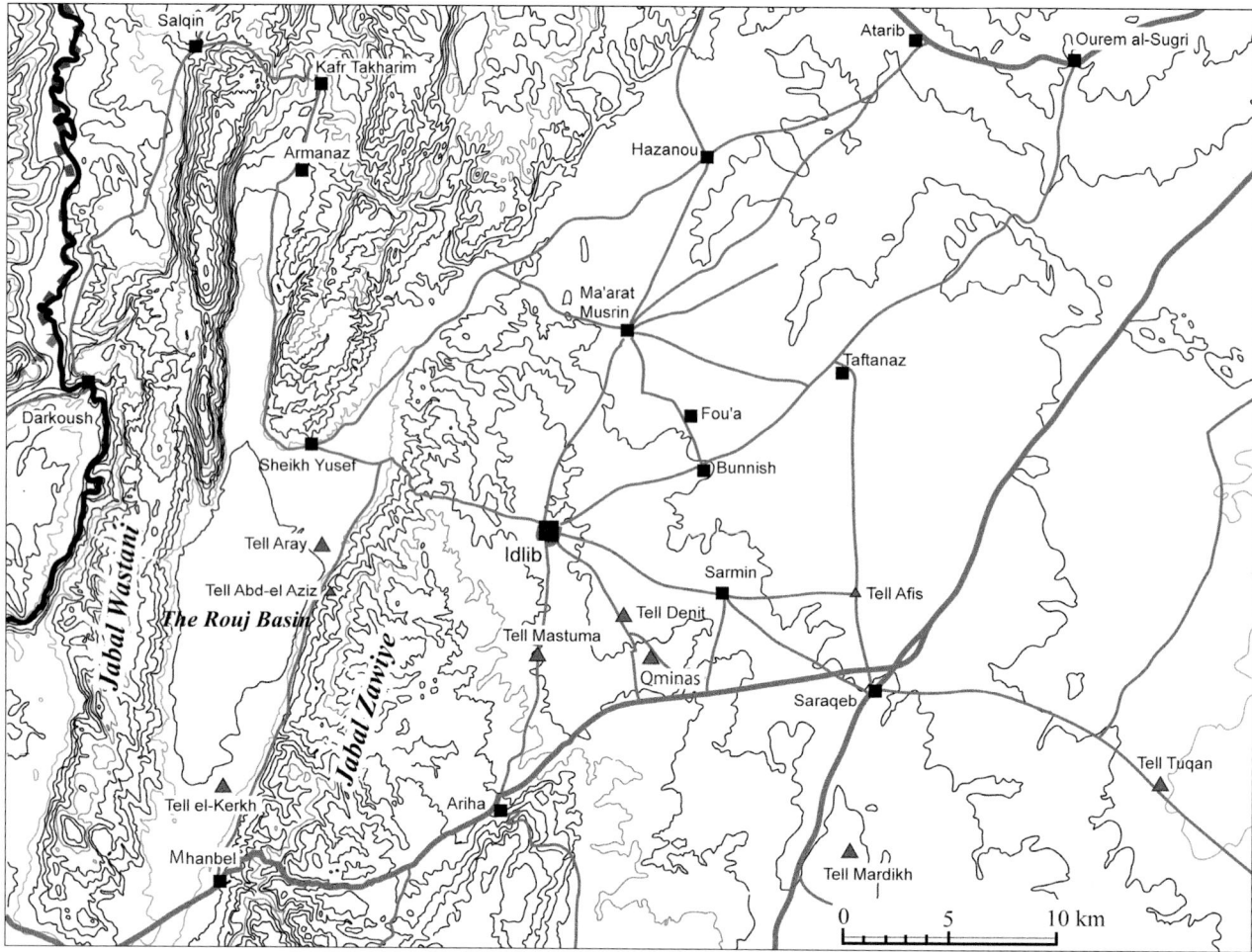

Figure 1-2. The Rouj Basin and its surroundings (revised drawing of Nishiyama).

Therefore, permission was sought from the DGAM to begin excavations at Tell el-Kerkh. After much negotiation, DGAM finally decided to begin a join archaeological mission with the University of Tsukuba to excavate Tell el-Kerkh. Based on their sincere goodwill, the new excavations started at Tell el-Kerkh in 1997, and continued until 2010, just before the conflict began in Syria.

The years of the twelve-season field campaign resulted in several unexpected archaeological results. The excavations revealed that there had been a series of large and complicated societies during the late Pre-Pottery Neolithic B and the early-middle Pottery Neolithic periods (c. 7600 – 6000 BC). In addition to the Neolithic inventories, Tell el-Kerkh produced a range of rich historical cultural properties as well.

One of the most conspicuous results of the investigation at Tell el-Kerkh was the discovery of a Neolithic cemetery. Though a few graves had been already discovered in the former excavation seasons at Tell el-Kerkh, 2007 season revealed the existence of an outdoor communal cemetery for the first time. Since then, over 240 burials had been discovered until

the 2010 season. It is clear that this cemetery is one of the oldest outdoor communal cemeteries not only in West Asia but also in the world; leading to increased understanding of its importance in human history. Investigation of the cemetery continued until 2010, but it has not been possible to completely excavate the whole area of the Neolithic cemetery. However, it was considered necessary to publish the known aspects of this precious Neolithic cemetery as soon as possible. So, the decision was made to publish the final report of the Kerkh Neolithic Cemetery as the second volume of the final report of excavations at Tell el-Kerkh.

2. Members and Operations of Each Excavation Season

1997 Season
Field duration: August 26 – October 9.

Operations: Paleo-environmental study (Landforms; geology; agricultural productivity potential); Excavations in Tell Ain el-Kerkh (Squares E270, E290 and E310 in the Central Area; Square E10 at the northern part of the mound; Square A386 at the northwestern fringe of the mound).

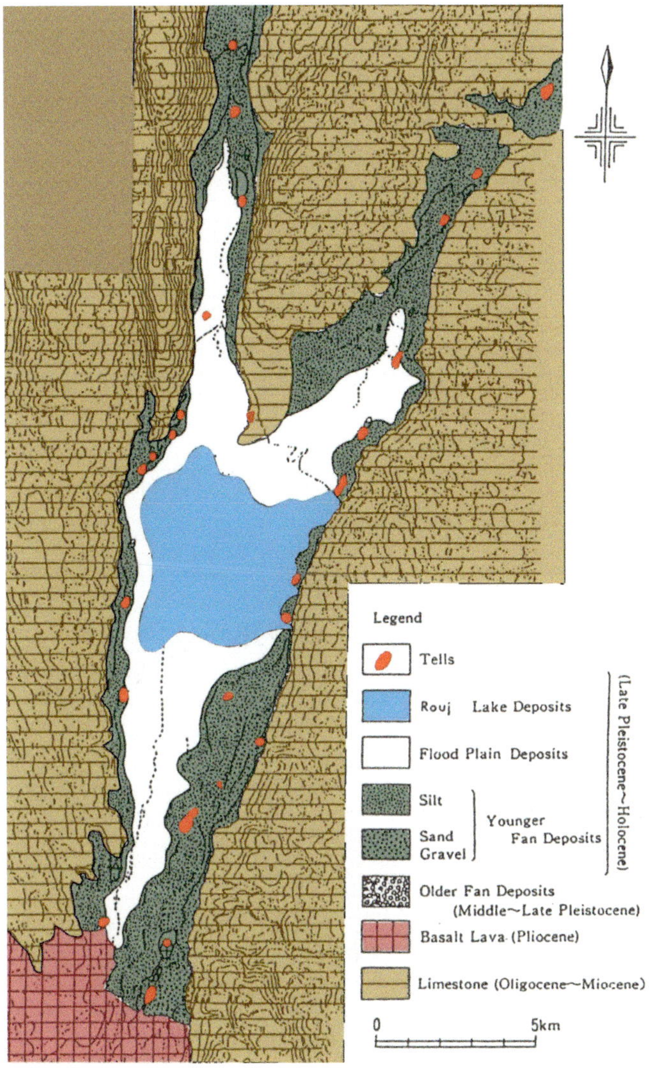

Figure 1-3. Geology of the Rouj Basin.

Legend

Tells

Rouj Lake Deposits } (Late Pleistocene~Holocene)

Flood Plain Deposits

Silt } Younger Fan Deposits
Sand Gravel

Older Fan Deposits (Middle~Late Pleistocene)

Basalt Lava (Pliocene)

Limestone (Oligocene~Miocene)

0   5km

Figure 1-4. Archaeological tells in the Rouj Basin.

1 Tell Fundo
2 Tell Douf
3 Tell Betraad
4 Tell Beshmaroun
5 Tell Failoun 1
6 Tell Fialoun 2
7 Tell Aray 1
8 Tell Aray 2
9 Tell Aray 3
10 Tell Abd el-Aziz
11 Tell Nahry
12 Tell Daoud
13 Tell Haila
14 Tell Hasan
15 Tell el-Kerkh 1
16 Tell el-Kerkh 2
17 Tell Ain el-Kerkh
18 Tell Telyla
19 Tell Marwan 1
20 Tell Marwan 2
21 Tell Izhan
22 Tell Hadad
23 Tell Qawaser
24 Tell Milis
25 Tell Qalyoun
26 Tel el-Ghafar 1
27 Tell el-Ghafar 2
28 Tell el-Mazoule
29 Tell Honmos
30 Tell Aqrabat
31 Tell Halaul
32 Tell Aswad
33 Tell el-Ghalbia
39 Tell Sheikh Bahry
40 Tell Innib
41 Tell el-Riz
42 Tlaylat al-Gab North
43 Tlaylat al-Gab Sough
44 Ard Jusr

Flood plain

Alluvial fans

Limestone mountains

Basalt lava

0   5km

Syrian side members: Jamal Hydar (co-director); Adel Habash; Taghrid Mohammad.

Japanese side members: Takuya Iwasaki (advisor); Akira Tsuneki (co-director); Yutaka Miyake; Makoto Takizawa; Etsuko Kurata; Sadayuki Akahane; Toru Nakamura; Makoto Arimura; Osamu Maeda; Shuich Sekine.

1998 Season

Field duration: July 25 – September 10.

Operations: Paleo-environmental study (Geology; ancient Rouj lake deposits); Excavations in Tell Ain el-Kerkh (Squares E270, E290 and E310 in the Central Area; Squares D6 and D26 in the Northwest Area; Sounding

Figure 1-5. General view of the Rouj Basin, looking north from Tell el-Kerkh 1.

3

trenches in Tell Ain el-Kerkh (Squares D11, D16, E1, F1, B230, B290, and E110); A Roman-Byzantine tomb excavation at the southern summit of Tell Ain el-Kerkh.

Syrian side members: Jamal Hydar (co-director); Adel Habash; Haifa Sha'baan; Hazem Jarkas,

Japanese side members: Takuya Iwasaki (advisor); Akira Tsuneki (co-director); Yutaka Miyake; Makoto Takizawa; Sadayuki Akahane; Takuro Adachi, Makoto Arimura; Toru Tomita; Shin-ichi Nishiyama; Tomoko Anezaki; Masaharu Nishizawa; Ken Hayase; Sachiko Yano; Atsunori Hasegawa.

1999 Season
Field duration: August 4 – August 30.

Operations: Excavations in Tell Ain el-Kerkh (Squares E270, E271 and E310 in the Central Area; Square D6 in the Northwest Area).

Syrian side members: Jamal Hydar (co-director); Haifa Sha'baan; Ghaith Sbeh; Saraa Saleh; Hazem Jarkas.

Japanese side members: Akira Tsuneki (co-director); Yutaka Miyake; Mark Hudson; Makoto Arimura; Osamu Maeda; Shin-ichi Nishiyama; Takahiro Odaka; Toshiko Matsuo; Sachiko Yano.

2000 Season
Field duration: August 5 – August 24.

Operations: Excavations in Tell Ain el-Kerkh (Squares E291, E310 and E311 in the Central Area).

Syrian side members: Jamal Hydar (co-director); Haifa Sha'baan; Ghaith Sbeh; Zeinab Ahmad.

Japanese side members: Akira Tsuneki (co-director); Yutaka Miyake; Makoto Arimura; Osamu Maeda; Ken-ichi Tanno; Takahiro Odaka; Atsunori Hasegawa; Daisuke Yamaguchi; Natsuko Kawazoe; Saori Katagiri (volunteer staff).

2001 Season
Field duration: July 21 – August 30.

Operations: Paleo-environmental study (Geology); Excavations in Tell Ain el-Kerkh (Squares E270, E271, E290, E291, E310 and E311 in the Central Area; Square D6 in the Northwest Area); Excavations in Tell el-Kerkh 1 (Square K-183 = the northern foot of Tell el-Kerkh 1)

Syrian side members: Jamal Hydar (co-director); Haifa Sha'baan; Adel Habassi.

Japanese side members: Takuya Iwasaki (advisor); Akira Tsuneki (co-director); Makoto Takizawa; Sadayuki Akahane; Mark Hudson; Makoto Arimura; Osamu Maeda; Ken-ichi Tanno; Takahiro Odaka; Atsunori Hasegawa; Sean Dougherty.

2002 Season
Field duration: July 29 – September 1.

Operations: Excavations in Tell Ain el-Kerkh (Squares E270, E271, E290, E291, E310 and E311 in the Central Area; Square D6 in the Northwest Area, Squares G191-G192 at the western outside of the tell); Excavations in Tell el-Kerkh 1 (Squares K-182, K183 and K163 = the northern foot of Tell el-Kerkh 1)

Syrian side members: Jamal Hydar (co-director); Haifa Sha'baan; Adel Habassi; Zeinab Ahmad; Basel Hamid.

Japanese side members: Akira Tsuneki (co-director); Yutaka Miyake; Makoto Takizawa; Makoto Arimura; Osamu Maeda; Ken-ichi Tanno; Takahiro Odaka; Tomoko Anezaki; Koji Miyazawa.

2005 Season
Field duration: August 13 – September 5.

Operations: Excavations in Tell Ain el-Kerkh (Squares E272, E273 and E274 in the East Trench); Excavations in Tell el-Kerkh 1 (Square O185 = the eastern foot of Tell el-Kerkh 1)

Syrian side members: Jamal Hydar (co-director); Haifa Sha'baan; Samaher Wannous.

Japanese side members: Akira Tsuneki (co-director); Takahiro Odaka; Ken-ichi Tanno; Atsunori Hasegawa; Mina Kosuge.

2006 Season
Field duration: August 11 – September 6.

Operations: Excavations in Tell Ain el-Kerkh (Squares E272, E273, E274, E275, E276 and E277 in the East Trench, Square A318 at Northern frontier of tell); Excavations in Tell el-Kerkh 1 (Squares O184 and O185 = the eastern foot of Tell el-Kerkh 1)

Syrian side members: Jamal Hydar (co-director); Haifa Sha'baan; Rudaena Harfoush.

Japanese side members: Akira Tsuneki (co-director); Takahiro Odaka; Atsunori Hasegawa; Ken-ichi Tanno; Tsuyoshi Maeda; Chie Akashi; Wataru Ando; Hiroki Takano; Yuki Tatsumi.

2007 Season
Field duration: July 17 – August 23.

Operations: Excavations in Tell Ain el-Kerkh (Squares E270, E271, E290, E291, E310 and E311 in the Central Area; Squares E274, E275, E276 and E277 in the East Trench, Square A318 at Northern frontier of tell); Excavations in Tell el-Kerkh 1 (Squares P110 and Q85 = the southern hilltop of Tell el-Kerkh 1)

Syrian side members: Jamal Hydar (co-director); Haifa Sha'baan; Mohamad Qantar.

Japanese side members: Akira Tsuneki (co-director); Takahiro Odaka; Atsunori Hasegawa; Ken-ichi Tanno; Hiroko Hashimoto; Naoko Murakami (Hironaga); Chie Akashi; Yuki Tatsumi; Maiko Nakamura; Tomoyuki Ishikawa; Morito Iizuka.

2008 Season

Field duration: July 16 – August 28.

Operations: Excavations in Tell Ain el-Kerkh (Squares E271, E291, and E311 in the Central Area; Squares E274, E275, E276 and E277 in the East Trench); Excavations in Tell el-Kerkh 1 (Square P110 = the southern hilltop of Tell el-Kerkh 1)

Syrian side members: Jamal Hydar (co-director); Haifa Sha'baan; Rudaena Harfoush; Mustafa Qador.

Japanese side members: Akira Tsuneki (co-director); Takahiro Odaka; Sean Dougherty; Atsunori Hasegawa; Ken-ichi Tanno; Naoko Murakami (Hironaga); Tomoyuki Ishikawa; Morito Iizuka; Yuji Matsushima.

2009 Season

Field duration: July 16 – August 28.

Operations: Excavations in Tell Ain el-Kerkh (Squares E271, E291, and E311 in the Central Area; Squares E274, E275, E276 and E277 in the East Trench); Excavations in Tell el-Kerkh 1 (Square P110 = the southern hilltop of Tell el-Kerkh 1)

Syrian side members: Jamal Hydar (co-director); Haifa Sha'baan; Rudaena Harfoush; Mustafa Al-Qador; Sari Jammo.

Japanese side members: Akira Tsuneki (co-director); Takahiro Odaka; Sean Dougherty; Atsunori Hasegawa; Ken-ichi Tanno; Naoko Murakami (Hironaga); Yuko Miyauchi; Tomoyuki Ishikawa; Morito Iizuka; Yuji Matsushima.

2010 Season

Field duration: July 4 – August 10, September 12 – September 29.

Operations: Excavations in Tell Ain el-Kerkh (Squares E251, E270, E271, E291 in the Central Area; Square A318 at Northern frontier of tell); Excavations in Tell el-Kerkh 1 (Squares P109 and P110 = the southern hilltop of Tell el-Kerkh 1; Squares M57 – M78 = Step trenches at northwest slope of Tell el-Kerkh 1).

Syrian side members: Jamal Hydar (co-director); Haifa Sha'baan; Rudaena Harfoush; Raed Badoura; Siham Ismail, Sari Jammo, Yahya Al-Amouri.

Japanese side members: Akira Tsuneki (co-director); Shigeo Wakita, Ken-ichiro Hisada; Takahiro Odaka; Sean Dougherty; Atsunori Hasegawa; Ken-ichi Tanno; Bérénice Chamel; Kaisho D. Masumori; Yuki Tatsumi; Morito Iizuka; Yu Itahashi; Masato Nagata, Yuji Matsushima; Yuko Miyauchi; Mariko Makino.

Affiliation of the members of the Tell el-Kerkh investigations between 1997 – 2010

(Position and affiliation at the time of latest participation)

Syrian side members

Co-director: Jamal Hydar: Director, Latakia Department of Antiquities

Members: Adel Habash: Architect, Latakia Department of Antiquities

Taghrid Mohammad: Staff, Latakia Department of Antiquities

Haifa Sha'baan: Archaeologist, Latakia Department of Antiquities

Hazem Jarkas: Architect, Idlib Department of Antiquities

Ghaith Sbeh: Architect, Latakia Department of Antiquities

Saraa Saleh: Architect, Latakia Department of Antiquities

Zeinab Ahmad: Archaeologist, Latakia Department of Antiquities

Basel Hamid: Architect, Jable Branch, Latakia Department of Antiquities

Samaher Wannous: Architect, Latakia Department of Antiquities

Rudaena Harhoush: Engineer, Latakia Department of Antiquities

Mohamad Qantar: Staff, Idlib Department of Antiquities

Mustafa Al-Qador: Archaeologist, Idlib Department of Antiquities

Raed Badoura: Archaeologist, Latakia Department of Antiquities

Siham Ismail: Architect, Jable Branch, Latakia Department of Antiquities

Sari Jammo: Student, Aleppo University

Yahya Al-Amouri: Student, Idlib Branch of Aleppo University

Japanese side members

Advisor: Takuya Iwasaki: Director, Matsudo City Museum

Co-director: Akira Tsuneki: Prof. in Archaeology, University of Tsukuba

Members: Yutaka Miyake: Assoc. Prof. in Archaeology, Tokyo Kaseigakuin University

Makoto Takizawa: Assoc. Prof. in Archaeology, Shizuoka University

Etsuko Kurata: Archaeologist, Matsudo City Museum

Sadayuki Akahane: Prof in Geology, Shinshu University

Toru Nakamura: Prof. in Botany, University of Tsukuba

Makoto Arimura: PhD candidate in Archaeology, University of Lyon

Osamu Maeda: PhD candidate in Archaeology, University of Tsukuba

Shuichi Sekine: PhD candidate in Biblical studies, University of Tsukuba

Takuro Adachi: PhD candidate in Archaeology, Aoyama Gakuin University

Toru Tomita: MA student in Archaeology, University of Tsukuba

Shin'ichi Nishiyama: PhD candidate in Archaeology, University of London

Tomoko Anezaki: Zoo Archaeologist, National Museum of Japanese History

Masaharu Nishizawa: MA student in Archaeology, Kokugakuin University

Ken Hayase: MA student, Shizuoka University

Sachiko Yano: Student, University of Tsukuba

Atsunori Hasegawa: Researcher in Archaeology, University of Tsukuba

Mark Hudson: Lecturer in Bio-Archaeology, University of Tsukuba

Takahiro Odaka: Research fellow, The Ancient Orient Museum, Tokyo.

Toshiko Matsuo: PhD candidate in Archaeology, Thessaloniki University

Ken'ichi Tan'no: Assoc. Prof. in Agriculture, Yamaguchi University.

Daisuke Yamaguchi: Research Student, University of Tsukuba

Natsuko Kawazoe: Student, University of Tsukuba

Saori Katagiri: Volunteer staff

Sean Dougherty: Instructor in Biological Sciences, Milwaukee Area Technical College

Koji Miyazawa: MA student, Shizuoka University

Mina Kosuge: Student, Shizuoka University

Ken Maeda: MA student, Shizuoka University

Chie Akashi: MA student, Waseda University

Wataru Ando: Student, Waseda University

Yuki Tatsumi: MA student, University of Tsukuba

Hiroki Takano: Student, Shizuoka University

Naoko Hironaga (Murakami): MA student, University of Tsukuba

Hiroko Hashimoto: Researcher, Nara Institute for Cultural Property

Kaisho Damonte Masumori: MA student, University of Tsukuba

Yuko Miyauchi: Student, University of Tsukuba

Maiko Nakamura: Student, University of Tsukuba

Tomoyuki Ishikawa: Student, University of Tsukuba

Morito Iizuka: Student, University of Tsukuba

Yuji Matsushima: Student, University of Tsukuba

Figure 1-6. People who participated in the 2010 season.

Kiyomi Mori: MA Student, Kokushikan University

Shigeo Wakita: Archaeologist, The Ancient Orient Museum

Ken-ichiro Hisada: Prof. in Geology, University of Tsukuba

Bérénice Chamel: PhD candidate in Bio-archaeology, University of Lyon II

Yu Itahashi: MA student in Prehistoric Anthropology, University of Tokyo

Masato Nagata: Student, Yamaguchi University

Mariko Makino: Student, University of Tsukuba

3. Chronology of the Rouj Basin

a. Relative Chronology

First, we will describe the Rouj Basin, where Tell el-Kerkh is located, and its local chronology. The Rouj Basin, located 10km west of modern Idlib city, is a small graben surrounded by limestone mountains. It extends north to south by about 37km and east to west by between 2 and 7km (Figure 1-3). An archaeological mission from the University of Tsukuba conducted the first intensive general survey in this basin from 1990 to 1992, including test pits at Tell Aray 1 and 2, Tell Abd el-Aziz, and Tell el-Kerkh 2 (Iwasaki and Nishino 1990, 1991, 1992; Iwasaki, Nishino and Tsuneki 1996).

Afterwards, archaeological study of the basin continued (e.g., Iwasaki and Tsuneki 2003; Tsuneki and Hydar 2007; Tsuneki et al. 2011). These studies formed the basis of the local Rouj Basin chronology. The Neolithic part of the Rouj Basin chronology is briefly summarized below (see Table 1-1, Figures 1-7 and 1-8).

Rouj 1 corresponds to the Pre-Pottery Neolithic B in the broad Levantine chronology. No PPNA site was discovered during the research in the Rouj Basin. The Early PPNB layers recovered at Tell Ain el-Kerkh

represent the earliest Neolithic evidence found in the Rouj Basin. The Rouj 1 era can be divided into two periods, Rouj 1a and 1c. As there must have been a hiatus between these two periods contemporary with the Middle PPNB period, the term Rouj 1b was created to indicate this period.

Rouj 1a (EPPNB): The lowest layers of the Northwest Area at Tell Ain el-Kerkh provide the indicator for this period. [14]C dating suggests that this area dates from c. 8700 to 8300 cal BC. Sophisticated naviform cores were used in blade production, and the stone tools were primarily made from the blades. The most characteristic tool-types are Aswad points and large blades with fine retouch on one lateral edge. Pressure flaking was frequently used to retouch the point.

Rouj 1c (LPPNB): This period corresponds to the Late PPNB period. Many test trenches which were set in each place of Tell Ain el-Kerkh and Test Pit A of Tell el-Kerkh 2 produced the Rouj 1c cultural layers. [14]C dating suggests that this period dates from c. 7600 to 7000 cal BC. The stone cores for blade production consisted of naviform cores and single platform cores. The Byblos point had become the main point type, with the Ugarit point also frequently appearing in the assemblage. Large sickle blades truncated at both ends, ordinary blades, and end scrapers on flakes were the main tool types.

Rouj 2 corresponds to the Pottery Neolithic (PN). This era can be divided into four periods.

Rouj 2a (Incipient PN): Layers 6–5 in the Test Pit A of Tell el-Kerkh 2, which produced the earliest type of pottery in the Levant, provides a typical assemblage for this period. The main chipped stone tool types are the Ugarit point, Amuq point, large sickle blades truncated at both ends, and end scrapers on blades and flakes; the technical continuity from Rouj 1c is remarkable. The most notable indicator for this period is the presence of so-called 'Kerkh Ware,' the prototype of Dark-faced

Table 1-1. The Rouj Basin chronology (2021 version).

Rouj Basin chronology	Supposed years based on ^{14}C dating (cal)	Levantine chronology
Rouj 2d	6000 - 5700 BC	Late Pottery Neolithic (Early-Halaf-related)
Rouj 2c	6600 - 6000 BC	Middle Pottery Neolithic
Rouj 2a-2b	7000 - 6600 BC	Early Pottery Neolithic
Rouj 1c	7600 - 7000 BC	Late Pre-Pottery Neolithic B
Rouj 1a	8700 - 8300 BC	Early Pre-Pottery Neolithic B

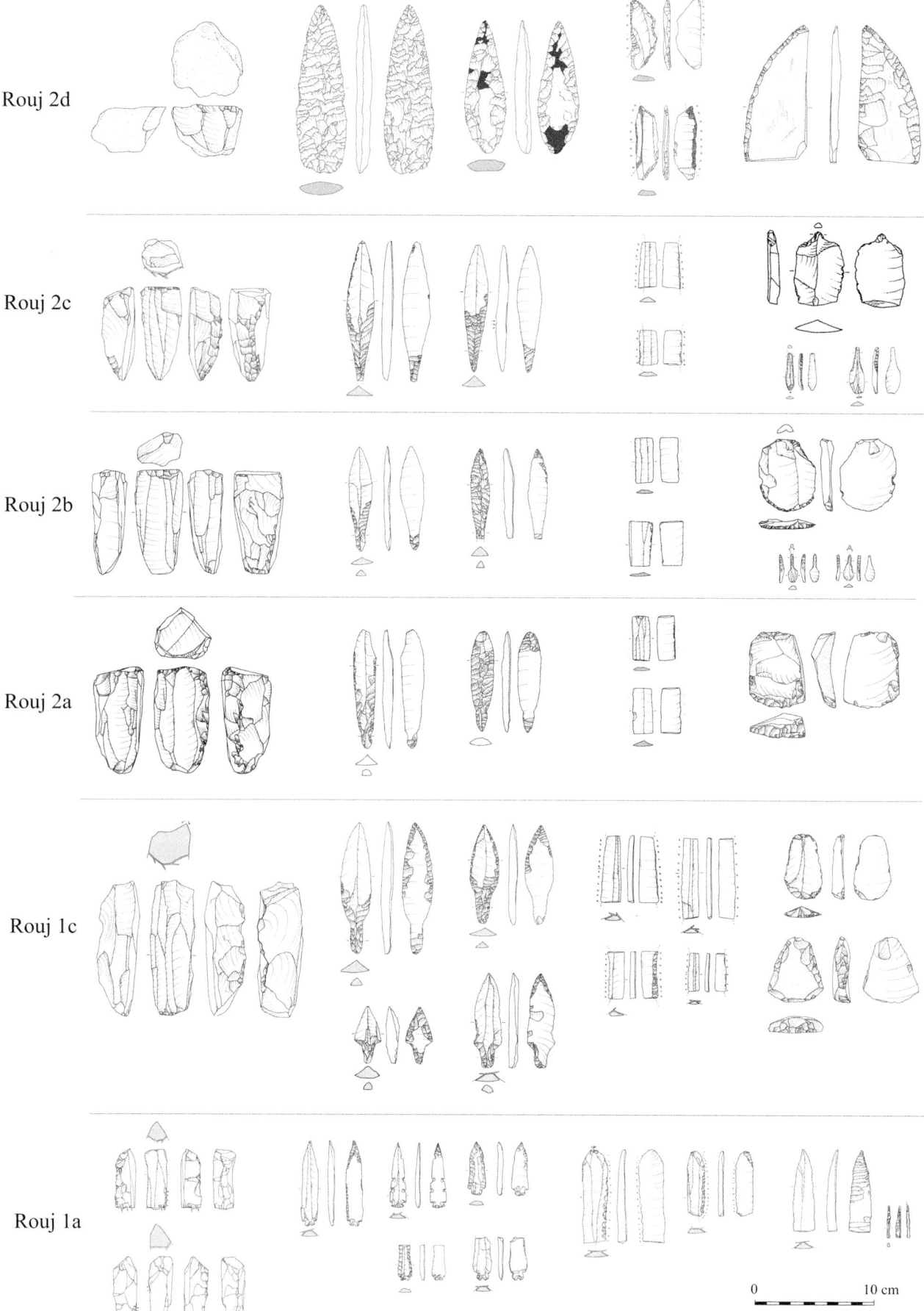

Figure 1-7. Neolithic lithic chronology of the Rouj Basin.

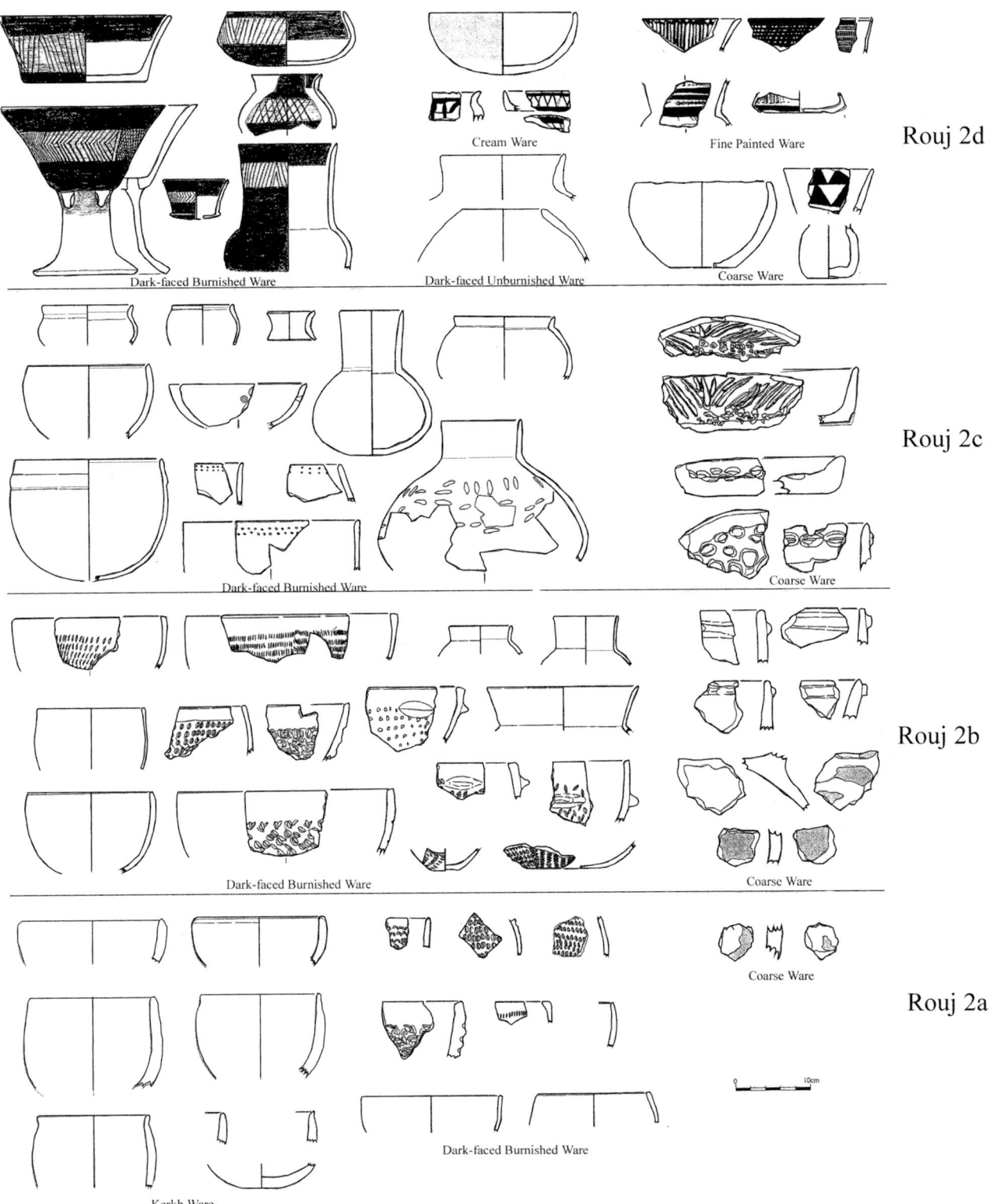

Figure 1-8. Neolithic pottery chronology of the Rouj Basin.

Burnished Ware (DFBW) (Tsuneki and Miyake 1996; Miyake 2003). In Layers 6–5 of Tell el-Kerkh 2, Kerkh Ware accounted for 33–42% of the pottery assemblage. However, a pure Kerkh Ware cultural layer has not yet been discovered in the excavations at Tell el-Kerkh. Kerkh Ware potsherds have always been discovered with early DFBW.

Rouj 2b (Early PN): The layers of this period were discovered in various trenches at Tell Ain el-Kerkh, Tell el-Kerkh 2, and Tell Aray 2. Although we do not have good ¹⁴C dating for the Rouj 2a-b period, Rouj 2a-b must be dated from between c. 7000 and 6600 cal BC based on the absolute dates of Rouj 1c and Rouj 2c. The chipped stone tools are similar to those of Rouj 2a. Kerkh Ware dwindled and finally disappeared, and the DFBW became the main pottery, with some accompanying Coarse Ware potsherds. The DFBW is a fine ware with grit tempering. In addition to the bowl, the jar became a significant pottery form. Applique bands and ridge handles were sometimes added to the outer surface of the pottery. Nail and pinch impressions are the most characteristic decorations for DFBW of this period. White plastering, with occasional reddish painting, is also a characteristic decoration for this pottery.

Rouj 2c (Middle PN): Layers 7–3 of the Central Area, the main excavated squares of Tell Ain el-Kerkh, provide the most typical objects for this period. ^{14}C dating of many of the organic samples indicates that this period spans between c. 6600 and 6000 cal BC. For the chipped stone tools, the Amuq point with pressure flaking retouch had become the main point type. Most sickle elements were truncated at both ends and of relatively short lengths. Small drills on blades for boring beads had become one of the main chipped stone tools. The number of scrapers on flakes had diminished less than in the previous period. DFBW and Coarse Ware were the main pottery types. The varieties of DFBW became richer and included carinated bowls, S-shaped bowls, hemispherical bowls, deep bowls, shallow bowls, short-necked jars, collar-necked jars, hole-mouthed jars, and stands. Low applique bands were frequently applied to the upper part of the outer surface of the pottery. In addition, fine stick impressions were observed as a decoration. Large and flat-based bowls and jars were the main forms of chaff-tempered Coarse Ware, which were mostly plain and rarely decorated. The husking tray is one of the most characteristic of Coarse Ware varieties.

Rouj 2d (Late PN): The last phase of the Pottery Neolithic dates from c. 6000 to 5700 cal BC. With few diagnostic imported potsherds, this period can be compared to the beginning of the Halaf period in Jazirah. This period was mainly represented by the material from Layers 2-1 of the Central Area at Tell Ain el-Kerkh. The chipped stone tools suddenly lost their definite forms and consisted mainly of rough flake tools. Although the point-type tool disappeared, a few very sophisticated stone daggers made with pressure flaking retouches were discovered. Crescent-shaped sickle elements and tile knives were also characteristic stone tools of this period. In addition to DFBW and Coarse Ware pottery, Dark-faced Unburnished Ware and Cream Ware (Red Washed Ware) appeared in this period. A few fine painted potteries, including Early Halaf painted potsherds, were also discovered. Remarkable forms, such as the flat-based bowl with a flared rim, the cream bowl, and the short-necked jar, all of which were typical of Early Halaf painted pottery, flourished among the Rouj 2d DFBW. Sophisticated pattern burnishing is a characteristic decoration of fine DFBW.

b. Absolute Chronology

We have many and various ^{14}C date results from Tell el-Kerkh, and these results were shown and discussed in the Chapter 7. Here the essence of the results is summarized to reconfirm the discussion for the Rouj Basin chronology.

Rouj 1a: There are five data samples from Square D6 of Tell Ain el-Kerkh. The oldest sample dates 8749-8470 cal BC (1σ) and the youngest dates 8426-8295 cal BC (1σ). The other three data samples show the ages between these two. Therefore, it is suggested that the Rouj 1a dates between 8700-8300 cal BC.

Rouj 1c: There are twelve data samples (five from charcoal and seven from human bones) from Square D6 of Tell Ain el-Kerkh and one datum from Test Pit A of Tell el-Kerkh 2. The oldest sample of the former dates to 7932-7585 cal BC (1σ), and the youngest one dates to 7177-6863 cal BC (1σ). Other samples from Square D6 date between 7578-7380 and 7312-7077 cal BC (1σ). The latter sample from Tell el-Kerkh 2 dates to 7345-6660 cal BC (1σ) (Yoneda 2003: 193-194). Therefore, it is suggested that the Rouj 1c dates between 7600-7000 cal BC.

Rouj 2a-b: There is just one old sample from the Test Pit A of Tell el-Kerkh 2. This sample is dated to 8280-7363 cal BC (1σ)(ibid). However, this date is too old for the beginning of the Pottery Neolithic period. The next, the Rouj 2c period started around 6600 cal BC. Therefore, it is suggested that the Rouj 2a-b period dates to 7000-6600 cal BC.

Rouj 2c: There are five samples from the Central Area (except human bone samples from Kerkh Neolithic cemetery), and five samples from the East Trench of Tell Ain el-Kerkh. There are also six samples from the Test Trench at Tell Aray (Yoneda 2003: 193-194). Ten samples from Tell Ain el-Kerkh date from 6748 to 5845 cal BC (1σ). However, middle six samples represent from 6570 to 6023 cal BC. In addition, all carbon ages of the twenty-five human bone samples from Kerkh Neolithic Cemetery fall within this range, especially from 6400 to 6100 cal BC (see Chapter 7: Table 7-4). Therefore, it is very probable that the Rouj 2c dates to between 6600-6000 cal BC.

Rouj 2d: There are one sample from the Central Area and five samples from the East Trench of Tell Ain el-Kerkh (except human bone samples). One sample dates to 6390-6260 cal BC (1σ), and the other five samples indicate a date between 5969 and 5669 cal BC (1σ). Four human bone samples from the Rouj 2d layers date 6057-5676 cal BC. Therefore, 6000-5700 cal BC is the most probable term for the Rouj 2d period.

Chapter 2
Geological Conditions of Tell el-Kerkh

Ken-ichiro Hisada

1. Introduction

The remains of Tell el-Kerkh, located in the northwestern part of Syria, are one of the largest vestiges of a colony from the Neolithic in West Asia. The remains of Tell el-Kerkh are considered to be a mega-site, which covers more than 10 ha, and is known to have contained the largest population in 7600-6600 cal BC (Tsuneki *et al.* 2006, Tsuneki 2012). In addition, the remains of Tell el-Kerkh may be critical for elucidating the mechanism of shifts from hunting and gathering to farming, livestock farming, and the expansion, as well as the complexity of the human society (Miyake 2017). It has been determined that a cultural unity had formed in the northwestern part of Syria while social complexity had advanced, frequently exchanging stone implement production techniques and volcanic glass (Maeda 2010, 2017, Arimura 2020, Arimura and Suleiman 2015). As one of the early human settlements, what were the conditions of settlement in the Rouj Basin? What resources were limited in the production of stone implements (stone blades in particular)? For these answers, it is probable that the geologic approach may be more desirable than an archaeological viewpoint (Hisada 2017).

I carried out two geological surveys in northwestern Syria (from April 25 to May 5, 2003, and July 9 to July 20, 2010). In this article, I discuss the geological features of the environment of Tell el-Kerkh based on those results. In addition, among stone implement materials, volcanic glass and flint, I examine the geologic significance of the latter.

2. Geological Outline from West Asia to East Africa

The northwestern part of Syria, including the Rouj Basin, is a continental geological environment, unlike an island arc, such as the Japanese Islands. The paradigm of plate tectonics is necessary for understanding the geological features around the Rouj Basin. The Eurasian, Arabian, and African plates form a line from north to south in West Asia, and the Anatolia and Indian plates are located on the sides (Hisada ed. 2018) (Figure 2-1). The Arabian plate separated from the African plate, forming the Red Sea and the Gulf of Aden, and collided with the Eurasian plate, shaping the Zagros Mountains. As an East-West boundary, leading to the Mediterranean Sea from the Zagros Mountains, substantially different geological environments occur in the north and south, representing an orogenic zone and a stable block, respectively. The orogenic zone is generally characterized by an earthquake zone with a geological feature structure due to intense and complicated crustal movement resulting from the Alps–Himalayas orogenic movement. However, for the stable block, the orogenic zone that was once active (a few billions of years ago) is now a stable continental Earth crust. The Precambrian zone made up of solid rocks is exposed in the stable block (Figure 2-1). This zone produced a relatively rugged topography, but the volcanic rock zone characterized by active volcanoes had spread to the Red Sea coast and the south as continent breakup had occurred. In addition, a fertile crescent moon zone, located along the border of the orogenic zone and the stable block, developed along the south side of the Zagros Mountains that were created by the collisions of plates (Figure 2-1). The fertile crescent moon zone was formed with huge amounts of debris due to transportation and deposition from the Tigris and Euphrates in the western extension of the Zagros Mountains.

However, a great mountain range did not form along the border between the Arabian plate and the African plate. This is because both plates were produced by divergent plate tectonics due to the continental breakup. It is known that the Arabian plate separated from the African plate tens of millions of years ago. The process of continental breakup is as follows: a large quantity of magma rose up in one area on the back side of the huge continent, the plate split in three directions from the center point that was lifted by the magma, and the continent was divided into three blocks (triple junction of Figure 2-1). In West Asia, the Red Sea, the Carlsberg Ridge (an extensional part of the Central Indian Ridge), and the East Africa Great Rift Valley were formed in the northwest, northeast, and southwest, respectively (Hisada ed. 2018). The center of this breakup is an area called the 'Afar Triangle' covering Ethiopia, Eritrea, and Djibouti. The African Great Rift Valley is divided into two lines of rift valleys.

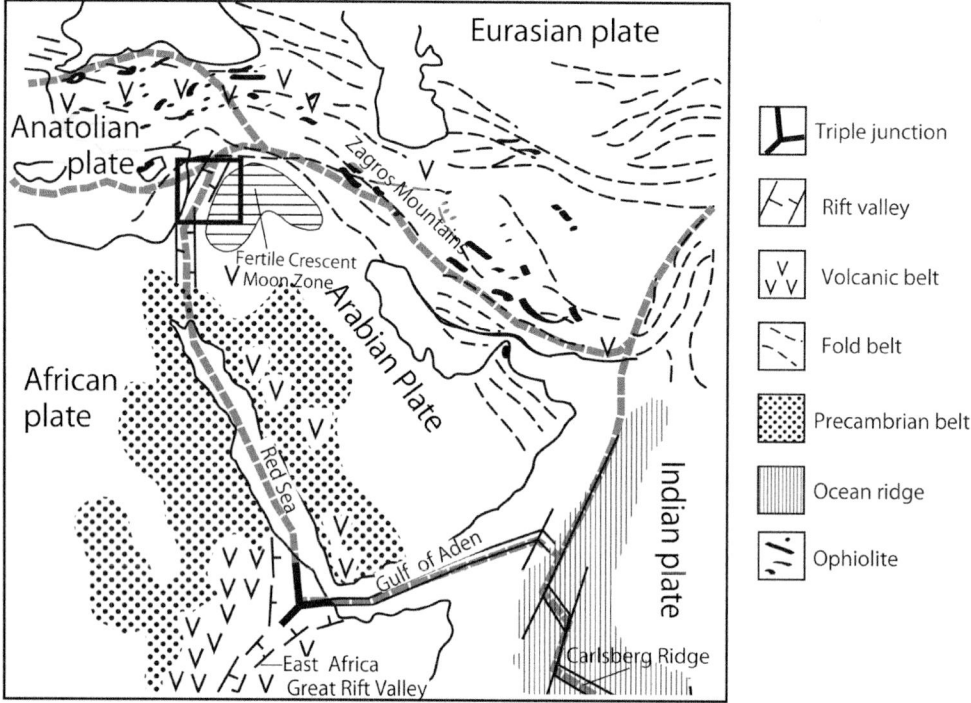

Figure 2-1. Outline of geology and plates in West Asia.
☐=Range of Figure 2-2.

The East Rift Valley runs from the Afar Triangle, via east of Lake Victoria, south through Kenya, and reaches Tanzania, whereas the West Rift Valley begins with the Afar Triangle, travels west of Lake Victoria, south to Lake Tanganyika and Lake Malawi, leading to the Indian Ocean. Furthermore, in the rift zone coming out of the Gulf of Aden to the Indian Ocean, the Carlsberg Ridge leads to the Central Indian Ridge. In addition, another rift leads to the Jordanian Dead Sea to the north via the innermost Gulf of Aqaba from the Red Sea, which changes the direction to the north by northeast a little after it travels through the Sea of Galilee from the Dead Sea to the north and reaches the Rouj Basin as a liner depression. Therefore, the Rouj Basin corresponds to the north end of the continent breakup, which had broken out from the Afar Triangle Zone. The Erta Al volcano and the neighboring volcanic activity remain active because the Afar Triangle is the center of the magma activity.

The 'East Side Story' by French anthropologist Yves Coppens proposing that the large topography of the African Great Rift Valley led to the birth of the initial human has attracted much attention, but has since been rejected with the discovery of the early Pithecanthropus from 7 million-6 million years ago in Central African Chad. However, the entire area of the Aruba Tyne trough between two parallel faults located at the north end of the West Rift Valley has drawn attention as the human birthplace because of the rich biological diversity that has been detected (Hisada ed. 2018). It is likely that the enclosed space and restrictive topography of the rift valley had a great influence on the history of hominization by producing biological diversity.

3. Role of 'the Bassit Ophiolite'

As mentioned, West Asia is comprised of an orogenic zone and a stable block, but the orogenic zone is relatively rich in mineral resources. This is because iron, copper, lead, and zinc condensed as ore bodies in the igneous rock mass or neighboring rock masses due to igneous activity (Hisada ed. 2018). Therefore, there is no doubt that the metal deposits of the orogenic zone were of great use for the ancient civilizations, especially ophiolite.

Ophiolite is a piece of the earth crust/mantle of the past ocean floor (Hisada ed. 2018). When an event such as a continental collision occurs between plates, one obducts (thrusts over) the continent despite the rock under the bottom of the sea. Therefore, the earth crust/mantle of the ocean floor that once existed between the continents obducted in the collision zone of the African plate (the Anatolia plate and Arabian plate) with the African Continent, which collided with the Eurasian plate containing the Eurasian Continent. The world's largest exposed ophiolite masses are on Cyprus Island (Troodos ophiolite) (Arai 1988) and in Oman (Oman ophiolite) (Miyashita 2018) of the Arabian Peninsula (Figure 2-1). The distribution of ophiolite is also known throughout Syria, which is located midway between the two masses.

Approximately 1,000km² of ophiolite is distributed over the Bassit district along the Mediterranean Sea in northwestern Syria (Figure 2-2), referred to as the 'Bassit ophiolite' hereafter. Ponikarov ed. (1968) described rocks constituting the Bassit ophiolite as follows: serpentinite and peridotite (Figure 2-3), intrusive rock, volcanic rock, and their covering rocks, such as radiolarite and limestone.

These rocks were formed before the Maastrichtian of the Late Cretaceous as the earth crust under the ocean floor, and it is thought that it obducted tens of millions of years ago by orogenic movement. The ophiolite consists mainly of the igneous rock of solidified magma, and the peridotite, stratified gabbro, sheet dyke group, and lava are equivalent to the parts from the upper mantle to the ocean crust. All the ophiolite thicknesses

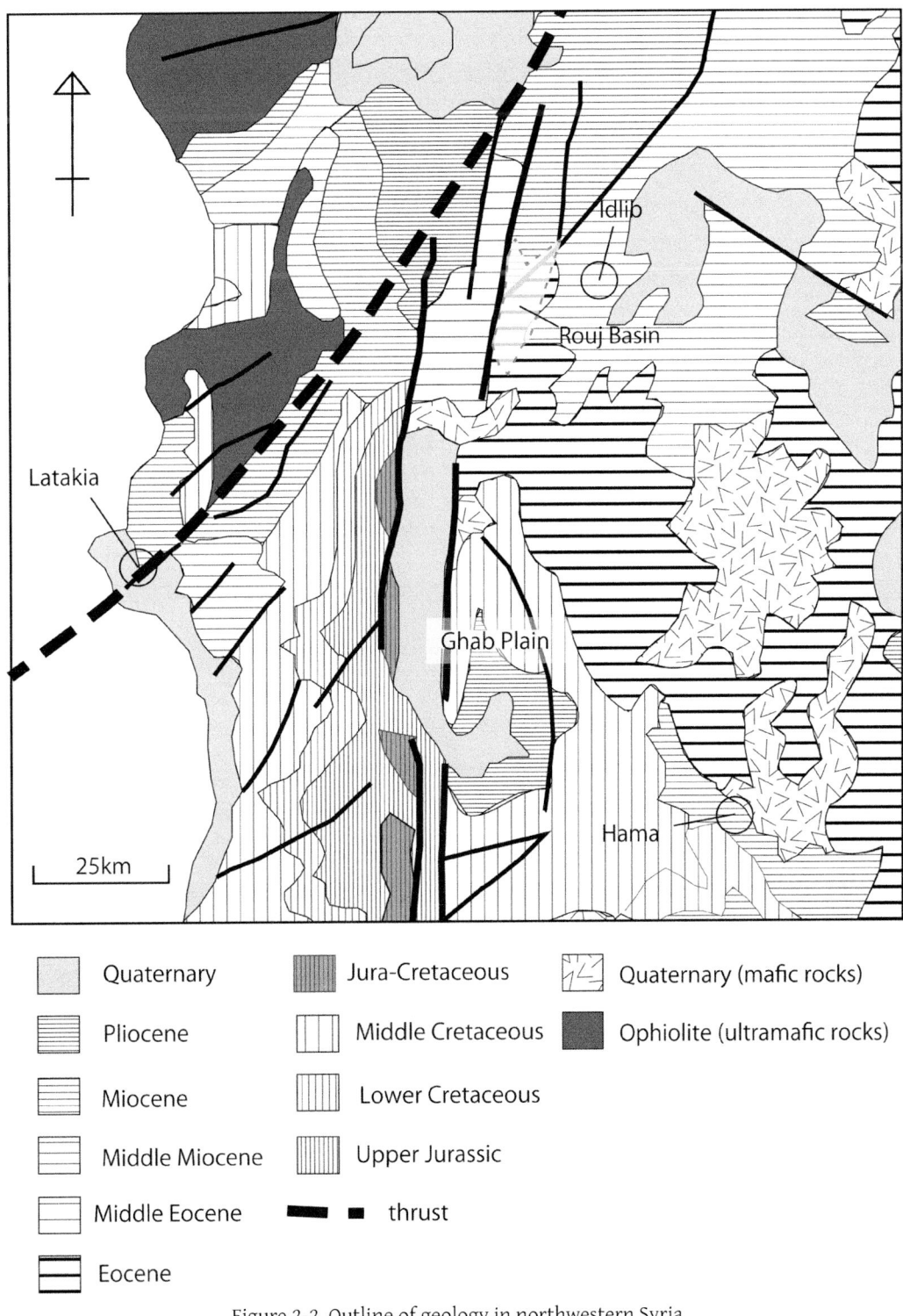

Figure 2-2. Outline of geology in northwestern Syria.
Based on Aghnabati (1986).

13

Figure 2-3. 'Bassit ophiolite'. a. Outcrop of serpentinite; b. Serpentinized peridotite.

range from a few kilometers to 10km. When the magma that occurred in a peridotite of the upper mantle ascended into the earth's crust, crystals were deposited in the space called a magma reservoir (accumulated) and erupted on the surface of the earth. The peridotite that generated the initial magma is called residual rocks.

The Bassit ophiolite is composed of peridotite-altered serpentinite, layered gabbro, a sheet-dyke group, lava of exclusive rocks, and covering sedimentary rocks. Among them, the layered gabbro, sheet-dyke group, and lava of exclusive rocks are mostly holocrystalline to hypocrystalline. As mentioned later, these rocks were used as raw materials for the ancient people's accessories.

The ophiolite often co-occurs with limestone and radiolarite (accumulation of radiolarian tests) (Mouty 2015). This radiolarite is similar to bedded chert, which is a significant component of the Jurassic accretionary prism known as the backbone of the Japanese Islands, but their sedimentary environments seem to be considerably different. It is inferred that bedded chert is from deep-sea sediments, but radiolarite may include shallower sediments. In other words, the formation by the difference in the depth of limestone–radiolarite–bedded chert may be recognized, with depositional depths ranging from very shallow to deep sea depths of a few thousand meters.

Dr. Shoji Arai in Hisada ed. (2018) mentioned that the tectonic event that deep-sea floor with underlying rocks obducted on land suggested that shallower sea sediments were also involved in this obduction and were emplaced on land. <omission> In this case, limestone is a shallow sediment, and radiolarite is categorized in the sediment of the deeper sea. When two continents collide, the trace becomes ophiolite. In other words, the existence of the ophiolite may

indicate the existence of the combinatorial rock of limestone-radiolarite. Radiolarite is a suitable material for stone blades, and limestone caves provided shelter for the ancients; therefore, limestone-radiolarite was an essential natural resource in the lives of the ancients (Hisada ed. 2018).

In addition, the ophiolite accompanies the jade of the peridotite and serpentine, yellow ocher (color of the yellow ocher mainly from iron hydroxide) in the umber (iron manganese ore) of eruptive rocks, and copper ore of the chromite deposit. It is worth noting that the distance between the Bassit ophiolite and the remains of Tell el-Kerkh is approximately 40km. This ophiolite has limited exposure in the collision zone of the plate, namely the Alps–Himalayas orogenic zone. Although the occurrence of rocks, such as the crystalline cumulates around the Rouj Basin on the Arabian plate, cannot be expected, the Bassit ophiolite might be available approximately 40km away.

4. Geological Features and Water Regime of the Rouj Basin

1) The Origin of the Rouj Basin

The Rouj Basin is in the extension of the rift valley lengthening north of the Dead Sea. The Rouj Basin itself is 37km from the north to south, 2–7km in width, and is surrounded by limestone. The limestone of the Rouj Basin is different on the west and east sides, with Miocene stratified limestone on the east (Figure 2-4b, Figure 2-5, Figure 2-6c), and, on the west, Eocene stratified limestone (Figure 2-4a, Figure 2-5, Figure 2-6b). In addition, the southernmost end of the west side contains basalt lava (Figure 2-5). Both Eocene and Miocene stratified limestones are gray to dark gray, micritic, and a single bed ranging from a few tens of centimeters to a few meters in thickness.

Figure 2-4. Distant view of Rouj Basin. a. western side; b. eastern side.

Garfunkel (1981) demonstrated the Dead Sea left-lateral transform with four lozenge troughs between two parallel faults from the Gulf of Aqaba to the Rouj Basin. The northernmost lozenge trough between two parallel faults includes the Rouj Basin and connects with the main Zagros thrust fault in the immediate north. This situation suggests that a rift valley formed by the left-lateral transform was thrust over by the Alps–Himalayas orogenic zone from the north. Manspeizer (1985) clarified the details of the lozenge trough between the two parallel faults of the southern Dead Sea area and the paleoclimate of the Dead Sea area in the Quaternary. The Rouj Basin was formed in conjunction with the Dead Sea transform, but it does not seem to be a typical lozenge trough between two parallel faults.

However, according to the geological map of the Middle East (1:5,000,000) published by the Geological Survey of Iran, the western fault of the Rouj Basin may correspond to a part of the fault zone, lengthening intermittently from the rift valley (Aghanabati 1986). The western side of the Rouj Basin was uplifted by a north-south trending fault, whereas the eastern side is thought to have had few gaps by faulting (Figure 2-5).

I carried out a geological survey around the Rouj Basin and found the possibility of the dome and basin structure, with a basin extending to the north and south. I confirmed that the stratified limestone of the east and west sides dip at 10–30° towards a basin center (Figure 2-5). In other words, the Rouj Basin, located at the north end of the Arabian plate, presents the features of a rift zone, but it is a half-graben (rift valley) only with the west dislocation. It seems that it is different from the rift valley of the neighborhood of the Dead Sea, not the rift valley where both sides were partitioned off in clear dislocation. This may be because it is located far from the triple junction and produced by plate divergence or because it was significantly affected by the Alps–Himalayas orogenic movement from the north.

2) Water Environment of the Rouj Basin

There was possibly some dislocation that developed in the west edge of the Rouj Basin, but the gap is not necessarily large. Therefore, the Rouj Basin is equivalent to the basin part of the dome and basin structure, and the groundwater drifts towards the center of the basin, which could have been easy to collect. In addition, large uvala in an oval of 1.3 × 1.0km, with a depth of more than 100m, developed in the southwestern part (Figure 2-6a), with the major axis in the northwest–southeast direction. It is a considerably large basin with an indefinite form from the combination of adjacent dolines, and the uvala was enlarged by the progress of the corrosion and collapse underground space (Urushibara ed. 1996). The existence of such a huge uvala means that there was once a large-scale water vein under the ground.

Although the Rouj Lake disappeared through reclamation, lake sediments are present in the central part of the basin in the Rouj Basin (Akahane 2003), with a thickness of several meters. Its lower part is greenish gray silt and green clay, with gypsum crystals formed in both layers. The top of the lower part includes freshwater shell fossils. The upper part consists of gray silt, dark gray silt, white silt, light brown silt, and peat. White silt is the primary bed including calcite crystals and shell fossils. It is indicated that the existence of the former Rouj Lake provided a good water environment in the Rouj Basin.

5. Flint Acquisition of Tell el-Kerkh

I was not able to find stone material suitable to produce a flake tool, particularly the stone blades, during my geological survey around the Rouj Basin. First, in this chapter, I show the origin of stone material suitable for stone blades, namely silicified rocks, and then examine stone material supply in Tell el-Kerkh.

According to the naked-eye observation of the stone blades, the material of the stone blades from West Asia is radiolarite and siliceous nodules (also known as concretions). These rocks are called flint archaeologically. Here, I introduce the geologic implication of the flint and examine the origin of siliceous nodules in limestone.

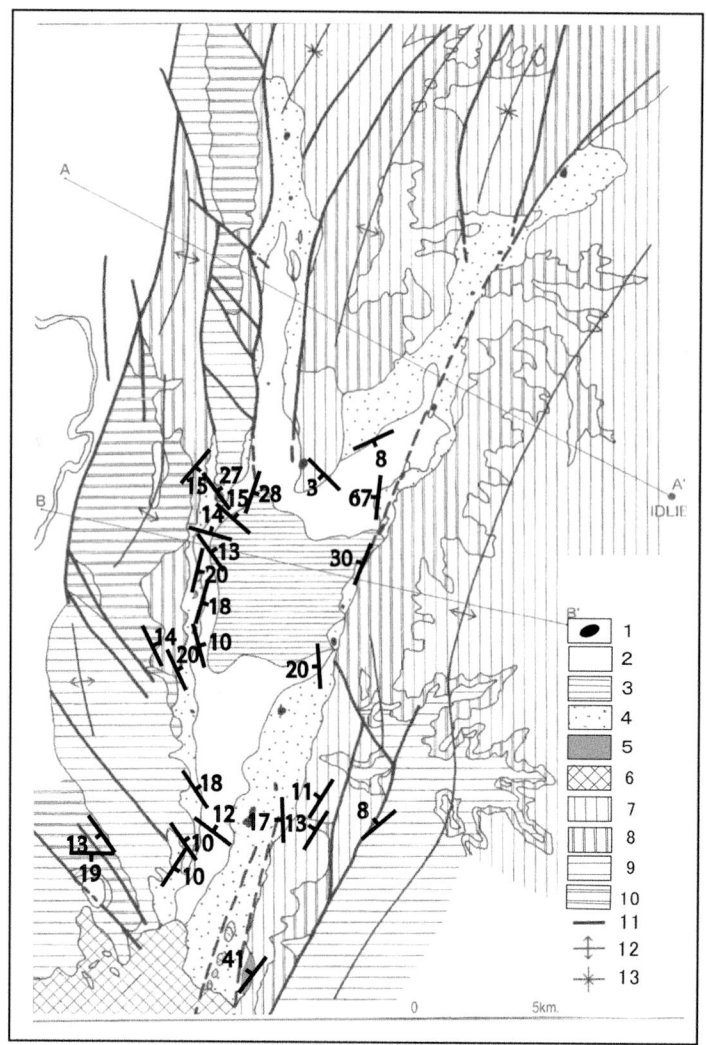

1:Tells, 2:Flood Plain Deposits, 3:Rouj Lake Deposits, 4:Younger Fan Deposits,
5:Older Fan Deposits, 6:Basalt Lava (Paleogene), 7: N1t Formation (Neogene),
8:N1h Formation (Neogene), 9:Pg3 Formation (Paleogene),
10:Pg2 Formation (Paleogene), 11: Faults, 12: Anticline Axis, 13:Syncline Axis

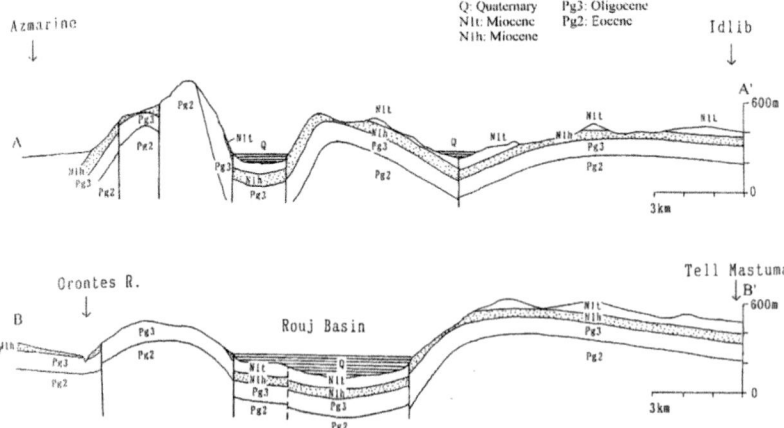

Figure 2-5. Geologic map and profile of Rouj Basin. Based on Akahane (2003).
Dip and strike are based on Hisada (unpublised data).

According to the 'New Publication Earth Science Dictionary Vol. 2' (Katayama *et al.* ed. 1970, 398), the flint is broken into a conchoidal fracture and makes a sharp ridge. It occurs in the lens-formed, nodular-formed, bed-formed, or vein-shaped in chalk layer. <omission> It is considered to be biogenic, while the others are partly inorganic sources; however, there is not necessarily an definite rock-forming model for

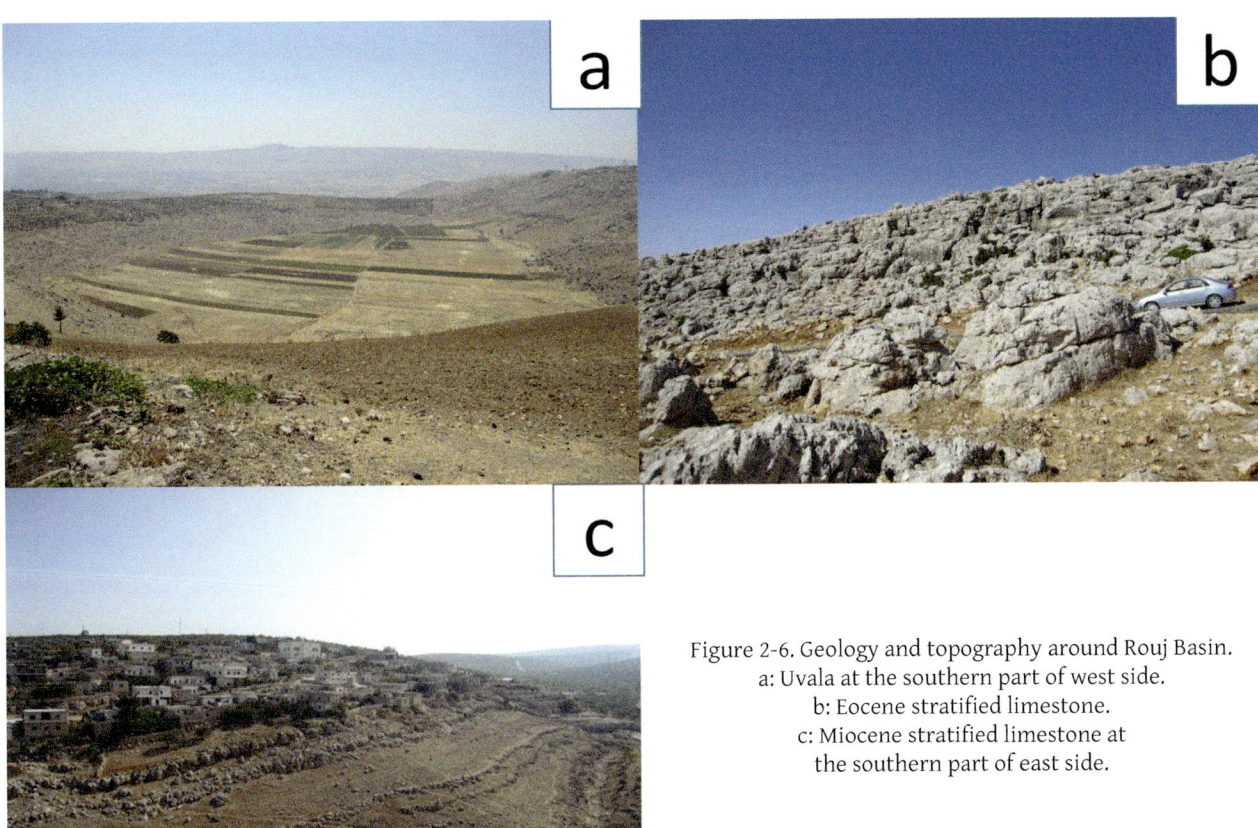

Figure 2-6. Geology and topography around Rouj Basin.
a: Uvala at the southern part of west side.
b: Eocene stratified limestone.
c: Miocene stratified limestone at
the southern part of east side.

them. It is said that this technical term is not currently used as geologic descriptions.

Hattori (2008) mentioned that flint is the same as a chert, and the name is only used for crafts, according to Tarr (1938), and, therefore, should not be used as a technical term. The technical term flint is not used in the present paper, following this suggestion. From the description, the term 'siliceous nodule' is appropriate because they are indefinite silicified rocks formed in the limestone. Thus, siliceous nodules are produced through lithification during diagenesis and formed by the movement of the interstitial water and diffusion of the ions. Accordingly, they are often densely developed on specific sedimentary surfaces.

The siliceous nodules in limestone are formed through three pathways: 1) hydrothermal processes on the ocean floor (Migaszewwski *et al.* 2006), 2) seawater dilution of rainwater in the shallow sea (James *et al.* 2000); and 3) diagenesis of the turbidity current sediments comprised of a mixture of siliceous and calcic tests (Bustillo and Ruiz-Ortiz 1987).

In the Eocene and Miocene limestone on the east and west sides of the Rouj Basin, siliceous nodules are scarce in stratified limestone. However, the occurrence of siliceous nodules with a short axis of 20cm and long axis of 30-50cm have been found in the stratified limestone of the Cretaceous formations in the suburbs of Latakia (Figure 2-7a, b), with many ellipsoidal nodules developed within the same horizon. Because there is no indication of hydrothermal effects on the stratified limestone or rainfall effects due to the close proximity to the land environment, the turbidity current origin 3) is thought to be the most appropriate for the siliceous nodules. The turbidity current sediment origin was proposed by Bustillo and Ruiz-Ortiz (1987) for the Late Jurassic limestone turbidite in the Petico Mountains, southern Spain. This limestone is composed of sand and calcic mud, including a piece of planktonic crinoid and radiolarian tests, and after their deposition from the turbidity current, through the diagenesis process, silica dissolved from the radiolarian tests capping the calcic mud, and as a result, the siliceous nodules were formed in the stratified limestone. This process would also be appropriate as the origin of the siliceous nodules found in the suburbs of Latakia.

Along the side of a farm road from the center of the Rouj Basin 50km south to the center of the Ghab Plain, a large quantity of siliceous nodules has accumulated

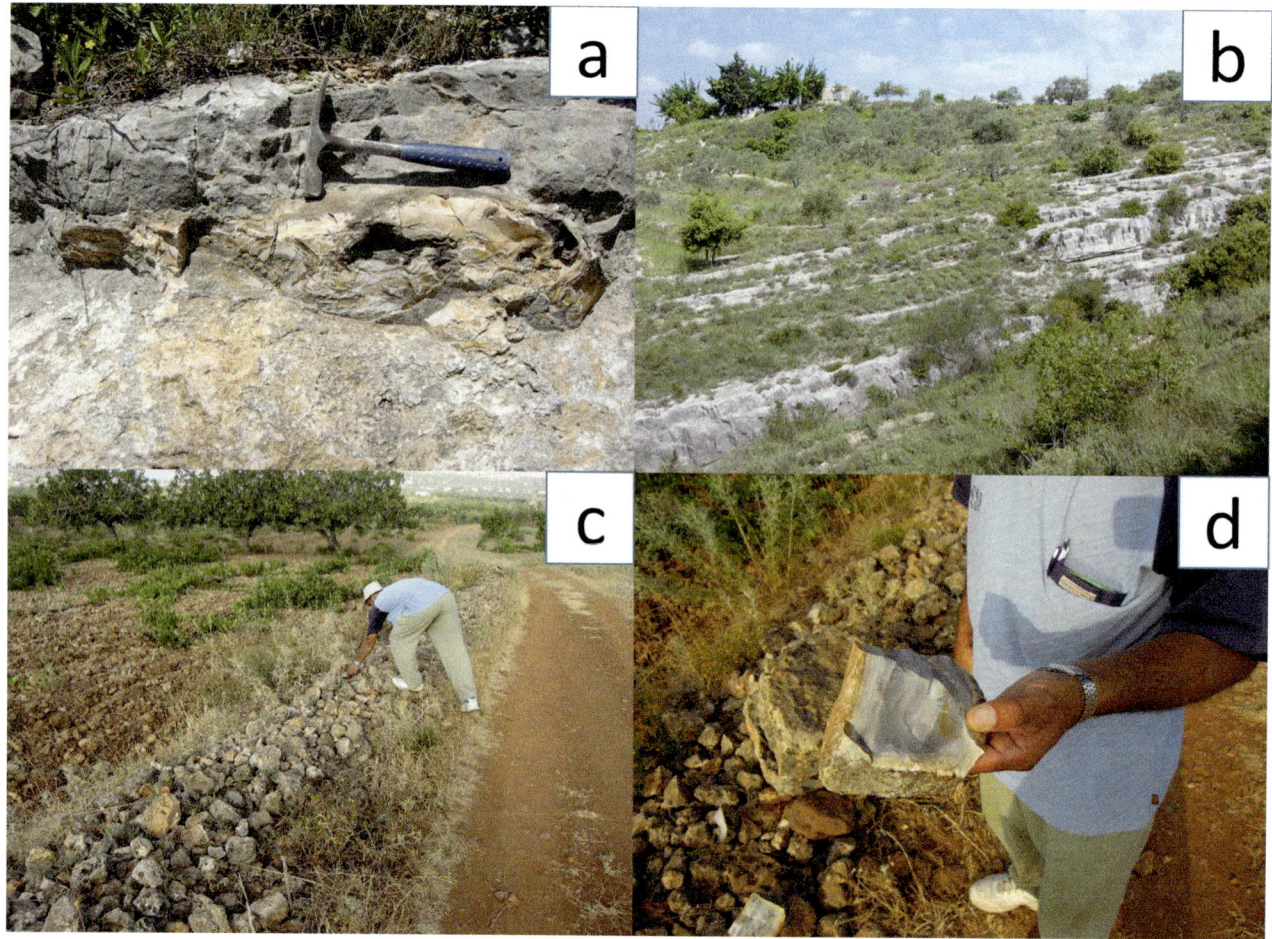

Figure 2-7. Siliceous nodules near Latakia and along farm road from Rouj Basin to Ghab Plain.
a: Siliceous nodule in Cretaceous limestone near Latakia.
b: Cretaceous stratified limestone near Latakia.
c & d: Siliceous nodules along the farm road from Rouj Basin to Ghab Plain.
(c: collection by local people, d: concentric design inside siliceous nodule).

artificially (Figure 2-7c, d; this location may be source 3 or its vicinity indicated by Arimura (2020)). Because this location is within the distribution area of the Mid-Cretaceous, the siliceous nodules were washed out after weathering or farmers removed them as debris from the farmland. Many of the nodules are 10cm in diameter and present a concentric design. There is a possibility that this Cretaceous limestone is the same horizon as the Latakia suburb limestone. Therefore, the siliceous nodules used as the material of the stone blades were unlikely to have originated in the Rouj Basin but were probably provided by the distribution area of the Mid-Cretaceous, as shown in Figure 2-2 (approximately 30km or more from the center of the Rouj Basin).

6. Conclusion

The Rouj Basin containing the remains of Tell el-Kerkh corresponds to the basinal part of a dome and basin structure, with a potentially good water environment. However, the occurrence of siliceous nodules suitable for stone blades from both sides of the stratified limestone is unexpected. The nodules used may have been from the distribution area dozens of kilometers south from the Cretaceous limestones. However, the cumulates that could have become the material of the accessories have been detected in the western Bassit ophiolite. Although the water environment was good in the Rouj Basin, the stone implement materials and the materials of the accessories may have been imported from dozens of kilometers away because it is unlikely that they originated within or near the basin. It is concluded that the archaeological situation around the Rouj Basin resulted from the Alps–Himalayas orogeny, caused by the collision with the Arabian plate, with sedimentation of the platform-type limestone.

Chapter 3
The Tell el-Kerkh Site and Stratigraphy

Akira Tsuneki

Tell el-Kerkh is a very large tell complex consisting of three artificial mounds: Tell el-Kerkh 1, Tell el-Kerkh 2, and Tell Ain el-Kerkh from south to north (Figure 3-1). The tell complex measures about 1km from north to south and about 400m from east to west. We set up eighteen 200 × 200m grids covering the entire tell complex along the axis, linking the two triangulation points of Tell el-Kerkh 1 and Tell Daoud, and we labelled each grid A to R. Then, we divided each grid into four hundred 10 × 10m squares and labelled 1 to 400. Each square was further subdivided into four 5 × 5m sub-squares labelled a to d.

Tell el-Kerkh 1 has an irregularly rectangular plan measuring ca. 400 × 400m. It stands over 30m above the surrounding plain. It seems to have had fortification walls dating to the Early Bronze, Middle Bronze, or Iron Age. A test trench along the western slope indicated that the site had fortification walls consisting of stones and mud bricks which date back to at least the MB and Iron Ages (Figure 3-2: M57-M78, Tsuneki and Hydar 2009). EB, MB, Late Bronze, and Iron Age buildings were discovered on the southern slope of Tell el-Kerkh 1 (Figure 3-2: P109-110, Q85, Tsuneki and Hydar 2008–2010). Roman-Byzantine era buildings and a cemetery were also excavated at the northern and eastern foot of Tell el-Kerkh 1 (Figure 3-2: K182-K183, O184-O185). Thus, the artificial mound of Tell el-Kerkh 1 was mainly formed during the Bronze Age, Iron Age, and Roman-Byzantine periods. However, as some Neolithic objects could be collected from the surface of Tell el-Kerkh 1, evidence of Neolithic occupation might have accumulated below thick post-Neolithic deposits.

The south end of Tell Ain el-Kerkh was also covered with Roman-Byzantine cultural layers. For example, a stone-vaulted chamber tomb from the Roman-Byzantine period was exposed near the southern summit of Tell Ain el-Kerkh. Excavations of the tomb have revealed that it belonged to the Late Byzantine era (Nishiyama and Sha'baan 1998) (Figure 3-2: H110). Numerous Roman-Byzantine potsherds have been found in the area around this tomb and the area was densely shared in the Roman-Byzantine era. However, most parts of Tell Ain el-Kerkh and the whole area of Tell el-Kerkh 2 contain only Neolithic layers. The University of Tsukuba

archaeological mission excavated a test pit at the central part of Tell el-Kerkh 2 in 1992 and discovered a good cultural sequence from the Late PPNB to the Early Pottery Neolithic periods. The Rouj Basin chronology, especially Rouj 1c, 2a, and 2b periods, were established based on this result (Iwasaki and Tsuneki 2003).

1. Investigating Neolithic Cultural Deposits in Tell Ain el-Kerkh

In 1992, we created a test pit measuring 25m² at the center of Tell el-Kerkh 2 (Iwasaki and Tsuneki 2003; Figure 3-2: Test Pit A). A Syro-Japanese joint archaeological mission, consisting of personnel from the Directorate-General of Antiquities and Museums and the University of Tsukuba, began excavations at Tell el-Kerkh in 1997. Since then, the main excavations have comprised about 650m² at the center of Tell Ain el-Kerkh (Central Area) and about 200m² in the northwest of Tell Ain el-Kerkh (Northwest Area), and 11 test pits and one long trench (60 × 2.5m, East Trench) have been excavated at various parts of Tell Ain el-Kerkh (Figure 3-2). Thick Neolithic cultural deposits have been discovered in all of these excavated areas. In the Northwest Area, the cultural layers date back to the Early PPNB (Rouj 1a period). At the summit of Tell Ain el-Kerkh, the latest Neolithic deposits date to the Late Pottery Neolithic period (Rouj 2d period). According to ¹⁴C dating, the Neolithic cultural deposits at Kerkh cover the period from ca. 8700 BC to ca. 5700 BC, and there is no material from the period between ca. 8300 BC and ca. 7600 BC (Rouj 1b = Middle PPNB).

Here, we summarize the results of the excavations in each area and square.

Northwest Area (Squares A386, D6, and D26)

We excavated a sounding trench measuring 9 × 2m (Square A386c-d) and two 9 × 9m squares (Squares D6 and D26) in the northwestern part of Tell Ain el-Kerkh from 1998 to 2002. This area produced the earliest Neolithic sequence at the site, dating from the Early PPNB (Rouj 1a) to the Early Pottery Neolithic periods (Rouj 2a-b) (Figure 3-3). We found the Rouj 2a-b layers (Layers 1 and 2) below the surface soil. Each had a thickness of

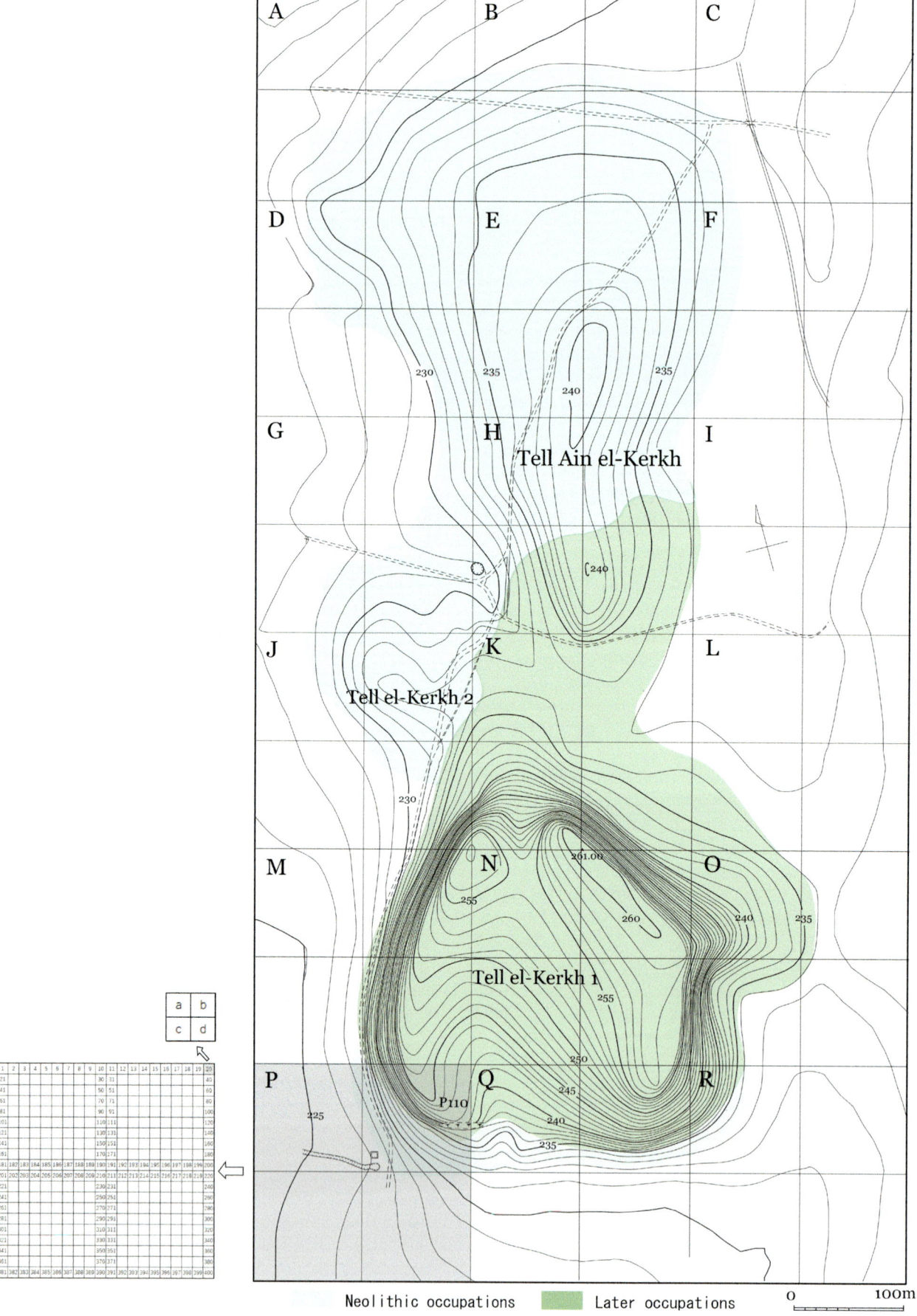

Figure 3-1. Mound complex of Tell el-Kerkh and grid system.

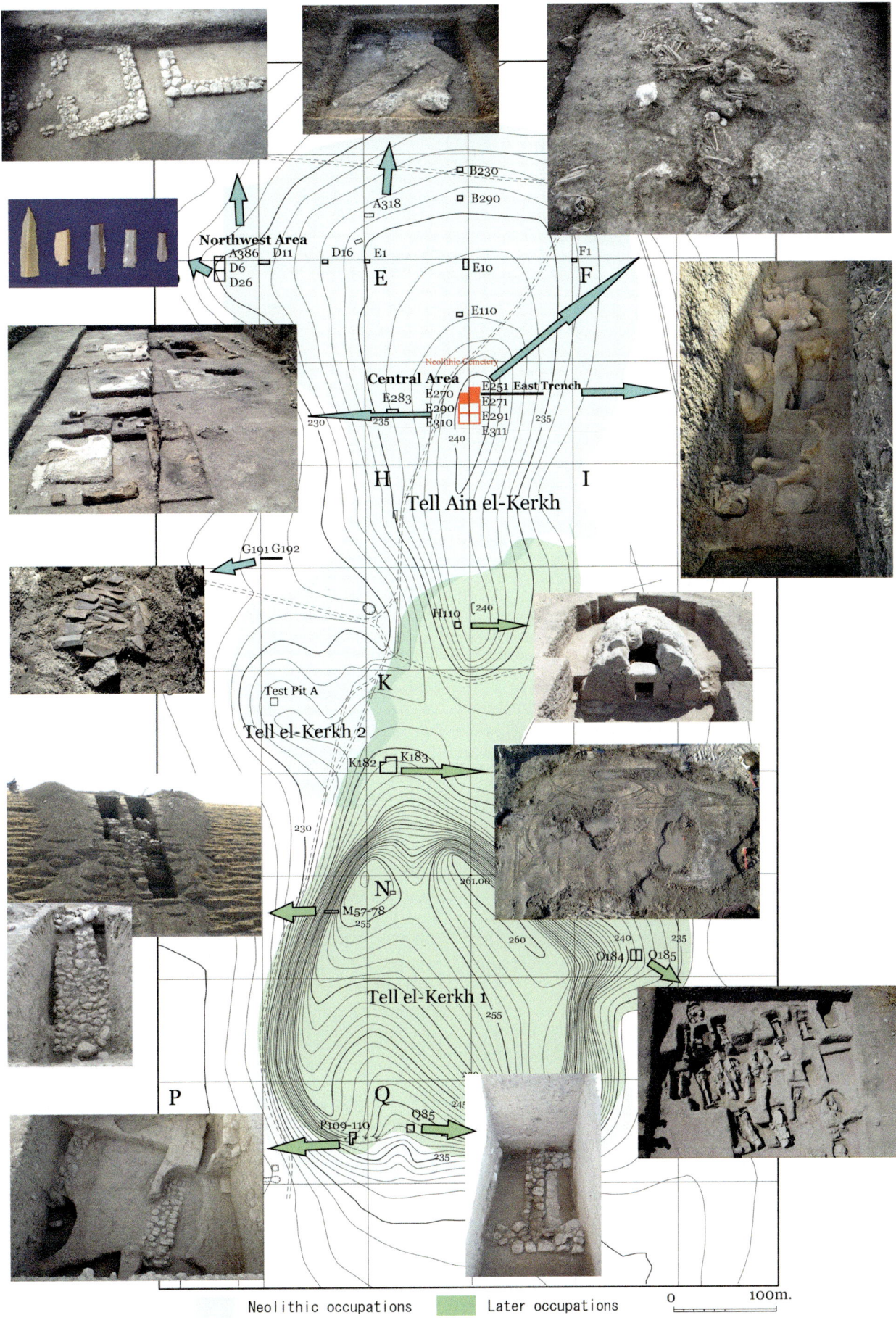

Figure 3-2. Excavated squares at Tell el-Kerkh.

Neolithic occupations   Later occupations   0   100m.

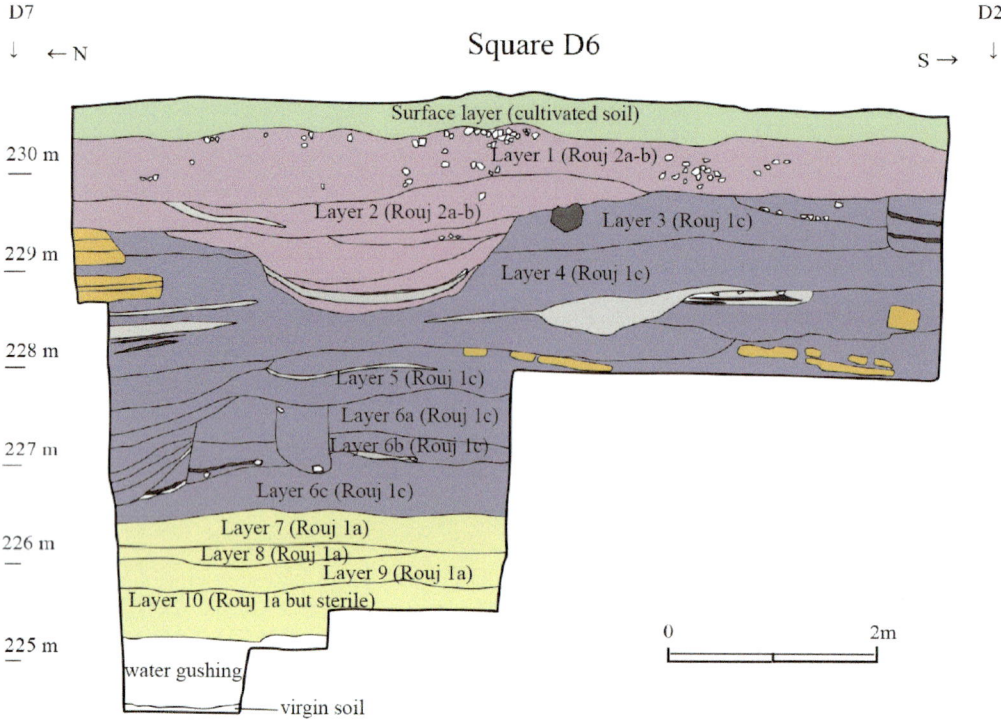

Figure 3-3. Square D6, eastern section.

about 0.5-0.9m. We discovered the stone foundation of a rectangular building (Str. 113) in Square D6 in Layer 1 and another row of stones in Square D26d in Layer 1 (Figure 3-4). The area under Str. 113 was packed with hard, reddish clay. This packed area may have been a building platform. The other main structures in Layer 1 are shallow pits full of stones and tannors. The most conspicuous structure of Layer 2 is a large expanse of stone floor in the northeastern corner of Square D26 (Str. 175), measuring approximately 5 × 4m (Figure 3-5). This floor consists of angular limestone, and its surface is extremely bumpy and unsuitable for living. Some animal bones were found in this structure. Thus, it seems that this structure's function might have been related to butchering meat or tanning hides, and that the stone floor's function might have been related to draining.

We continued digging in Square D6 below Layer 2. We found thick Rouj 1c deposits about 3.2m thick in Square D6 (Layers 3 to 6). Layer 3 produced many small circular areas consisting of stones (Figure 3-6). These circular areas contain ash and animal bones, but the stones themselves are not burnt. We believe that they were used for butchering and cooking. We also found tannors and hearths in Layer 3. Although we discovered a fragmented pisé wall and a row of stones, traces of residential buildings were relatively faint in Layer 3. We continued digging in the eastern half of Square D6 from Layer 4. Layer 4 produced pisé walls, clustered stones, shallow ash pits, and infant burials (Figure 3-7).

We found two solid stone foundations of buildings in Layer 5 (Figure 3-8a, b). Although the western half of the buildings were out of the excavated squares, both buildings (Strs. 215 and 244) may have had rectangular plans. They were built side by side, facing the same direction. Str. 244 is probably a multiple-roomed building that stretches to the south. We also discovered a cache of flints, consisting of 83 blade blanks for sickle elements, at the northeastern corner of the southern room of Str. 244 (Figure 3-8c, Tsuneki et al. 1999: Pl. 2, 7). Considering the place of their discovery, the blades were probably brought into the building and buried under the floor. This is an exciting finding because we can reconstruct blade-flaking techniques from these blades (Arimura 2020: 91-94). The number of blade blanks could produce dozens of sickles, and therefore this deposit was too large to be consumed by one domestic family. Therefore, it seems that the cache was prepared for community consumption.

We also found some buried infants and children among the buildings and other facilities in Layers 4 and 5. They are Strs. 211, 216, 220, 232, 234, 242 and 411 (Figure 3-7, 8a, 9). Str. 211 is a perinatal burial discovered in Layer 4. The remains were not well-preserved and the original burial posture was not fixed. Str. 216 is the burial of a child about four years of age discovered in the eastern part of Square D6b-d in Layer 4. The child was buried in a flexed position, lying on its left side, and its arms held a bent knee. The body lies north-south, with its head pointing north and facing east. Str. 220 is the burial of an infant discovered below the burnt soil, probably

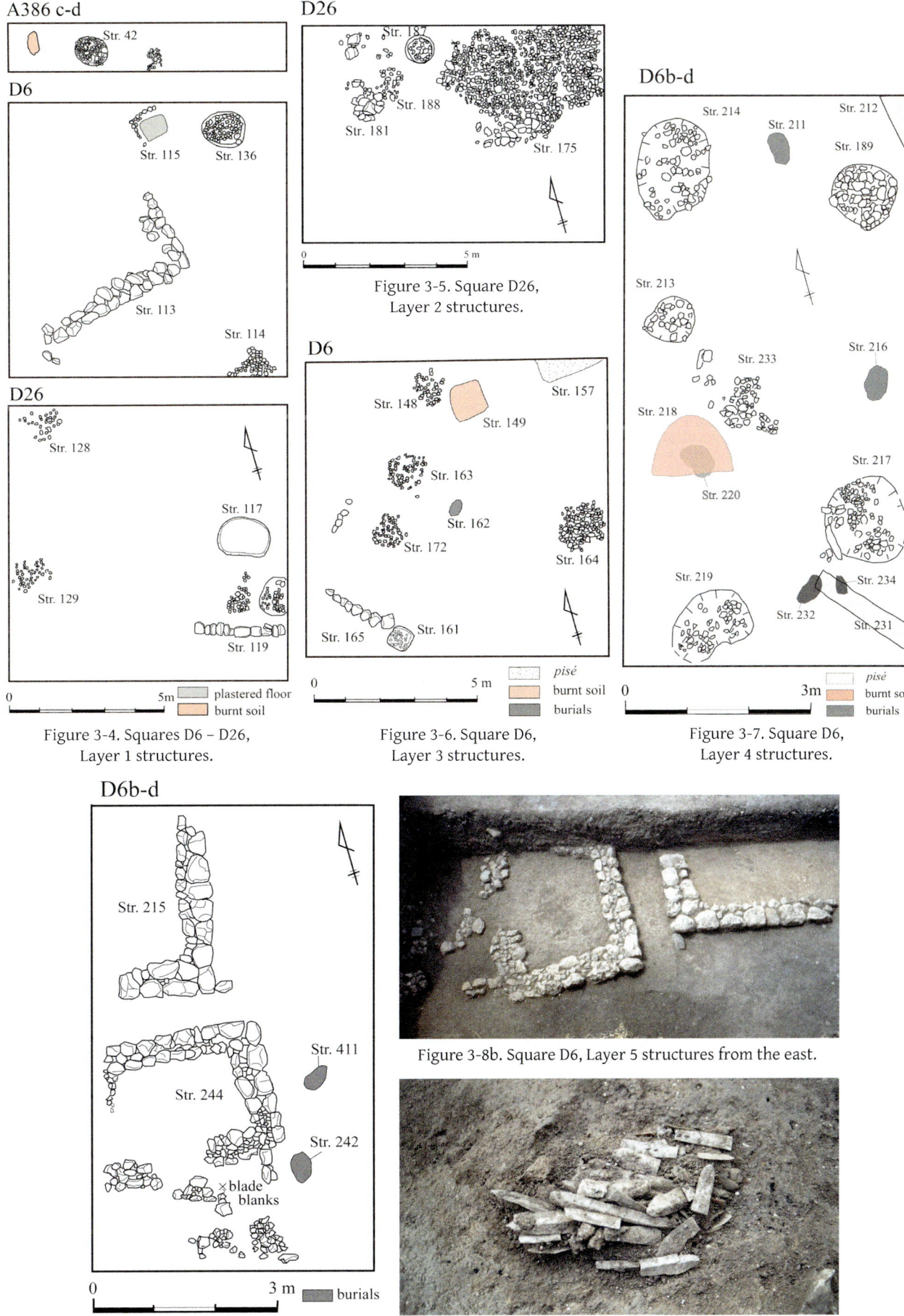

A386 c-d

D6

D26

D26

D6

D6b-d

D6b-d

Figure 3-4. Squares D6 – D26, Layer 1 structures.

Figure 3-5. Square D26, Layer 2 structures.

Figure 3-6. Square D6, Layer 3 structures.

Figure 3-7. Square D6, Layer 4 structures.

Figure 3-8a. Square D6, Layer 5 structures

Figure 3-8b. Square D6, Layer 5 structures from the east.

Figure 3-8c. A cache of blade blanks from the west.

Str. 216   Str. 220   Str. 232

Str. 242   Str. 411

Figure 3-9. Square D6, Layers 4 and 5 burials.

tannor (Str. 218) in Square D6d in Layer 4. Though disturbed, the infant seemed to have been buried in a flexed position, lying on its right side. The burial pit measured 0.85 x 0.55m and the body lies southeast-northwest, with its head pointing southeast and facing northeast. A large number of flint and obsidian blades and flakes were discovered above the lower half of the body – it is possible that these were buried along with this small child. We discovered two more burials (Strs. 232 and 234) side by side below the pisé wall (Str. 231) in the southeastern part of Square D6d in Layer 4. The child buried in Str. 232 was about four years old, and the child buried in Str. 234 was perinatal. Both of them were buried in a flexed position on their left side, and both bodies lay north-south. The head of the child buried in Str. 232 points northeast and the head of the child buried in Str. 234 points north. The former faces southeast and the latter east. No grave goods were discovered with Str. 232. However, we discovered a flint point with a missing tip in front of Str. 234. Strs. 242 and 411 are the burials discovered east of the foundation of Building Str. 244 in Layer 5. Str. 242 contains the burial

of a child aged four or five years old in the eastern part of Square D6d in Layer 5. This child is lying on its left side, was bent and buried, and its body lies south-north. There were no grave goods found with this burial. Str. 411 is a small infant burial. It was located ca. 1.5m north of Str. 242.

All of these infants and children located near buildings and other facilities in Layers 4 and 5 were buried in flexed positions and laid on one side. Therefore, we presume that in the Late Pre-Pottery Neolithic B period at Tell el-Kerkh, people buried perinatal babies and children up to five or six years old near residential buildings and courtyards.

Early PPNB layers (Layers 7 to 10) about 1.6m thick had accumulated between the Rouj 1c layers and the virgin soil at 224.5m asl. We identified these layers as belonging to the Rouj 1a period (Figure 3-3). In the lower layers below Layer 5, we reduced the size of the excavation area to 3 × 3m. We detected no building remains in Layers 6-10 except for hearths and ash pits.

Figure 3-10. Square D6, northern section and Aswad points discovered from Layers 7-10.

Therefore, we did not find any good or Early PPNB architectural remains in Square D6. However, Layers 7 to 9 produced a good amount of lithic and other objects that could be identified as belonging to the EPPNB, the oldest phase of the Rouj Basin Neolithic chronology to date. Aswad points are among the most eloquent lithics found here, and indicate the existence of EPPNB deposits (Figure 3-10). These EPPNB layers are among the oldest Neolithic cultural deposits discovered in northwest Syria and provide a lot of information about Neolithization in this region (Tsuneki *et al.* 2006, Arimura 2020). No remains were excavated below an altitude of 224.5m, indicating that we reached the virgin soil. Groundwater also sprang near this altitude.

Square A318

We set a 5 × 5m trench in Square A318d to investigate the northern frontier of the LPPNB and early PN settlement. We excavated only the top two layers, digging 0.6-0.8m from the tell's surface (Figure 3-11). After removing the surface soil, we directly encountered Layer 1 building structures with burnt mud plastering (Figure 3-12). These buildings have a rectangular plan with pisé walls approximately 0.9m wide. We discovered some notable objects on the mud plastering floor, including a frog-shaped stone pendant, an ironstone axe, and a small female figurine (Figure 3-13).

Layer 2 produced many stone clusters, including broad scattering of limestone pieces and small circles of limestone (Figure 3-14). We presume that these might represent cooking facilities, draining places, or disposal areas.

Layer 1 produced only five small potsherds, and Layer 2 produced three potsherds. These layers did not include any potsherds that could help us date the remains. Some of them seem to be Neolithic potsherds, but there are no obvious Rouj 2 potsherds. By contrast, we found a large number of flints, some obsidian, and many animal bones in both layers. Byblos and Ugarit-type points

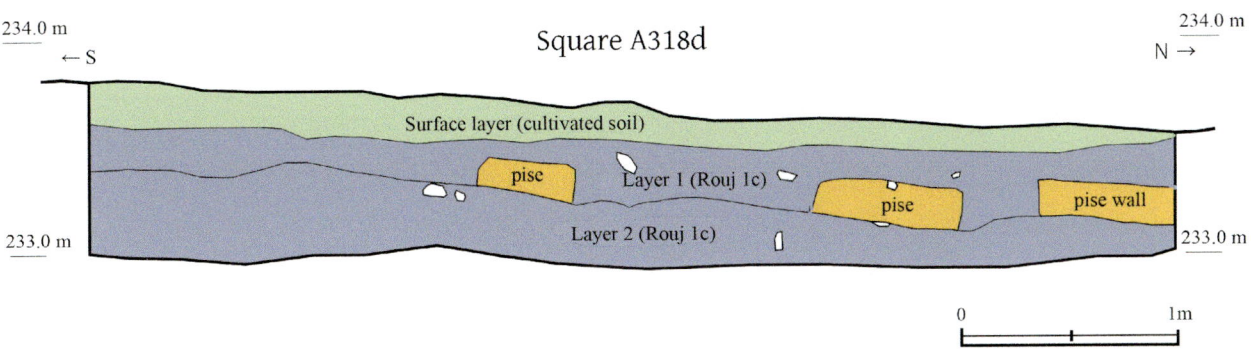

234.0 m
← S

Square A318d

234.0 m
N →

Surface layer (cultivated soil)

pise
Layer 1 (Rouj 1c)
pise
pise wall

Layer 2 (Rouj 1c)

233.0 m

233.0 m

0   1m

Figure 3-11. Square A318d, western section.

Figure 3-12. Square A318d, Layer 1 structures from the west.

a. Frog shaped peridotite pendant.

b. Ironstone axe.

c. Female figurine.

Figure 3-13. Objects discovered from Layer 1,
Square A318d.

predominated here, and we found no Amuq points. We also found conspicuously large blades detached from the naviform cores. All these characteristics indicate that Layers 1 and 2 of Square A318d might date to the Rouj 1c (Late PPNB) period.

Square B230

This is one of the northernmost trenches. It measured 2 × 1m and was located in Square 230d along the middle axis between Grids B and E (Figure 3-15). Below the surface cultivated soil layer, we found the Layer 1 measuring approximately 0.5m thick which is dark brown colored weathered soil. We obtained late Chalcolithic potsherds which date to the fourth millennium BC from Layer 1. Below this layer we found a yellowish-brown layer containing many carbons and limestones. This layer was at least 0.7m thick and produced many potsherds dating to Rouj 2c. On the western side of the trench we encountered a rough row of limestones, which we figured might be a part of the structure. We stopped digging at the limestone level. Layer 1 is a mixed deposit that may have flowed from elsewhere. Layer 2 is solid and contains thick cultural deposits dating to the Rouj 2c period. It is highly possible that the settlement of the Rouj 2c period flourished in this area.

Square B290

We set a 2 × 1m trench 60m south of Square B230. The trench was dug to a depth of 1.8m from the tell surface in Square B290d (Figure 3-16). Layer 1, just below the surface, contained naturally accumulated weathered soil – a mixed, thick, dark-brown layer

Figure 3-14. Square A318d, Layer 2 structures from the south.

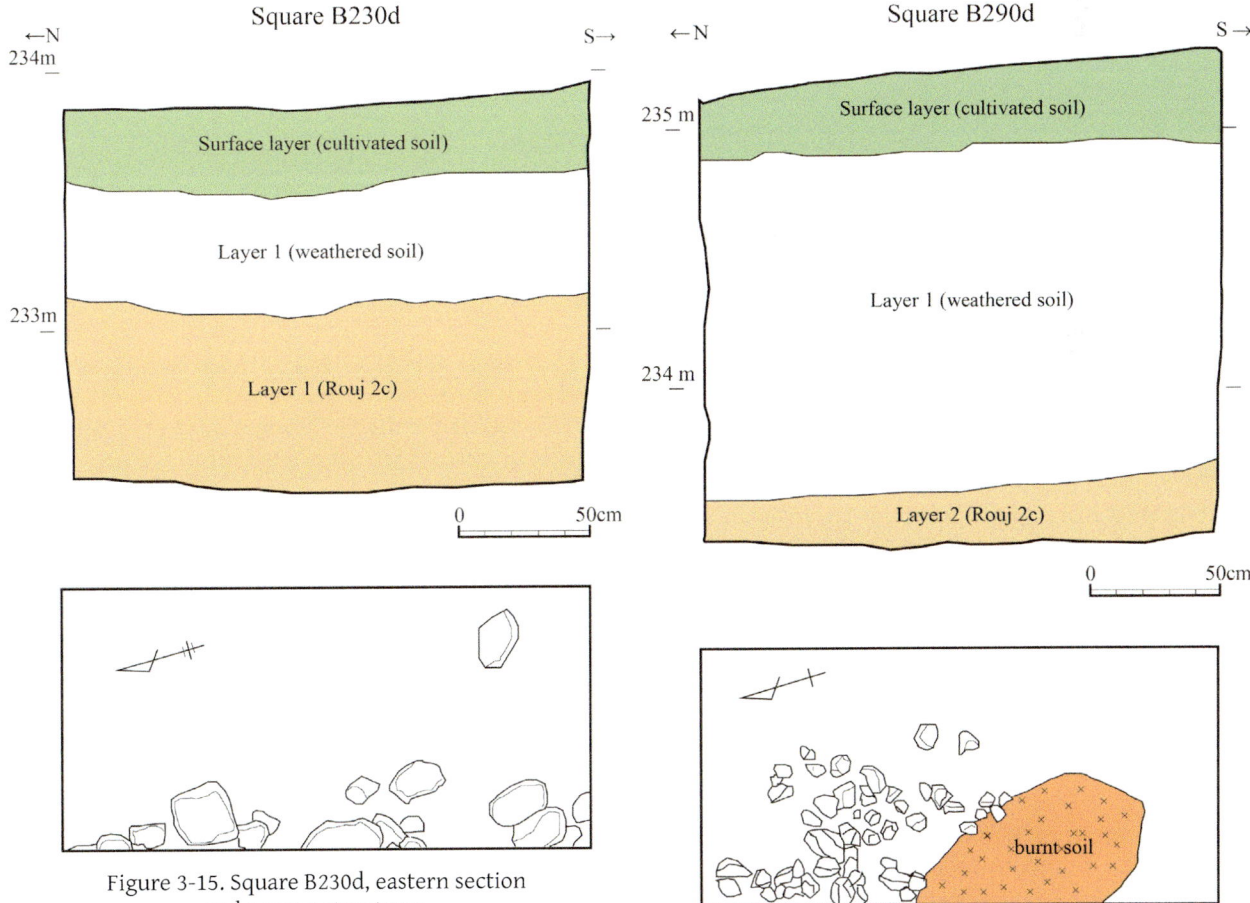

Figure 3-15. Square B230d, eastern section
and Layer 2 structures.

Figure 3-16. Square E290d, eastern section
and Layer 2 structures.

measuring about 1.3m thick. This layer produced both Roman-Byzantine era and Neolithic potsherds. After removing this thick mixed layer, we found a yellowish-brown layer and immediately encountered structures dating to Rouj 2c, including a stone cluster and a hearth. Therefore, we stopped the excavation at this level.

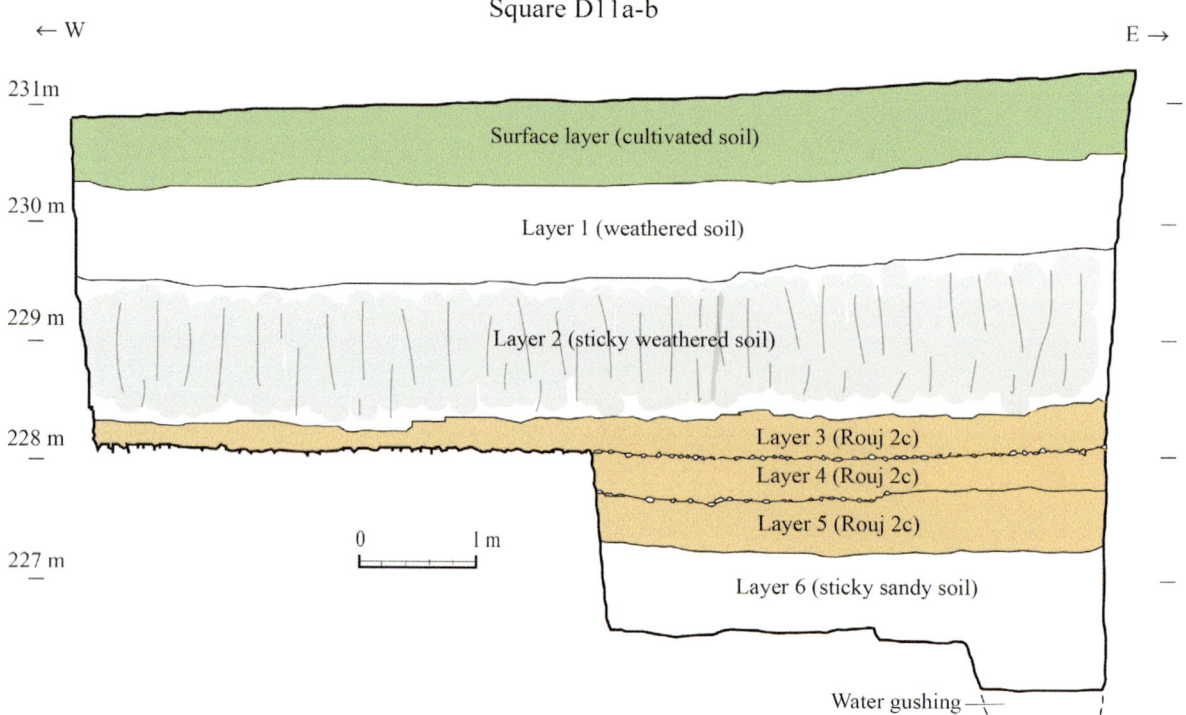

Figure 3-17. Square D11a-b, northern section.

Square D11

A 9 × 2m trench was set in Square D11a-b, 40m east of Square D6. This trench was dug 5.2m deep from the tell surface (Figure 3-17). The uppermost 1.5m, containing both the surface layer of cultivated soil and Layer 1, produced weathered potsherds, flint fragments, and animal bones. Below these layers, we found a sticky, 1.2m thick grayish-brown layer of accumulated soil (Layer 2). These three layers were sterile and produced a small amount of mixed potsherds from the Roman-Byzantine and Neolithic eras. We detected no solid structures in these layers. These layers were probably formed by soil which was carried by wind and water from other parts of the tell and eventually accumulated there. Below these sterile upper layers, we found three continuous occupation layers (Layers 3-5) measuring over 1.2m thick. We discovered pavement consisting of small limestones at the bottom of Layer 3. We also found some stone clusters in Layer 4. These layers produced only materials dating to the Neolithic period, and the Rouj 2c period in particular. Therefore, most of Neolithic cultural deposits here belong to the Rouj 2c period. Below Layer 5 we found an accumulation of sticky, sandy, black-brown soil. We stopped digging at 226m asl, when water gushed out. Therefore, we could not determine whether cultural layers which date to an even earlier time are present below this layer. However, as the water level was similar to that of Square D6, the bottom of this trench seemed to almost reach the virgin soil.

Square D16

We set a 2 × 1m trench in Square D16a along the northern axis of Grids D, E, and F. The upper two layers (Layers 1 and 2) were about 2.5m thick and were similar to the upper two layers of Square D11. These were probably weathered and naturally accumulated soil. Cultural deposits dating to the Rouj 2c era were continuously accumulated below these layers (Figure 3-18). Traces of domestic living, such as ash layers and pisé walls, were detected even in our small trench. To avoid destroying the pisé walls and lime-plastered floor, we stopped digging at approximately 3.5m below the surface.

Square E1

We set a 2 × 1m trench in Square E1a along the northern axis of Grids DEF. After removing the surface layer (cultivated soil), we encountered cultural layers dating to the Rouj 2c period (Figure 3-19). Therefore, the weathered, sterile soil did not accumulate in this part of the tell. We also detected traces of many structures; for example, the floor of the tannor in Layer 1, a plastered floor in Layer 2, and a pisé wall in Layer 3. As these layers produced the Rouj 2c potsherds and other objects, we presume that all of these structures belong to the Rouj 2c period. We stopped digging at 234m asl, about 1.4m below the tell's surface.

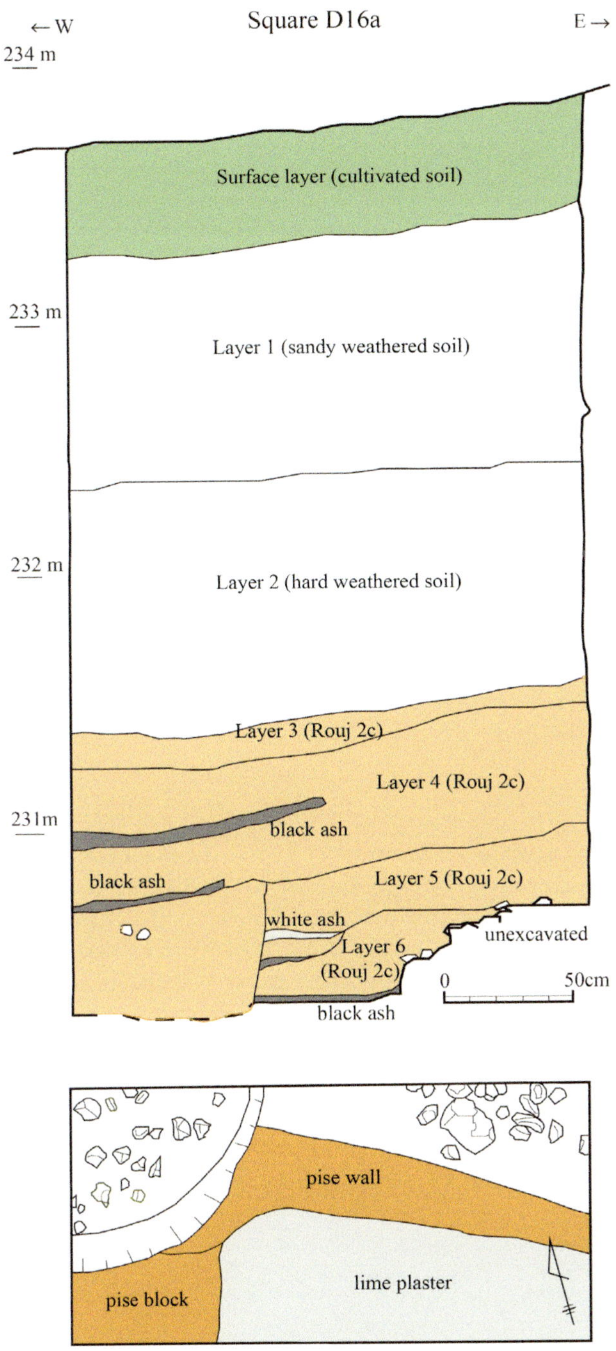

Square D16a

234 m
←W　　Square D16a　　E→

233 m

Surface layer (cultivated soil)

Layer 1 (sandy weathered soil)

232 m

Layer 2 (hard weathered soil)

Layer 3 (Rouj 2c)

Layer 4 (Rouj 2c)

231m

black ash

black ash

Layer 5 (Rouj 2c)

white ash

Layer 6 (Rouj 2c)

unexcavated

black ash

0　　50cm

Square E1a

←W　　Square E1a　　E→

235 m

Surface layer (cultivated soil)

Layer 1 upper (Rouj 2c)

tannor floor

Layer 1 lower (Rouj 2c)

Layer 2 (Rouj 2c)

plaster floor

234 m

Layer 3 (Rouj 2c)

pise wall

0　　50cm

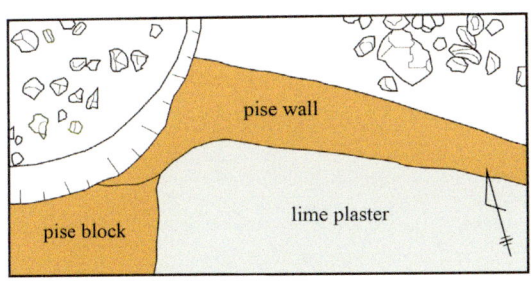

pise wall

pise block

lime plaster

Figure 3-18. Square D16a, northern section and Layer 5 structures.

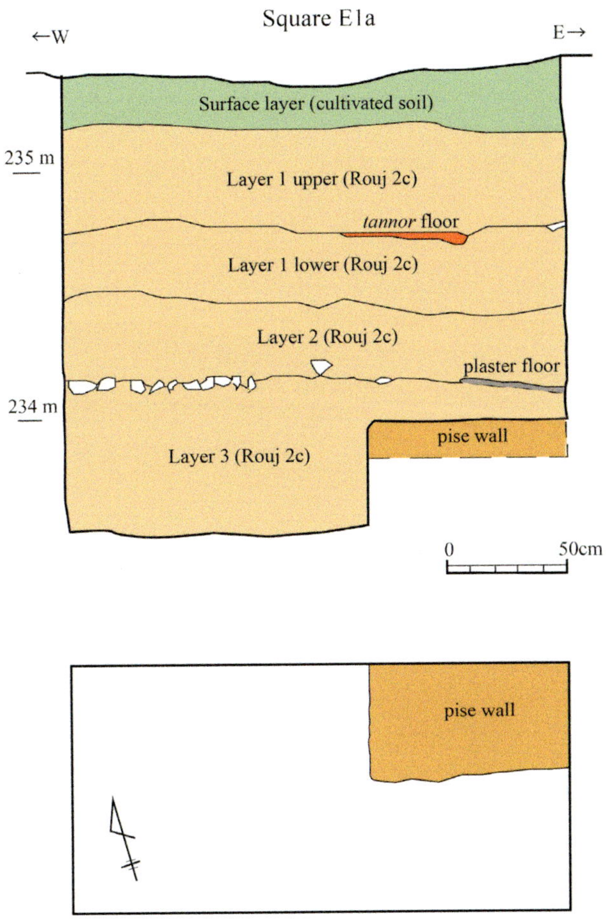

pise wall

Figure 3-19. Square E1a, northern section and Layer 3 structures.

stone foundations (Figure 3-21). The objects obtained from this layer belong to the Rouj 2c period. Although we expected to find more Rouj 2c buildings and structures dating to an even earlier period below Layer 7, excavation of this section was halted and the trench buried for preservation because of the thick sterile deposits above the Rouj 2c settlement in this area. Nevertheless, it is clear that the Rouj 2c settlement expanded into this area and was densely inhabited, and that it was covered with sterile brown soil from other parts of the tell and from outside.

Square F1

This is the easternmost trench in Square F1a. It measured 2 × 1m and was located along the northern axis of Grids D, E, and F at the northeastern foot of Tell Ain el-Kerkh. We found very thick artificially accumulated continuous Neolithic layers at least 3.4m thick just below the surface layer of cultivated soil (Figure 3-22). Some layers produced traces of pisé walls, and we detected ash deposits in many layers. Thus, it appears that Neolithic people were very active in this area. Thus, the area around Square F1 was inhabited by Neolithic people. The excavated materials indicate that

Square E10

We set a 9 × 9m square in the northern terrace of Tell Ain el-Kerkh. Similar to the trenches in Squares B290, D11, and D16, the upper 2.2m deposits of this square (the surface layer through to Layer 5) were quite sterile (Figure 3-20). We discovered no solid structures or mixed objects in these upper deposits. However, the inside of the trench changed drastically in Layer 6. The excavated square was full of structures, such as pisé walls and stone rows. These structures are rectangular residential buildings made of pisé walls on

29

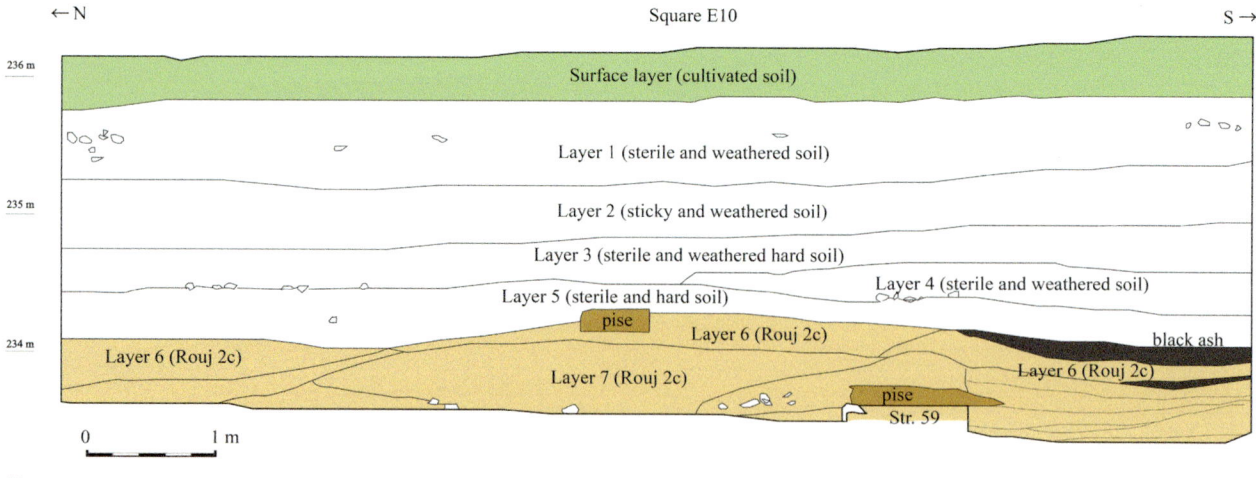

Figure 3-20. Square E10, eastern section.

Figure 3-21. Square E10, Layer 6
structures from the east.

the upper six layers belong to the Rouj 2a-b period, and the lowest two layers belong to the Rouj 1c period. We detected a red-brown fan deposit of soil below Layer 8, which might be virgin soil.

Square E110

This trench in Square E110b is located between the Central Area and Square E10. We discovered Neolithic structures below the surface soil and Layer 1 of weathered soil (Figure 3-23). The trench was full of limestone pebbles, and the structures seems to have been crowded. Thus, we stopped digging 1.2m below the tell's surface. Layer 2 certainly belongs to the Rouj 2c period.

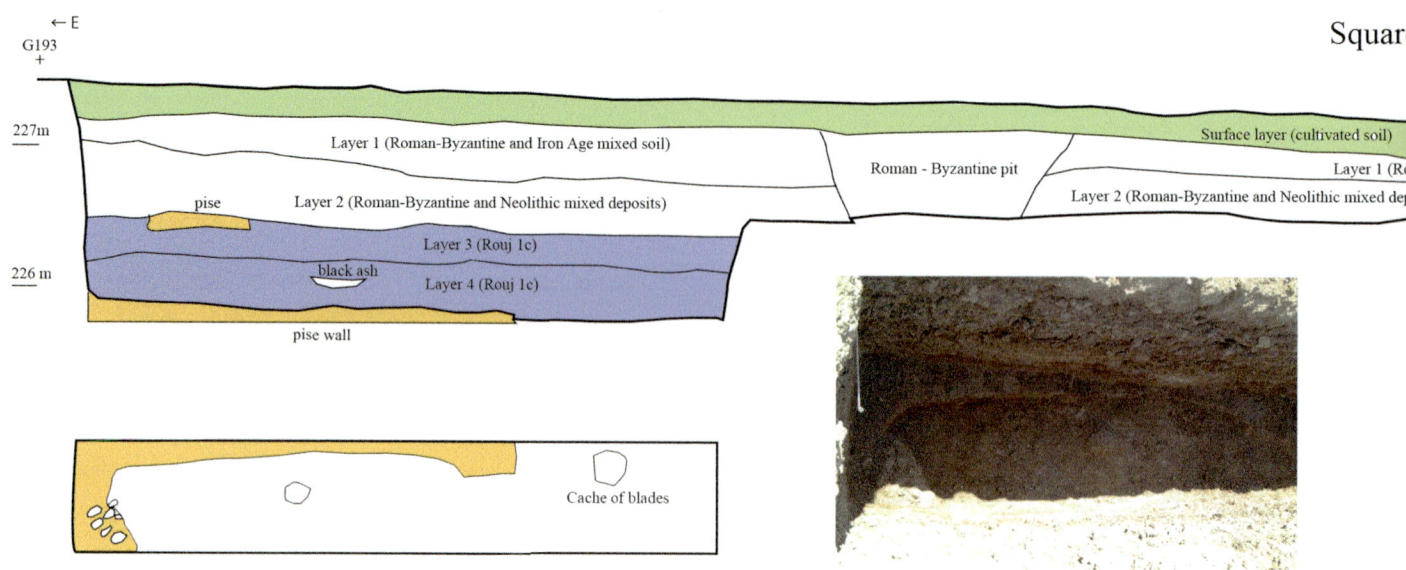

Figure 3-24. Squares G191-G192, southern section

30

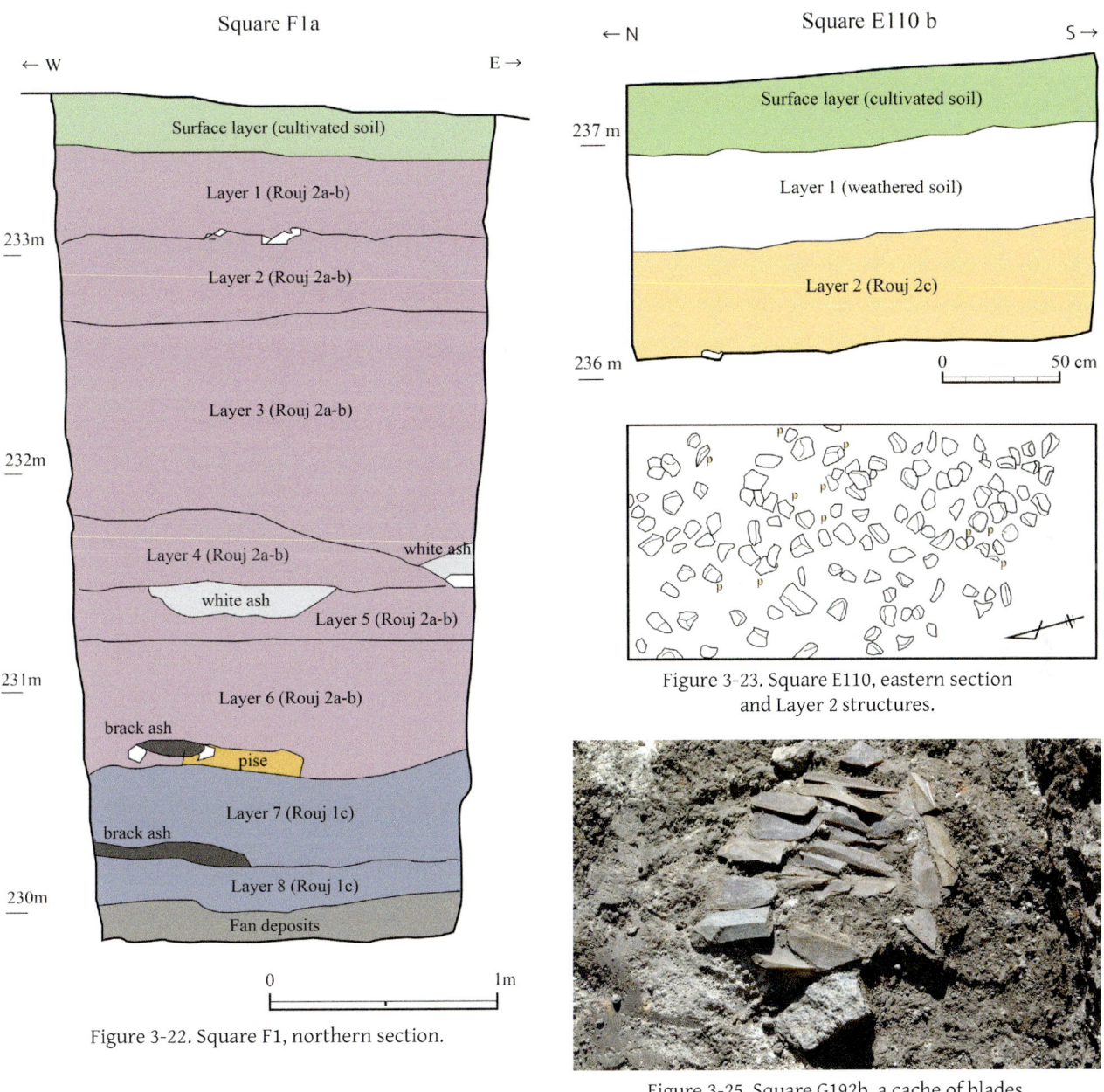

Square F1a

← W   E →

Surface layer (cultivated soil)

Layer 1 (Rouj 2a-b)

233m

Layer 2 (Rouj 2a-b)

Layer 3 (Rouj 2a-b)

232m

Layer 4 (Rouj 2a-b)   white ash

white ash   Layer 5 (Rouj 2a-b)

231m

Layer 6 (Rouj 2a-b)

brack ash

pise

Layer 7 (Rouj 1c)

brack ash

Layer 8 (Rouj 1c)

230m

Fan deposits

0   1m

Figure 3-22. Square F1, northern section.

Square E110 b

← N   S →

237 m

Surface layer (cultivated soil)

Layer 1 (weathered soil)

Layer 2 (Rouj 2c)

236 m

0   50 cm

Figure 3-23. Square E110, eastern section
and Layer 2 structures.

Figure 3-25. Square G192b, a cache of blades.

191-G192

92

W →
G191
+

zantine and Iron Age mixed soil)

Surface layer (cultivated soil)

Roman - Byzantine pit   Layer 1 (Roman-Byzantin)

0   5 m

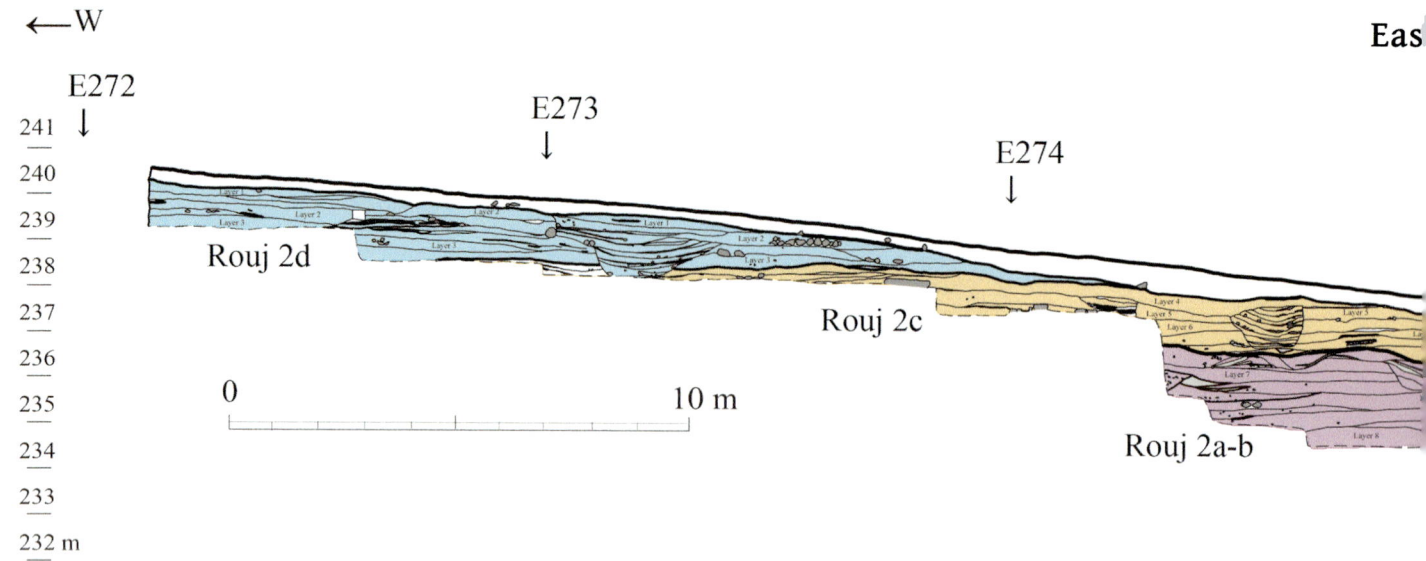

← W

E272
241 ↓
240
239
238
237
236
235
234
233
232 m

E273
↓

E274
↓

Eas

Rouj 2d

Rouj 2c

Rouj 2a-b

0   10 m

Figure 3-26. East Trench, northern sectio

Squares G191 and G192

We prepared a 1 × 20m trench in the southwestern part of the tell – that is, Squares G191a and b and Squares G192a and b – in order to look for the limit of the Neolithic settlement between Tell el-Kerkh 2 and Tell Ain el-Kerkh. The trench in Squares G 191a was only about 60cm deep, to the bottom of Layer 1, and the trench in Squares G192b was dug down to Layer 4, approximately 1.5m below the surface (Figure 3-24). The top layer (between the surface and 0.4m deep) produced large amounts of Roman-Byzantine era potsherds, which were scattered from the southern summit of Tell Ain el-Kerkh. Byzantine coins and Iron

Figure 3-27a. Square E273, Str. 602-605
from the east (Layer 2).

Figure 3-27b. Square E273, Strs. 623-624
from the north (Layer 4).

Figure 3-27c. Square E274, Strs. 657, 659, 660, 662
from the northwest (Layer 8).

Trench   E⟶

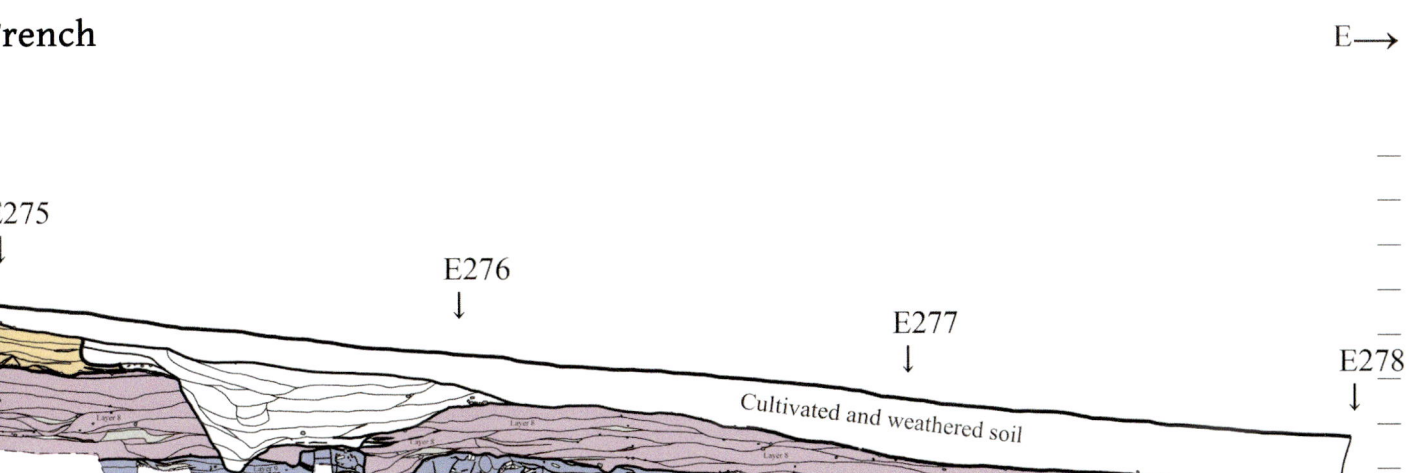

E275   E276   E277   E278

Cultivated and weathered soil

Rouj 1c   Rouj 2a-b   Rouj 1c

Age style bronze fibula were also discovered in Layer 1.

In contrast, we collected very few potsherds below Layer 2. Roman-Byzantine and Neolithic potsherds were mixed in Layer 2, and the potsherds disappeared completely in Layers 3 and 4. These layers contained a large number of chipped stones and animal bones. We also discovered a few diagnostic flint tools, most of them with relatively large blades and flakes, in this layer. We encountered broken pisé walls and a stone concentration in Layer 3 and red pisé walls in Layer 4. Our most striking finding here was a deposit of flint blades in Layer 4 of Square G192b.

Figure 3-28a. Squares E275-E276, Str. 655 from the west (Layer 9).

Figure 3-28b. Str. 655, from the southeast.

Figure 3-28c. Str. 655 from the south.

Figure 3-29. One of the bins facilitated in Str. 655 produced many mud shell beads.

Thirty-one blades were bare in the same direction in situ (Figure 3-25). All blades, except one, were flaked from the same brown-colored flint core. Most of them are thin, wide, and short blades, and they are by-products of flint blade knapping. They seem to have been packed in a sack and placed there for later use. Although they lack eloquent tools, the presence of chipped stones indicates that Layers 3 and 4 belong to the Rouj 1c period, that is, the Late PPNB period. Therefore, the Rouj 1c settlement at Tell Ain el-Kerkh extended in the western direction far beyond the limit of the visible artificial mound. We stopped our digging at Layer 4 because we did not want to break the Neolithic pisé walls in this layer. Therefore, we did not reach the virgin soil in this trench.

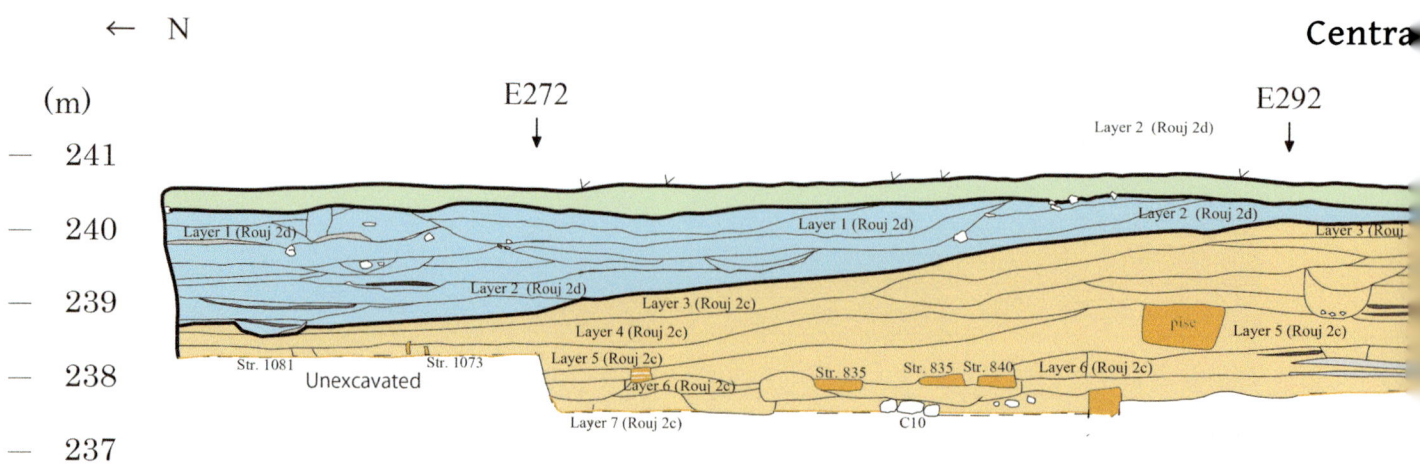

Figure 3-30. Central Area, Squares E251-E271-E-291-E311, eastern section

Tell el-Kerkh 2 Test Pit A

This test pit (TP-A) was set on the summit of Tell el-Kerkh 2 in 1992. The TP-A measured 5 × 5m and was dug down to virgin soil, 4.8m from the tell's surface (Iwasaki and Tsuneki 2003: 48; Fig. 15). The deposits were divided into 12 layers. Layers 1 to 4 (about 1 to 1.2m thick) belong to the Rouj 2b period. Layers 5 to 6 (about 1.0m thick) belong to the Rouj 2a period. Layers 7 to 12 (between 2.2 and 2.6m thick) belong to the Rouj 1c period. As mentioned before, the chronology for Rouj 1c, 2a, and 2b was established largely on the excavation results of this TP-A (Iwasaki and Tsuneki 2003).

East Trench (Squares E272, E273, E274, E275, E276, and E277)

This long trench was set on the eastern slope of Tell Ain el-Kerkh, just east of the Central Area. It was 2.5m wide and 60m long and divided into six squares, E272 to E277, following Tell el-Kerkh's grid system. Each square was dug to a depth of approximately 1.4 to 3.6m from the tell's surface (Figure 3-26). The cultural deposits were divided into nine layers. Each area of the step trench was limited, and each step trench produced a few imposed layers. A sterile surface layer, which seems to have been driven and accumulated by wind and agricultural activities, was randomly distributed throughout the trench. Removing this surface layer revealed superimposed Rouj 2d buildings in Layers 1 to 3 – namely, a series of tannors and fireplaces with stone foundations of rectangular and plastered floors (Figure 3-27a). As Layer 3 disappeared in Square E274, we presume that the Rouj 2d era settlement extended to this point.

The lower layers, Layers 4–6, produced a series of buildings dating to the Rouj 2c period (Figure 3-27b). These layers were cut by a large, post-Neolithic pit in Square E275 and disappeared east of this square. Layers 7 and 8 belong to the Rouj 2a-b period (Figure 3-27c) and sometimes reach a thickness of nearly 2m, whereas Layer 8 disappeared at the eastern end of the trench. Layer 9, the Rouj 1c layer, appeared in Squares E275 to E277. Some impressive buildings were discovered in this layer, including a burnt, but well-preserved storehouse (Str. 655) at the bottom of Squares E275 and E276 (Figure 3-28). The storehouse was made with pisé walls. It measured 5.6m in length and consists of many small rectangular rooms, each containing large clay bins. At least 14 large clay bins were installed in the storehouse, and one of the bins contained nearly 200 pieces of rare mussel beads (fossil species: *Viviparus syriacus*. According to the appraisal of Dr. Taiji Kurozumi) (Figure 3-29). This evidence suggests that the storehouse was used communally, that the Rouj 1c settlement must continue further east, and that the extent of the Rouj 1c settlement is not only large but that it also contained complex societies.

Central Area (Squares E251, E270, E271, E290, E291, E310 and E311)

At the northern summit of Tell Ain el-Kerkh, we set six 10 x 10m squares and dug with leaving section banks to a depth of about 2.2-3.5m from the tell's surface. We later added one 10 × 5m square (Excavation range is exactly 9.5 × 4.5m) (Square E251c-d) to these excavated squares in an attempt to detect the northern boundary of the Neolithic Cemetery. We named these excavated squares the 'Central Area,' and encountered more than seven building layers here. Layers 1 and 2 belong to the

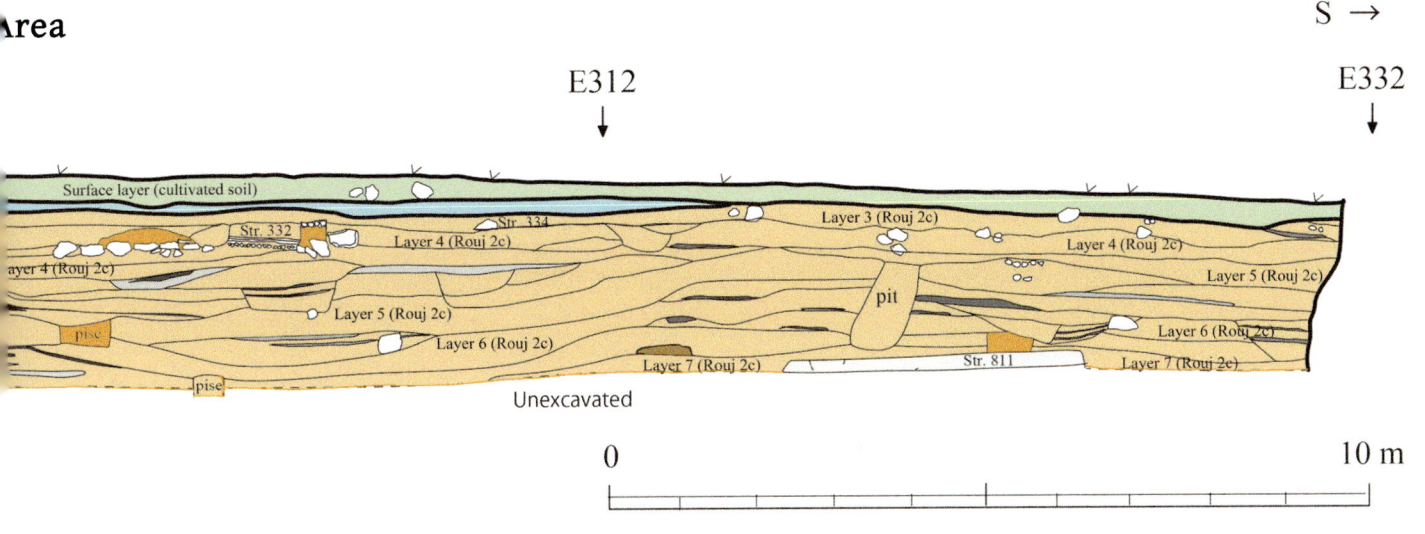

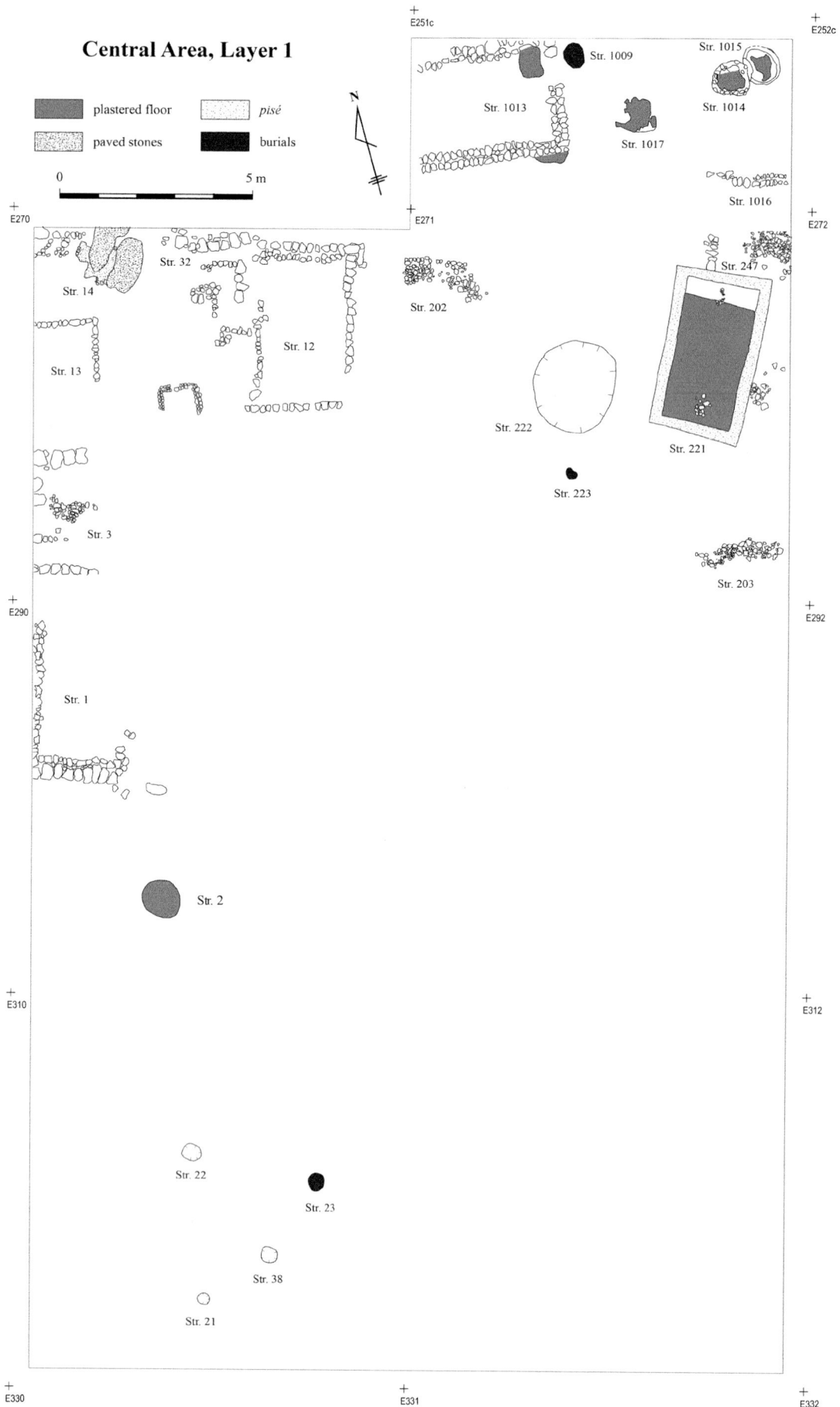

Central Area, Layer 1

plastered floor　　　pisé

paved stones　　　burials

0　　　　　　5 m

N

Str. 1009

Str. 1015

Str. 1013

Str. 1014

Str. 1017

Str. 1016

Str. 32

Str. 14

Str. 247

Str. 202

Str. 12

Str. 13

Str. 222

Str. 221

Str. 3

Str. 223

Str. 203

Str. 1

Str. 2

Str. 22

Str. 23

Str. 38

Str. 21

E251c
E252c
E270
E271
E272
E290
E292
E310
E312
E330
E331
E332

Figure 3-31. Central Area, Layer 1 structures.

Rouj 2d period and were about 0.3 to 1.5m thick. Layers 3 to 7 belong to the Rouj 2c period, and were over 2 m thick (Figure 3-30).[1] The deposits in Layers 1 and 2 are relatively thick in the northern end of the Central Area (Squares E251, E270, and E271) but thin out rapidly toward the southern end. The layers are less than 0.5m thick in Squares E291 and E311. This finding is thought to reflect the miniaturization of Neolithic settlements during the Rouj 2d period.

The building structures detected in Layer 1 were distributed densely in the northern part of the Central Area (Figure 3-31). Except for a few Hellenistic burials, which were found just below the surface (see Tsuneki *et al.* 1997, 2000), the Layer 1 and all of other cultural layers below the surface layer belong to the Neolithic period. There is no doubt that most of the artificial mound of Tell Ain el-Kerkh belongs to the Neolithic period, and that thick Neolithic layers still remain below the excavated squares.

Layer 1 structures

The building remains of Layer 1 were mostly damaged by the rebuilding activities discovered in the successive layers. Most of the structures were discovered in the thick Rouj 2d deposits in the northern part of Central Area, i.e., Squares E251, E270 and E271 (Figure 3-31). In many cases, we can only observe partially preserved rows of stones, which were used as stone foundations of the houses (Strs. 1, 3, 12, 13, 1013). These stone foundations indicate that rectangular rooms were constructed during Layer 1. We found a one-roomed pisé building with lime-plastered floor and walls at the northeastern corner of Square E271 (Str. 221) (Figure 3-32). Therefore, most building structures in Layer 1 consist of rectangularly planned one-room residences. We also detected round plastered tannors measuring approximately 1m in diameter and fragments of stone pavements (Strs. 2, 1014, 203, and 247).

The most conspicuous findings in Layer 1 were three ritual pits (Strs. 21, 22, and 38) discovered in Square E310. These consist of small shallow pits full of broken pottery and a few burnt bones (Figures 3-33, 34). We found a pedestal bowl, a cream bowl and a cylindrical necked jar in Str. 21, a pedestal bowl and a cylindrical necked jar in Str. 38, and a shallow bowl and a hole-

Figure 3-32. Str. 221 from the north.

mouthed jar in Str. 22. All of these were restorable pieces and they all seemed to have been intentionally broken and carefully placed in these shallow pits. The red pedestal bowl of Str. 21 was broken into the bowl part and the pedestal part, and then the bowl part was broken again and placed around the pedestal part, which was placed upside down (Figure 3-33: middle, Figure 3-34: top row). The black pedestal bowl of Str. 38 was also broken into two parts, and the bowl and pedestal parts were laid sideways separately (Figure 3-33: left, Figure 3-34: third row). The small, dark-faced burnished (DFBW) shallow bowl of Str. 22 was carefully broken and combined with a larger painted jar like a puzzle ring (Figure 3-33: right, Figure 3-34: bottom row).

These three pits were also filled with carbonized ash and burnt clay. We also discovered a few burnt human infant bones in Str. 22. Although we cannot decisively determine the function of these shallow pits from this evidence, the evidence indicates that they must have been used for ritual purposes, such as making offerings on behalf of the dead. Most of the pottery found in the pits are quite elaborate specimens, especially two pedestal bowls (Figure 3-34: second row) and one cream bowl. These high-quality pieces of pottery also indicate

---

[1] Some of the layers in the Central Area have changed since the preliminary reports of the site (Tsuneki *et al.* 1997, 1998, 1999, 2000). We started the excavations at the northern squares of the Central Area in 1997. The Rouj 2d cultural deposits at Squares E 270 and E271 are thick, and we divided them into four building phases at first. However, the Rouj 2d cultural deposits in the southern squares are very thin, and we summarized that the Rouj 2d deposits belonged to two distinct phases at last. Therefore, we attributed Layers 1 and 2 to the Rouj 2d period and Layers 3 to 7 to the Rouj 2c period. The layers to which each structure belong to have been reexamined and changed along with the excavated objects.

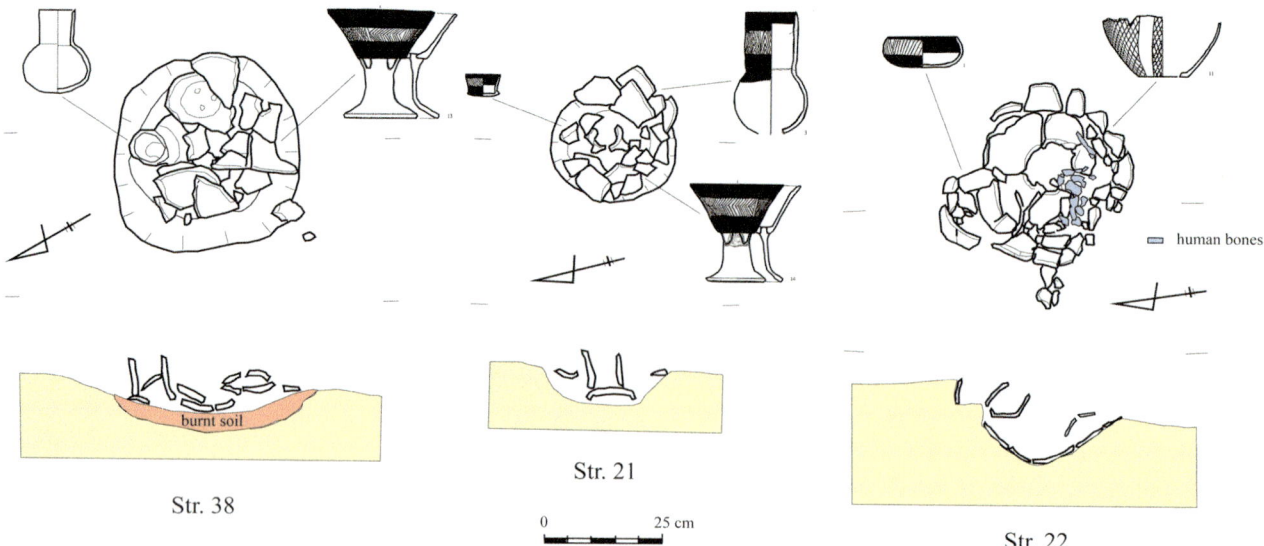

Figure 3-33. Three ritual pits (Strs. 21, 22 and 38).

that the pits had a special purpose. The pedestal bowls immediately remind us of similar specimens that were reported in the Tell al-Judaidah excavations in the Amuq Plain by Braidwood *et al.* (1960: Fig. 81). In addition to these three ritual pits, we found one infant burial (Str. 23) near the ritual pits in the same Square E310. This burial contained grave goods, including a small stone vessel which was placed near the skull of the infant (Figure 3-35).

Layer 2 structures

Unlike the Layer 1 structures which we found on the northern side of the Central Area, we discovered structures in Layer 2 throughout the excavation area (Figure 3-36). However, the structures' appearance differs between the north and south portions of Central Area. In the northern Squares E270 and E271, the structures' preservation is limited. We identified stone rows running northwest to southeast (Strs. 201 and 206) and the stone foundation of a rectangular-planned multi-chamber building (Str. 24). We also detected circular-planned large tannors with plastered floors on stone pavements here (Strs. 54 and 204).

In southern Squares E291 and E311, we detected the stone foundations of structures which consisted of multiple small rectangular rooms (Strs. 304, 308, and 312; Figure 3-37). We also found a stone row with a fragmented plastered floor (Str. 15) and some tannors and clustered stones on the outside of these stone foundations. The clusters of structures in the southern squares have different main axis directions from the structures of the northern squares. As the structures of the southern cluster produced potsherds dating to both the Rouj 2d and Rouj 2c periods, it is possible that these structures are older than the structures found in the northern cluster.

Some human infant skeletons were discovered at various locations in relation to these stone foundations (Figure 3-38. Str. 35 was found under the stone foundation, Strs. 307, 319, 339, and 320 were discovered within the stone foundation areas, and Strs. 60 and 309 came from just outside the stone foundation area. All the skeletons took a contracted position and none of their burials contained grave goods. One urn burial containing a perinatal skeleton (Str. 19) was discovered near the stone wall of Str. 201.

Layer 3 structures

All the building structures discovered in the Central Area from Layer 3 on down belong to the Rouj 2c period. The most recent deposits from this period were found in Layer 3. In this layer, most of the stone foundations were partially preserved (Figure 3-39). As most of them did not seem to have partition walls, they were probably the foundations of single-roomed rectangular residences (Strs. 17, 311, 314, 334, and 346). Str. 334 contained a square-planned hearth facility along the western wall (Figure 3-40). Str. 346 contained a similar hearth. The structure in Str. 346 was only partially preserved, but it is considered to be the rebuilt structure of the building found in Layer 4 of Str. 332.

We found many tannors in open spaces among the stone foundations – i.e., among the residences. Therefore, the square-planned hearths located inside these rooms seem to have been used for heating and cooking, and the tannors outside the residence seem to have been used for baking bread.

We found some human burials related to the residences in Layer 3. One infant burial (Str. 331) found near the corner of rectangular-planned stone

Str. 21 upper

Str. 21 lower

Pedestal bowl from Str. 21

Pedestal bowl and jar from Str. 38

Str. 38 from the northwest

Str. 38 from the south

Str. 22 upper

Str. 22 lower

Figure 3-34. Three ritual pits (Strs. 21, 22 and 38) and discovered objects.

Figure 3-35. Str. 23 Burial.

foundation (Str. 311) is notable because it was buried with a small DFBW bowl (Figure 3-41), 113 small flat, mostly serpentinite stone beads, and six small blue spherical beads. During the funeral practice, the corpse was covered with a large body fragment of DFBW. Therefore, this corpse seems to have been buried with respect more than other infants, which were buried without grave goods.

Layer 4 structures

The preservation of residential buildings in this layer is not very good, with the exception of Str. 332. Instead of residential structures, we encountered many tannors, fire installations, paved stones, stone clusters, pits, and other domestic facilities in this layer. Layer 4 is composed of two imposed sub-layers, Layer 4a and 4b. Both layers produced similar structures (Figures 3-42, 43). The most well-preserved building among them is Str. 332, northeast of Square E291 in Layer 4a. This building is a rectangular-planned one-room pisé residence with a white lime-plastered floor (Figure 3-44). We observed small round pits on the floor. These small pits produced limestone pebbles, and one of them produced fragments of basalt grinding slabs. These small pits were probably used for storage purposes. We also discovered thick layers of limestone pebbles, about 20cm thick, under the two-stage thick lime plastering (Figure 3-45). The square-planned hearth along the southern wall of Str. 332 was carefully made. Large flat limestone cobbles were paved for the hearth's foundation. Pisé walls in the main room were also constructed on limestone foundations. We also discovered one stamp seal and 47 beads just south of Str. 332. This residence was rebuilt afterward (Str. 346 in Layer 3). Some parts of the western pisé wall were covered with new foundation stones, and the southern wall was rebuilt in a slightly inner position across the hearth.

Besides Str. 332, the residences of this layer were poorly preserved. The main domestic structures here include broken stone foundations (Str. 55), paved stones (Strs. 106, 184, 434, and 444), many large tannors, and large fire installations (Strs. 341, 410, 439) (Figure 3-46), and ash pits. We also found some shallow, circular pits which were filled with animal bones and limestone (e.g., Str. 431) and sometimes filled with broken pottery (Str. 510; Figure 3-47). The stone floorings were probably used as workshops, and shallow pits were either used as dump places or used for ritual purposes. These structures indicate that the Central Area was used for some domestic communal activities instead of personal residential areas during Layer 4.

In this respect, it is quite notable that the northeastern part of the Central Area – i.e., Squares E251 and E271 – continued to be used as communal burial ground or Neolithic outdoor cemetery (Figure 3-48a, b). As we discuss in detail later on, Kerkh Neolithic people made their first outdoor communal cemetery some time after Layer 7. Layer 4 was the last stage of the communal cemetery, and it is believed that burials were performed in spaces in the settlement where people performed common domestic activities (rather than in residences).

However, we did find some deceased (mostly children, but some adults) buried in connection with the residential buildings that we discovered in this layer. For example, we found two adult corpses and one infant body together under the plastered floor of Str. 55 at the southeastern corner of Square 290d. The most well-preserved adult, probably male (Str. 29), was buried in a highly contracted position, with their head bent forward and their knees toward his forehead (Figure 3-49). Although most adults and children were buried in the communal cemetery, some were buried in connection with residences. We were very interested in the differences between their burial places.

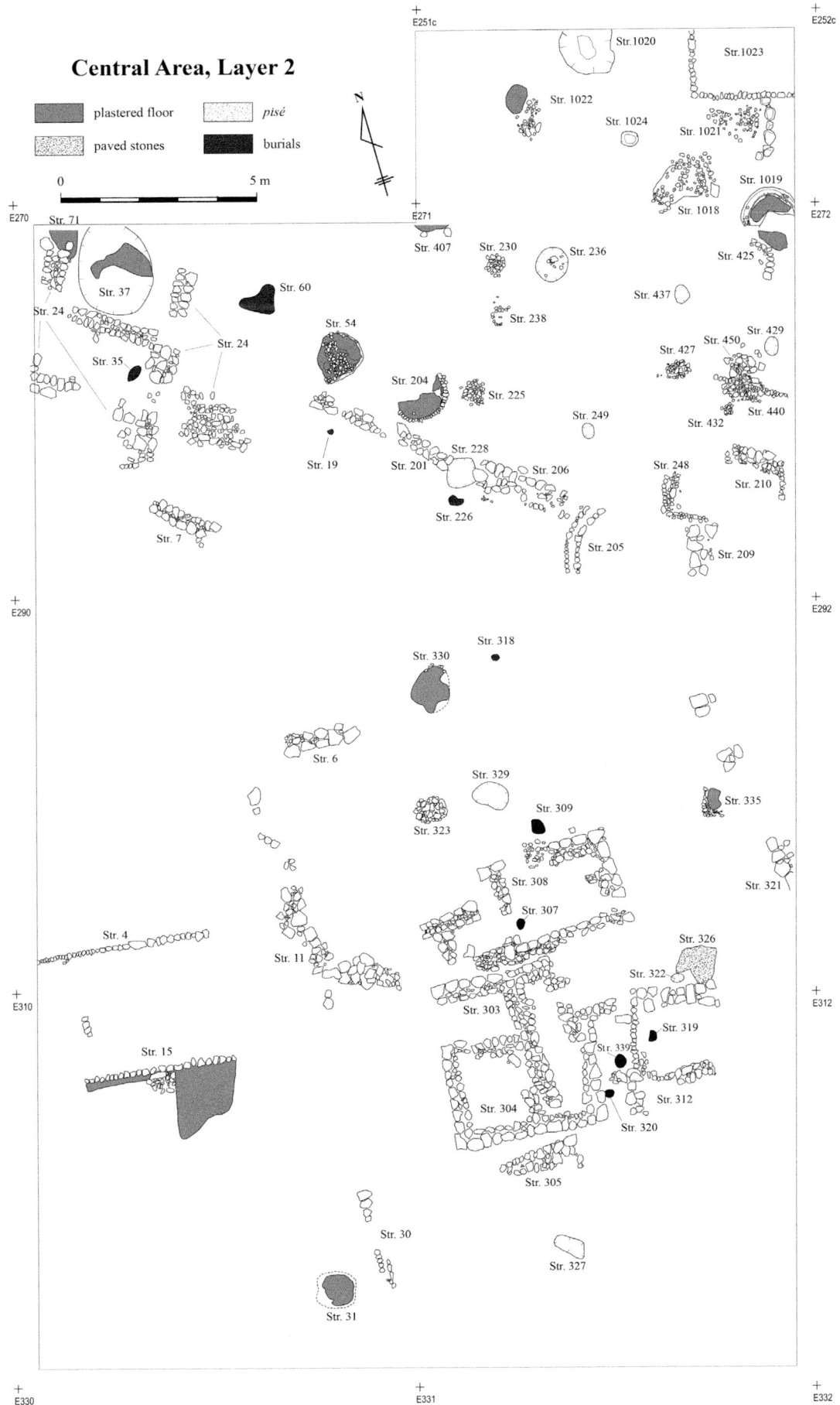

Central Area, Layer 2

Figure 3-36. Central Area, Layer 2 structures.

Figure 3-37. Central Area, Layer 2 southern structures from the north.

Str. 19

Str. 35

Str. 60

Str. 307

Str. 309

Figure 3-38. Infant burials in Layer 2.

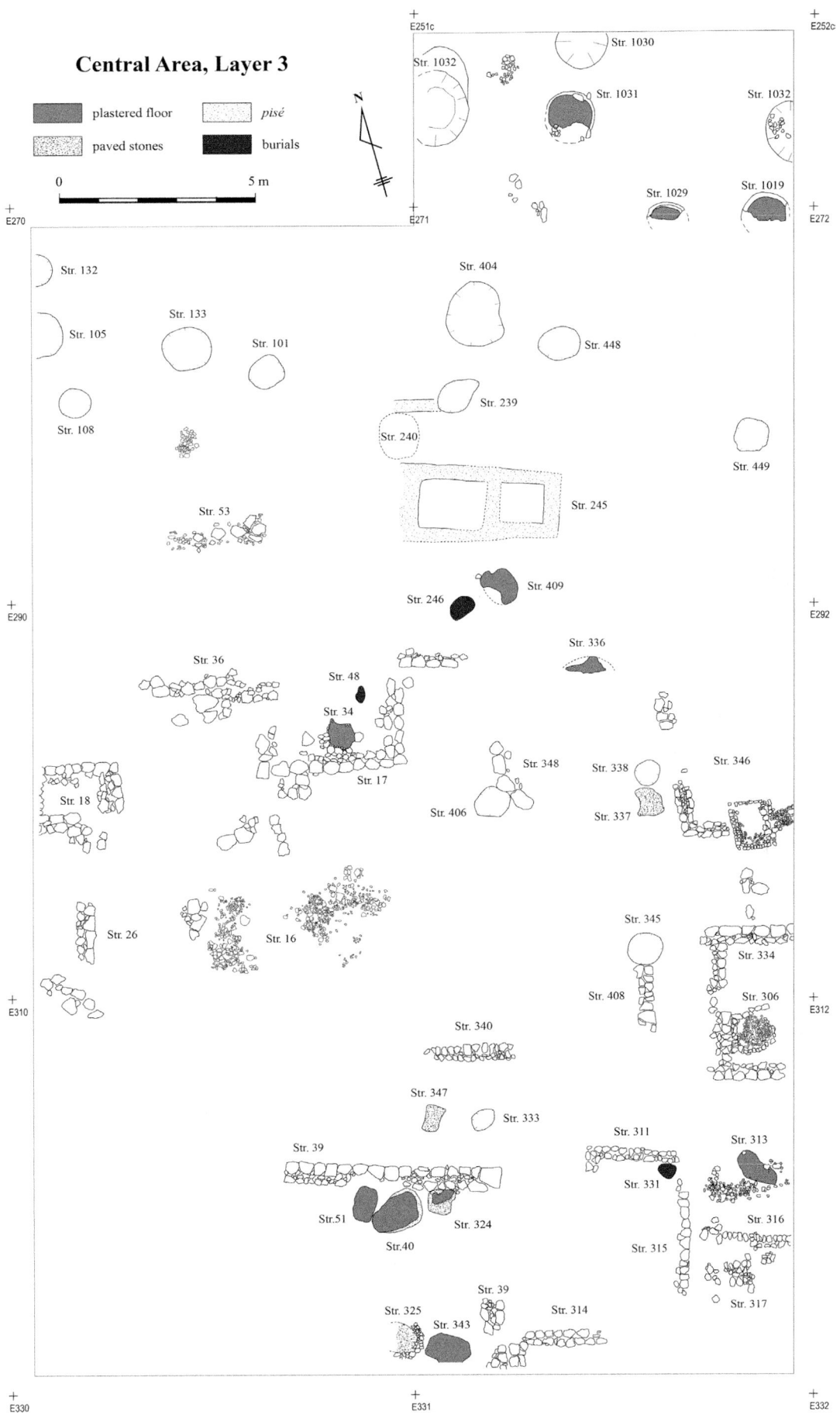

Figure 3-39. Central Area, Layer 3 structures.

Figure 3-40. Str. 334 from the west.

Figure 3-41. Str. 331, an infant burial and grave goods.

Layer 5 structures

The plans and structures of residential buildings found in Layers 5 and 6 are different from those of the upper layers. The buildings in these layers are also better preserved than those in the upper layers. This might be because of the heavy use of plaster in these buildings' construction and the fact that the buildings were frequently burnt after usage.

The common characteristics of these buildings are noteworthy (Figures 3-50, 3-51). Residential buildings found in these layers consist of several types of structures. The first type is a large rectangular-planned pisé building with a two-story structure. In this type of building, the first floor is divided into small rooms, which are thought to have been used for domestic purposes, such as storage. The second floor was not divided, and it must have been for residential use with a well-plastered floor. The second type of residential building is a relatively small square-planned one-room building.

Str. 72 discovered in Square E310 is probably the first floor of the first type of residential building (Figure 3-52a, b). It is well preserved because it was completely burnt by fire. This burnt building consisted of a narrow, rectangular room, seven small square rooms and one circular room. The central narrow room (Room 1) measures 3.0 x 1.1m, and its long side walls are made of two rows of square-shaped pisé lumps. The eastern short side wall is made of pebble stones and clay. It seems that this side was open at first and then closed later. A 0.65m wide doorway opens to Room 5 at the western part of the north wall of Room 1. As the floor level of Room 1 is lower than that of Room 5, this doorway is like a step. All the square rooms around Room 1 have small sides about 0.7-1.3m long. Rooms 3, 4, 6, and 7 are paved with pebble stones. The stone floors were covered with layers of black ash. The southern wall of this burnt building is relatively narrow compared to the other walls. We discovered a broken tannor at the southeastern corner of Room 7. It is probable

Central Area, Layer 4a

plastered floor

paved stones

pisé

burials

0   5 m

N

Figure 3-42. Central Area, Layer 4a structures.

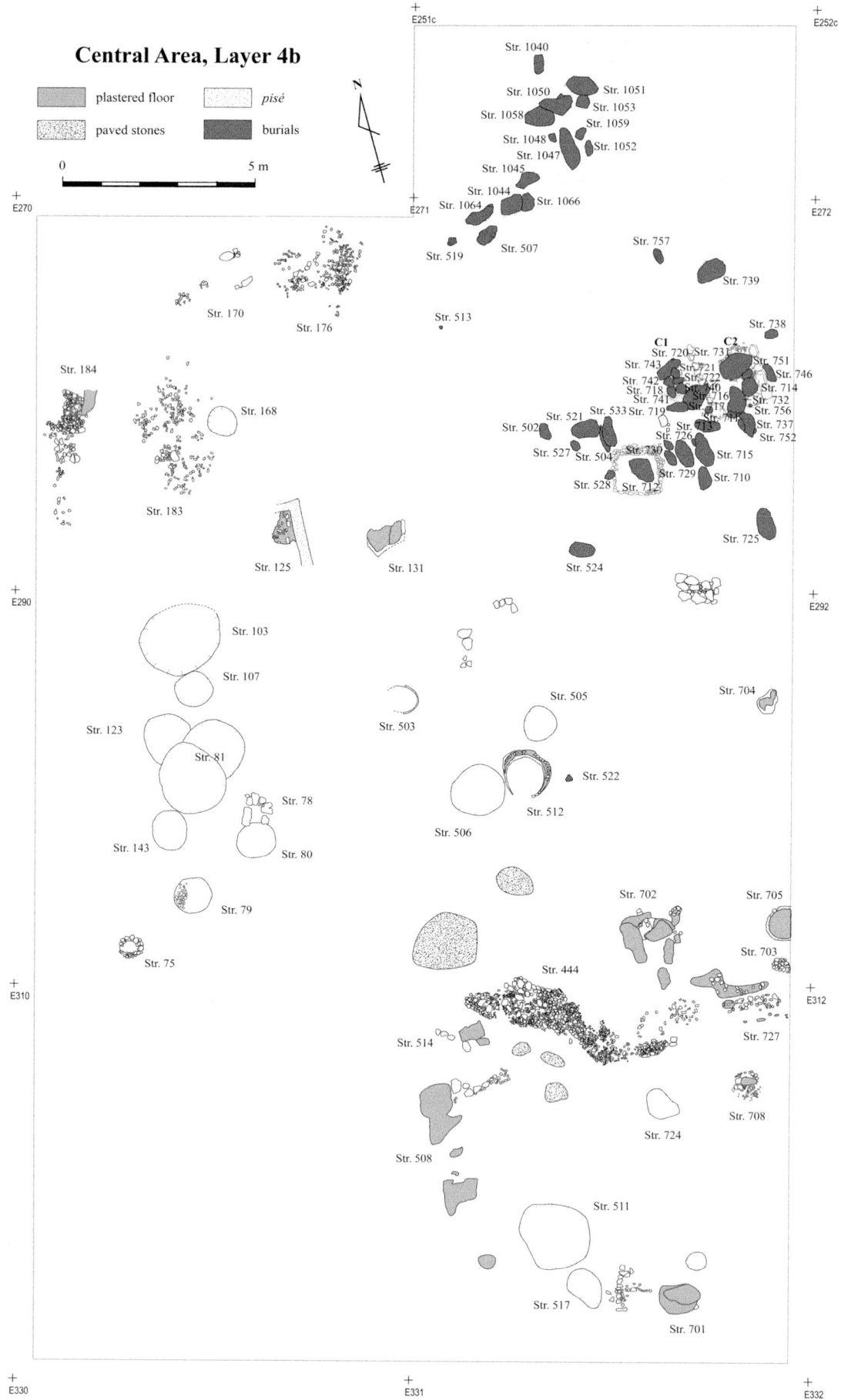

Figure 3-43. Central Area, Layer 4b structures.

Figure 3-44. Str. 332 from the north.

Figure 3-45. Str. 332, thick lime plastering on stone

Figure 3-46. Str. 341, tannor.

Figure 3-47. Str. 510 from the south.

Figure 3-48a. Square E271, cemetery of Layer 4 from the south.

Figure 3-48b. Square E251, cemetery of Layer 4-5 from the west.

Figure 3-49. Str. 29 Burial.

that this tannor was the cause of the fire because it was heavily burnt. Although the western part of this building was severely burnt, the eastern part was not burnt. Room 12, at the northeast corner of the building, produced a large complete cow mandible on the floor. It seems that a large cow was butchered elsewhere, and the lower jaw was cut off and placed on the floor of Room 12. Some other animal bones, the pelvis of a small cow, and the ulna of a pig were also found in the same room.

Str. 74 in Square E290c is typical of the second type of residential building. It measures 3 × 2.6m and is made of pisé walls (Figures 3-50, 3-53). This building is characterized by a carefully made lime-plastered floor above a fist-sized layer of stone pavement. The preservation of its pisé wall is poor, but the building might have a 0.6m wide doorway on the eastern part of the northern wall.

We discovered a unique and notable structure in the southern part of the building while removing the floor of Str. 74. This structure was a small square-planned pit (Str. 153) measuring 0.9 × 0.8m and 0.74m deep (Figure 3-54). Its four walls were covered by small limestone, flint pebbles piled up in between 15 and 17 rows, and

Figure 3-50. Central Area, Layer 5 structures.

Figure 3-51. Central Area, Layers 5-6 structures from the north.

a. Under digging.

b. Complete digging.

Figure 3-52. Str. 72 from the west.

its floor was paved with large flat limestones. One skeleton of a human perinatal was discovered in its southwestern corner. It was buried in a contracted position near the top level of the pit. One Amuq-type flint point was placed on the corpse. We also discovered many animal bones in the uppermost layer of the same pit, including one complete six-month-old suid skeleton and a capra horn. The animal bones seemed to have been gathered and buried in the pit. Although we can interpret this structure in various ways, we suppose that it was probably used for a ritual ceremony before the construction of the residence of Str. 74. I have also interpreted it as a ritual structure for a ground-breaking ceremony for the residence in previous publications (Tsuneki 2002).

A square planned one-room residential building (Str. 516) was also located east of Str. 74. Only the northern pisé wall remained of this building, but we could observe that the floor was covered with white lime plaster with sporadic stone spread underneath (Figure 3-55). This plastered floor spreads at least 3 × 3m, almost same size as other one-room buildings.

We detected another pisé building with a layout that differed slightly from the two aforementioned types of residential buildings around the boundary between Squares E270 and E271. This building (Str. 109) had an almost square plan with a side of approximately 6m. It

Figure 3-53. Str. 74 from the north.

consisted of an eastern lime-plastered room and three small rooms on its western side (Figure 3-56a-c). A rough square-planned hearth was built at the eastern end of the lime-plastered room. After removing the thick white lime plastering, we encountered a layer of dense stone pavement. The area of the stone pavement was approximately 4.0 × 2.5m (Figure 3-56b). The stone pavement and plastering were supported by the pisé walls, and the soil was filled between the walls. The extent of supporting walls indicated that the original paved and plastered area measured approximately 5.4 × 4.0m. This paved and plastered area must have been

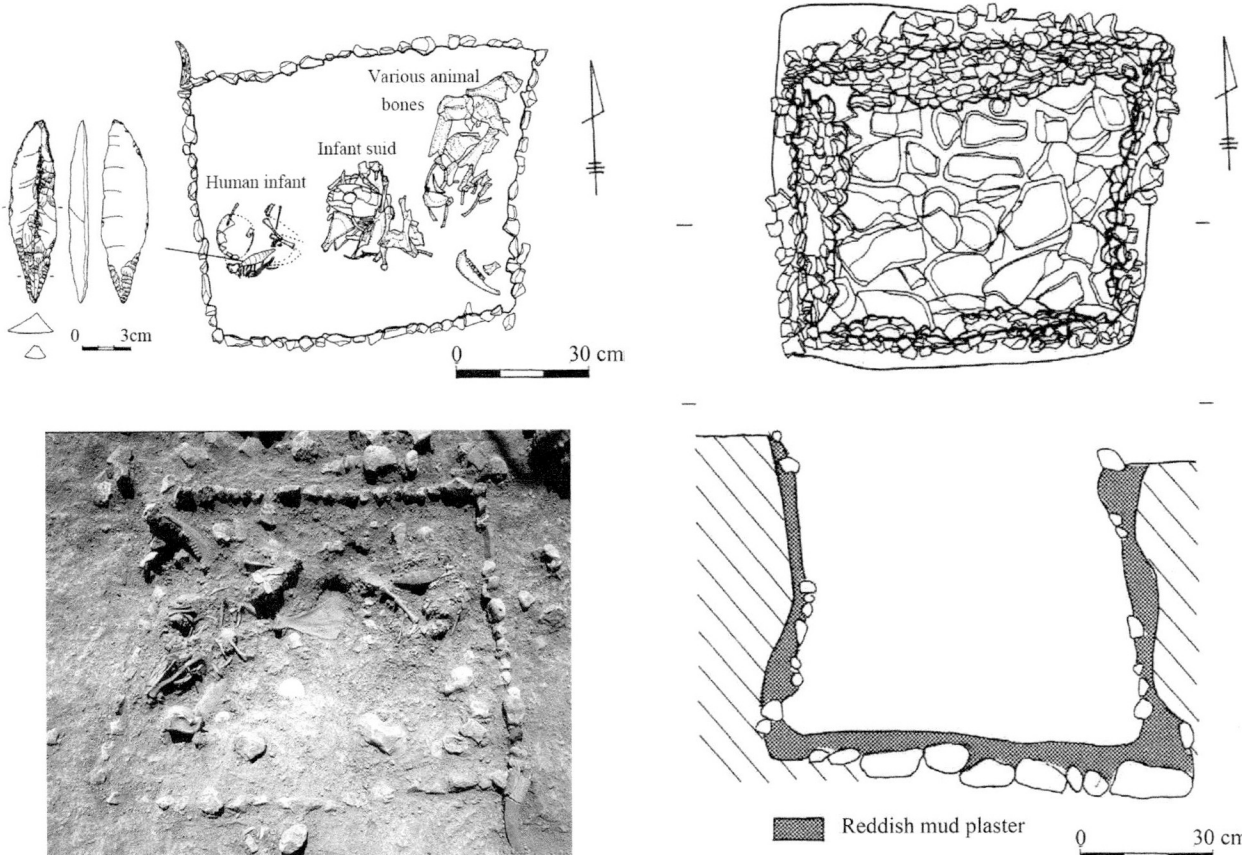

Various animal bones

Infant suid

Human infant

0   3cm

0   30 cm

Reddish mud plaster   0   30 cm

Figure 3-54. Str. 153 (Photograph: from the north).

Figure 3-55. Str. 516 from the east.

Figure 3-56a. Str. 109 from the east.

Figure 3-56b. Str. 109 from the west.

Figure 3-56c. Str. 109, base bottom from the west.

the main residential space. Three small square rooms are arranged in rows west of this space. A circular-planned, bin-like structure was installed in the middle room of the western series of small rooms facing the southern wall. This circular-planned structure is similar to a tannor, but its inner wall is not burnt and we found no ashy layers here. It did not have a stone-paved floor like a tannor; therefore, it appeared to be a bin. Structurally, it is possible that Str. 109 was also a two-story building (Figure 3-56c). However, the extent of the plastered floor was limited to the eastern part of the structure.

Therefore, we have a few different types of residential buildings: 1) relatively large rectangular buildings in which the first floor consists of a group of small, square-planned rooms, 2) relatively small, square-planned, one-room residences, and 3) relatively large square-planned building with a style similar to the eclectic style of the two mentioned above. In addition to residential buildings, we detected some clustered stones, tannors, and parts of plastered floors in Layer 5. We also discovered some infant burials on the residential floors (Strs. 76, 141, 145 and 901).

Our most striking discovery from this layer was a Neolithic cemetery in Squares E251 and E271 and the surrounding area. The cemetery stretched from the north to the east of Str. 109 (Figure 3-50), and Str. 109 was the southwestern limit of the cemetery during Layer 5. As mentioned above, the Neolithic cemetery continues from the lower part of Layer 6 through Layer 4, and it is clear that the outdoor space in Square E 271 and around was used as a cemetery for hundreds of years during the Rouj 2c period.

Layer 6 structures

The buildings found in Layer 6 are similar to those of Layer 5 (Figure 3-57). We found the same two types of residential buildings in this layer. We were also able to glean additional details about the buildings in this layer. Str. 167 is the most eloquent example of the first type of residential building (Figure 3-58). It was a large building and featured a 7.6 × 4.4m plastered floor surrounded by pisé walls. We also found a square-planned hearth on the lime-plastered floor near the eastern end of the structure. Because the hearth was covered with at least three strictly burnt layers of ash, we suppose that it was used repeatedly over a long period of time.

We found similar, square-planned hearths inside other residential buildings. For instance, we discovered a similar basin-like structure (Str. 532) made of lime plaster outside the eastern edge of Str. 167. However, the interior of this structure was not burnt, and it seemed to have been used as a trough (Figure 3-59). The plastered floor of Str. 167 was well preserved, but the western part of the floor was remarkably depressed (Figure 3-58: 1). Therefore, we suppose that Str. 167 had a basement beneath the plastered floor. We started to remove the plastered floor in order to examine the first floor of the building. The plastered floor was approximately 10cm thick and consisted of densely placed pebbles packed with lime plaster several millimeters in thickness. We encountered a well-packed layer of clay land sporadically placed

pebbles beneath the plastered floor (Figure 3-58: 3). Neatly arranged burnt timbers were found at regular intervals in the western part of the building below this clay layer (Figure 3-58: 4). These timbers were passed over the pisé walls of the small rectangular-planned rooms on the first floor. There were two small rooms on the western side measuring 2.3 × 1.5m. Timbers, packed clay with limestone pebbles, and thick lime plastering were imposed to make the ceiling of the first floor and the flooring of the second floor. This makes it clear that the large rectangular-planned buildings with well-plastered floors were in fact two-story buildings. We excavated only three rooms on the western side of the first floor. These excavations produced many objects, including six stamp seals, a mace head, a lamp-shaped stone vessel, and a large limestone weight (Figure 3-60). As the size of each room was too small and the room stood only one meter in height, the first floor of Str. 167 was likely used as a warehouse.

We detected a similarly large and rectangular residential building at the western end of Square E290 (Figure 3-57). This building (Str. 151) was made of pisé walls. We could only detect the eastern wall of this building. This wall ran 8.5m long, north to south. The inside of the building was divided into at least three parts. The southernmost room has a stone-paved floor like the first floor small rooms of Str. 72. Therefore, Str. 151 seems to be the first floor of a two-story residential building.

Str. 124 in Square E290 is typical of the second type of residences (small, square-planned, one-room residences). It has a square plan measuring 4 × 3.6m (Figure 3-61). Although its reddish clay pisé walls were poorly preserved, the white lime-plastered floor was still well preserved. The floor was paved with fist-sized limestone before the lime plaster was carefully spread over the stones. We observed two different floor layers inside Str. 124; thus, this structure was rebuilt at least once. We also discovered a rectangular hearth measuring 0.8 × 0.5m on the later floor along the eastern wall, and the remnant of another hearth on the earlier floor along the northern wall.

In Square E271, we discovered the remnants of a large building (Str. 827) below the base bottom of Str. 109 of Layer 5. This Str. 827 itself seems to have been used in the previous period. However, it is notable here that we found a skeleton aged 11-13 years old in Room 5 (Figure 3-62). The burial indicated that this person was buried during Layer 6 after Str. 827 had been abandoned completely. It is also notable that Str. 916 pisé building with stone foundation on the northern side of Str. 827 across a narrow street also produced two clusters of human bones (Concentration 7-1 and 7-2). As the building basement level of Str. 916 is as same as that of Str. 827, these two buildings were built

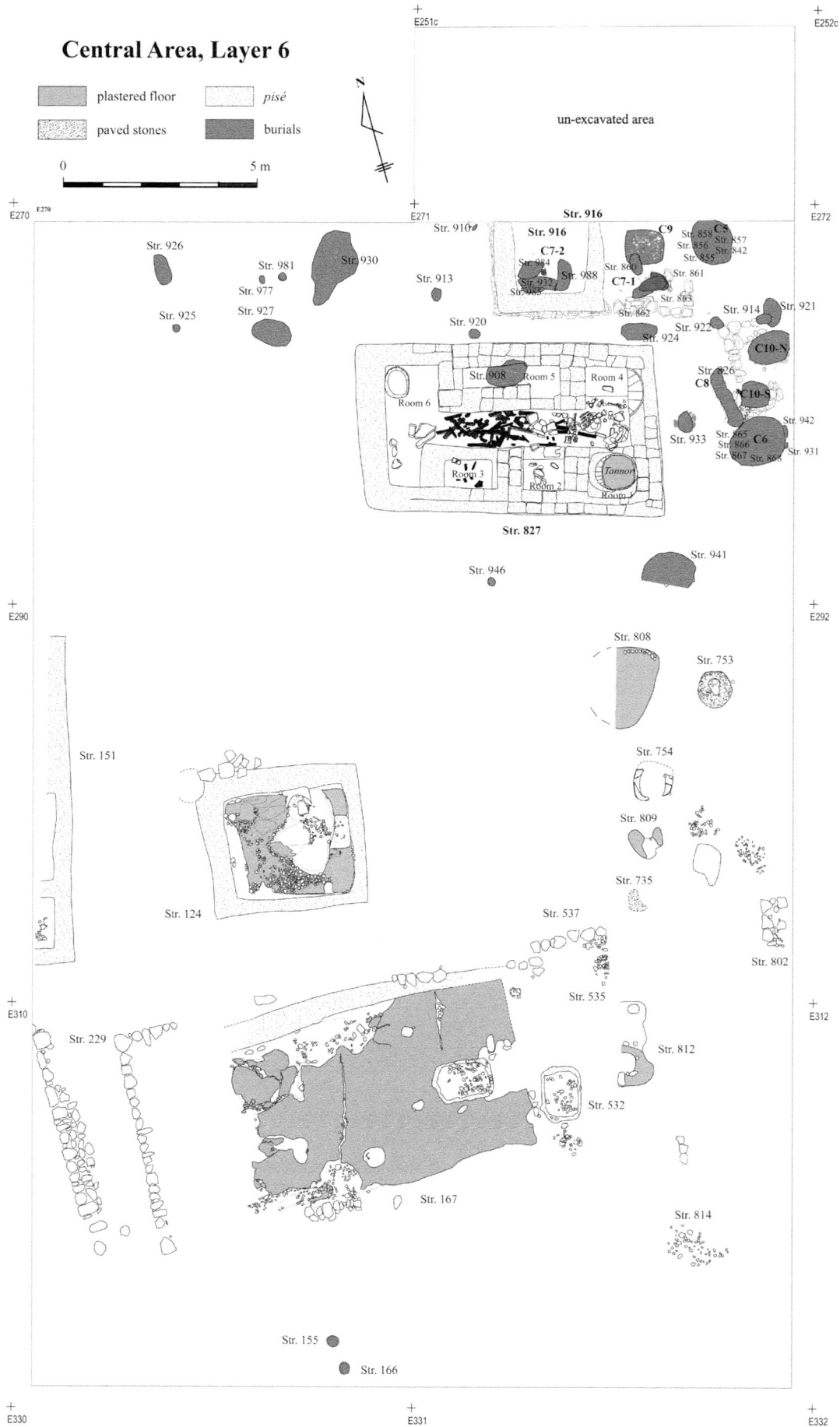

Figure 3-57. Central Area, Layer 6 structures.

Figure 3-58. Str. 167 from the west.

Figure 3-59. Str. 167 and Str. 532 from the east.

and used during the previous Layer 7 era. However, the remnants of these buildings still remained during the Layer 6 era, and the people might use these abandoned buildings as a graveyard. The detail of Strs. 827 and 916 will be discussed in the next Layer 7 section.

As we will discuss in Chapter 4, Kerkh people began to build full-scale outdoor communal cemeteries from this layer onward. Most of the Layer 6 burials in the

cemetery were dug down below the level of buildings in Layer 6, and the bottom of the burial pits sometimes reached the level of Layer 7 buildings. Therefore, we encountered many human skeletons in the upper deposits of Layer 7, but almost all of these were burials dug down from Layer 6.

Besides the Neolithic Cemetery in the northern squares of the Central Area, we also found some infant burials in the residential area of this layer. Strs. 155 and 166 were the burials of perinatal infants discovered in Square E310d (Figure 3-63). Both skeletons were buried in a contracted position and discovered near the poorly preserved pisé walls. This indicates that that they were buried in connection with the residences. Although many children were buried in the communal cemetery in Squares E251, E270, and E271, some children were buried close to residential buildings.

Layer 7 structures

We dug deeper in Squares E270 and E271 and in the eastern half of Squares E291 through E311 to order to find Layer 7 structures and therefore determine the extent and origin of the Neolithic Cemetery. Although

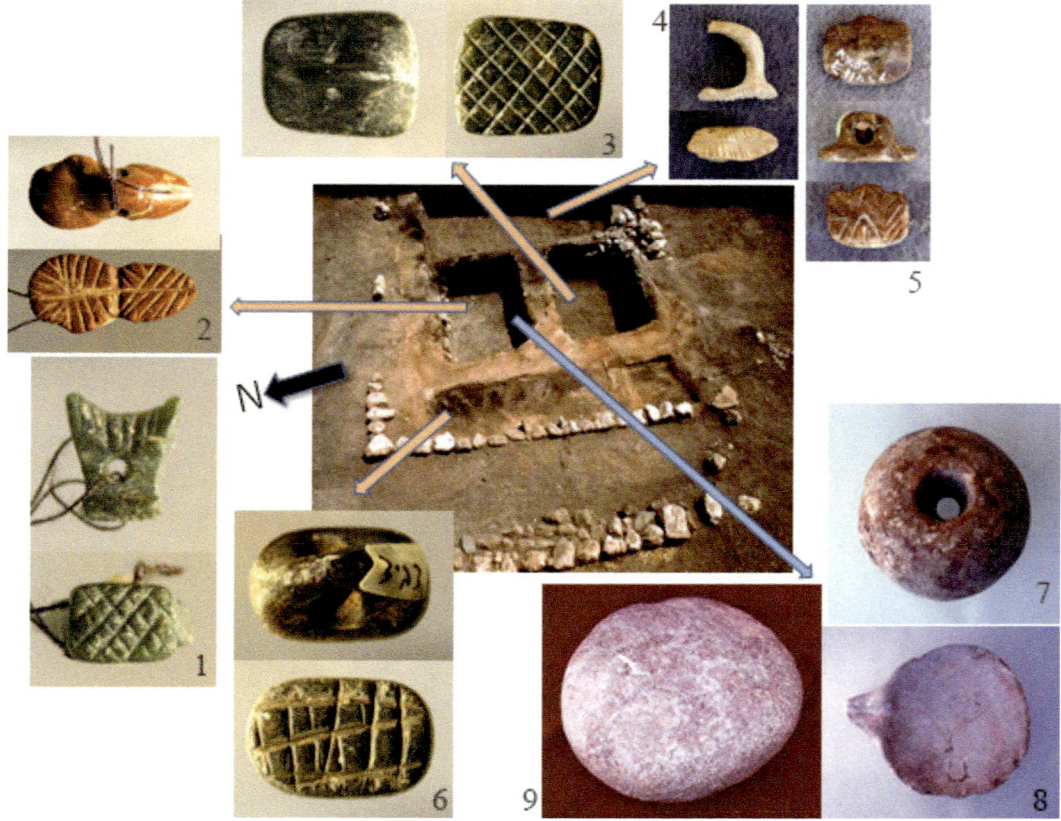

Figure 3-60. Objects found from the first floor of Str. 167.

Figure 3-61. Str. 124 from the west.

Figure 3-62. The uppermost layer of Str. 827 from the west. Str. 908 burial was discovered in Room 5.

Str. 155

Str. 166

Figure 3-63. Strs. 155 and 166 Burials.

we only excavated a limited area of Layer 7, we encountered several well-preserved building structures (Figures 3-64, 3-65).

Str. 827 was discovered below the Str. 109 in Square E271. Str. 827 was well-preserved because it was completely burnt (Figures 3-66). The building has a rectangular plan measuring 4.2 × 6.2m long in an east-west direction. It was originally built as a tripartite building, but some partitions were added later. A narrow corridor runs east-west in the center of the building and this corridor is flanked on both sides by six small rooms. A small room at the southeastern corner (Room 1) featured a well-preserved tannor having the ceiling. As the building had been burnt, many objects were discovered in situ. For example, we found a large saddle quern made of porous basalt, a plano-convex griding stone (upper stone of saddle quern), two other griding stones, a beautiful limestone vessel, a large clay basin, two pot stands, and a hammer stone in the eastern end of the corridor. All of these objects were complete, and some were broken by fire. In addition to these objects, we also discovered three fragments of the upper stone of the saddle quern. We found another large saddle quern made of porous basalt together with an upper stone of the saddle quern in the middle-south room (Room 2). A large broken mortar, a large amorphous stone with a ground surface, a grinding stone, a stone axe, and some fragments of grinding stones were also discovered in this room. The southwestern room (Room 3) and the northeastern room (Room 4) also produced a complete upper stone of the saddle quern. The narrow north-middle room (Room 5) produced a stone axe. As mentioned in the section of Layer 6, we found a skeleton aged 11-13 years old in this room (Figures 3-62). However, the burial indicated that this person was buried during Layer 6 after Str. 827 had been abandoned – we discuss this in more detail in Chapters 4 and 5. We found another stone axe in the Room 6, in the northwestern corner of the building. These found objects, especially the ground stones, are summarized in Figures 3-66d and Table 3-1. The most remarkable objects here are a series of food-processing tools.

These findings indicate that this building was used for food-processing activities. The number of objects found here, including the two large objects, indicate that this structure was not an ordinary dwelling. In addition, the tannor in Room 1 is unusual, the clay basin furnished in the eastern part of the central corridor had an unusual shape, and a large flint scraper was discovered in the basin. The two complete pot stands found here were also extraordinary objects. All of these findings and situations indicate that this building was not a personal dwelling but a communal mill and kitchen.

We found many carbonized timbers distributed on the floor of the building, especially in the central corridor. Most of them had a thickness of 10cm and seemed to be ceiling materials which had been burnt down to the floor by fire. These materials indicate that Str. 827 was a first floor of a two-story building, such as Str. 167 in Layer 6, before it was burned down and abandoned.

We discovered Str. 916 on the northern side of Str. 827 across a narrow range of 0.7m wide streets (Figures 3-67). The direction and long axis of this building were same as those of Str. 827. The northern half of this building was not excavated; we could only excavate the southern half of the building. It might have had a rectangular plan. The excavated portion measured approximately 5.2m from east to west. The building consisted of at least two rooms. The eastern room was severely destroyed by two crematorium pits (C5 and C9) from Layer 6, and only its stone foundation remained. However, we found at least four adult human skeletons inside the stone foundation. As the level of these human skeletons is almost same as the bottom of crematorium pits from Layer 6, and the skeletons seemed to have buried after Str. 916 was abandoned, we identified them as a cluster of burials dug down from Layer 6 in the Neolithic Cemetery. We named them Concentration 7-1. The details of Concentration 7-1 are discussed in the following chapters.

The western room of Str. 916 was relatively well preserved. The pisé walls remained on their stone foundation, which consisted of three to four stages of limestone. The width of the pisé wall is approximately 0.6m. We found at least nine human skeletons below some thin, white, bark- or hide-like organic materials stretched in the room. As in Concentration 7-1, these human bones were buried as graves after Str. 916 was abandoned, and we identified them as Concentration 7-2, a burial cluster from the Neolithic Cemetery. We discuss these in detail later as well.

These pisé buildings were discovered mainly in Square E271. We discovered two lime-plastered buildings in Square E311b-d (Figures 3-68). Both of these buildings extended outside the excavated area and so we could only excavate parts of them. Beautiful lime plaster was applied repeatedly to the floor of Str. 804 at least three times. Str. 811 also had a beautiful, white plastered floor, but only part of the floor remains. Both structures must have been residential buildings, but the layout of their rooms is unknown.

We detected some tannors in Square E291b-d. Here again, tannors were ordinally built not inside the house but in the open spaces among buildings. We also detected a serpentinite bead workshop, consisting of unfinished beads and flint drills, near the tannors.

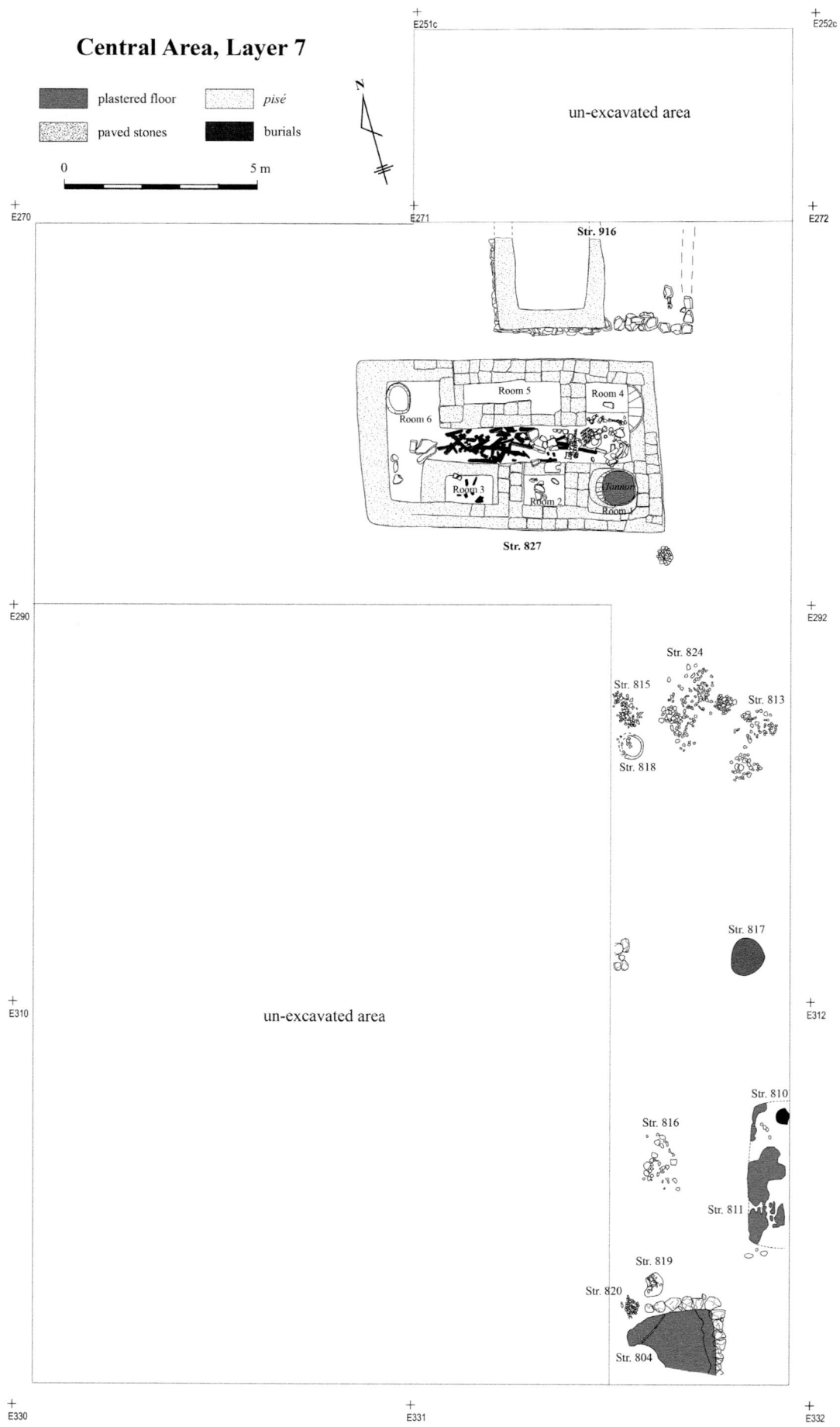

Figure 3-64. Central Area, Layer 7 structures.

Figure 3-65. Square E271 and beyond, Layer 7 from the north.

Figure 3-66a. The upper layer of Str. 827 from the west.

Figure 3-66b. The middle layer of Str. 827 from the west.

Figure 3-66c. The lower layer of Str. 827 from the west.

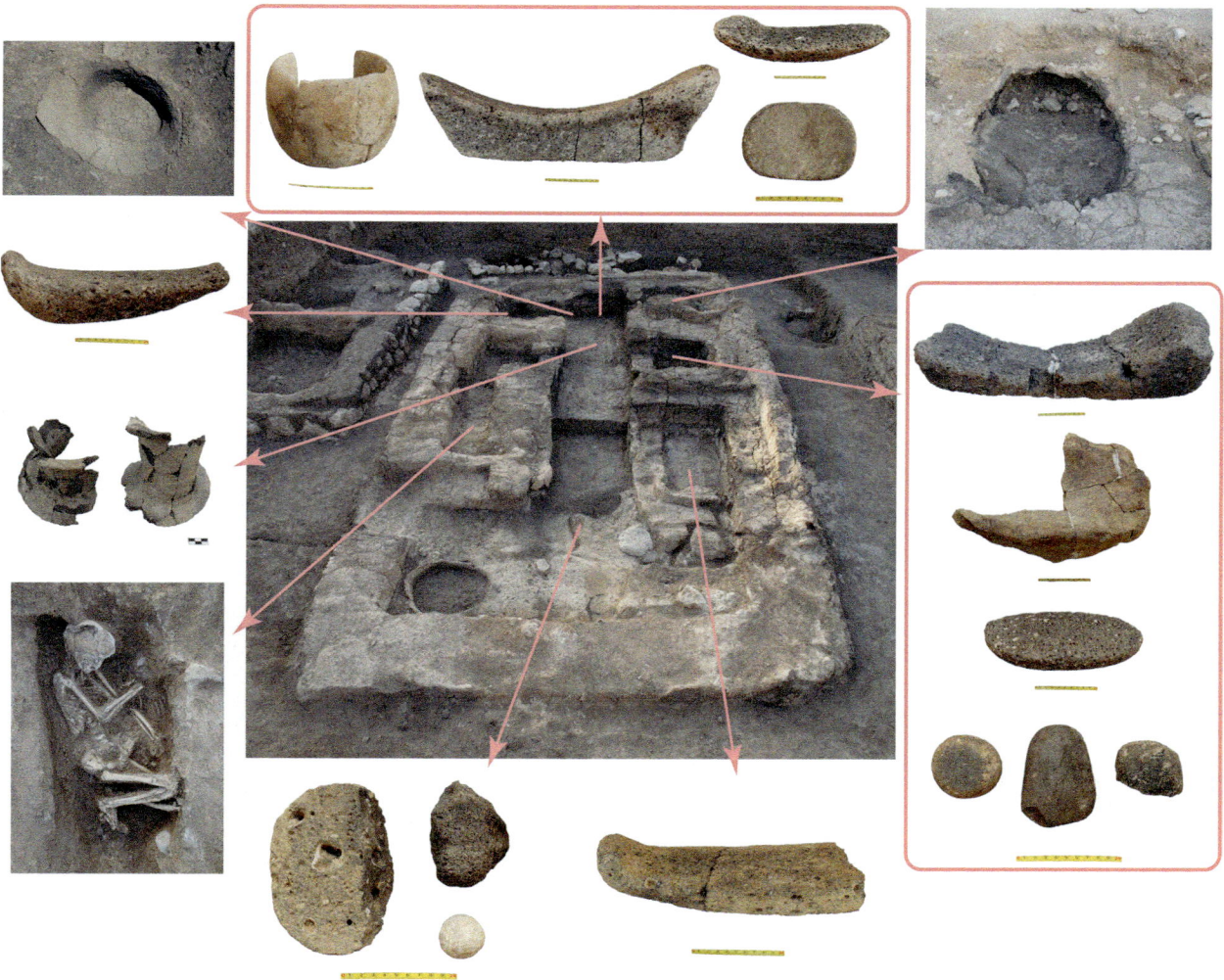

Figure 3-66d. Str. 827, discovered objects.

Table 3-1. Number of ground stone objects discovered from Str. 827.

objects find spots	mortar	saddle quern (lower stone)	saddle quern (upper stone)	grinding stone	stone axe	hammer stone	stone vessel	others
Room 1								
Room 2	1	1	1 + f1	1	1 + f1			
Room 3			1 + f1					
Room 4			1					
Room 5								
Room 6								
Eastern part of the central corridor		1	1 + f3	2		1	1	pot stand 2, clay bin 1, flake scraper 1
Western part of the central corridor				f1		1		pumice (f2)
Total	1	2	4 + f5	3 + f1	3 + f1	2	1	

Number of complete ground stone objects, f = framgemts

The cultural deposits in the central area are very thick. They measure over 10m from the virgin soil to the surface. All of the cultural deposits, excluding the Hellenistic burial pits dug down from the surface, belong to the Neolithic period. We have only exposed the top three meters, consisting of cultural deposits from the Rouj 2c and 2d periods. Based on the results of excavations below these layers in the Northwest Area, East Trench, Squares A318, F1, and G192, we believe that the thick early Pottery Neolithic (the Rouj 2a-b)

Figure 3-67. Str. 916 from the west.

Figure 3-68. Str. 804 from the east.

and LPPNB (the Rouj 1c) layers must have accumulated in the Central Area of Tell Ain el-Kerkh.

2. The Size of the Neolithic Settlement

In addition to these excavations, we performed a detailed surface collection for the entire tell complex in 1994. We collected the Rouj 1 and Rouj 2 lithics and Rouj 2 potsherds from all of the fixed squares in the northern half of Tell Ain el-Kerkh and everywhere in Tell el-Kerkh 2. We also collected a few Rouj 1 and Rouj 2 lithics and Rouj 2 potsherds from the southern end of Tell Ain el-Kerkh and the southern slope of Tell el-Kerkh 1. Therefore, it is probable that most parts of Tell Ain el-Kerkh and the whole of Tell el-Kerkh 2 were occupied during some of the Neolithic periods. The

results of excavations, test pits, and surface collection were used to estimate the settlement size during each Neolithic period at Tell el-Kerkh. (Tsuneki 2012). Here is a summary of the size transitions of Neolithic settlements in Tell el-Kerkh.

Rouj 1a period

Only the Northwest Area of Tell Ain el-Kerkh has produced cultural layers from the Rouj 1a period. No other excavations that reached virgin soil produced cultural layers belonging to this period. Therefore, we conclude that the area of the Rouj 1a period settlement was quite limited, around the low summit of the Northwest Area of Tell Ain el-Kerkh – perhaps less than 1ha (Figures 3-69).

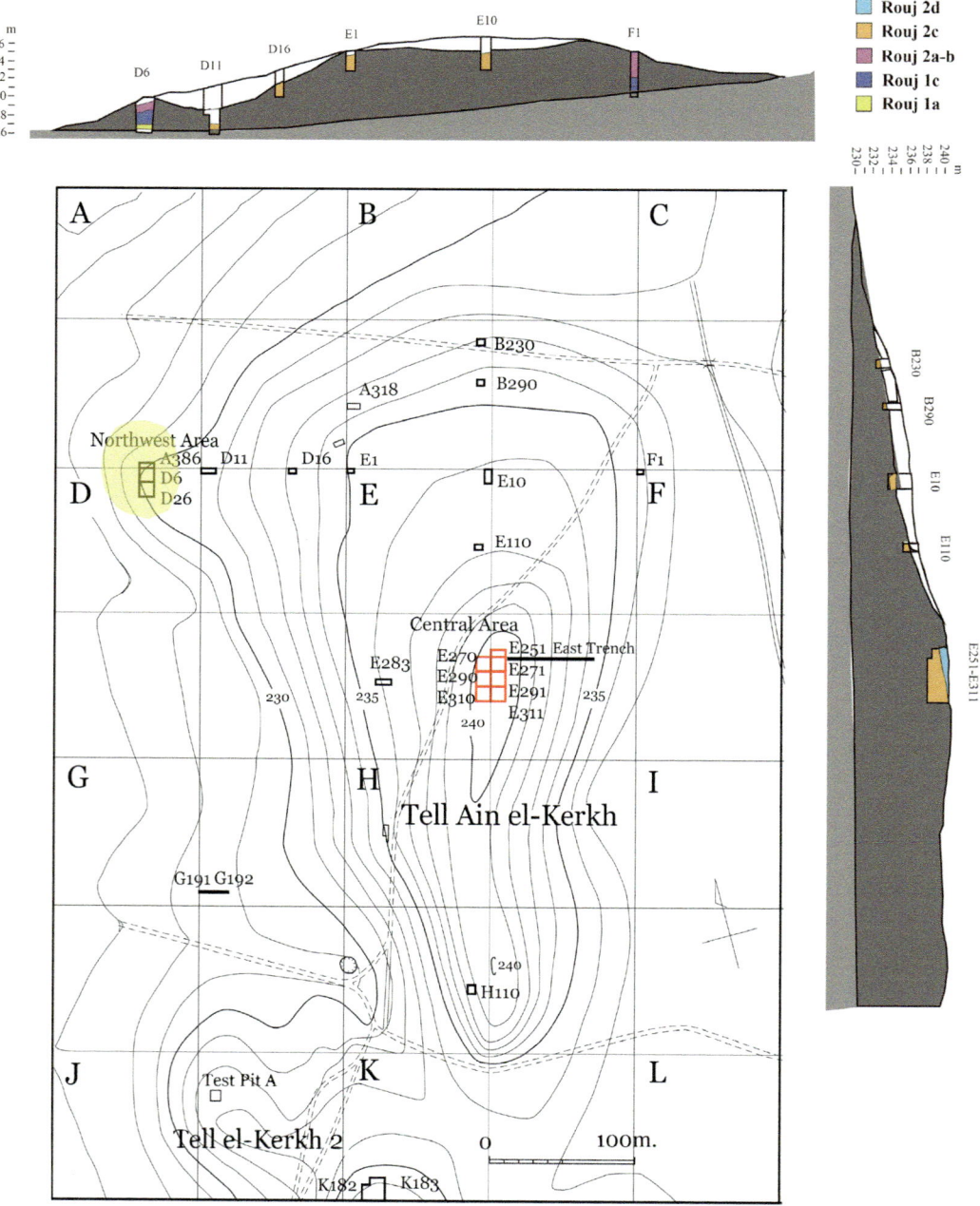

Figure 3-69. Estimated settlemnt range for Rouj 1a period.

62

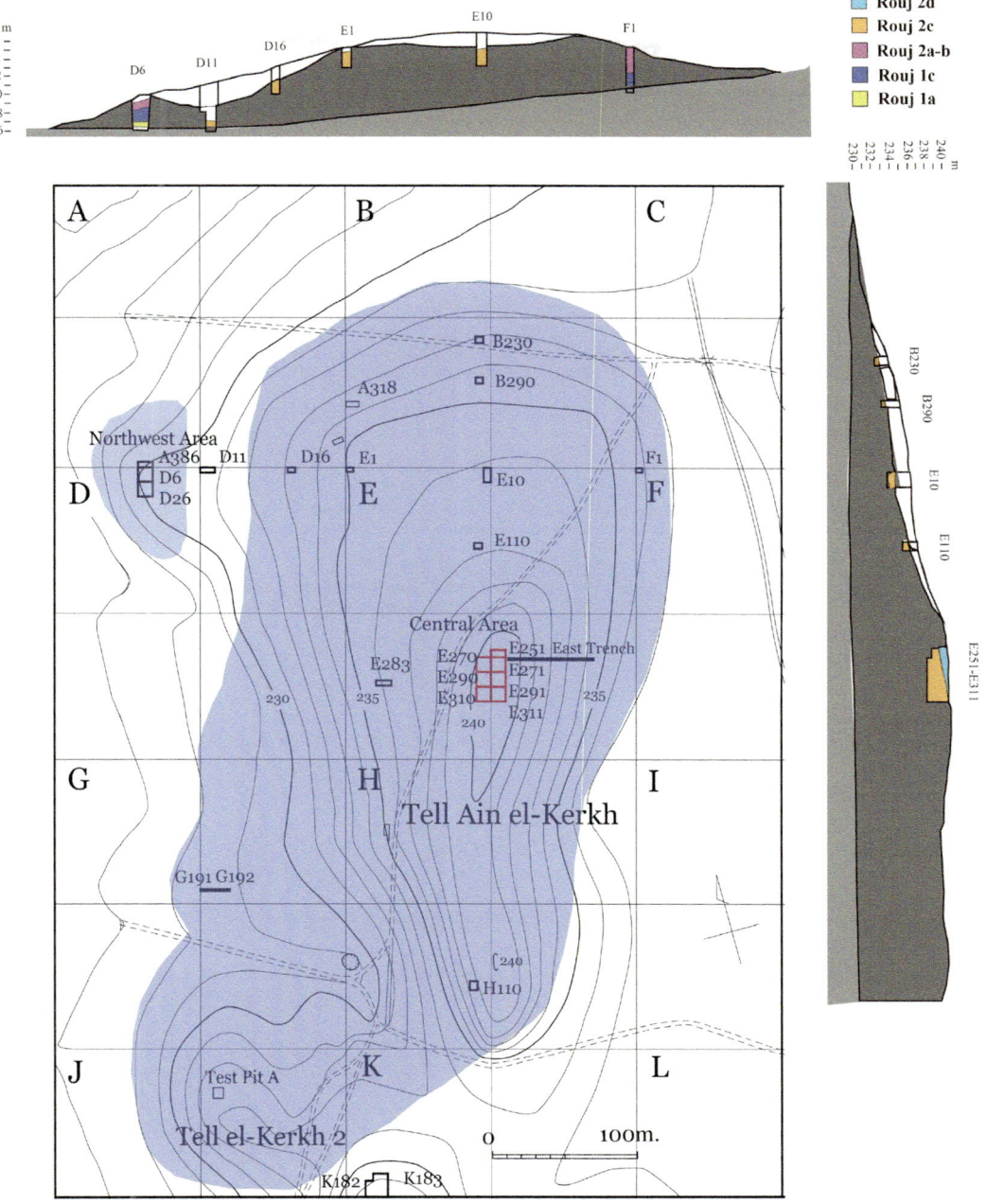

Figure 3-70. Estimated settlemnt range for Rouj 1c period.

Rouj 1c period

The settlement from this period is the largest in the history of the Tell el-Kerkh. All of the excavated squares that reached virgin soil (except Square D11) produced cultural layers dating to the Rouj 1c period. This clearly indicates that a large LPPNB settlement lay at the basement of the whole Tell el-Kerkh 2 area and almost the entire Tell Ain el-Kerkh area. The southern foot of Tell el-Kerkh 1 might have been an isolated patch of a Rouj 1c period settlement because of the Rouj 1c era materials there. As the deep test pit of Square D11 did not produce layers dating to the Rouj 1c period, the Rouj 1c settlement of the Northwest Area of the site was probably separated from the main Rouj 1c settlement at Tell Ain el-Kerkh. On the other hand, because Squares G191–G192 produced cultural layers dating to the Rouj 1c period, it might be possible that Tell el-Kerkh 2 and Tell Ain el-Kerkh formed one large settlement. The evidence testifies to the simultaneity of the deposits found at the site, and that the Rouj 1c period settlement was quite large, covering over 16 ha (Figures 3-70).

Rouj 2a-b period

The excavation did not extend to the lower deposits below the Rouj 2c period layers in most of the excavated squares. Layers dating to the Rouj 2a-b period were encountered only in the Test Pit of Tell el-Kerkh 2, and the Northwest Area, the East Trench, and Square F1 of Tell Ain el-Kerkh. As the thick Neolithic cultural layers must have accumulated below the Rouj 2c period layers, we assume that there was a relatively large Rouj 2a-b settlement. On the other hand, no layers dating to the Rouj 2a-b period were found in Squares G191–G192, D11, or A318. Therefore, the settlement might have been separated into at least three areas: Tell el-Kerkh 2, the Northwest Area, and the main part of Tell Ain el-Kerkh (Figures 3-71). We estimate that these settlements covered 2ha, 0.6ha, and 7ha, respectively – a total of <. 10ha. It is not easy to determine if these areas were occupied simultaneously.

Rouj 2c period

Although we encountered layers dating to the Rouj 2c period in most of the excavated squares set in the northern part of Tell Ain el-Kerkh, these layers were not found at Tell el-Kerkh 2 or in the Northwest Area of Tell Ain el-Kerkh. This means that the settlement area during the Rouj 2c period was mostly limited to within the main part of Tell Ain el-Kerkh (Figure 3-72). The southern and eastern edges of the settlement were clearly reduced. In other words, the people concentrated their habitation area in the north-central part of Tell Ain el-Kerkh during the Rouj 2c period. The results of excavations in the Central Area revealed a densely populated settlement of about 6ha during this period.

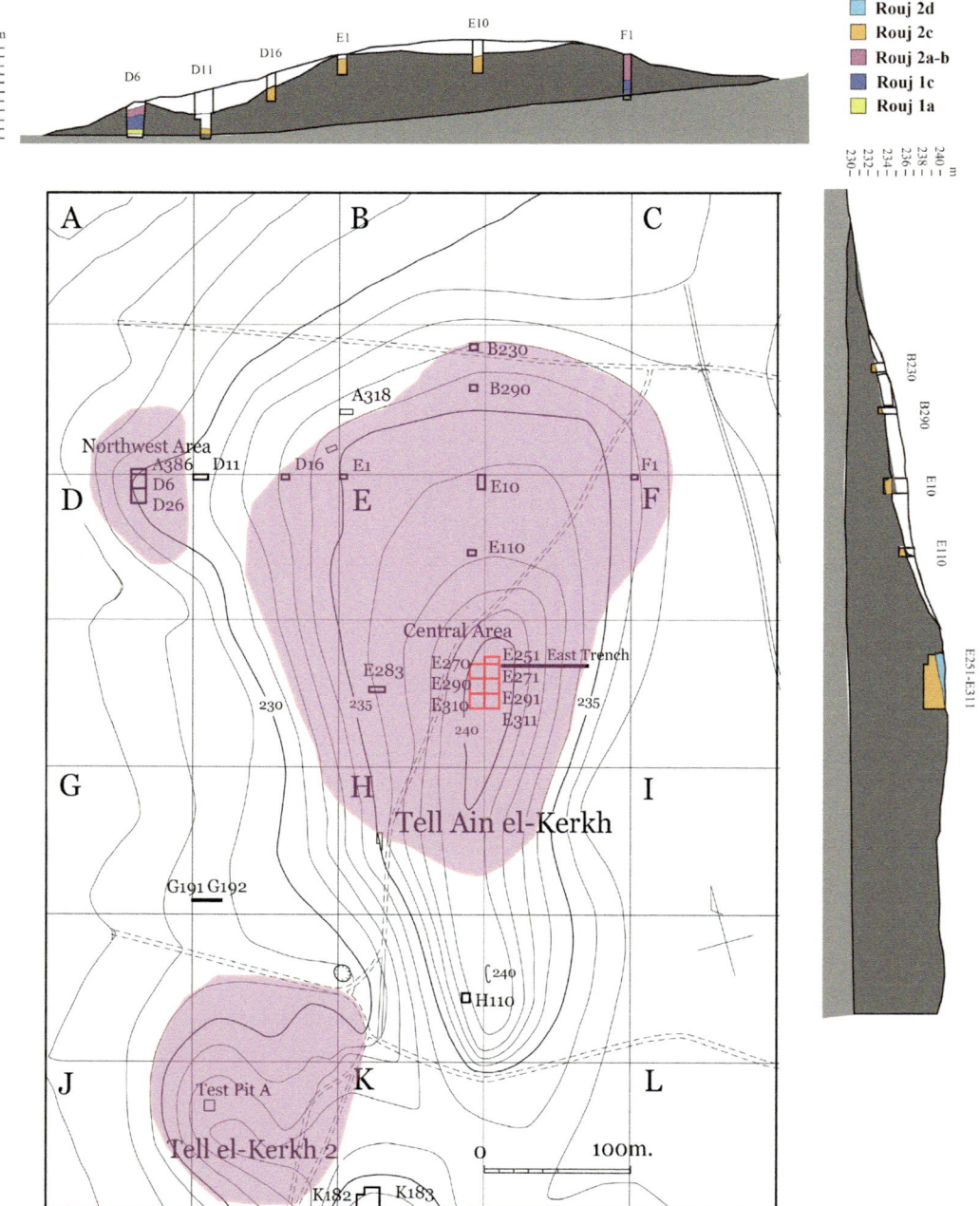

Figure 3-71. Estimated settlemnt range for Rouj 2a-b period.

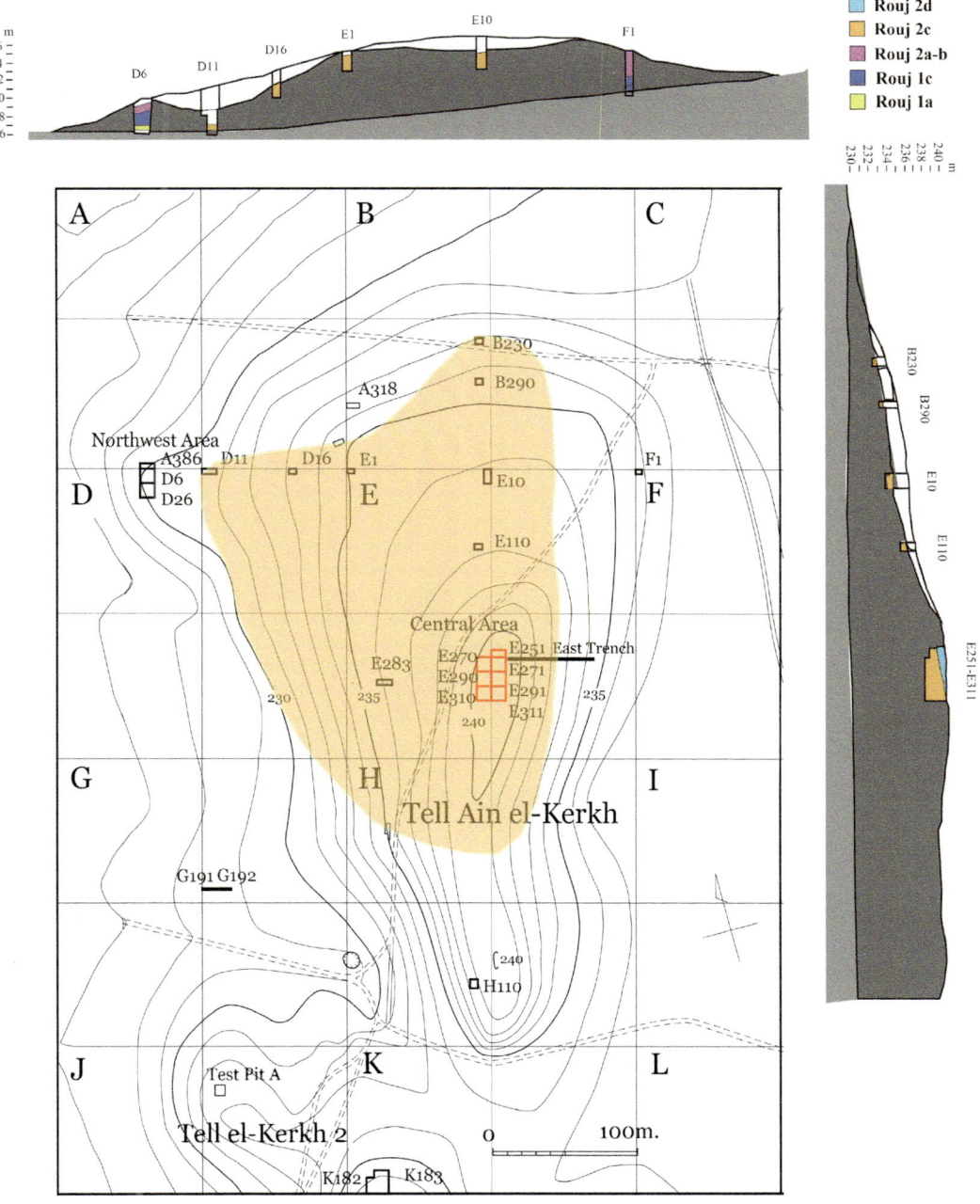

Figure 3-72. Estimated settlemnt range for Rouj 2c period.

Rouj 2d period

Only the Central Area and the East Trench produced layers dating to the Rouj 2d period. Thus, the Rouj 2d settlement was clearly much smaller than the previous settlements. As the Rouj 2d layer disappears below 238m asl contour line in the East Trench, this level might be the eastern limit of the settlement. It is supposed that the settlement's size did not exceed 1 ha in this period (Figure 3-73).

Considering the grid sections of Tell Ain el-Kerkh, we recovered relatively thick sterile surface layers, especially in the northern part of Tell Ain el-Kerkh. The original tell surface might have been rugged, and later natural and human activities may have leveled it. Therefore, the tell complex of Kerkh originally consisted of a few separated habitation areas, and each area seems to have been occupied successively. However, the size of the settlement was quite large between 16-6ha during Rouj 1c, Rouj 2a-b Rouj 2c periods.

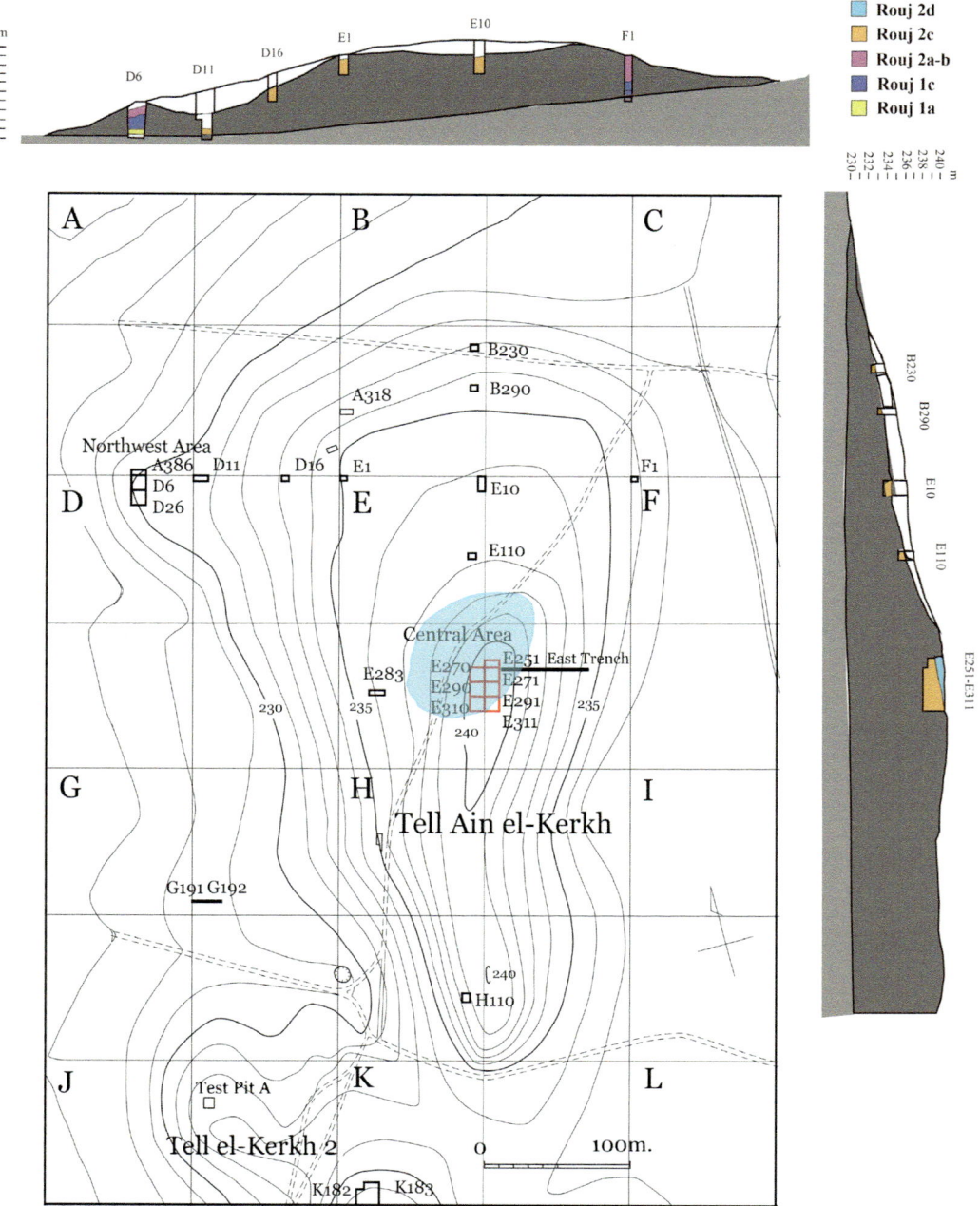

Figure 3-73. Estimated settlemnt range for Rouj d period.

Chapter 4
Burial Types and the Transition of Kerkh Cemetery

Sari Jammo

Tell el-Kerkh revealed 244 individuals in an outdoor communal cemetery located in Squares E251, E270, and E271, adjacent to the habitation zone in the Central Area (Figure 4-1). Deceased of both sexes, from all age groups, were uncovered, and the cemetery had been used for hundreds of years in the late 7th millennium BC. The deceased in the cemetery were categorized into four burial types showing simple and complex interment patterns. The deceased were buried individually or in groups aggregated in different burial contexts. Stratigraphically, the cemetery is divided into three main layers, Layers 4, 5, and 6, from the top to the bottom. Each layer of the cemetery is distinguished by the number of deceased, burial customs, and funerary practices.

In this chapter, we first introduce the burial types in the cemetery and cover details related to age, sex, and interment pattern in each burial type. Next, we describe the transition of the cemetery and the distribution of burials in each layer.

1. Burial Types in Kerkh Cemetery

In total, 244 individuals had been discovered in the Kerkh cemetery until the 2010 season. The deceased were interred within the cemetery in various ways. Various funerary practices have also been observed within the cemetery. However, burials in the cemetery have been classified into four main types (Figure 4-2):

1. Primary burials;
2. Secondary burials/pits;
3. Cremation burials/pits;
4. Urn burials;
5. Some burials were too disturbed to be classified into a type, so they were categorized as unknown type burials.

A total of 244 individuals were distributed in various places in the cemetery from three main layers. Deceased from all ages and both sexes were discovered, however, indeterminate sex were also present. Primary burials were the largest burial type uncovered in the cemetery, next were secondary burials, cremation burials, unknown type burials and urn burials. Most of the individuals were buried individually on the surface of the cemetery, however, in many instances they were clustered in 'household' group burials. Further, other burials were buried in a specific location or special burial contexts such as in collective burials and crematorium pits.

A large number of the individuals in the cemetery (107 individuals = 44%) were recovered from a collective context. These collective burials were called 'Concentration (C1, C2... etc.)' at the site. In total, eleven concentrations were uncovered at Kerkh cemetery. A concentration is a type of burial, in which several individuals were buried within one pit or area surrounded by stone rows. Each concentration has very different characteristics and includes several burial types.

A large number of individuals lacked skeletal parts or their remains were fragmented after exposure to the air, which prevented identification of the sex of the deceased. Further, the investigations indicate that many skeletal remains were re-located and removed from their original interment into other contexts for subsequent treatments such as in collective burials, cremation and skull/cranium removal.

Burials of all ages were uncovered in the cemetery, and the ages for most of the burials have been identified (Table 4-1). Adults were the largest age category at Tell el-Kerkh cemetery and represent over half of the individuals (124 individuals = 51%) (Figure 4-3). Nearly a quarter of the burials are juveniles and represent the second largest age category. Whereas, the number of other age categories is limited.

A large number of individuals' sex is indeterminate. Of 244 individuals, the sex for 158 individuals (65%) is indeterminate. However, the number of identified males is slightly larger than females. They were 46 individuals (19%) who were male/probable male and 40 individuals (16%) female/probable female.

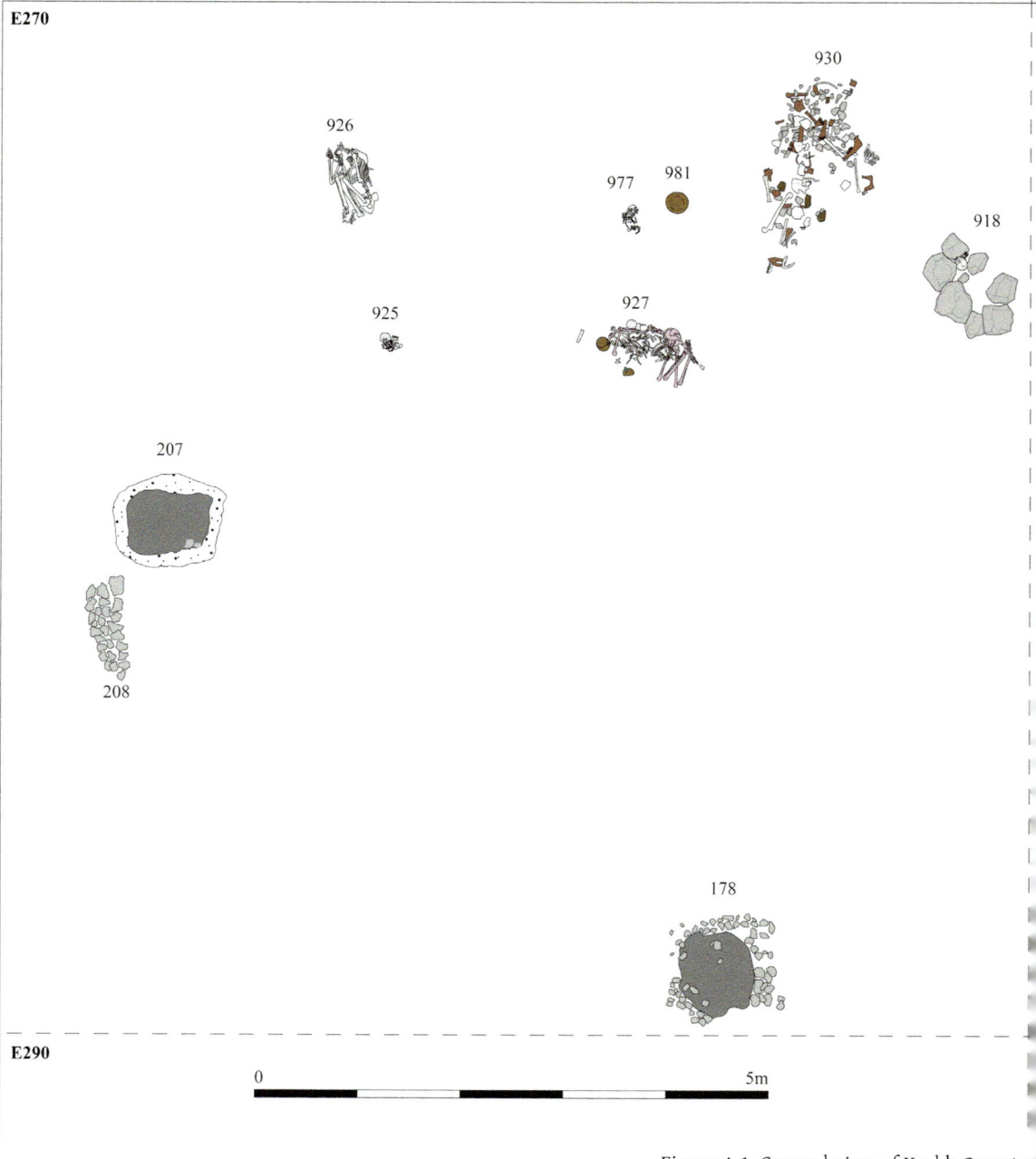

Figure 4-1. General view of Kerkh Cemete

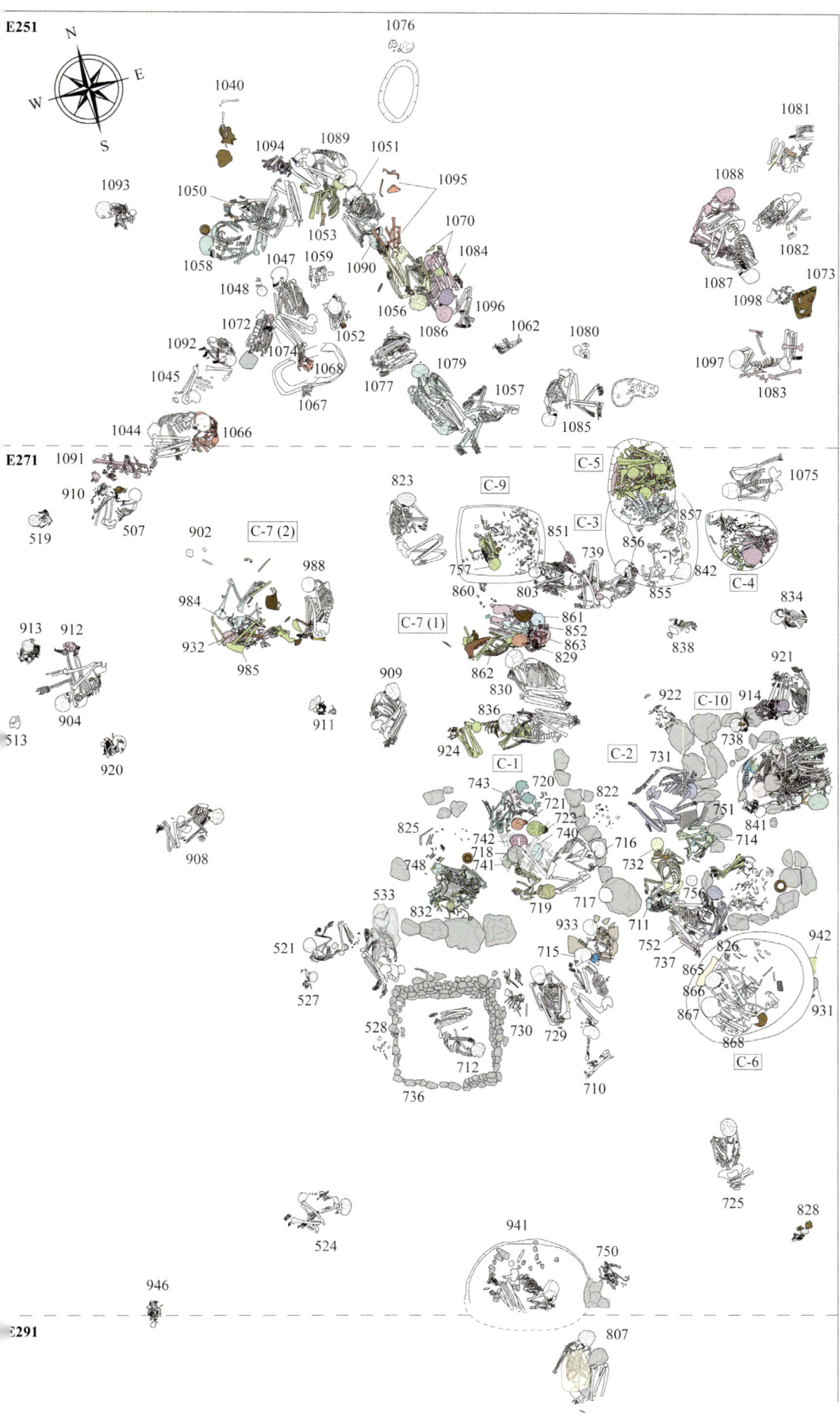

Table 4-1. Sex and age-based distribution of deceased at Kerkh Cemetery.

Sex/Age	Fetal	Perinatal	Infant	Juvenile	Subadult	Adult	Young adult	Middle adult	Old adult	Unknown	Total
Male							2	4			6
Probable Male						13	14	10	3		40
Female						1	2	3			6
Probable Female				1		13	14	5	1		34
Unknown	7	12	14	57	15	33	2		4	14	158
Total	7	12	14	57	16	60	34	22	8	14	244

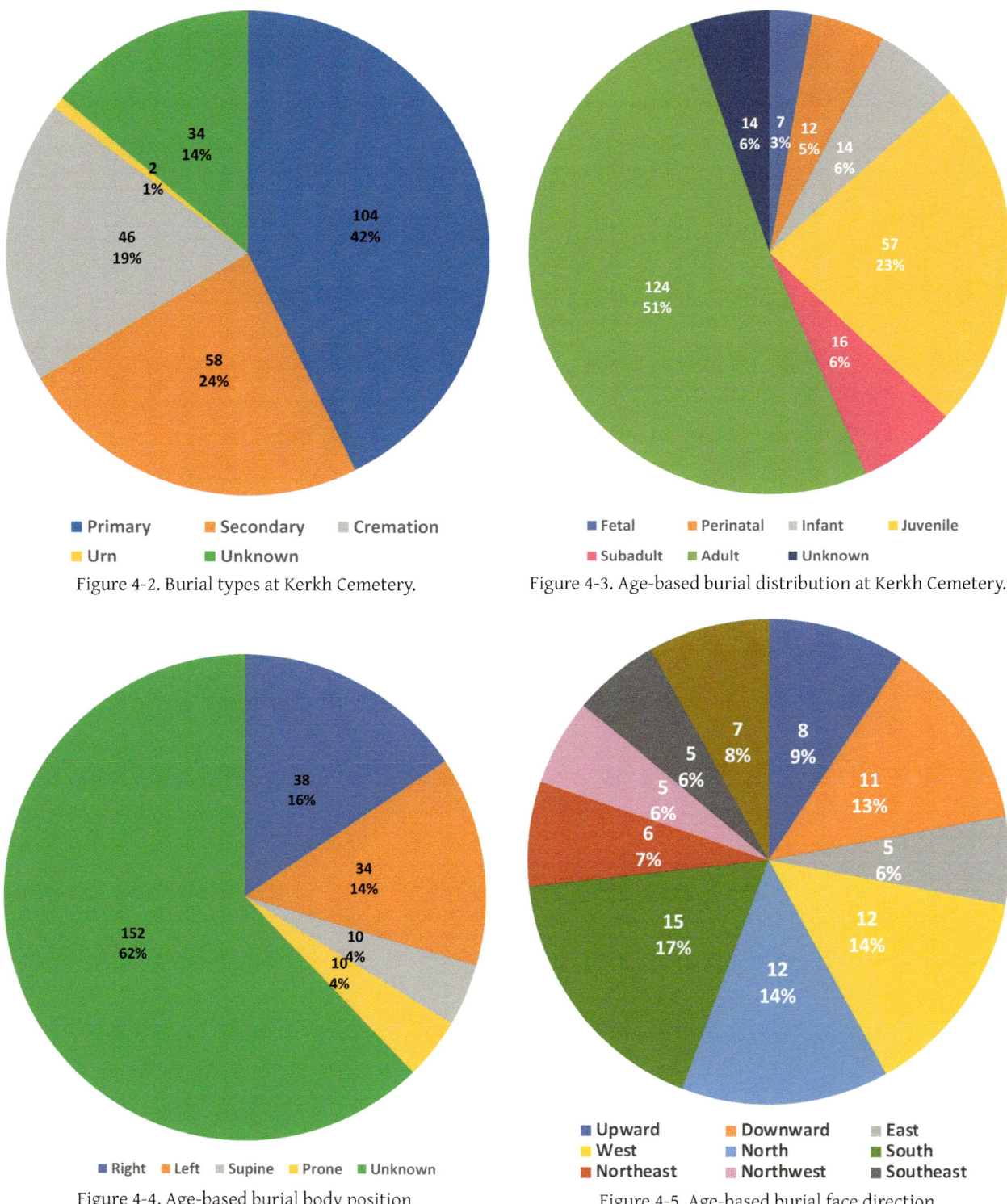

Figure 4-2. Burial types at Kerkh Cemetery.

Figure 4-3. Age-based burial distribution at Kerkh Cemetery.

Figure 4-4. Age-based burial body position at Kerkh Cemetery.

Figure 4-5. Age-based burial face direction at Kerkh Cemetery.

Deceased were interred in various body positions; on one side (right or left) is the most common and adults and juveniles were often buried in this way. However, deceased buried in prone and supine position were also uncovered (Figure 4-4). The heads of the burials were pointed in various directions and so was face direction. In general, it was difficult to identify a common or preferable head or face direction, however, exceptions were documented amongst the group burials. The face direction for 86 individuals (35%) could be identified. Although it is difficult to identify a common face direction, the largest number of deceased faced south (Figure 4-5). Curiously, of those whose face direction has been determined, none of the males/probable males was facing east or southeast, whereas, the females/ probable females did not face west or northeast. This may suggest that the people of Tell el-Kerkh were considering the direction of the face based on sex. However, further investigation is needed to illustrate this suggestion.

1) Primary Burials

Primary burials refer to skeleton in complete or nearly complete anatomical articulations discovered in its original place at the time of interment (Figure 4-6).

Primary burial is the main burial type uncovered in the Kerkh Cemetery (104 individuals = 42%). Most of the individuals were buried intact in a small shallow pit. However, some were disturbed, with loose or disarticulated human bones, and the bones were mostly recovered from the grave fill. The disturbance could have occurred due to the removal of body parts or successive burial activities conducted by the Neolithic people.

The burial pit was simple and shallow, and in many instances is unclear. A number of burials were structured burials surrounded by a row of stones, enclosing the burial completely or partially. Most of the primary burials were discovered intact, however some

Figure 4-6. Primary burials at Kerkh Cemetery.

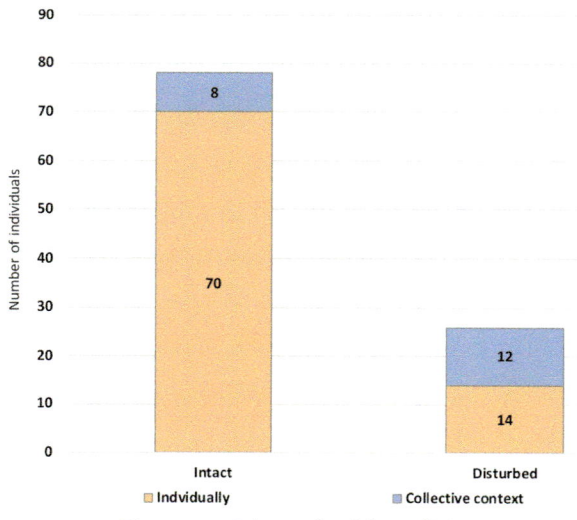

Figure 4-7. Primary burial conditions.

The number of primary males is larger than females; males comprised 26 individuals (25%), females 23 individuals (22%) and the rest 55 individuals (53%) are indeterminate (Table 4-2). Notably, most identified primary individuals were buried in a flexed position. They were mainly buried on one side on the right or the left side, supine and in a prone position (Figure 4-8). Adult males, females and children were all buried in various body positions and axil directions. Although right and left side down position is the most common, no remarkable position was noticeable in regard to age and sex.

The most common face directions among the primary burials were north, south and downward (Figure 4-9). Notably, none of the males faced east or southeast, whereas, females did not face the west, northeast or northwest directions.

A few deceased were covered fully or partly with lime plaster or stone. Some individuals were disturbed

were disturbed. In both conditions, primary burials were found even individually, or within the collective burials (Figure 4-7).

Table 4-2. Sex and age-based distribution of deceased in the primary burials at Kerkh Cemetery.

Sex/Age	Fetal	Perinatal	Infant	Juvenile	Subadult	Adult	Young adult	Middle adult	Old adult	Unknown	Total
Male							2	4			6
Probable Male						5	10	6			21
Female						1	2	3			6
Probable Female						4	9	4			17
Unknown	5	6	5	19	7	9	1		1	1	54
Total	5	6	5	19	7	19	24	17	1	1	104

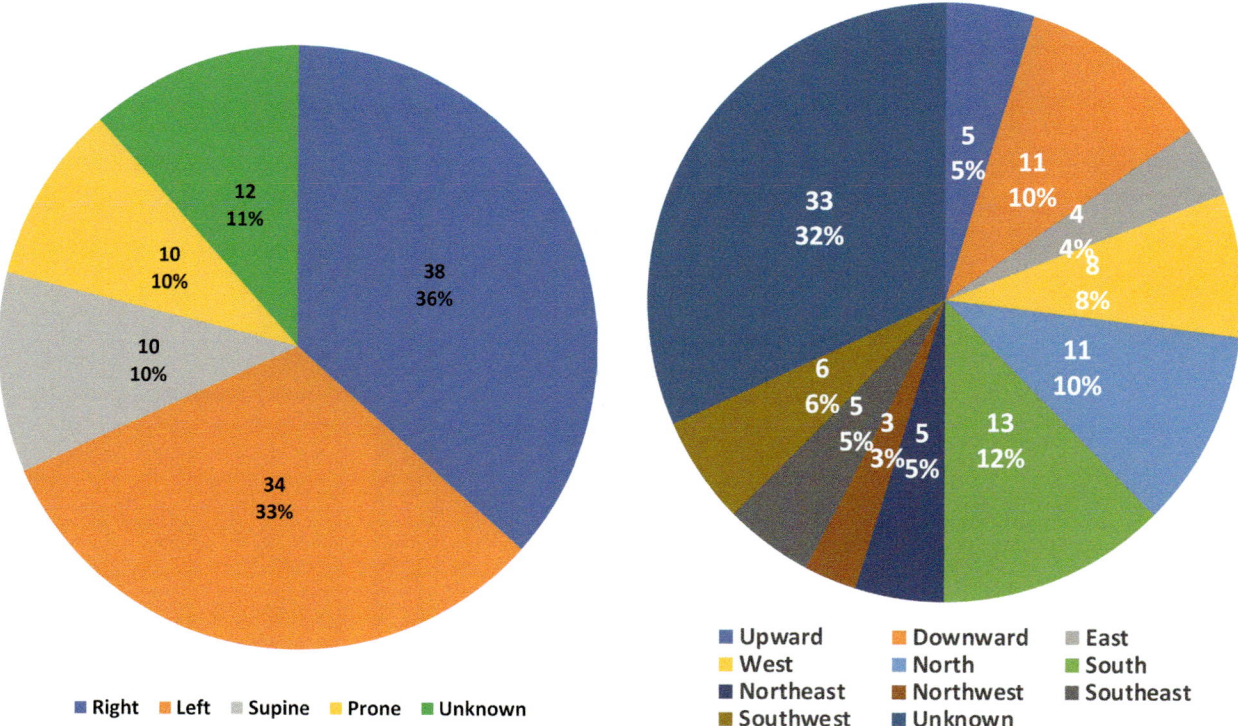

Figure 4-8. Primary burials' age-based body position.

Figure 4-9. Primary burials' age-based face direction.

or lacking body parts including skulls or long bones. In total, 26 primary individuals were discovered in a disturbed condition, some of them were discovered in the collective burials. It is suggested that the disturbance occurred during the removal of body parts. The retrieved parts were relocated into another burial deposit in the cemetery, where several dismembered and articulated bodily parts were uncovered on the cemetery ground and within the collective burials.

2) Secondary Burials/Pits

Secondary burials refer to skeletons, partial or complete, removed from their original interment context and relocated and reinterred in ultimate location or context.

Secondary burials are the second largest burial category uncovered at Kerkh Cemetery (58 individuals = 24%) (Table 4-3). The secondary burials are categorized into two basic types:

a) Secondary single inhumation.
b) Collective burial comprising large number of deceased.

The first type indicates typical secondary burials contain incomplete human remains inhumated individually in the cemetery (Figure 4-10). The number of deceased in this type is 17 individuals (29%). Most of these individuals were incomplete, and in a fragmented condition with separated skulls/ crania, long bones, and fragmented body parts, which seem to have been retrieved from its original interment context and relocated to another context. Detached skulls and separated long bones were found in different places in the cemetery. These remains were even buried in ground of the cemetery in shallow pit, or beside primary burials. In some instances, they were buried together with animal bones, stones and pottery fragments. Seemingly, some of the body parts were removed by the Neolithic people from their primary context and relocated to a secondary context.

The second type indicates a number of deceased buried collectively in different forms of burial context. The size of the collective burials different depending on the number of burials and the layout is varied as well. The collective burials are (Figure 4-11):

Table 4-3. Sex and age-based distribution of deceased in the secondary burials at Kerkh Cemetery.

Sex/Age	Fetal	Perinatal	Infant	Juvenile	Subadult	Adult	Young adult	Middle adult	Old adult	Unknown	Total
Male						3	1	1	1		6
Probable Male						1	1		1		3
Female						1	1		1		3
Probable Female						2	3	2			7
Unknown	1	3	4	15	3	4	1			8	39
Total	1	3	4	15	3	11	7	3	3	8	58

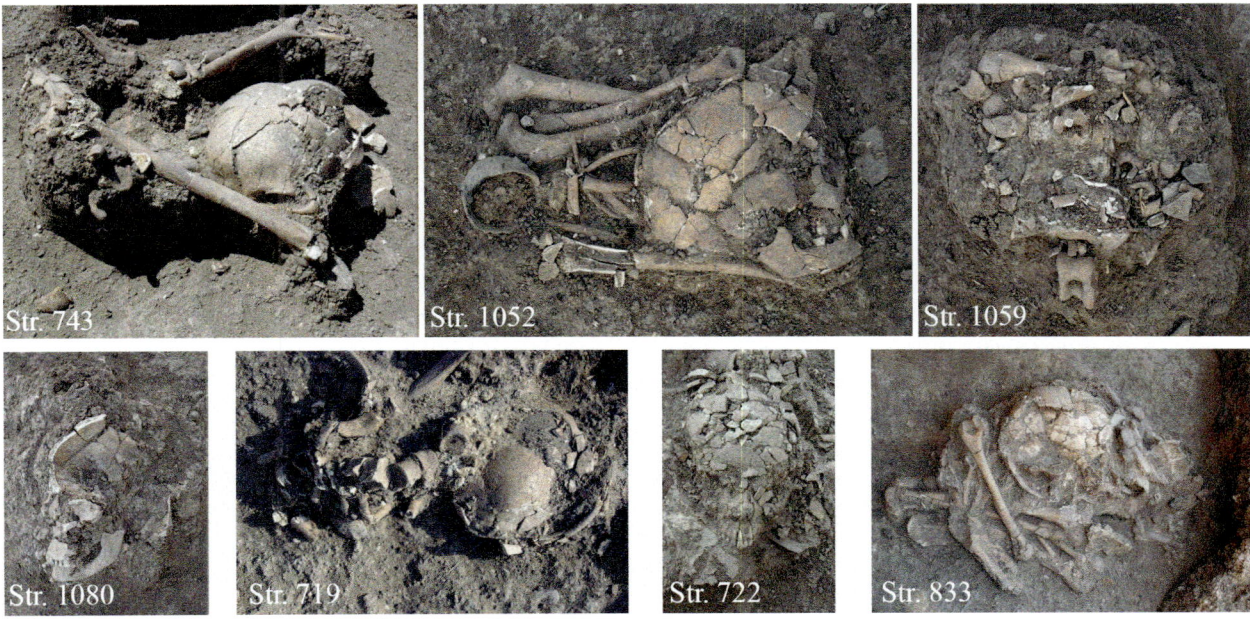

Figure 4-10. Secondary burials at Kerkh Cemetery.

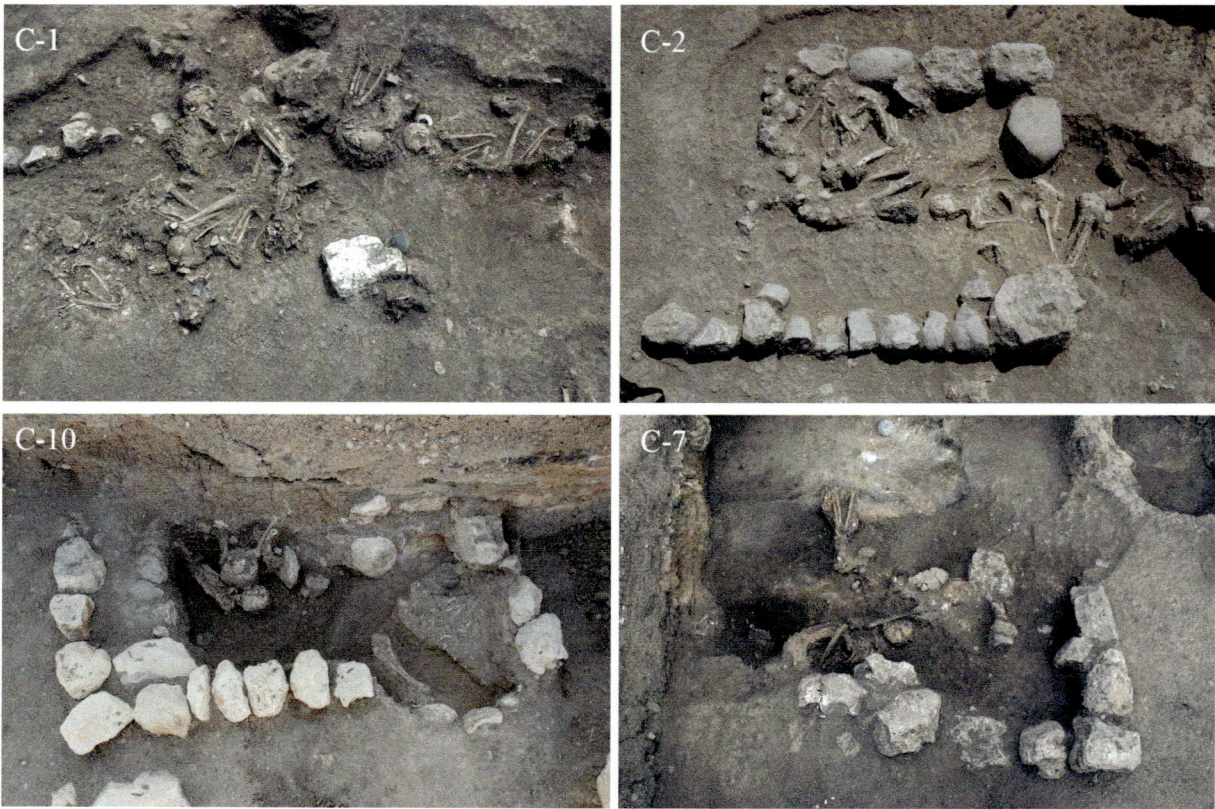

Figure 4-11. Collective burials at Kerkh Cemetery.

1. Collective burial pits are surrounded partially or completely by rows of limestones (e.g., C10).
2. Shallow collective burials enclosed partially or completely by rows of limestones (e.g., C2).
3. Collective burials constructed in the remnant of abandoned buildings (e.g., C7).
4. Collective burials located adjacent to the former burials and not enclosed by stones (e.g., C1).

The majority of secondary burials were uncovered from the collective context (41 individuals = 71%). Individuals of all ages and both sexes were present, which may indicate that the collective burials were not associated with specific people. Furthermore, the age distribution and the sex ratio indicate that the individuals were not intentionally selected by age or sex, which may indicate the use of the area for a specific household for a period of time. Some individuals in the collective burials were buried intact, however, some were partly articulated, and others were represented only by skull and/or long bones. The collective burial structural features range in size depending on the number of individuals buried within. The presence of a large number of individuals in the collective burials (between 4 – 22) suggests the use of the same pit for a long time, likely for several generations.

Adults and juveniles were the largest age group uncovered in the secondary burials. Most were fragmented and lacking skeletal parts to facilitate identifying the body position, body axis, and face directions. Thus, none of deceased's body direction was identified in the secondary burials. Only 13 of the individuals face direction was identified, whereas, 45 were unknown.

3) Cremation Burials/Pits

Cremation burials refer to the intentional manipulating of the dead body using fire and burning it to ashes, cremated and fragmented skeleton parts that found in the crematorium pit, or remains that have burnt traces removed from the crematorium pit and relocated to a different interment context.

A total of 46 individuals (19%) were discovered from nine different locations in the Kerkh cemetery (Table 4-4). Most of the cremation burials belong to Layers 5-6, and notably, no cremated fetus was discovered. Cremated human remains were discovered from two different contexts and hence classified into two categories:

a) Crematorium pit (primary cremation): Skeletons or corpses were cremated in the pit and reduced to ashes or heavily burnt fragments, and the pit was covered afterward with soil.

b) Removed burnt bones (secondary cremation): Burnt bones were removed from a crematorium

Table 4-4. Sex and age-based distribution of deceased in the cremation burials at Kerkh Cemetery.

Sex/Age	Perinatal	Infant	Juvenile	Subadult	Adult	Young adult	Middle adult	Old adult	Unknown	Total
Male										
Probable Male					4	2	2			8
Female										
Probable Female				1	6					7
Unknown	1	1	11	4	12			1	1	31
Total	1	1	11	5	22	2	2	1	1	46

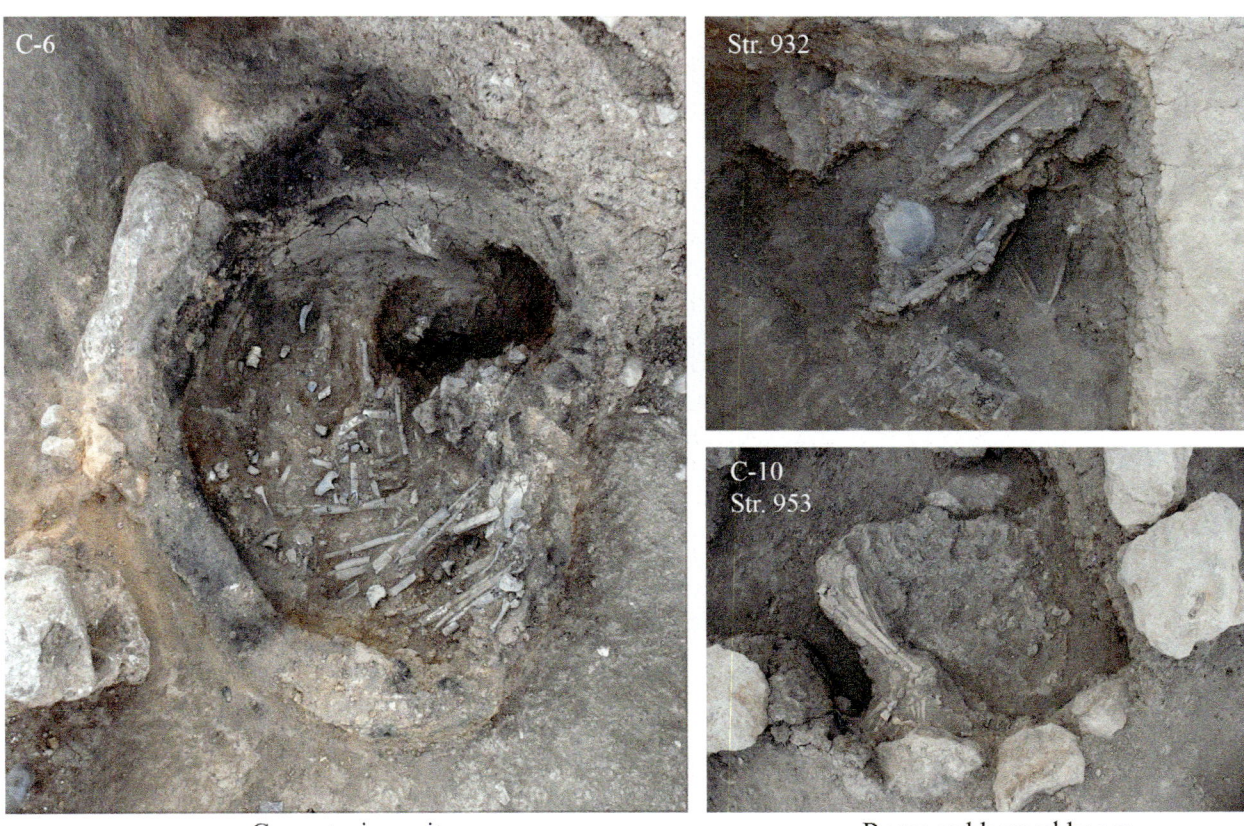

Crematorium pit   Removed burned bones

Figure 4-12. Cremation burials at Kerkh Cemetery.

pit and relocated to another place in the cemetery (Figure 4-12).

3-a) Crematorium Pits

Three crematorium pits were uncovered in the Kerkh cemetery; they are C5, C6 and C9 (further details and descriptions for each pit will be provided in Chapter 5). The three crematorium pits revealed the remains of 17 individuals (37%), whereas the rest of burnt remains 29 individuals (63%) were uncovered with other individuals in the collective burials or in other sections of the cemetery beside intact individuals. The interior wall and bottom of the pits were burnt and changed into an orange color. The pits were full of burned soil, black and white ash, charcoal and cremated human remains. The size of the crematorium pits was relatively

small to accommodate intact bodies, however, the number of individuals in each pit ranges from five to seven individuals. Given the small size of the pit, cremating a number of intact and fresh human bodies simultaneously is not possible. Therefore, the human remains were decomposed or nearly decomposed before retrieved from the original burial and then placed into the crematorium pit for cremation.

The crematorium pits contain remains of individuals of various age groups, but not fetus was cremated. The burnt human bones exhibit a white, gray or bluish black color due to the high temperature. However, some skulls such as at C5 and C6 retained their original shape and a lot of burnt long bones were placed around them. Some articulated bones and a few remnants of un-burnt bones were also found from C9.

Figure 4-13. Urn burials
at Kerkh Cemetery.

3-b) Removed Burned Bones

Besides crematorium pits, some cremated human bones were discovered from various locations within the cemetery (29 individuals = 63%). The cremated remains were uncovered solo on the cemetery ground, or in secondary burial pit, or in collective burials where intact and un-burnt burials were buried. No traces of fire or cremation were observed neither in the place where the cremated remains were uncovered nor on the intact burials remains. Thus, these burned human remains must have been cremated elsewhere and subsequently removed from that place. Therefore, the evidence suggests that some burned bones were removed from the crematorium pit after the end of cremation and relocated into its ultimate interment position beside other individual remains in a different interment context.

Exceptionally, C8 uncovered a cluster of small, fragmented and cremated human bones from at least eight individuals. Most of these bones turned white, which indicates that the bones were burnt at high temperatures. Some burned skull fragments were also covered with DFBW sherds. Unlike the removed burnt bones uncovered in some instances in burials contains intact human remains, all the remains in this cluster were cremated and no intact bones were uncovered.

Almost all cremation burials in both types were discovered in the lower layers and in the eastern part of the cemetery (Figure 4-1 and Chapter 9). The discovery of a number of cremation pits indicates that cremation activities took place in Kerkh cemetery and human bones were intentional manipulated using fire on a large scale.

The cremated human remains were heavily dismembered and fragile due to high temperature. Most of the remains were analyzed through the skulls, mandibles and long bones that retained their shape after cremation. Thus, the age, sex, and body axis direction or interment position for most of the individuals were indeterminate, however, adult and juvenile were the most cremated burials. Of those whose sex was determinate, eight individuals (17%) were probable male, seven individuals (15%) were probable female and 31 individuals (68%) were unknown. All of the individuals' body position was indeterminate. Also, most of the individuals' face direction was not identified except for two specimens; one faces north and another south.

4) Urn Burials

Urn burials refer to individuals buried inside different shaped pottery vessels.

Two specimens of urn burials were uncovered in the Kerkh cemetery belong to a fetus and juvenile (Figure 4-13). The fetus (Str. 981) was buried within a DFBW bowl. An intact fetus was placed in the bottom of the pottery, filled with soil and then placed upside down. The juvenile (Str. 1073) was represented by fragmented bones buried within unique square-shaped pottery.

Interestingly, another fetus (Str. 933) was buried on its right side, but its body was covered with DFBW pottery sherds. The way in which this individual was buried suggests that people aimed to protect its body by covering it with pottery sherds (like a lid).

Kerkh cemetery provides one of the oldest evidences of urn burials in the Neolithic period. However, this practice continued into subsequent periods and is attested in many sites.

5) Unknown Burials

Unknown burials refer to disarticulated and isolated skeletons removed from the original interment context or lacking skeletal elements that help to determine the origin deposition and the burial type (Figure 4-14).

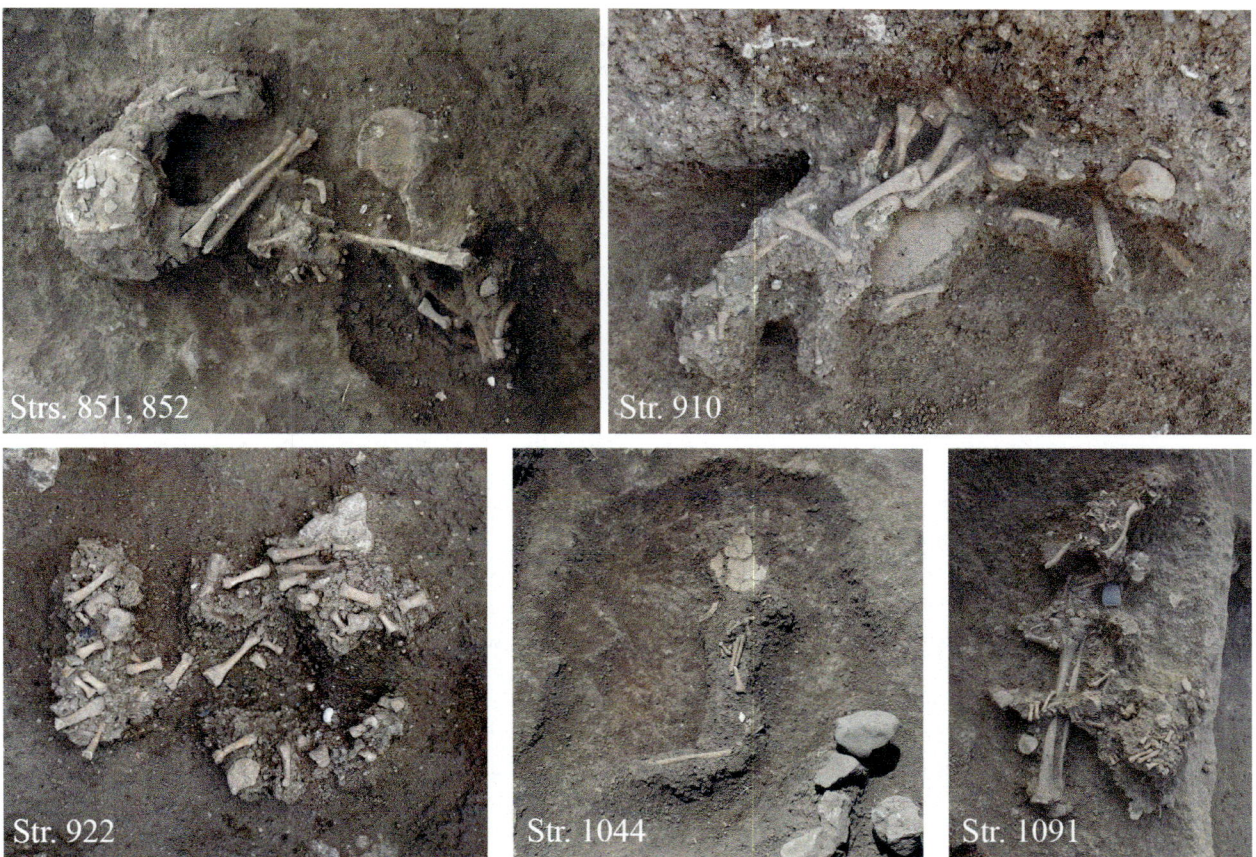

Figure 4-14. Unknown burials at Kerkh Cemetery.

Table 4-5. Sex and age-based distribution of deceased in the unknown burials at Kerkh Cemetery.

Sex/Age	Perinatal	Infant	Juvenile	Subadult	Adult	Young adult	Old adult	Unknown	Total
Male									
Probable Male					1				1
Female									
Probable Female						1			1
Unknown	2	4	11	1	9		1	4	32
Total	2	4	11	1	10	1	1	4	34

Unknown burials comprise 34 individuals (14%) of the total number of burials in the cemetery (Table 4-5). The most identified burials were adults and juveniles. All of the individuals' sex is indeterminate except two adult individuals, one is probable male and the other is probable female. None of the burial's body position or axis and face direction were identified.

The deceased in this burial type was represented by different skeletal parts and there were no particular body parts were uncovered. The human remains in this type were separated skull or skull fragments, long bones, small bones and phalanges, and heavily disturbed and dismembers long and small bones. Some of these remains seem to have been interred in its original place where excavated, but many skeletal parts were missing, which indicate removing and relocating the missing parts. Other cases showed evidence for detached skulls,

fragments of skulls, long or small bones individually interred in the cemetery, which may indicate retrieval of these bones from its original interment context and relocated to another.

2. The Transition of the Cemetery and the Distribution of Burials

This section describes the transition of the cemetery and the distribution of burials in each layer. We discuss general information about the burials in each layer of the Kerkh Neolithic cemetery. Detailed information on each burial in the Kerkh cemetery can be found in Chapter 5.

A Neolithic cemetery, located in the habitation zone of the Rouj 2c settlement, was clearly recognized in 2007 in the Central Area of Tell Ain el-Kerkh. Up to 2010, 244 individuals have been recovered from the cemetery (Figure 4-1). The area of the cemetery comprises Squares E251, E270, and E271 (each square is 10 × 10 m) in the overall grid system of Tell el-Kerkh and it covers approximately 200m². Based on pottery chronology and extensive ¹⁴C dating of the Rouj 2c layers, the cemetery dates to the late 7th millennium BC. A dozen ¹⁴C dates taken directly from human bone samples in the burials date between 7,550±80 and 7,115±70 uncal BP, with most concentrated dates being around 7,400s and 7,300s uncal BP, suggesting that the cemetery was most likely used for several centuries around 6,400-6,100cal BC (see Chapter 7). This is one of the oldest outdoor communal 'cemeteries' in West Asia.

As mentioned in Chapter 3, the Rouj 2c layers from Squares E251 – E311 can be divided into at least five layers (Layers 3 to 7 from top to bottom). The burials within the cemetery, the 244 individuals, were confined to three layers (Layers 4 – 6 from top to bottom) of Squares E251, E270, and E271, and a few burials were from Square E291. Each square measured 10 × 10m, excluding Square E251, of which only the southern half was excavated (Figure 4-1). Pits were dug for most of the burials in the cemetery; the individuals were buried in them. However, cases in which the pits are clearly visible are few; in many cases, only human skeletons were detected. Therefore, in many cases, the attribution period of each burial had to be judged from the level of the basal plane of the burial, and in these cases, the precise contemporaneousness remains controversial. However, there is no doubt about the order of the overlapping burials in the cemetery. To identify the attribution layer of each burial, the cemetery at Tell el-Kerkh was subdivided into three main layers for the revealed burials. They are Layers 4, 5, and 6 (from top to bottom). Layer 7 is the habitation layer, and only residential buildings were detected in this area. The Kerkh people assigned a specific part of their settlement located to the north and east of the excavation area as a cemetery, and used it continuously for hundreds of years during the Layers 6 to 4 eras.

Each layer has produced a large number of deceased individuals, and various burial types have been uncovered. Remains of 85, 98, and 61 human skeletons have been excavated from Layers 6, 5, and 4, respectively. Each layer of the cemetery has a particular layout including the existence or absence of structures, collective burials, cremation burials/pits, and grouping of individuals.

Layer 7 (Before becoming a cemetery)

Layer 7 of this area mainly consisted of habitation structures (Str. 916 and Str. 827), which were used for daily activities (Figure 4-15). Some burials were uncovered in this layer; however, most of them seemed to be from the upper layer. People at Tell el-Kerkh buried their dead in residential dwellings. However, they did so after the buildings were abandoned. In Squares E270 – 271, people used the remnants of these abandoned habitation buildings to bury their dead, and the buildings and surrounding spaces became a part of the cemetery in Layer 6.

As mentioned in Chapter 3, Str. 827 was one of the most notable houses discovered in the Central Area of Tell Ain el-Kerkh. It was a large building extending over Square E271 and the neighboring Square E270. It has a rectangular plan consisting of two stories measuring 4.2 × 7.7m. Many objects were discovered from this building, and the most remarkable objects were a series of food processing tools, such as saddle querns and grinding stones. These finds indicate that this building was used as a communal mill and/ or kitchen. The black residue and burnt accumulation remain in Str. 827, indicate that a fire burnt caused the building down to the floor level and collapse of the wood which supported the roof. The remains of carbonized timbers, burnt deposits, and soil can be seen on the building's floors and along its east-west corridor. Str. 827 was abandoned after burning down. A young individual (Str. 908) was found buried inside Room 5 of Str. 827, but no traces of burning were observed on the skeleton. In addition, the burial pit of Str. 908 had partially broken the wall of Room 5. Therefore, it is clear that the burial of Str. 908 was dug from the upper level and that the deceased was buried near the walls of Room 5 after Str. 827 was abandoned. Therefore, at the location of the wreckage of Str. 827, people were aware of the walls of Room 5 for a burial place. The burial pit of Str. 908 was probably dug during the following Layer 6 era and a deceased juvenile was buried there.

The Str. 916 building was discovered north of Str. 827 in the same layer, beyond a narrow 0.7m wide street. It was excavated in two successive seasons from 2009 to 2010. The direction and long axis of this building are similar to those of Str. 827. As the northern half of this structure extends beyond the excavated area, only the southern half of the building was uncovered. It possibly has a rectangular plan, measuring 5.2m from east to west. The building was divided into at least two rooms. Str. 916, with walls of pisé on a stone foundation, seems to have functioned as a residential building based on its size and structure. However, after this residential building was abandoned, it seemed to have been used as a graveyard. The eastern room was severely damaged by two cremation pits (C5 and C9) from Layer 6, and most of the walls were destroyed, excluding the western pisé wall and the southern stone foundation. Near this southern stone foundation, we discovered a cluster of primary burials consisting of four individuals

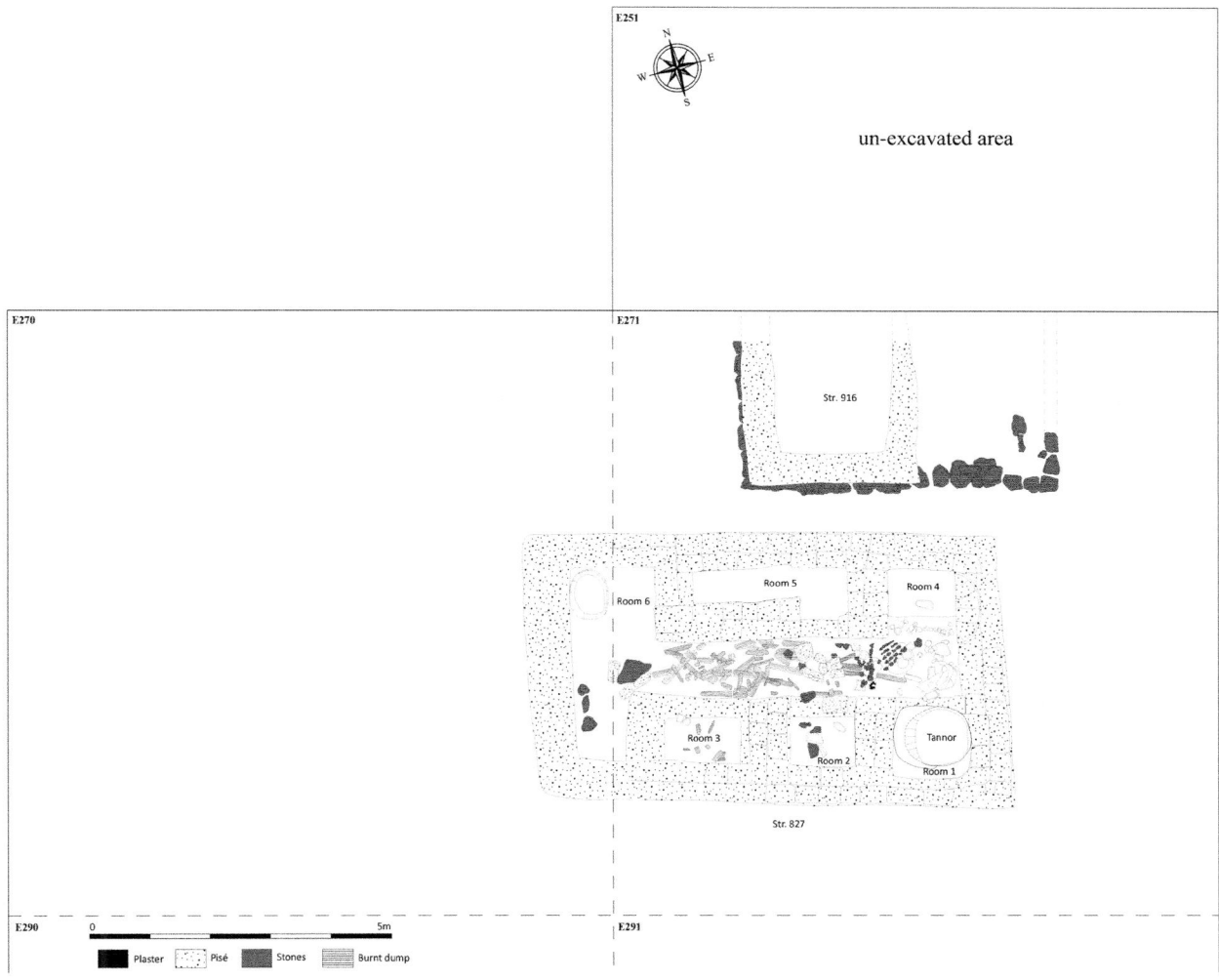

Figure 4-15. The area of Kerkh Cemetery, Layer 7.

(Concentration 7-1). Since the basal planes of these human skeletons and the basal planes of the C5 and C9 crematorium pits, which were clearly dug from the upper layer, were at almost the same level, the C7-1 burials were conducted considering the southern wall of the Str. 916 eastern room. Therefore, it is believed that the C7-1 burials occurred during the Layer 6 era. In the western room of Str. 916, some bark or white, hide-like, thin organic material was found stretched. Below this organic material, a few carbonized timbers and many human skeletons were detected. They were clearly buried in the Str. 916 western room after this building was no longer used as a residence. We call this cluster of human skeletons C7-2; it includes at least nine human individuals (Strs. 932, 984, 985, and 988). The basal planes of the human skeletons belonging to C7-2 are similar to those of the C7-1 skeletons, and these burials probably occurred during the Layer 6 era as well.

In summary, during the Layer 7 period, the area around Squares E251 – E271 was used for residential purposes. There was a residential building and a communal mill/

kitchen. However, after these buildings burned down and they were abandoned, it is assumed that their ruins were used as a burial ground in the next era.

Layer 6 (The beginning of the cemetery)

The area of Squares E270 – E271 suddenly became a graveyard in the Layer 6 era (Figure 4-16). It is probable that after Strs. 827 and 916 were abandoned, their remnants were not removed. People used these remnants to bury the deceased. As mentioned above, an 11-13-year-old subadult (Str. 908) was buried in a pit dug in Room 5 of Str. 827. The burial pit damaged the wall of Room 5, and the skeleton of the subadult had no burn marks. Four adults (Concentration 7-1; Strs. 860-863) were buried near the southern wall of the eastern room of Str. 916. Nine individuals were buried in the western room of Str. 916 (Concentration 7-2). Three of them are primary burials, including a young adult male (Str. 984), a middle-aged female (Str. 988), and a 6-7-year-old juvenile (Str. 985). Three are cremated individuals (adult, subadult, and juvenile), and the remaining three are secondary burials (fetal and two juveniles) (Str.

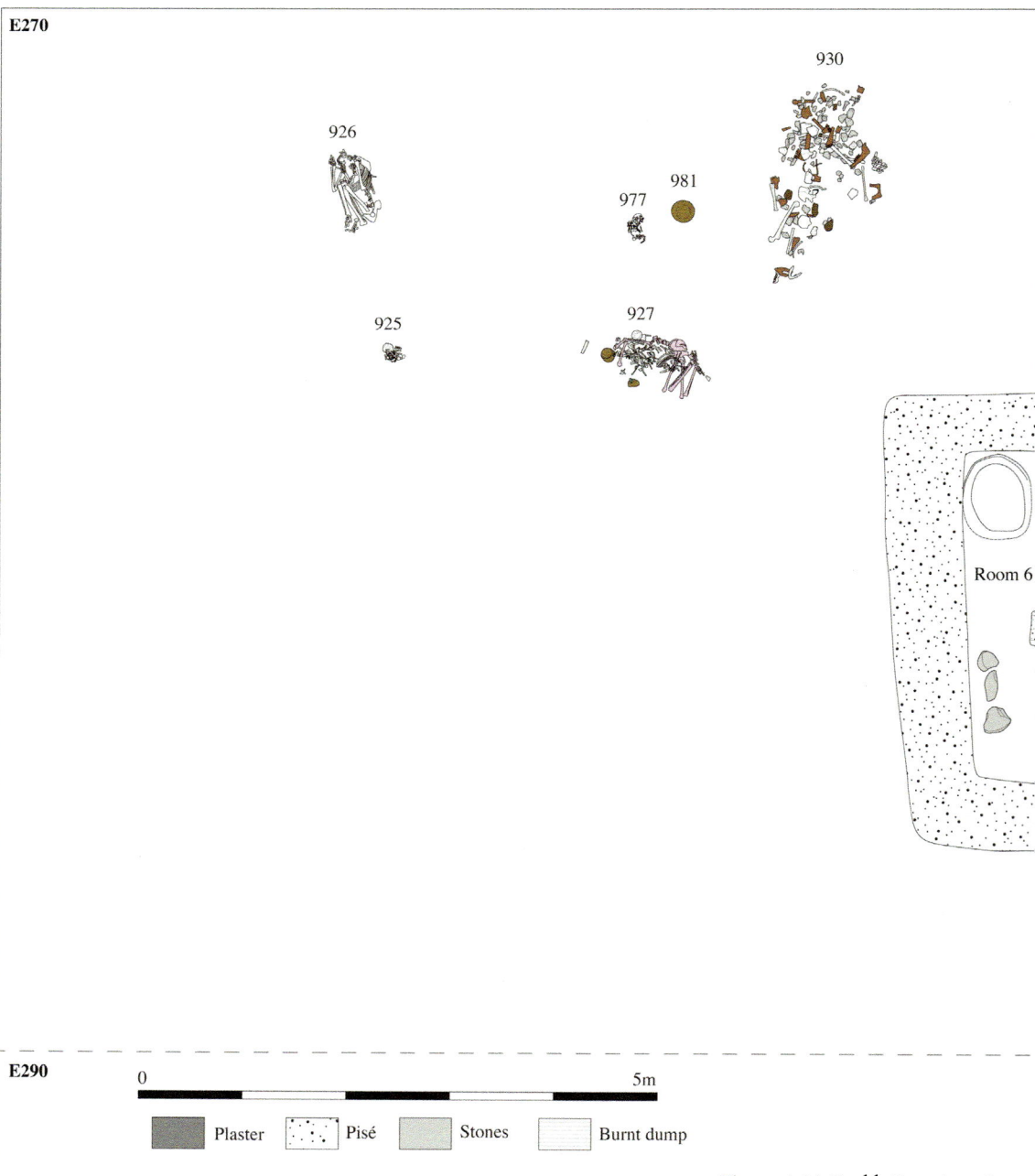

Figure 4-16. Kerkh Cemetery, Layer

E251

un-excavated area

E271

910

932 984 985

C-9

C-5

858 857

856

855 842

C-7 (2)

988

860 861 C-7 (1)

862

863

913

922 914 921

916

924

C-10

920

Room 5

908 Room 4

933

C-8

Room 3

942

865

866

867 931

Tannor

868

Room 2

C-6

Room 1

827

941

946

E291

81

932). Some of the adults were buried with a wealth of burial goods (Strs. 860, 862, 984, and 988). We do not know the relationship between these buildings and people buried. However, it is assumed that they were connected in some way with these buildings.

A young adult female (Str. 924) and a 3-4-year-old juvenile (Str. 920) were discovered along the narrow street between Strs. 827 and 916. It is clear that the walls of these building structures were standing when their burial pits were dug and they were buried along the street.

An impressive collective burial was discovered at the eastern edge of Square E270. It is a pit grave of Concentration 10 North; it produced at least 15 individuals (Strs. 943, 947, 962, 971, 972, 978, 979, 980, 983, 991, 993, 995, 996, 998, and 999). The deceased are diverse in age and sex, and they were buried successively over a long period in the small pit. The grave pit seems to have been used as a collective burial for an extended family. C10 North was located east of Strs. 827 and 916, and the pit grave was surrounded with another pit grave (C10 South) by rows of stones. These rows of stones do not seem to be the wall foundation of the residential building. In other words, in order to divide the C10 graveyard, stone rows were aligned like the stone foundation of residential buildings. It could be called a pseudo house grave.

One of the striking burial types in Layer 6 is the crematorium pit. Concentrations 5, 6, and 9 (C5, C6, and C9) are of this burial type, and they were discovered in Square E271b. As each crematorium pit had 5 – 7 cremated individuals, a large number of cremated skeletons were discovered in these three crematorium pits in the Layer 6 at the cemetery. As we will discuss in Chapter 8, the Kerkh Neolithic people did not burn fresh corpses in these pits; they disinterred bodies from the cemetery and burned them in these pits. Hence, we suggest that the cremation practice at Kerkh was a type of secondary burial practice. Nevertheless, the Kerkh Neolithic people undoubtedly practiced cremation, and these crematorium pits could be considered one of the earliest pieces of clear evidence of cremation in West Asian archaeology.

In addition to these crematorium pits, a characteristic secondary burial was detected in Square E270b. It is Str. 930, which produced some human skulls and mandibles mixed with many animal bones, especially cattle mandibles. The human remains from this deposit belong to three adult females. Moreover, two female adult primary burials without skulls were discovered beside Str. 930 (Strs. 926 and 927). We examined the connection between these structures, but there was no connection between these human bones. Regardless, they suggest that various rituals were held in association with the burial practices in the cemetery.

Layer 6 is the first layer forming the Kerkh Neolithic cemetery. A total of 85 individuals (35%) were uncovered in this layer (Table 4-6). Various types of burials existed since the cemetery was formed. People used the abandoned houses to bury their dead, and this type of 'house grave' was a part of the cemetery. The deceased were buried not only in the building structures, but also in the available spaces around and between them. Some were uncovered in the western part of the cemetery, and fewer were found south of Str. 827; the majority was discovered east of Str. 827. C10 burial pits were deliberately surrounded by stone rows, which looked like a stone foundation for residential buildings (Figure 4-11).

Interestingly, all the crematorium pits (C5, C6, and C9) that were uncovered in the cemetery were from this layer, the oldest. Hence, a large number of cremated skeletons were uncovered in this layer. One urn burial of a fetus (Str. 981) and two skull removal specimens (Strs. 926 and 927) were discovered in the western area. Four collective burials (C7-1, C7-2, C8, and C10) were also discovered in this layer.

The collective burials revealed 43 individuals, and 17 individuals were discovered from the crematorium pits. However, cremated burials uncovered from the crematorium pits and other parts of the cemetery were the largest type in this layer. All burial types were discovered from this layer, however, primary individuals were the largest category (Figure 4-17). Many of the skeletons were fragmented or in a bad condition due to severe commingling or cremation conditions, thus

Table 4-6. Sex and age of deceased in the Layer 6 at Kerkh Cemetery.

Sex/Age	Fetal	Perinatal	Infant	Juvenile	Subadult	Adult	Young adult	Middle adult	Old adult	Unknown	Total
Male							1	1			2
Probable Male						2	4	2			8
Female							2	1			3
Probable Female				1		5	6	2			14
Unknown	5	3	3	19	6	18			2	2	58
Total	5	3	3	19	7	25	13	6	2	2	85

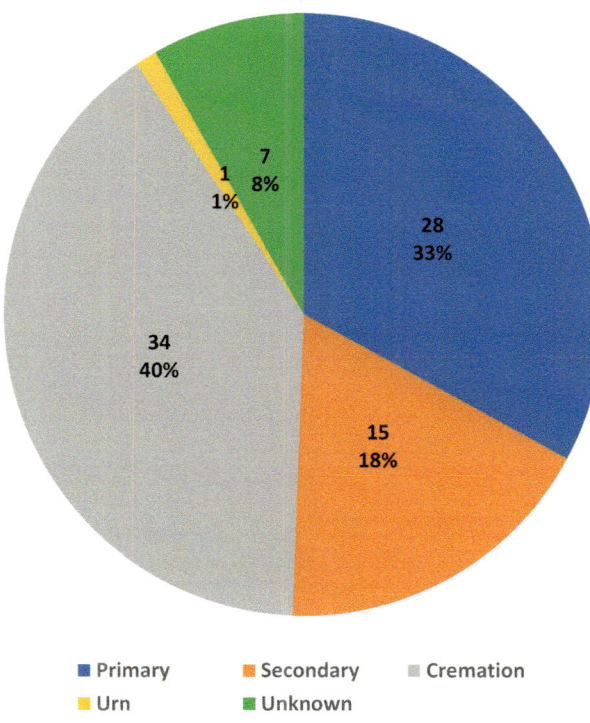

Figure 4-17. Burial types at Layer 6.

Archaeological investigation shows that the feature of grouping burials in this layer is obvious. The number of individual burials in this layer was limited (15 burials) compared to the group burials. Eight burial groups comprising 70 individuals were identified including the collective burials and crematorium pits (Figures 4-18, 4-19). In the western part of the cemetery in Square E270, ten individuals were uncovered. Both Str. 927 and 930 were comprised of three individuals, whereas the other burials were individual. All the individual burials in this layer were inhumed in a shallow pit except for Str. 941, which was buried within a deeper pit and Str. 908, which was buried inside room 5 of the abandoned building structure (Str. 827). The burials in groups 1 and 7 were placed on the surface of the cemetery in a shallow pit, whereas all other group burials took place in a determined location. The burials took place even in the abandoned structures such as group 2 and 3, or they were partly enclosed by rows of limestone such as groups 6, or the human remains were left in the crematorium pits after the end of cremation such as groups 4, 5 and 8.

Group 2 in Str. 916, for example, contains nine burials comprising three adults, one sub-adult, four juveniles and one fetus. Three individuals were cremated; an adult male, a subadult and a juvenile. Among the adults whose sex was identified, only one mid-adult female (Str. 988) was identified in this accommodation and was accompanied by several grave goods. Eight of the deceased were buried in the western part of the structure over and beside each other. Based on the number of the deceased in this group, an extended household may have used this place for interring their deceased for at least two generations. Seemingly, the number of grave goods dedicated to the female and interring her alone beside the other members may indicate that she is relevant to the group and had played an important role in sustaining her household.

Layer 5

Layer 5 is the mid layer of the Kerkh cemetery (Figure 4-20). In total, 61 interment context comprising (98 individuals = 40%) were discovered in this layer, and it contains the largest number of burials (Table 4-7). In this layer, only one building structure, Str. 109 was discovered, and it was constructed at the southern limit of the cemetery. However, no deceased were buried inside. All of the deceased from this layer were uncovered to the north and east of Str. 109. The dead were inhumed individually and in groups. One urn burial and five specimens of skull removal were uncovered. Two collective burials (C3 and C4) came from this layer.

All burial types were uncovered from this layer. Primary individuals were the largest category whereas

a large number (58 individuals = 68%) of individuals' sex was not determined, whereas, 10 individuals (12%) are male/probable male and 17 individuals (20%) are female/probable female. Deceased of all ages were discovered, however, adults and juveniles were the largest.

Deceased were buried in various body positions and direction and more than half of the individuals' body position is indeterminate (62 individuals = 73%). Whereas nine individuals (11%) of those whose age has been determined were buried on their right side down, six individuals (7%) on their left side down, three individuals (3%) in a supine position and five individuals (6%) in a prone position. The face directions of many individuals have not been identified (65 individuals = 76%). Hence, no unique face or body directions based on age and sex were identified among the individuals in this layer.

The dead were adorned by various kinds of grave goods. Grave goods accompanied with 24 of the 85 individuals. The grave goods accompanying the deceased were personal grave goods (most common), or they were dedicated to a group of deceased buried in particular context such as the crematorium pits or collective burials. About 106 different grave goods were uncovered in Layer 6. About 96 grave goods were accompanied the dead, and ten were dedicated to deposits containing the commingled remains or to the collective burial/ cremation pits. Grave goods were found with fifteen adults, one subadult, four juveniles, one perinatal, two fetuses and one unknown individual.

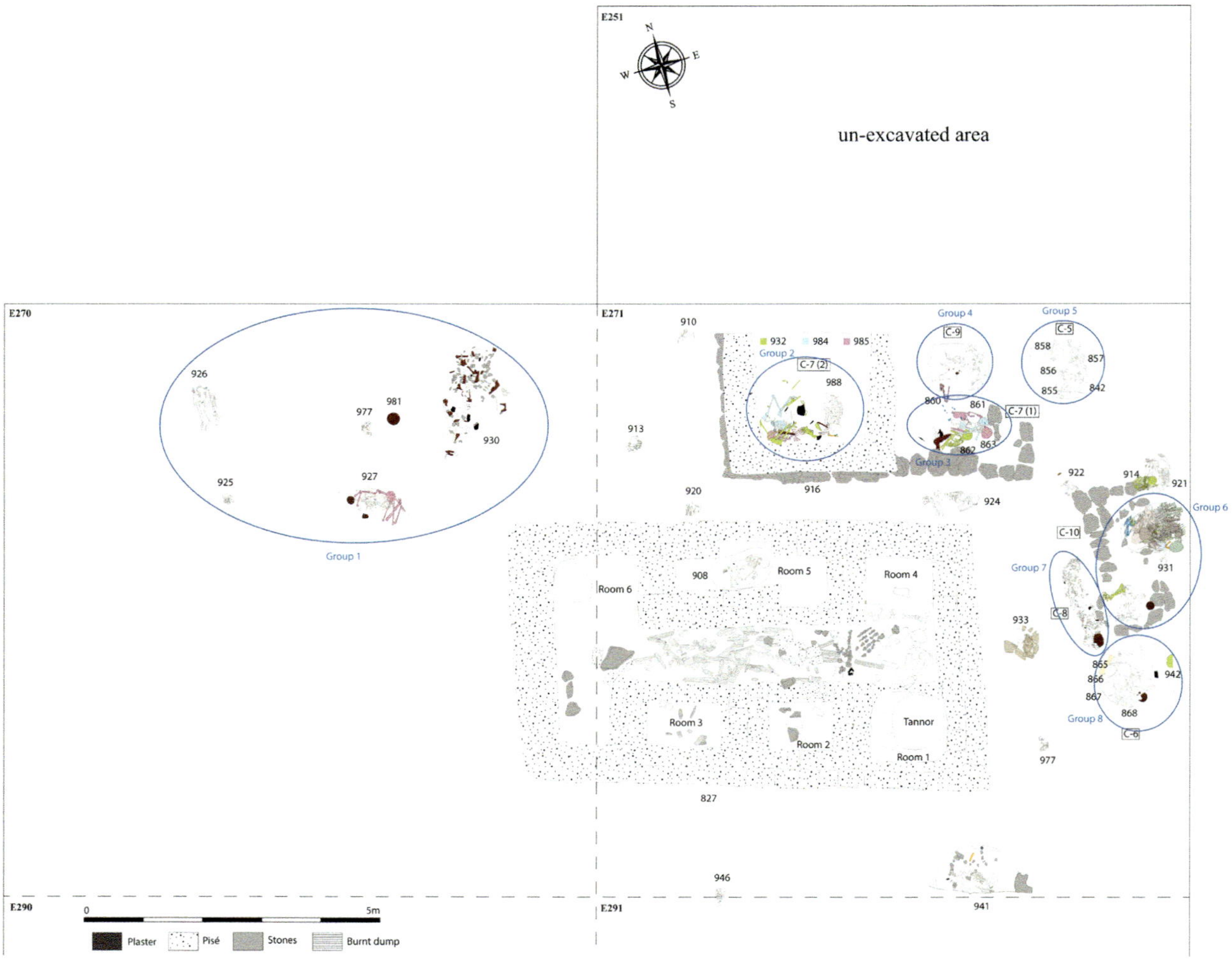

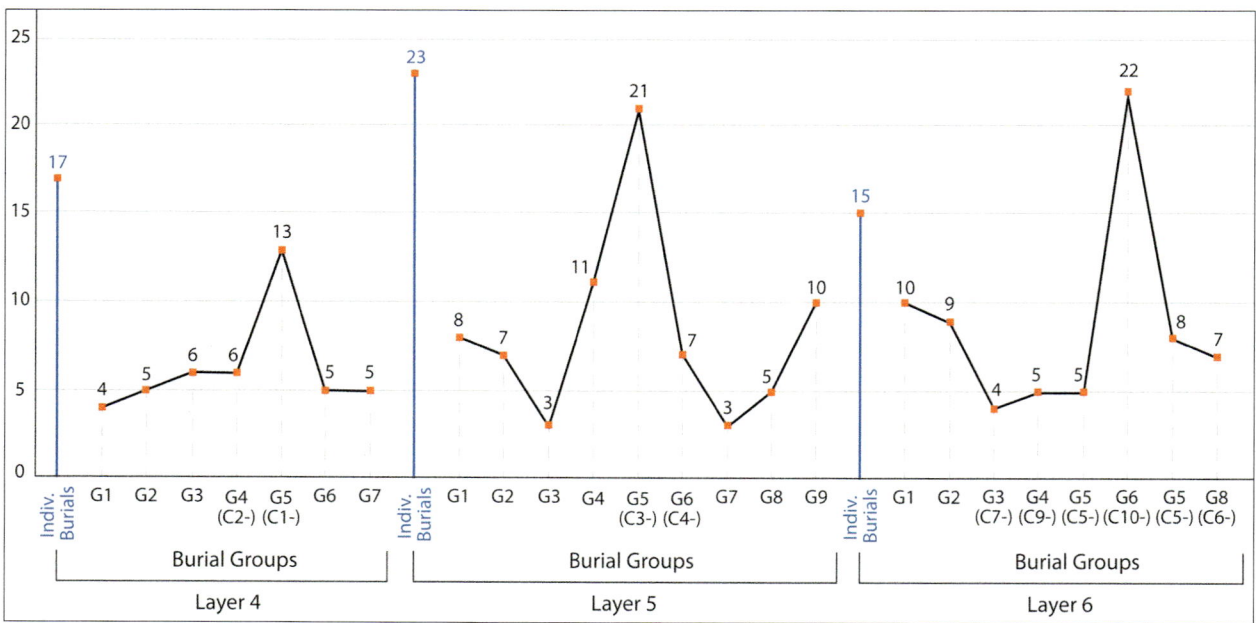

Figure 4-18. Burial groups in Kerkh Cemetery Layer 6.

Figure 4-19. Individual burials and burial groups in
layers 4, 5 and 6 of Kerkh Cemetery.

Table 4-7. Sex and age of deceased in the Layer 5 at Kerkh Cemetery.

Sex/Age	Fetal	Perinatal	Infant	Juvenile	Subadult	Adult	Young adult	Middle adult	Old adult	Unknown	Total
Male								2			2
Probable Male						7	5	3	1		16
Female						1					1
Probable Female						7	6		1		14
Unknown	1	6	7	20	3	13	1		2	12	65
Total	1	6	7	20	3	28	12	5	4	12	98

the number of secondary and unknown burials were almost the same, and greater than cremation burials (Figure 4-21). Many skeletons were in a fragmented or degraded condition, thus the sex was not determined in many instances (65 individuals = 66%). However, 18 individuals (19%) are male/probable male and 15 individuals (15%) are female/probable female.

Deceased of all ages were discovered and adults were the largest age group (49 individuals = 50%). The dead were buried in various body positions. More than half of the individuals' body direction is indeterminate (59 individuals = 60%). Whereas 17 individuals (18%) of those whose age has been determined were buried on their left side down and 13 individuals (13%) were buried on their right side down, which indicates a preferred body position. However, five individuals (5%) were buried in a supine position and four individuals (4%) in a prone position. About 69% of the individuals' face direction has not been identified. Hence, no unique face direction based on age or sex was identified among the rest of the individuals in this layer.

Various kinds of grave goods were discovered in Layer 5. In total, 76 gave goods were uncovered in this layer (including 294 flat stone beads around the neck of Str. 1087). Grave goods accompanied 20 of the individuals. The majority of grave goods (63 objects) were discovered with the deceased, whereas 13 objects were dedicated to a group or collective burials. Grave goods were discovered with 14 adults, two subadults, five juveniles. Remarkable number of grave goods were discovered near the hipbone with an adult probable female (Str. 1081). Investigation have illustrated that these objects might have been used for weaving and boring, which suggest that this female was engaged in weaving.

Grouping individuals was a common feature in this layer. Remains of 75 individuals clustered in nine burial groups were identified. In contrast, twenty-three deceased were buried individually (Figures 4-22, 4-19). Unlike the burials in Layer 6, which were found within a determined or specific location, most of the burial groups in this layer were clustered adjacent to each other in different places in the cemetery. However, group 5 (C3) and group 6 (C4) were only clustered

within collective pits. Also, a short limestone row was constructed in the southern section of the burials for group 9. Deceased in all groups – except for groups 5 and 6 – were buried next to each other and they partly overlapped in some instances. This way of interment suggests that people who participated in the funeral were aware of the location of the former grave, or it might have been partially visible; hence overlapping was avoided as much as possible. The other individual burials were interred in various positions like the other deceased in a shallow pit and dispersed in the vacant places near and between the grouped burials.

The interment pattern for group 1 was distinctive in this layer. Remains of eight individuals were interred in this group burial. Four completed skeletons were buried in a unified body axial position. The deceased in this group were accumulated in a small area and buried beside each other. They partly overlapped except for Str. 1090, which was buried under Str. 1089. Seemingly, this household followed a unified interment pattern represented as a distinctive custom to their dead members distinguishing them from other groups.

The stone row in the southern part of the group 9 area indicates that this grave pit was surrounded by stones to identify the border of the grave. The age categories of the deceased may indicate a household burial in this location. A notable number of objects accompanied the deceased representing richness in the grave goods compared to other groups. Further, one complete short-necked jar, a typical Rouj 2c DFBW pottery, was placed upright at the northeastern corner of this spot. It was probably dedicated to this mass burial.

Layer 4

Layer 4 is the upper most layer in the Kerkh cemetery (Figure 4-23). Notably, all the space in this area was used just for inhumation, and building structures were not discovered. In total, 61 individuals (25%) were discovered in this layer. Three skull removal specimens, two cremation specimens and two collective burials (C1 and C2) were uncovered.

Primary individuals were the most numerous in this layer, secondary burials were the second largest,

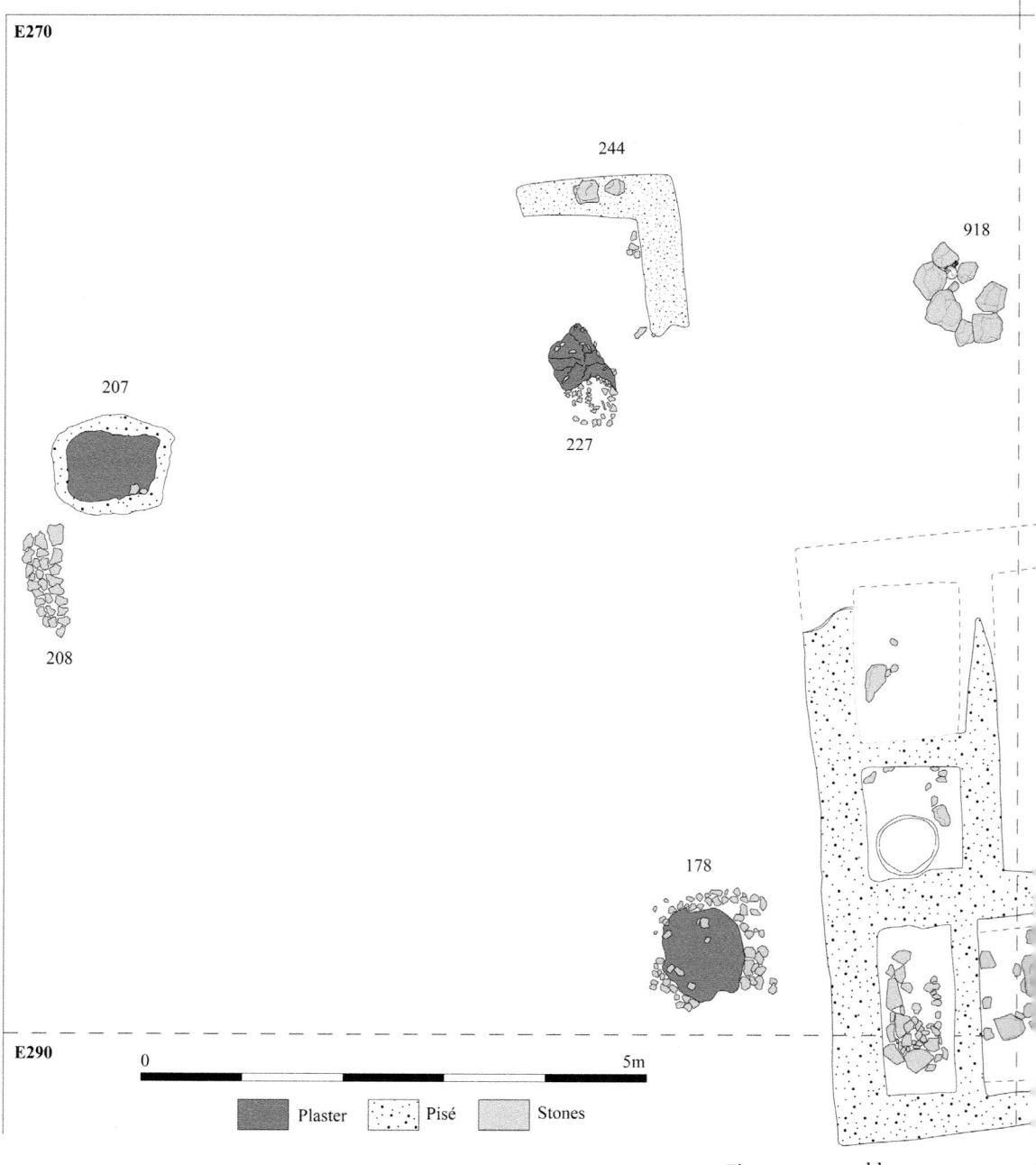

E270

E290

244

918

207

227

208

178

0   5m

Plaster   Pisé   Stones

Figure 4-20. Kerkh Cemetery, Layer

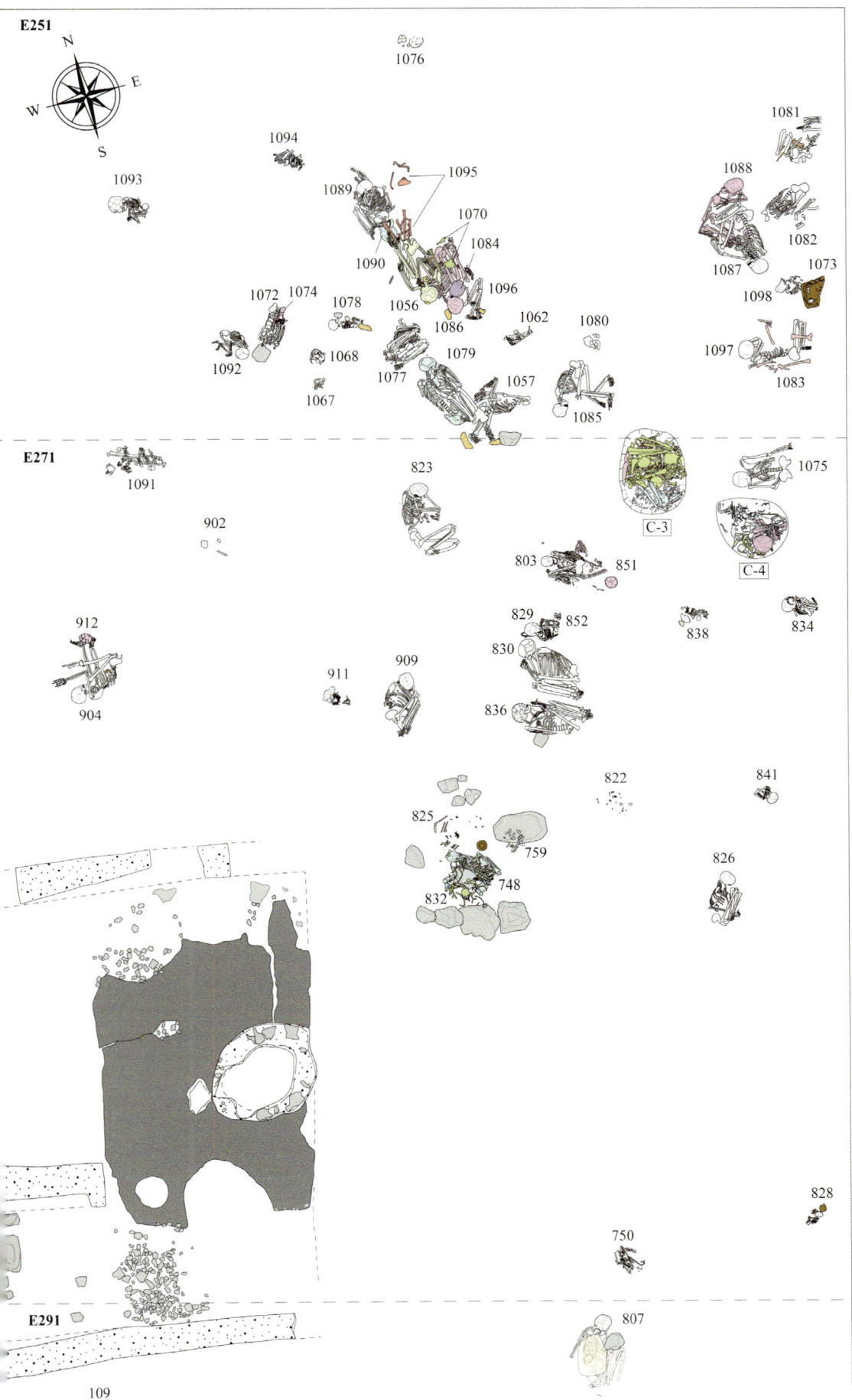

87

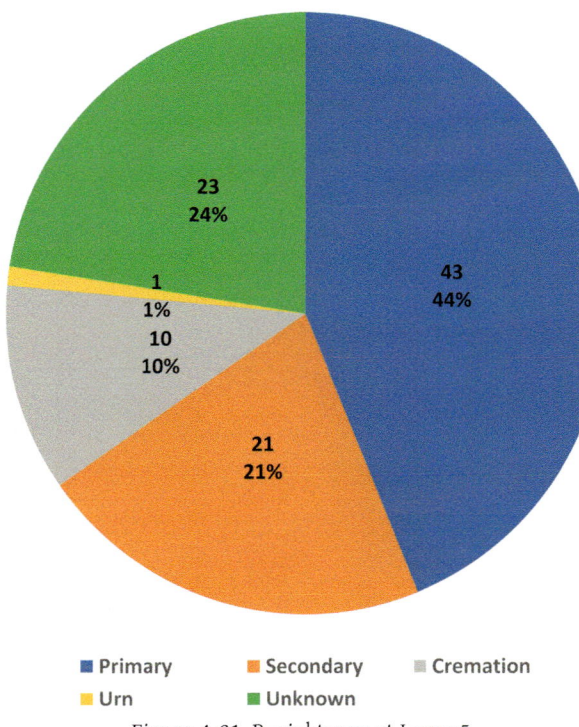

■ Primary   ■ Secondary   ■ Cremation
■ Urn   ■ Unknown

Figure 4-21. Burial types at Layer 5.

and only a few cremation and unknown burials were uncovered (Figure 4-24). Of those whose sex has been identified, the number of males/probable male (17 individuals = 28%) is larger than female/probable female (eight individuals = 13%), whereas 36 individuals (59%) were unknown due to preservation condition or were lacking skeletal parts.

Deceased of all ages were uncovered, and the adult remains were the most numerous in this layer (29 individuals = 47%) (Table 4-8). They were buried in various body directions. Half of the individuals' body direction is indeterminate (31 individuals = 51%). More than half of those whose age has been determined were buried on their right side down (16 individuals = 26%) which seems to be the preferred side of interment. However, 11 individuals (18%) were buried on their left side down, two individuals (3%) in supine position and one individual (2%) in a prone position. The face direction for 24 individuals (39%) has not been identified. Among those whose face direction has been identified, the south direction was predominant (eight individuals = 13%). Notably, none of the deceased's faces in this layer oriented to the east.

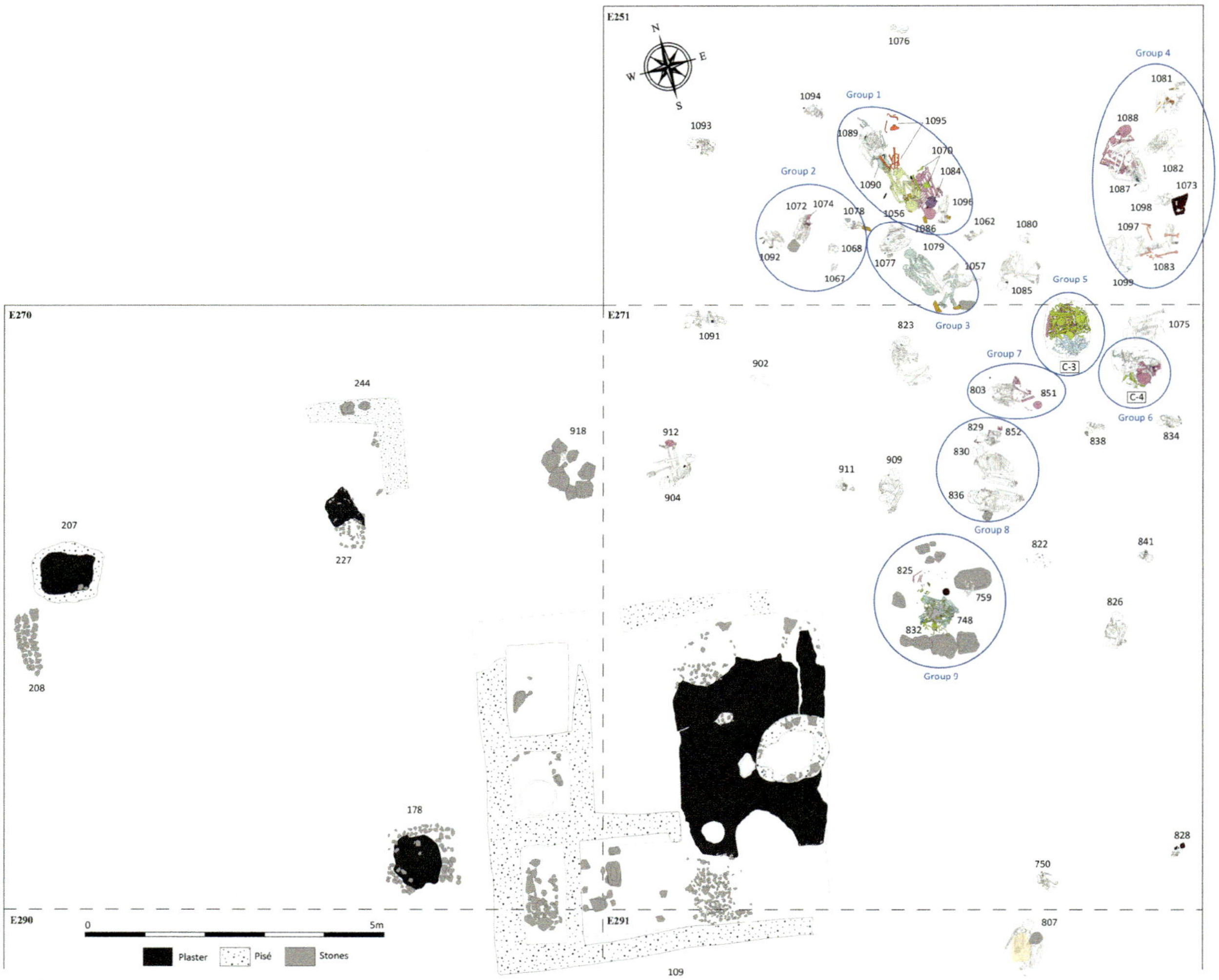

Figure 4-22. Burial groups in Kerkh Cemetery Layer 5.

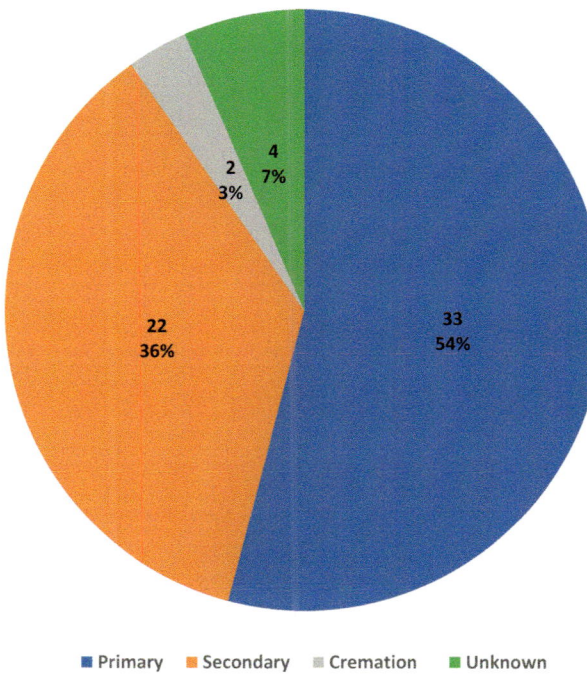

Figure 4-24. Burial types at Layer 4.

stone implement production and personal belonging indicates that these tools were used chipped stone knapping and the tomb owner was relied upon as a master of knapping (Tsuneki 2017; Arimura 2019). Investigations at Tell el-Kerkh provide us information about craft specialization and provides new insight about the lithic production technology. The evidence derived from the burials in the cemetery illustrate the division of labor based on sex in the Kerkh Neolithic society.

The dead in this layer were mainly buried in two separated clusters: in the north side and the south. Seven burial groups were identified, three in the north and four in the south (Figures 4-25 and 4-19).

Remains of forty-four individuals were uncovered from seven burial groups, whereas seventeen deceased were buried individually. The group burials were even, clustered adjacent to each other or within a determined location surrounded by a row of limestone such as group 4 (C2).

Grouping of burials in all layers indicate that inhabitants selected a part of the cemetery to bury their dead. In some instances, they have surrounded it with rows of limestone such as in (C-2) to identify the grave. Archaeological investigation suggests that the households at Tell el-Kerkh were using this structured burial to bury the dead over generations.

It is assumed that, from the beginning, the Kerkh Neolithic cemetery consisted mainly of several group burials. Each group burial often contains diverse individuals of all ages and both sexes. This evidence seems to suggest that these group burials were a family or an extended family graveyard.

Deceased were adorned with various kinds of grave goods. In total, 81 grave goods were uncovered in this layer. Notably, most of the grave goods were dedicated as a grave goods to deceased, and a few were dedicated to the burial deposits. In total, 17 individuals were accompanied with grave goods and most of them were adults. Grave goods were discovered with 10 adults, three subadults, four juveniles and one perinatal. Similar to the former layer, one middle adult male (Str. 1058) was accompanied with remarkable number of grave goods near his lower back. The objects uncovered with this individual including tools for

Table 4-8. Sex and age of deceased in the Layer 4 at Kerkh Cemetery.

Sex/Age	Fetal	Perinatal	Infant	Juvenile	Subadult	Adult	Young adult	Middle adult	Old adult	Total
Male							1	1		2
Probable Male						3	5	5	2	15
Female								2		2
Probable Female						1	2	3		6
Unknown	1	3	4	18	6	3	1			36
Total	1	3	4	18	6	7	9	11	2	61

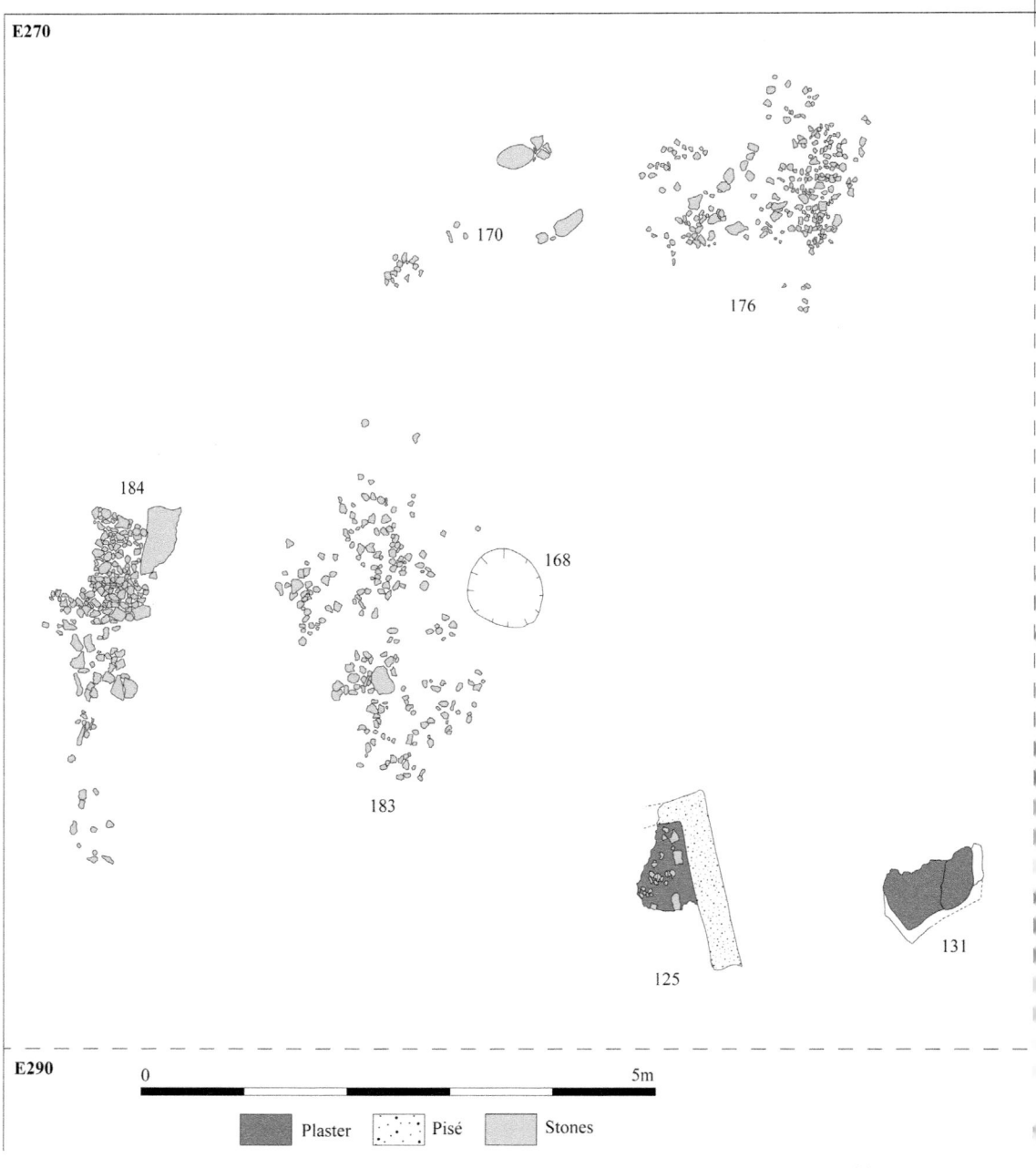

Figure 4-23. Kerkh Cemetery, Layer

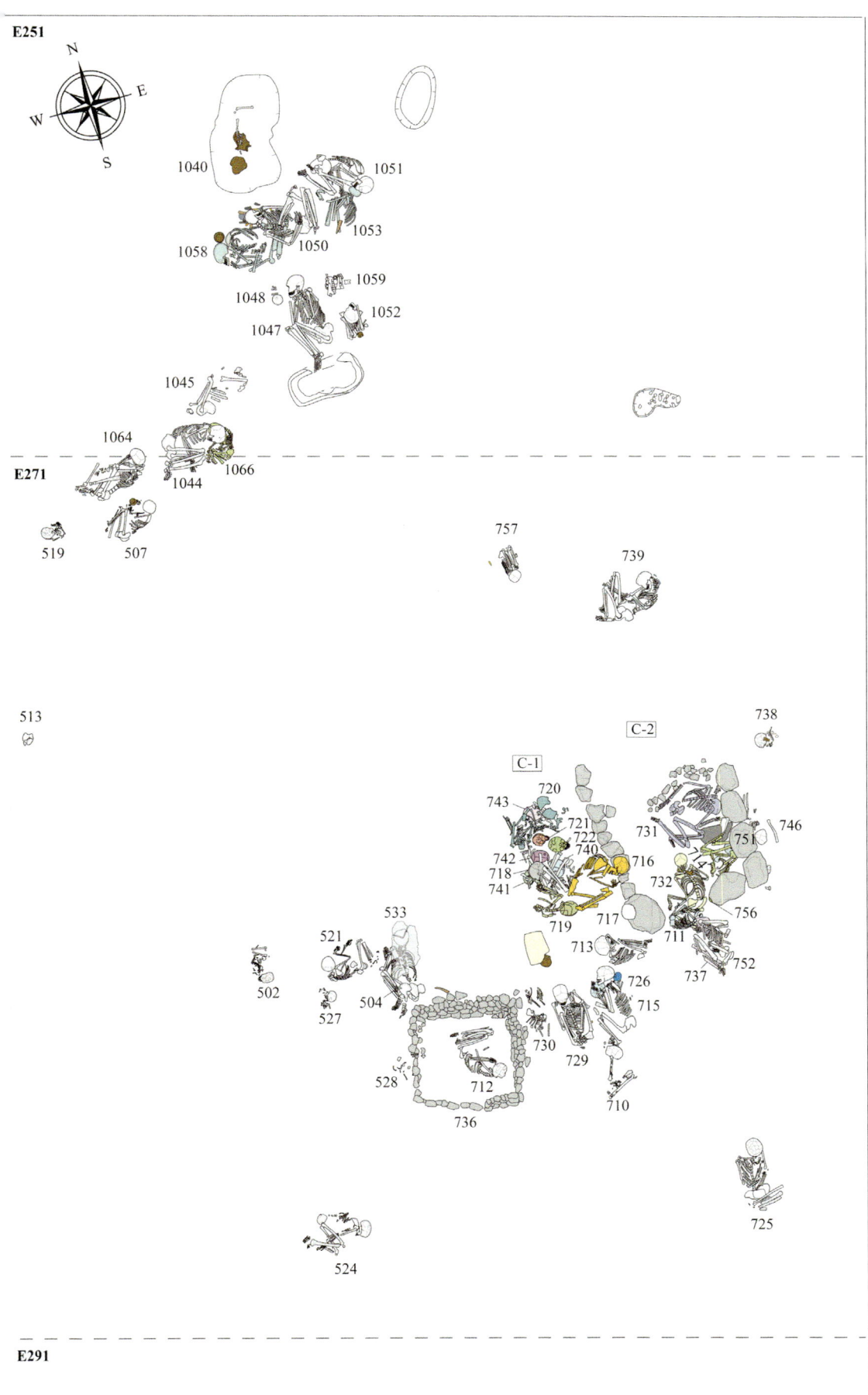

E251

N
W — E
S

1040
1051
1053
1058 1050
1048 1059
1047 1052

1045

1064
E271
1044 1066

519 507

757
739

513
738
C-2
C-1
743 720
721
731
722
746
742 740 751
718 716
741 732
756
717 711 752
719 713 737
521 533
726
502 504 715
527
730
528 712 729
736 710
524

725

E291

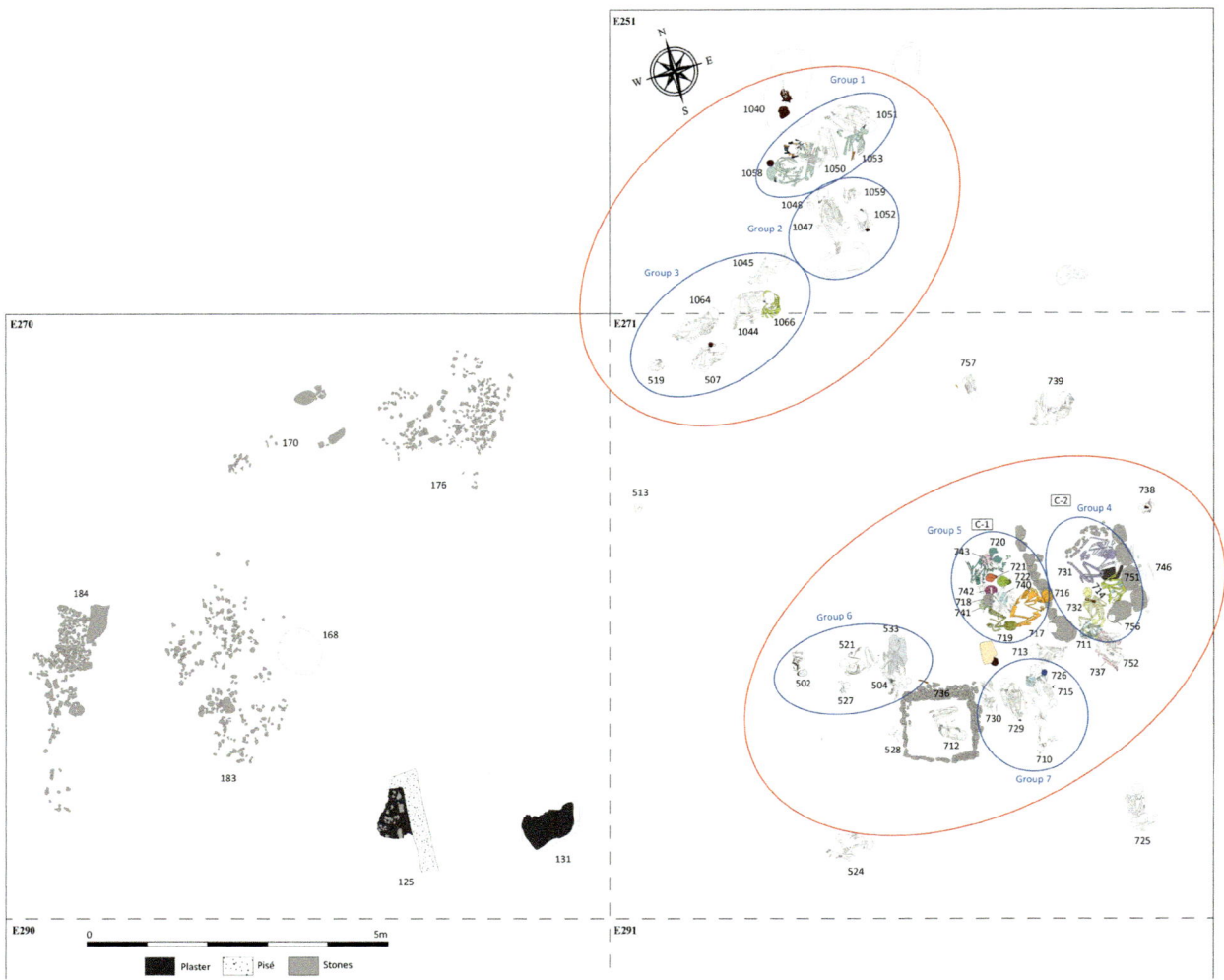

Figure 4-25. Burial groups in Kerkh Cemetery Layer 4.

Chapter 5
Burial Catalogue of Kerkh Cemetery

Akira Tsuneki, Naoko Hironaga, Sari Jammo,
Yuko Miyauchi and Yuki Tatsumi

Table 5-1. Burial list of Kerkh Cemetery.

	Concent-ration	Str. No.	Square	Year	Layer	Age	Sex	Burial type	Dedicated gave goods	
									Deceased	Concentration
1	—	502	E271c	2002	4	Juvenile, 2–3yrs.	—	Primary	—	—
2	—	504	E271c	2002	4	Perinatal, 30–40wks. ges.	—	Unknown	—	—
3	—	507	E271a	2002	4	Juvenile, 8–10yrs.	—	Primary	DFBW bowl: 1	—
4	—	513	E271a	2002	4	Perinatal	—	Secondary	Animal-shaped stone pendant: 1	—
5	—	519	E271a	2002	4	Fetal	—	Primary	—	—
6	—	521	E271c	2002	4	Subadult, 12–15yrs.	—	Primary	—	—
7	—	524	E271c	2002	4	Middle adult	Probable female	Primary	—	—
8	—	527	E271c	2002	4	Infant, birth–3mths.	—	Primary	—	—
9	—	528	E271c	2002	4	Juvenile, 1–3yrs.	—	Unknown	—	—
10	—	533	E271c	2002	4	Middle adult, 40–50yrs.	Female	Primary	—	—
11	—	710	E271d	2007	4	Old adult	Probable male	Secondary	—	—
12	—	712	E271d	2007	4	Middle adult	Probable female	Primary	Flint blade: 2	—
13	—	713	E271d	2007	4	Juvenile, 10–12yrs.	—	Primary	—	—
14	—	715	E271d	2007	4	Young adult	Probable male	Primary	Flint blade: 1 Shell bead: 1 Stone vessel: 1	—
15	—	716	E271b	2007	4	Middle adult	Probable male	Primary	—	—
16	—	717	E271d	2007	4	Juvenile, 1–2yrs.	—	Secondary	—	—
17	—	725	E271d	2007	4	Young adult	Probable female	Primary	—	—
18	—	726	E271d	2007	4	Infant, 9–18mths.	—	Primary	—	—
19	—	729	E271d	2007	4	Young adult	Probable female	Primary	Flint core: 1 Stone stamp seal: 1	—
20	—	730	E271d	2007	4	Juvenile, 2–3yrs.	—	Primary (disturbed)	—	—
21	—	738	E271b	2007	4	Infant, birth–3mths.	—	Primary (disturbed)	—	—
22	—	739	E271b	2007	4	Middle adult	Probable male	Primary	Stone bead: 2 Shell bead: 2 Clay bead: 3	—
23	—	746	E271b	2007	4	1. Juvenile, 1–2yrs.	—	Cremation	—	—
						2. Juvenile, 6–8yrs.	—		—	

Table 5-1. Continued.

	Concent-ration	Str. No.	Square	Year	Layer	Age	Sex	Burial type	Dedicated gave goods	
									Deceased	Concentration
24	—	748	E271b	2007	5	1. Young adult	Probable male	Primary	Flint borer: 1 Stone bead: 1	DFBW bowl: 1
						2. Juvenile, 2–3yrs.	—	Unknown	—	
						3. Infant	—	Unknown	—	
25	—	750	E271d	2007	5	Juvenile, 5–6yrs.	—	Primary	—	—
26	—	752	E271d	2007	4	Adult	Probable female	Primary	—	—
27	—	756	E271b	2007	4	Juvenile	—	Secondary	—	—
28	—	757	E271b	2007	4	Juvenile, 7–8yrs.	—	Primary	Bone awl: 1	—
29	—	759	E271b	2007	5	Adult	—	Unknown	—	—
30	—	803	E271b	2008	5	Young adult	Probable female	Primary	Bone bead: 1 Shell adornment: 1	—
31	—	807	E291b	2008	5	Middle adult, 35–40yrs.	Male	Primary	Flint drill: 1 Stone bead: 1	—
32	—	822	E271b	2008	5	Juvenile, 10–12yrs.	—	Unknown	Stone bead: 19 Shell bead: 1	—
33	—	823	E271a,b	2008	5	Subadult, 14–16yrs.	—	Primary	Bone needle: 1 Shell bead: 1	—
34	—	825	E271d	2008	5	Juvenile, 10–12yrs.	—	Unknown	—	—
35	—	826	E271d	2008	5	Subadult, 14–15yrs.	—	Primary	—	—
36	—	828	E271d	2008	5	Fetal, 28–32wks. ges.	—	Primary	—	—
37	—	829	E271b	2008	5	Juvenile, 2–3yrs.	—	Primary	—	—
38	—	830	E271b	2008	5	Middle adult	Probable male	Primary	Stone bead: 1	—
39	—	832	E271d	2008	5	1. Perinatal	—	Unknown	—	DFBW jar: 1
						2. Juvenile, 10–12yrs.	—	Unknown	—	
						3. Juvenile	—	Unknown	—	
						4. Adult	—	Primary (disturbed)	Stone bead: 6 Shell bead: 1	
						5. Adult	—	Unknown	—	
40	—	834	E271b	2008	5	Juvenile, 2–3yrs.	—	Primary	—	—
41	—	836	E271b	2008	5	Middle adult	Male	Primary	Shell bead: 1	—
42	—	838	E271b	2008	5	Perinatal	—	Primary	—	—
43	—	841	E271b	2008	5	Perinatal, 37–41wks. ges.	—	Primary	—	—
44	—	851	E271b	2008	5	1. Infant, 10–12mths.	—	Unknown	—	Shell bead: 1
						2. Adult	—	Primary (disturbed)	—	
45	—	852	E271b	2008	5	1. Adult	Probable male	Unknown	—	—
						2. Juvenile, 1–2yrs.	—	Unknown	—	
46	—	902	E271a	2009	5	Juvenile, 1–2yrs.	—	Unknown	—	—
47	—	904	E271a	2009	5	Young adult, 30–35yrs.	Probable male	Primary	—	—
48	—	908	E271a	2009	6	Subadult, 11–13yrs.	—	Primary	Flint blade: 1	—
49	—	909	E271a	2009	5	Young adult	Probable female	Primary	Stone stamp seal: 1	—

Table 5-1. Continued.

	Concent-ration	Str. No.	Square	Year	Layer	Age	Sex	Burial type	Dedicated gave goods	
									Deceased	Concentration
50	—	910	E271a	2009	6	1. Adult	—	Unknown	—	—
						2. Old adult	—	Unknown	—	
						3. Infant, 6mths.–1yr.	—	Unknown	—	
51	—	911	E271a	2009	5	Perinatal, birth–1mth.	—	Primary	—	—
52	—	912	E271a	2009	5	Infant	—	Secondary	—	—
53	—	913	E271a	2009	6	Juvenile, 1–2yrs.	—	Primary	Stone bead: 20	—
54	—	914	E271b	2009	6	Juvenile, 3–4yrs.	—	Primary	Stone bead: 8	—
55	—	918	E270b	2009	5	Infant, 4–6mths.	—	Primary (disturbed)	—	—
56	—	920	E271a	2009	6	Juvenile, 3–4yrs.	—	Primary	—	—
57	—	921	E271b	2009	6	Young adult, 30–35yrs.	Male	Primary	—	—
58	—	922	E271b	2009	6	Adult	—	Unknown	Stone bead: 2 Shell bead: 1	—
59	—	924	E271b	2009	6	Young adult	Female	Primary	Stone bead: 1	—
60	—	925	E270a	2009	6	Fetal, 34–38wks. ges.	—	Primary	—	—
61	—	926	E270a	2009	6	Adult	Probable female	Primary	Stone bead: 1 Shell bead: 4 Bone bead: 2	—
62	—	927	E270b	2009	6	1. Young adult, 30–40yrs.	Female	Primary Secondary	DFBW bowl: 1 DFBW sherd: 1 Stone bead: 3 Shell bead: 2 Bone bead: 1 Shell: 1	—
						2. Perinatal, 38–40wks. ges.	—	Secondary		
						3. Juvenile, 4–5yrs.	—	Secondary		
63	—	930	E270b	2009	6	1. Young adult	Probable female	Secondary	—	—
						2. Young adult	Probable female	Secondary	—	
						3. Adult	Probable female	Secondary	—	
64	—	931	E271d	2009	6	Adult	—	Secondary	—	—
65	—	933	E271d	2009	6	Fetal	—	Primary	DFBW fragments	—
66	—	941	E271d	2010	6	Middle adult	Probable female	Primary	Flint point: 1 Hammerstone: 1 Bone spatula: 1	—
67	—	942	E271d	2010	6	Adult	—	Unknown	—	—
68	—	946	E271c, E291a	2010	6	Perinatal, 36–40wks. ges.	—	Primary	Stone bead: 1	—
69	—	977	E270b	2010	6	Fetal	—	Primary	—	—
70	—	981	E270b	2010	6	Fetal	—	Urn burial (primary)	—	—
71	—	1040	E251c	2010	4	1. Adult	—	Unknown	—	—
						2. Juvenile, 5–6yrs.	—	Unknown	—	
72	—	1044	E251c	2010	4	Middle adult	Probable male	Primary	Bead: 1	—
73	—	1045	E251c	2010	4	Adult	Probable male	Primary (disturbed)	—	—
74	—	1047	E251c	2010	4	Young adult	Probable male	Primary	—	—
75	—	1048	E251c	2010	4	Perinatal	—	Secondary	—	—

Table 5-1. Continued.

	Concent-ration	Str. No.	Square	Year	Layer	Age	Sex	Burial type	Dedicated gave goods	
									Deceased	Concentration
76	—	1050	E251c	2010	4	Young adult, 30–35yrs.	Probable male	Primary	—	—
77	—	1051	E251c	2010	4	Middle adult	Female	Primary	—	—
78	—	1052	E251c	2010	4	Subadult, 12–13yrs.	—	Secondary	Coarse pottery bowl: 1	—
79	—	1053	E251c	2010	4	Adult	Probable male	Primary (disturbed)	Goat horn: 1 Stone stamp seal: 1 Stone bead: 2 Clay bead: 2	—
80	—	1056	E251c	2010	5	Young adult	Probable male	Primary	Flint blade: 1 Stone bead: 2	—
81	—	1057	E251d	2010	5	Adult	Female	Primary	—	—
82	—	1058	E251c	2010	4	Middle adult	Male	Primary	DFBW bowl: 1 Flint point: 1 Flint blade: 5 Flint axe: 3 Flint flake: 18 Burin: 2 Hammerstone: 4 Whetstone: 1 Bone awl: 3 Deer horn: 5 Clay stamp seal: 1	—
83	—	1059	E251c	2010	4	1. Subadult, possibly 15–17yrs.	—	Secondary	—	Animal talus: 1
						2. Juvenile	—	Secondary	—	
84	—	1062	E251d	2010	5	—	—	Unknown	—	—
85	—	1064	E271a	2010	4	Young adult, 18–20yrs.	Male	Primary	Shell bead: 3	—
86	—	1066	E251c	2010	4	Juvenile, 2–3yrs.	—	Primary	Bead (imitation turquoise bead): 1	—
87	—	1067	E251c	2010	5	1. Juvenile	—	Unknown	—	—
						2. Adult	—	Unknown	—	
88	—	1068	E251c	2010	5	Infant, birth–2mths.	—	Unknown	—	—
89	—	1070	E251d	2010	5	—	—	Unknown	—	—
90	—	1072	E251c	2010	5	Juvenile, 11–12yrs.	—	Primary (disturbed)	—	—
91	—	1073	E251d	2010	5	Juvenile, 1–2yrs.	—	Urn burial (secondary)	Bead: 1	—
92	—	1074	E251c	2010	5	Infant	—	Primary (disturbed)	—	—
93	—	1075	E271b	2010	5	Young adult, 21–30yrs.	—	Primary	—	—
94	—	1076	E251c	2010	5	—	—	Unknown	—	—
95	—	1077	E251c	2010	5	Young adult	Probable female	Primary	Stone bead: 1 Shell bead: 2	—
96	—	1078	E251c	2010	5	Perinatal	—	Primary	—	—
97	—	1079	E251d	2010	5	Young adult	Probable male	Primary	Shell bead: 1	—
98	—	1080	E251d	2010	5	Old adult	—	Secondary	—	—
99	—	1081	E251d	2010	5	Adult	Probable female	Primary	Bone awl: 7 Cattle metatarsal: 1 Stone bead: 3	—

Table 5-1. Continued.

	Concent-ration	Str. No.	Square	Year	Layer	Age	Sex	Burial type	Dedicated gave goods Deceased	Dedicated gave goods Concentration
100	—	1082	E251d	2010	5	Old adult	—	Primary (disturbed)	—	—
101	—	1083	E251d	2010	5	Adult	—	Unknown	—	—
102	—	1084	E251d	2010	5	Adult	Probable female	Secondary	—	—
103	—	1085	E251d	2010	5	Young adult	Probable female	Primary	—	—
104	—	1086	E251d	2010	5	Adult	Probable male	Primary	Flint blade: 2 Stone stamp seal: 1	—
105	—	1087	E251d	2010	5	Young adult, 18–22yrs.	Probable female	Primary	Stone bead: 294	—
106	—	1088	E251d	2010	5	1. Adult	Probable male	Primary (disturbed)	—	Stone stamp seal: 1
						2. Adult	—	Primary (disturbed)	—	
						3. Juvenile	—	Unknown	—	
107	—	1089	E251c	2010	5	Juvenile, 8–12yrs.	—	Primary	—	—
108	—	1090	E251c	2010	5	Middle adult	Probable male	Primary	—	—
109	—	1091	E271a	2010	5	Subadult, 16–20yrs.	—	Unknown	Stone axe: 1 Stone bead: 1	—
110	—	1092	E251c	2010	5	Juvenile	—	Primary	—	—
111	—	1093	E251c	2010	5	Juvenile, 2–3yrs.	—	Primary	Stone stamp seal: 1	—
112	—	1094	E251c	2010	5	Juvenile	—	Primary	—	—
113	—	1095	E251c	2010	5	Adult	—	Unknown	—	—
114	—	1096	E251d	2010	5	Adult	—	Primary (disturbed)	—	—
115	—	1097	E251d	2010	5	Adult	Probable female	Primary	—	—
116	—	1098	E251d	2010	5	Perinatal	—	Primary	—	—
117	—	1099	E251d	2010	5	Adult	—	Primary (disturbed)	—	—
118	1	718	E271b	2007	4	1. Young adult, 25–30yrs.	Probable female	Secondary	—	DFBW jar: 1
						2. Infant	—			
		719				1. Adult	—	Secondary		
						2. Juvenile, 1–2yrs.	—			
		720				1. Old adult	Probable female	Secondary		
						2. Adult	—			
						3. Young adult	—			
		721				Subadult, 11–13yrs.	—	Secondary		
		722				Middle adult	Probable female	Secondary		
		740				Juvenile, 10–12yrs.	—	Secondary		
		741				Juvenile, 5–7yrs.	—	Secondary		
		742				Juvenile, 6–8yrs.	—	Secondary		
		743				Middle adult	Probable male	Secondary		

Table 5-1. Continued.

Concent-ration		Str. No.	Square	Year	Layer	Age	Sex	Burial type	Dedicated gave goods	
									Deceased	Concentration
119	2	711	E271b	2007	4	Subadult, 15–18yrs.	—	Primary (disturbed)	—	Stone ball: 1
		714				Adult	Probable male	Primary (disturbed)	Shell bead: 2	
		731				Young adult	Probable male	Primary	Stone bead: 1	
		732				Subadult, 12–15yrs.	—	Primary	Cattle metacarpal: 1	
		737				Middle adult	Probable male	Secondary	—	
		751				Juvenile, 5–6yrs.	—	Primary (disturbed)	Stone stamp seal: 1 Stone bead: 2	
120	3	831	E271b	2008	5	1. Adult	Probable female	Cremation	—	—
						2. Adult	Probable female		—	
						3. Adult	Probable male		—	
						4. Juvenile	—		—	
						5. Adult	—		—	
						6. Adult	—		—	
		847				1. Adult	1. Probable male	Secondary	—	
						2. Old adult	2. Probable male		—	
		848				3. Adult	3. Probable male		—	
						4. Infant	4. —		—	
		850				5. Adult	5. Probable female		—	
		854				Juvenile, 5–7yrs.	—	Secondary	Stone bead: 1	
		—		2010		—	—	1. Secondary 2. Secondary 3. Secondary 4. Secondary 5. Cremation 6. Secondary 7. Secondary 8. Secondary 9. Secondary	—	Stone bead: 1 Clay disc: 1
121	4	833	E271b	2008	5	Young adult	Probable male	Secondary	—	Unfinished stone stamp seal: 1 Stone bead: 2 Shell bead: 2
		839				1. Middle adult	Probable male	Cremation	—	
						2. Adult	Probable male	Cremation	—	
		845				Adult	Probable male	Secondary	—	
		846				Young adult	Probable female	Secondary	—	
		853				Adult	Probable female	Cremation	—	
		859				Old adult	Probable female	Secondary	—	

Table 5-1. Continued.

	Concent-ration	Str. No.	Square	Year	Layer	Age	Sex	Burial type	Dedicated gave goods Deceased	Concentration
122	5	842	E271b	2008	6	Middle adult	Probable male	Cremation	—	DFBW jar: 2 Bone stamp seal: 1
		855				Young adult	Probable male		—	
		856				Adult	Probable female		—	
		857				Young adult	Probable male		—	
		858				Subadult	Probable female		—	
123	6	865	E271d	2008	6	1. Adult	Probable female	Cremation	—	DFBW jar: 1 Wheat
						2. Adult	Probable female		—	
		866				Adult	—		—	
		867				1. Juvenile	—		—	
						2. Juvenile	—		—	
		868				1. Juvenile	—		—	
						2. Juvenile	—		—	
124	7-1	860	E271b	2008	6	Adult	—	Primary (disturbed)	Stone stamp seal: 1 Bone stamp seal: 3 Stone bead: 7 Shell bead: 5 Bone bead: 1 Miniature stone vessel: 1	Flint point: 1
		861				Young adult	Probable female	Primary (disturbed)	Coarse pottery ware: 1	
		862				Young adult	Probable female	Primary (disturbed)	DFBW jar: 1 Animal jaw: 1	
		863				Middle adult	Probable female	Primary	Stone bead: 1	
	7-2	932	E271a	2009	6	1. Adult	Probable male	Cremation	—	—
						2. Subadult	—		—	
						3. Juvenile	—		—	
						4. Fetal	—	Secondary	—	
						5. Juvenile	—		—	
						6. Juvenile, 1–2yrs.	—		—	
		984		2010	6	Young adult	Probable male	Primary (disturbed)	Flint blade: 1 Flint point: 1 Stone bead: 1	
		985		2010	6	Juvenile, 6–7yrs.	—	Primary (disturbed)	Animal scapula: 1	
		988		2010	6	Middle adult	Female	Primary	Obsidian blade: 1 Flint blade: 1 Bone spatula: 1 Stone bead: 2 Goat horn: 1 Shell: 1	

Table 5-1. Continued.

Concent-ration		Str. No.	Square	Year	Layer	Age	Sex	Burial type	Dedicated gave goods	
									Deceased	Concentration
125	8	835	E271b, d	2008	6	1. Infant, birth–3mths.	—	Cremation	—	Flint dril: 1
						2. Juvenile	—		—	
						3. Juvenile, 4–6yrs.	—		—	
						4. Subadult	—		—	
						5. Old adult	—		—	
						6. Adult	—		—	
						7. Adult	—		DFBW fragments	
						8. Adult	Probable male		—	
126	9	919	E271b	2009	6	1. Subadult, 13–16yrs.	—	Cremation	—	Stone ball: 1
						2. Juvenile	—		—	
						3. Adult	—		—	
						4. Adult	—		—	
						5. Adult	—		—	
127	10 North	943	E271b	2010	6	Young adult	Probable male	Primary	Flint blade: 1	Stone bead: 1
		947				Middle adult	Probable male	Primary	Clay disc: 2	
		962				Middle adult	Male	Primary	—	
		971				Juvenile, 3–4yrs.	—	Secondary	—	
		972				Juvenile, 11–12yrs.	—	Secondary	—	
		978				Young adult	Probable female	Unknown	—	
		979				Subadult, 12–13yrs.	—	Primary	—	
		980				—	—	Unknown	—	
		983				Young adult	Probable female	Secondary	—	
		991				Juvenile, 5–6yrs.	—	Secondary	—	
		993				Infant, 9–12mths.	—	Secondary	—	
		995				Adult	—	Primary (disturbed)	Stone stamp seal: 1 Bone stamp seal: 1 Animal tusk: 1	
		996				Juvenile, 4–5yrs.	—	Secondary	—	
		998				Adult	—	Primary (disturbed)	—	
		999				—	—	Primary (disturbed)	Stone bead: 3	
	10 South	953				1. Adult	—	Primary (disturbed)	—	DFBW bowl: 1
						2. Adult	—	Cremation	—	
						3. Adult	—		—	
						4. Adult	—		—	
						5. Adult	—		—	
						6. Perinatal	—		—	
						7. Subadult, 10–14yrs.	—		—	

1. Str. 502 (Figure 5-1)

Str. 502 is a primary burial of a 2–3-year-old juvenile uncovered in Square E271c in Layer 4. The juvenile was buried in a shallow grave pit in a flexed position on its left side. Body axis direction was south-north and the skull faced upward. Sex was indeterminate, and no grave goods were uncovered.

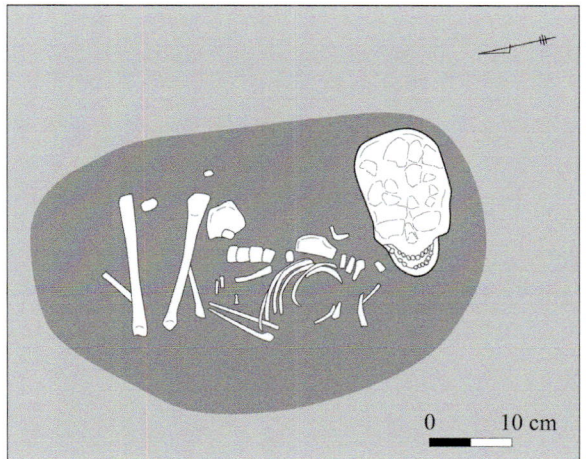 

from the west

Figure 5-1. Str. 502 Burial.

2. Str. 504 (Figure 5-2)

Str. 504 is a perinatal individual, classified as an unknown burial, uncovered in Square E271c in Layer 4. It was difficult to determine the deposition of the bones, so sex, body axis orientation, and face direction were indeterminate. No grave goods were uncovered.

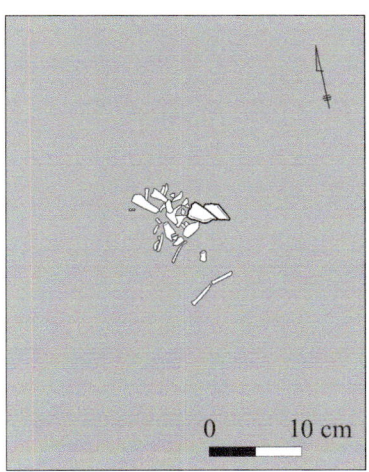 

from the west

Figure 5-2. Str. 504 Burial.

3. Str. 507 (Figure 5-3)

Str. 507 is a primary burial of a 8–10-year-old juvenile, but sex was indeterminate. It was uncovered in the northwestern part of Square E271a in Layer 4. It was buried in a flexed position in a shallow pit on its right side. The body axis direction was northeast-southwest. The skull pointed to northeast and its face look northwest. A small DFBW bowl (H = 6.9cm, D = 8.3cm) was placed on its right palm.

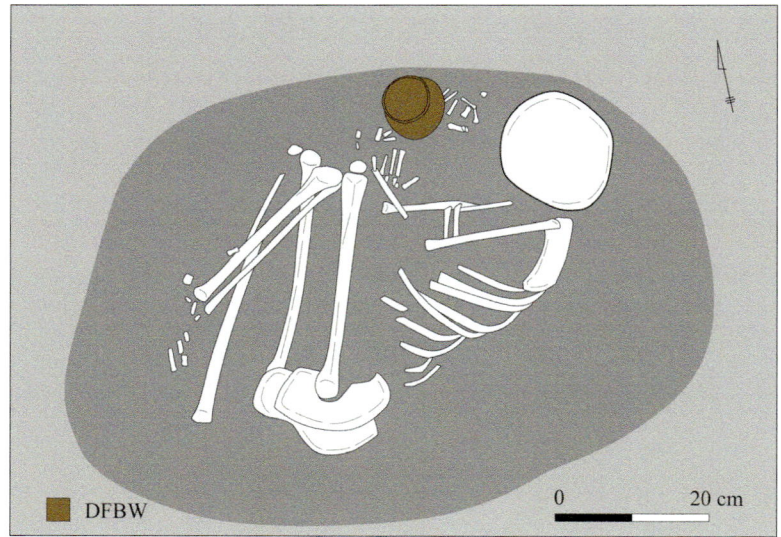

from the south

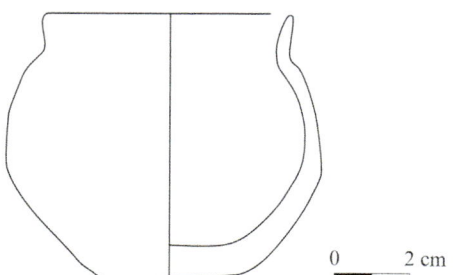

Figure 5-3. Str. 507 Burial and grave goods: DFBW bowl.

102

4. Str. 513 (Figure 5-4)

Str. 513 is a secondary burial of a perinatal individual. It comprised a portion of the skull uncovered on the ground of the cemetery in Square E271a in Layer 4. It was isolated from neighboring burials in the same location. This skull was likely moved from its original place and relocated to this final deposit. Sex was indeterminate. A small animal-shaped mottled limestone pendant was found nearby.

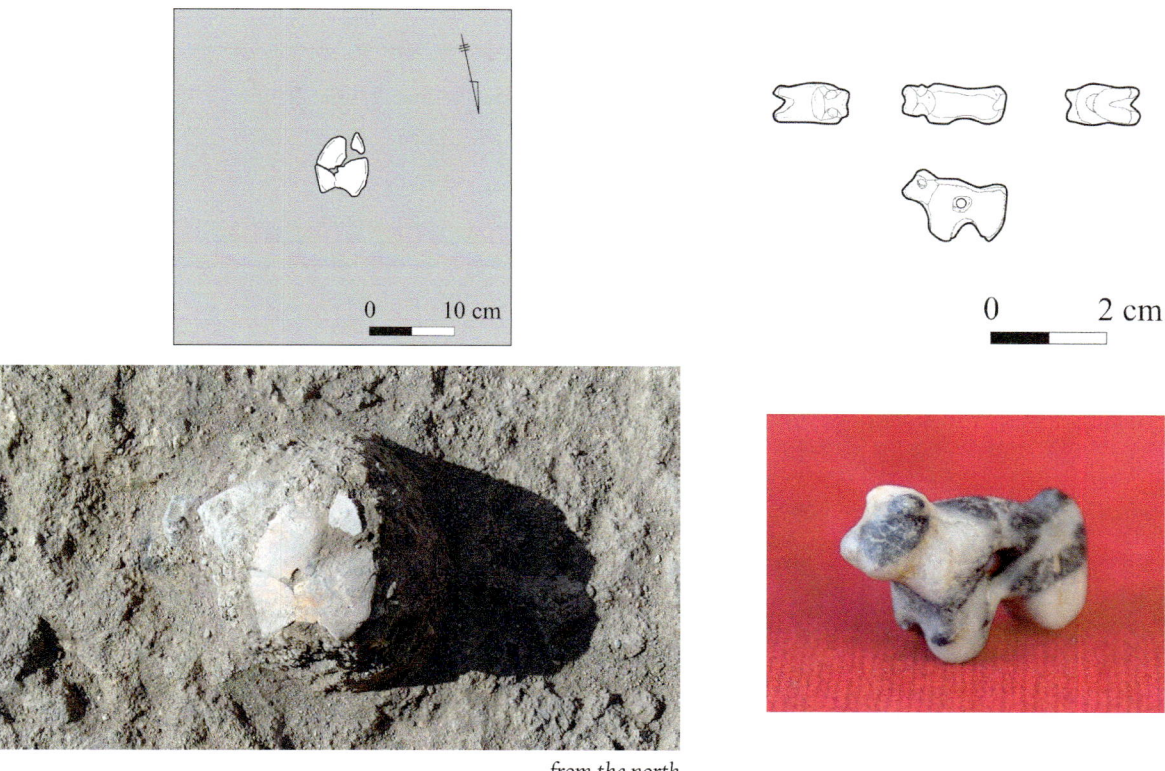

from the north

Figure 5-4. Str. 513 Burial and grave goods: Stone animal-shaped pendant.

5. Str. 519 (Figure 5-5)

Str. 519 is the primary burial of a fetus discovered in the northwestern part of Square E271a in Layer 4. It was buried within a shallow pit in a flexed position on its right side. The body axis direction was west-east, and the skull pointed to the west and faced southeast. Sex was indeterminate, and no grave goods were uncovered.

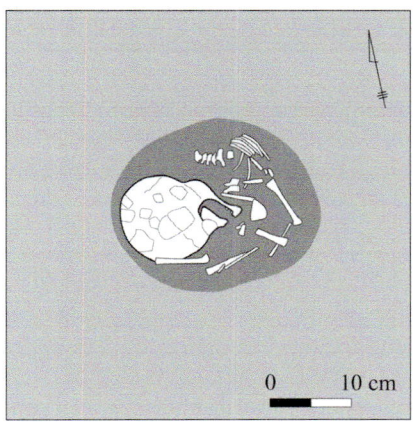

from the south

Figure 5-5. Str. 519 Burial.

6. Str. 521 (Figure 5-6)

Str. 521 is a primary burial of a 12-15-year-old subadult. Sex was indeterminate. It was buried in a flexed position on its left side in a shallow pit in Square E271c in Layer 4. The left arm was extended along the body axis, while the right one was folded and crossed over the left arm. The body axis direction was west-east, but the face direction could not be determined due to the lack of skull parts. No grave goods were uncovered.

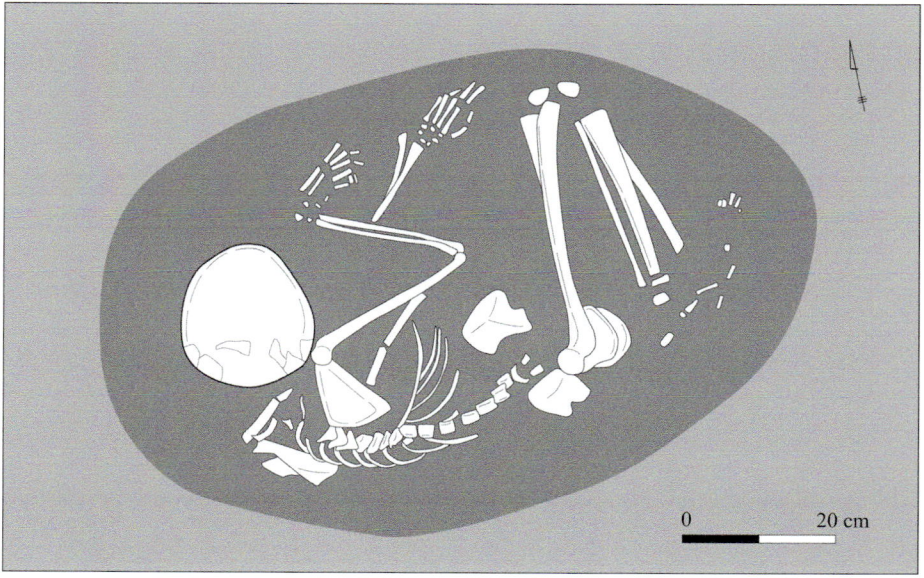

from the south

Figure 5-6. Str. 521 Burial.

7. Str. 524 (Figure 5-7)

Str. 524 is a primary burial of a middle-aged adult, probably female. She was buried on her left side in a shallow pit in Square E271c in Layer 4. The hands extended along her body axis through the femur bones, and the phalanges reached and were placed between the tibia bones. Her body axis direction was east-west and the skull faced south. No grave goods were uncovered.

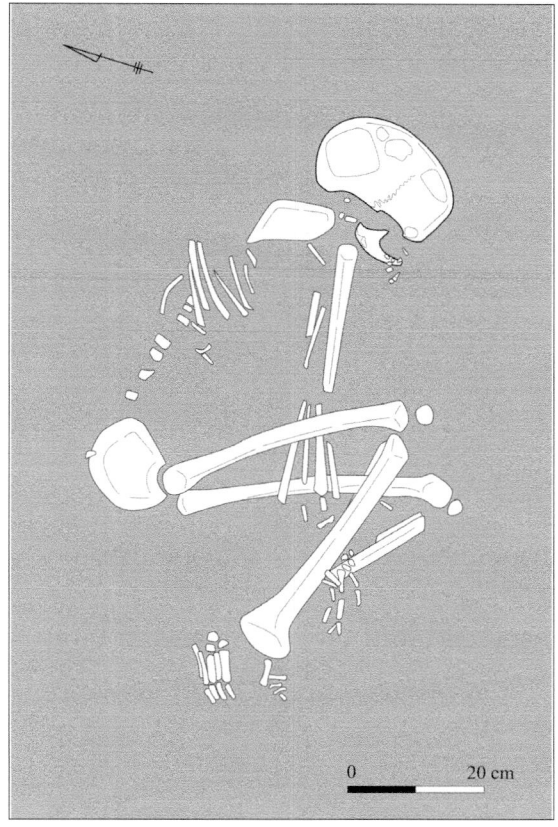 

from the southwest

Figure 5-7. Str. 524 Burial.

8. Str. 527 (Figure 5-8)

Str. 527 is a primary burial of an infant (birth–3 mths.) discovered in Square E271c in Layer 4. Sex was indeterminate. Body axis direction was north-south, but it was difficult to determine its position due to partial disarticulation of the skeleton. The face direction was not determined. No grave goods were uncovered.

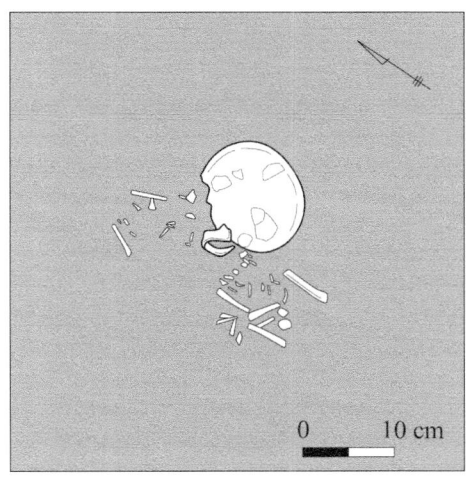 

from the southwest

Figure 5-8. Str. 527 Burial.

9. Str. 528 (Figure 5-9)

Str. 528 is a burial of a juvenile (1–3 yrs.) uncovered in a shallow pit in Square E271c in Layer 4. Burial type is unknown. Just the ribs, tooth, and other bones were present. It was difficult to determine the deposition of the bones, so sex, body axis orientation, and face direction were not determined. No grave goods were uncovered.

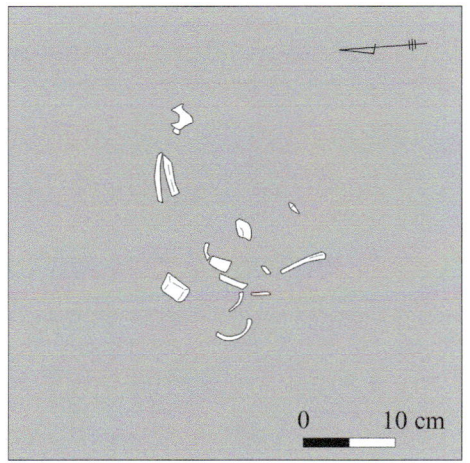

from the west

Figure 5-9. Str. 528 Burial.

10. Str. 533 (Figure 5-10)

Str. 533 is a primary burial of a middle-aged adult female (40–50 yrs.) discovered in Square E271c in Layer 4. She was buried in a shallow pit in a flexed position on her right side. Her upper body was twisted toward the right, and her body axis direction was north-south. The skull pointed to the north and faced downward. A big stone had been placed over her upper body covering the skull and chest before the grave was closed. The reason for this action is not clear. No grave goods were uncovered.

A   *from the south*   B   *from the south*

Figure 5-10a. Str. 533 Burial: A. The upper body covered with a large stone; B. The skeleton under a large stone.

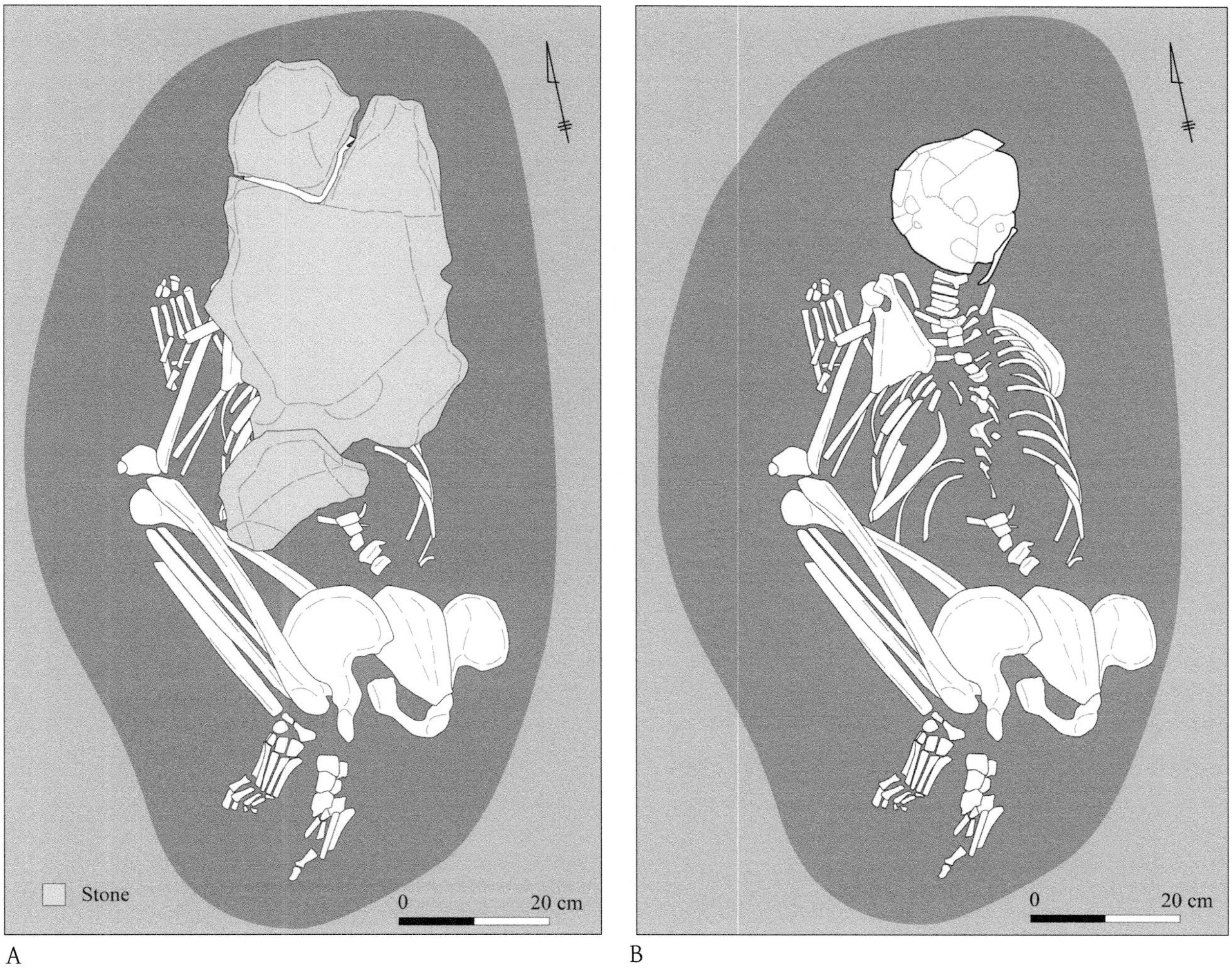

Figure 5-10b. Str. 533 Burial: A. The upper body covered with a large stone; B. The skeleton under a large stone.

11. Str. 710 (Figure 5-11)

Str. 710 is a secondary burial of an old adult (probably male) uncovered in Square E271d in Layer 4. It is one of a series of burials that includes Str. 713 and Str. 715. This skeleton was fragmented and mainly represented by a large skull and legs. The skull was placed first and the legs were later heaped up south of the skull. As the other parts of the skeleton were not discovered, the remains were repositioned bones. The body axis direction could not be determined. The skull faced a northwestern direction, and no grave goods were uncovered.

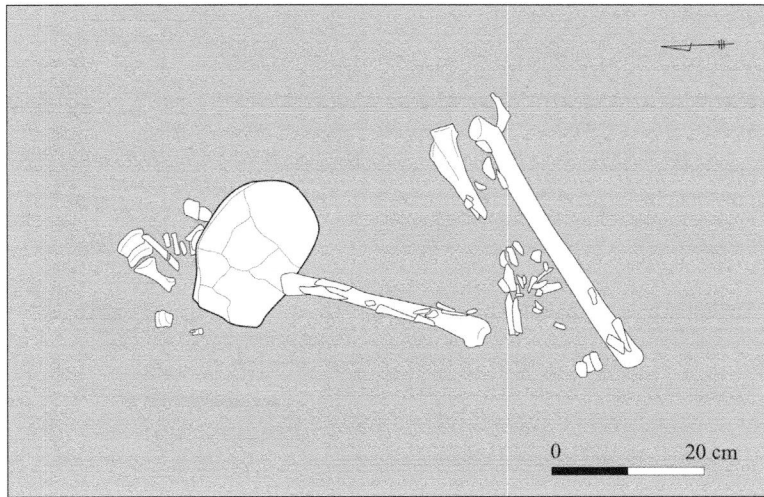

Figure 5-11a. Str. 710 Burial.

from the west

Figure 5-11b. Str. 710 Burial.

12. Str. 712 (Figure 5-12)

Str. 712 is a primary burial of a middle-aged adult, probable female, discovered above the square-planned pit in the northwestern part of Square E271d in Layer 4. It was buried in a flexed position on its right side. The leg bones were extremely contracted, the left arm was folded, and the fingers were placed near the skull. Judging from the pelvis, this adult had experienced childbirth. Her body axis direction was southeast-northwest.

The most conspicuous element of this burial was the twisting of the head. The head pointed to the northeast direction, and the skull was twisted and the face looked downward. It is also notable that two flint blades were discovered, one in the skull and another near the waist. The former flint blade measures 4cm long, and one end seems to have been stuck into her left eye, though it did not reach the orbital bone. The latter flint blade is 5cm long and one end almost reached the lowest rib. The square-planned pit below Str. 712 measures about 1.1 x 1.2m and 0.35m deep. The pit walls were covered by small-sized pebbles piled up in around five rows. These extraordinary elements evoke an image of the dead being buried with special treatment.

A   *from the north*   B   *from the south*

Figure 5-12a. Str. 712 Burial: A. Middle adult skeleton; B. The square-planned pit. Grave goods:
1. Flint blade in the skull; 2. Flint blade near the waist.

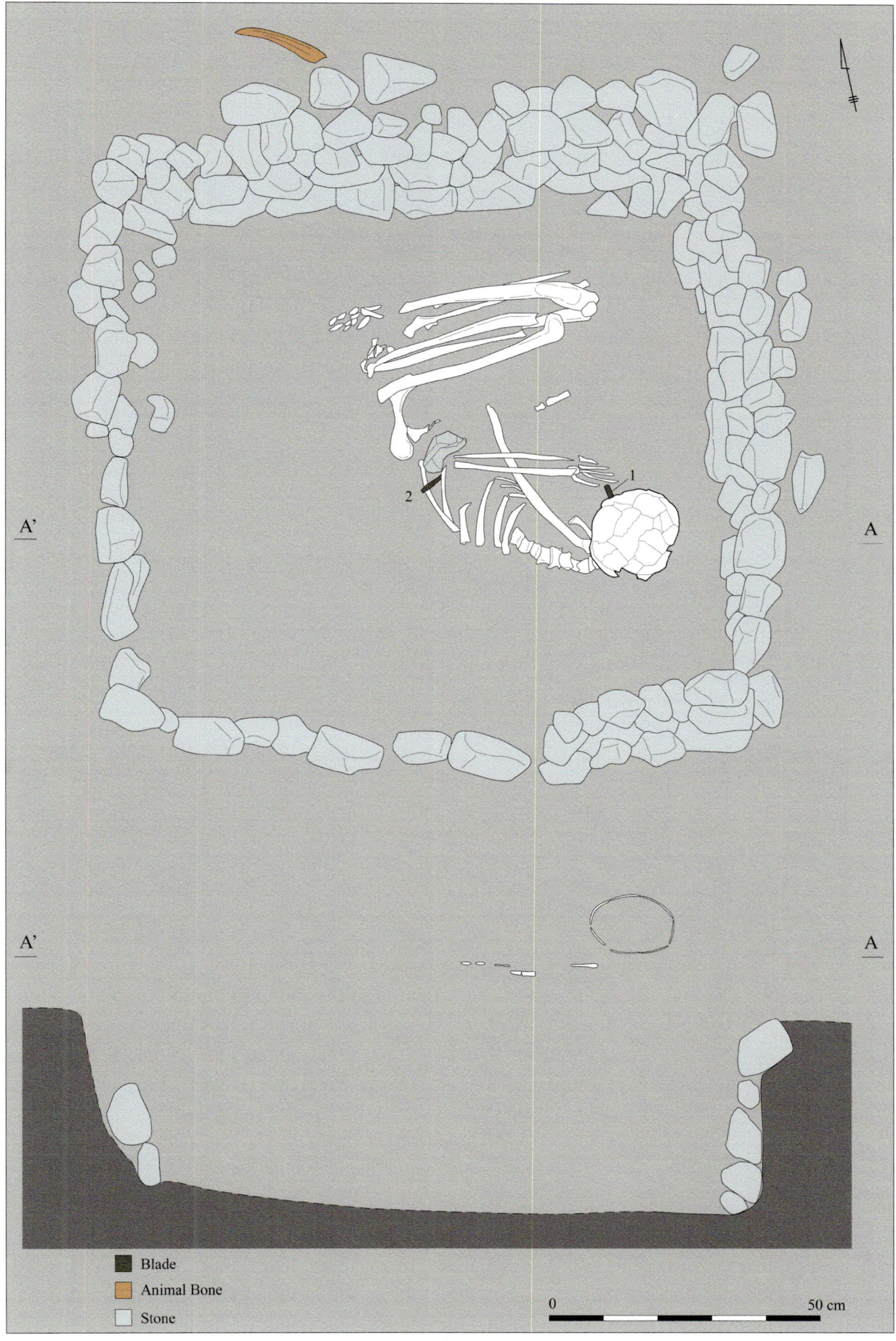

Blade
Animal Bone
Stone

0   50 cm

Figure 5-12b. Str. 712 Burial.

13. Str. 713 (Figure 5-13)

Str. 713 is a primary burial of a 10–12-year-old juvenile uncovered in the northern part of Square E271d in Layer 4. It was discovered near Str. 715. It was buried in an extremely flexed position on its left side. The body axis direction was west-east, the head pointed west, and the skull faced northeast. No grave goods were uncovered.

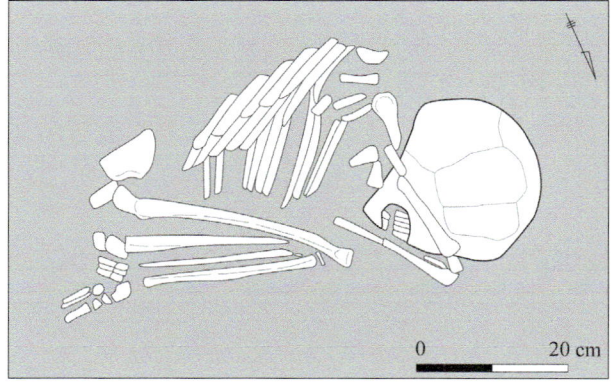

from the northeast

Figure 5-13. Str. 713 Burial.

14. Str. 715 (Figure 5-14)

Str. 715 is a primary burial of a young adult, probably male, discovered between Str. 710 and Str. 713 in Square E271d in Layer 4. He was buried in a flexed position on his right side. His body axis position was north-south, and the head pointed toward north and looked toward west. His arms were contracted and the fingers were placed in front of his face. He was buried with a remarkable bio-clastic limestone vessel recovered near the back of his head. The limestone vessel has a spherical shape, measuring 9.7cm in height and 10.8cm in width. It is rather heavy and weighs 888g. A conch shell bead and a flint blade were discovered together near his back. These objects indicate that the dead individual was buried with remarkable care.

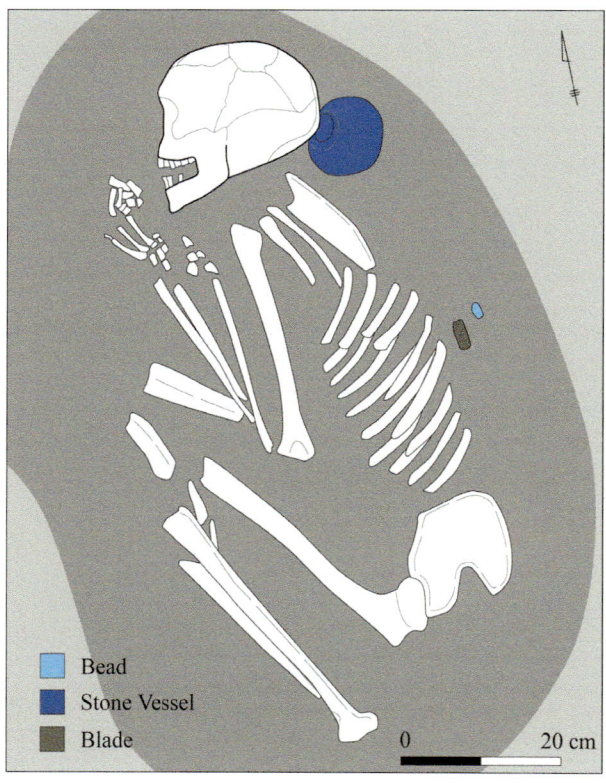

Bead
Stone Vessel
Blade

from the south

Figure 5-14a. Str. 715 Burial.

Figure 5-14b. Str. 715 Burial and grave goods:
1. Stone vessel; 2. Shell bead; 3. Flint blade.

15. Str. 716 (Figure 5-15)

Str. 716 is a primary burial of a middle-aged adult, probably male, uncovered in Square E271b in Layer 4 on the top of a collective burial comprising a number of burials (C1). He was buried in a flexed position on his left side. His body axis direction was east-west. The left side of his head rested on his left arm and a stone pillow, which is one of the stone rows surrounds C2. His head pointed to the east, while looking toward the southern direction. His right arm was also contracted, and the fingers of his right hand were placed in front of his face. Even though he was buried on top of C1, some of his skeletal parts were superimposed with other human remains buried beneath in C1. No grave goods were uncovered.

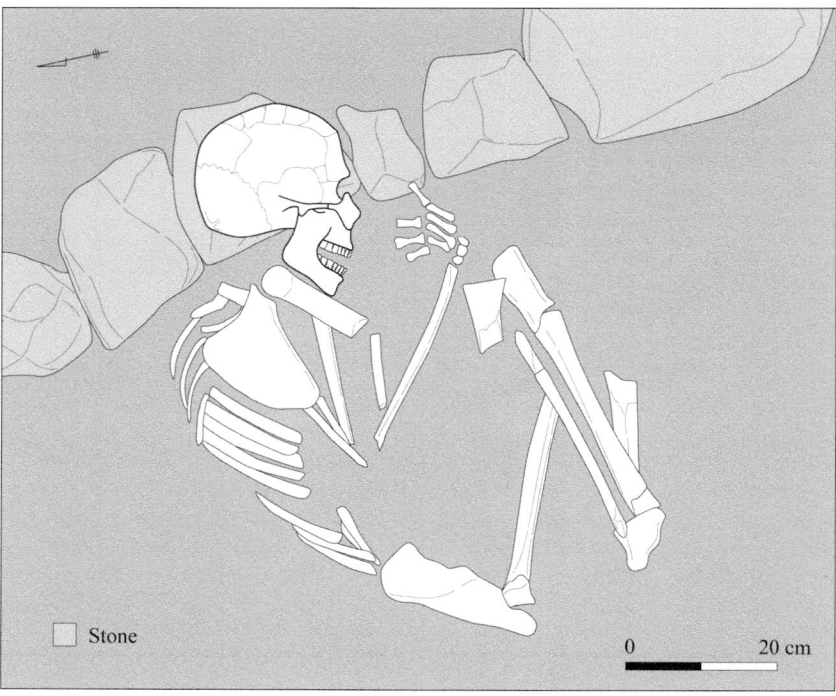

from the west

Figure 5-15. Str. 716 Burial.

16. Str. 717 (Figure 5-16)

Str. 717 is a secondary burial of a juvenile (1–2 yrs.) discovered in Square E271d in Layer 4. It is an isolated skull discovered between Str. 716 and Str. 713 and placed on one of the flat stone courses of C2, but the upper part of the skull had almost disappeared. The diameter of the skull measures 18cm. The remains comprise the parietal part of the skull and lack teeth and the jaw. The head pointed to the east, although the face direction was not defined. No grave goods were uncovered.

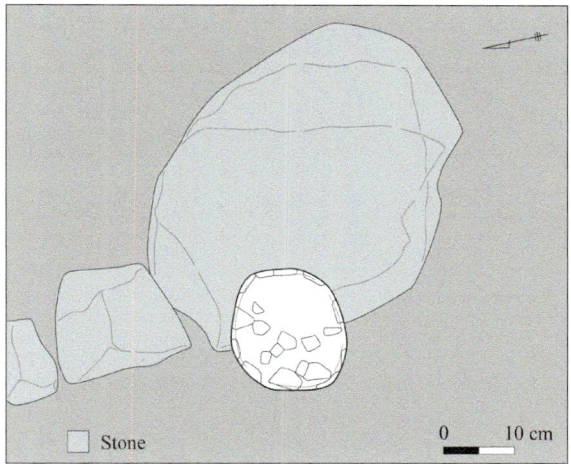

from the west

Figure 5-16. Str. 717 Burial.

17. Str. 725 (Figure 5-17)

Str. 725 is a primary burial of a young adult discovered alone in the southeastern part of Square E271d in Layer 4. Judging from the pelvis and gracile bones, this adult was probably female. Her jaw had all the permanent teeth without third molars, indicating that she was a young adult. She was buried in a flexed position on her back. Her legs were tightly folded on the left side. Her body axis direction was north-south, and the head pointed to the north but the vertex pointed upward. Her skull faced south. It is notable that she held her left elbow with her right hand. No grave goods were uncovered.

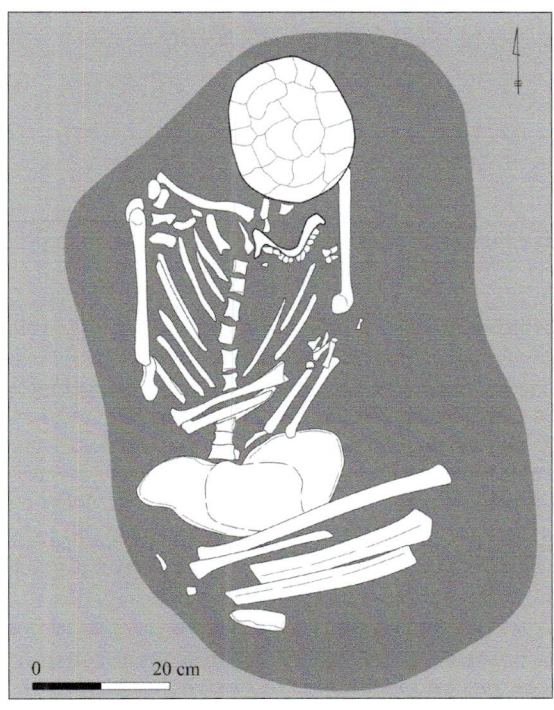

from the south

Figure 5-17. Str. 725 Burial.

18. Str. 726 (Figure 5-18)

Str. 726 is a primary burial of an infant (9-18 mths.) discovered below Str. 715 in Square E271d in Layer 4. It was buried in a flexed position on its right side. The body axis direction was west-east. The head pointed to the west and faced south. Sex was indeterminate, and no grave goods were uncovered.

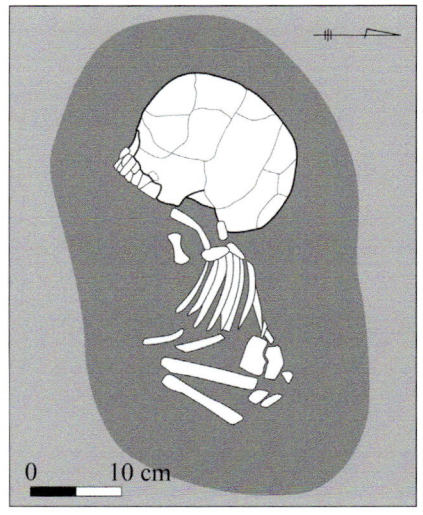

from the east

Figure 5-18. Str. 726 Burial.

19. Str. 729 (Figure 5-19)

Str. 729 is a primary burial of a young adult, probably female, discovered in Square E271d in Layer 4. She was buried in a supine position between Str. 715 in the east and Str. 730 in the west. The remains are gracile, and judging from the teeth and pelvis, it was a young female. She was lying on her back and her legs were tightly bent in front of her abdomen. She seems to have held her breast with her right hand. The body axis direction was north-south. Her head pointed to the north, but the vertex pointed upward and her face looked southward. Beside her left femur, a stamp seal made of serpentinite was recovered. It is 2cm in height and 1.9cm in diameter. It is a 'bullet-shaped' seal and the design can be classified into the 'cross and parallel lines' category. This stamp seal was popular among the Neolithic stamp seals in Tell el-Kerkh, though the seven circles were added to the simple 'cross and parallel lines' impression design. Further, a flint core was also uncovered beside her pelvis.

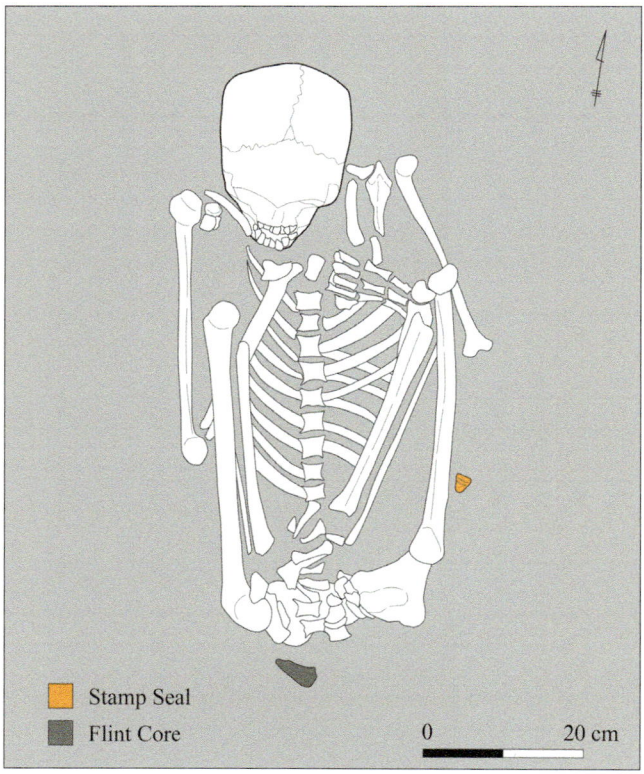

■ Stamp Seal
■ Flint Core

from the south

Figure 5-19a. Str. 729 Burial.

from the north

from the south

Figure 5-19b. Str. 729 Grave goods: 1. Stone stamp seal; 2. Flint core.

20. Str. 730 (Figure 5-20)

Str. 730 is a disturbed primary burial of a 2–3-year-old juvenile discovered in Square E271d in Layer 4. Sex was indeterminate. It was discovered just west of Str. 729. A fragment of the pelvis and spine indicated that the head probably pointed to the south, but the skeleton was too fragmented to determine the burial position and the head alignment. No grave goods were uncovered.

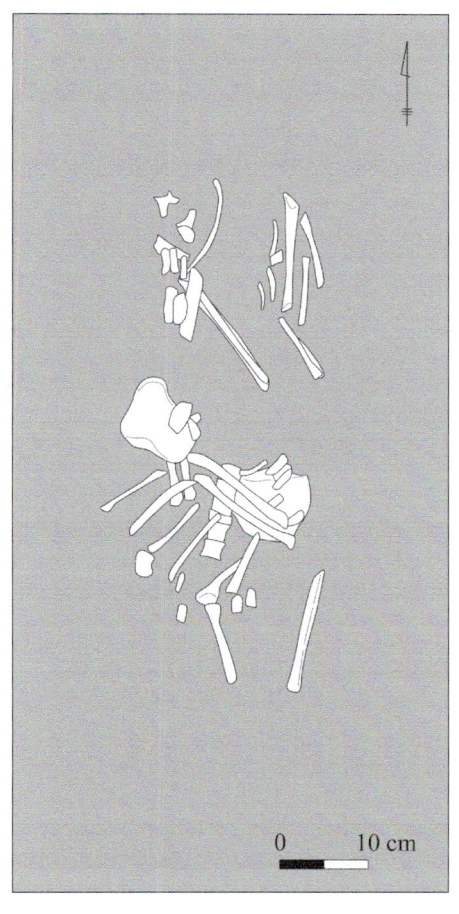

from the south

Figure 5-20. Str. 730 Burial.

21. Str. 738 (Figure 5-21)

Str. 738 is a disturbed primary burial of an infant (birth–3 mths.) discovered in Square E271b in Layer 4. The infant was buried in a flexed position on its left side. It was buried alone in the northeastern corner of the stone square of C2. The body axis direction was west-east. The head pointed to the west. However, the skull was twisted and faced south. Sex was indeterminate. A small potsherd was found on the skull, but it does not seem to be grave goods.

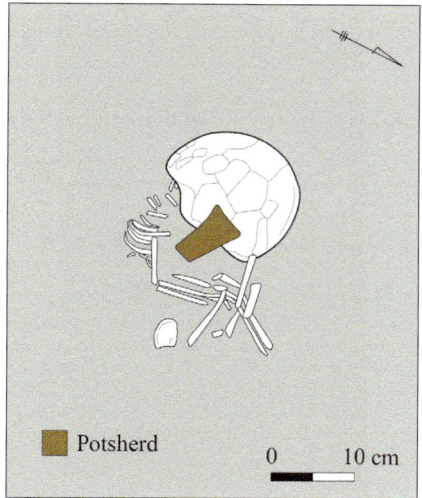

from the northeast

Figure 5-21. Str. 738 Burial.

22. Str. 739 (Figure 5-22)

Str. 739 is a primary burial of a middle-aged adult, probably male, discovered alone in the northern part of Square E271b in Layer 4. The relatively well-preserved skeleton obviously belonged to a mature adult. The femurs were huge, but the upper parts of the body skeleton were relatively delicate. The mandible was large and the other parts of the skull had masculine characteristics. It was buried in a flexed position on its right side. The body axis direction was northeast-southwest. The neck was bent at a right angle. Therefore, the head pointed to the northwest and faced southwest.

Seven beads were discovered at the back of the head and were aligned under the neck. A serpentinite butterfly bead was at the bottom, and then two barrel-shaped terracotta beads, a barrel-shaped limestone bead, a conch shell bead, a tube-shaped tusk shell bead, and a barrel-shaped terracotta bead lined up near the head. It is very certain that the deceased wore a necklace made of these beads.

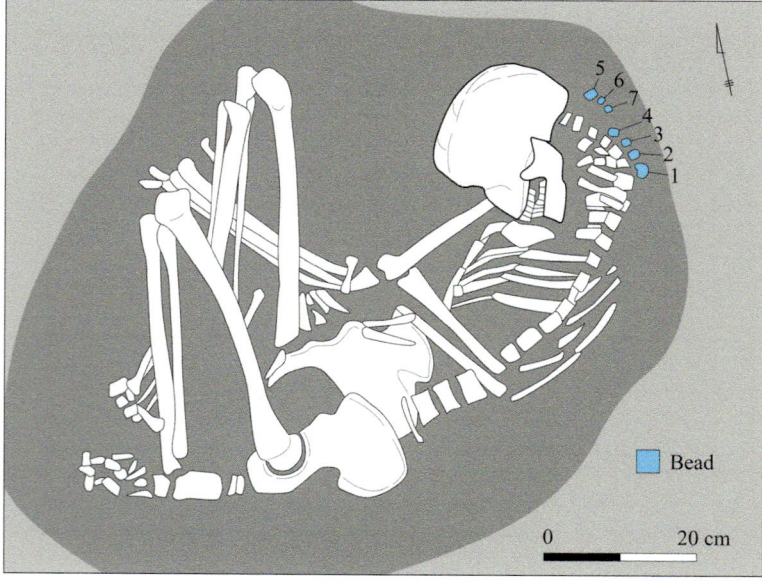

Figure 5-22a. Str. 739 Burial.

116

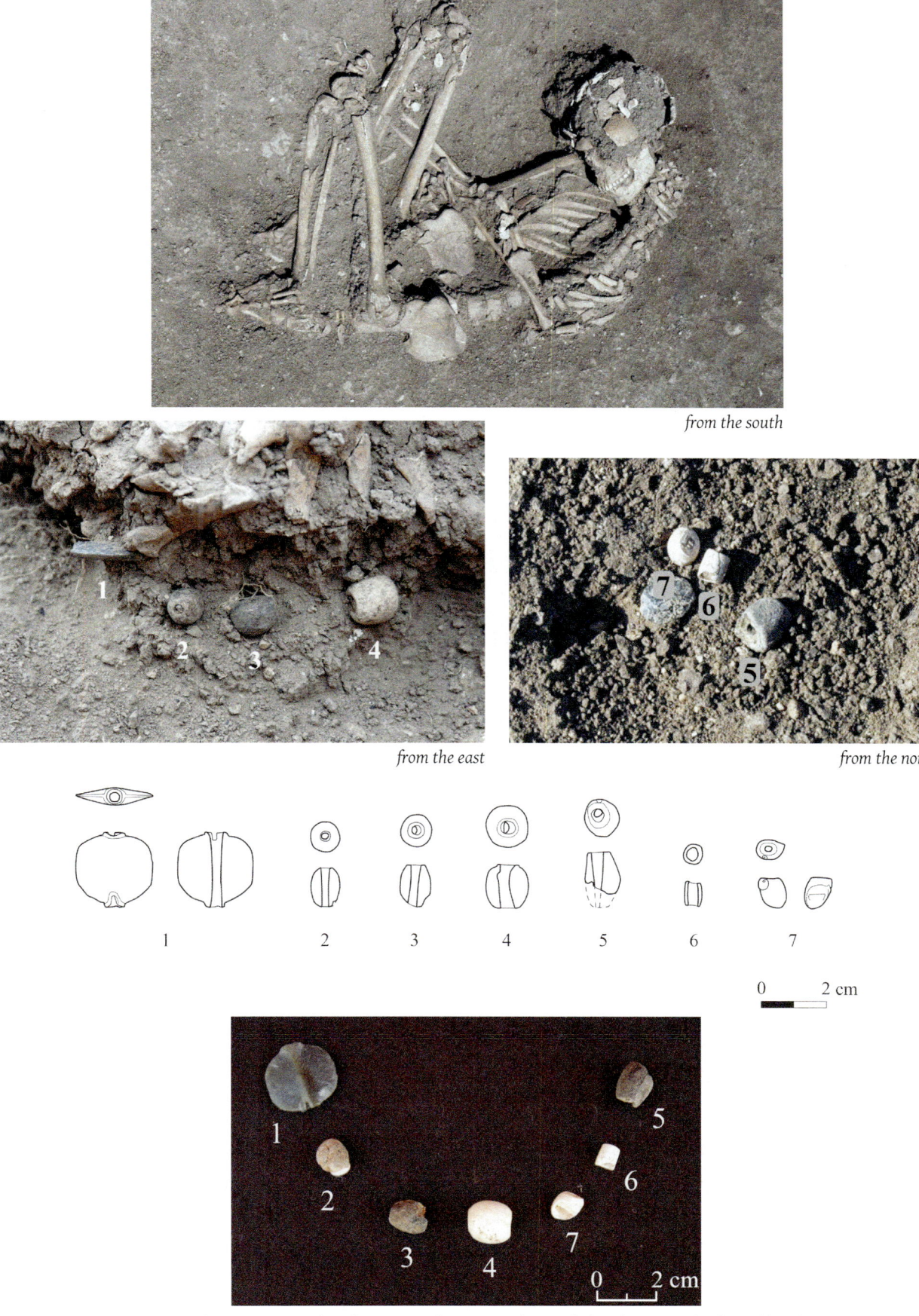

from the south

from the east

from the north

0   2 cm

Figure 5-22b. Str. 739 Burial and grave goods: 1. Stone butterfly bead; 2, 3, 5. Clay barrel beads; 4. Stone barrel bead; 6. Tusk shell bead; 7. Conch shell bead.

23. Str. 746 (Figure 5-23)

Str. 746 is a cremation burial (removed burnt bones) and contained the comingled remains—mainly cremated—of two juveniles discovered in Square E271b in Layer 4. One was 1–2 year-old, and the other was 6–8 year-old. Two skulls, arms, other long bones, and small fragments of human bones were discovered beside and under the eastern side limestone course of C2. The most remarkable characteristic of these bones was that they were burnt. One of the isolated skulls was heavily burnt and black in color. Another fragmented skull had turned grayish in color due to burning. The black-colored skull was almost complete, and it rested upright and faced north. No grave goods were uncovered.

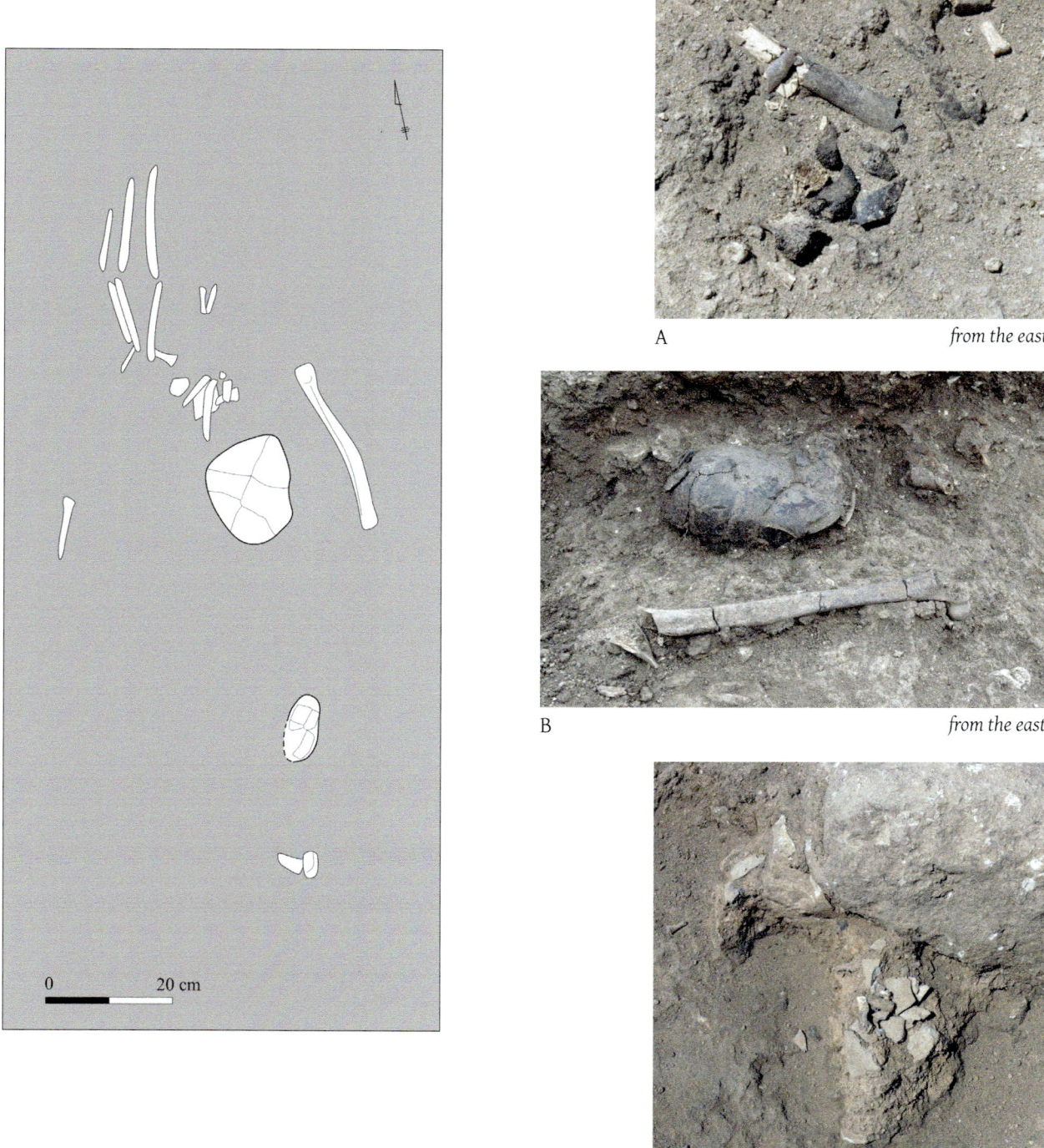

A   *from the east*

B   *from the east*

C   *from the east*

Figure 5-23. Str. 746 Burial: A. Northern part; B. Central part; C. Southern part.

24. Str. 748 (Figure 5-24)

A small plastered floor, measuring 1.2 × 0.8m, was discovered at the center of the excavation area in Square E271 in Layer 5. This floor was partly surrounded by a row of limestone blocks. The room does not seem to have been part of the habitation area as the surrounding rows were very crude and no other rooms were attached to this floor. The remains of three individuals were discovered from a crack in the center of this plastered floor. Therefore, this structure, although not part of a house, was probably made for the dead. It is certain that the dead were buried first and the floor was later plastered over them.

The first individual is a primary burial of a young adult, probably male. He was buried in a prone position, with his legs folded in front of his chest. His body was tightly bent at the waist with the right knee touching his face. The body axis direction was northwest-southeast. His head pointed northwest and faced downward. Both arms were folded, and both hands were clasped in front of his chest. Interestingly, his left arms seem to have been holding the maxilla of a juvenile aged 2–3 years. Also, part of an infant mandible was discovered near his left elbow. The infant and juvenile burial types were unknown. Body axis and face direction were indeterminate.

A mottled limestone bead (L = 0.9cm, W = 0.6cm) was found near the adult right arm and a complete flint borer (L = 3.2cm, W = 1.0cm) was also found at his tightly bended waist. Both objects seemed to belong to the adult. The flint borer might have been a clasp such as the cloth that wrapped the adult, or the rope that tied the bent body.

As mentioned above, this burial was covered with white lime plaster. A small shallow DFBW bowl, measuring 9cm in diameters and 4.2cm in height, was placed upright above the plaster. A few centimeters of soil were deposited between the plaster and the pottery. Therefore, it is probable that this bowl was placed sometime after the burial act. Anyhow, this DFBW bowl was dedicated to the persons of Str. 748.

from the east

Figure 5-24a, Str. 748 Burial: General view.

DFBW
Bead
Borer
Stone
Plaster
Animal Bone

0   50 cm

Figure 5-24b. Str. 748 Burial: Upper level.

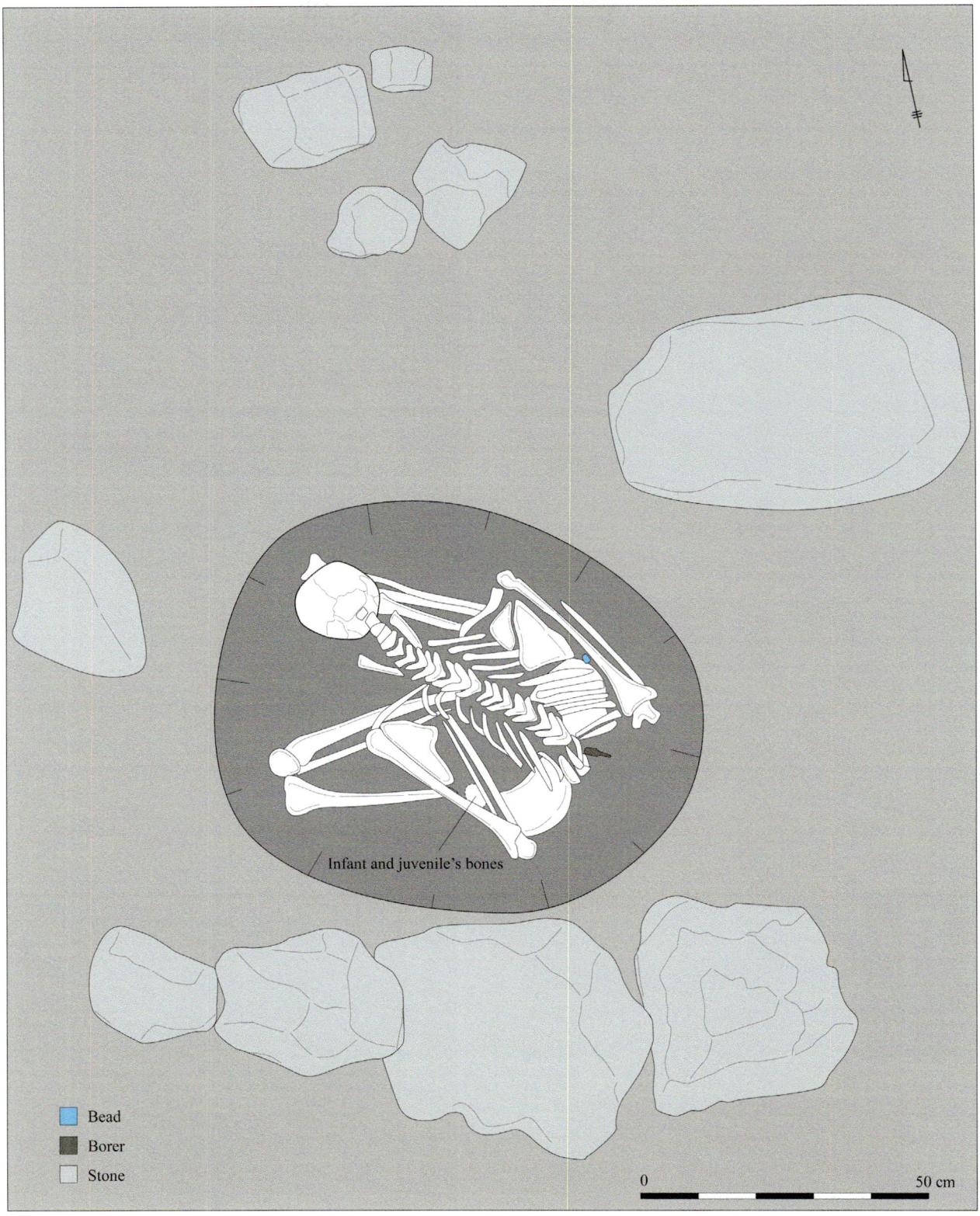

Figure 5-24c. Str. 748 Burial: Lower level.

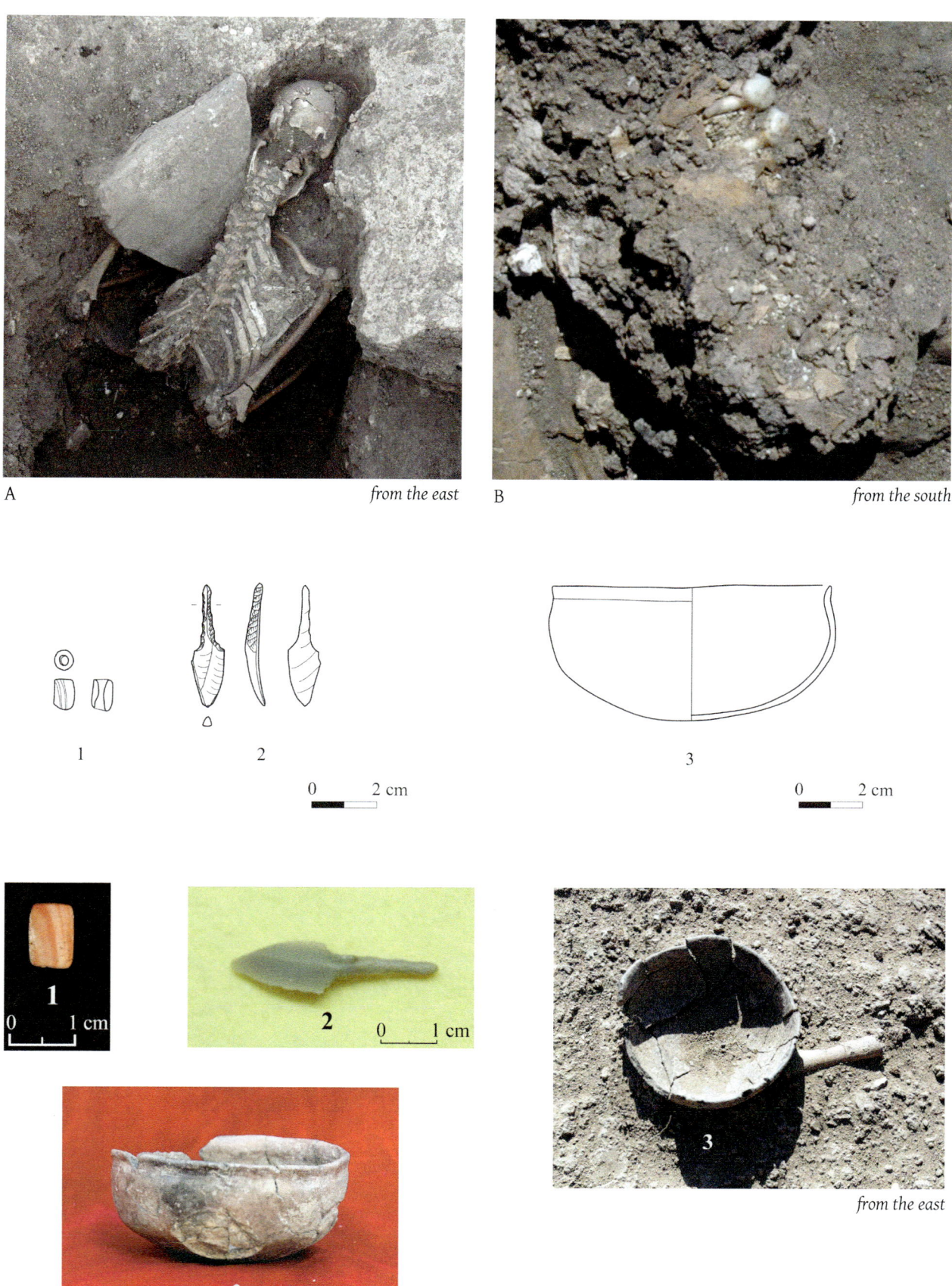

A   *from the east*   B   *from the south*

1   2   0   2 cm   3   0   2 cm

1   0   1 cm   2   0   1 cm   3   *from the east*

3

Figure 5-24d. Str. 748 Burial: A. Young adult skeleton; B. Infant bones.
Grave goods: 1. Stone bead; 2. Flint borer; 3. DFBW bowl.

122

25. Str. 750 (Figure 5-25)

Str. 750 is a primary burial of a 5–6-year-old individual lacking its cranium, discovered in Square E271d in Layer 5. The body axis direction was northwest-southeast. The position of the mandible and the visibility of posterior skeletal elements of the torso suggest that it was buried in a flexed, but prone position. There were three maxillary deciduous teeth present and they seemed to be in the proper anatomical location. Further, the second cervical vertebra, though damaged, was in situ. So, the cranium could have been removed after flesh decomposition. No grave goods were discovered.

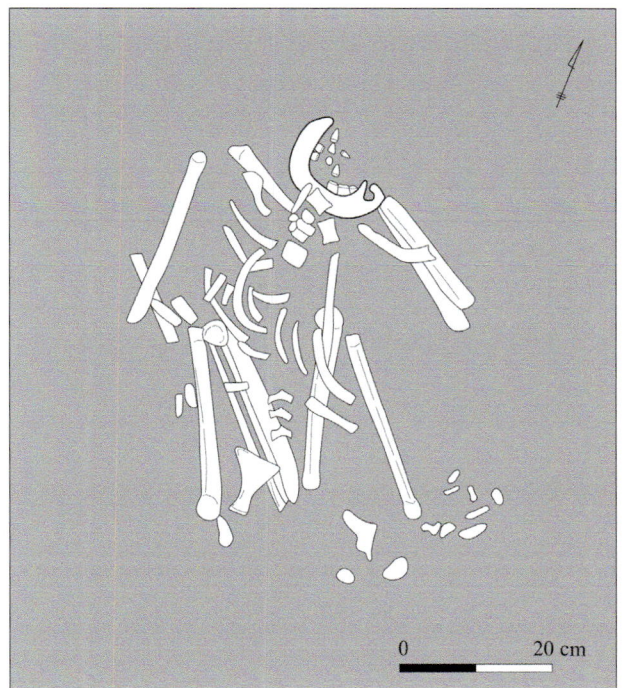 

from the southeast

Figure 5-25. Str. 750 Burial.

26. Str. 752 (Figure 5-26)

Str. 752 is a primary burial of an adult, probably female, discovered south of the stone courses of C2 in Square E271d in Layer 4. She was buried in a shallow pit on her right side. Her body axis oriented northwest-southeast. It was a highly fragmented skeleton lacking cranial elements. Remarkably, her skull was completely removed from the grave and the cervical vertebrae were missing. No grave goods were present.

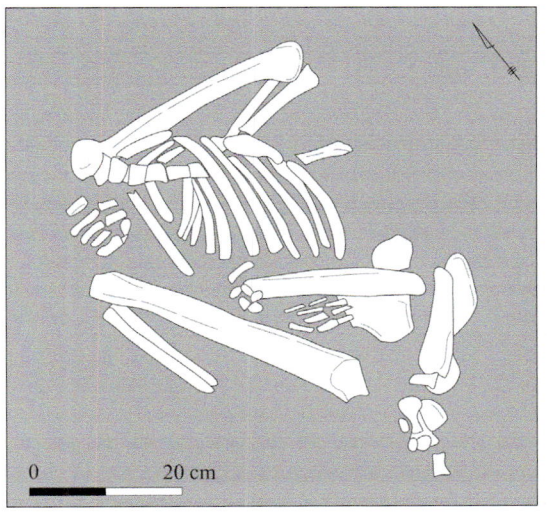 

from the southwest

Figure 5-26. Str. 752 Burial.

123

27. Str. 756 (Figure 5-27)

Str. 756 is an isolated skull of a juvenile discovered in Square E271b in Layer 4. This individual was represented by skull fragments discovered under the southern part of the square stone course of C2. As only half of the skull remained, the orientation of the head and face were not detectable. Judging from the excavated situation, this skull looks like a secondary burial. No grave goods were discovered.

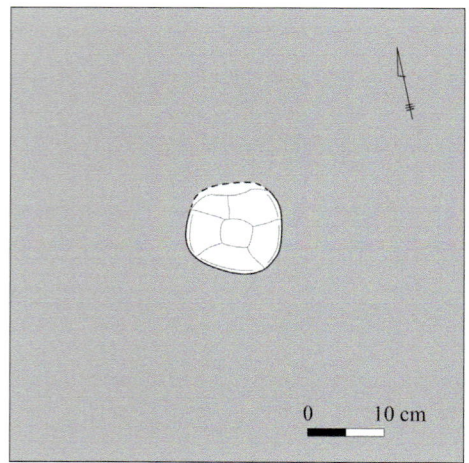

from the southeast

Figure 5-27. Str. 756 Burial.

28. Str. 757 (Figure 5-28)

Str. 757 is a primary burial of a juvenile aged 7–8 years. It was discovered alone in the northwestern part of Square E271b in Layer 4. Sex was indeterminate. It was buried in a flexed position on its right side. Its legs were tightly bent in front of the abdomen. The body axis direction was south-north. The head pointed to the south, but was placed slightly upright. The face looked toward the northeast. This individual had 16 enamel hypoplasia as well as dental caries affecting the remaining deciduous molars. Beside the skeleton, a bone awl (L=5.2cm, W=1.1cm), possibly a grave good, was recovered.

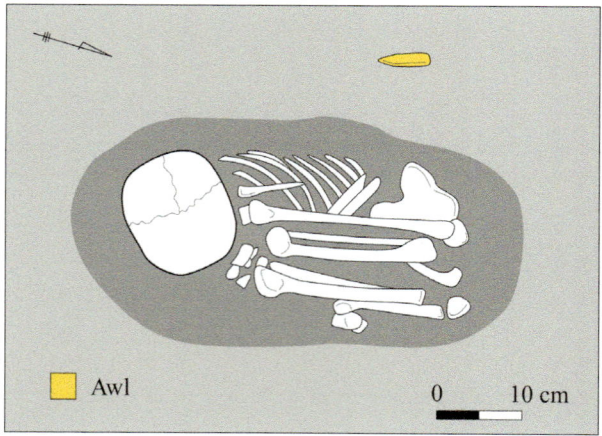

from the northeast

Figure 5-28a. Str. 757 Burial.

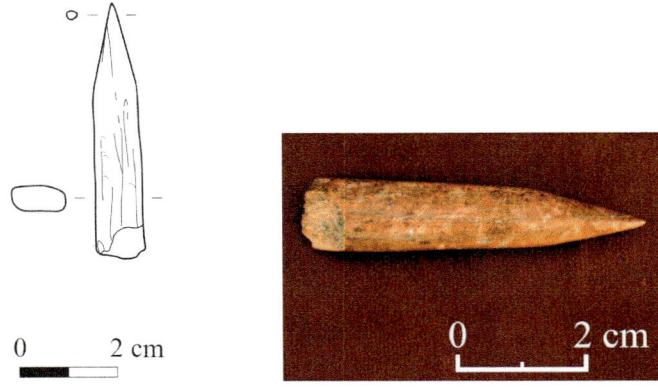

Figure 5-28b. Str. 757 Grave goods: Bone awl.

29. Str. 759 (Figure 5-29)

Str. 759 is a deposit containing the remains of an adult. It was discovered in the southwestern part of Square E271b near Str. 748 in Layer 5. Burial type is unknown. This individual was identified by the presence of disarticulated left and right adult feet. No grave goods were uncovered.

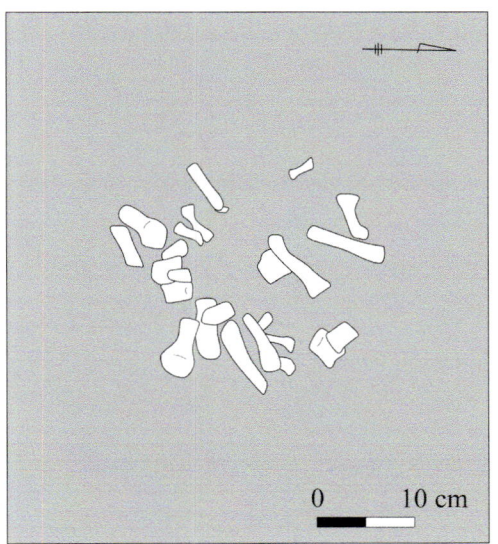

from the east

Figure 5-29. Str. 759 Burial.

30. Str. 803 (Figure 5-30)

A small limestone-paved platform area was discovered in the northern part of Square E271b in Layer 5. This platform area, made of many small coarse and weathered reddish limestone pieces, measures c. 1 x 1m. Another limestone pavement was also discovered on its eastern side, though the structure was longer and narrower.

Str. 803 is a primary burial of a young adult, probably female, discovered in the former limestone pavement area. The relationship between Str. 803 and the limestone pavement is not clear. She was buried in a tightly flexed position on her right back. Her lower back and legs inclined to her right. Her body axis direction was west-east. Her face looked upward with the mouth open. She was buried with her knees drawn up, and the ends of the tibia and fibula were destroyed. Her shoulder inclined extremely. Her left arm was bent near her hipbones and placed below her legs. Her right arm was bent under her hipbones and the fingers were placed in front of her face. Her legs were bent tightly that her tibias and fibulas extended upward.

A conch shell and a bone bead were discovered beside Str. 803. The conch shell, which was found near her right shoulder, was a relatively large shell of which both sides were ground. It was used as an adornment like a pendant. The bone bead was a tiny cylindrical one and found beside the legs.

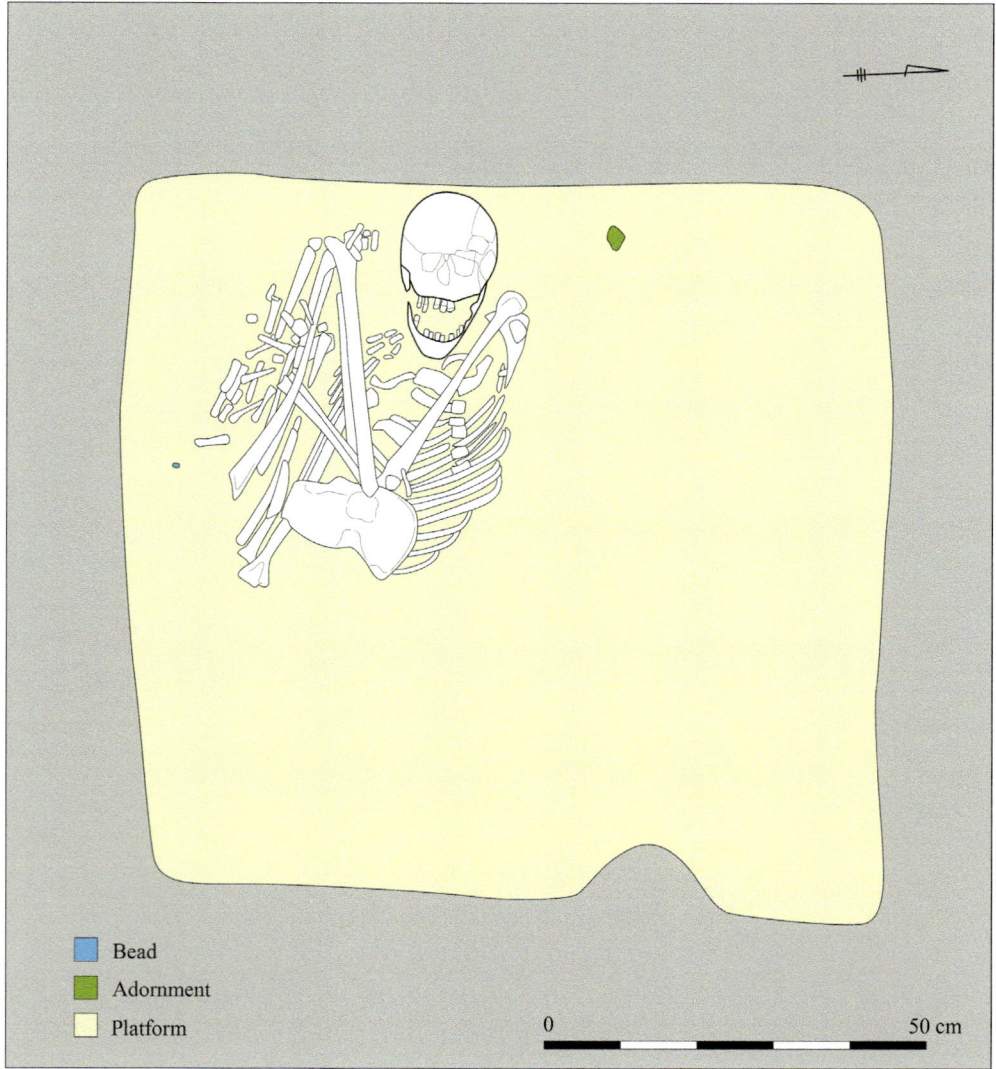

Bead
Adornment
Platform

0   50 cm

Figure 5-30a. Str. 803 Burial.

from the east

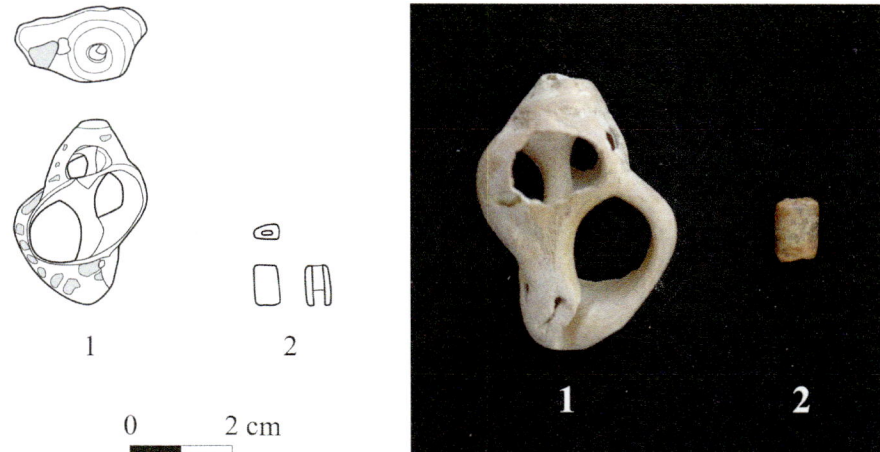

Figure 5-30b. Str. 803 Burial and grave goods:
1. Conch shell adornment; 2. Bone bead.

31. Str. 807 (Figure 5-31)

Str. 807 is a primary burial of a middle-aged adult male (35–40 yrs.) discovered south of Str. 750 at the northern end of Square E291b in Layer 5. He was buried in a tightly flexed position on his back. Both legs were folded down on the left side. His body axis direction was north-south. The head pointed to the north. His face looked upward, though his head was slightly inclined to the left. The right arm was bent tightly, and his right hand was placed in front of his face. His left arm was extended and his left hand was placed under his hips. Physical anthropological observation revealed that he had suffered catastrophic perimortem fractures of the mandible and cranium.

A grayish-black colored cylindrical bead (probably made of basalt) was discovered at the right side of the skull. A flint drill was discovered on the pelvis. When the skeleton was discovered, most of the body, except the legs, was covered with lime plaster, and a large limestone was placed at the knees. These materials had been used to cover the body after interment.

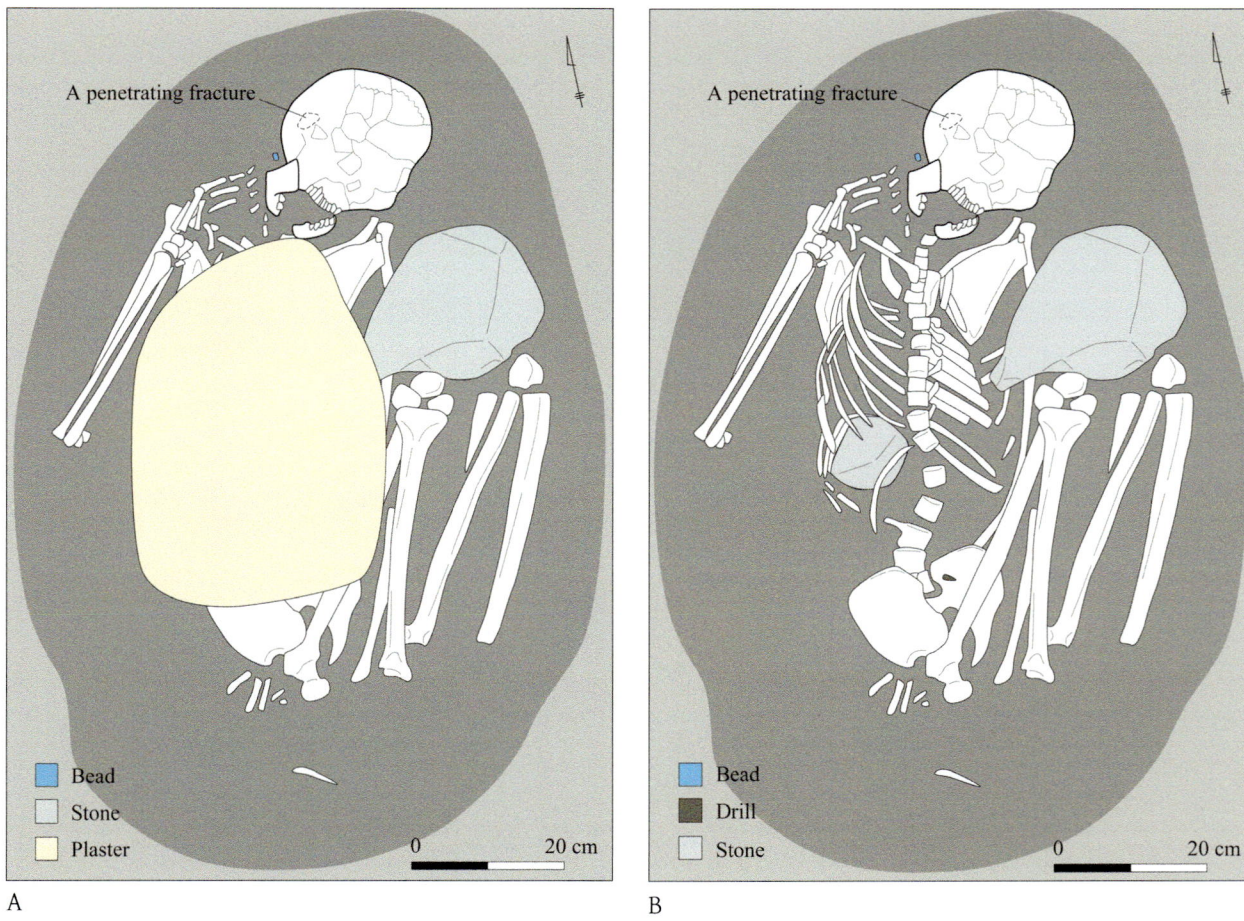

Figure 5-31a. Str. 807 Burial: A. The body covered with lime plaster and limestone;
B. The skeleton under lime plaster.

A   *from the south*   B   *from the south*

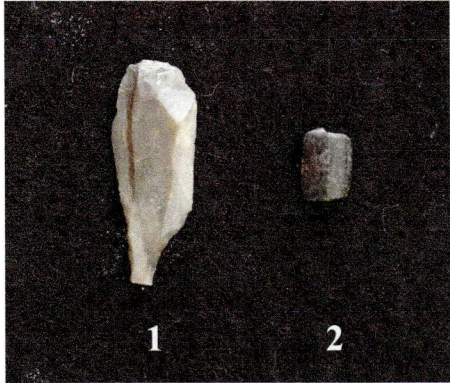

Figure 5-31b. Str. 807 Burial: A. The body covered with lime plaster and limestone;
B. The skeleton under lime plaster. Grave goods: 1. Flint drill; 2. Stone bead.

32. Str. 822 (Figure 5-32)

Str. 822, a cluster consisting of hand bones, teeth, and some vertebrae, was found at the southern part of Square E271b in Layer 5. Burial type is unknown. The bones were parts of a juvenile between ten and twelve years of age. Most parts of the rest of the skeleton were not recovered and, therefore, sex was not identified.

Twenty beads were discovered among these small fragments of the skeleton. They were 15 agate, four basalt, and one conch shell beads. The agate and basalt beads were found together in groups of three to five in the cluster. The agate beads were the small flat type, measuring 6-7mm in diameter and 2mm in thickness, and the basalt beads were the tiny short cylindrical types, measuring 4mm in diameter and 3mm in thickness. This burial seemed to be a secondary and disturbed one.

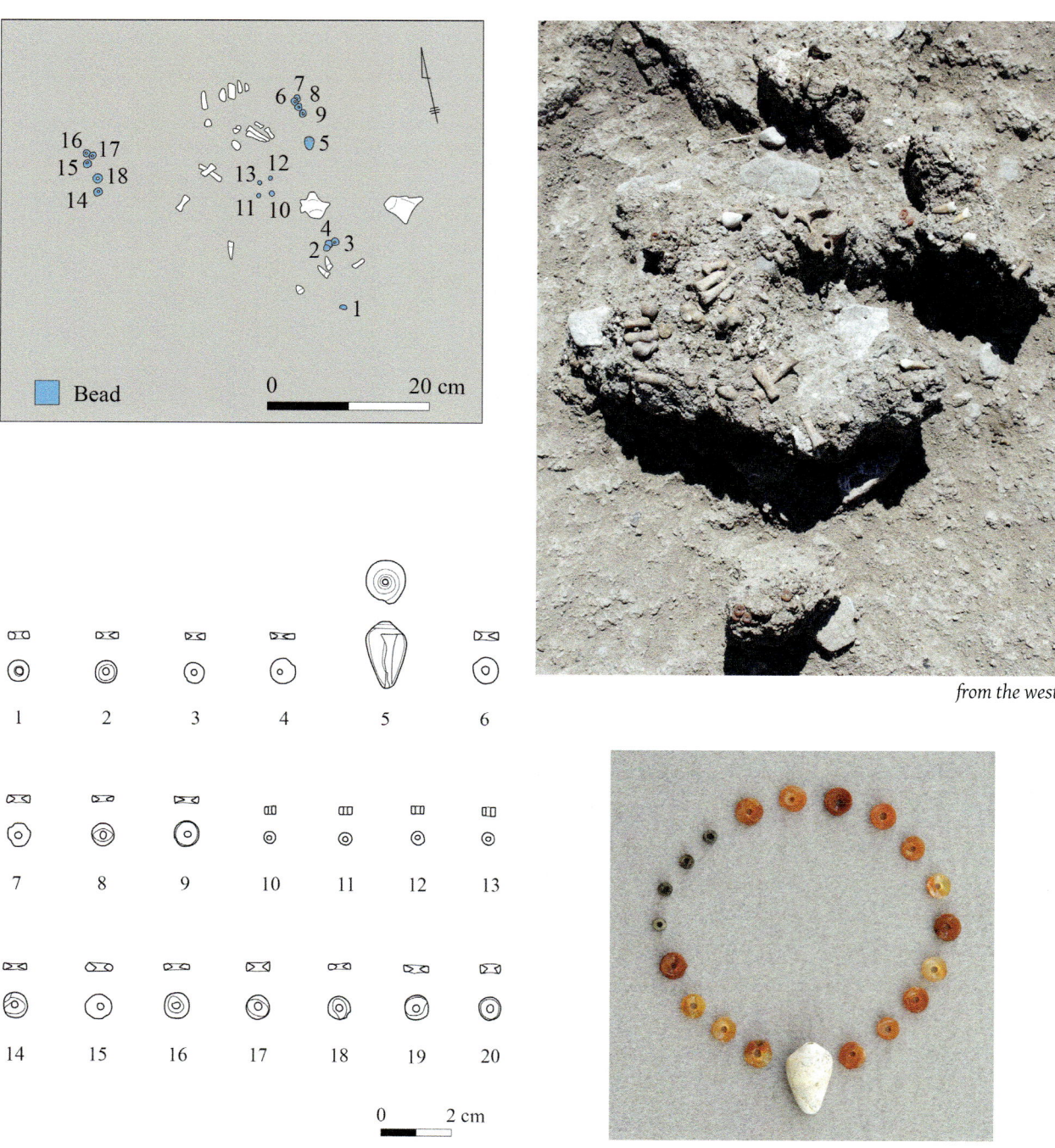

from the west

Figure 5-32. Str. 822 Burial and grave goods: 1–4, 6–20. Stone beads; 5. Shell bead.

33. Str. 823 (Figure 5-33)

Str. 823 is a primary burial of a subadult (14–16 yrs.) discovered at the northern end of the border between Square E271a and b in Layer 5. The body position could be observed completely, but the skeleton was poorly preserved, so sex was not identified. It was buried in a flexed position on its left side. The body axis direction was north-south, and the skull pointed to the north and faced southeast. Its left arm was bent and the hand was placed on its breast.

A fragment of a shell bead was found beside the scapula. A broken bone needle with an eye was discovered at its right foot.

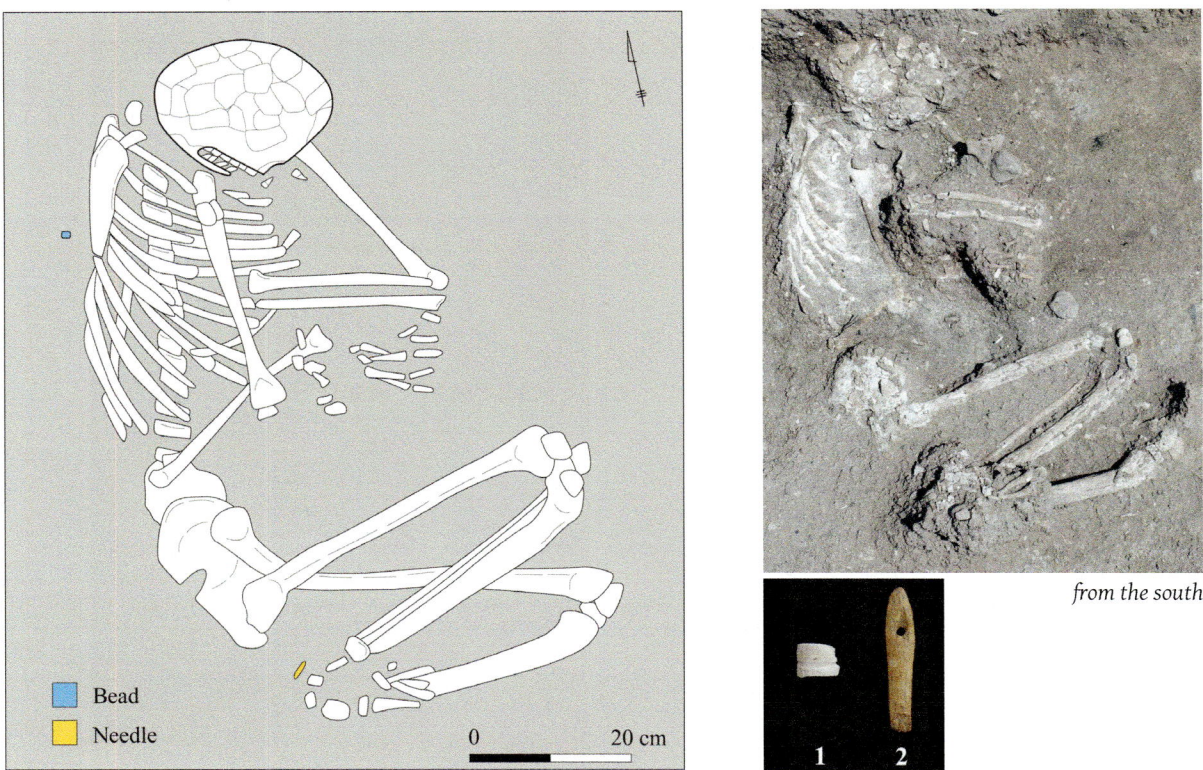

from the south

Figure 5-33. Str. 823 Burial and grave goods: 1. Shell bead; 2. Bone needle.

34. Str. 825 (Figure 5-34)

Some long bones, pelvis fragments and fingers were discovered in the southwestern part of Square E271b in Layer 5. They were parts of a juvenile (10–12 yrs.) and seemed to be the remnants of a disturbed burial. Burial type is unknown. Sex was indeterminate, and no grave goods were discovered.

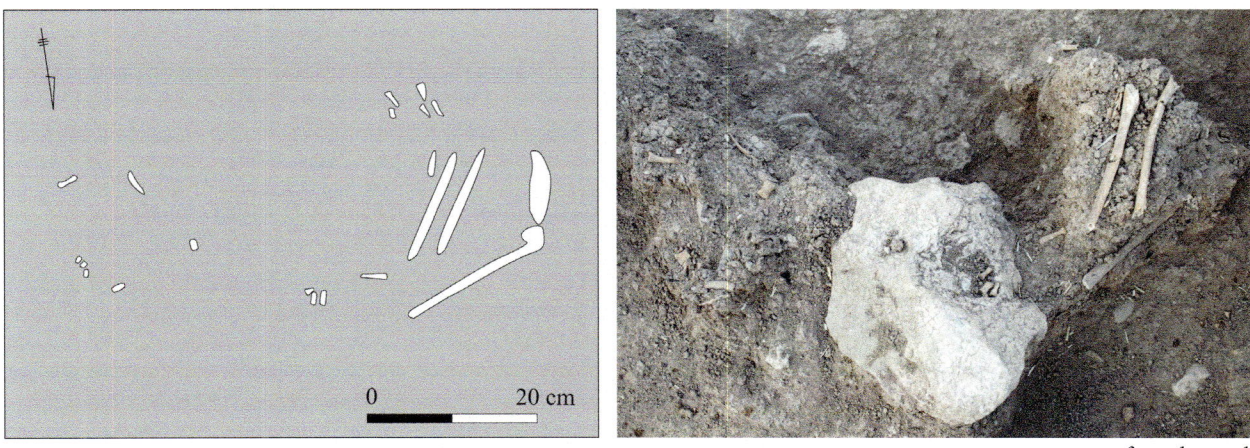

from the north

Figure 5-34. Str. 825 Burial.

35. Str. 826 (Figure 5-35)

Str. 826 is a primary burial of a subadult (14–15 yrs.) discovered in the northeastern part of Square E271d in Layer 5. Sex was indeterminate. As a rough stone and potsherd scatter were present on its western side, it was originally thought that the remains were buried on a stone-potsherd pavement. However, the scatter was not observed below the skeleton itself, suggesting that it did not represent a stone pavement. It was buried in a tightly flexed position on its left side. The legs were flexed in front of the abdomen. The body axis direction was northeast-southwest, and the skull faced southeast. Its right hand seemed to hold the left elbow under its folded legs. No grave goods were recovered.

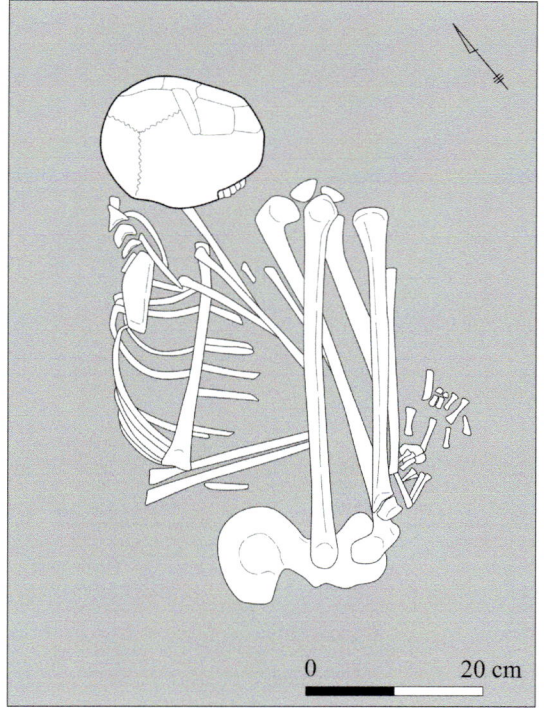 

from the southwest

Figure 5-35. Str. 826 Burial.

36. Str. 828 (Figure 5-36)

Str. 828 is a primary burial of a fetus discovered at the southeastern corner of Square E271d in Layer 5. It was a small fetus measuring only 35cm in height, and sex was indeterminate. It was buried in a flexed position on its right side. The body axis direction was northeast-southwest, the head pointed to the northeast, and the face looked to the northwest. A large potsherd was found to the north of the skull and smaller potsherds were found in front of its face. No grave goods were recovered.

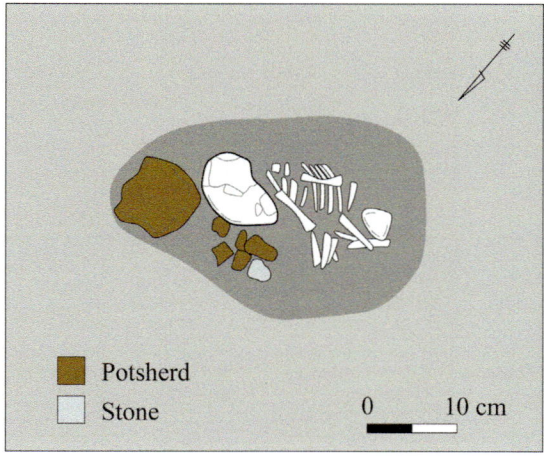 

Potsherd
Stone

from the northwest

Figure 5-36. Str. 828 Burial.

37. Str. 829 (Figure 5-37)

Three primary burials—Str. 836, 830, and 829—were discovered side by side at the center of Square E271b in Layer 5. They were closely aligned from south to north. Str. 829 is the northernmost of these three burials. It is a primary burial of a juvenile (2–3 yrs.). It was buried in a flexed position on its left side. The body axis was in the west-east direction, and the head was slightly bent and pointed toward north. The face looked to the east. No grave goods were recovered.

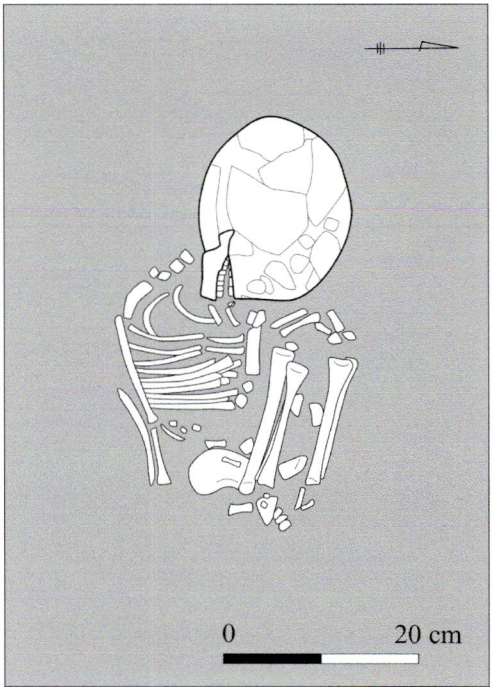

from the east

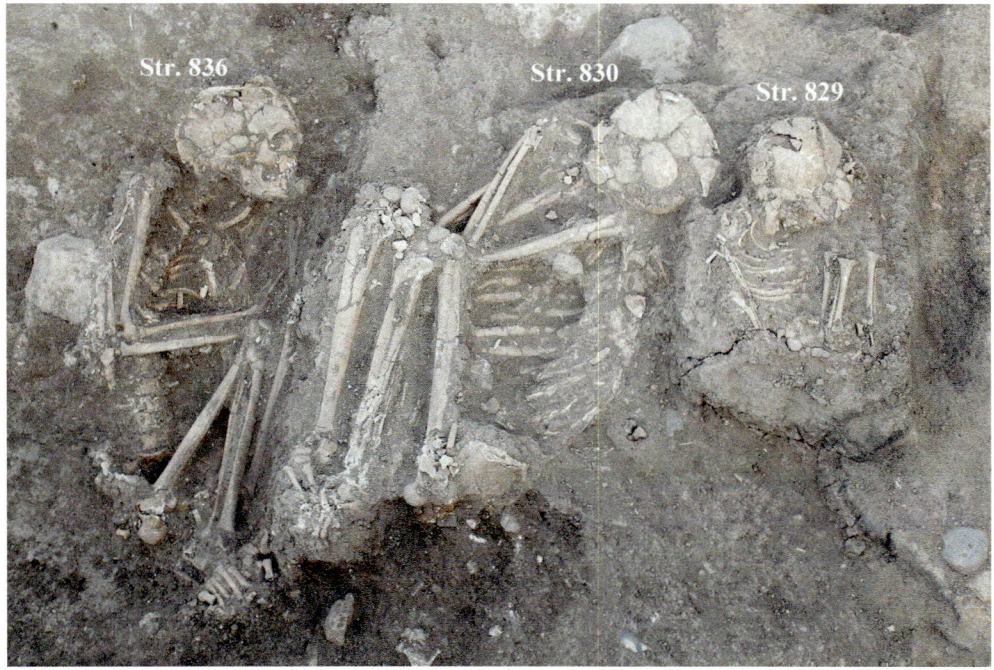

from the east

Figure 5-37. Str. 829 Burial.

38. Str. 830 (Figure 5-38)

Str. 830 is a primary burial of a middle-aged adult, probably male. He was buried back to back with Str. 829 (Figure 5-37). He was buried in a tightly flexed position on his right side. He seemed to have placed his hands together in front of his face. His body axis direction was northwest-southeast, the head pointed to the northwest, and his face looked southwest. A barrel-type dark-green stone (probably gabbro) bead was discovered beside his left femur.

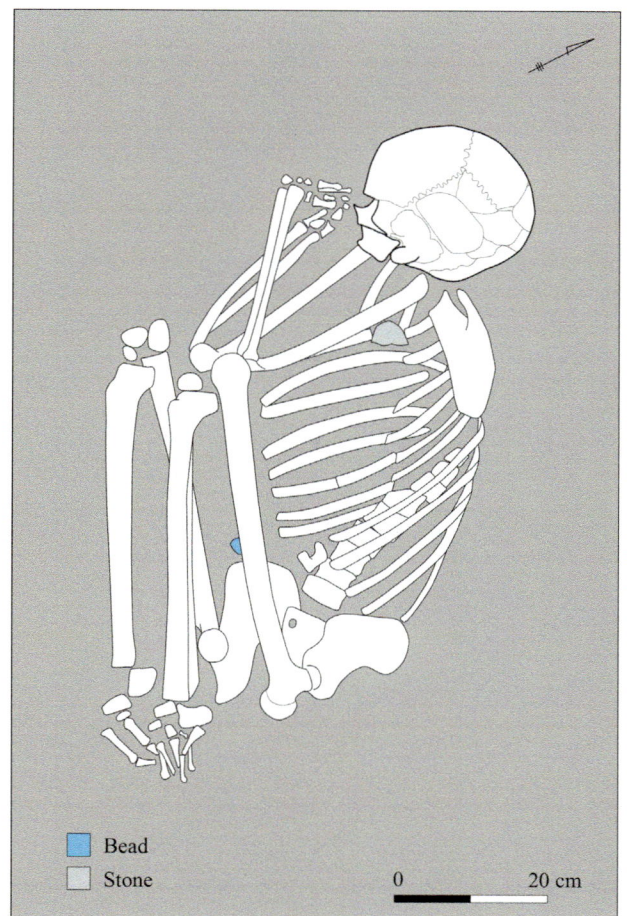

Bead
Stone

0   20 cm

from the southwest

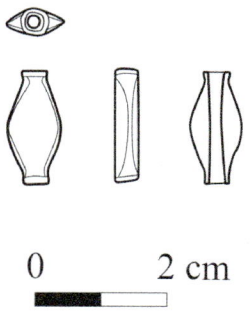

0   2 cm

Figure 5-38. Str. 830 Burial and grave goods: Stone bead.

39. Str. 832 (Figure 5-39)

Dismembered human bones were discovered at the northwestern corner of Square E271d in Layer 5. The distribution of the juvenile ribs was the most conspicuous feature of this deposit. A skull, vertebrae, and fingers were the other main elements. Physical anthropological analysis indicated that the deposit contained at least five individuals: a perinatal baby, two juveniles, and two adults. The human skeletons were heavily disturbed and they did not remain in their original positions. As it was very difficult to distinguish each skeletal remnant in the field, the remains were grouped together and treated as one grave. However, one is a disturbed primary burial of an adult. The burial types of the other individuals are unknown.

One complete short-necked jar, a typical Rouj 2c DFBW, was placed upright at the northeastern corner of the deposit. Seven beads were discovered around the cervical vertebrae of an adult. They were two flat agate beads, a barrel-shaped serpentinite bead, a barrel-shaped obsidian bead, an oval gypsum bead, a barrel-shaped limestone bead, and a cowrie shell bead. As six of the seven beads were found in a row along the cervical vertebrae, they were probably worn as a necklace by the adult.

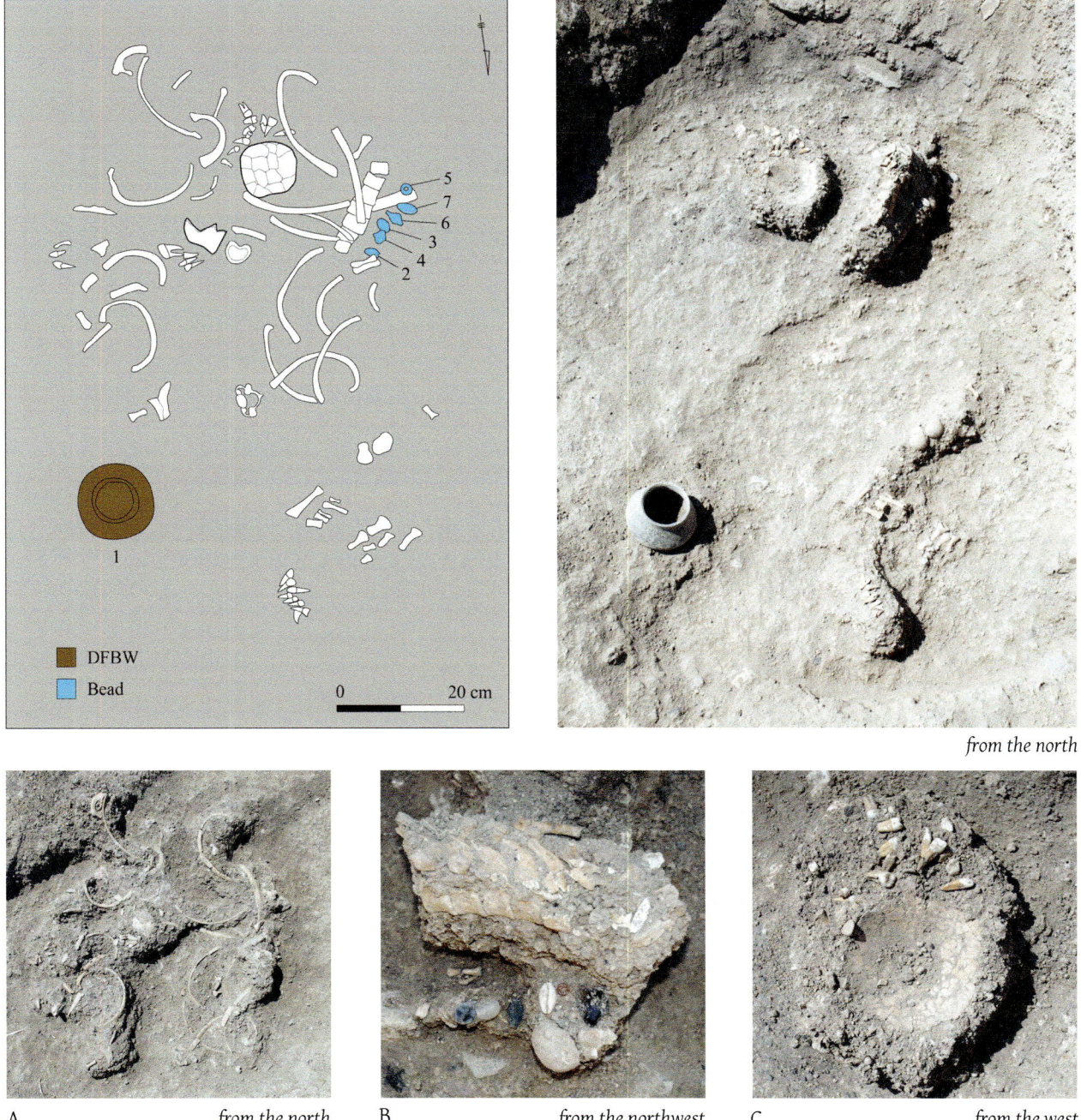

from the north

A   *from the north*   B   *from the northwest*   C   *from the west*

Figure 5-39a. Str. 832 Burial: A. Northern part; B. Western part; C. Southern part.

135

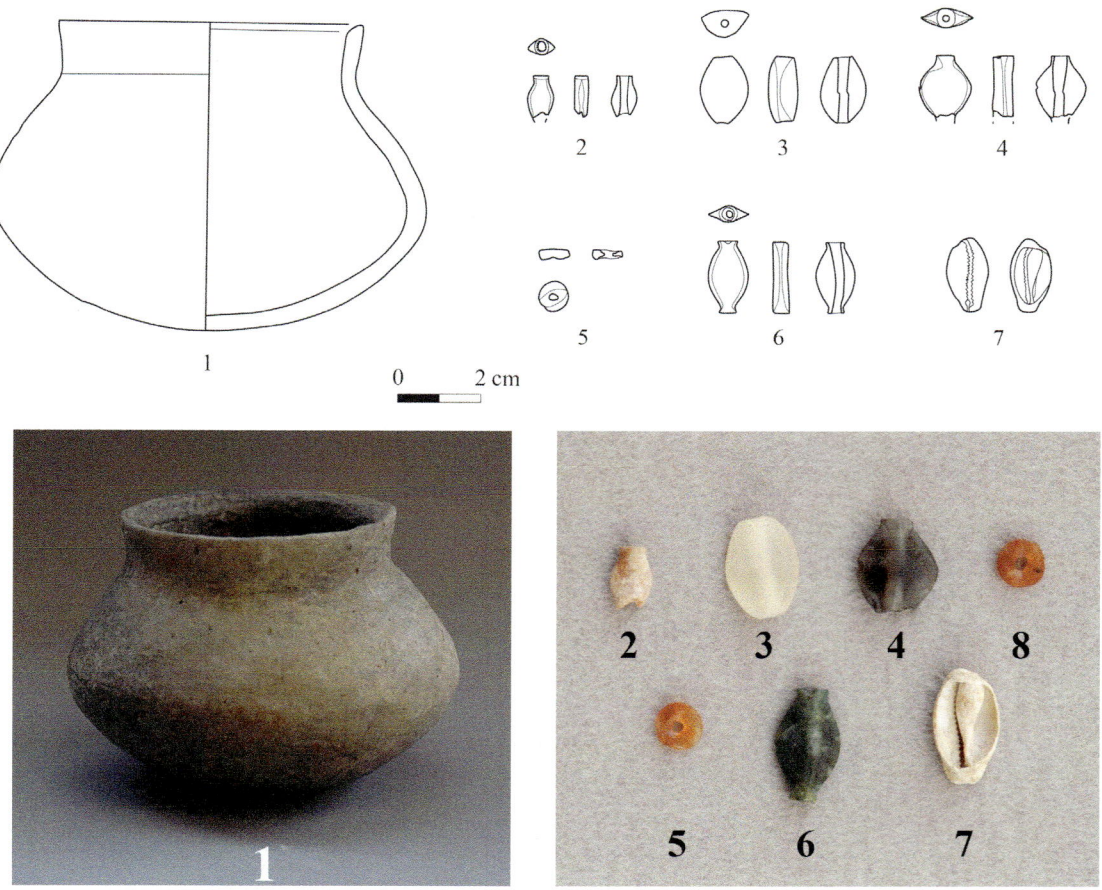

Figure 5-39b. Str. 832 Grave goods: 1. DFBW jar; 2. Limestone barrel bead; 3. Gypsum oval bead;
4. Obsidian barrel bead; 5, 8. Agate flat beads; 6. Serpentinite barrel bead; 7. Cowrie shell bead.

40. Str. 834 (Figure 5-40)

Str. 834 is a primary burial of a juvenile (2–3 yrs.) discovered at the eastern end of Square E271b in Layer 5. The juvenile was buried in a flexed position on its left side. The body axis direction was northwest-southeast and it faced northeast. Interestingly, the skull of this juvenile was clearly in an upside-down position. However, it could not be determined whether the skull was decapitated or not and if there were cut marks on the cervical vertebrae. Thus, the skull of this individual was intentionally manipulated. There were no grave goods.

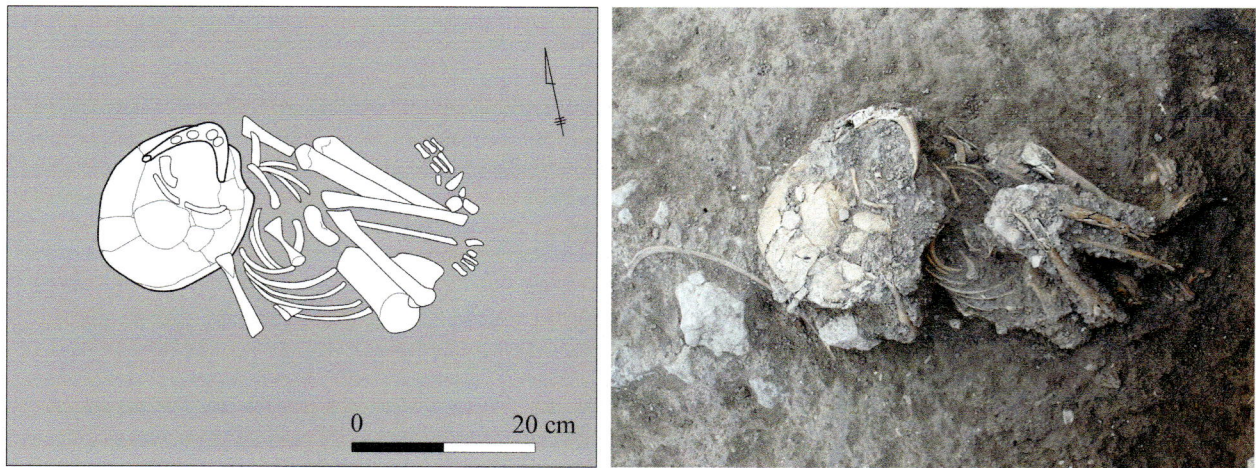

from the south

Figure 5-40. Str. 834 Burial.

41. Str. 836 (Figure 5-41)

Str. 836 is the southernmost burial in a series of three parallel primary burials discovered in the western part of Square E271b in Layer 5. It is a primary burial of a middle-aged adult male facing Str. 830, though the recovery level of this skeleton was c. 10cm lower than that of the latter. He was buried in a tightly flexed position on his left side. The body axis direction was west-east, the head pointed to the west and faced north. The left arm was bent, and his left hand was placed in front of his face. His right hand was placed on his left arm. A small conch shell bead was discovered near his back.

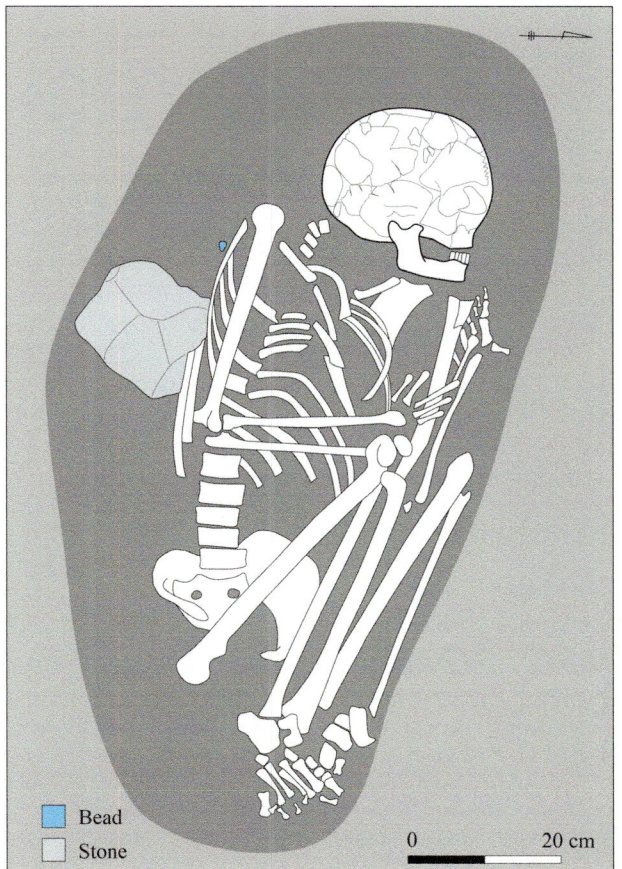

Bead
Stone

0   20 cm

from the east

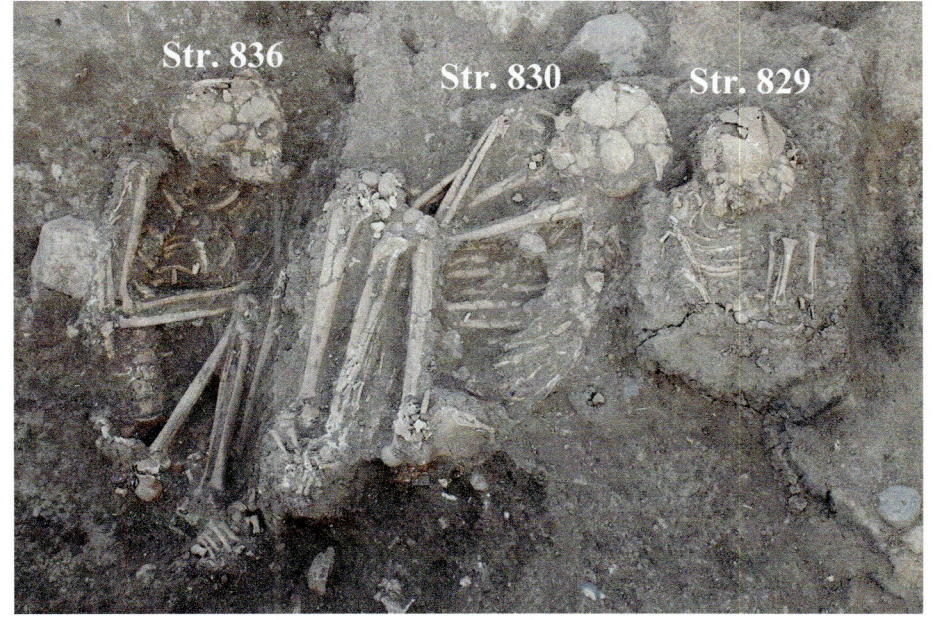

Str. 836   Str. 830   Str. 829

Figure 5-41. Str. 836 Burial and grave goods: Conch shell bead.

42. Str. 838 (Figure 5-42)

Str. 838 is a primary burial of a perinatal baby discovered in Square E271b in Layer 5. Most of the skeleton was preserved, but in poor condition, so sex could not be determined. It seems to have been buried in a flexed position on its left side. The body axis direction was west-east, and the head pointed to the west and faced north. A stone was found adjacent to the skull. There were no grave goods.

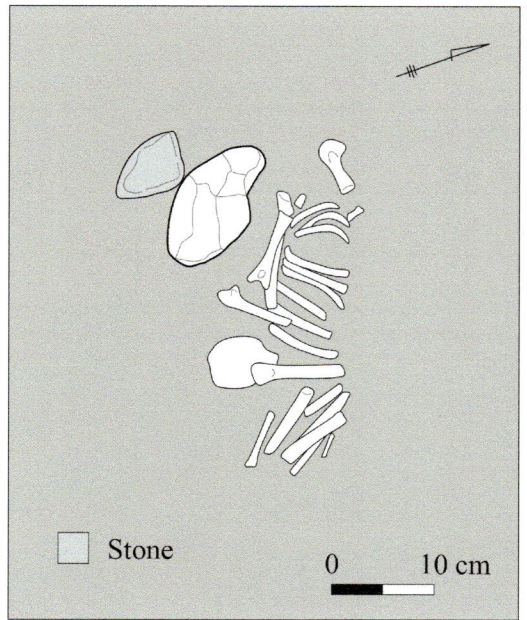 

from the east

Figure 5-42. Str. 838 Burial.

43. Str. 841 (Figure 5-43)

Str. 841 is a primary burial of a perinatal individual discovered in the southeastern part of Square E271b in Layer 5. There were traces of burnt soil on the grave walls and the floor. However, the skeletal remains exhibited no traces of burning, which rules out the possibility of cremation. It was buried lying on its back. The body axis direction was southeast-northwest. Due to skull fragmentation, the face direction has not been determined. No grave goods were recovered.

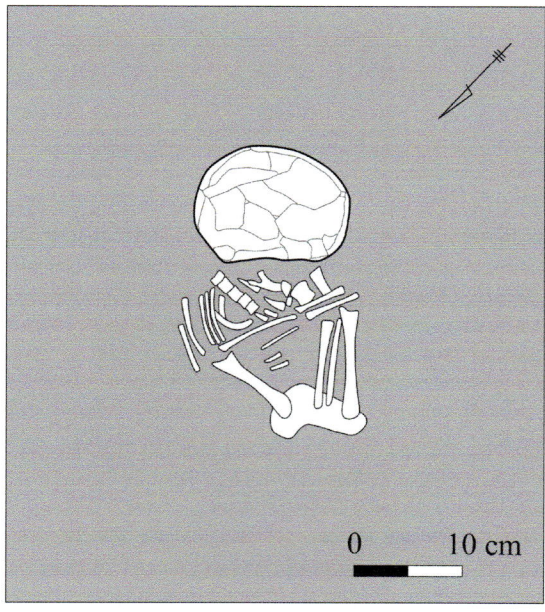 

from the northwest

Figure 5-43. Str. 841 Burial.

44. Str. 851 (Figure 5-44)

This deposit contains the disturbed remains of two human skeletons, including a skull, pelvis, and other bones, in the northwestern part of Square E271b in Layer 5. The first individual is an infant (10–12 mths.), but the remains were heavily disturbed. Therefore, the burial type is unknown, and sex was not determined. The second is a primary burial of an adult, but these remains were also disturbed. The body axis and face direction for both these individuals were not identified. One cowrie shell bead was uncovered near the adult hip bone.

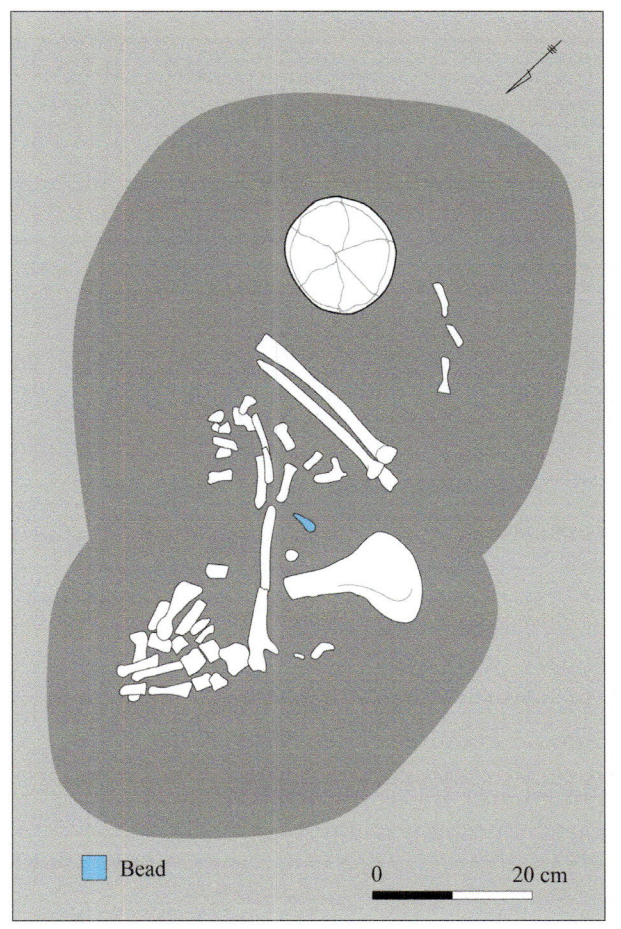

Bead

0   20 cm

from the northwest

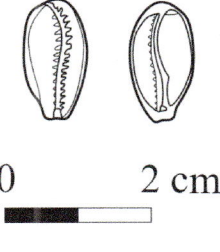

0   2 cm

Figure 5-44. Str. 851 Burial and grave goods: Shell bead (front and back).

45. Str. 852 (Figure 5-45)

This deposit contains commingled remains of two individuals, including a mandible and other bones, discovered in Square E271b in Layer 5. It represents partial evidence of a burial, and was heavily disturbed. Some of the human remains were partly burnt. The burnt mandible suggests that the owner was an adult, probably male, but the other bones belonged to a juvenile (1–2 yrs.). The remains were heavily disturbed, so the burial type is unknown and sex was not determined. No grave goods were uncovered.

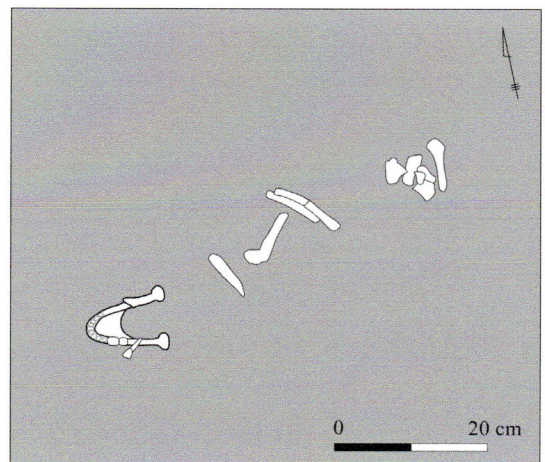 

from the south

Figure 5-45. Str. 852 Burial.

46. Str. 902 (Figure 5-46)

Str. 902 contains a part of a skull discovered in the northern part of Square E271a in Layer 5. It belonged to a juvenile (1–2 yrs.), but sex was indeterminate. Burial type is unknown. It was difficult to determine if this was the site of original inhumation and the rest of the body parts were removed to another location in the cemetery or vice versa. Some animal bones were also recovered from the same spot. No grave goods were discovered.

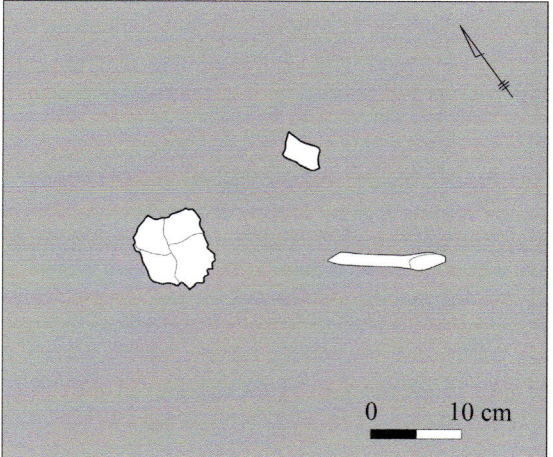 

from the southwest

Figure 5-46. Str. 902 Burial.

47. Str. 904 (Figure 5-47)

Str. 904 is a primary burial of a young adult male (30–35 yrs.) discovered in the western part of Square E271a in Layer 5. He was buried in a flexed position on his left side. His right hand was placed in front of his face. His left leg was stretched parallel to his right forearm. His right leg was bent along the body and crossed with the left leg from behind. His body axis direction was southwest-northeast. The head pointed to the southwest and his face looked to the north. A part of the skull of Str. 912 was discovered beside his feet. A fragment of a pottery handle was discovered near his waist, but this may not be grave goods.

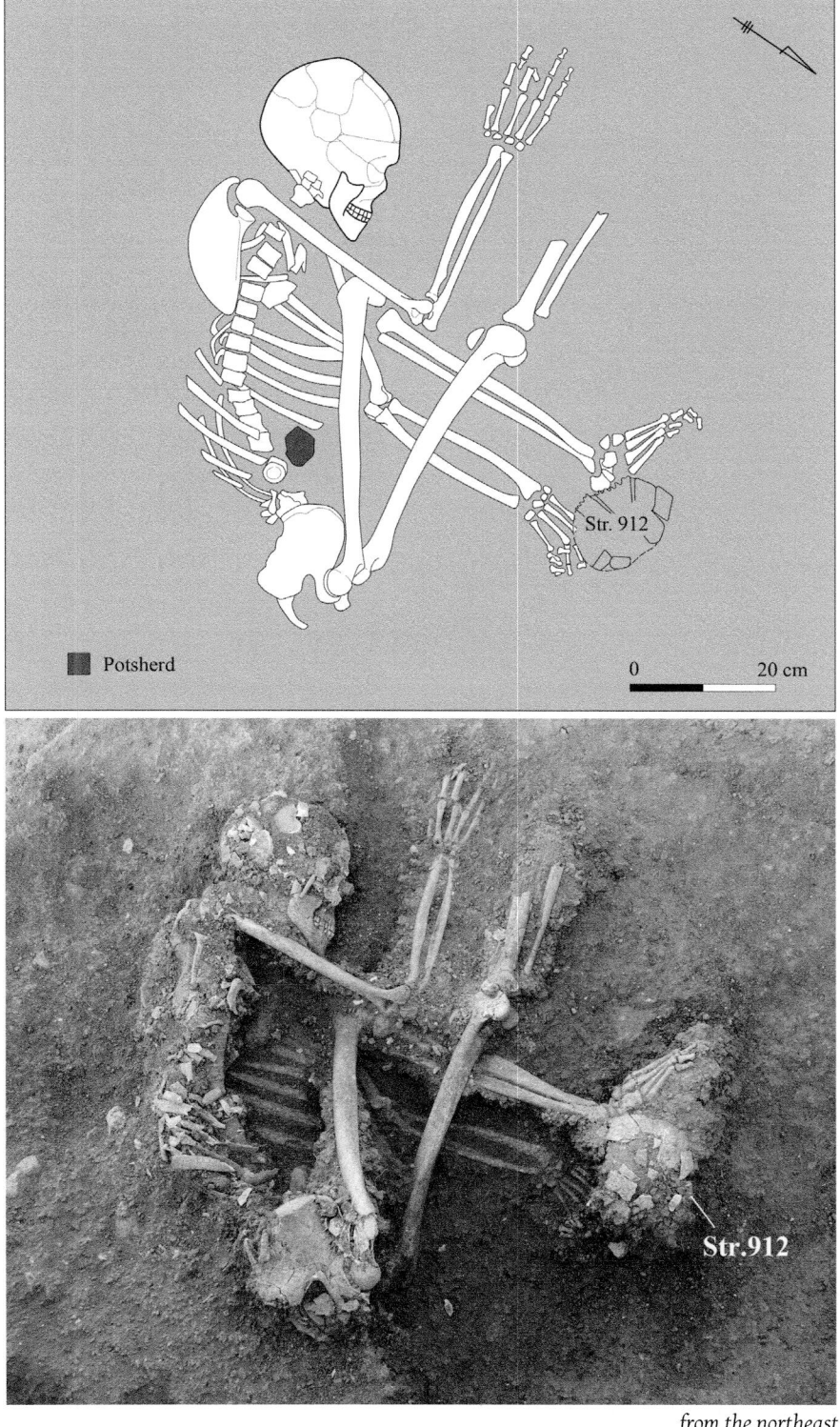

from the northeast

Figure 5-47. Str. 904 Burial.

48. Str. 908 (Figure 5-48)

Str. 908 is a primary burial of a subadult (11–13 yrs.) discovered in room 5 of the Str. 827 building in Square E271 in Layer 7. Sex was indeterminate. It was buried in this room after the building was abandoned. No fire traces were observed on this skeleton, which suggests that the deceased was placed in this room after the Str. 827 building was burnt down. Therefore, Str. 908 was an interment that happened during the Layer 6 era. It was buried in a flexed position on its left side. Its head, bust, and legs were inclined to its left side. Its right hand was twisted, and its left arm was stretched along its body. The body axis direction was east-west. Its face was inclined to the lower left and looked to the southwest direction. A flint blade was discovered near its pelvis.

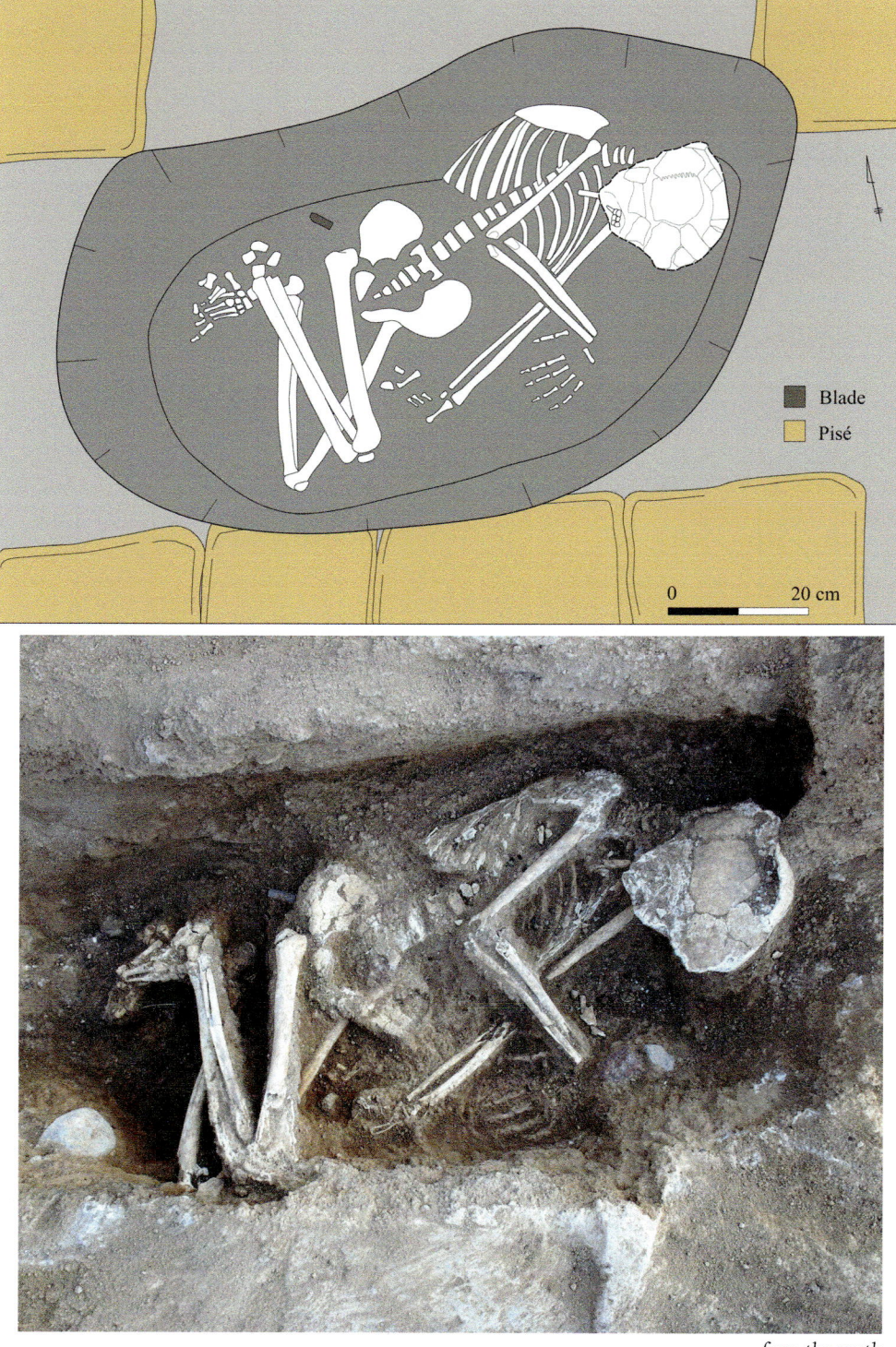

■ Blade

■ Pisé

0   20 cm

from the south

Figure 5-48. Str. 908 Burial.

49. Str. 909 (Figure 5-49)

Str. 909 is a primary burial of a young adult, probably female, discovered in the eastern part of Square E271a in Layer 5. The cranial indicators of sex were, unfortunately, ambiguous. However, general skeletal gracility would seem to suggest that this individual was a young adult female. She was buried in a tightly flexed position on her left side. Her right hand was placed on the back of her head. Her left arm was stretched and the hand was placed near her pelvis. Her body axis was in the northeast-southwest direction and her face looked to the south. A limestone stamp seal was discovered beside her waist. It is shaped like a gourd with a straight and parallel line impression design.

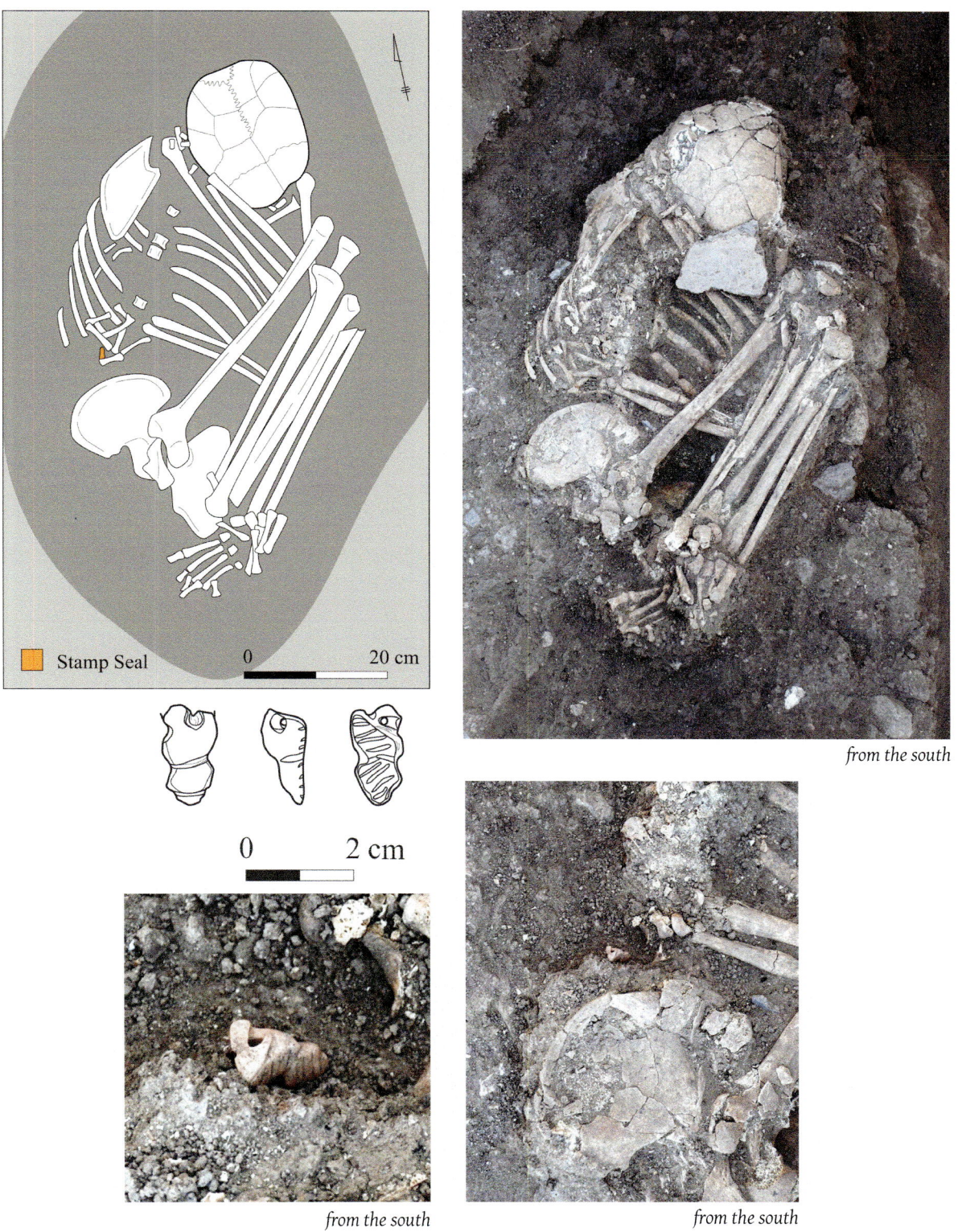

from the south

from the south

from the south

Figure 5-49. Str. 909 Burial and grave goods: Limestone stamp seal.

50. Str. 910 (Figure 5-50)

This burial contains the fragmentary remains of at least three individuals—two adults, including an old one, and an infant (6 mths.–1yr.). These remains include part of a skull, some long bones, fingers, and feet and were discovered in the northern edge of Square E271a in Layer 6. The remains were disturbed and mixed, so the burial type was unknown. No grave goods were discovered.

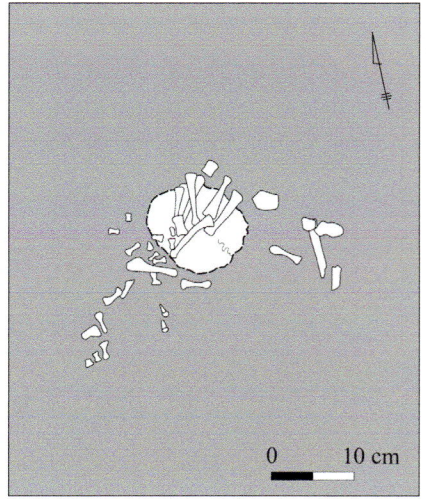

from the south

Figure 5-50. Str. 910 Burial.

51. Str. 911 (Figure 5-51)

Str. 911 is a primary burial of a perinatal baby discovered in the eastern part of Square E271a in Layer 5. It was buried in a flexed position on its back. The skeleton was poorly preserved, and sex was indeterminate. Both of its arms could not be defined and its skull was crushed. Its body axis was in the northwest-southeast direction. No grave goods were uncovered.

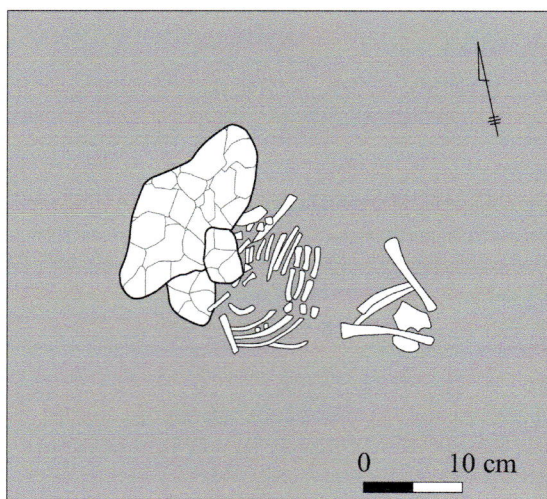

from the south

Figure 5-51. Str. 911 Burial.

52. Str. 912 (Figure 5-52)

Str. 912 contains a part of an isolated skull discovered near the foot of a skeleton (Str. 904). It is a secondary burial containing an infant skull. The rest of the body was not discovered. The skull seems to have been moved from its original deposit and relocated here. There were no grave goods.

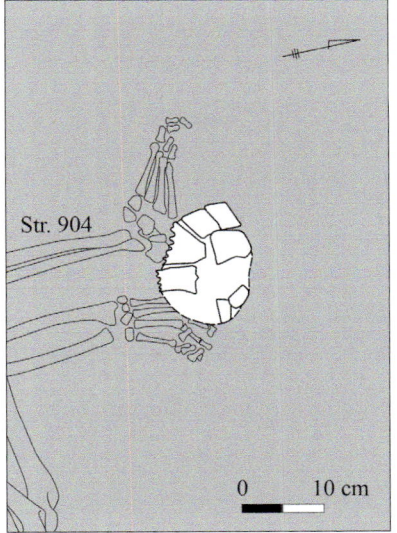 

from the southeast

Figure 5-52. Str. 912 Burial.

53. Str. 913 (Figure 5-53)

Str. 913 is a primary burial of a juvenile (1–2 yrs.) discovered in the western part of Square E271a in Layer 6. It was buried in a flexed and prone position. Its arms were stretched along its body. Its body axis was in the northeast-southwest direction. Its head was raised and inclined to the left. Therefore, its face looked to the north.

Notably, 20 beads were discovered in this grave. Eighteen beads were found near its waist and two near its left wrist. They were three flat agate beads, 13 butterfly/barrel-shaped serpentinite beads, two oval blue-colored beads, and two fragmented beads.

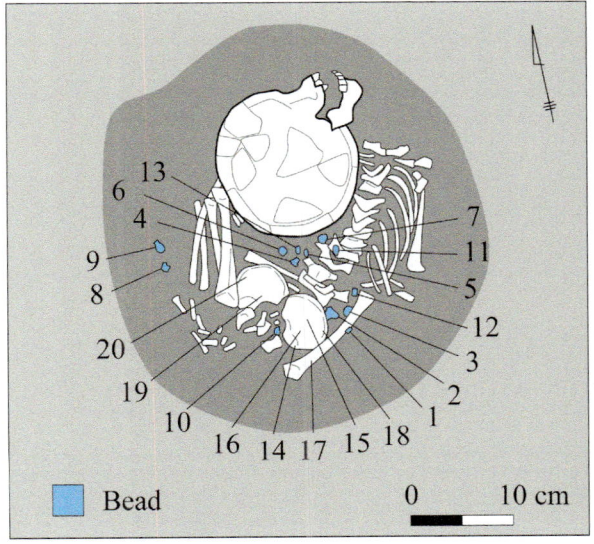 

from the southwest

Figure 5-53a. Str. 913 Burial.

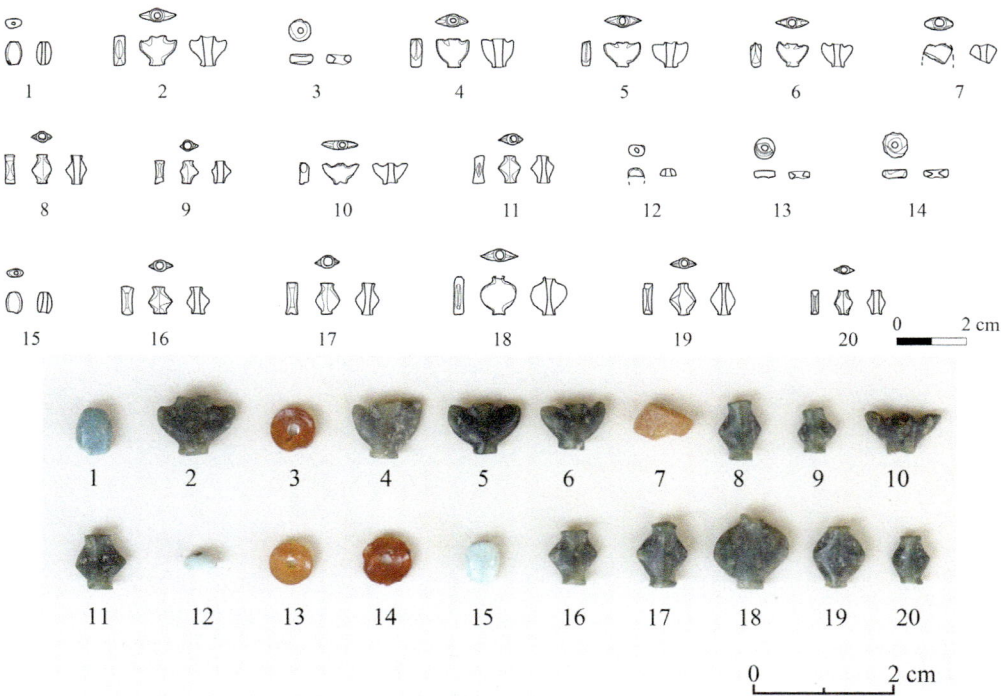

Figure 5-53b. Str. 913 Grave goods: 1, 15. Oval stone beads; 2, 4–6, 8–11, 16–20. Serpentinite butterfly/barrel beads; 3, 13–14. Agate flat beads; 7, 12. Fragments of stone beads.

54. Str. 914 (Figure 5-54)

Str. 914 is a primary burial of a juvenile (3–4 yrs.) discovered in the eastern part of Square E271b in Layer 6. It was buried on the limestone course of the collective burial (C10) beside the Str. 921 burial. Even though these two structures had a different body axis, the skulls were very close. It was buried in a flexed position on its right side. Its right elbow was bent beside its head, and its right hand was placed near its back. Its left hand was placed on the front of its face. The body axis direction was northeast-southwest, the head pointed northeast, and its face looked to the west.

Eight stone beads were discovered around its neck, and they seemed to be a necklace. They were stone beads of different shapes made of agate, serpentinite, and other materials.

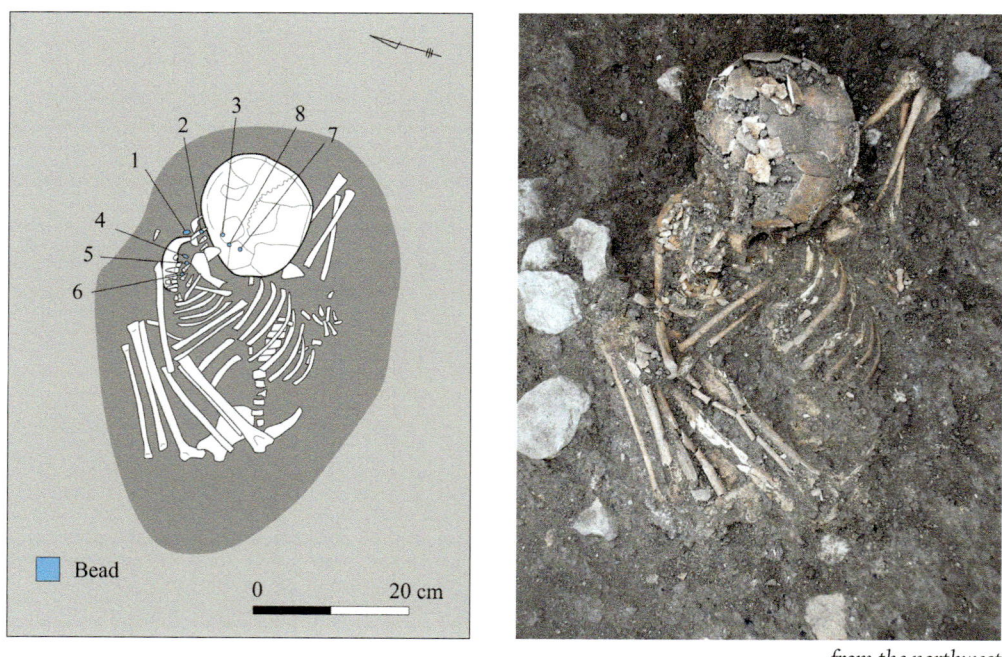

from the northwest

Figure 5-54a. Str. 914 Burial.

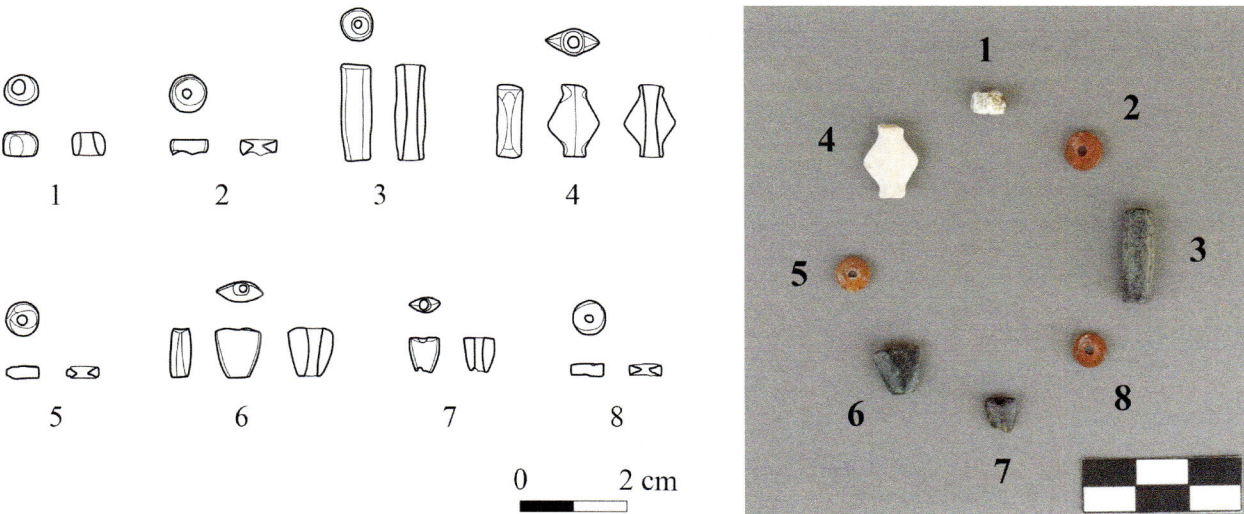

Figure 5-54b. Str. 914 Grave goods: 1. Stone short-cylindrical bead; 2, 5, 8. Agate flat beads; 3. Stone cylindrical bead; 4. Stone barrel bead; 6. Serpentinite trapezoid bead; 7. Stone trapezoid bead.

55. Str. 918 (Figure 5-55)

Str. 918 is a disturbed primary burial of a small infant (4–6 mths.) discovered in the eastern end of Square E270b in Layer 5. Though its cranium was noticed easily, the body parts were poorly preserved. However, it seems to have been accidentally placed among the stones. The body position and the direction of the body axis were not clear. Sex was indeterminate. The skull pointed to the southeast direction and it faced east and looked downward. Therefore, it must have been buried in a flexed position on its right side. It seems that there was no relation between the infant burial and the surrounding stones. There were no grave goods.

from the north

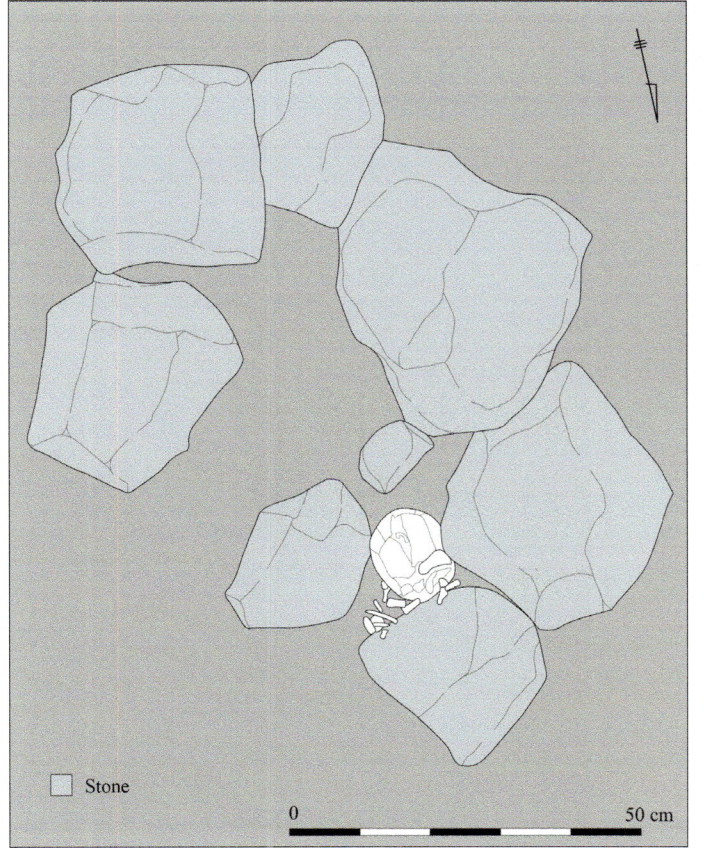

Figure 5-55. Str. 918 Burial.

56. Str. 920 (Figure 5-56)

Str. 920 is a primary burial of a juvenile (3–4 yrs.) discovered in the southwestern part of Square E271a in Layer 6. Sex was indeterminate. It was buried in a flexed position on its back. Its left leg was tightly bent and placed on its head. The right arm was bent at its elbow and the right hand was placed near its neck. Its body axis was in the southeast-northwest direction. The head was twisted to the northeast and its face looked to the southeast. A small stone was found in front of its head. There were no grave goods.

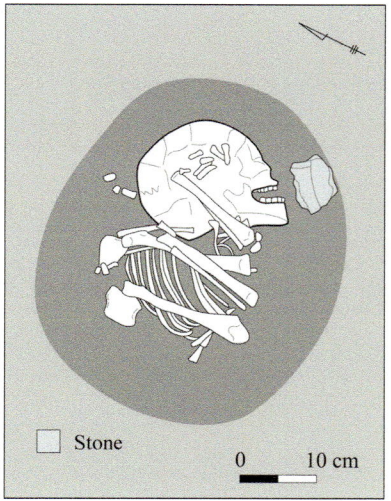

from the southwest

Figure 5-56. Str. 920 Burial.

57. Str. 921 (Figure 5-57)

Str. 921 is a primary burial of a young adult male discovered in the eastern edge of Square E271b in Layer 6. The skeleton was found on the limestone of C10. He was buried beside Str. 914 in a tightly flexed position on his back. Both arms were stretched along his body. His body axis was in the south-north direction. His face looked to the west. There were no grave goods.

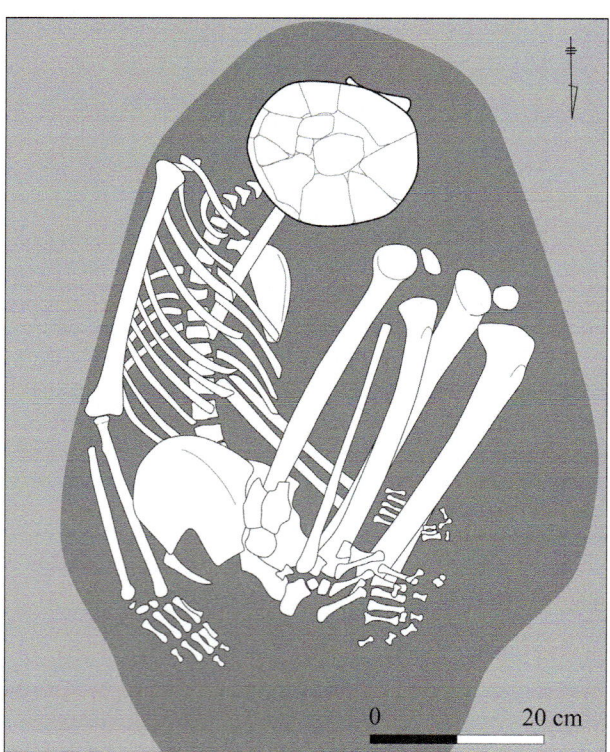

from the north

Figure 5-57. Str. 921 Burial.

148

58. Str. 922 (Figure 5-58)

This deposit contains some finger and foot bones discovered in the central part of Square E271b in Layer 6 beside the northwestern corner of the limestone enclosure of C10. There were some articulated bones, though most bones were disturbed. All of these bones are attributed to the same adult individual. Sex was indeterminate. The burial seemed to be a remnant of a disturbed primary burial. However, this burial type is unknown.

Three beads were discovered among the bones. They are an oval serpentinite bead, a short cylindrical limestone bead, and a shell bead.

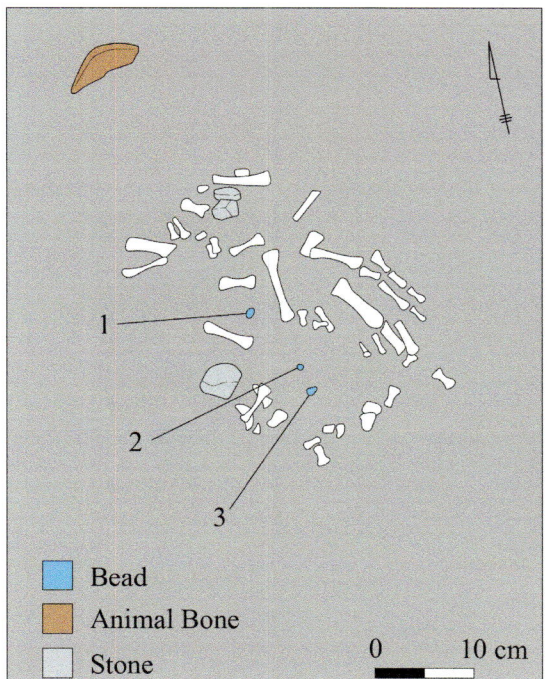

from the northwest

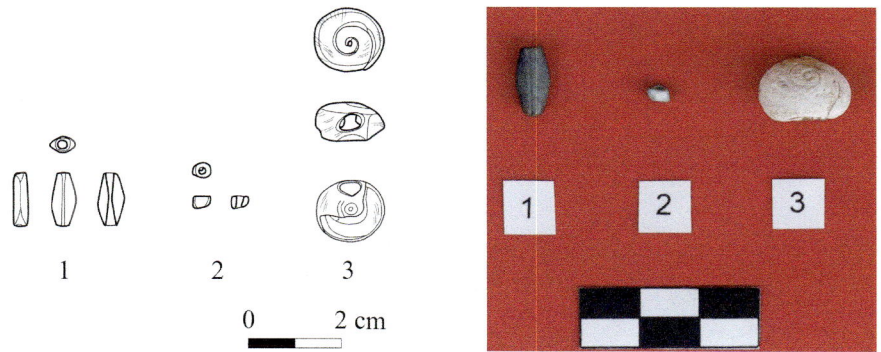

Figure 5-58. Str. 922 Burial and grave goods: 1–2. Stone beads; 3. Shell bead.

59. Str. 924 (Figure 5-59)

Str. 924 is a primary burial of a young adult female discovered in the southwestern part of Square E271b in Layer 6. This burial was located in an alleyway between two rectangular buildings: Str. 827 and Str. 916. She was buried in a flexed position on her left side. Both her hands were placed under her head. Her body axis was in the east-west direction. Her face looked to the south. A limestone bead was discovered under her lower jaw.

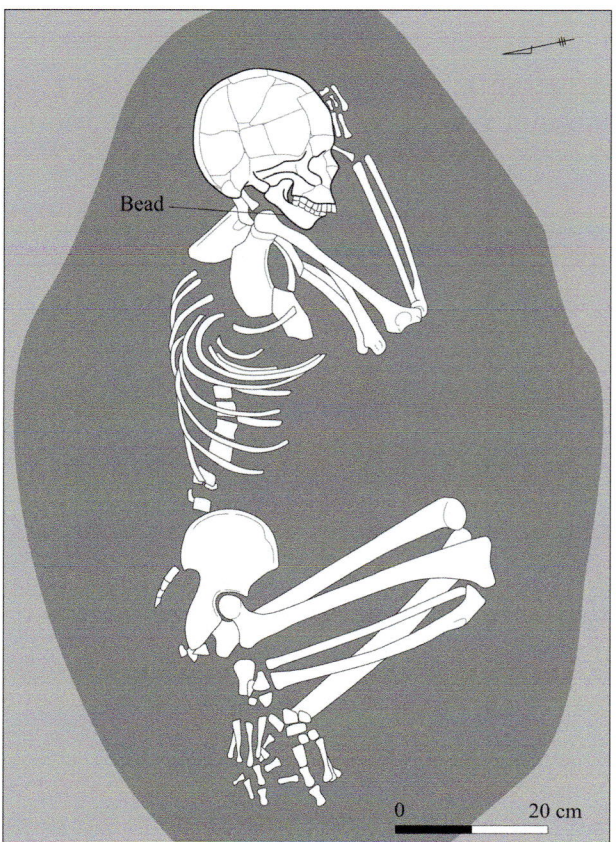

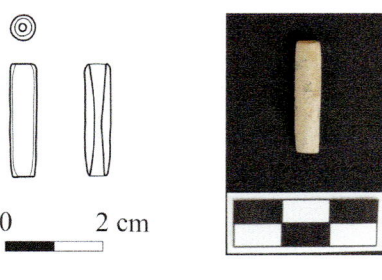

from the west

Figure 5-59. Str. 924 Burial and grave goods: Stone bead.

60. Str. 925 (Figure 5-60)

Str. 925 is a primary burial of a fetus discovered in the southeastern part of Square E270a in Layer 6. Though the skeleton was very small, its skull and most body parts were discernible. It was buried in a supine position. The left arm was folded in front of the skull, and leg bones were placed over the ribs. The body axis direction was northwest-southeast and the skull pointed toward the north. There were no grave goods.

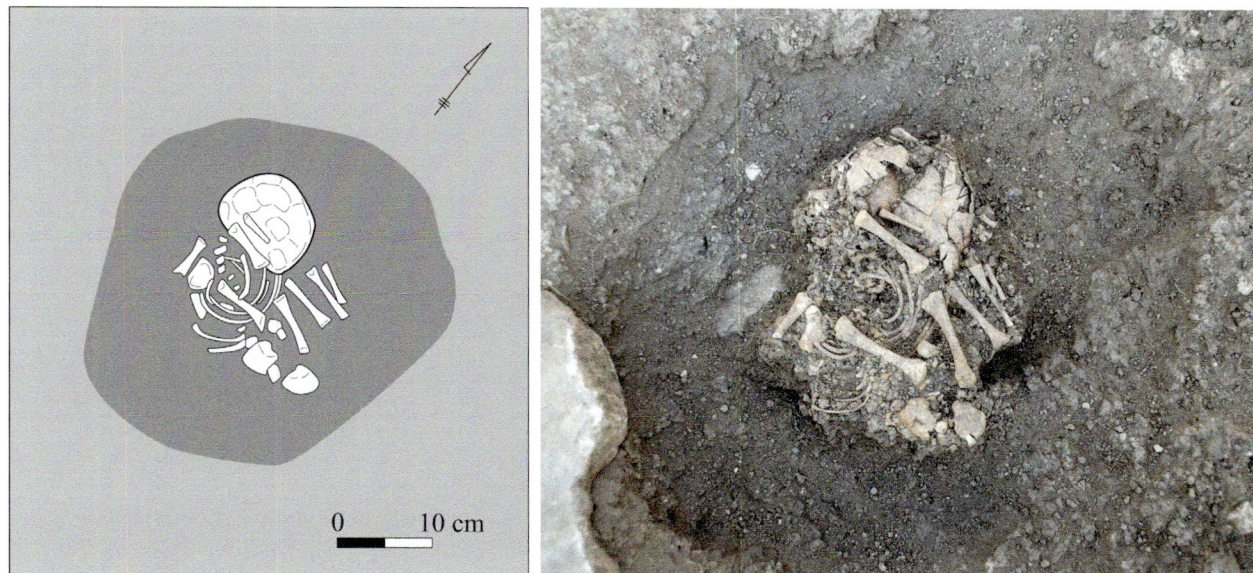

from the southeast

Figure 5-60. Str. 925 Burial.

61. Str. 926 (Figure 5-61)

Excavations in the western part of the cemetery in Square E270 uncovered six graves of ten individuals in Layer 6. Two of the primary burials exhibited clear skull/cranium treatment (Strs. 926 and 927).

Str. 926 is a primary burial found beneath lime plaster in the northeastern part of Square E270a in Layer 6. Its location is about 2m north of the Str. 925 burial. The long bones, pelvis, and mandible indicated that the remains were of an adult, probably female. She was buried in a flexed position on her right side. The body axis was oriented north to south, and the lower limbs were tightly flexed, with knees positioned close to the chest. Her left hand was close to the chin—seeming to hold it, while the right hand was positioned parallel to the left hand and placed in front of the face.

Notably, the cranium was missing, but the mandible was present in its natural anatomical position. The intact mandible and the absence of any cut marks on the mandible and cervical vertebrae indicate that her skull was removed after the flesh had decomposed completely. This indicates that the cranium removal was deliberate in order to fulfill the funerary practices of removing the skull. Physical anthropological observation indicates that this individual had highly unusual mandibular teeth wear that is suggestive of the use of dentition as a gripping tool.

This female was adorned with seven beads distributed in various locations along her body within the grave: a shell and bone bead above her left arm; tusk shell, limestone, and bone beads near her lower spine; and two conch shell beads around her neck.

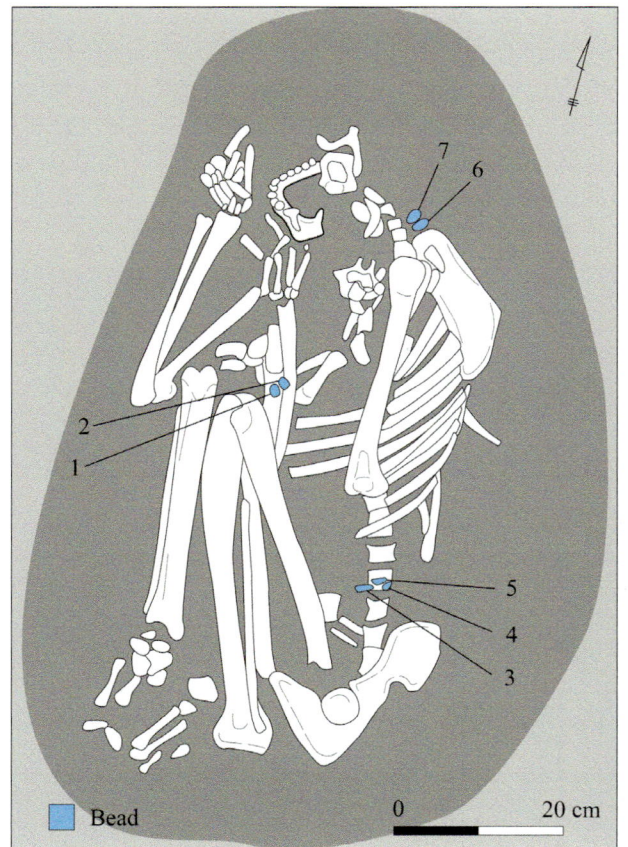

from the south

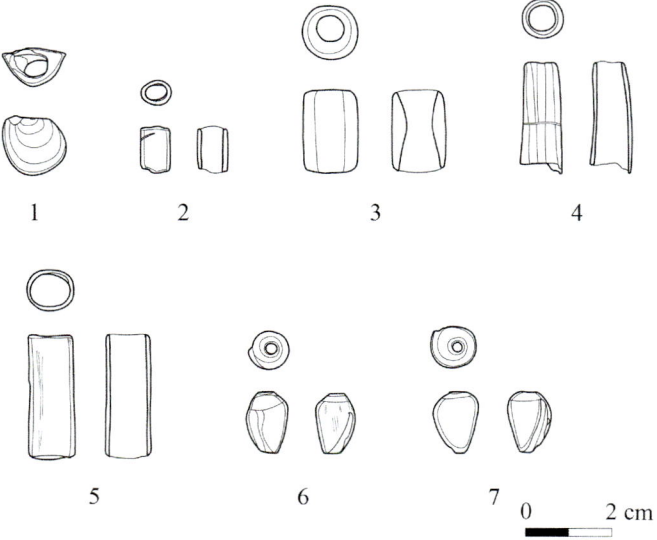

Figure 5-61. Str. 926 Burial and grave goods: 1. Shell bead; 2. Bone bead; 3. Limestone bead;
4. Tusk shell bead; 5. Bone bead; 6–7. Conch shell beads.

62. Str. 927 (Figure 5-62)

Str. 927 is a primary burial located in the southwestern part of Square E270b in Layer 6. Str. 927 contained three individuals, whose remains were disturbed and buried together in the same grave. The main individual was a young adult female, and the other individuals were a perinatal baby and juvenile (4–5 yrs.). The female body axis was oriented west-east, while the perinatal and juvenile body positions could not be determined.

The adult female was buried in a flexed position on her right side. The lower part of her body was articulated and the upper part was disturbed. Notably, her skull was completely removed, but the first cervical vertebra was present. The skull was removed after the flesh had decomposed completely. Interestingly, a small Dark-Faced Burnished Ware (DFBW) bowl was placed near the missing skull. The skull of the juvenile was found at the back of the adult female, while the perinatal mandible was discovered at the abdomen of the young female, suggesting that this female was perhaps pregnant when she died. The long bones of the adult female are notably gracile.

It is not clear if the remains belong to the same family, but it seems they were buried together at the same time. The disturbance of the grave most likely suggests that it was a result of human interference in the context of rituals when the skull was removed some time after interment.

This assemblage was supplied with various grave goods, including a small DFBW bowl placed near the missing skull of the adult female, and a pottery fragment with a bivalve shell. Five beads made of agate, mottled-limestone, blue material, and shell were found near the female's abdomen and beneath the perinatal baby, and a beautiful incised and burnt bone bead was found near the female's pelvis.

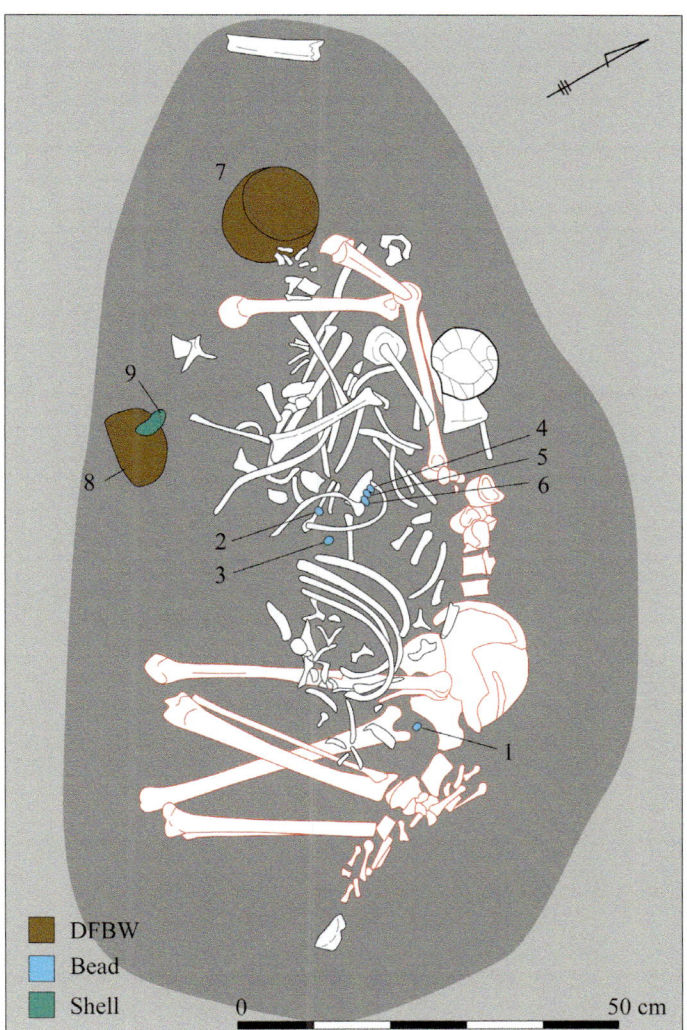

It is assumed that the placement of the pottery bowl near the original skull position is an intentional act aimed at marking the place of the removed skull by using a round-shaped object (Pottery in PN) that to some degree resembles the human skull. Alternatively, this DFBW bowl could have been placed right next to the removed skull. However, this suggestion needs further consideration.

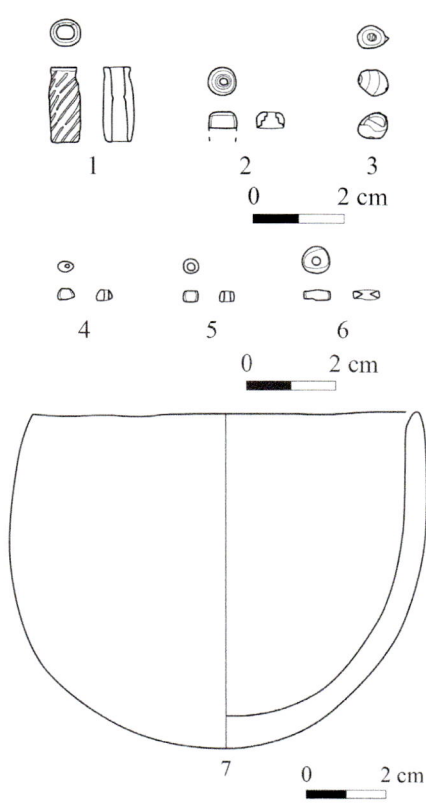

Figure 5-62a. Str. 927 Burial and grave goods: 1. Incised and burnt bone bead; 2. Shell bead;
3. Conch shell bead; 4. Blue bead; 5. Stone bead; 6. Agate bead; 7. DFBW bowl.

A   *from the southeast*   B   *from the southeast*

Figure 5-62b. Str. 927 Burial: A. Upper level; B. Lower level. Grave goods: 1. Incised and burnt bone bead; 2. Shell bead; 3. Conch shell bead; 4. Blue bead; 5. Stone bead; 6. Agate bead; 7. DFBW bowl; 8. Pottery fragment; 9. Bivalve shell.

63. Str. 930 (Figure 5-63)

Str. 930 burial contained mainly human crania, mandibles, animal mandibles, and postcranial bones, and was located in the northern part of Square E270b in Layer 6. The human remains belong to three adult individuals, and the others were animal bones. Tell el-Kerkh presented clear evidence for the inhumation of humans along with animal bones in the same deposits. It is an accumulation of human and animal bones extending one to two meters. This assemblage is comprised of disarticulated human bones mixed with many animal bones, most of them belonging to cattle. Potsherds and stone rubble were the most abundant in the deposits. They were scattered and mixed together. The heap of human skulls, long human bones, and many animal bones gave these deposits the characteristics of a secondary burial. It is not clear if this deposit was a burial in the truest sense or a ritualistic deposit.

Two human mandibles were documented in the southern end of this accumulation, while two human skulls, some skull fragments, and various human bones were uncovered at the center. Skulls were placed in the deposits facing east. Human phalanges, femora, and humeri were placed around the skulls. This is obvious evidence of the mixture of human-animal bones at the cemetery.

The human remains from this deposit belong to three individuals. Two individuals were represented by crania, mandibles, and several postcranial elements, while the third individual was represented by one occipital bone.

1. The first individual is a young adult, probably female.
2. The second individual is a young adult, probably female.
3. The third individual is an adult, probably female.

At first glance, the general pattern of Square E270b suggested that there is a connection or relationship between Str. 926 and Str. 927 with Str. 930. The skulls were missing from Str. 926 and 927, while two skulls were found in Str. 930, which may suggest that the skulls were removed from their primary context and reburied in the secondary place. This was the primary hypothesis for skulls missing from structures and present in others. This hypothesis was rejected after an analysis of the human skeletal remains. The long bones, skulls, mandibles, and phalanges discovered in Str. 930 indicate that these individuals were buried with their bodies and have no relation to structures 926 and 927.

The relationship between the individuals was ruled out based on the following evidence:

1. The mandibles of the individuals in Str. 930 were not associated with the skulls, but were found in the southern part of the accumulation next to cattle bone. Also, the tooth wear in Str. 926 was very advanced, while the maxillary tooth wear for both crania in Str. 930 was light to moderate.
2. Cervical vertebrae were present in both Str. 926 and Str. 927, and at least one vertical vertebra was present in Str. 930.
3. The estimated age of the individuals differs between the structures.

from the east

Figure 5-63a. Str. 930 Burial: Secondary burial contained human bones and animal bones.

Figure 5-63b. Str. 930 Burial.

A *from the southeast*

B *from the east*

C *from the west*

Figure 5-63c. Str. 930 Burial: A. Animal jaw and human bones;
B. Human skulls in situ; C. Human mandible and animal bones.

64. Str. 931 (Figure 5-64)

Str. 931 is a secondary burial represented by an isolated skull discovered in the eastern edge of Square E271d in Layer 6. It is an adult skull lacking a lower jaw (cranium). Sex was indeterminate. No other skeletal remains from this individual were recovered. As it was an isolated skull, no further details were recovered. However, there is a possibility that it was moved from its original deposit and relocated here. No grave goods were found.

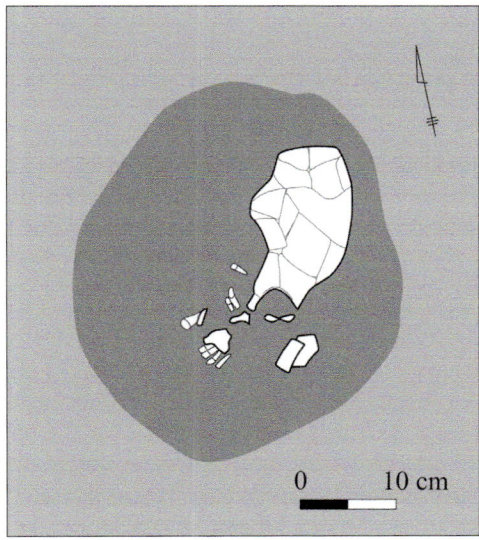

from the southwest

Figure 5-64. Str. 931 Burial.

65. Str. 933 (Figure 5-65)

Str. 933 is a primary burial of a fetal skeleton covered with DFBW potsherds, discovered in the northern part of Square E271d in Layer 6. The fetus was buried in a flexed position on its right side. Sex was indeterminate. Both hands were placed on the front of the face. Its body axis was in the northwest-southeast direction. The head pointed to the northwest, but face direction was indeterminate. The whole of the fetal skeleton was covered with DFBW potsherds. This burial suggests that people who interred this individual aimed to protect its body by covering it with pottery sherds.

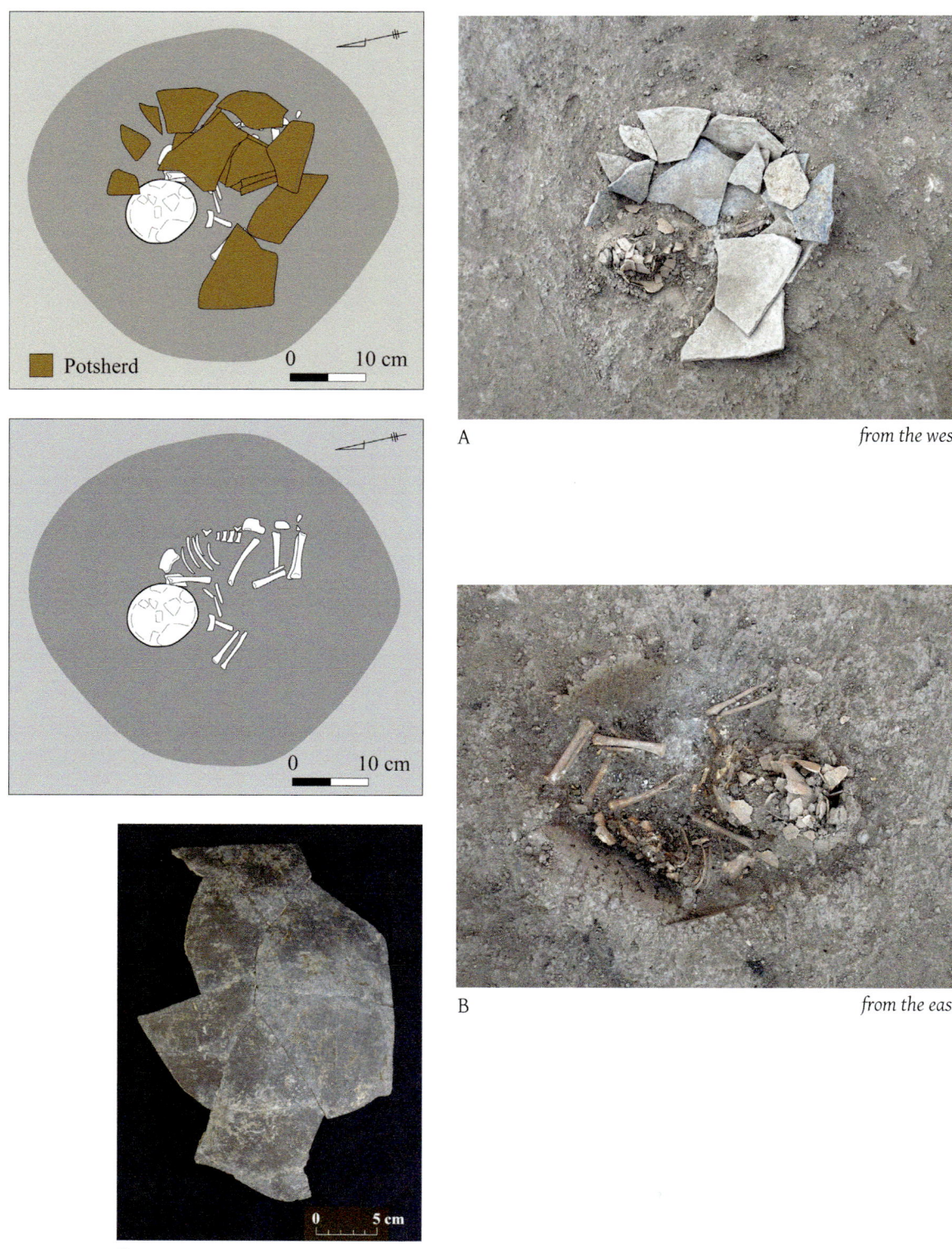

A   *from the west*

B   *from the east*

C

Figure 5-65. Str. 933 Burial: A. The body covered with DFBW potsherds;
B. The skeleton under DFBW potsherds; C. Restored a part of DFBW potsherds.

66. Str. 941 (Figure 5-66)

Str. 941 is a primary burial of a middle-aged adult, probably female, discovered at the southern edge of Square E271d in Layer 6. As it was located at the edge of the square, it was possible to identify the section and a rough plan of this grave pit. The pit seems to be c. 1.4m in diameter, and it is at least 0.6m deep. The section tells us that the pit was refilled after the dead body was placed in the pit. She was buried in a flexed position on her left side. Her body axis direction was southeast-northwest, but her head was bent and oriented in a counterclockwise direction. Therefore, the skull pointed to the north and it faced south. Both her arms were folded in front of her face.

A bone spatula near her hipbone, a flint point at her feet, and a hammer stone were uncovered in the grave.

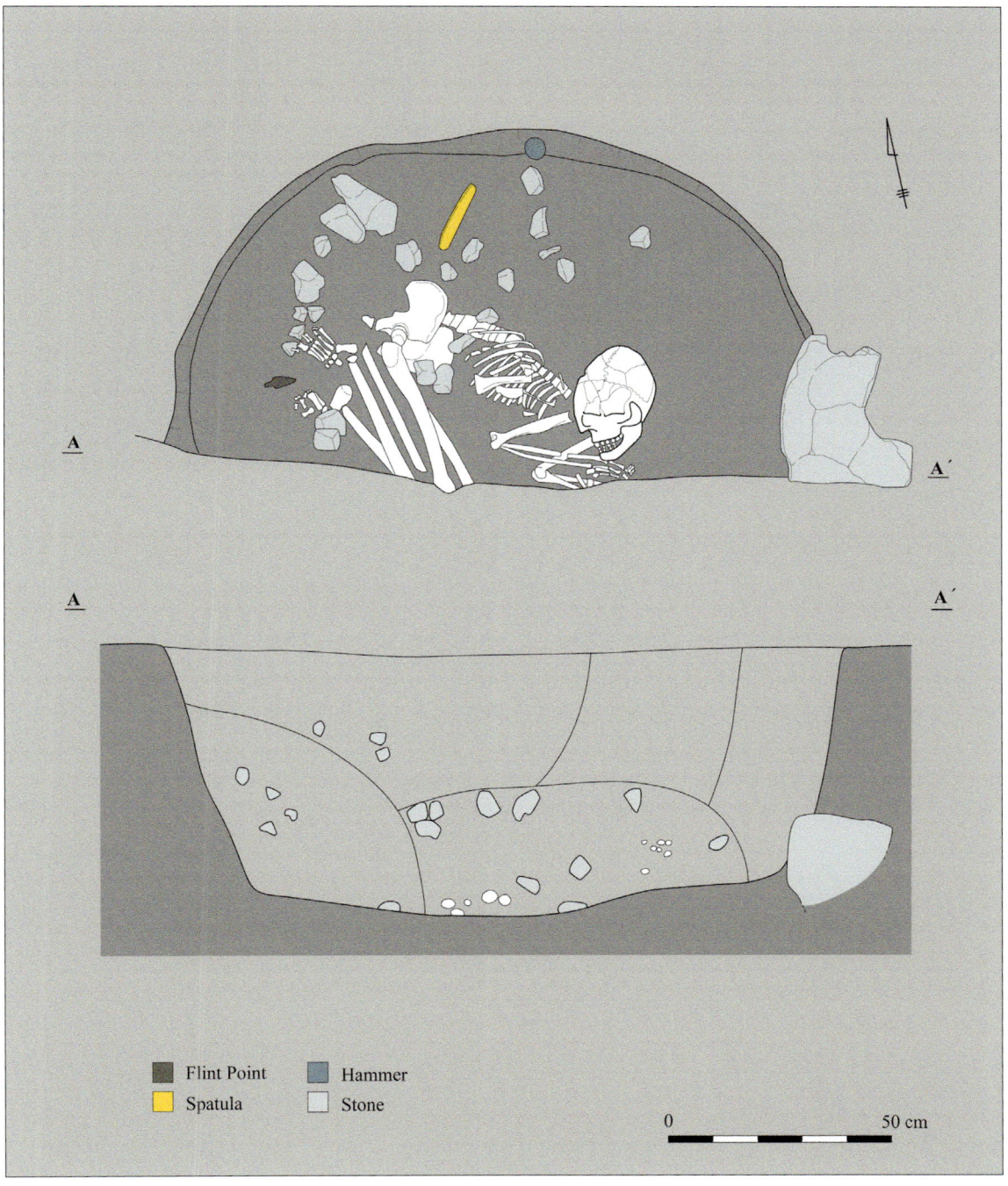

Figure 5-66a. Str. 941 Burial.

from the west

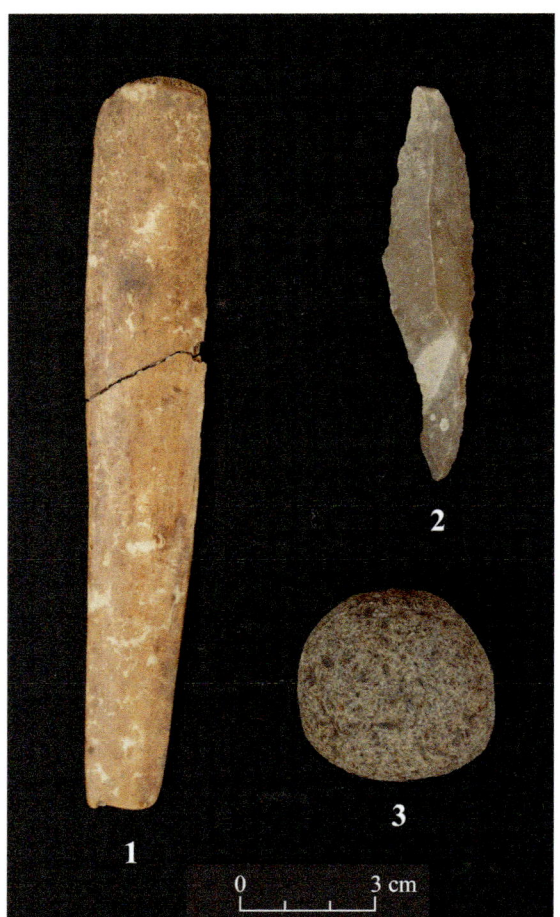

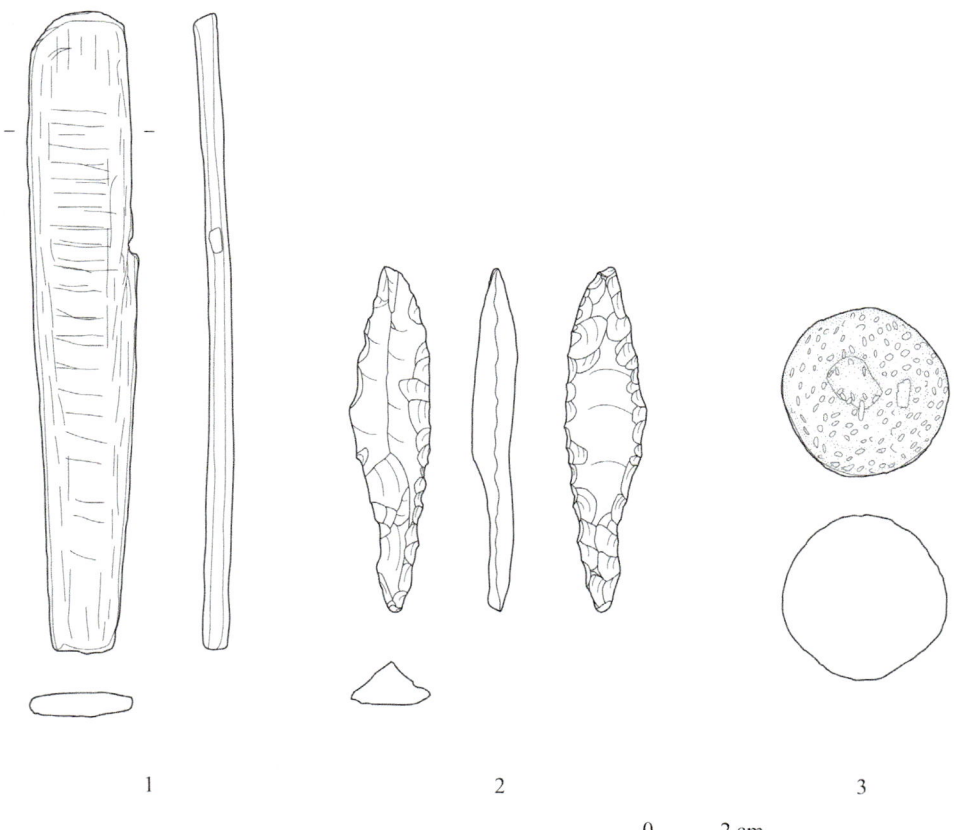

Figure 5-66b. Str. 941 Burial and grave goods: 1. Bone spatula; 2. Flint point; 3. Hammer stone.

67. Str. 942 (Figure 5-67)

Str. 942 is an isolated adult skull discovered on the eastern edge of Square E271d in Layer 6. It is located to the south of C10. The rest of the body was not excavated because it extruded out of the excavation area. Thus, the burial type was unknown. The fragmentary condition of this cranium prohibited successful estimation of sex or age. As the postcranial skeleton was under the balk, it was not possible to determine the type of this burial. The skull seemed to face northeast. No grave goods were found.

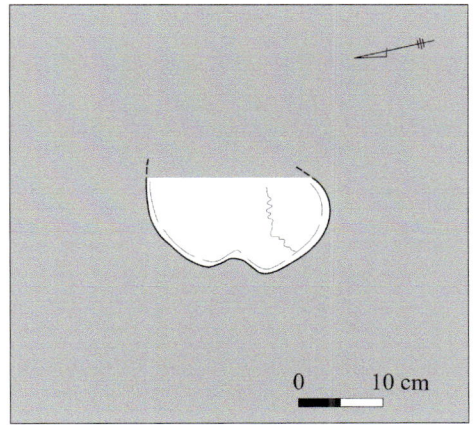

from the west

Figure 5-67. Str. 942 Burial.

68. Str. 946 (Figure 5-68)

Str. 946 is a primary burial of a perinatal baby discovered along the border between Square E271c and E291a. It belongs to Layer 6. Some bones were discovered in a disarticulated condition, and it was partly disturbed. Sex was indeterminate. The remaining skeleton was buried on its right side. The body axis direction was south-north. The head pointed to the south and faced eastward. A flat quartz bead was discovered near the neck.

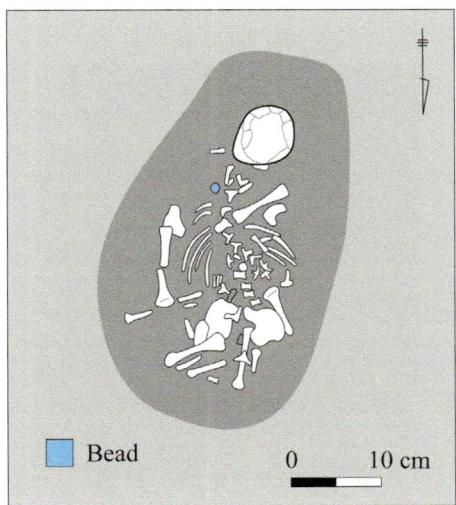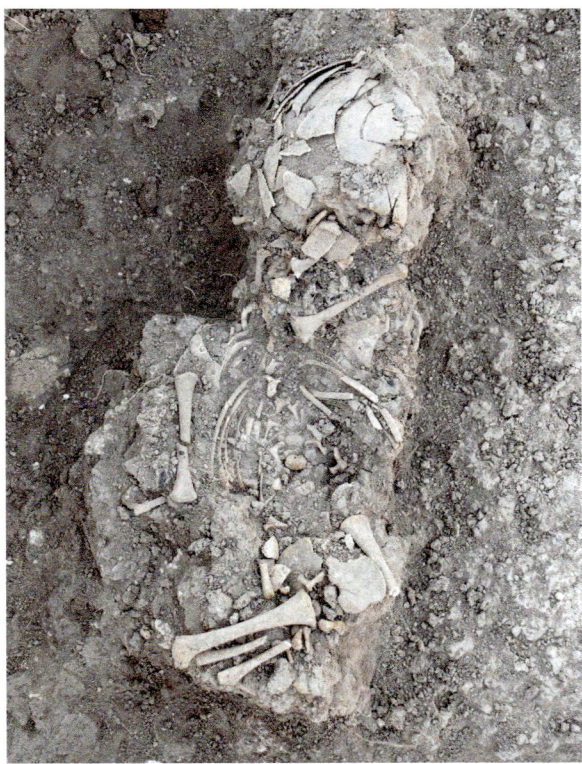

Bead

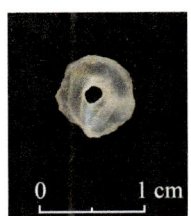

from the north

Figure 5-68. Str. 946 Burial and grave goods: Stone bead.

69. Str. 977 (Figure 5-69)

Str. 977 is a primary burial of a fetus discovered in the northwestern part of Square E270b in Layer 6. It seems to have been buried in a flexed position on its left side. Its left hand was folded and placed in front of the face. Its body axis direction was south-north. The head and face direction were not identified. There were no grave goods.

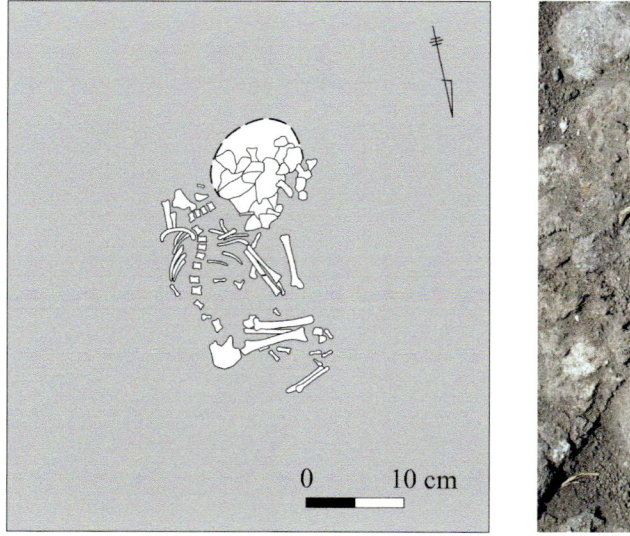

from the north

Figure 5-69. Str. 977 Burial.

70. Str. 981 (Figure 5-70)

Str. 981 is an urn burial (primary) discovered near the center of Square E270b in Layer 6. The DFBW bowl used as an urn is not sophisticated pottery. It is a medium-sized, globular-shaped brown bowl, measuring 21.5cm in diameter and 14.5cm in height. The bowl was upside down, and a complete fetus was discovered underneath the pottery. This suggests that the dead fetal body was placed at the bottom of bowl. The bowl was probably lidded with some organic material. Finally, the bowl was buried upside down. This is one of the oldest urn burials discovered in the Near East so far. No grave goods were recovered.

A *from the west* B *from the west*

Figure 5-70. Str. 981 Burial: A. Upside-down urn; B. Fetal skeleton in an urn.

71. Str. 1040 (Figure 5-71)

This deposit contains the disturbed remains of two human skeletons, discovered in Square E251c in Layer 4. The first individual is an adult of unknown age, represented by the bones of the right upper limb. The second individual is a juvenile (5–6 yrs.), represented by a right mandible, but sex for both individuals was indeterminate. This burial type is unknown. There were no grave goods.

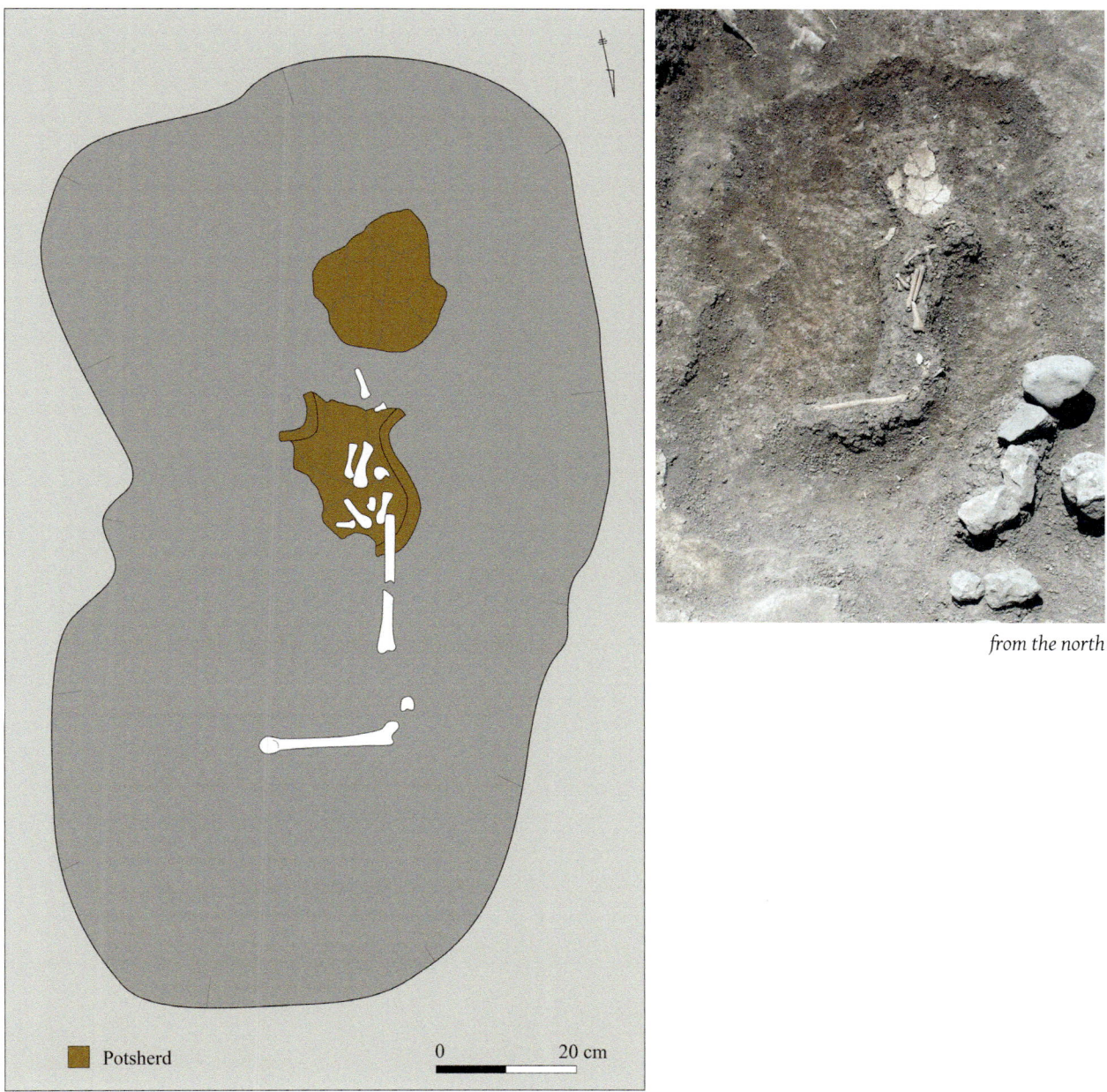

from the north

Potsherd

0   20 cm

Figure 5-71. Str. 1040 Burial.

72. Str. 1044 (Figure 5-72)

Str. 1044 is a primary burial of a middle-aged adult, probably male, discovered in the southern end of Square E251c in Layer 4. He was buried in a flexed position on his left side. The body axis direction was east-west, and the head pointed to the east and faced south. Notably, both hands were placed under his folded legs, but the wrist of the right hand was bent downward. A small blue bead accompanied him.

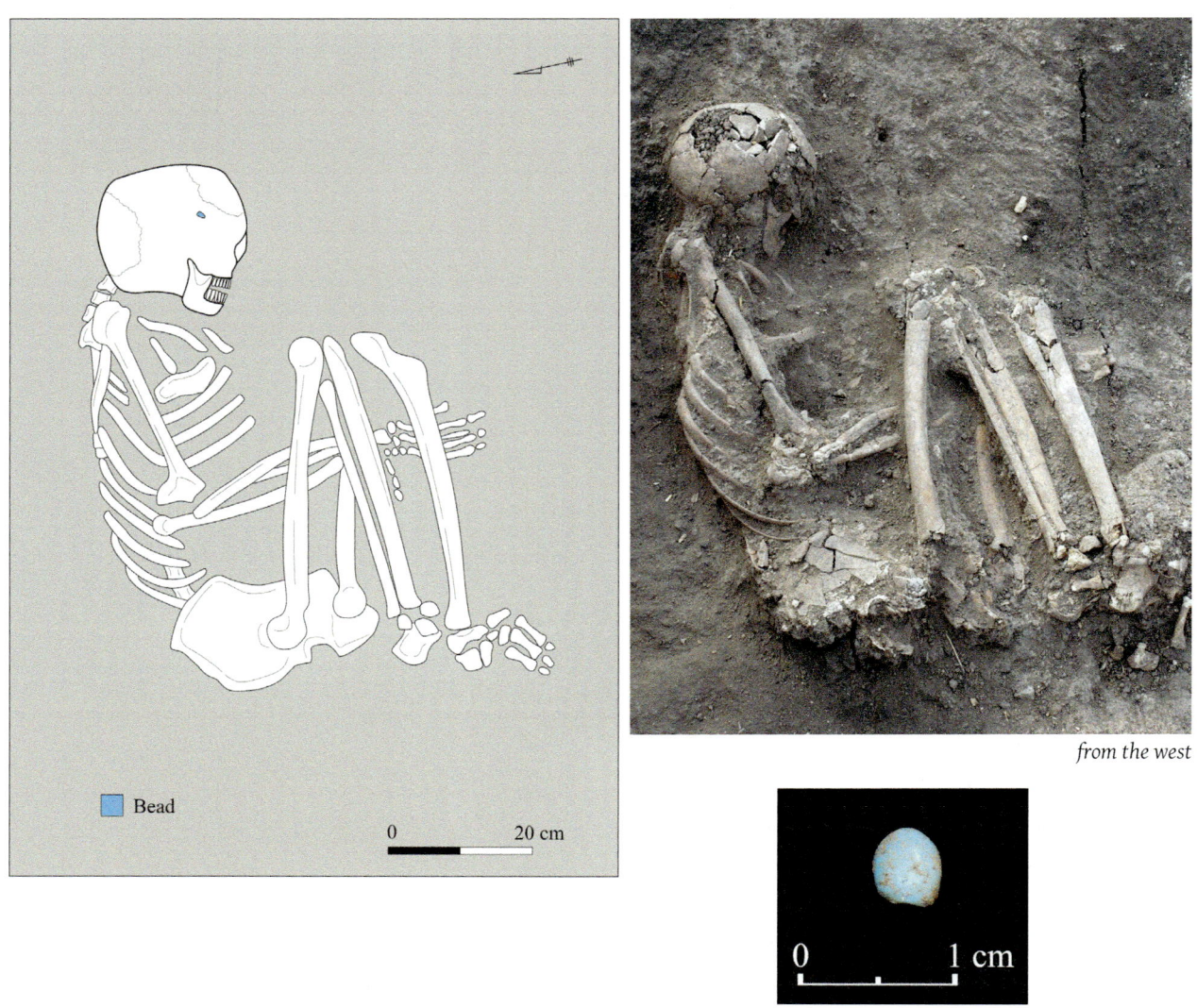

from the west

Bead

0   20 cm

Figure 5-72. Str. 1044 Burial and grave goods: Blue bead.

73. Str. 1045 (Figure 5-73)

Str. 1045 is a disturbed primary burial of an adult, probably male, discovered in the southern part of Square E251c in Layer 4. This burial was discovered behind the Str. 1044 burial. It was represented by one arm and one leg with pelvis, ribs, and jaw, while some fragmentary bones were discovered northeast of Str. 1044, seemingly belonging to the same individual. The leg was articulated with the pelvis. The leg and the remaining parts of this individual indicated that he was buried in a flexed position on his right side. The axis of the body was in the northeast-southwest direction. No grave goods were discovered.

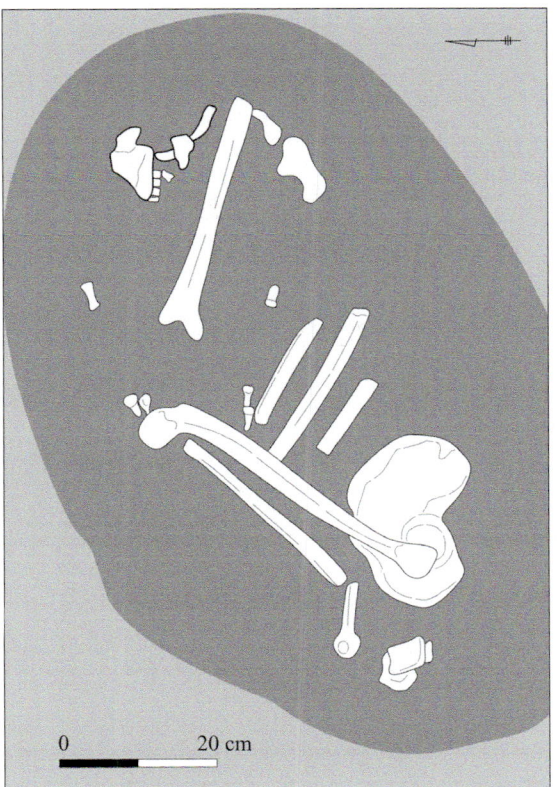 

from the west

Figure 5-73. Str. 1045 Burial.

74. Str. 1047 (Figure 5-74)

Str. 1047 is a primary burial of a young adult, probably male, discovered in Square E251c in Layer 4. This individual was buried at the center of a cluster of five burials surrounded by the others. They likely belonged to one family buried in the same place. This skeleton was well preserved. He was buried in a flexed position on his right side. His body axis direction was north-south, the head pointed to the north, and his face looked to the west. Both arms were bent, with the right-hand elbow touching the left knee, and both hands were placed under his chin. There were no grave goods.

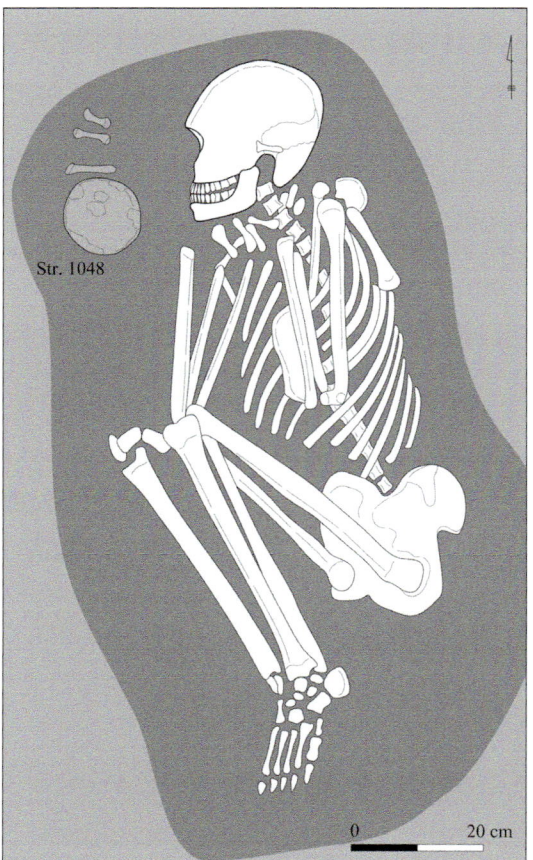

from the south

Figure 5-74. Str. 1047 Burial.

75. Str. 1048 (Figure 5-75)

Str. 1048 is a secondary burial represented by a portion of an isolated skull of a perinatal baby discovered in Square E251c in Layer 4. It was discovered just in front of the facial bones of Str. 1047. Since postcranial bones were not uncovered, it was difficult to identify the characteristics of this isolated skull (age, sex, and direction). However, the skull of this perinatal baby appeared to have been consciously placed near the face of a young adult male.

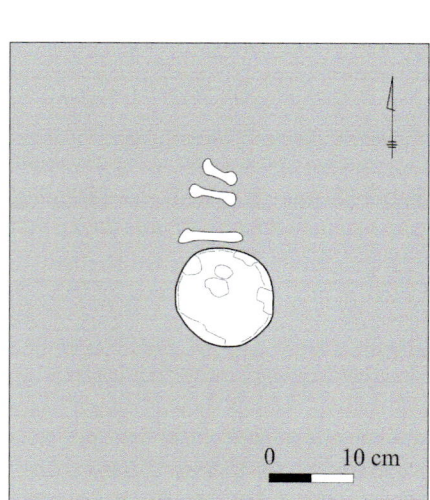

from the south

Figure 5-75. Str. 1048 Burial.

76. Str. 1050 (Figure 5-76)

Str. 1050 is a primary burial of a young adult, probably male. He was discovered in a cluster of four individuals buried close to each other (Strs. 1050, 1051, 1053, and 1058). He was found between Strs. 1051, 1053, and 1058 in the eastern part of Square E251c in Layer 4. This young adult male seemed to have been buried in a strange position. Based on his bone positions—with the exception of his left leg—he was buried in a flexed position on his left side. The body axis direction was northwest-southeast, his head pointed to the northwest, and he faced a northeastern direction. While his right leg was folded in a normal position, his left leg was placed in an opposite position and the toe tips were placed in an abnormal position near his right shoulder. The reason for this unusual positioning was understood after the right leg was removed. His left femur was articulated with his pelvis at one end and with the tibia and fibula on the other, but it was broken in half and bent conversely. There is little doubt that he died from heavy bleeding from this femur fracture. His people had tried to bury his dead body in a normal flexed position, but they likely could not fold his left leg. There were no grave goods.

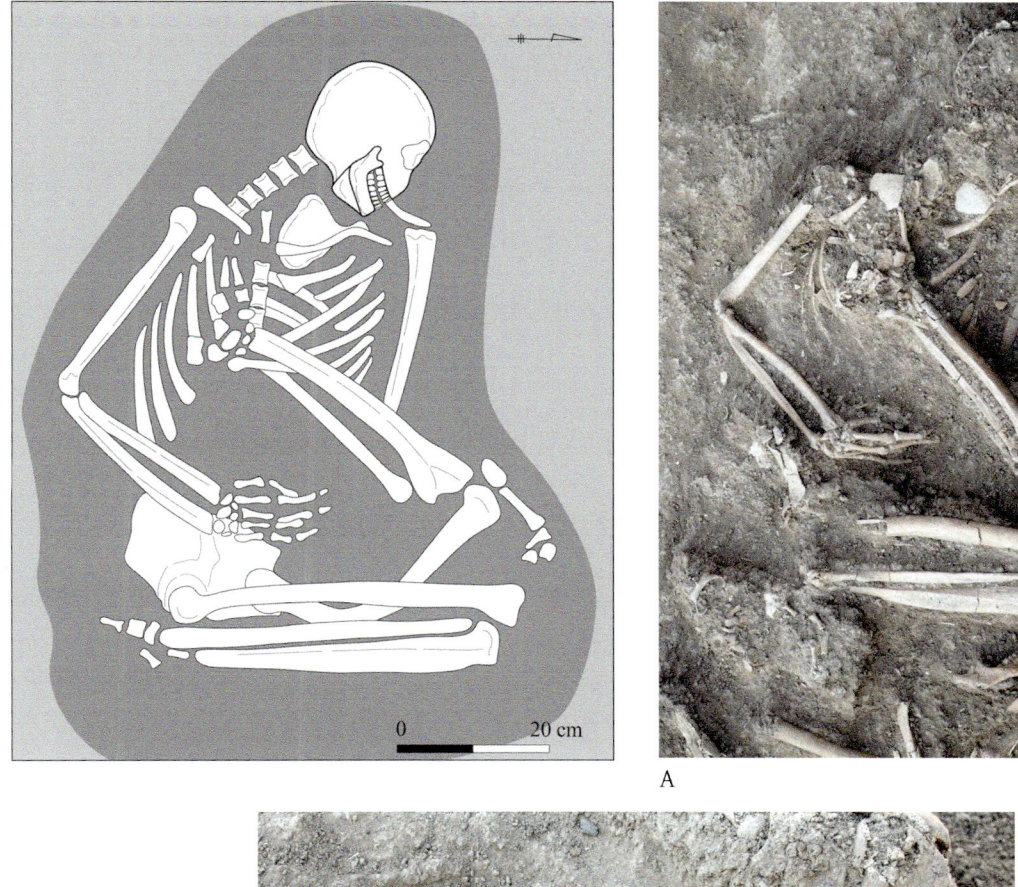

A

from the east

B

Figure 5-76. Str. 1050 Burial: A. Young adult skeleton; B. Broken left femur.

77. Str. 1051 (Figure 5-77)

Str. 1051 is a primary burial of a middle-aged adult female discovered just to the northeast of Strs. 1050 and 1053 in the eastern part of Square E251c in Layer 4. She was buried in a point symmetrical arrangement with Str. 1050 in a tightly flexed position on her left side. Her body axis direction was southeast-northwest, the head pointed to the southeast, and she faced southwest. Her legs were folded, but her right knee reached the chin. Both arms were placed under her folded legs. There were no grave goods.

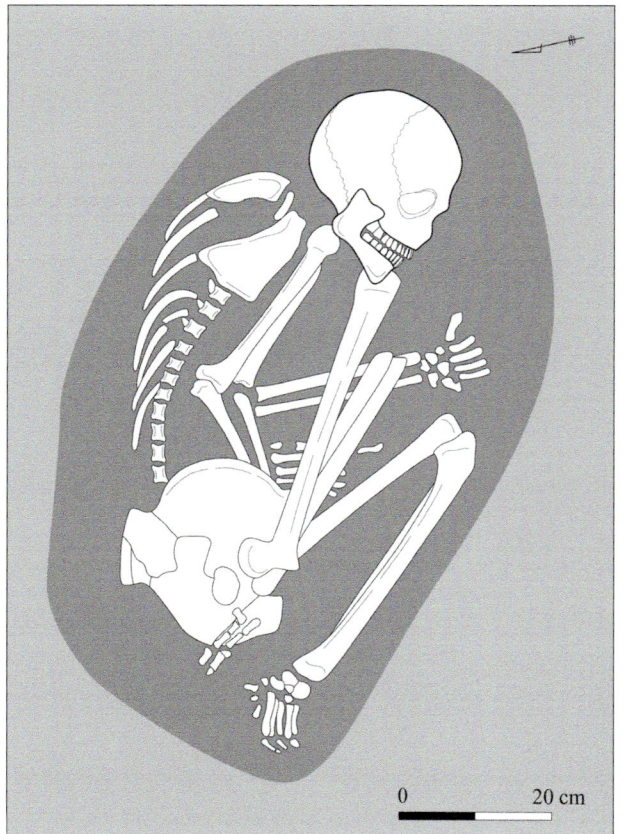

from the west

Figure 5-77. Str. 1051 Burial.

78. Str. 1052 (Figure 5-78)

Str. 1052 is a secondary burial of a subadult (12–13 yrs.) discovered in Square E251c in Layer 4. This individual was part of the cluster burial where Str. 1047 was uncovered. Sex was indeterminate. Interestingly, its bones were disarticulated, but showed intentional arrangement as follows: the femurs and the humerus were first placed in the same direction, the ribs and other bones were then placed above, and the skull was placed on its left side facing the northwest at the top. A small coarse pottery bowl with three vertical handles was discovered with it.

Coarse Pottery   0   10 cm

A   *from the east*

B   *from the east*

0   2 cm

Figure 5-78. Str. 1052 Burial: A. Upper level; B. Lower level;
Grave goods: Coarse pottery bowl.

79. Str. 1053 (Figure 5-79)

Str. 1053 is a disturbed primary burial of an adult, probably male, discovered in Square E251c in Layer 4. Part of the skull was buried below Str. 1051. It was partly disturbed, seemingly when the burial pit of Str. 1051 was dug. Most parts of the skull were found just beside the skull of Str. 1051. However, the mandible and the remainder of the skull were found 40cm away to the west. He was buried in a flexed position on his right side. The body axis direction was north-south, and the head pointed to the north and faced northwest.

He was accompanied by a number of grave goods. A goat horn was found near his hip bone. One stamp seal and four beads were discovered together near his breast. This stone seal is bullet-shaped, having a 'cross and parallel lines' impression design. Four cylindrical type beads, two made of stone (one of them has diagonal engraved patterns) and two made of clay, seem to have been hung together from the neck.

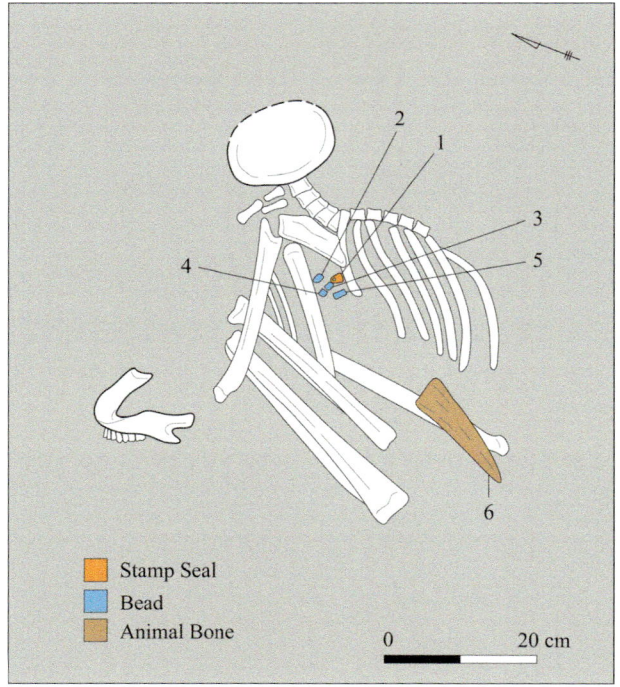

from the southwest

from the southwest

Figure 5-79. Str. 1053 Burial and grave goods:
1. Stamp seal; 2–3. Clay beads; 4–5. Stone beads; 6. Goat horn.

80. Str. 1056 (Figure 5-80)

Str. 1056 is a primary burial of a young adult, probably male, discovered at the border between Squares E251c and d in Layer 5. He was buried in a flexed position on his left side. His body axis direction was south-north, his head pointed to the south, and he faced west. His right hand was placed on his mouth, and his left arm bent near the knee and hung limply. Two agate beads and a flint blade were discovered near his left arm.

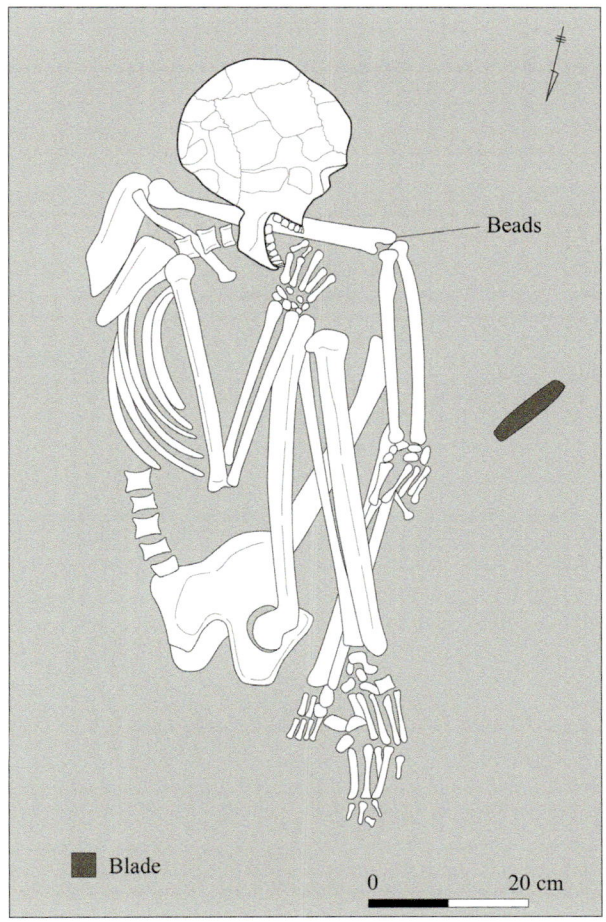

Beads

Blade

0   20 cm

from the north

Figure 5-80. Str. 1056 Burial and grave goods:
1-2. Stone beads; 3. Flint blade.

81. Str. 1057 (Figure 5-81)

Str. 1057 is a primary burial of an adult female discovered in Square E251d in Layer 5. She was buried in a flexed position on her right side. Her body axis was east-west and her missing head must have pointed to the east. The long bones were thin and gracile. The right arm was stretched down in front of her chest, and her left arm formed an N shape with her hand. The lower limbs were tightly folded. The skull was completely removed from the grave, but some cervical vertebrae were present in situ. Her right humerus was above the scapula near the top of the cervical vertebrae. No grave goods were recovered.

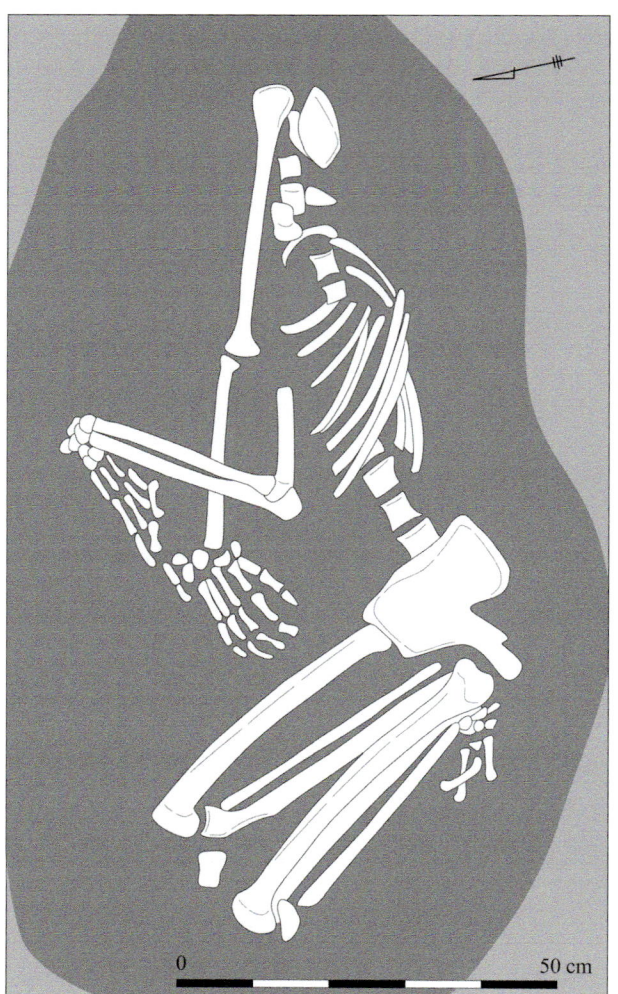

from the west

Figure 5-81. Str. 1057 Burial.

82. Str. 1058 (Figure 5-82)

Str. 1058 is the southernmost burial of the four-burial cluster that comprised Strs. 1050, 1051, 1053, and 1058. It is a primary burial of a middle-aged adult male discovered in the middle part of Square E251c in Layer 4. The lower body was covered with the upper part of Str. 1050. He was buried in a flexed position on his right side. The body axis direction was west-east, his head pointed to the west, and he faced south.

It is noticeable that he was buried with many objects. A small DFBW bowl was placed at the back of his head. A flat clay stamp seal, three flint axes (they were reductions from bipolar-blade cores), three bone awls, five deer (probably fallow deer) horns, an Amuq-type flint point, five long flint blades, two burins, four soft stone hummers, a small whetstone, and 18 chipped flint flakes unearthed in a cluster as if they had been placed in a bag were discovered near his lower back. The number and variety of these offerings are conspicuous and indicated the importance of the tomb owner. These objects were the tools and products of chipped stone knapping, indicating that the tomb owner was relied upon as a master of knapping, especially a blade producer.

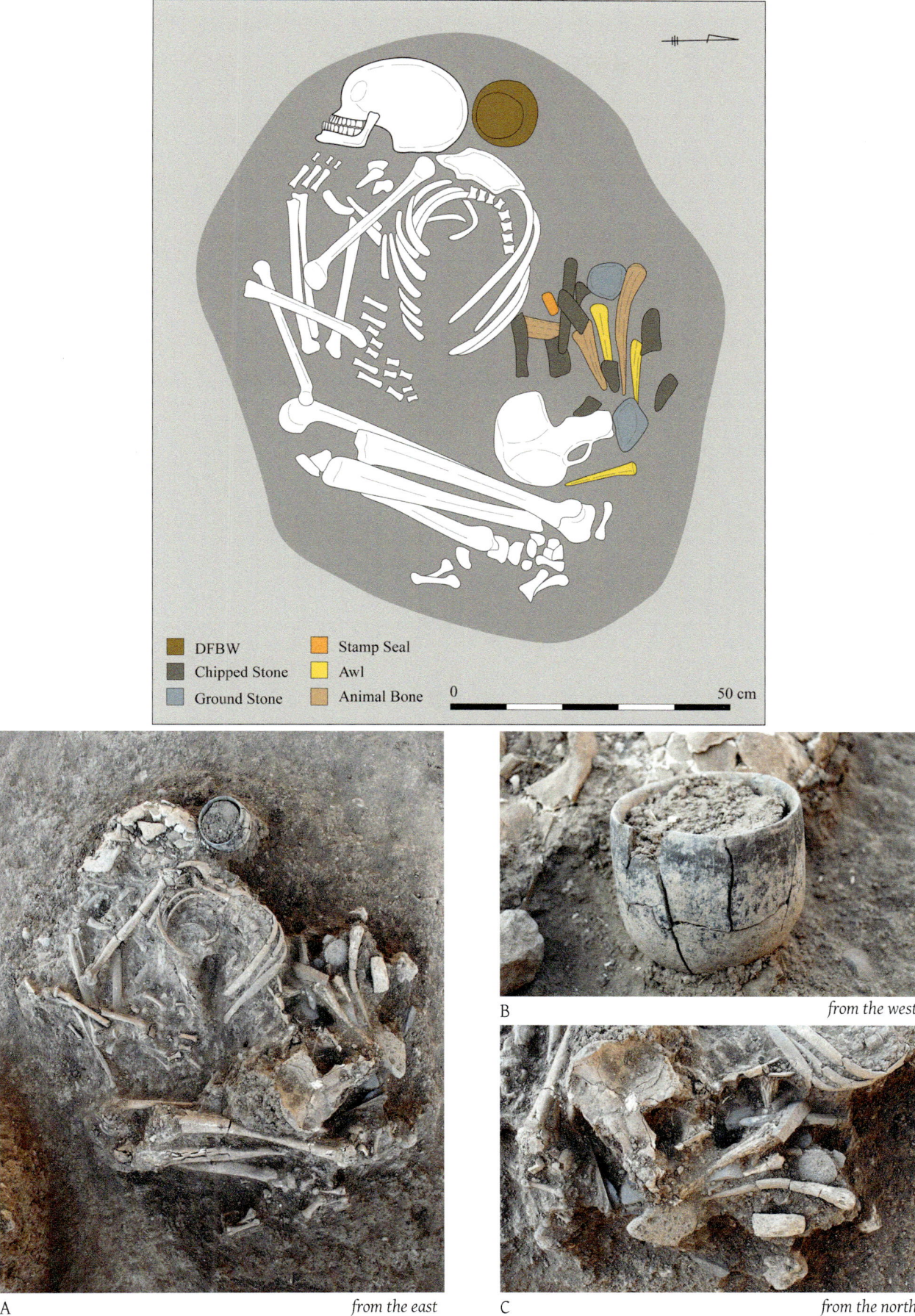

DFBW
Chipped Stone
Ground Stone
Stamp Seal
Awl
Animal Bone

0   50 cm

A   from the east

B   from the west

C   from the north

Figure 5-82a. Str. 1058 Burial: A. Adult skeleton and grave goods; B. DFBW bowl from the back of his head;
C. Grave goods near his lower back.

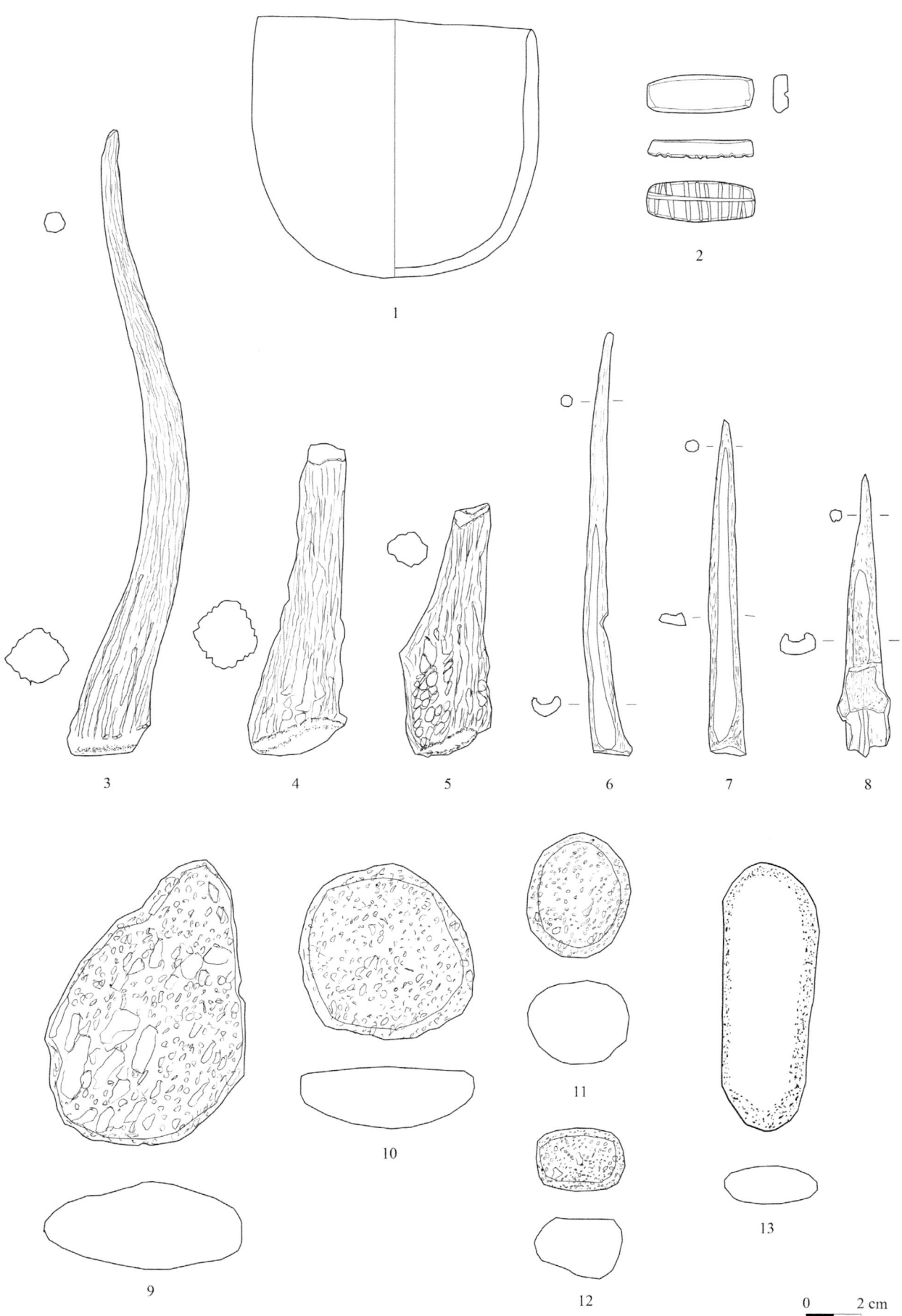

Figure 5-82b. Str. 1058 Grave goods: 1. DFBW bowl; 2. Clay (DFBW potsherd) stamp seal; 3–5. Deer horns; 6–8. Bone awls; 9–12. Soft stone hammers; 13. Whetstone.

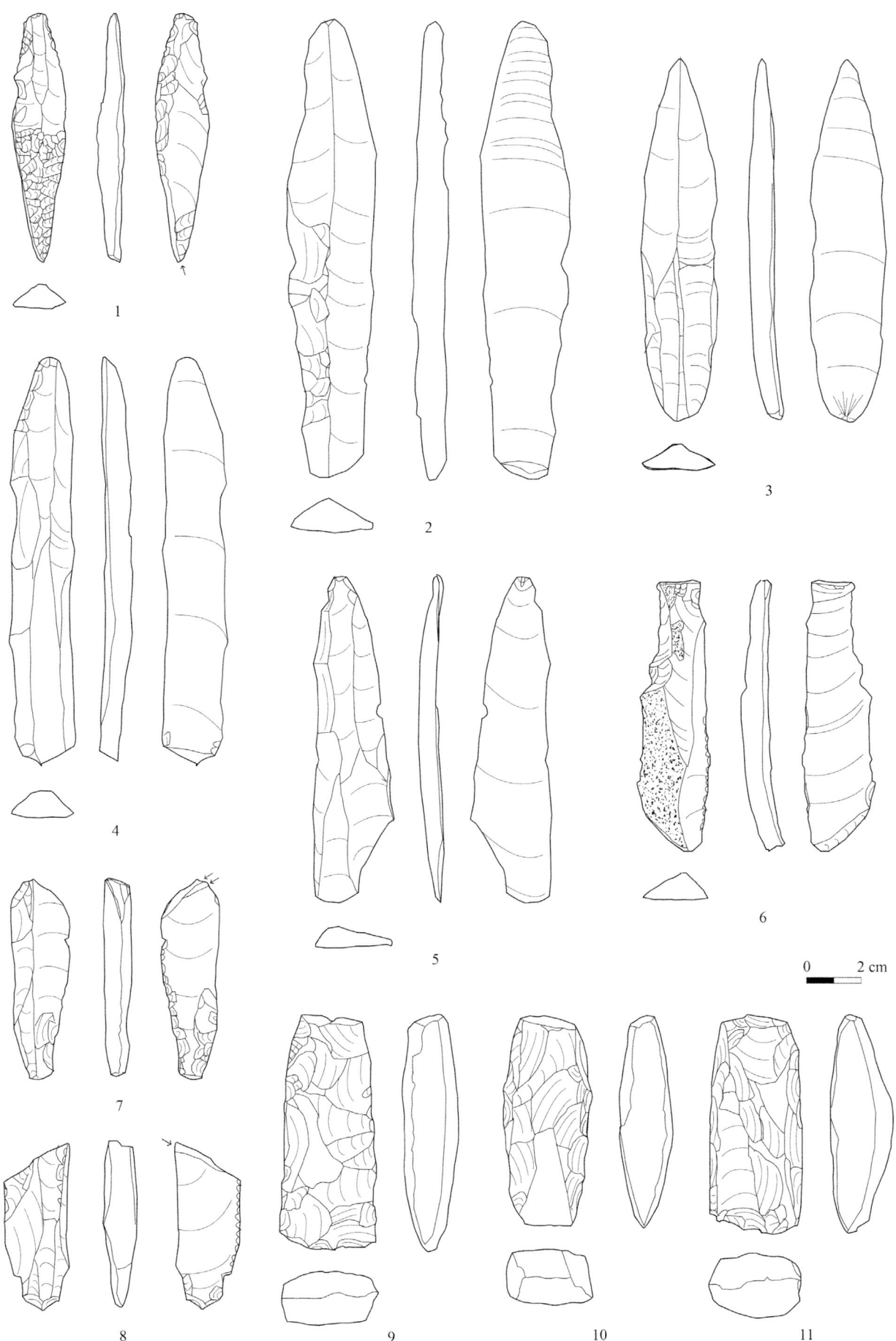

0   2 cm

Figure 5-82c. Str. 1058 Grave goods: 1. Amuq-type flint point; 2–6. Flint blades; 7–8. Burins; 9–11. Flint axes.

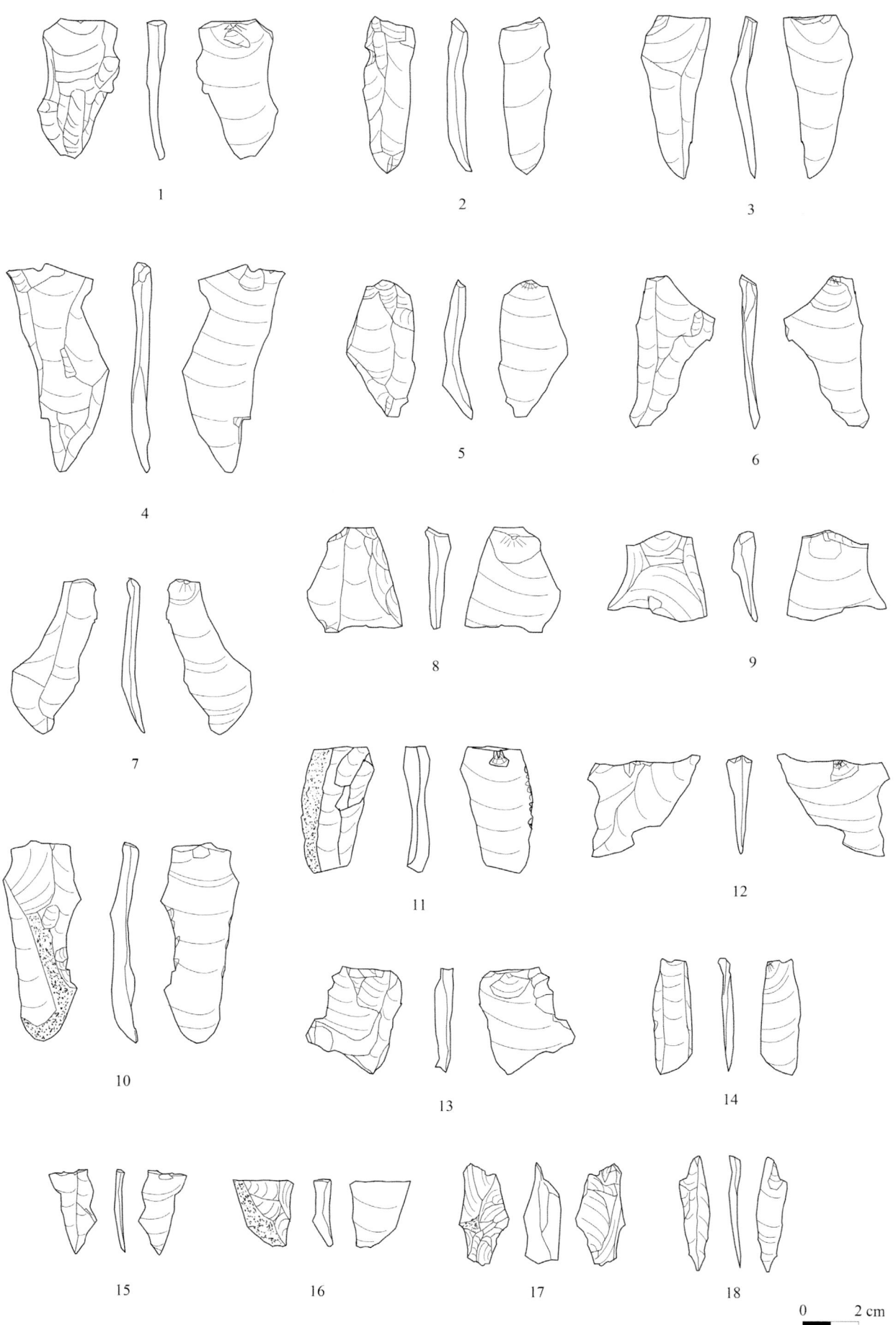

Figure 5-82d. Str. 1058 Grave goods: 1–18. Flint flakes.

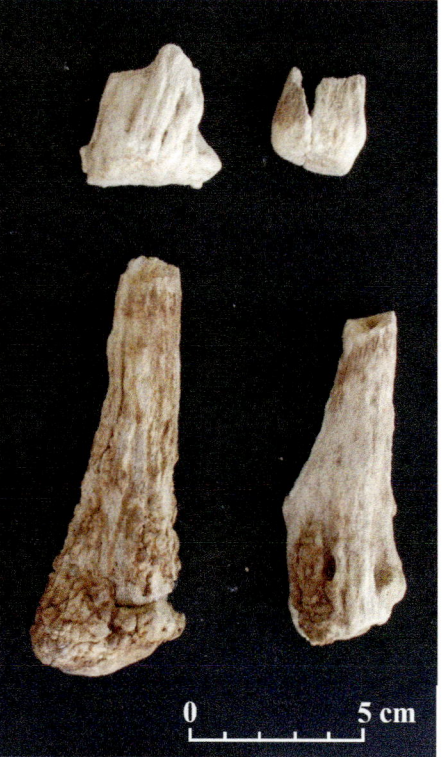

Figure 5-82e. Str. 1058 Grave goods.

83. Str. 1059 (Figure 5-83)

Str. 1059 is a typical secondary burial discovered behind Str. 1047 in Square E251c in Layer 4. This burial comprises the remains of two individuals identified through long bones and pelvises, which were placed first. The other long bones and vertebrae were then placed on the pelvis. Sex of both individuals was indeterminate. The first individual was a subadult, possibly 15–17 yrs., whereas the second one was a juvenile. A large animal talus was also uncovered.

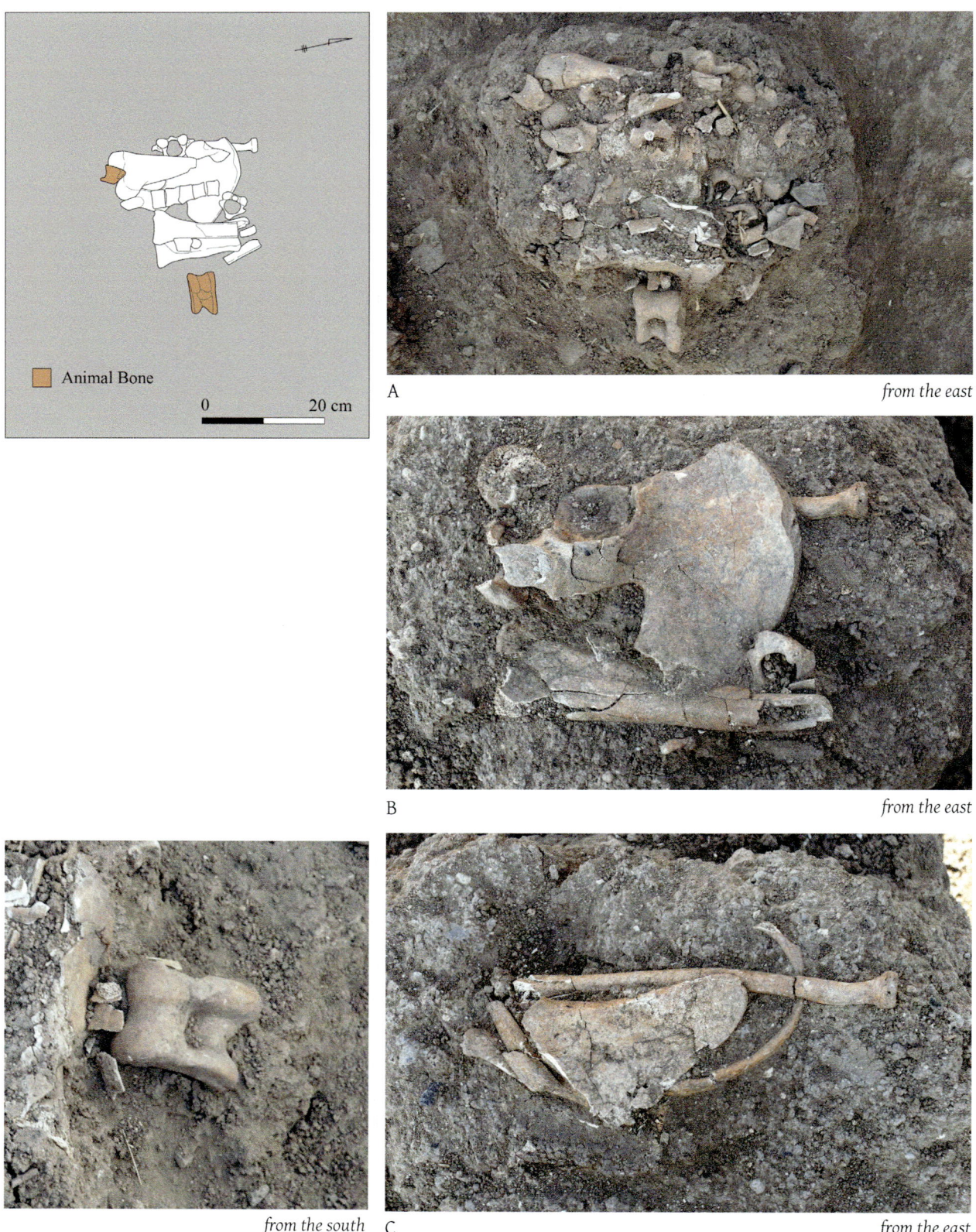

Animal Bone

0   20 cm

A   *from the east*

B   *from the east*

from the south   C   *from the east*

Figure 5-83. Str. 1059 Burial: A. Upper level; B. Middle level; C. Lower level. Grave goods: Animal talus.

84. Str. 1062 (Figure 5-84)

This deposit contains heavily disturbed human remains, discovered in the southwestern part of Square E251d in Layer 5. Only one arm and a few ribs were discovered. Based on the position of the arm, the tomb owner might have been buried on the right side. However, the burial type is unknown. There were no grave goods.

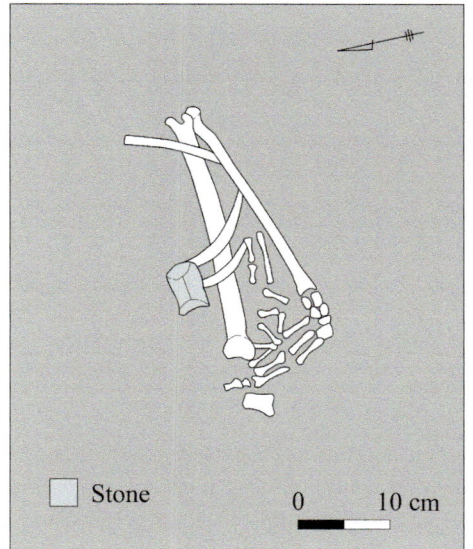

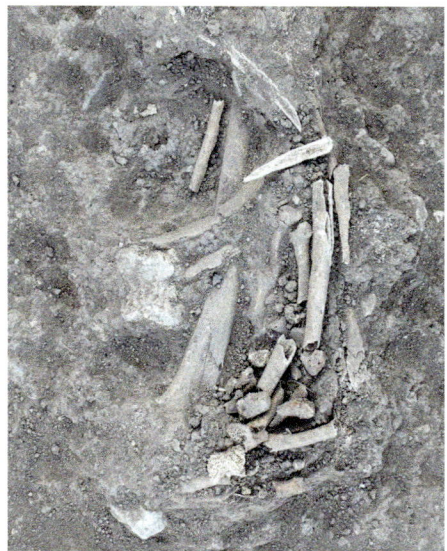

from the west

Figure 5-84. Str. 1062 Burial.

85. Str. 1064 (Figure 5-85)

Str. 1064 is a primary burial of a young adult male discovered along the border between Square E251c and E271a in Layer 4. He was buried in a flexed position on his right side. His body axis was northeast-southwest, his head pointed to the northeast, and he faced west. Three conch shell beads were discovered at his feet.

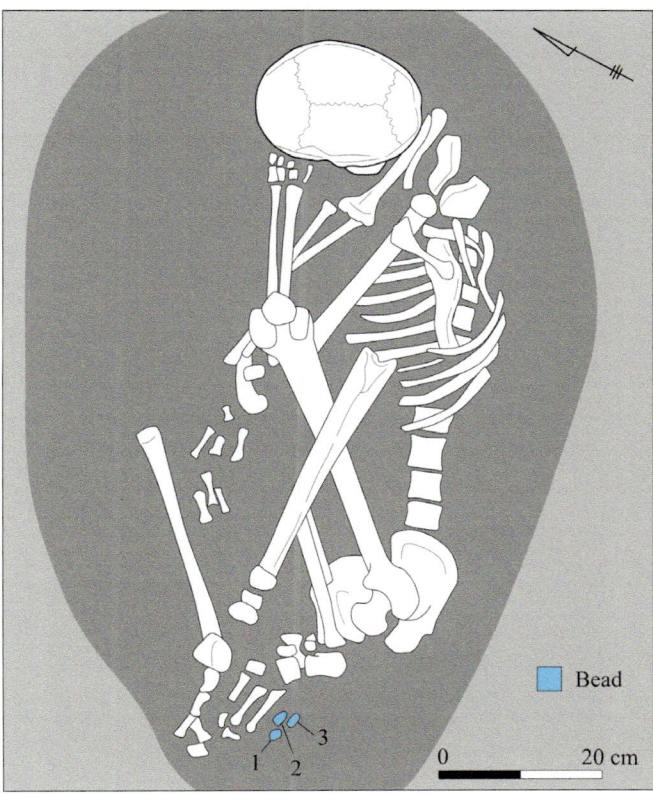

from the west

Figure 5-85a. Str. 1064 Burial.

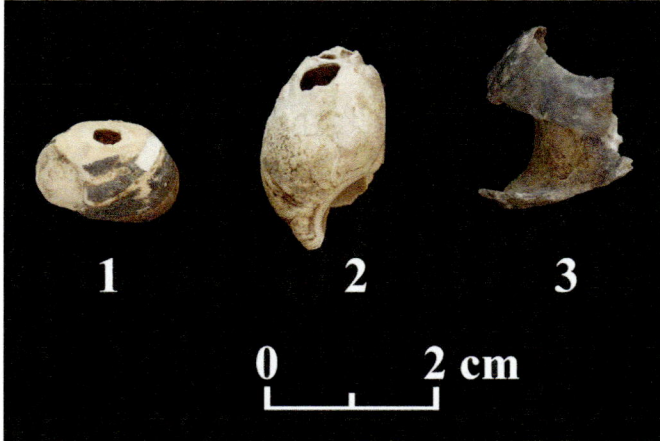

Figure 5-85b. Str. 1064 Grave goods: 1–3. Shell beads.

86. Str. 1066 (Figure 5-86)

Str. 1066 is a primary burial of a 2–3-year-old juvenile discovered in the southern end of Square E251c in Layer 4. Sex was indeterminate. The upper part of this individual was located partly beneath Str. 1044. It was buried in a flexed position on its right side. The body axis direction was north-south, and the head pointed to the northwest and looked downward. A blue-coated bead (so-called imitation turquoise bead) was discovered near the wrist of his left hand (Taniguchi *et al.* 2002).

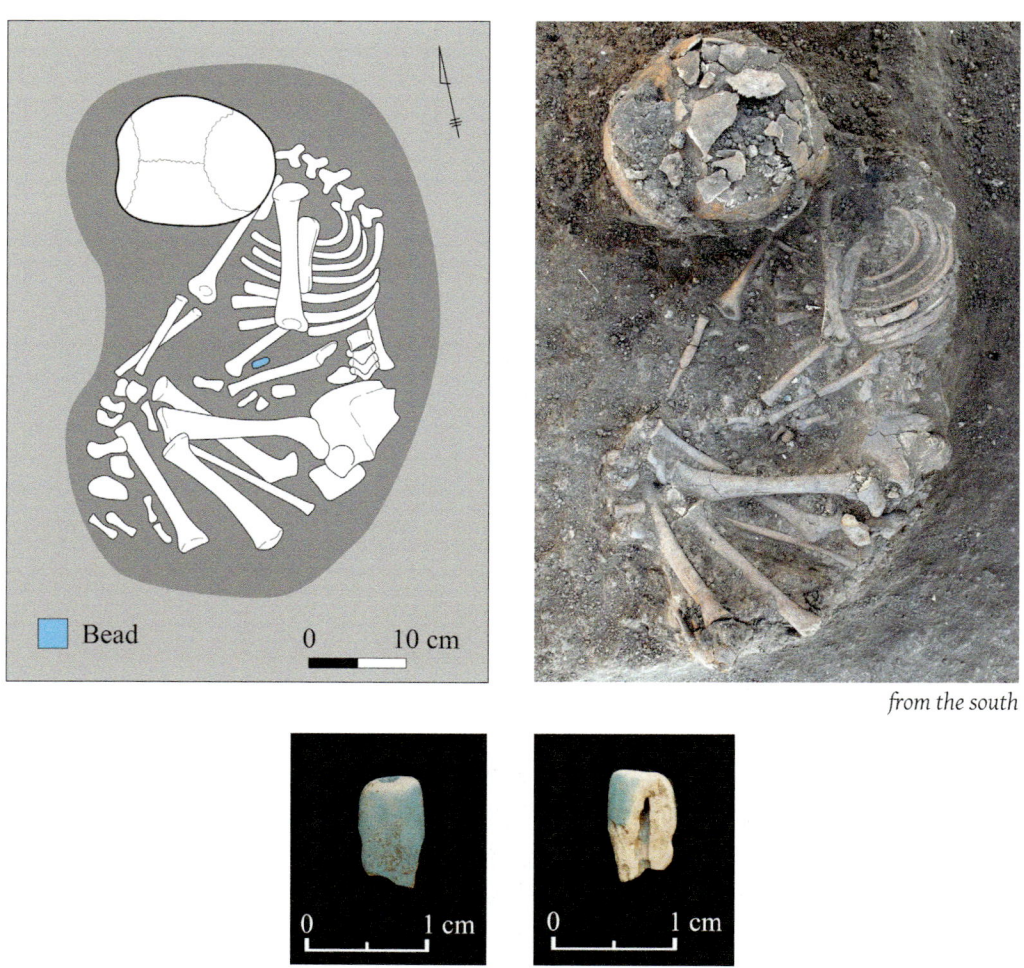

from the south

Figure 5-86. Str. 1066 Burial and grave goods:
Imitation turquoise blue bead (front and back).

87. Str. 1067 (Figure 5-87)

Str. 1067 was discovered in the southeastern part of Square E251c in Layer 5. This deposit contains the human remains of two individuals, including toes and legs. The burial type is unknown. Sex of both individuals was indeterminate. The first individual is a juvenile represented by a left foot. The second individual is an adult also represented by a left foot. There were no grave goods.

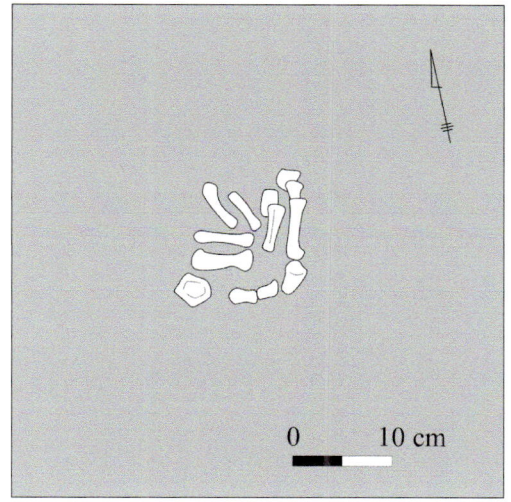

from the south

Figure 5-87. Str. 1067 Burial.

88. Str. 1068 (Figure 5-88)

Str. 1068 was discovered just north of Str. 1067 in Square E251c in Layer 5. This deposit contains human remains of an infant (birth – 2 mths). It was represented by a few skull fragments, ribs, and some other bones. The burial type is unknown. No grave goods were recovered.

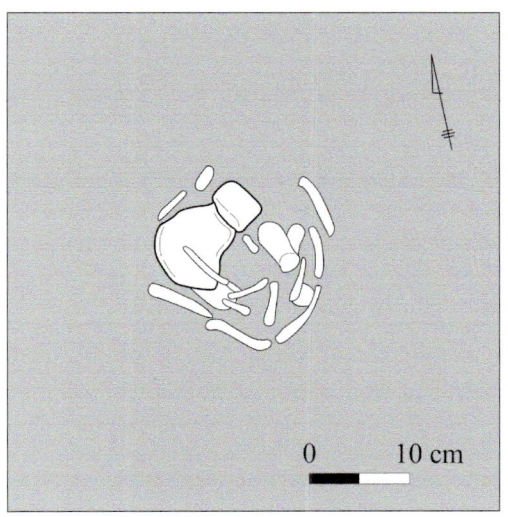

from the north

Figure 5-88. Str. 1068 Burial.

89. Str. 1070 (Figure 5-89)

Str. 1070 was discovered in the area where burials were concentrated at the border of Square E251c and d in Layer 5. The burial type is unknown. It was represented by a few fragmented and disturbed bones placed over the remains of Str. 1086. No grave goods were recovered.

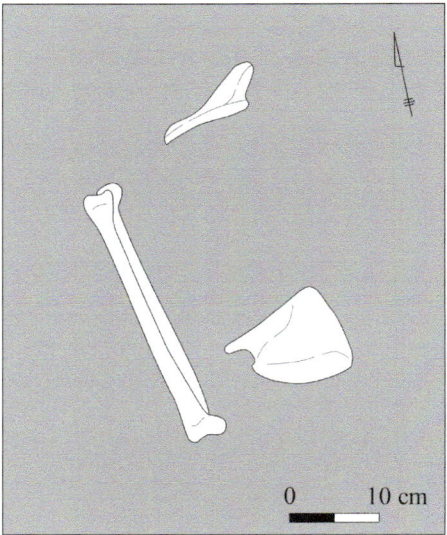

Figure 5-89. Str. 1070 Burial.

90. Str. 1072 (Figure 5-90)

Str. 1072 is a disturbed primary burial discovered in the southern part of Square E251c in Layer 5. The lower part of its body was found beneath Str. 1047. It was a juvenile aged 11–12 years, but sex was indeterminate. It was buried in a supine position on its back. The body axis direction was southwest-northeast. Notably, the entire skull was missing and the first and second vertebrae were also missing, which suggests that the head was removed while the soft tissue was still intact. No cut-marks were observed on the remaining articulated cervical vertebrae, but their poor condition may have obscured such evidence. Although the axial skeleton was articulated and intact, both lower limbs and the left upper limb, except for a few hand bones, were missing. No grave goods were uncovered.

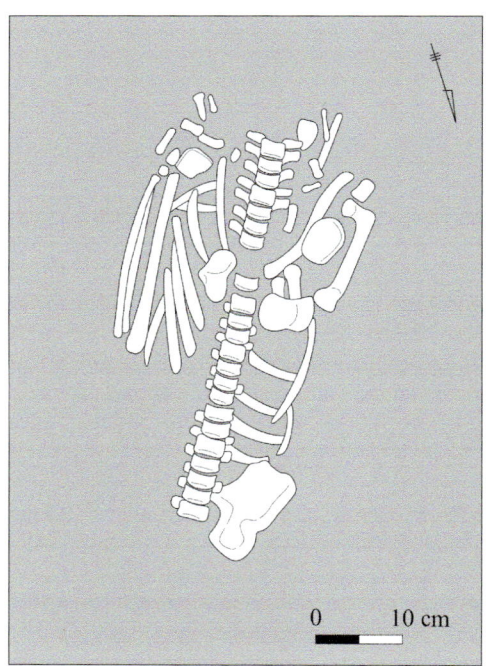 

from the north

Figure 5-90. Str. 1072 Burial.

91. Str. 1073 (Figure 5-91)

Str. 1073 is an urn burial discovered at the eastern end of Square E251d in Layer 5. Some bone fragments of a juvenile aged 1–2 years were discovered in a unique rectangular-planned coarse pottery. The short side of the rectangle measures at least 30cm. The long sides extend beyond the excavation square. Inside the pottery urn, all of the human bones were disarticulated, and they seemed to be secondarily deposited bones. A small blue bead was discovered with the human bones inside the pottery urn.

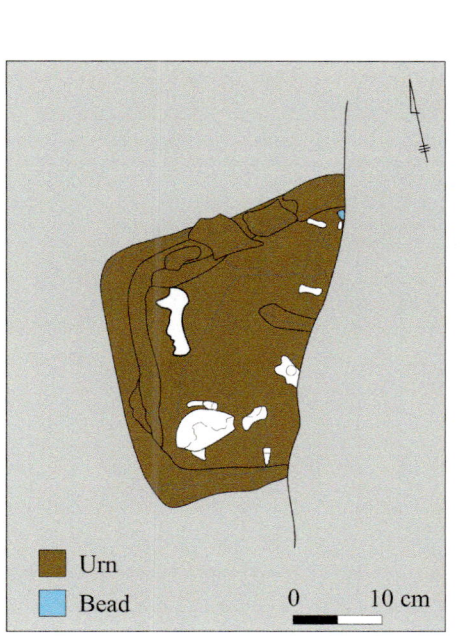

Urn
Bead

0   10 cm

from the south

from the southwest

Figure 5-91. Str. 1073 Burial and grave goods: Blue bead.

92. Str. 1074 (Figure 5-92)

Str. 1074 is a disturbed primary burial of an infant discovered in the southern part of Square E251c in Layer 5. Sex was indeterminate. Due to the disturbed condition, it was difficult to determine the burial position, but it was likely discovered in a prone position. It was buried beneath Str. 1072 and a large part of its remains were covered by the former burial. Its body axis direction was north-south. Notably, it lacked most parts of the skull. There were no grave goods.

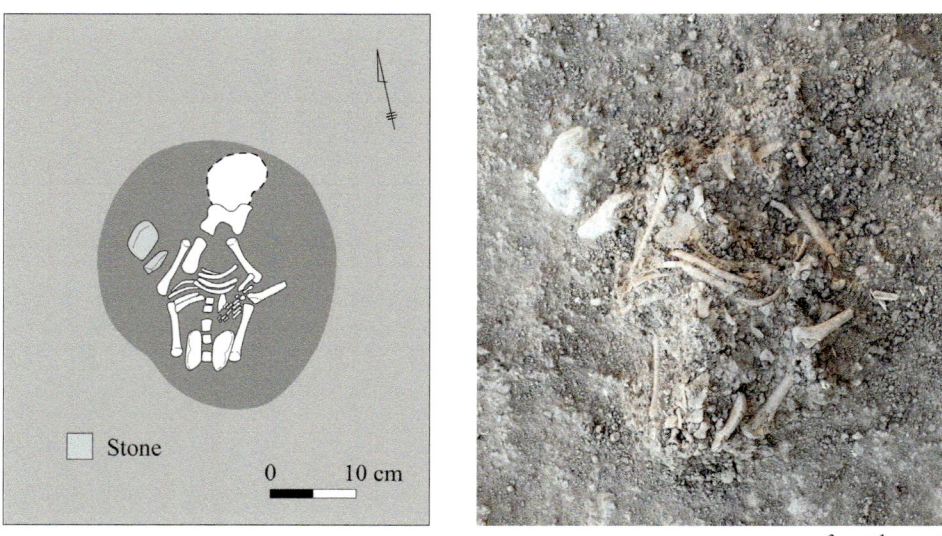

from the south

Figure 5-92. Str. 1074 Burial.

93. Str. 1075 (Figure 5-93)

Str. 1075 is a primary burial of a young adult discovered in the northeastern corner of Square E271b in Layer 5. It was buried in a prone position. A few pieces of orange pisé lined the skeleton. The skull was in contact with a large limestone on the left side. The body axis direction was west-east. The head pointed to the west and looked downward. Its right hand hung limp and extended along the body axis, and its left hand was half folded and placed under the hipbones. Curiously enough, the bones of the lower limbs were completely missing. There were no grave goods.

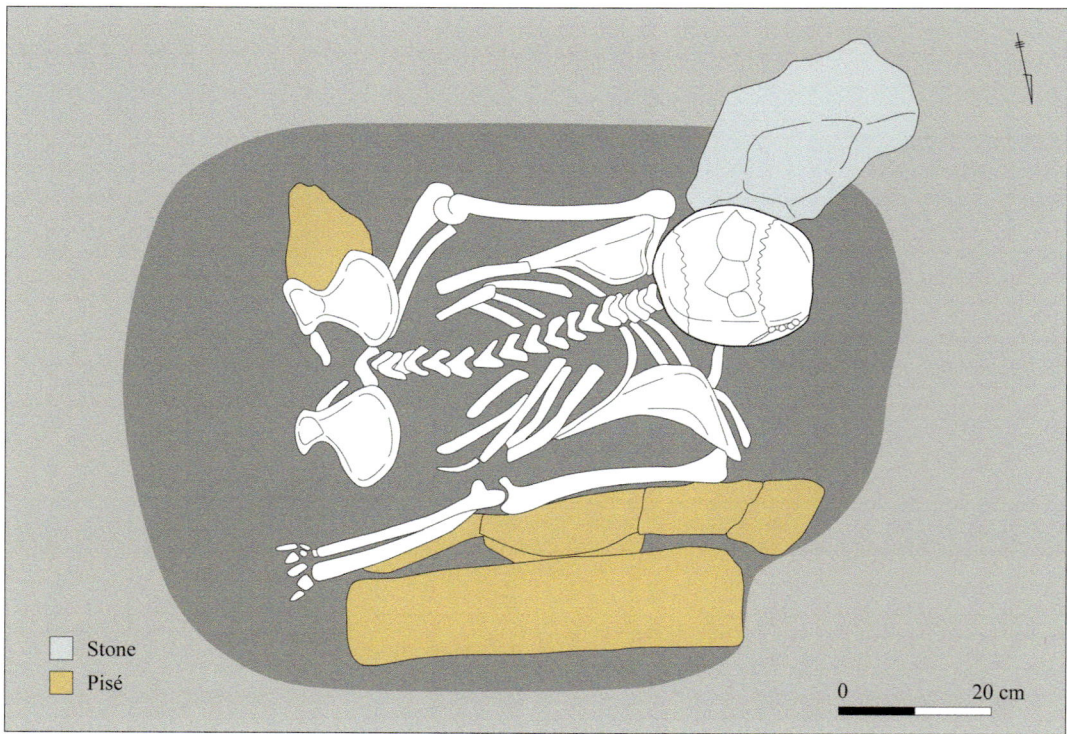

Figure 5-93a. Str. 1075 Burial.

from the north

Figure 5-93b. Str. 1075 Burial.

94. Str. 1076 (Figure 5-94)

Broken isolated skull fragments were discovered in the northeastern corner of Square E251c in Layer 5. Sex was indeterminate. However, open sutures indicate a young age. The burial type is unknown. There were no grave goods.

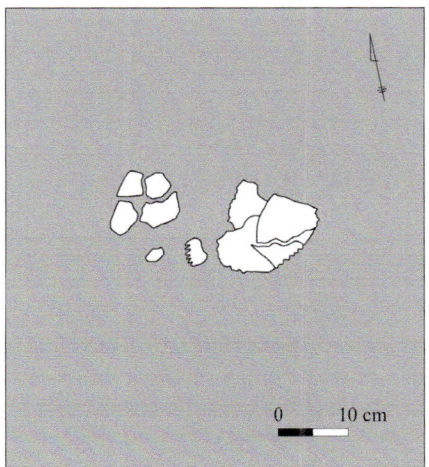

from the south

Figure 5-94. Str. 1076 Burial.

95. Str. 1077 (Figure 5-95)

Str. 1077 is a primary burial of a young adult, probably female, discovered in the southeastern part of Square E251c in Layer 5. She was buried in a tightly flexed position on her back. Her head was bent under the body. It is impossible to bury the human body in such a compact position without tying with a rope. The body axis direction was east-west, but the skull was bent. Both her legs were bent over her abdomen. A short-cylindrical stone bead and a tusk shell bead were discovered under her left leg. A conch shell bead was also discovered near her toes.

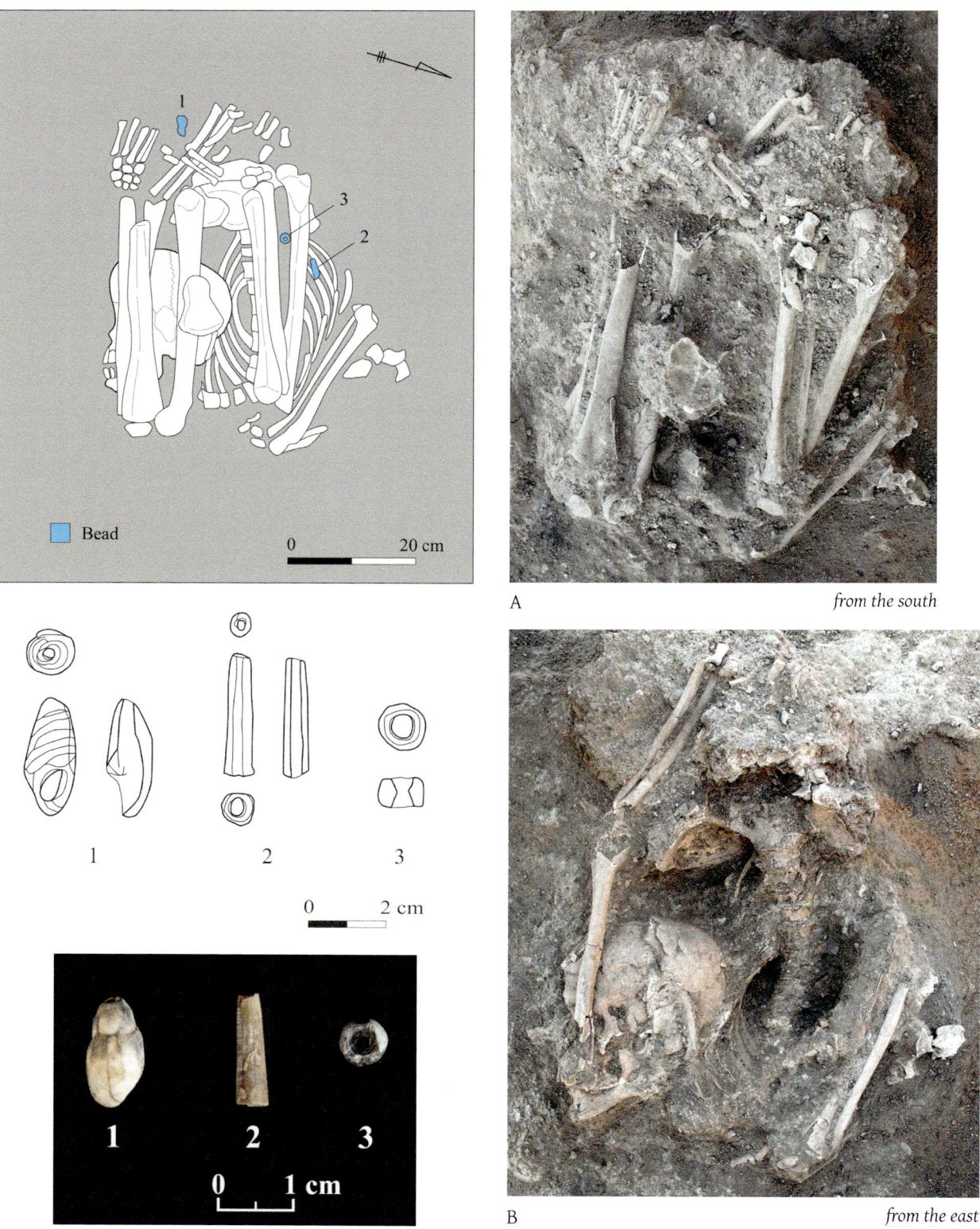

Figure 5-95. Str. 1077 Burial: A. Upper level. B. Lower level. Grave goods:
1. Conch shell bead; 2. Tusk shell bead; 3. Stone short-cylindrical bead.

96. Str. 1078 (Figure 5-96)

Str. 1078 is a primary burial of a perinatal baby discovered in the southeastern part of Square E251c in Layer 5. The skeletal remains were not well preserved. It was buried in a flexed position on its left side. The body axis direction was west-east, and the head pointed to the west and faced north. There were no grave goods.

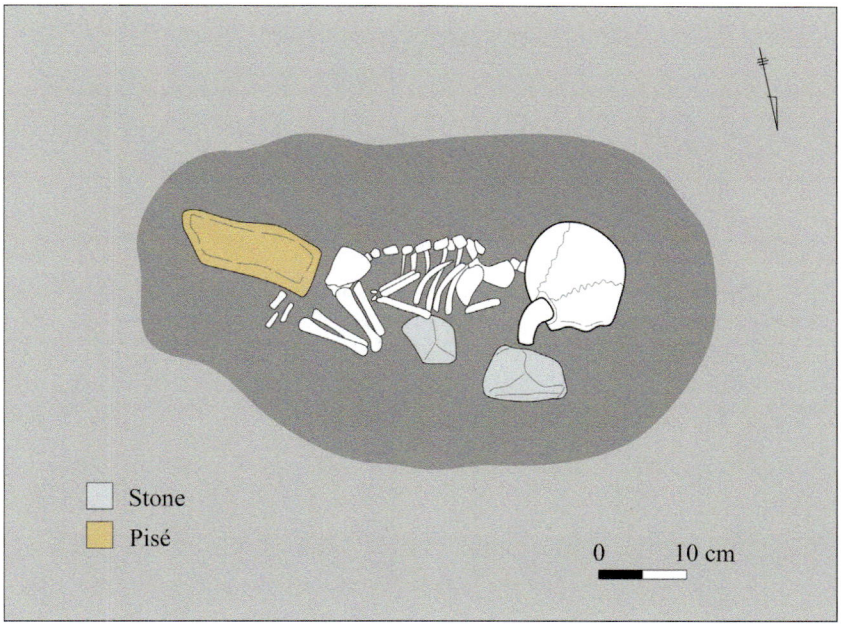

from the north

Figure 5-96. Str. 1078 Burial.

97. Str. 1079 (Figure 5-97)

Str. 1079 is a primary burial of a young adult, probably male, discovered in the southwestern corner of Square E251d in Layer 5. He had a large skeleton and his length was greater than 170cm. He was buried in a flexed position on his left side. His upper body reflected a near prone position. Both of his arms were bent and his right hands were placed near his face. His body axis direction was northwest-southeast, and his head pointed to the north and faced downward toward the east. A small conch shell bead was discovered near his skull.

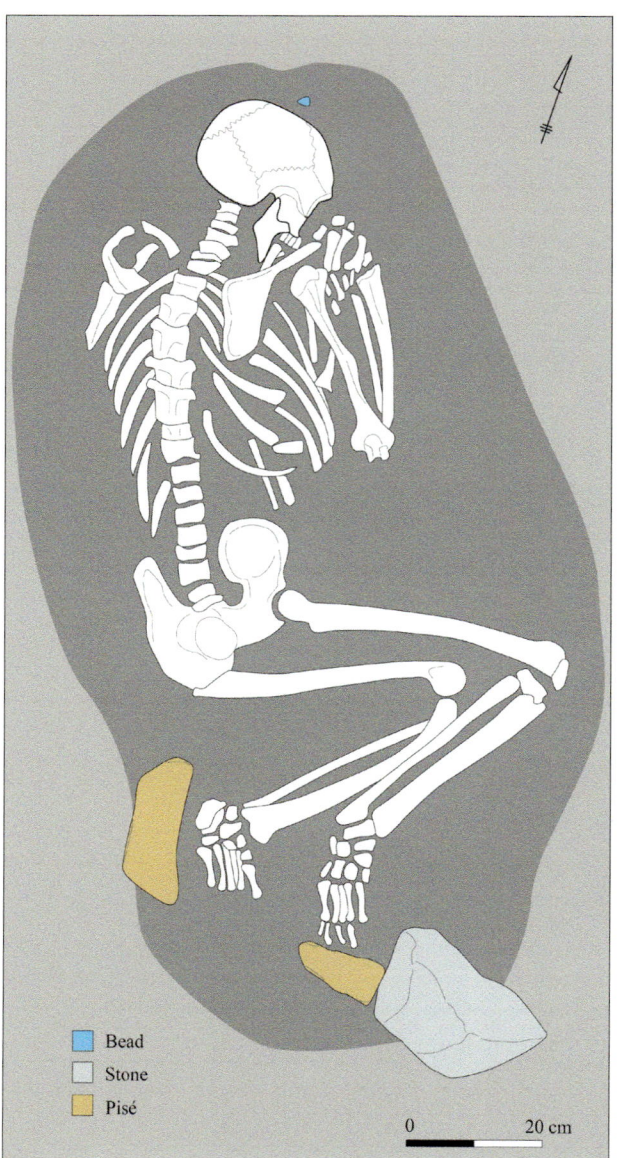

from the southeast

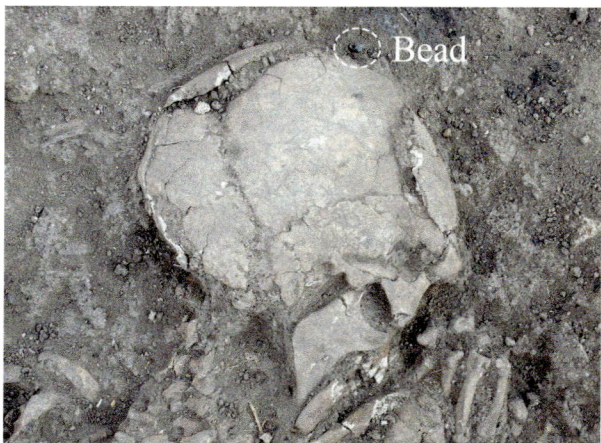

Figure 5-97. Str. 1079 Burial.

98. Str. 1080 (Figure 5-98)

Str. 1080 is an isolated adult skull discovered in the southern part of Square E251d in Layer 5. It seems to be a secondary burial. Most of the skull and the face skeletal remains were present. The head pointed to the west and faced south. There were no grave goods.

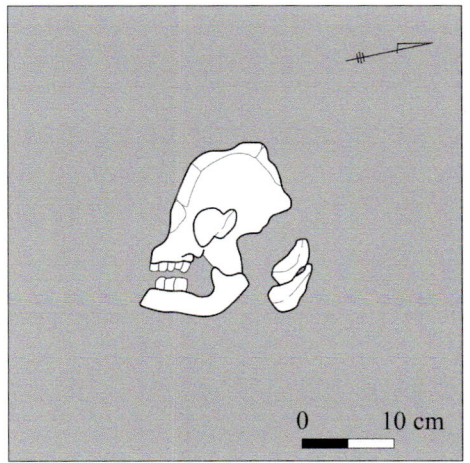

from the east

Figure 5-98. Str. 1080 Burial.

99. Str. 1081 (Figure 5-99)

Str. 1081 is a primary burial of an adult, probably female, discovered in the northeastern part of Square E251d in Layer 5. This individual was only partly excavated because the upper part and the head extended beyond the excavated square, and as such have not yet been excavated. She was buried in a flexed position on her right side. The body axis direction was northeast-southwest. The most remarkable finding was the presence of numerous burial goods. Four bone awls were discovered under the legs with one stone bead, and three bone awls were discovered under the arms with two stone beads. In addition, a cattle metacarpal was discovered near the hipbone. The combination of bone awls and cattle metacarpal indicates that the tomb owner might have been engaged in weaving.

The cattle metacarpal was also discovered at another subadult burial (Str. 732). In ethnographical documents, animal metacarpals are often used to tighten cords for a loom (Saito 2010). The metacarpi were found with bone awls, which might have been used for weaving and drilling. Therefore, it was supposed that women and girls were engaged in weaving.

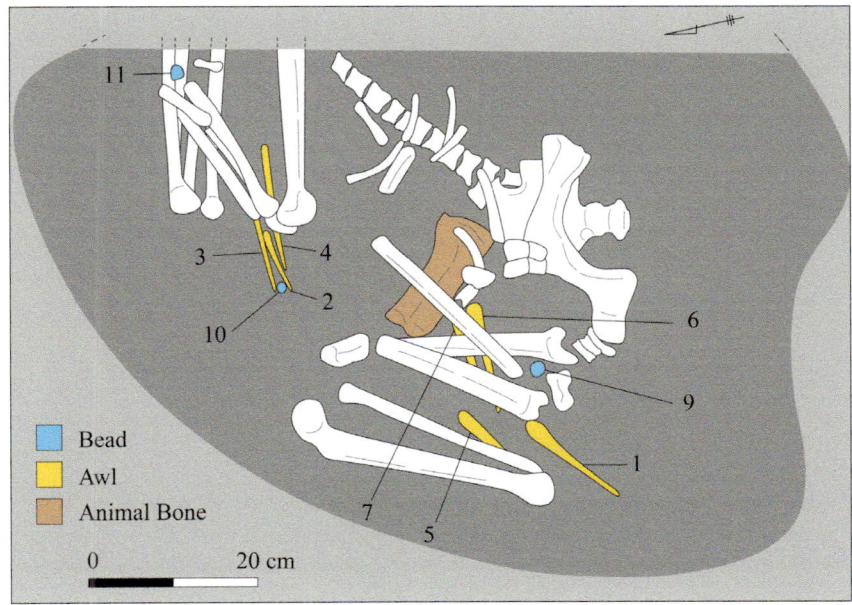

Figure 5-99a. Str. 1081 Burial.

A   *from the west*

B   *from the west*

C   *from the north*

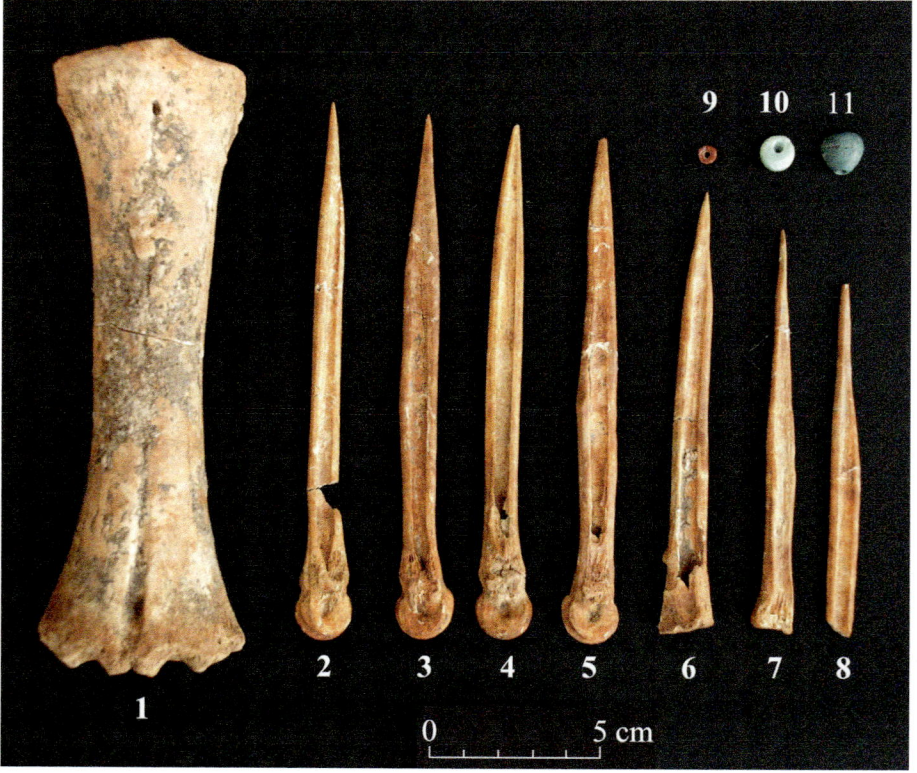

Figure 5-99b. Str. 1081 Burial: A. Adult skeleton; B. Cattle metacarpal and bone awls; C. Bead and bone awls.
Grave goods: 1. Cattle metacarpal; 2–8. Bone awls; 9–11. Stone beads.

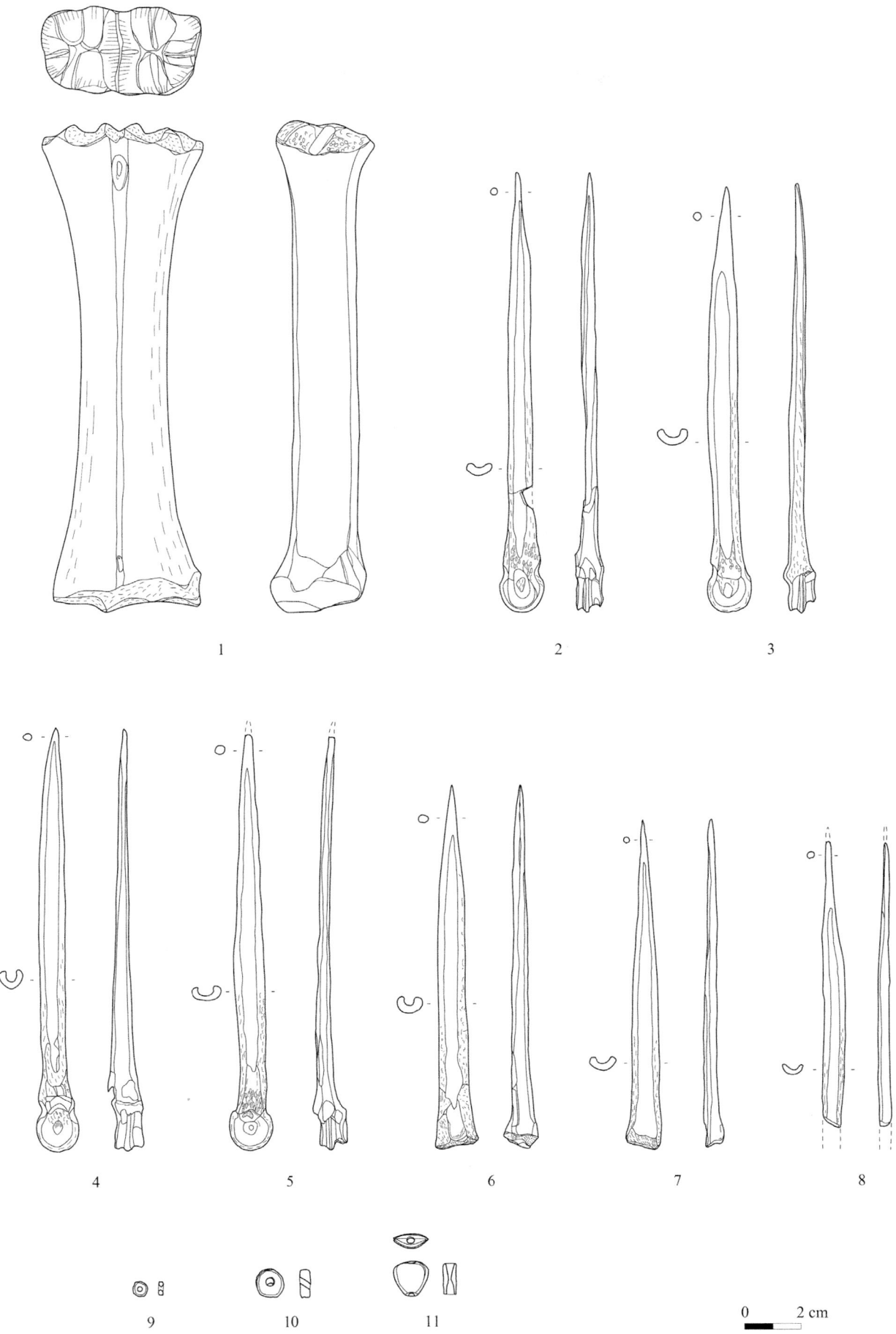

Figure 5-99c. Str. 1081 Grave goods: 1. Cattle metacarpal; 2–8. Bone awls; 9–11. Stone beads.

100. Str. 1082 (Figure 5-100)

Str. 1082 is a disturbed primary burial of an old adult discovered in the eastern part of Square E251d in Layer 5. Sex was indeterminate. It was buried to the south of the Str. 1081 Burial. It was buried in a tightly flexed position on its right side. The body axis direction was southwest-northeast and the head pointed to the southeast. The skull was very fragmented, so the direction of the face could not be determined. There were no grave goods.

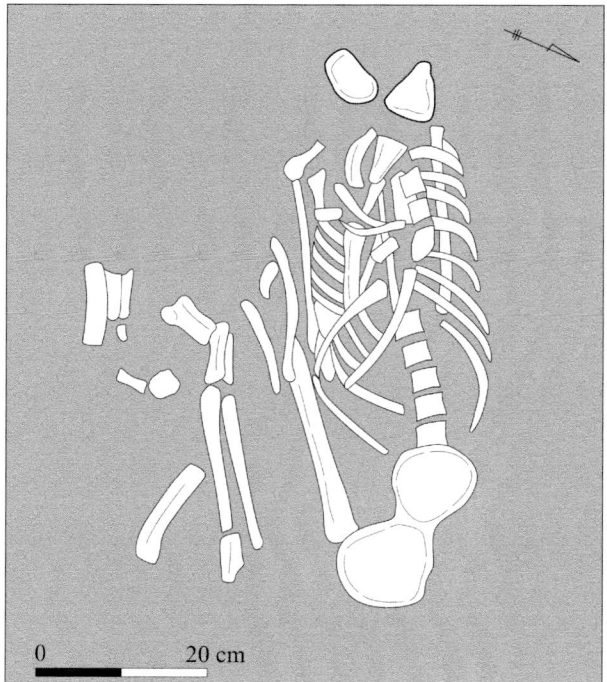 

from the northeast

Figure 5-100. Str. 1082 Burial.

101. Str. 1083 (Figure 5-101)

Str. 1083 was found at the eastern part of Square E251d in Layer 5. This burial was represented by some long bones of an adult individual, such as the femur and humerus, which remained in a disarticulated position. This burial was above the Str. 1097 burial. It was difficult to reconstruct the original figure, so the burial type is unknown. There were no grave goods.

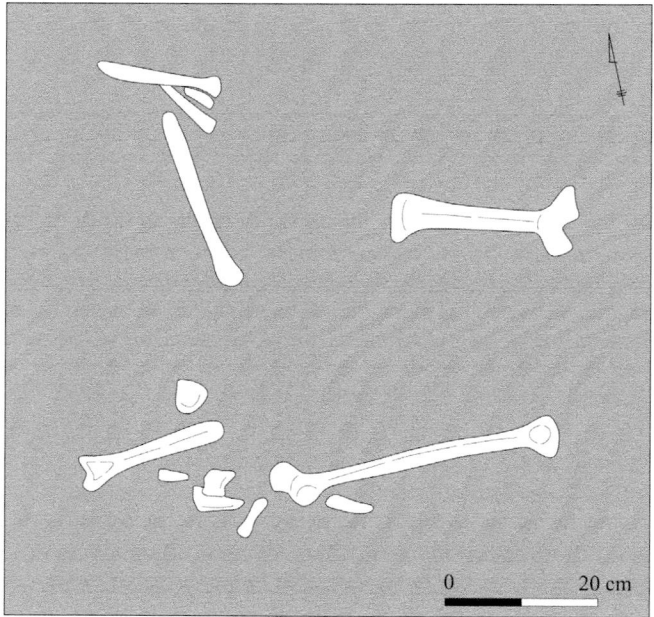

Figure 5-101. Str. 1083 Burial.

102. Str. 1084 (Figure 5-102)

Str. 1084 is a secondary burial containing an isolated cranium of an adult, probably female, discovered in the western part of E251d in Layer 5. It was placed over the knees of the Str. 1086 individual and lacked a mandible. The cranium was facing upward. This cranium possibly belonged to one of the headless individuals uncovered in the cemetery. The cranium must have been removed from its original grave and placed in this location. No grave goods were found.

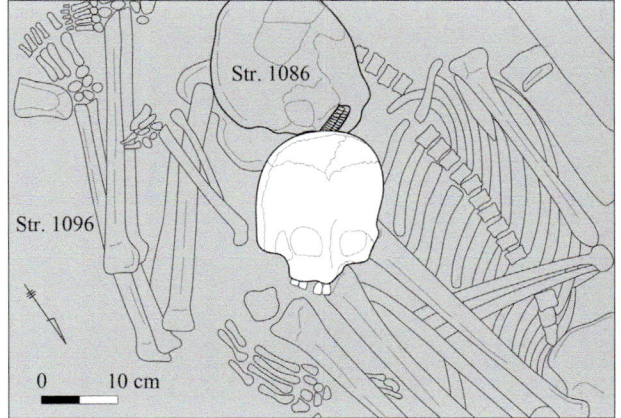

from the northeast

from the northwest

Figure 5-102. Str. 1084 Burial.

103. Str. 1085 (Figure 5-103)

Str. 1085 is a primary burial of a young adult, probably female, discovered in the southern part of Square E251d in Layer 5. She was buried in a flexed position on her right side. The body axis direction was southwest-northeast, and the head pointed to the southwest and faced southeast. Its left arm was bent and the hand was placed under the left knee, though its right arm was stretched under the right leg. There were no grave goods.

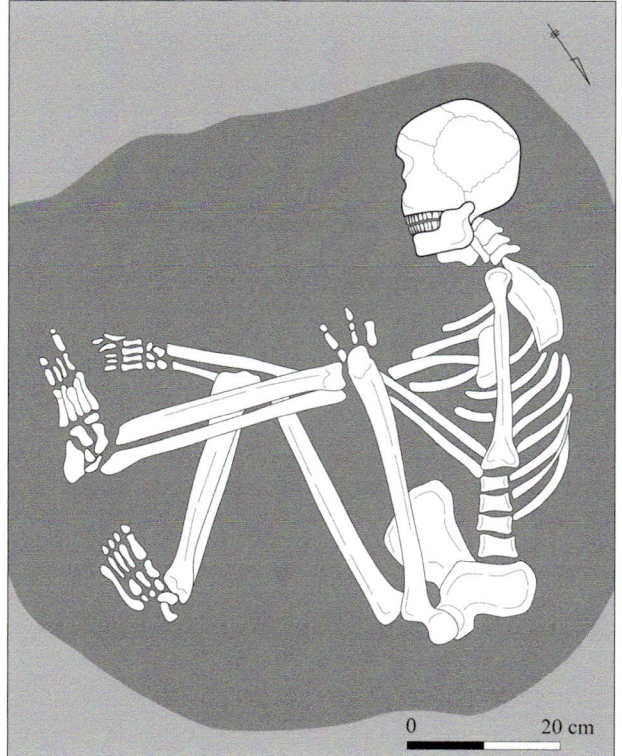

from the northeast

from the southeast

Figure 5-103. Str. 1085 Burial.

104. Str. 1086 (Figure 5-104)

Str. 1086 is a primary burial of an adult, probably male, discovered in Square E251d in Layer 5. He was buried in a tightly flexed position on his right side. However, the upper body tended to lie supine. The body axis direction was south-north, and the head pointed to the south and faced northeast. Both legs were tightly bent, and the arms were placed under the legs. The isolated cranium of an adult female (Str. 1084) was placed on the knees in front of the Str. 1086 skull. A stone stamp seal and a flint blade were discovered on his left pelvis. Another flint blade was discovered near his back.

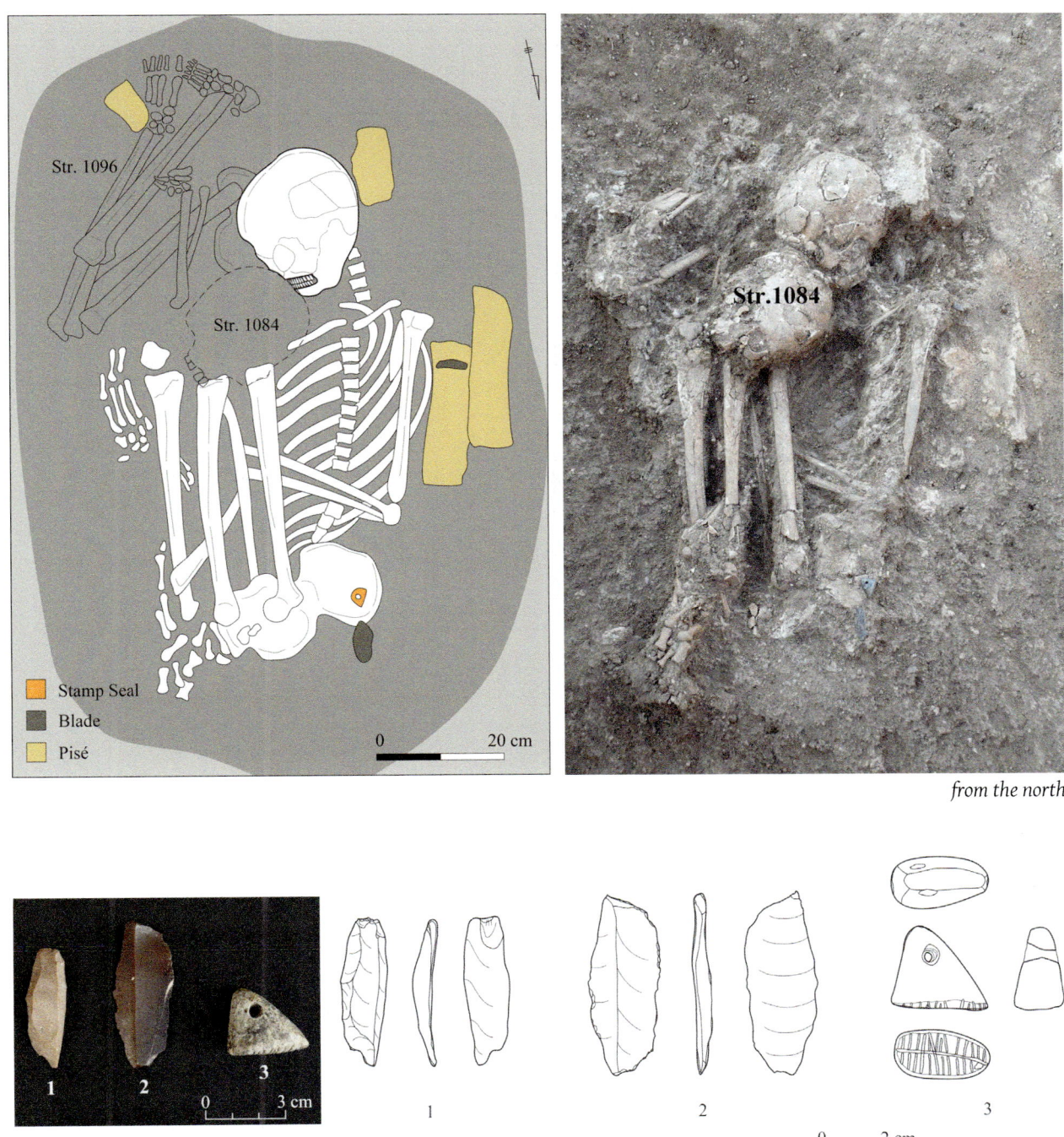

from the north

Figure 5-104. Str. 1086 Burial and grave goods: 1–2. Flint blades; 3. Stamp seal.

105. Str. 1087 (Figure 5-105)

Str. 1087 is a primary burial of a young adult, probably female, discovered in the eastern part of Square E251d in Layer 5. It was discovered superimposed on another burial (Str. 1088). She was buried in a flexed position on her left side. However, her upper body tended toward being supine. Her right arm was bent on her chest. The left arm stretched beyond the left knee. The body axis direction was south-north, and the head pointed to the south and faced southwest. The most striking discovery was 294 pieces of flat basalt beads around her neck. The beads were discovered in double lines. It is clear that the beads were tied in a line with string and wound around her neck.

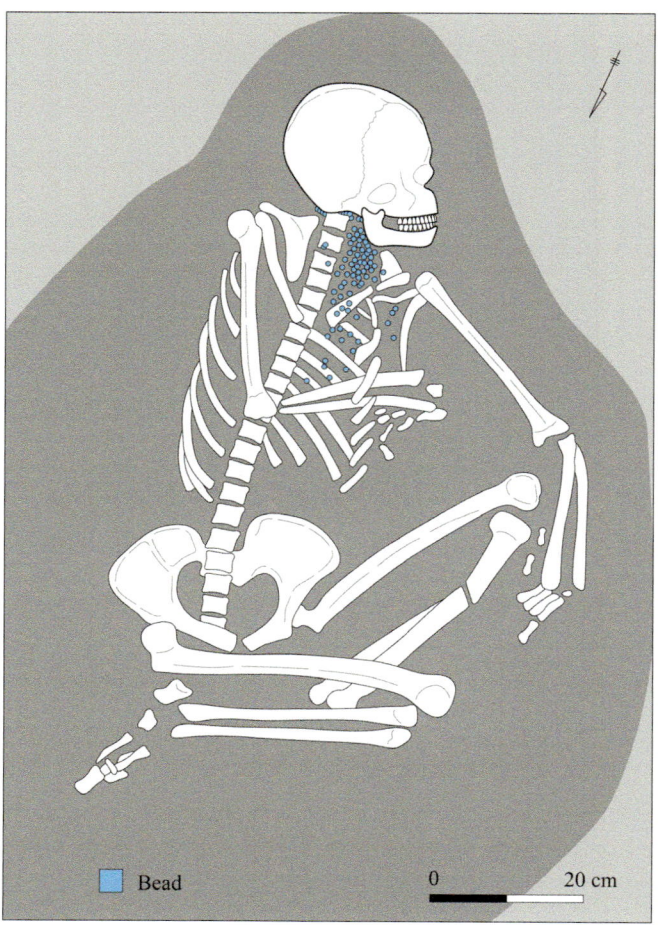

Bead   0   20 cm

from the northwest

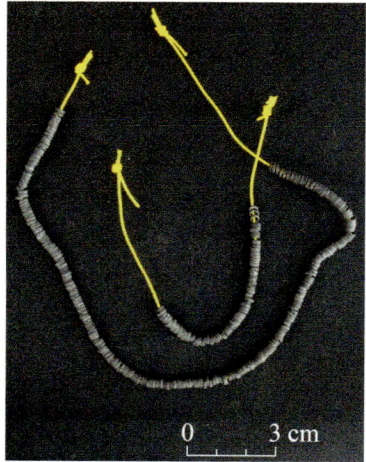

0   3 cm

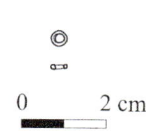

0   2 cm

from the northwest

Figure 5-105. Str. 1087 Burial and grave goods: Flat basalt beads.

106. Str. 1088 (Figure 5-106)

Beneath Str. 1087, another human bone deposit was discovered in Square E251d in Layer 5. This deposit contains the skeletons of three individuals, i.e., two adults and one juvenile. The first is the disturbed primary inhumation of an adult, represented by a complete skull and right upper limb. The skull faced upward. A part of the skeleton had heat marks. The second was an unburnt adult, represented by the lower limbs, the right upper limb, and the left hand and forearm. The remainder of the skeleton was disturbed and buried in a flexed position on its right side. The third individual was a juvenile, represented by an ulna and toe phalanges. Its burial type was unknown.

One limestone stamp seal was discovered between the distal end of the upper limb of the first individual and the proximal end of the lower limb of the second individual. Therefore, it is unclear which burial this seal belongs to.

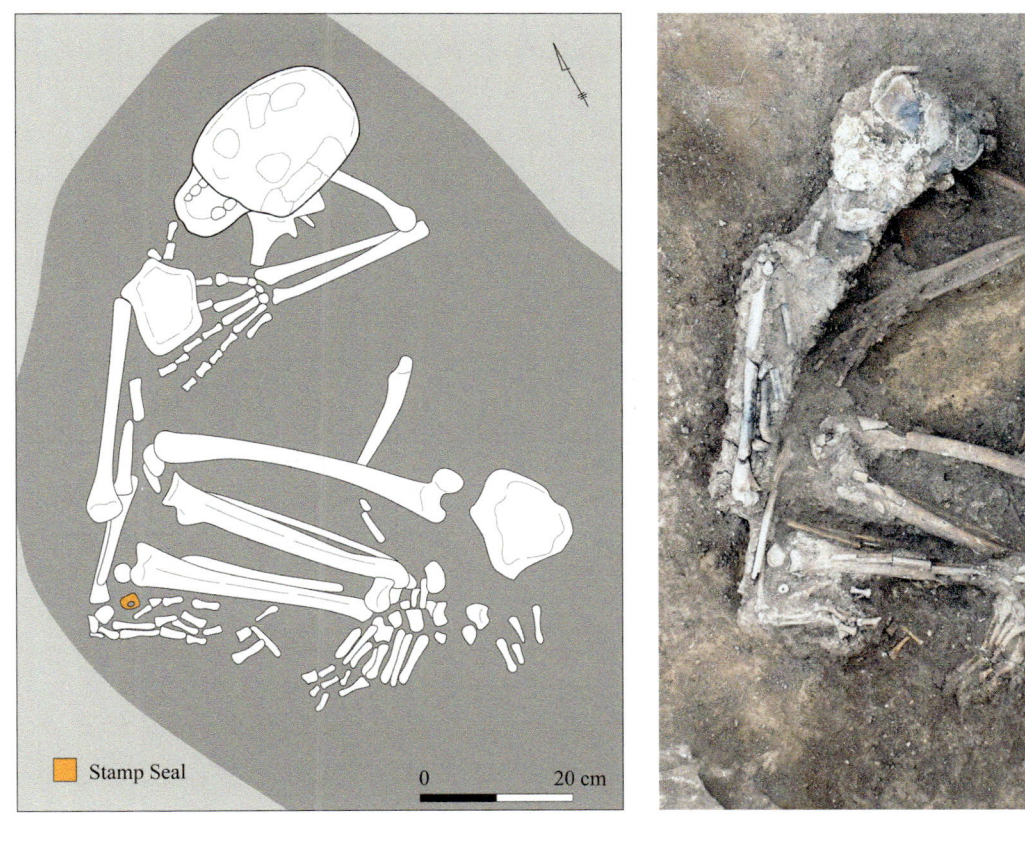

from the southwest

Figure 5-106. Str. 1088 Burial and grave goods: Stamp seal.

107. Str. 1089 (Figure 5-107)

Str. 1089 is a primary burial of a 8–12-year-old juvenile discovered in the eastern end of Square E251c in Layer 5. It was superimposed on another skeleton (Str. 1090). It was buried in a flexed position on its right side. The body axis direction was north–south, and the head pointed to the north and faced west. The right hand was folded and placed under the skull, and the left hand was placed in front of the face. There were no grave goods.

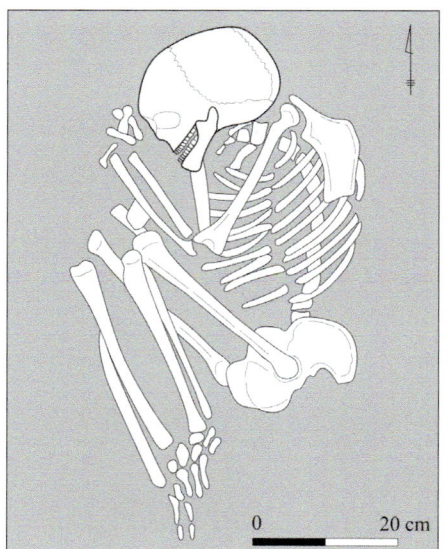

from the south

Figure 5-107. Str. 1089 Burial.

108. Str. 1090 (Figure 5-108)

Str. 1090 is a primary burial of a middle-aged adult, probably male, discovered at the eastern end of Square E251c in Layer 5. It was buried beneath Str. 1089. This burial was likely disturbed when the Str. 1089 burial was constructed. Only the skull, arm, and leg remained in a relatively good condition. The backbones, ribs, and hipbone had disappeared completely. It was buried in a flexed position on its left side. The body axis direction was south-north, and the head pointed to the south and faced west. There were no grave goods.

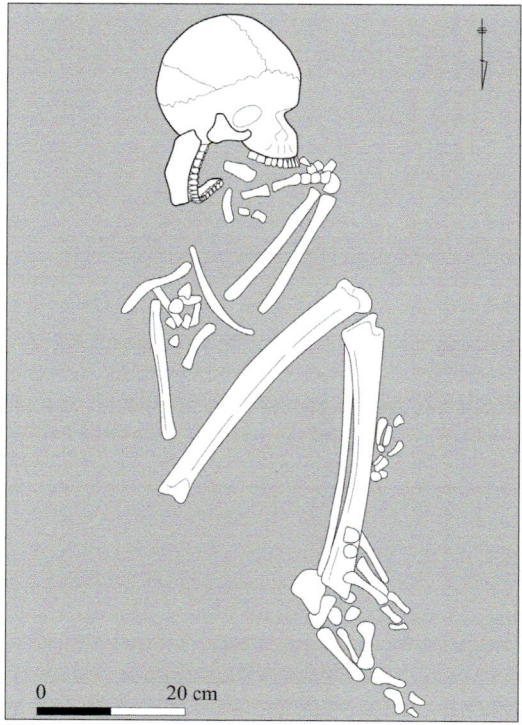
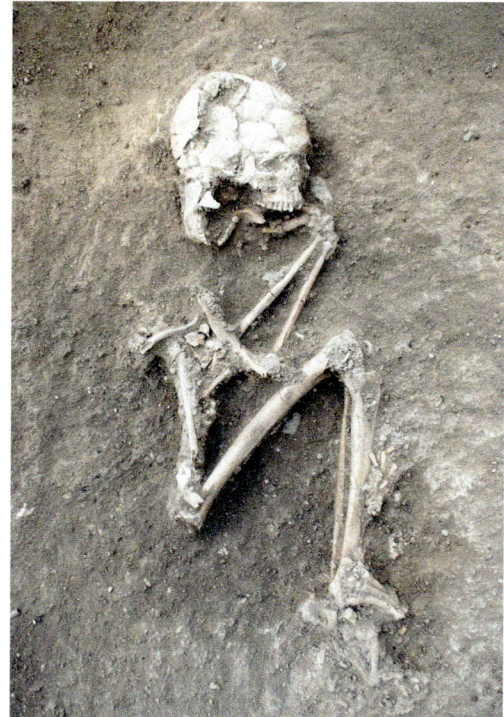

from the north

Figure 5-108. Str. 1090 Burial.

109. Str. 1091 (Figure 5-109)

This deposit contained a mass of human bones of a subadult (16–20 yrs.) discovered in the northern end of Square E271a in Layer 5. An articulated leg, the collarbones, fingers and toes, and a fragment of the skull were present. The articulated leg tells us that it was originally a primary burial. However, it was extensively disturbed, so it was not possible to recognize the original position of the deceased. Thus, the burial type is unknown. A stone axe (probably gabbro) and a quartz bead were discovered near one of the collarbones.

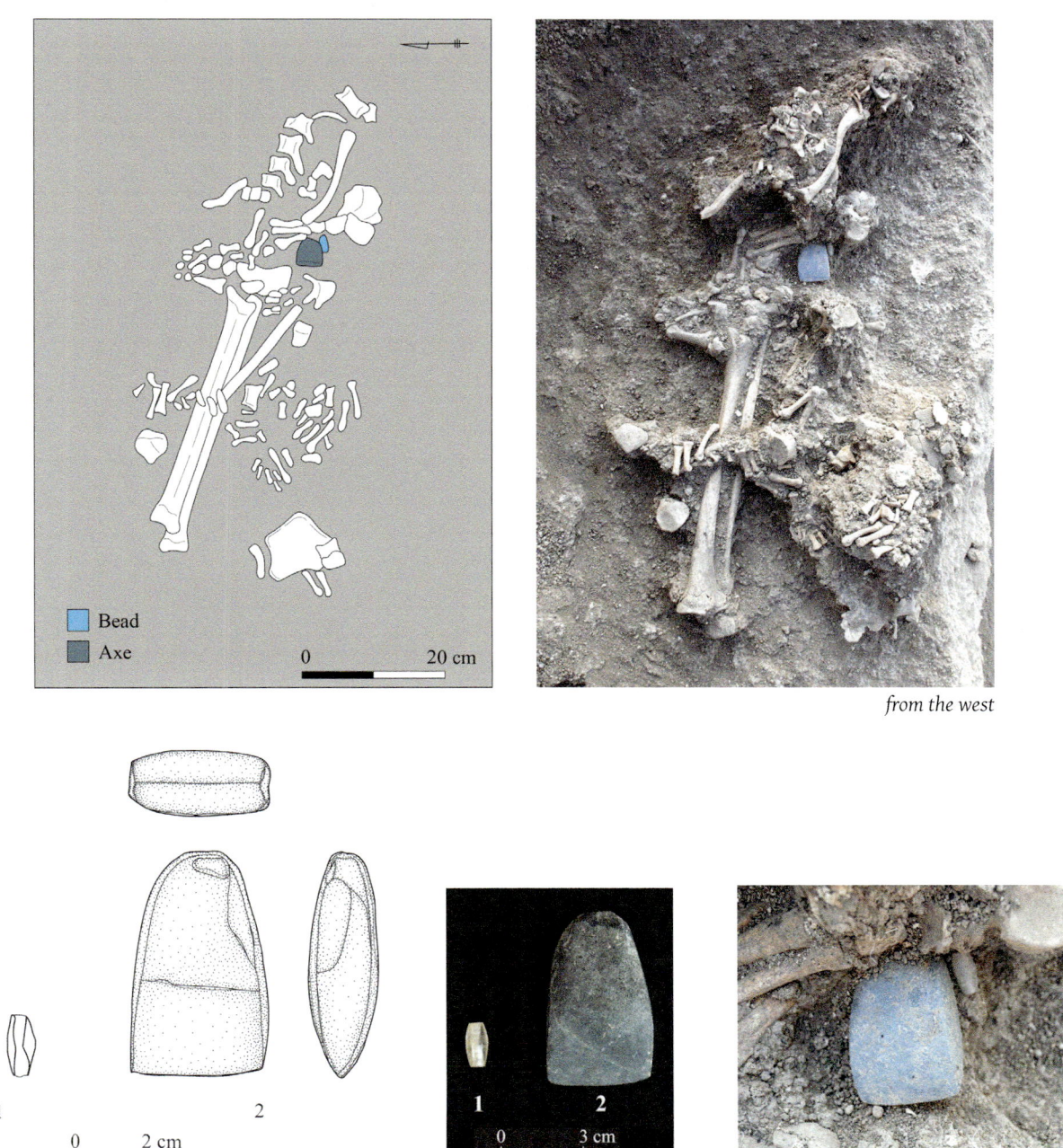

from the west

from the west

Figure 5-109. Str. 1091 Burial and grave goods: 1. Stone bead; 2. Stone axe.

110. Str. 1092 (Figure 5-110)

Str. 1092 is a primary burial of a juvenile aged below 12 discovered in the southern part of Square E251c in Layer 5. It was buried in a flexed position on its left side. The body axis direction was southeast-northwest, and the head pointed to the southeast and faced west. The left leg was tightly bent and the right arm was half folded in front of the head. There were no grave goods.

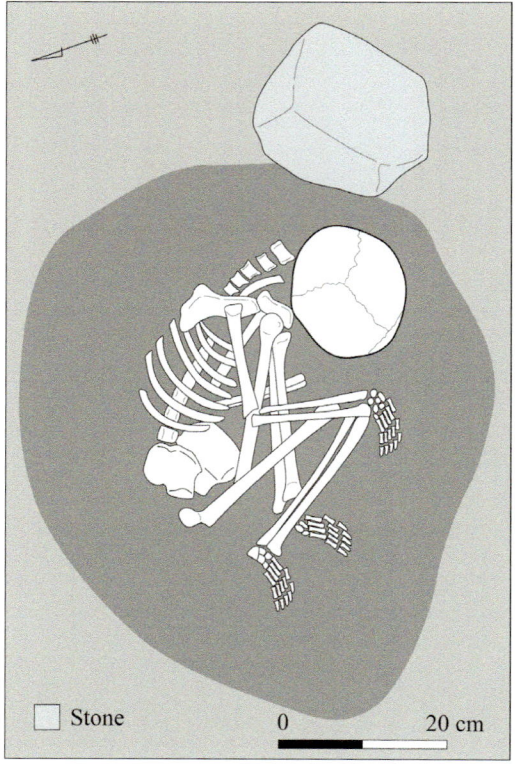 

from the west

Figure 5-110. Str. 1092 Burial.

111. Str. 1093 (Figure 5-111)

Str. 1093 is a primary burial of a 2–3-year-old juvenile discovered in the western part of Square E251c in Layer 5. It was buried in a flexed position on its right side. The body axis direction was west-east, and the head pointed to the west and faced south. Both legs were tightly bent, and they must have been tied up to the body with rope. The arms were free and extended. Among the fingers of its left hand, a small gabbro stamp seal was discovered. This is the second specimen of a stamp seal buried with a child. Therefore, this suggests that even a small child carried a stamp seal in the Neolithic society of Tell el-Kerkh.

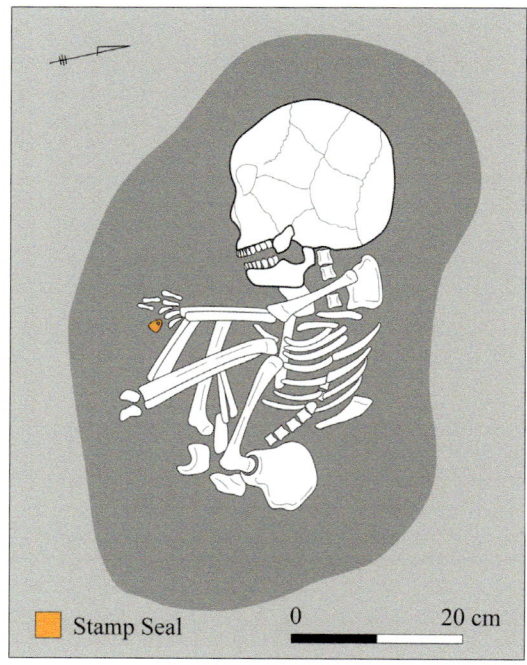

Figure 5-111a. Str. 1093 Burial.

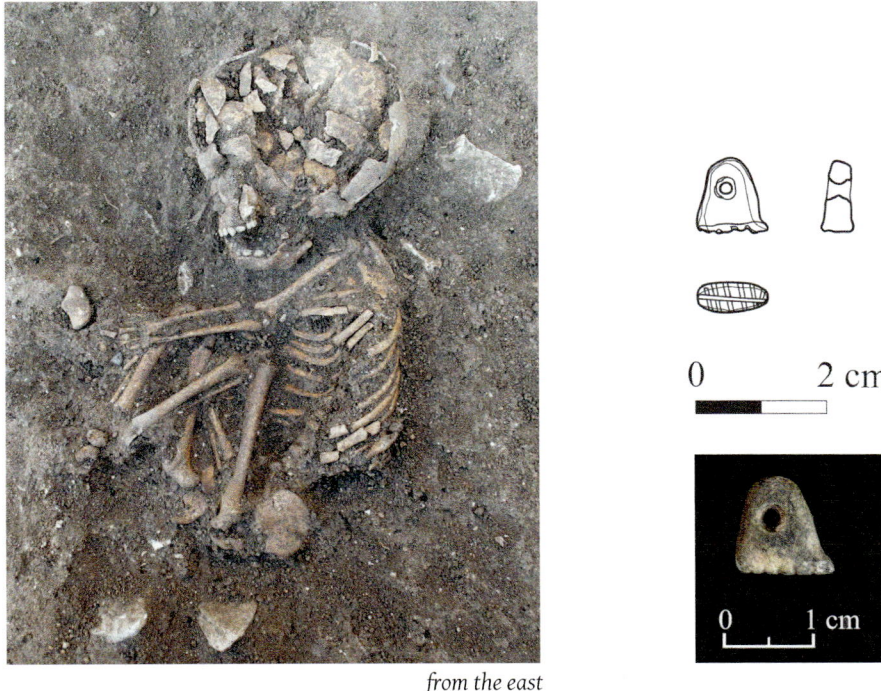

from the east

Figure 5-111b. Str. 1093 Burial and grave goods: Stone stamp seal.

112. Str. 1094 (Figure 5-112)

Str. 1094 is a primary burial of a juvenile discovered in Square E251c in Layer 5. Sex was indeterminate. It was buried in a flexed position on its right side. The body axis direction was southeast-northwest and the skull was completely missing. What appears to be an isolated maxillary lateral incisor is visible in the photo, as is the incomplete root of another unidentifiable tooth. Unfortunately, it was difficult to determine if the skull removal occurred before or after the flesh decomposed. A small flint flake was uncovered near its feet.

In general, small children and infants were usually buried intact during the Neolithic periods, but some specimens reflected exceptional treatment. Str. 1094 from Tell el-Kerkh represents evidence of skull removal practiced on small children, whilst similar specimens are scarce in the PN period.

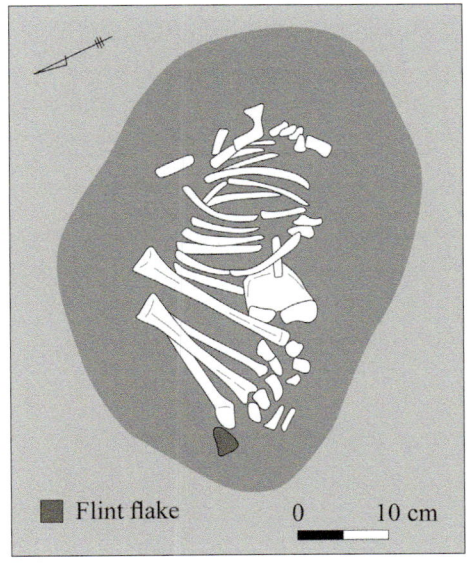

Flint flake

from the northwest

Figure 5-112. Str. 1094 Burial.

113. Str. 1095 (Figure 5-113)

This deposit contained the disturbed remains of human bones discovered just east of Strs. 1089 and 1090 in the eastern end of Square E251c in Layer 5. The human remains belonged to an adult whose sex was indeterminate. The long bones, including femur and tibia, and ribs were located in the south, and a hipbone and a collarbone in the north of the square. However, the burial type is unknown. A large cattle horn was discovered on the northeastern side. There were no grave goods.

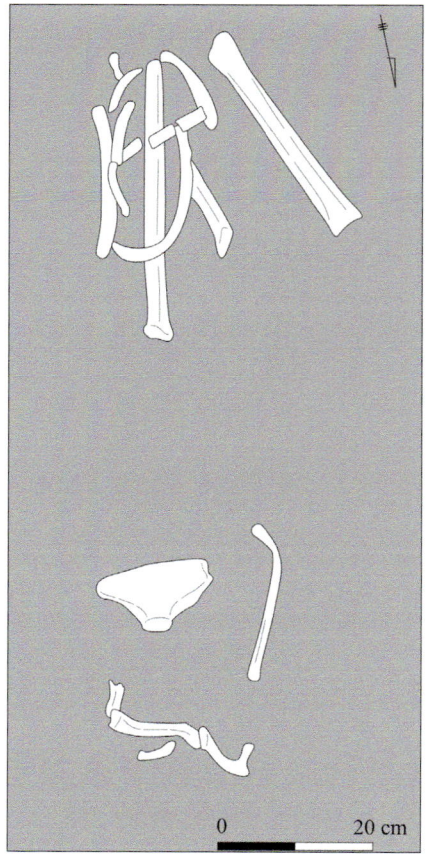 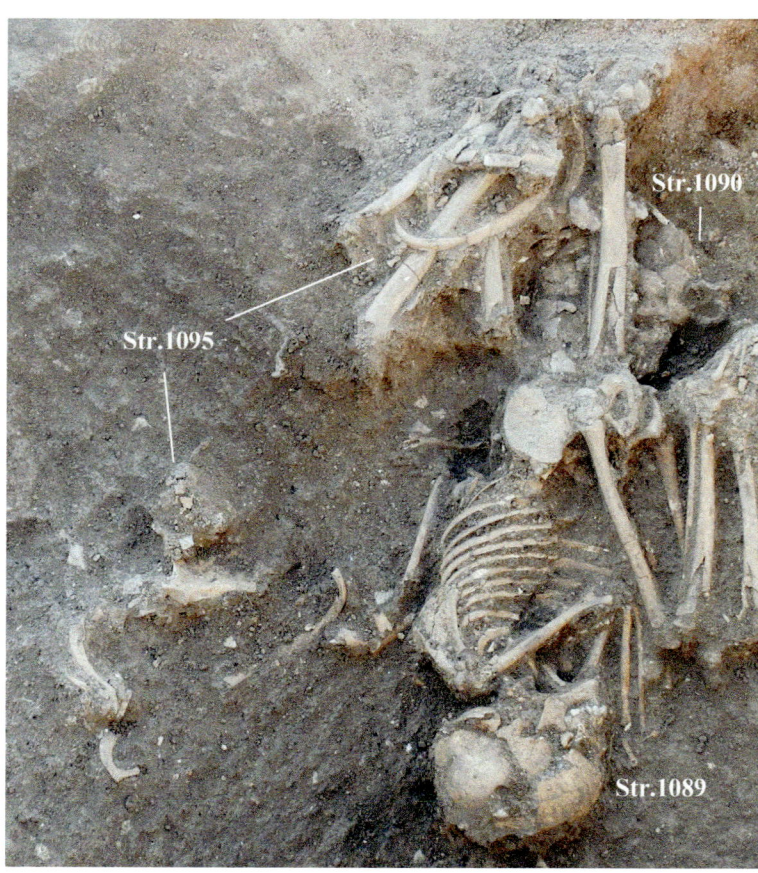

from the north

Figure 5-113. Str. 1095 Burial.

114. Str. 1096 (Figure 5-114)

Str. 1096 is a disturbed primary burial of an adult containing a set of articulated human legs discovered just east of and beneath Str. 1086 in Square E251d in Layer 5. Sex was indeterminate. The rest of the skeletal remains of this individual were completely missing, probably due to the construction of Str. 1086. From its legs it was concluded that it was an adult buried in a flexed position on its left side. There were no grave goods.

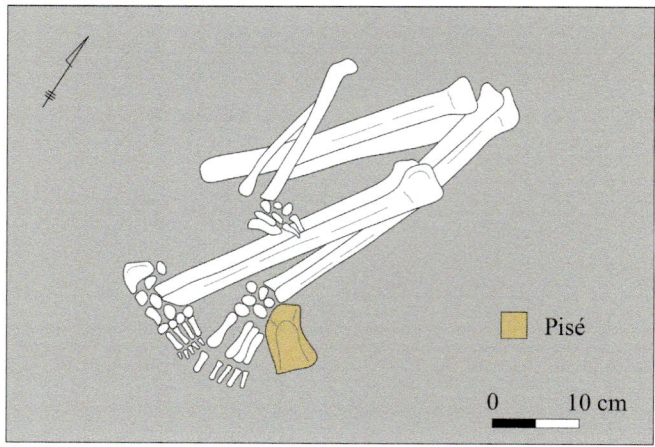

Figure 5-114a. Str. 1096 Burial.

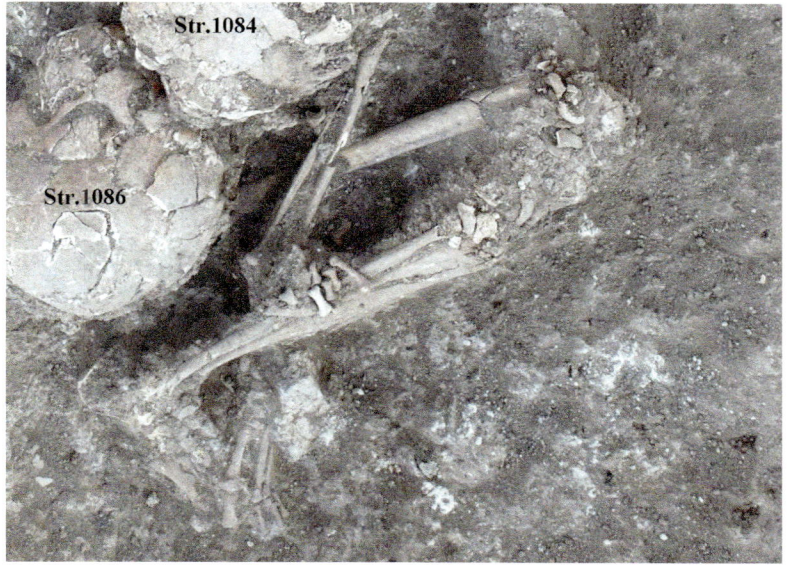

from the southeast

Figure 5-114b. Str. 1096 Burial.

115. Str. 1097 (Figure 5-115)

Str. 1097 is a primary burial of an adult, probably female, discovered with a series of graves in the southeastern part of Square E251d in Layer 5. This grave was constructed below Str. 1083. She was buried in a flexed position on her left side. The body axis direction was west-east, and the head pointed to the west and faced north. The legs were folded very tightly as if they had been tied with rope. Its right arm was bent, and the hand was placed below the head. There were no grave goods.

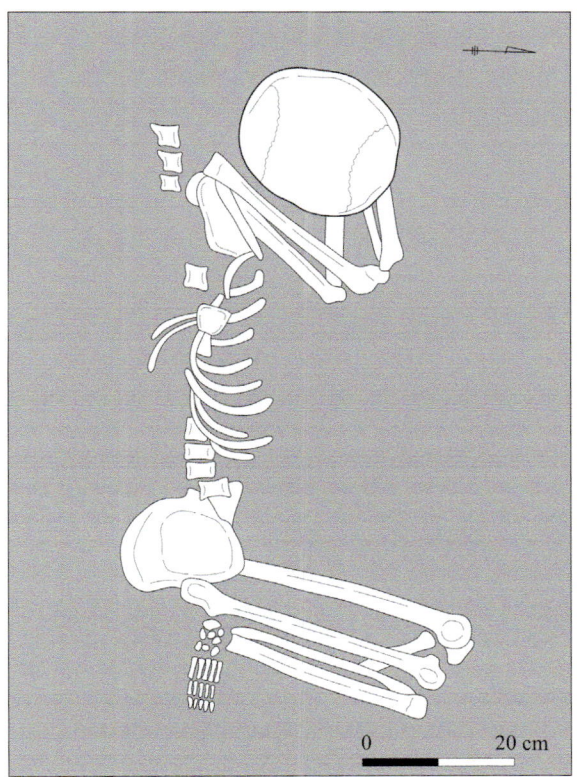

from the east

Figure 5-115. Str. 1097 Burial.

116. Str. 1098 (Figure 5-116)

Str. 1098 is a primary burial of a perinatal baby discovered between Strs. 1082 and 1083 at the eastern part of Square E251d in Layer 5. This burial was discovered partly beneath the urn burial of Str. 1073. It seems to have been buried in a flexed position on its left side. The body axis direction was west-east, and the head pointed to the west and faced north. There were no grave goods.

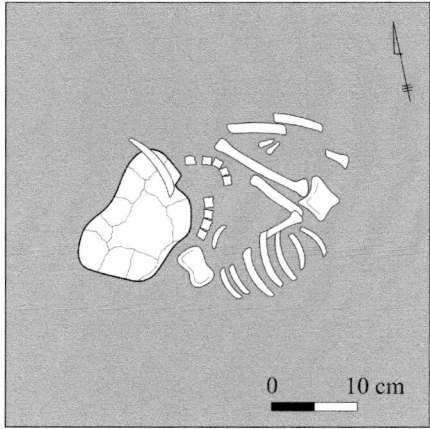

Figure 5-116. Str. 1098 Burial.

117. 1099 (Figure 5-117)

Str. 1099 is a disturbed primary burial of an adult discovered with a series of graves from the eastern part of Square E251d in Layer 5 to the west of Str. 1097. Due to the disturbed condition, sex was indeterminate. The bone deposits of this individual include the skull, teeth, femur, tibia, fibula, ribs, vertebrae, and left elbow. There were no grave goods.

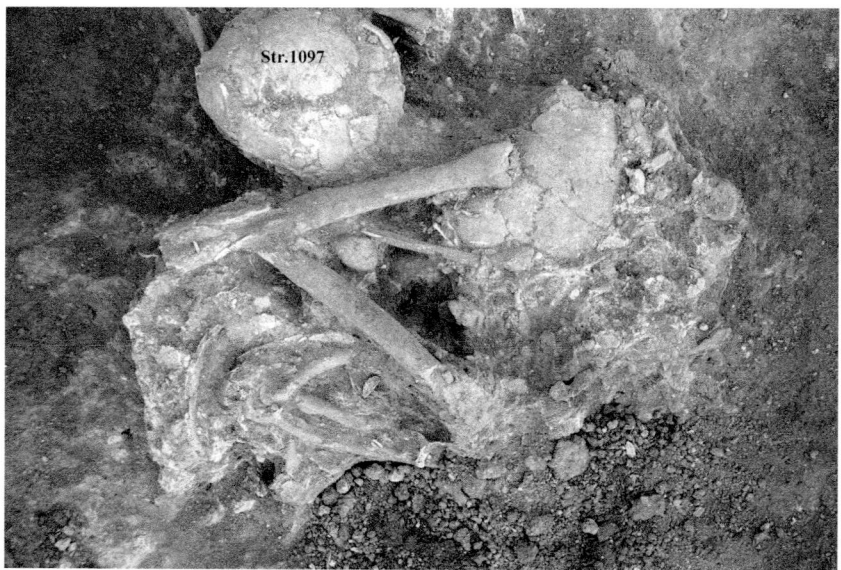

from the west

Figure 5-117. Str. 1099 Burial.

118. Concentration 1 (C1) (Figure 5-118)

C1 is a collective burial containing the remains of at least 13 individuals discovered in Square E271b in Layer 4. It measures about 1.5m from north to south and 0.8m from east to west. The human remains were fragmented and superimposed on each other. The deceased were identified mainly by their skulls, mandibles, long bones, and other fragmented bones. The deceased in this concentration were distributed in two levels: upper and lower. In the upper level, two accumulations contain the remains of at least seven individuals (Strs. 718, 719, and 720). At least six individuals were discovered in the lower level (Strs. 721, 722, 740, 741, 742, and 743). All of the burials were secondary.

No grave goods that directly accompanied the human skeletons were excavated from C1. However, a complete DFBW jar was discovered 0.4m to the south. It is highly possible that this pottery vessel were dedicated to the C1 burials.

Str. 718

Str. 718 is a secondary burial containing the remains of two individuals identified by a set of leg bones, including two femurs and two tibias, discovered in the western part of C1. They were discovered on the top of the bone heap. The pelvis and other bone parts near these legs probably belong to the same skeleton. The size of the femurs indicates that the owner was a young adult, probably male. One of the four skulls recovered under these leg bones may also belong to this skeleton. This skull was located on the top of those four skulls. The skull was lying on its right side. The head pointed to the northwest and faced southwest. The second individual is an infant, represented only by a right petrous and a developing mandibular first molar. It is obvious that these bones were removed from their original burial context and placed on the heap of human bones.

Str. 719

Str. 719 is a secondary burial containing the commingled remains of an adult and a juvenile (1–2 yrs.), discovered in the southern part of the C1. A skull, long bones, and other parts of a human skeleton were recovered. The remains of the two individuals were mixed. The adult was identified via vertebrae bones and skull fragments, whereas the juvenile was identified by a skull and some teeth. The head of the juvenile pointed to the east. In regard to the other parts of the skeleton, a twisted vertebra was the most conspicuous. If these bones are associated with the skull, the twist probably happened during the replacement of this human skeleton.

Str. 720

Str. 720 is a secondary burial containing the commingled remains of at least three individuals as evident from repetitive skeletal elements. It was discovered in the northern part of C1. A pelvis was recovered in prone position, and the vertebrae and some long bones were uncovered nearby. These bones were not connected directly to the pelvis and they were secondarily deposited. These individuals are as follows:

1.   An old adult, probably male, with a healed fracture of the left fourth metacarpal.
2.   An adult of indeterminate sex.
3.   An adult of indeterminate sex, with the light dental attrition suggesting a young age.

Str. 721

Str. 721 is a secondary burial of a 11–13-year-old subadult. It was discovered in the northern part of C1. This burial comprised a skull only, and sex was indeterminate. As no bones relating to this skull were recovered, it may have been relocated here after removal from the original context. The head pointed to the west and the skull faced upward.

Str. 722

Str. 722 is a secondary burial containing an isolated skull, probably of a middle-aged adult female, discovered just east of Str. 721. The orientation of the skull was almost the same as that of Str. 721, i.e., the head pointed to the west and the skull faced upward. It was likely removed from the original burial and relocated to C1.

Str. 740

Str. 740 is a secondary burial identified by an isolated skull, located in the central part of C1 south of Strs. 721 and 722. The orientation of this skull was different from that of Str. 721 and Str. 722. The skull seemed to stand upright and faced west. Sex was indeterminate. The remaining teeth indicate that it is a 10–12-year-old juvenile.

Str. 741

Str. 741 is a secondary burial containing another skull discovered in the skull cluster in the southwestern part of C1. Sex was indeterminate. It lay on its right side. The head pointed to the northwest and faced southwest. This skull belongs to a 5–7-year-old juvenile.

Str. 742

Str. 742 is also a secondary burial represented by an isolated skull in the cluster of skulls in C1. It was discovered just northwest of Str. 740, and both skulls had similar orientation. The skull stood upright and faced west. The skull condition and the teeth indicate that it is a 6–8-year-old juvenile.

Str. 743

Str. 743 is a secondary burial of a middle-aged adult, probably male, represented by various skeletal remains. The burial contains a skull and arms discovered in the northern part of C1. The skull stood upright, but leaned slightly to the right side. It faced northeast. The arms were placed on both sides of the skull in a V-shape. At the point of the V-shape, the mandible was discovered. Some other bones found near the skull and arms probably belong to the same person.

The skulls excavated from C1 indicate that three skulls were paired with three others (Strs. 718 and 741, Strs. 740 and 742, and Strs. 721 and 722) in that they were placed in almost the same orientation and posture, whereas three skulls (Strs. 719, 720, and 743) were laid out differently. It is possible that every pair was placed at the same time. However, the orientations and postures are different as a whole. Therefore, not all three paired-skulls would have been placed at the same time.

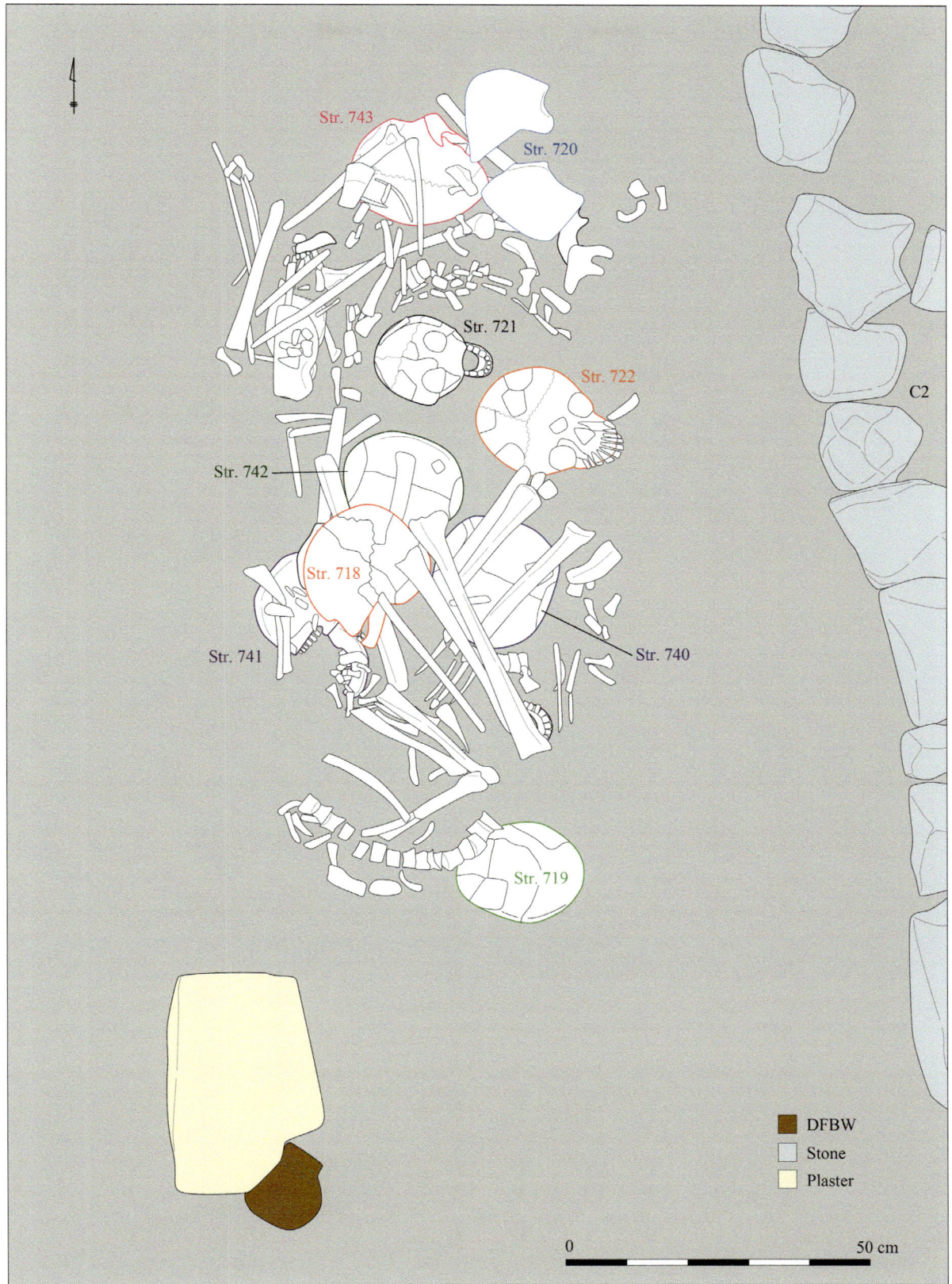

Figure 5-118a. Concentration 1 Burial.

A   *from the west*

B   *from the east*

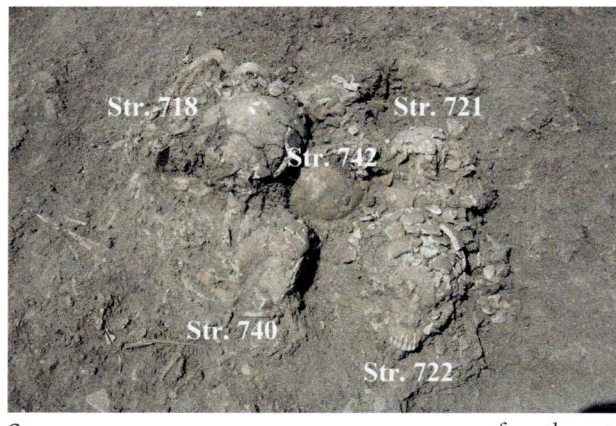

C   *from the east*

D   *from the south*

E   *from the north*

Figure 5-118b. Concentration 1 Burial: A. General view; B. Strs. 740, 741 and 742;
C. Strs. 718, 721, 722, 740 and 742; D. Str. 719; E. Str. 720.

F   *from the north*

G   *from the south*

0   2 cm

Figure 5-118c. Concentration 1 Burial: F. Str. 743; G. DFBW jar. Grave goods: DFBW jar.

119. Concentration 2 (C2) (Figure 5-119)

C2 is a collective burial containing the remains of six individuals discovered in Square E271b in Layer 4. C2 was surrounded by limestone rows (courses) from the eastern and western sides. A smaller stone row was also constructed on the northern side and one big stone on the southern side. Thus, C2 is surrounded by a stone structure in three directions, forming a square-shaped burial field opened partly from the south. The concentration measures about 1.5m from north to south and 0.7m from east to west. The human remains in C2 were discovered in two levels. Two individuals were buried in the top concentration (Strs. 711 and 714). Their level was slightly higher than the stone row beneath them, which suggests that they were buried on the top after C2 was filled with dead bodies or sealed. However, their remains are superimposed with the other individual remains buried beneath them.

In the lower level, four individuals were buried in and around the stone structure (Strs. 731, 732, 737, and 751). All of the identified burials were primary or disturbed primary burials, except one secondary burial. A big limestone ball was discovered beneath the western row of the stone square.

Str. 711

Str. 711 is a disturbed primary burial of a 15–18-year-old subadult discovered in the southern part of C2. It was buried on the top of the stone structure entrance in the southern side. Its remains were placed over and superimposed with the lower limbs of Str. 732. Sex was indeterminate. However, it was buried in a flexed position on its right side. Most of the skeletal remains were recovered, but the cranium was missing and only part of the mandible could be seen. The body axis direction was east-west. No grave goods were uncovered.

Str. 714

Str. 714 is a disturbed primary burial of an adult, probably male, discovered to the northeast of the Str. 711 burial. This individual was poorly preserved. It was buried in a flexed position on its left side. The body axis direction was southwest-northeast. Notably, it lacked the cranium, but the mandible was almost completely preserved. Two sea conch beads were discovered between the upper ribs and the lower jaw, and they seem to have been a necklace worn by the dead.

Str. 731

Str. 731 is a primary burial discovered in the northeastern part of C2. The skeleton had massive femurs and tibias, and all the other characteristics of the skeleton indicate that it was a young adult, probably male. His upper body was buried in a flexed position on his left side. His legs were folded on the left side. His head seems to have been buried with a big bend from the beginning, and the skull seems to have slid down below his right shoulder. Though his right arm was folded, his left arm remained stretched. The body axis direction was east-west, and his head pointed to the east and faced downward. An agate bead was discovered near his right hand.

Str. 732

Str. 732 is a primary burial of a 12–15-year-old subadult discovered in the southern part of C2 to the south of Str. 731. It was discovered at the entrance of the burial stone square. The upper part, from the head to the pelvis, was inside the stone square, but the portion from the pelvis to the feet was outside. Sex was indeterminate. Its upper body was buried in a prone position, with folded legs on the right side. The right arm was bent and the right hand was placed under the chest. The left arm was similarly bent, but the left wrist was bent downward. The body axis direction was north-south, and the head pointed to the north and faced downward. Curiously enough, a toe was placed on the skull of Str. 737. It is also notable that the deceased was holding a cattle metacarpal bone by the right hand and the chin.

Str. 737

Str. 737 is a secondary burial of a middle adult, probably male, represented mainly by a skull and legs. It was discovered outside of the C2 stone square at the foot of Str. 732. The skull was placed upright and faced west. The legs were found just south of the skull. It is obvious that the skull and legs were removed from the original context and relocated here.

Str. 751

Str. 751 is a disturbed primary burial of a 5–6-year-old juvenile represented by a skull, pelvis, jaw, and a few other bones, discovered under the eastern side of the stone square. These bones were found in the same place but separated. It was difficult to understand its original burial posture, but it seemed that the body axis direction was east-west. The most remarkable findings relating to this individual are a stamp seal and two beads. The stamp seal, which was found near the hip bone, is a tiny 'boot-shaped' limestone stamp having a 'straight and parallel lines' design for impression. This tiny 'boot-shaped' type is not very popular among the stamp seals of the Kerkh Neolithic material, but a few specimens have been discovered. This finding indicates that these tiny seals might have been the property of small children. A small blue stone bead and a serpentinite bead were found near the jaw and probably belonged to this juvenile.

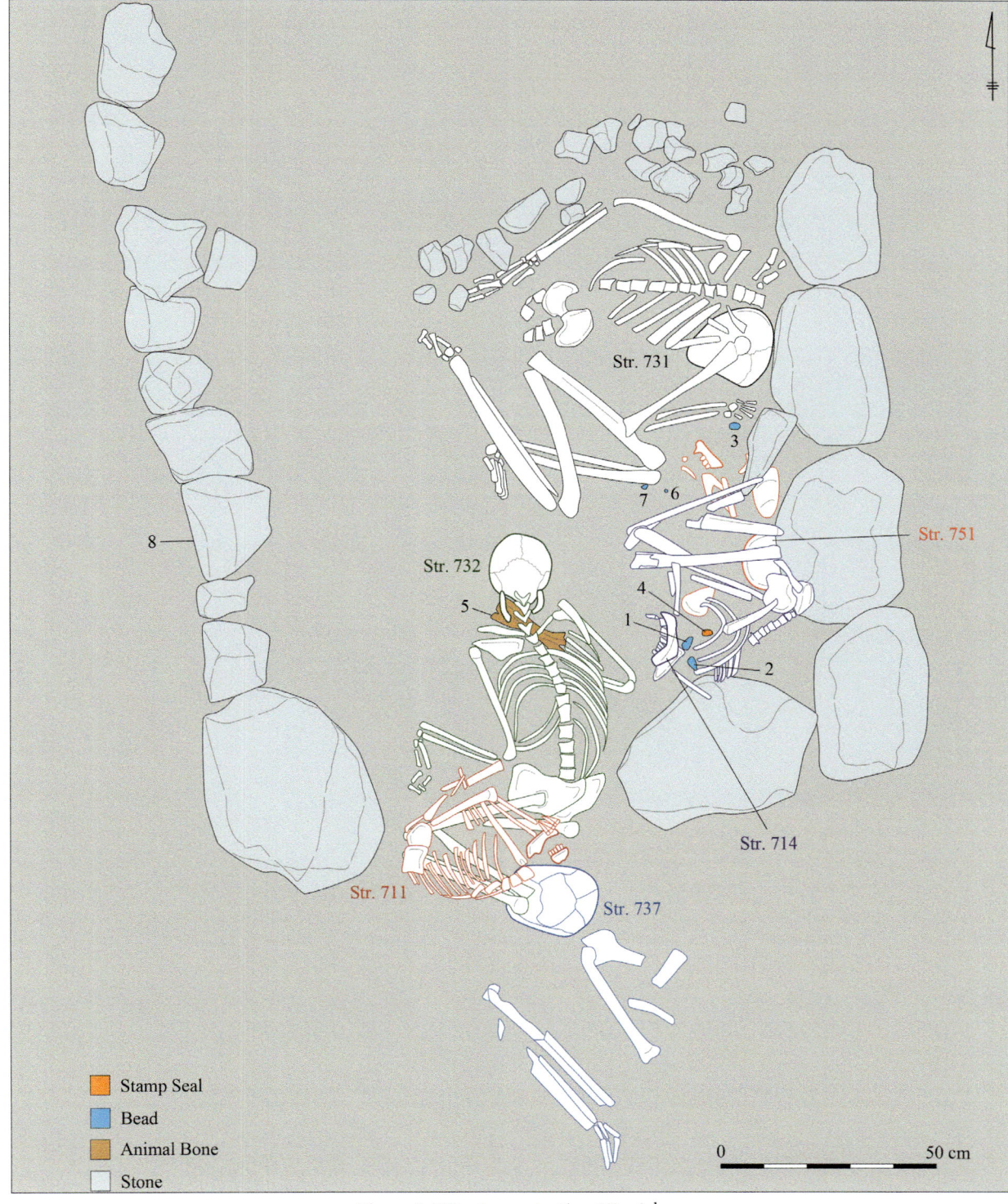

Figure 5-119a. Concentration 2 Burial.

211

A   *from the west*

B   *from the north*

C   *from the northeast*

Figure 5-119b. Concentration 2 Burial: A. General view; B. Str. 711; C. Str. 714.

D *from the west*

E *from the west*

F *from the west* G *from the north*

Figure 5-119c. Concentration 2 Burial: D. Str. 731; E. Strs. 732 and 737; F. Str. 751; G. Limestone ball.

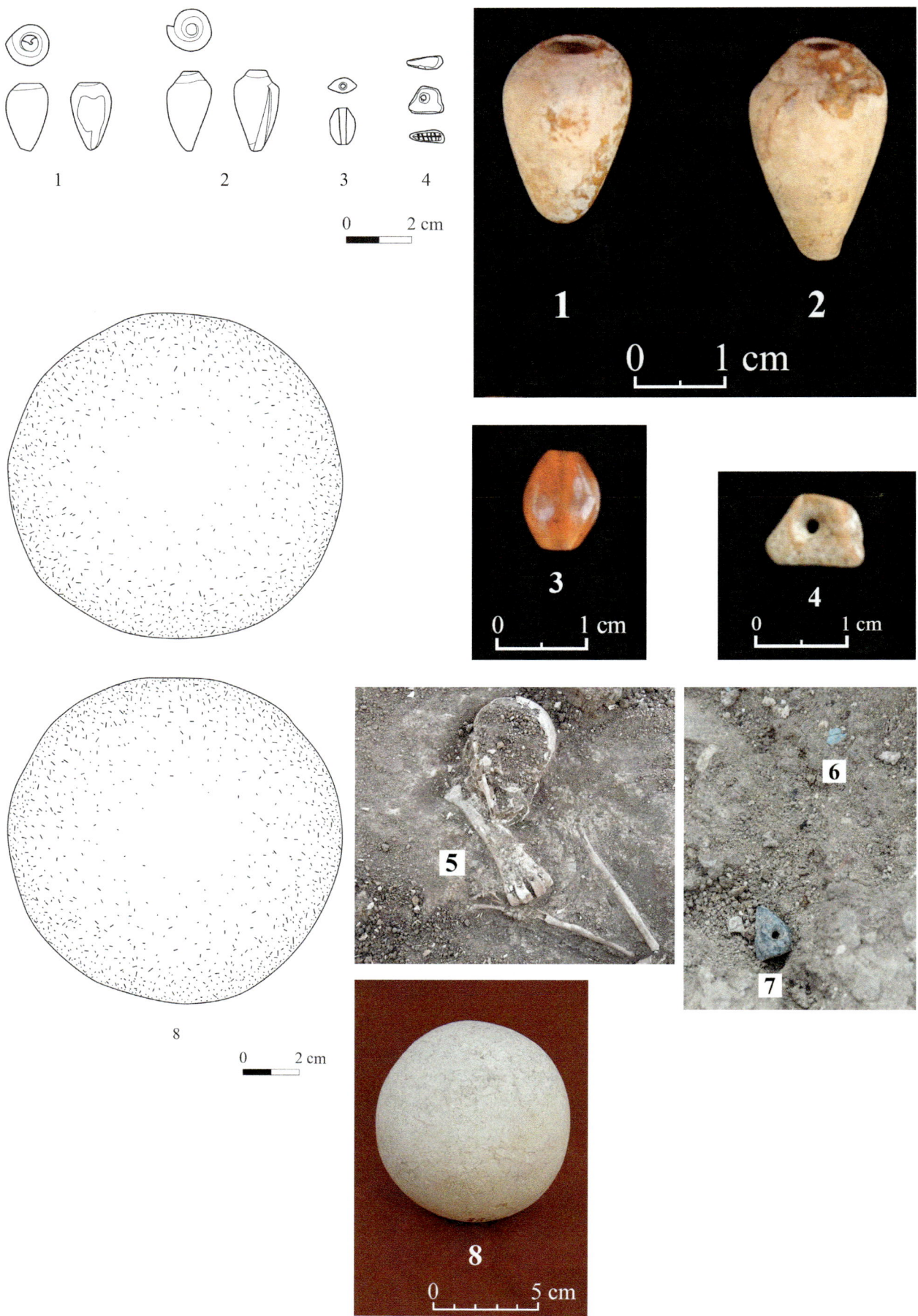

Figure 5-119d. Concentration 2 Grave goods: 1–2. Shell beads (Str. 714); 3. Stone bead (Str. 731); 4. Stamp seal (Str. 751); 5. Cattle metacarpal (Str. 732); 6–7. Stone beads (Str. 751); 8. Limestone ball.

120. Concentration 3 (C3) (Figure 5-120)

C3 is a typical burial pit used for secondary burials discovered at the northern edge of Square E271b in Layer 5. At least 21 individuals were discovered from this pit, measuring 0.8-1.0m in diameter and c. 0.3m in depth. Many human bones were piled up within the pit. This concentration was excavated in two different seasons. The southern half of C3 was first excavated in the 2008 season. After that, the northern half was excavated two years later in 2010.

In 2008, in the southern half, at least 12 individuals were uncovered (9 adults, 2 juveniles, and one infant), and six of them had been cremated (Str. 831 1–6). At least nine human skulls were discovered in the 2010 season. Most of the human remains were disarticulated and fragmented. Skulls, mandibles, long bones, and other fragmented human skeletons can be clearly seen. A stone bead and a clay disc were found between the piled bones. Though the pit size is small, it seems that these deceased were removed from their original grave and part of their skeletons were relocated and buried in this heap.

Str. 831

Str. 831 was the uppermost accumulation found in the southern part of the pit. In the spot, some remains of at least six individuals were uncovered, and notably all of them had been cremated. Thus, we named them Str. 831 (1–6). This accumulation contains one juvenile and five adults (two probably females, one probably male, and two of indeterminate sex). Notably, some of these human bones were heavily cremated.

Strs. 847, 848 and 850

Strs. 847, 848, and 850 are secondary burials represented mainly by skulls, mandibles, and long bones, which were discovered under the skeletons of Str. 831 in the southern part of the pit. In this accumulation, remains of at least five individuals were discovered. They were four adults and one infant. One of the adults was an elderly probably male. Of the other three adults, two were probably male and one was probably female.

Str. 854

Str. 854 is a secondary burial of a 5–7-year-old juvenile discovered below Str. 850. A small cylindrical serpentinite bead was discovered near the skull.

Excavation in the 2010 season revealed at least nine individuals in the northern half of C3. All of them were secondary burials, including one cremated skeleton. They were represented by skulls, mandibles, and long bones. The remaining human bones were also piled in a complex way. Some of the human bones in the piled deposits were thoroughly cremated, and sometimes the human bones had turned into a bluish white color because of the high cremation temperature. People piled the cremated and un-cremated bones within the pit. Such a comingled situation could be observed not only in C3 but also in C4.

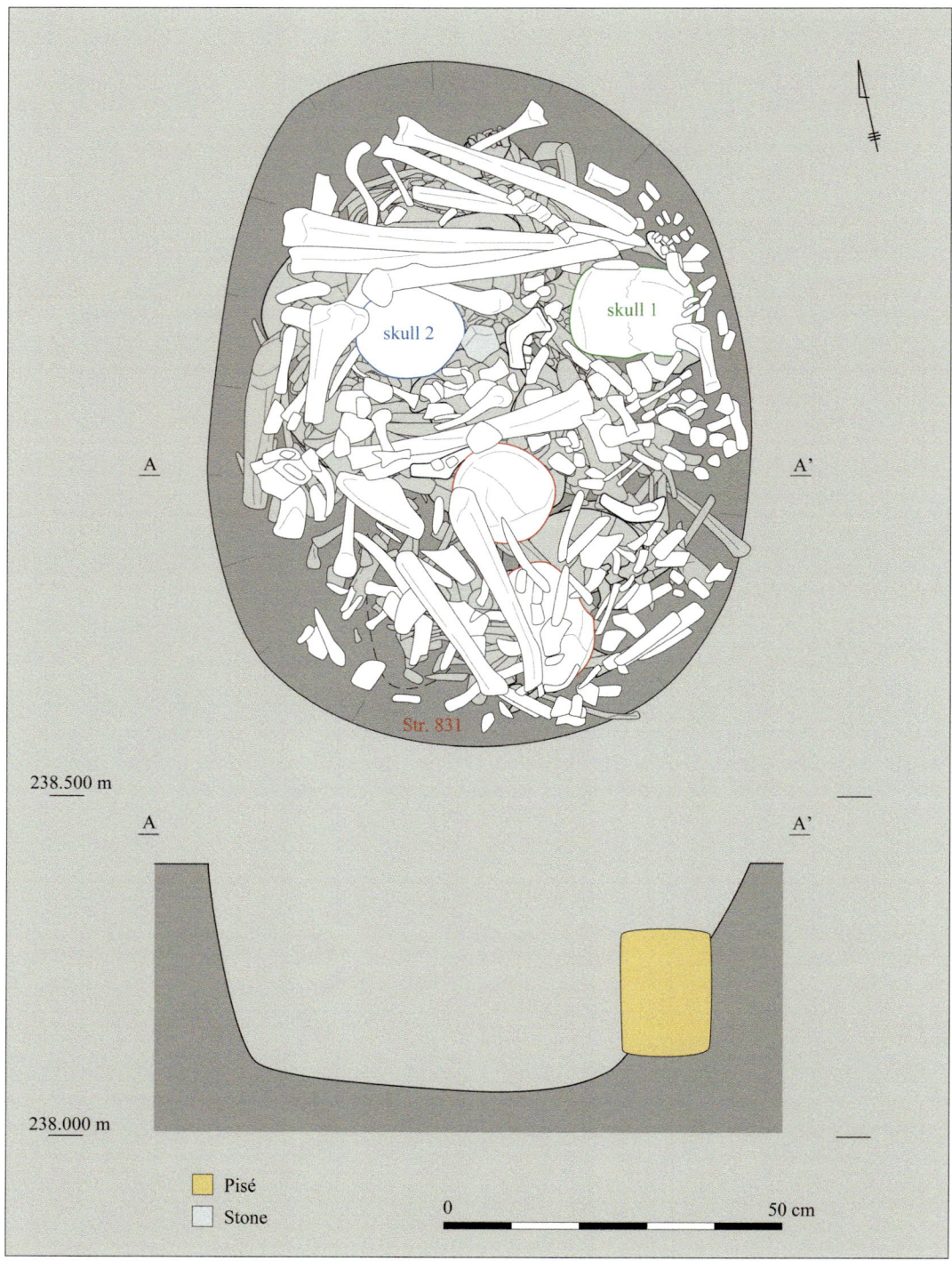

238.500 m

238.000 m

Pisé
Stone

0   50 cm

A

Figure 5-120a. Concentration 3 Burial: A. Uppermost level and the elevation of the pit.

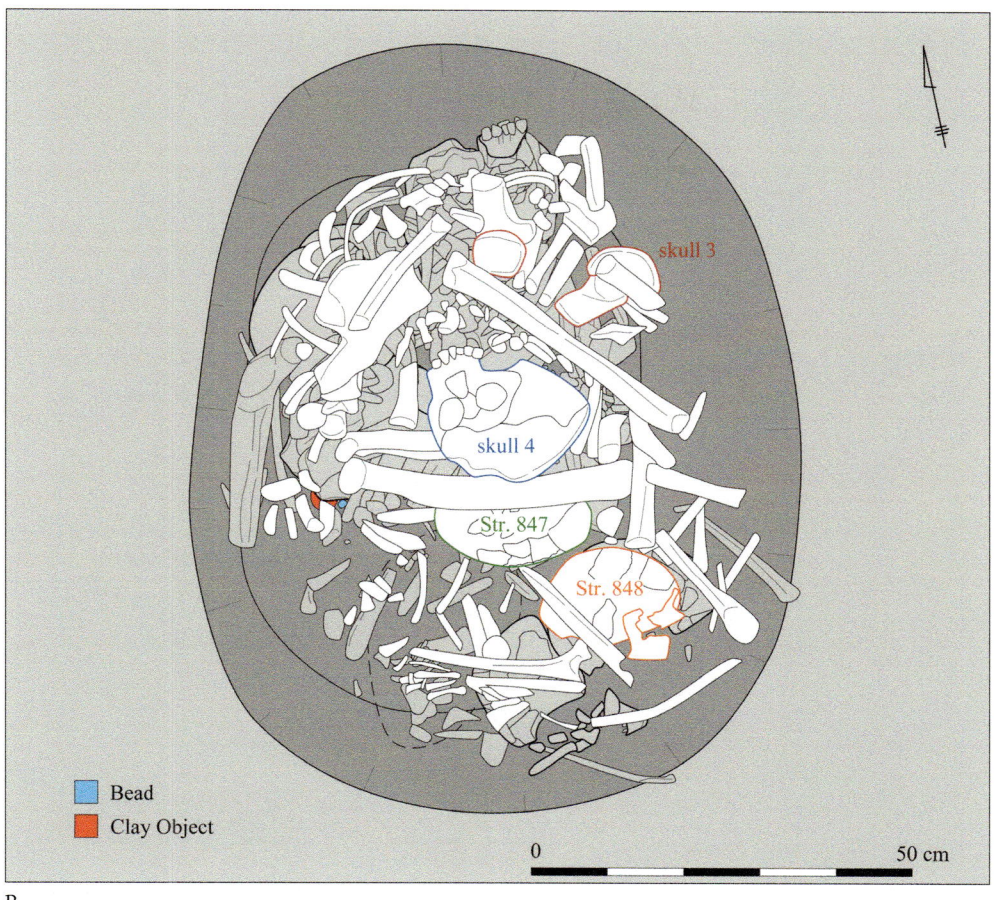

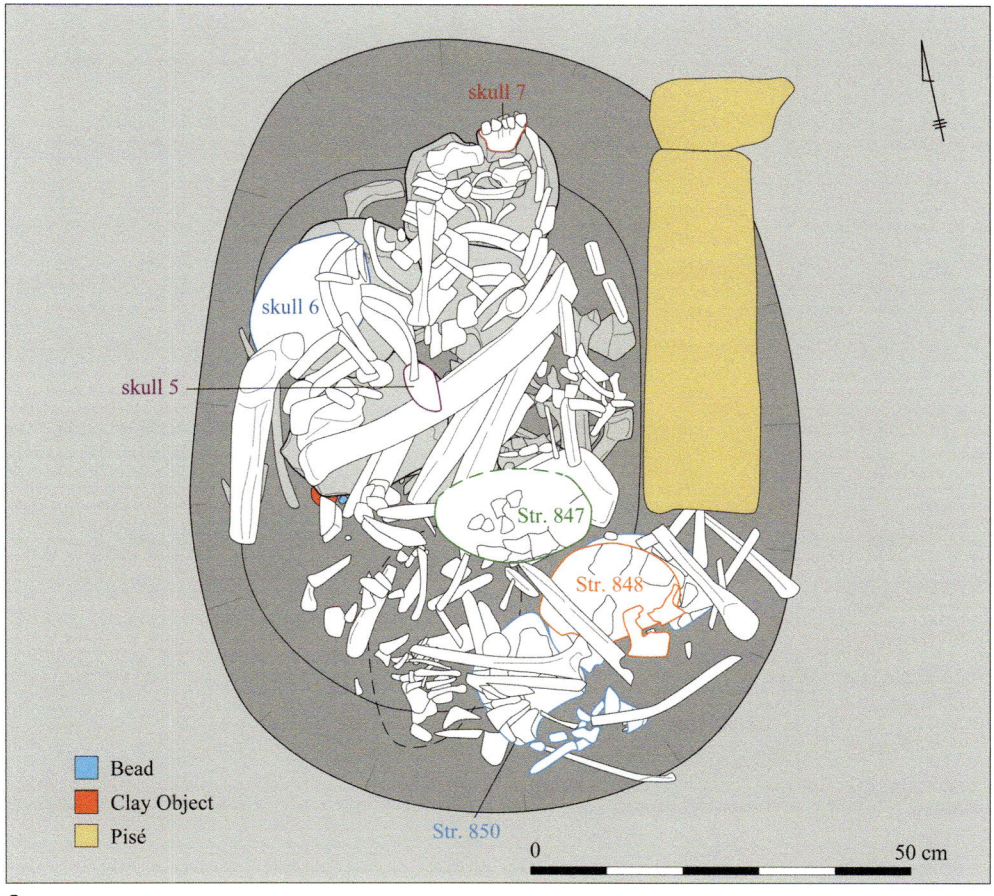

Figure 5-120b. Concentration 3 Burial: B. Upper level; C. Middle level.

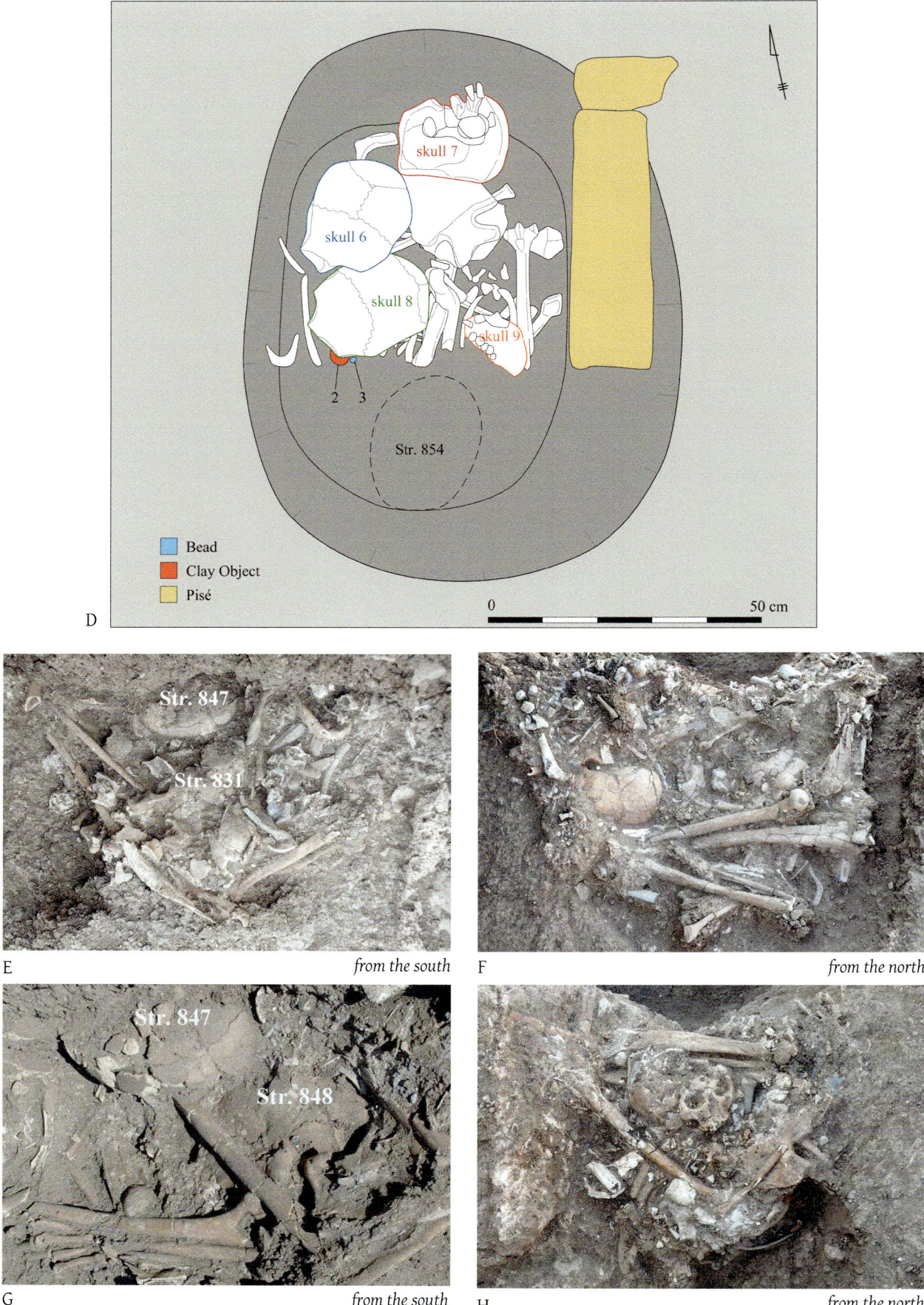

Figure 5-120c. Concentration 3 Burial; D. Lower level; E. Uppermost level of southern half of the pit (Strs. 831 and 847);
F. Uppermost level of northern half of the pit; G. Upper level of southern half of the pit (Strs. 847 and 848);
H. Upper level of northern half of the pit.

Figure 5-120d. Concentration 3 Burial: I. Middle level of southern half of the pit (Strs. 848 and 850);
J. Middle level of northern half of the pit; K. Lower level of southern half of the pit (Str. 854);
L. Lower level of northern half of the pit. Grave goods:
1. Stone bead (Str. 854); 2. Clay disc; 3. Stone bead.

121. Concentration 4 (C4) (Figure 5-121)

Concentration 4 (C4) is a collective burial containing the remains of at least seven individuals. It was discovered immediately southeast of C3 at the northeastern corner of Square E271b in Layer 5. C4 measures 0.9m from east to west and 0.7m from north to south. The condition and contents of the skeletal concentration are very similar to those of C3. Therefore, this concentration must have been a burial pit, but the pit itself was not clearly defined. A pile of human bones extending 0.8m in diameter and 0.3m in thickness was the feature discovered here. Though the skulls and long bones were the most remarkable remnants of this pile, other skeletal material were also piled in the bone heap. A mixture of cremated and un-cremated skeletons was recovered from the pit. A structure number was given for each skull here. The directions of the skulls and jaws uncovered in C4 were various and there was no regulation. Each skull or jaw was usually accompanied with long bones.

Concerning grave goods, a short cylindrical blue bead, a flat agate bead, a conch shell bead, and an unfinished gabbro stamp seal were discovered near the skull of Str. 845. A cowrie shell bead was discovered near a mandible of Str. 846. All of these grave goods were found in the middle level of C4.

Str. 833

Str. 833 is a secondary burial of a young adult, probably male, discovered on the top of the heap of bones in C4. A skull and folded long bones were placed in the southeastern part of the concentration.

Str. 839

Str. 839 is a cremation burial containing two individuals discovered in the southwestern part of C4. Str. 839(1) is a skull fragment of a middle-aged adult, probably male. Str. 839(2) is another skull fragment of an adult, probably male, discovered in the same place. Both burials represent cremated skulls with other cremated human bones piled alongside. The comingled cremated and un-cremated human bones were visible in the lower parts of the concentration.

Str. 845

Str. 845 is another skull and long bones, relocated and placed at the western end of C4. It is a secondary burial of an adult, probably male.

Str. 846

Str. 846 is a jaw and some long bones discovered beneath the skull of Str. 833. It is a secondary burial of a young adult, probably female.

Str. 853

Str. 853 is a jaw and some long bones recovered from the southeastern part of C4. The bones were cremated, and the owner was an adult, probably female.

Str. 859

Str. 859 is a jaw and some long bones discovered at the bottom of the pit. It is a secondary burial of an old adult, probably female.

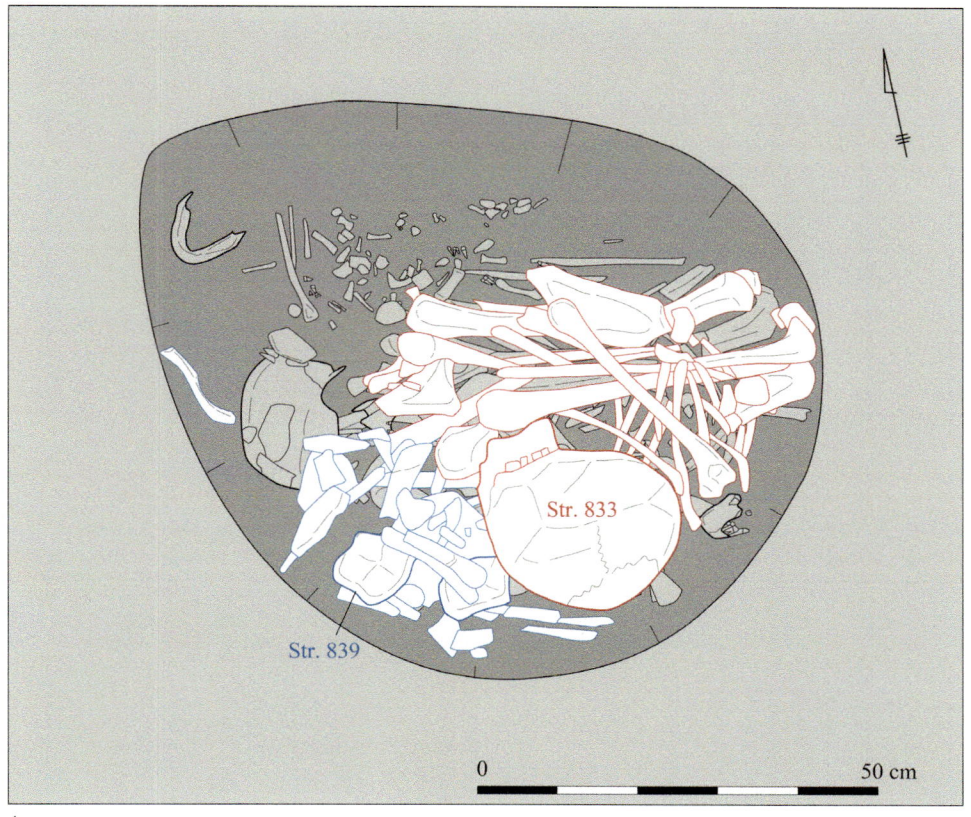

A

B

Figure 5-121a. Concentration 4 Burial: A. Upper level (Strs. 833 and 839);
B. Middle level (Strs. 845, 846 and 853).

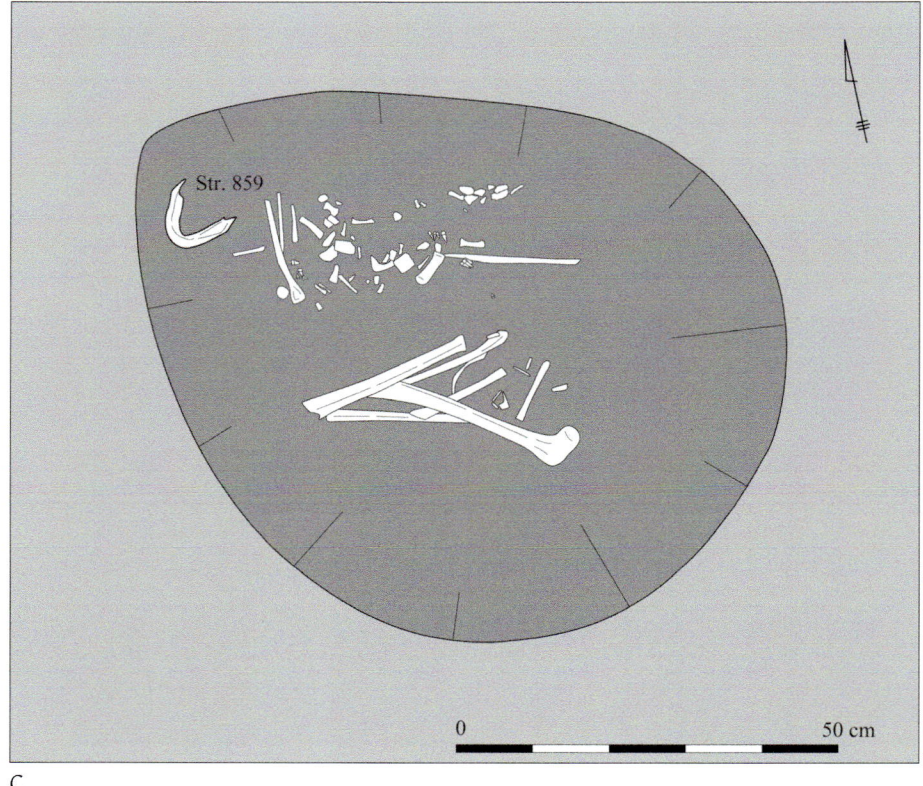

C

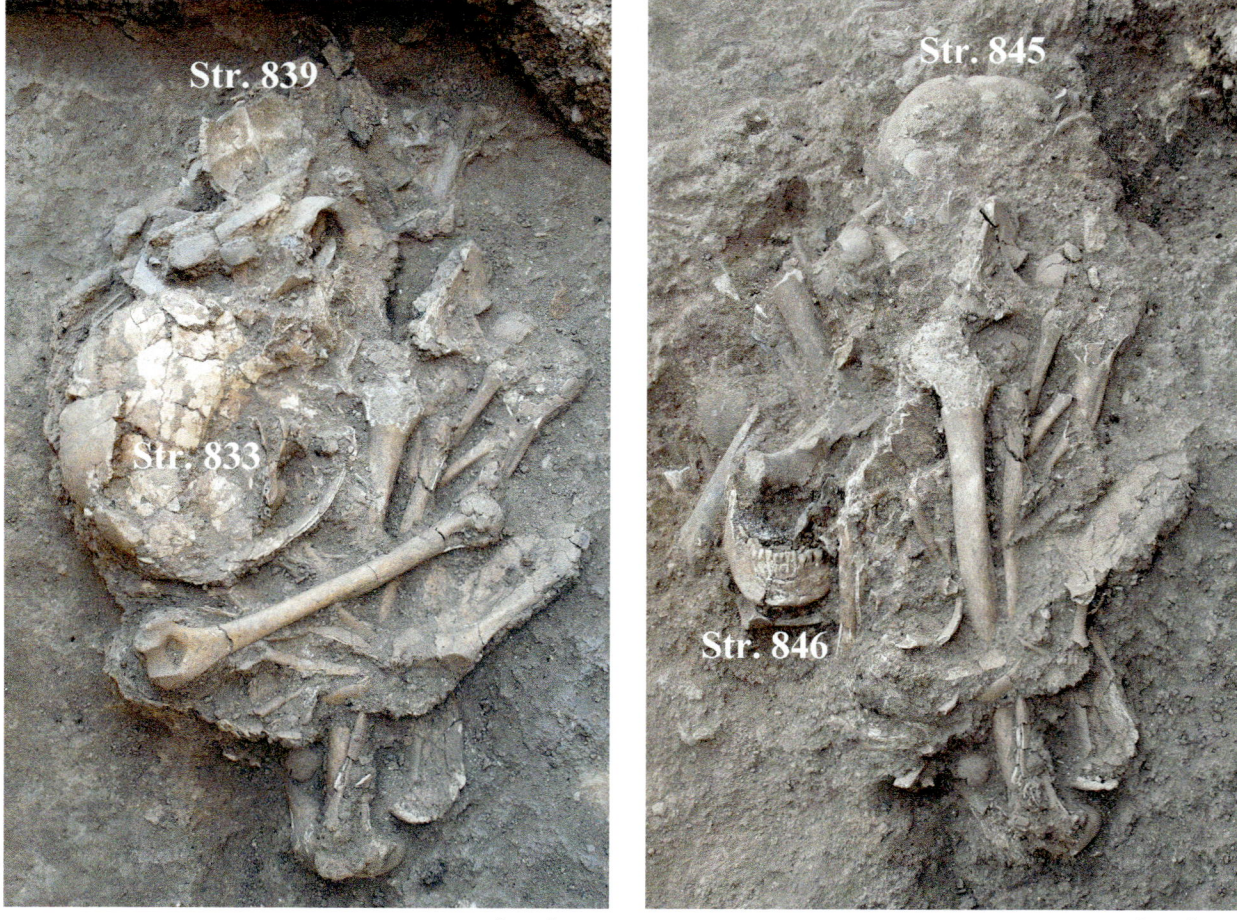

D *from the east* E *from the east*

Figure 5-121b. Concentration 4 Burial: C. Lower level (Str. 859);
D. Strs. 833 and 839; E. Strs. 845 and 846.

Figure 5-121c. Concentration 4 Burial: F. Str. 845; G. Str. 853; H. Str. 859; I. Stamp seal and beads;
J. Shell bead. Grave goods: 1, 4. Stone beads; 2. Unfinished stone stamp seal; 3, 5. Shell beads.

122. Concentration 5 (C5) (Figure 5-122)

Concentration 5 (C5) is a crematorium pit containing cremated human skeletons of at least five individuals. It was discovered in the northern part of Square E271b in Layer 6.

The characteristic of this concentration is very different from previously mentioned concentrations. The pit shape is oval and measures 1.05 x 1.25m in diameter and 0.4m in depth. The pit is surrounded by a pisé wall measuring c. 0.2m wide. The pisé wall was also burnt. The walls and bottom of the pit were thoroughly burnt and had turned an orange color. The inside of the pit was full of highly burnt soil, and carbonized pieces of wood were found at the bottom of the pit. The pit characteristics and the thoroughly burnt human bones uncovered inside suggest that C5 was used as a crematorium pit for cremating human remains. Some of these skeletons had turned white and the others had turned black due to cremation. The cremated individuals were mainly identified by five skulls uncovered inside C5. The skulls of Strs. 855, 856, 857, and 858 were not as well-preserved as the Str. 842 skull, but had maintained their basic shape. Also, many other parts of the skeletons were dispersed within the pit, and it was not easy to identify their relationship with each skull within the pit.

No grave goods were discovered with the human bones. However, two complete DFBW vessels were discovered above the pit, at the level of the mouth of the pit. It is almost certain that this crematorium pit was filled with soil after the cremation, and the two pieces of pottery were then placed on the crematorium pit. One is a short-necked and squat type DFBW jar, measuring 17cm in diameter and 10.5cm in height. It has a thin wall and highly burnished surface. The other pottery piece is a short straight-necked DFBW jar, measuring 11cm in both diameter and height. Surprisingly, a stamp seal was discovered from this short-necked jar. It is a bullet type seal, having a cross-hatched design. The seal was made of bone, but the surface color had turned gray due to burning. Anyhow, retrieval of such complete and sophisticated pottery is unusual from the excavation of dwellings, and it is probable that these two pottery jars and the stamp seal were dedicated to the dead who were cremated in this pit.

Str. 842

Str. 842 is a cremated skeleton of a middle-aged adult, probably male. An astonishingly well-preserved cremated skull was discovered in the southeastern corner of the pit. The skull was placed on his left side and faced south. Though the remains had been thoroughly cremated, the skull had not fallen into pieces but had remained whole. This condition indicates that the skull was cremated and left untouched in the pit. Some remnants of cremated body parts like fingers, ribs, and long bones were discovered around the skull and ashes as well. It is difficult to infer if these bones belong to the same individual or not.

Str. 855

Str. 855 is also a cremated skeleton of a young adult, probably male. It was discovered in the southwestern part of the crematorium pit. It was a cremated skull but not as well preserved as Str. 842. It seems that the high temperature caused its fragmentation, but it maintained its basic shape, and the mandible can be seen.

Str. 856

Str. 856 is also a cremated skull of an adult, probably female, discovered in the western part of the cremation pit to the north of Str. 855. The upper half of the skull remained, but it was fragmented and heavily burnt.

Str. 857

Str. 857 is also a cremated skeleton of a young adult, probably male, discovered in the northeastern part of the crematorium pit. It was heavily fragmented and included a burnt skull. Moreover, due to the high cremation temperature, both surfaces of the skull fragments had turned into a whitish color.

Str. 858

Str. 858 is also a cremated skeleton of a subadult, probably female, discovered in the northwestern part of the cremation pit. It was also heavily fragmented and had a burnt skull.

Figure 5-122a. Concentration 5 Burial: A. Upper level; B. Cremated cranium (Str. 842).

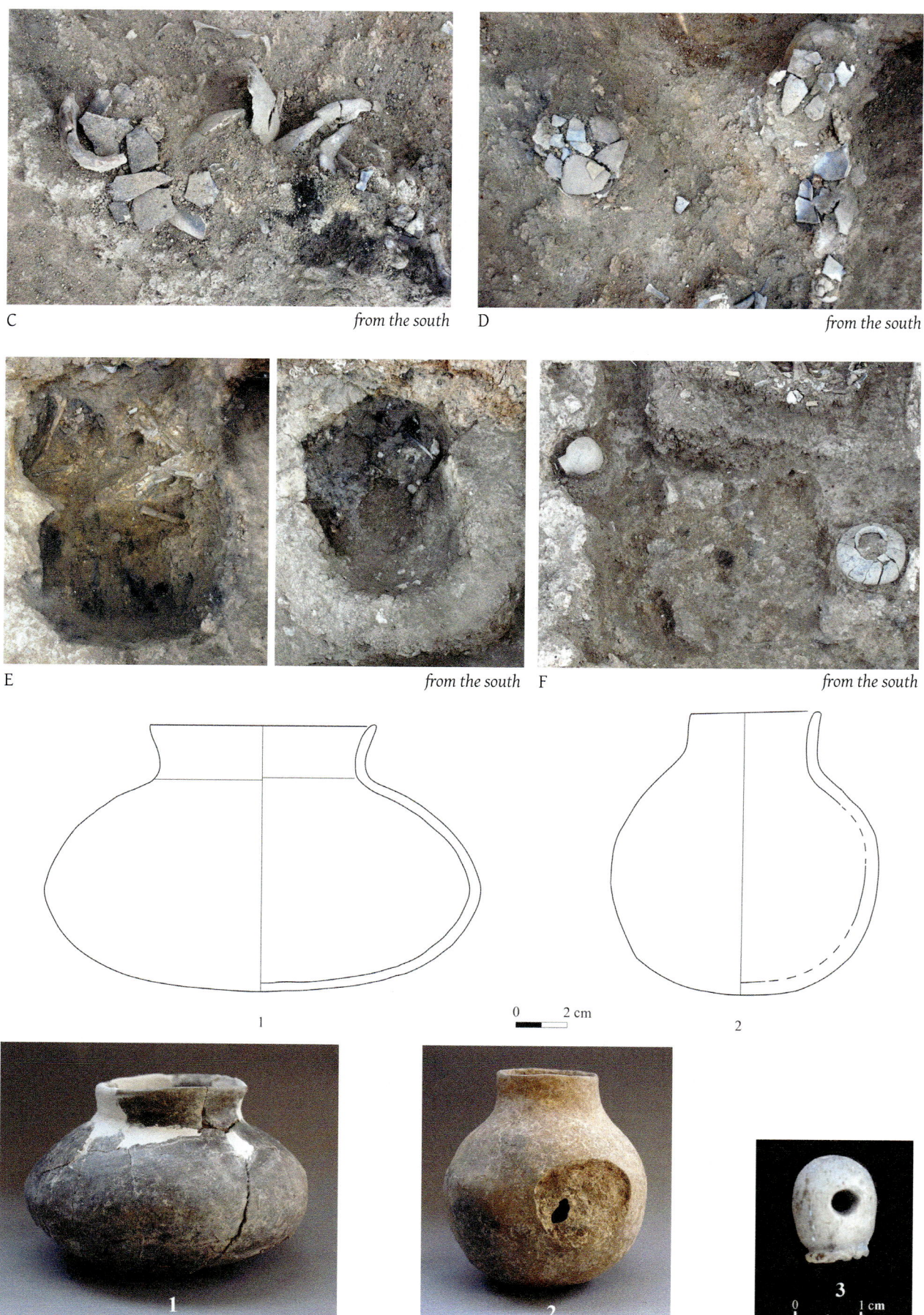

C   *from the south*   D   *from the south*

E   *from the south*   F   *from the south*

1   0   2 cm   2

1   2   3

Figure 5-122b. Concentration 5 Burial: C. Cremated cranial bones (Str. 855); D. Cremated cranial bones (Strs. 856 and 857); E. Lower level and bottom of the pit; F. DFBW jars on the top of the pit. Grave goods: 1–2. DFBW jars; 3. Bone stamp seal.

123. Concentration 6 (C6) (Figure 5-123)

Concentration 6 (C6) is another crematorium pit discovered approximately 5m south of C5. It is located near the eastern side of Square E271d in Layer 6. Remains of seven individuals were identified in the pit, and they had all been cremated. Interestingly, the characteristics of the C6 pit suggest that it was used for cremation twice. Two different floor levels were observed within the pit. The older pit was dug in the western part of the crematorium pit. It has a circular shape, measuring 0.6m in diameter and 0.3m in depth.

The upper pit was expanded to the east and wider. It covered and superimposed the old lower pit. The upper pit has an oval shape, measuring 1.0 x 0.8m in diameter and 0.2m in depth. Many long bones were found along the southwestern wall of the upper pit, and belong to other identified individuals. Four skulls were discovered in the lower pit. All of the human bones from the crematorium pit, including the skulls, had been thoroughly cremated and had turned white and black in color. The wall and bottom of the crematorium pit were heavily burnt. Mud plaster remained on a part of the wall in the upper pit.

This crematorium pit had been filled with soil after cremation. A short row of small stones and a large volume of carbonized wheat were discovered at the level just above the upper pit. It is possible that the stone row was a facility accompanying this cremation pit and the wheat was dedicated to the dead. One small-necked DFBW jar was discovered at the southeastern edge of the lower pit. It measures 9.6cm in diameter and 8.3cm in height. It was almost complete. Further, two grains of carbonized emmer wheat were found in the jar. It is likely that the jar and the wheat inside were dedicated to the dead before cremation.

Str. 865

Str. 865 represents two cremated individuals discovered in the northwestern part of the crematorium pit. This burial includes a cremated skull and remains of at least two adults, probably both female.

Str. 866

Str. 866 is a cremated adult discovered in the northwestern part of the crematorium pit. Sex was indeterminate. A portion of the cremated skull was discovered beneath the skull of Str. 865.

Str. 867

Str. 867 represents cremated individuals discovered in the southwestern part of the crematorium pit. This burial includes commingled skeletons of at least two juveniles. However, their sex was indeterminate. One of them was represented by a cremated skull.

Str. 868

Str. 868 represents cremated individuals discovered in the southern part of crematorium pit. They include commingled cremated skeletons of at least two juveniles. However, their sex was indeterminate.

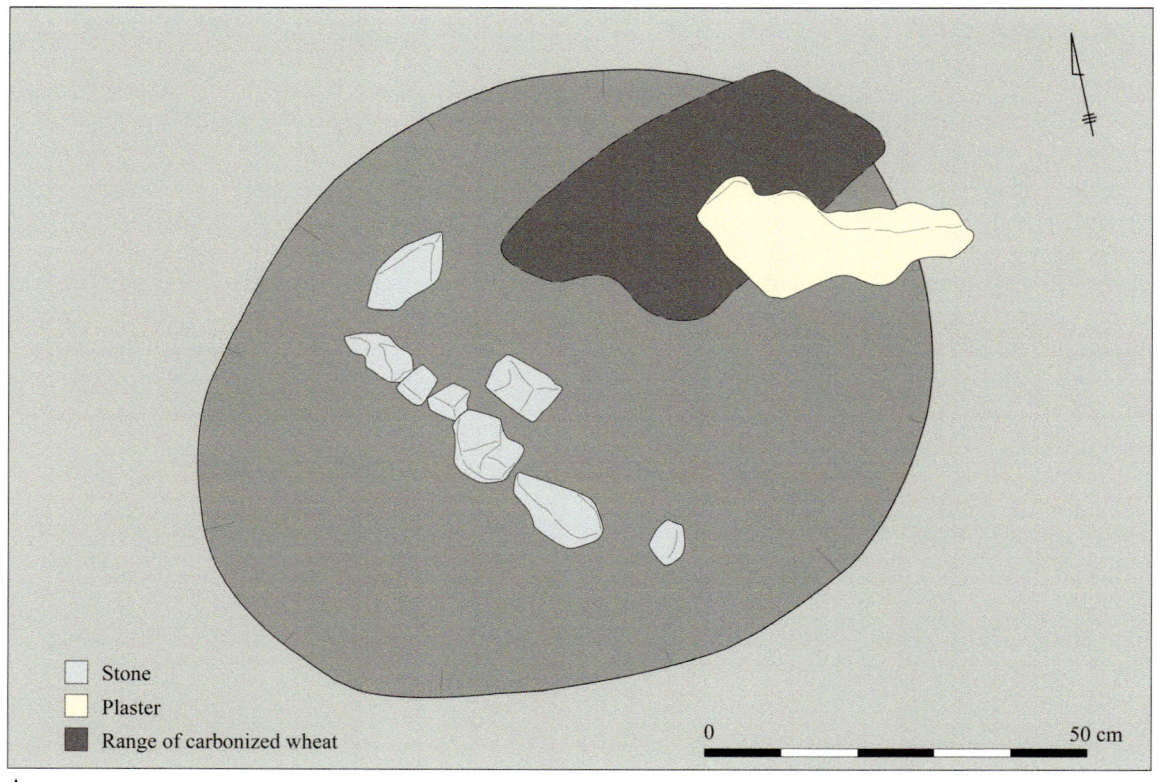

A

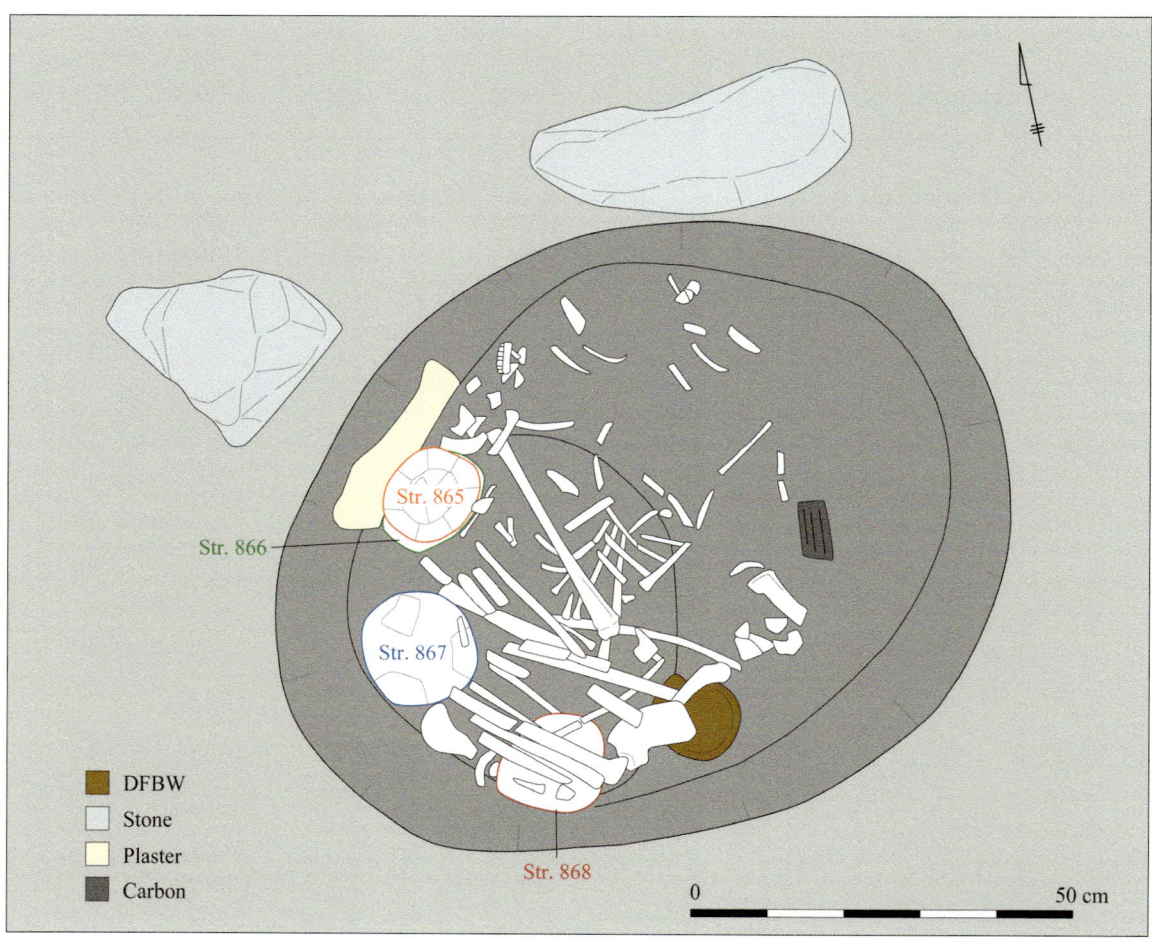

B

Figure 5-123a. Concentration 6 Burial: A. Just above the upper pit; B. Upper and lower pits.

C   *from the south*

D   *from the west*

E   *from the south*

F   *from the south*

G   *from the west*

Figure 5-123b. Concentration 6 Burial: C. General view; D. Upper pit; E. Plaster and cranium bones (Str. 865);
F. Strs. 866, 867 and 868; G. Bottom of the lower pit.

H *from the south*   I *from the west*

Figure 5-123c. Concentration 6 Burial: H. Mass of carbonized wheat just above the upper pit;
I. DFBW jar at the lower pit. Grave good: DFBW jar.

124. Concentration 7 (C7) (Figure 5-124)

Concentration 7 (C7) is two collective burials found in each of the two rooms of the building structure (Str. 916) of Layer 7 in Square E271a, b. Str. 916 is believed to have been a habitation building during the Layer 7 era, but it is presumed that the building was used as a graveyard after the residence was abandoned. In this building, two collective burials (C7) were created during the following Layer 6 era. Of the two collective burials, the one found in the eastern room is designated as C7-1, and the other found in the western room is designated C7-2.

Concentration C7-1

C7-1 contains the human skeletons of at least four individuals. Though most of the skeletons were severely disturbed, all individuals seem to be primary burials. This concentration was limited by a 2.4m long course of limestone at the southern end and a 1m long course on the eastern side. These limestone courses were the foundation of the eastern room of the Structure 916 building. Therefore, this collective burial was formed near the southern side of the eastern room of Str. 916. Three of the four individuals (Strs. 861, 862, and 863) were piled up and superimposed on each other in the southern part, whereas Str. 860 was buried separately further to the north.

Str. 860

Str. 860 is a heavily disturbed primary burial of an adult represented by the bones of the left upper limb and six teeth (linear enamel hypoplasia was present on three teeth), but sex was indeterminate. The arm was articulated, comprising the humerus, radius, ulna, and hand, and all parts were severely bent. This arm seemed to be a remnant of a primary burial, while all other skeletal parts had been removed. It is not sure why only the arm part was left in situ in this way.

The most astonishing finding about this arm was the three stamp seals that overlapped in the palm of the hand. All of them were sophisticated bone seals, but their shapes and designs were different. In addition to these three seals, a stone stamp seal was also discovered beside the ulna. It was a boot-shaped seal with a 'straight and parallel lines' impression design. This stone seal was a good specimen, probably made of gabbro. Besides the four stamp seals, 13 beads and one miniature stone vessel were discovered around this arm. The shape and material of the beads varied. There were four butterfly-shaped serpentinite beads (one of them was severely burnt), two trapezoid limestone beads, one oval quartz bead, one burnt bone bead, one dentalium bead, and four large cowrie beads.

The miniature stone vessel had a lamp-like handle, measuring 6.3cm long and 4.2cm wide. Reddish alabaster-like stone was used as material. Some of these objects were located near the pelvis of Str. 863, and there is a possibility that they were the burial goods for Str. 863. However, the level and condition of these objects suggested that they were an assortment of grave goods for the same person. In this case, there is a strong possibility that all of them belonged to Str. 860.

Str. 861

Str. 861 is a disturbed primary burial of a young adult, probably female, discovered on the top of three piled up burials in the southern part of C7. Sex was indeterminate. The remnant long bones indicate that it was buried in a flexed position on its left side. The body axis direction was indeterminate. The skull was buried on its left side and faced east, but it seems to have been bent at this angle. A coarse pottery bowl was placed on its shoulder.

Str. 862

Str. 862 is a disturbed primary burial of a young adult, probably female. It was the westernmost of these three burials. It was buried in a flexed position on its right side. The body axis direction was east-west, and the head pointed to the east and faced north. Interestingly enough, the left mandible of a large animal, probably cattle, was placed on the flexed legs. Below the legs, a complete DFBW necked jar was discovered. It is 8.5cm in diameter and 11cm in height. It has a narrow, long neck and ball-like body. This kind of shape is rare among the jars of the Rouj 2c period.

About 20cm west of Str. 862, a complete Amuq-type flint point was discovered. There is a possibility that this was also a burial good dedicated to this accumulation.

Str. 863

Str. 863 is a primary burial of a middle-aged adult, probably female. She was discovered just below Str. 861. She was buried in a prone position, and her legs were tightly folded under the pelvis. Her body axis direction was east-west, and her head was pointed to the east and faced north. Her arms seemed to be folded across her chest. One flat black stone bead, probably made of gabbro, was discovered near her chin.

Concentration C7-2

C7-2 is a collective burial containing at least nine individuals excavated from the western room of the Str. 916 building. The human bone heap measures 1.5m × 1.2m. This collective burial consists of a commingled deposit of six individuals (Str. 932) and three primary burials (Strs. 984, 985, and 988). Human skeletons were found to be in an overlapping and disturbed condition, except for Str. 988, which was discovered from the eastern side at a distance from the other human skeletons. Therefore, it is probable that many of the previously buried human bones were disturbed due to the build-up of new human remains one after another.

Str. 932

A commingled deposit containing cremated, unburnt remains and dismembered human bones was discovered in the northwestern part of the collective burial. Almost all of the human skeletons were disarticulated and disturbed. At least six individuals were identified. Three of them had been cremated: one adult (probably male), a subadult, and a juvenile. The skeletons of a fetus and two juveniles, one of whom was 1–2 years old, were not burnt. It is probable that some skeletons were burnt when Str. 916 was burnt in a fire.

Str. 984

Str. 984 is a disturbed primary burial of a young adult, probably male, discovered in the southwestern corner of Str. 916. The skull faced upward. The vertebrae were not attached to the skull. A completely bent but articulated right arm, from the clavicle through the scapula, humerus, and forearm to the hand, was discovered north of the skull. An articulated leg also appeared above the arm. Therefore, it is supposed that it was disturbed post mortem. It is difficult to speculate on the body axis direction. A small flat stone bead, a flint point, and a flint blade were discovered near his leg.

Str. 985

Str. 985 is a disturbed primary burial of a 6–7-year-old juvenile that was discovered just south of Str. 984 along the southern wall at the southwestern corner of Str. 916. It seems to have been buried in a flexed position on its right side. The body axis direction was west-east. The skull pointed to the west, and it faced south. An animal (probably cattle) scapula was placed on its left shoulder.

Str. 988

Str. 988 is a primary burial of a middle-aged adult female discovered in the eastern side of C7-2. She was buried in a flexed position on her right side. Her body axis direction was north-south, but her head was bent and pointed to the west. Her face looked downward. Her legs were strictly flexed in front of her abdomen, and both hands were crossed between her legs.

At her feet, a bone spatula, a flat stone bead, and a shell were placed together. They seemed to be funeral gifts. Another cylindrical stone bead was found near her legs. A goat horn was also discovered above her legs. An obsidian blade and flint blade were found nearby.

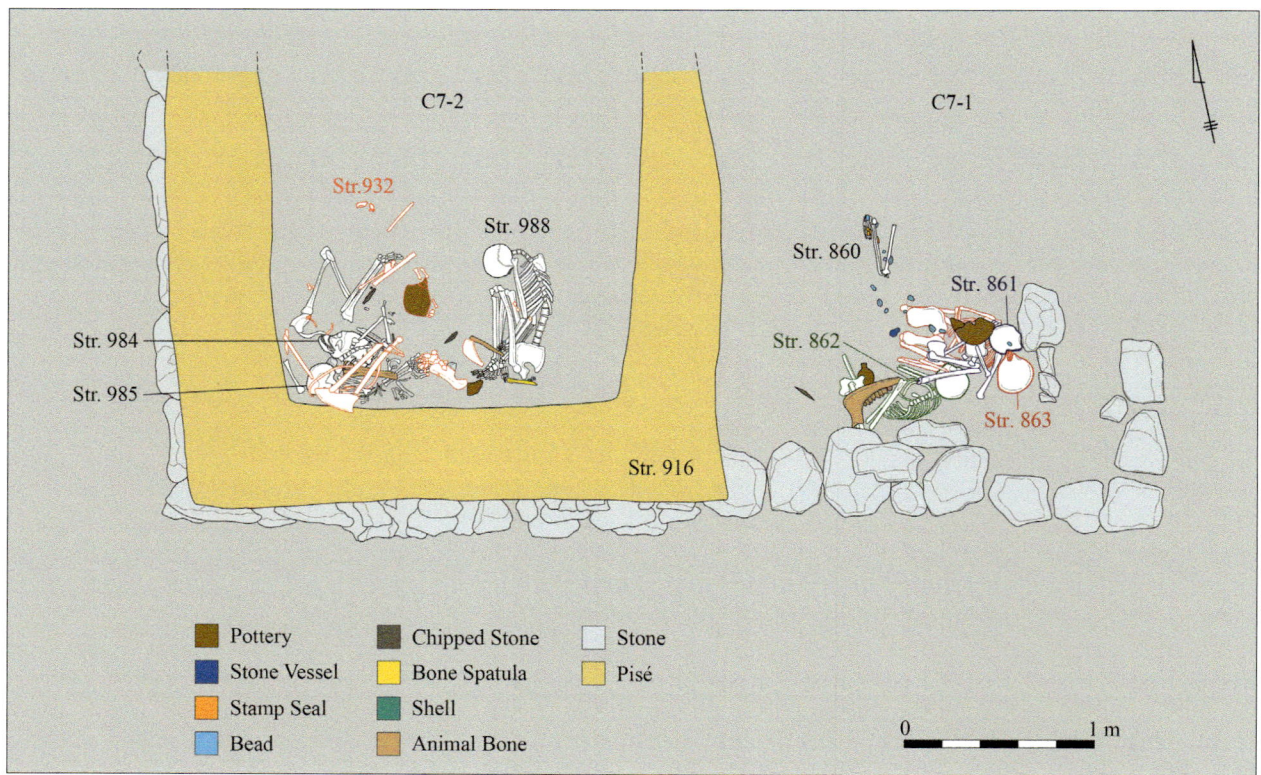

A

Figure 5-124a. Concentration 7 Burial: A. General view.

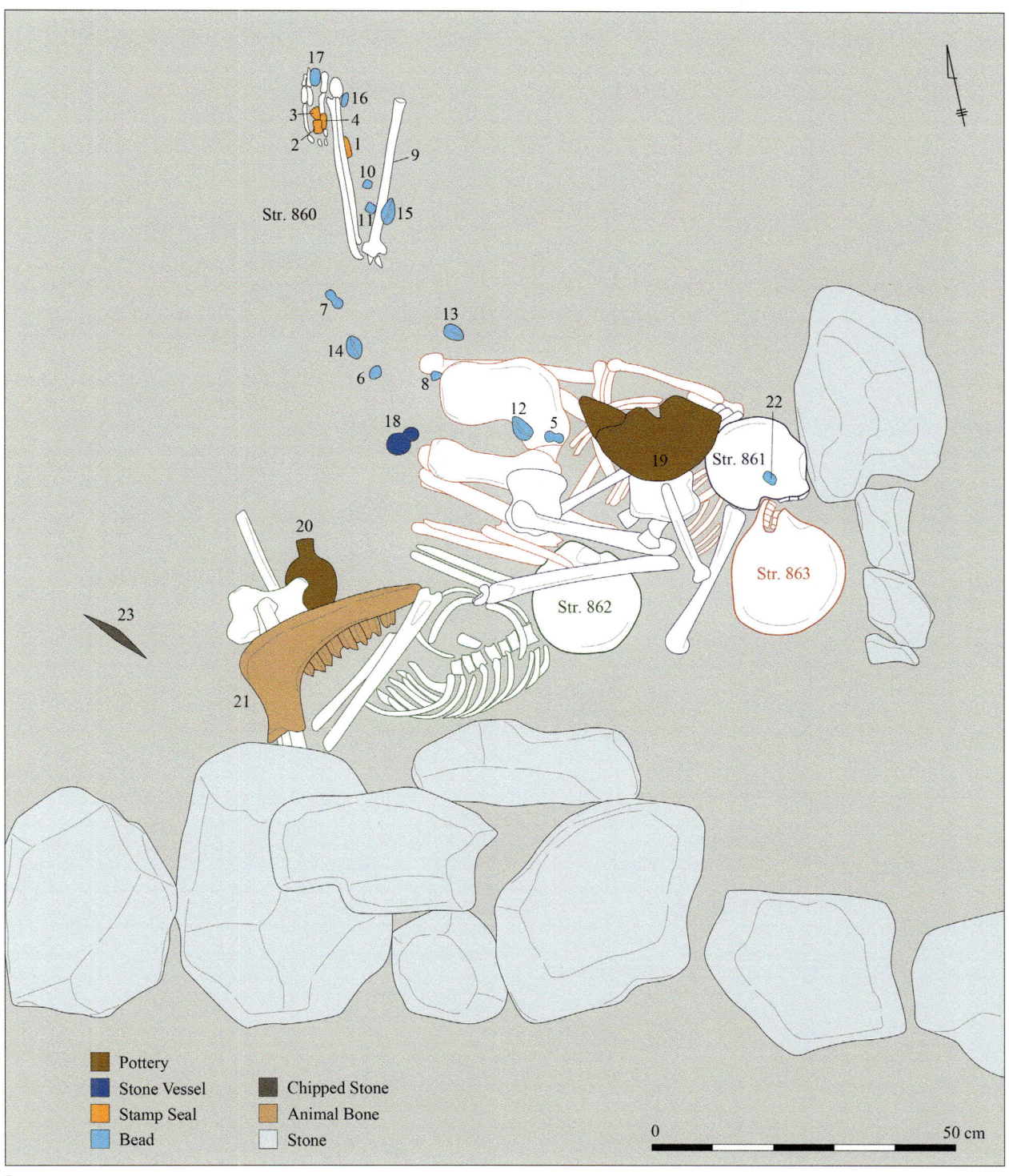

Figure 5-124b. Concentration 7 Burial: B. Strs. 860, 861, 862 and 863 (C7-1).

C

D

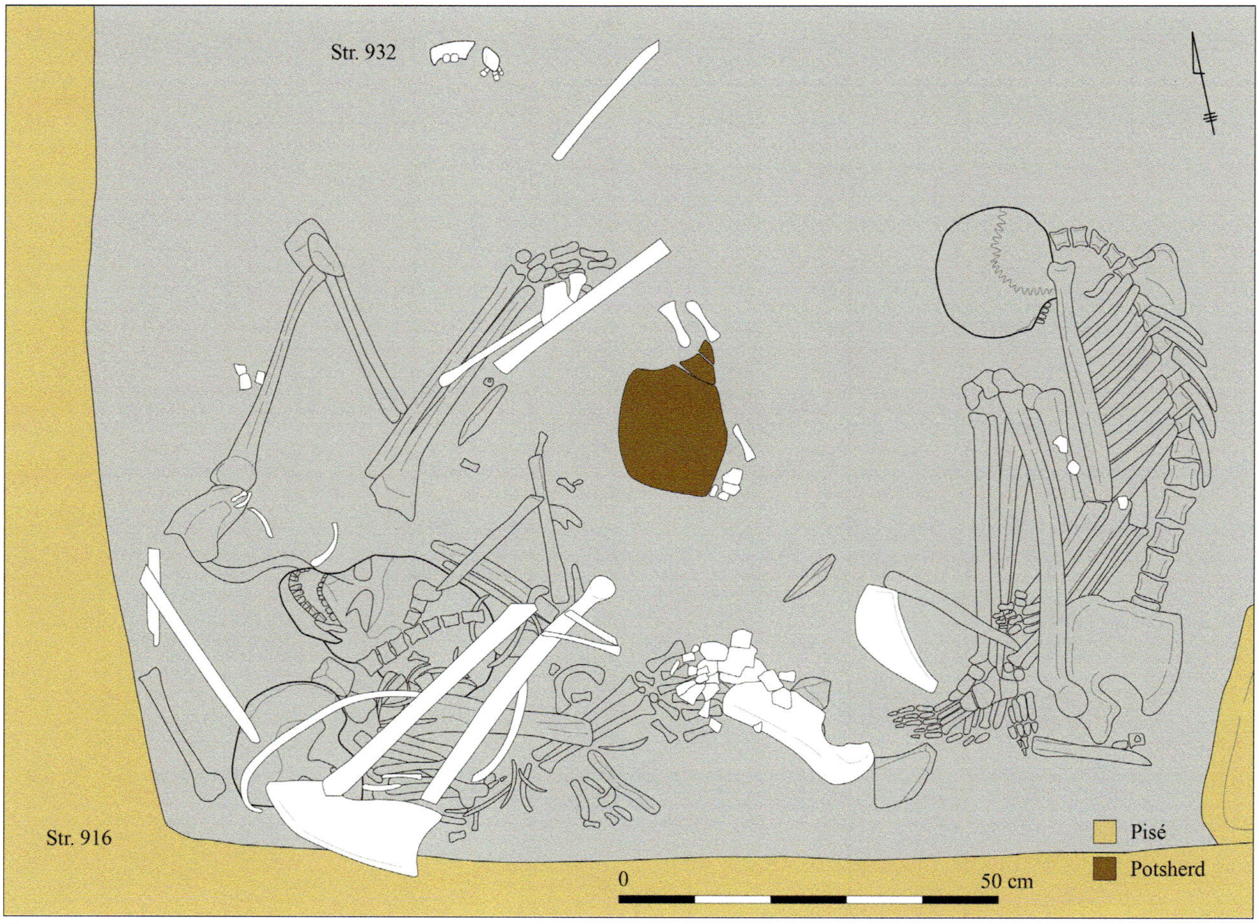

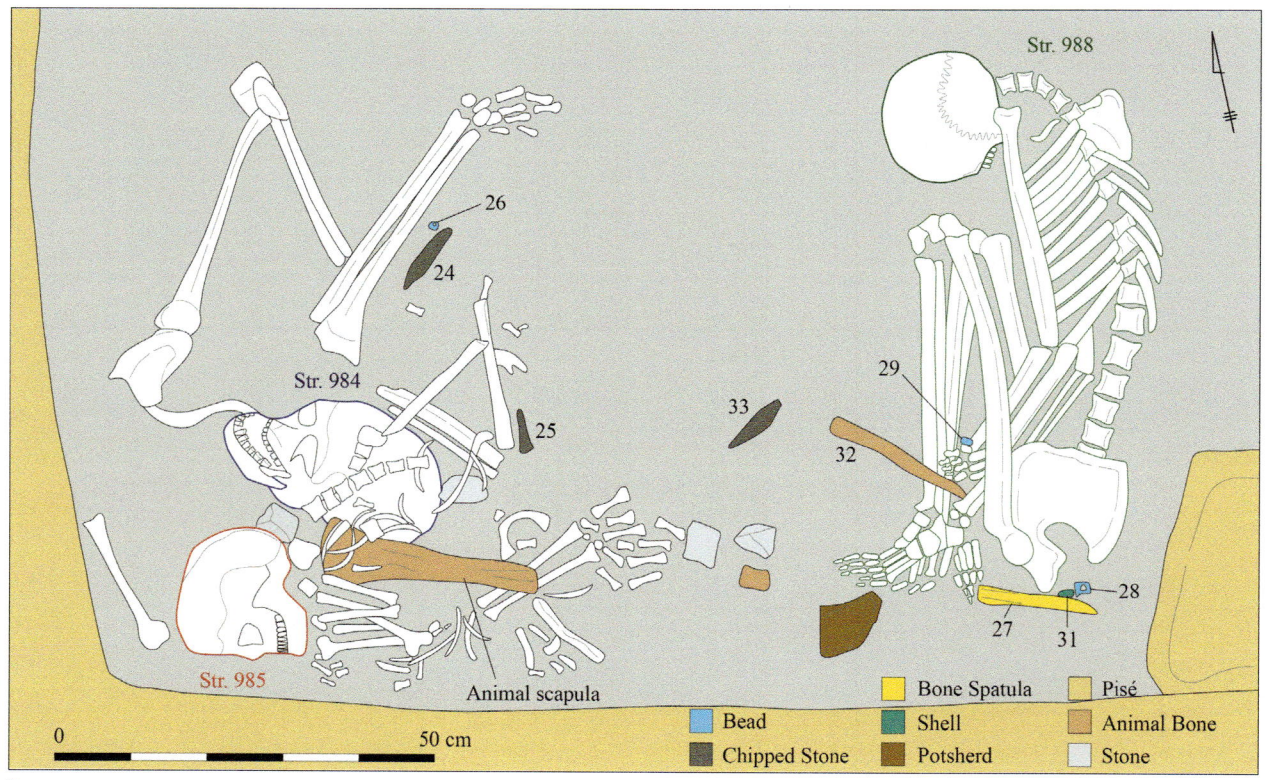

Figure 5-124c. Concentration 7 Burial: C. Str 932 (C7-2); D. Strs 984, 985 and 988 (C7-2).

E   *from the south*

F   *from the north*    G   *from the west*

Figure 5-124d. Concentration 7 Burial: E. General view (C7-1); F. Str 860 (C7-1); G. Str 861 (C7-1).

H   *from the west*   I   *from the west*

J   *from the west*

K   *from the west*

Figure 5-124e. Concentration 7 Burial: H. Str. 862 (C7-1); I. Str. 863 (C7-1); J. Str. 932 (C7-2); K. Str. 984 (C7-2).

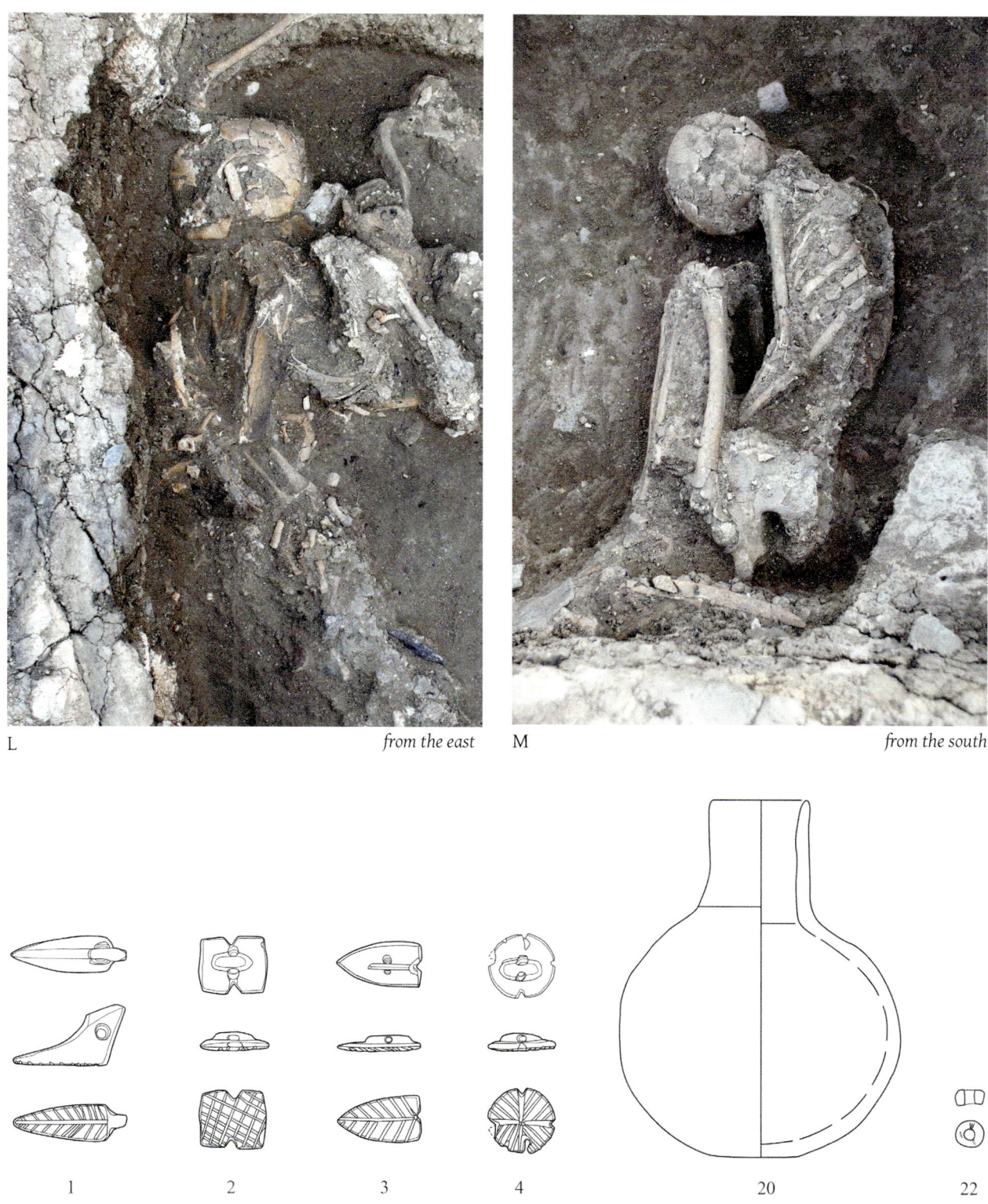

L   *from the east*   M   *from the south*

Figure 5-124f. L. Str. 985 (C7-2); M. Str. 988 (C7-2). Grave goods: 1. Stone stamp seal (Str. 860);
2-4. Bone stamps seals (Str. 860); 20. DFBW jar (Str. 862); 22. Stone bead (Str. 863).

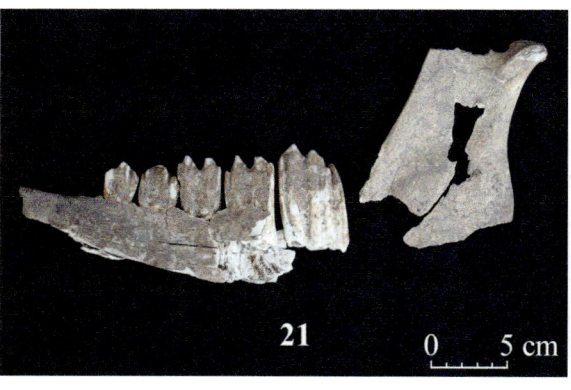

Figure 5-124g. Concentration 7 Grave goods: 1. Stone stamp seal (Str. 860); 2–4. Bone stamp seals (Str. 860); 5–8. Butterfly stone beads (Str. 860); 9–10. Trapezoid stone beads (Str. 860); 11. Bone bead (Str. 860); 12–15. Cowrie beads (Str. 860); 16. Tusk shell (Str. 860); 17. Oval quartz bead (Str. 860); 18. Miniature stone vessel (Str. 860); 19. Coarse pottery bowl (Str. 861); 20. DFBW jar (Str. 862); 21. Animal left mandible (Str. 862); 22. Stone bead (Str. 863); 23. Amuq-type flint point (C7-1).

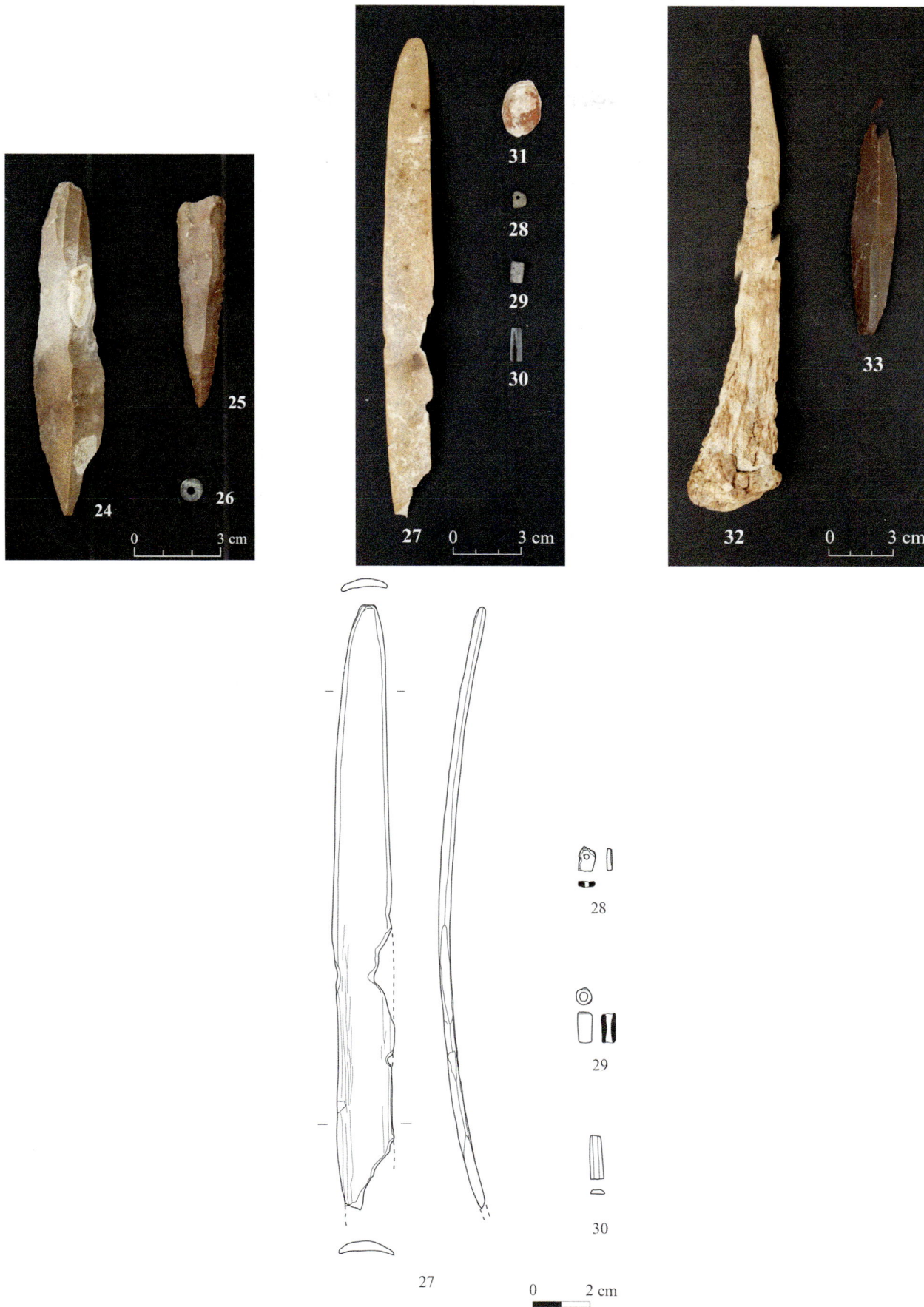

Figure 5-124h. Concentration 7 Grave goods: 24. Flint blade (Str. 984); 25. Flint point (Str. 984); 26. Stone bead (Str. 984); 27. Bone spatula (Str. 988); 28. Flat stone bead (Str. 988); 29. Cylindrical stone bead (Str. 988); 30. Obsidian blade (Str. 988); 31. Shell (Str. 988); 32. Goat horn (Str. 988); 33. Flint blade (Str. 988).

125. Concentration 8 (C8) (Figure 5-125)

Concentration 8 (C8) is a cluster of heavily cremated human bones found north of the crematorium pit C6 of Square E271b, d in Layer 6. Two parallel ditches full of burnt soil and ash, measuring 0.6m wide and 0.4m deep, were discovered. The bone cluster was discovered at the western end of these two ditches. The area of bone spread was c. 1.5m x 0.5m, which traversed the western end of both ditches. Human remains were not found in the ditches as they perhaps had been used for cremation. The cremated bones seemed to have been swept and accumulated at the western ends. This deposit contains the commingled cremated remains of at least eight individuals (Str. 835 1–8): an infant (birth–3 mths), two juveniles, one subadult, and four adults, one of which is probably male. One of the adults was elderly.

At the southern end of the concentration, some large fragments of a DFBW bowl covered the skull of an adult of unknown sex. A flint drill was discovered in the concentration.

A   *from the west*

B   *from the west*   C   *from the west*

Figure 5-125a. Concentration 8 Burial: A. Cremated bones and DFBW bowl; B. Cremated skull under the DFBW bowl (upper level); C. Cremated bones under the skull (lower level). Grave goods: Flint drill.

Skull

Potsherd
Stone

0   50 cm

Figure 5-125b. Concentration 8 Burial.

126. Concentration 9 (Figure 5-126)

Concentration 9 (C9) is a crematorium pit discovered in the northwestern part of Square E271b in Layer 6. It is a small rectangular pit, measuring c. 1.0m x 0.9m. It is shallow with a depth of 0.15m. The pit was filled with burnt soil and black- and white-colored ash. Very thin black organic matter was noticed at the bottom of the pit. There were a lot of human bones, which had turned white due to the high-temperature fire. However, some bones remained black and dark red/brown in color, due to exposure to lower-temperature fire. Though most bones were fragmented, some skeletal parts were still articulated. This indicated that the dead had been cremated in this pit soon after the corpses had decayed in other places. No grave goods were discovered in the pit. However, one limestone ball was discovered above the pit. The ball measures 14cm in diameter. The ball was dedicated to the dead who were cremated in this pit.

At least five individuals (three adults, a subadult, and a juvenile) were discovered in this pit. The first adult was represented by foot bones. It is unclear if these bones were exposed to low-temperature fire or were discolored by the soil and ash within the pit. The second adult was represented by grayish-white cremated cranial and postcranial remains. The fragments display color changes and drastic morphological modifications that are indicative of high-temperature exposure. The last adult was represented by an unpaired first metacarpal. The subadult was represented by metacarpals, carpals, and phalanges showing a partial fusion of the epiphyses. The juvenile was represented by a fragment of developing sternum and a vertebral body.

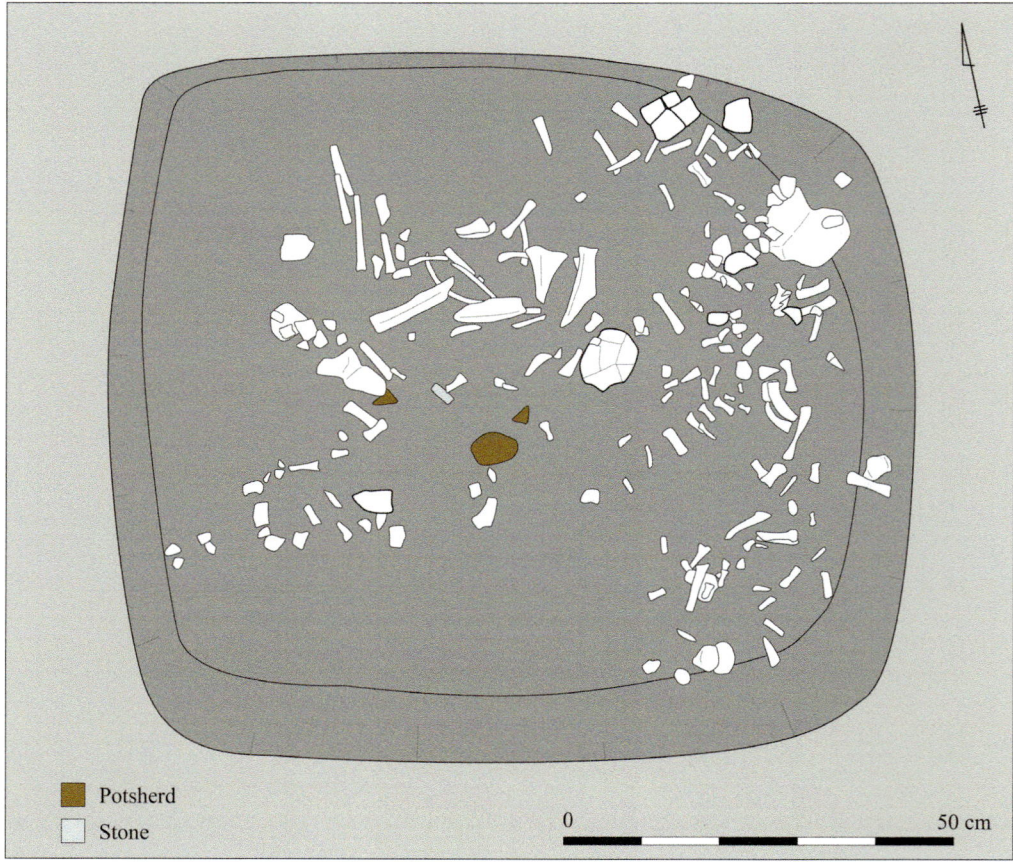

Potsherd
Stone

0   50 cm

Figure 5-126a. Concentration 9 Burial.

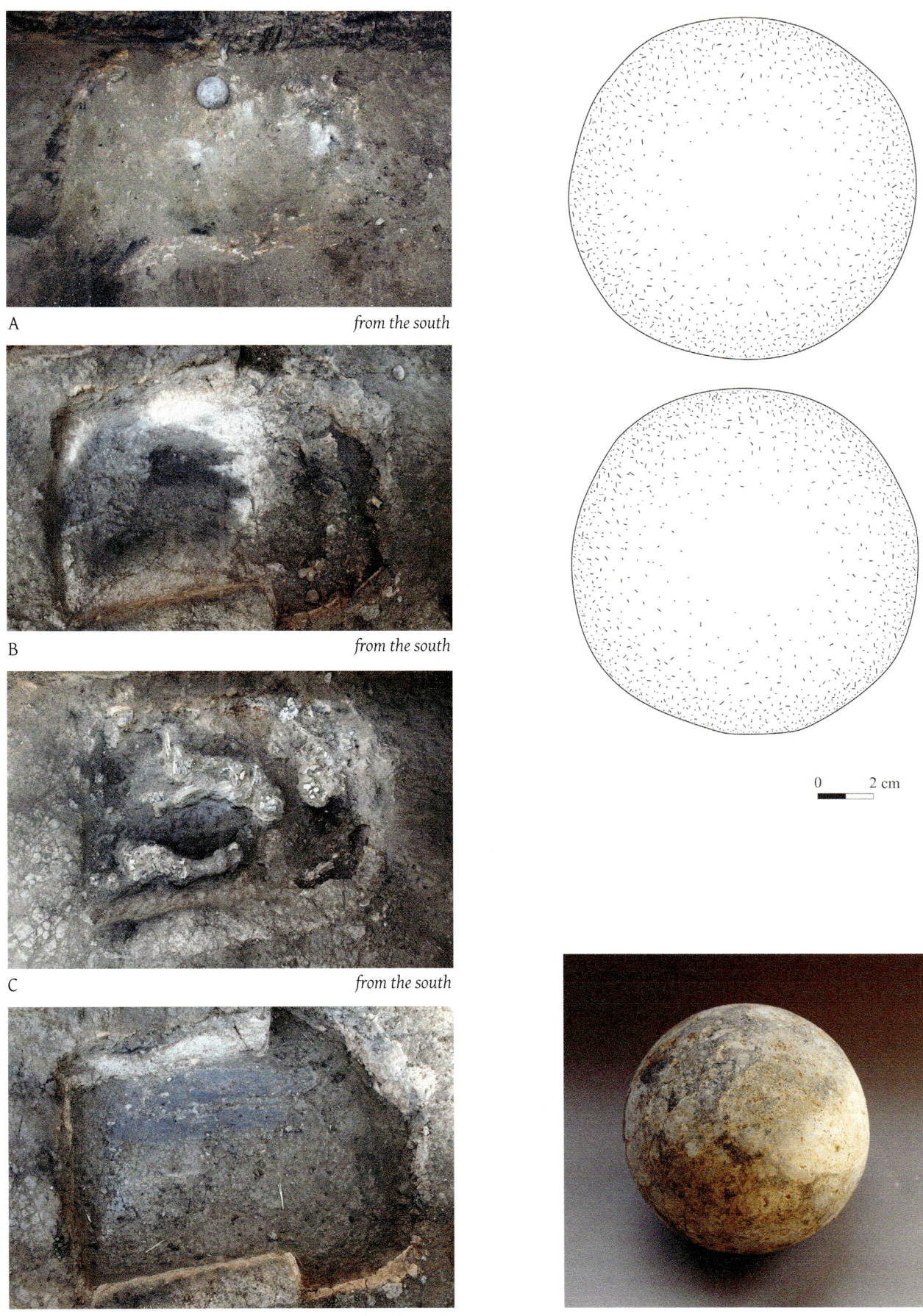

A *from the south*

B *from the south*

C *from the south*

D *from the south*

0   2 cm

Figure 5-126b. Concentration 9 Burial: A. Just above a crematorium pit and a stone ball;
B. Upper level; C. Lower level; D. Bottom of the pit. Grave goods: Stone ball.

127. Concentration 10 (C10) (Figure 5-127)

Concentration 10 (C10) is a collective burial discovered in the southeastern corner of Square E271b in Layer 6. C10 has unique characteristics among the collective burials. It is enclosed by rows of limestone rocks, measuring 2.5m x 1.5m. Inside this small area, there were two accumulations of human remains belonging to at least 22 individuals.

The northern accumulation (C10 north) is a small pit measuring 0.8m x 1.0m in diameter and 0.8m in depth. At least 15 individuals were found here, of which four individuals were in a complete primary context. Some individuals remained partly articulated, while others were represented by part of the skull and long bones. The age distribution of these individuals is seven adults, one subadult, four juveniles, one infant (possibly young juvenile), and two individuals of unknown age. The deceased included three males / probably males and two probably females. A flint blade, clay discs, a bone stamp seal, a stone stamp seal, an animal tusk, and stone beads were found as grave goods. They mostly accompanied intact or disturbed primary burials.

The three complete primary individuals, interred in the uppermost layer of C10 north, overlapped each other in a small pit. This suggests that these individuals were not buried in a single event. A mass of long bones and isolated skulls were discovered on the side of the pit. Therefore, the burial process can be hypothesized as follows: First, one of the deceased was buried in a primary condition. Second, during the burial of the next deceased, only the long bones and skull (or other parts of the body) of the former individual were left in the pit and put aside. Third, these two steps were repeated. Thus, in the last stage of C10 north, three complete primary individuals were interred and overlapped each other.

This northern accumulation is a very special mass burial and the first of its kind discovered in the Tell el-Kerkh excavations. In addition, the pit was too small to bury the 15 individuals together at the same time. Therefore, the conclusion is that the people buried the deceased in this small pit consecutively over a considerable interval. In fact, the excavation revealed intermediate soil layers of a few centimeters thickness between individuals. After burying a deceased person, the pit seemed to have been covered with a clay plaster. The yellow color clay remnant remained here and there in the pit. For burying the newly dead, the clay cover was removed and the dead person was buried on top of the previous skeletons. Then, the pit was covered again with clay plaster. If the burial space was limited, the former accumulated skeletons were put away within the pit. In this way, at least 15 individuals were accumulated within this small pit.

C10 north

Str. 943

Str. 943 is a primary burial of a young adult, probably male, discovered on the top of the primary burials in the northern accumulation in C10. Age could not be determined precisely. He was buried in a flexed position on his left side. The body axis direction was west-east, and the head pointed to the west and faced north. His legs were tightly bent in front of the chest. The arm was disturbed, and the left arm was not found. He was accompanied by one flint blade.

Str. 947

Str. 947 is a primary burial of a middle-aged adult, probably male, discovered directly beneath Str. 943. He was also buried in a flexed position, but his upper body tended toward a prone position. His body axis direction was southwest-northeast, and the skull pointed southwest and faced downward. Two disk-type clay objects were uncovered over his pelvis.

Str. 962

Str. 962 is a primary burial of a middle-aged adult male discovered below Strs. 943 and 947. He was buried in a flexed position on his abdomen. His body axis direction was west-east and the skull pointed west and faced north. There were no grave goods.

Str. 971

Str. 971 is a secondary burial of a 3–4-year-old juvenile discovered below Str. 962. Sex was indeterminate. It was represented by a skull.

Str. 972

Str. 972 is also a secondary burial of a juvenile aged 11–12 years discovered near the bottom. Sex was indeterminate. It was represented by a skull.

Str. 978

Str. 978 is a young adult, probably female, discovered in the eastern part of C10. This burial was represented by a skull found from the eastern section wall of the excavation area, which was not fully excavated. Therefore, it was not possible to determine the type and position of this burial. This skull was found at the highest level of C10 north.

Str. 979

Str. 979 is a primary burial of a 12–13-year-old subadult discovered in layer C10 north. The legs were flexed and tightly bent, and it was buried in a prone position. The body axis direction was south-north, and the head pointed to the south and faced downward.

Str. 980

Str. 980 is represented only by the skull, which was found from the eastern section wall of the excavation area. Therefore, it was not possible to determine the type and position of this burial.

Str. 983

Str. 983 is a secondary burial of a young adult, probably female, discovered beneath the Str. 979 skull. This individual is represented by an isolated mandible.

Str. 991

Str. 991 is a secondary burial of a 5–6-year-old juvenile discovered beneath Str. 983. It is represented by a skull, ribs, and phalanges. The skull pointed to the southeast and faced east.

Str. 993

Str. 993 is a secondary burial of an infant. It is represented by a skull and was found by the foot of Str. 995. Sex was indeterminate.

Str. 995

Str. 995 is a disturbed primary burial of an adult, but sex was indeterminate. It was buried in a flexed position on its right side. The body axis direction was east-west and the head, which was missing, pointed to the east. Two stamp seals and an animal tusk were dedicated to this burial as grave goods.

Str. 996

Str. 996 is a secondary burial of a 4–5-year-old juvenile discovered next to the legs of Str. 995. Sex was indeterminate.

Str. 998

Str. 998 is a disturbed primary burial of an adult discovered at the bottom of C10. It is represented by articulated ribs, vertebrae, and a pelvis. The body axis was determined as south-north. Sex was indeterminate.

Str. 999

Str. 999 is a disturbed primary burial discovered beside Str. 995. It is represented by spinal vertebrae and other long bones. The body axis was east-west. Sex was indeterminate. Three stone beads were discovered beside the vertebrae.

As mentioned here, at least 15 human individuals have been excavated from C10 north. Based on the overlapping of human bones, it is estimated that they were buried in the following order, from oldest to newest.

Str. 998 → Str. 972 → Str. 996 → Str. 995 → Str. 993/Str. 999 → Str. 991 → Str. 971/Str. 983 → Str. 979 → Str. 962 → Str. 978/Str. 947/Str. 980 → Str. 943

C10 south

The southern accumulation is a small spot, measuring 0.8m in diameter, partly encircled by limestone rocks. This location produced a complete DFBW bowl, many fragments of burnt human bones, and a set of unburnt adult leg bones.

Str. 953 (1)

Str. 953 (1) is a disturbed primary burial of an adult of indeterminate sex, represented by the left and right tibia, fibulae, and feet, which were found on the northern fringe of the location. The lower leg bones were not burnt and were found over the distribution of burnt bones. These articulated legs indicate that the adult was buried in a flexed position on its right side over the burnt human bones. However, the skeleton was missing except the lower legs. A DFBW bowl was uncovered in the east side of this accumulation. It must have been dedicated to the adult or the burnt human bones.

Strs. 953 (2–7)

Strs. 953 (2–7) are an accumulation of disarticulated and fragmented burnt human bones. These burnt bones belong to at least six individuals, though no skulls or mandibles were found. No further details were obtained due to the cremated and fragmented conditions of the bones. However, the burnt remains belong to four adults, one perinatal baby, and a subadult, probably 10–14 years old.

Therefore, the southern accumulation consists of a strange combination of human bones, i.e., fragments of burnt bones and a set of unburnt legs. We do not know the symbolic meaning of such bone accumulations. However, the bones of at least seven individuals were placed in the southern accumulation.

Str. 943

Str. 980

Str. 947

1

2

3

10

Pottery
Chipped Stone
Animal Bone
Clay Object
Stone

0   50 cm

A

Figure 5-127a. Concentration 10 Burial: A. Uppermost level of C10 north and C10 south.

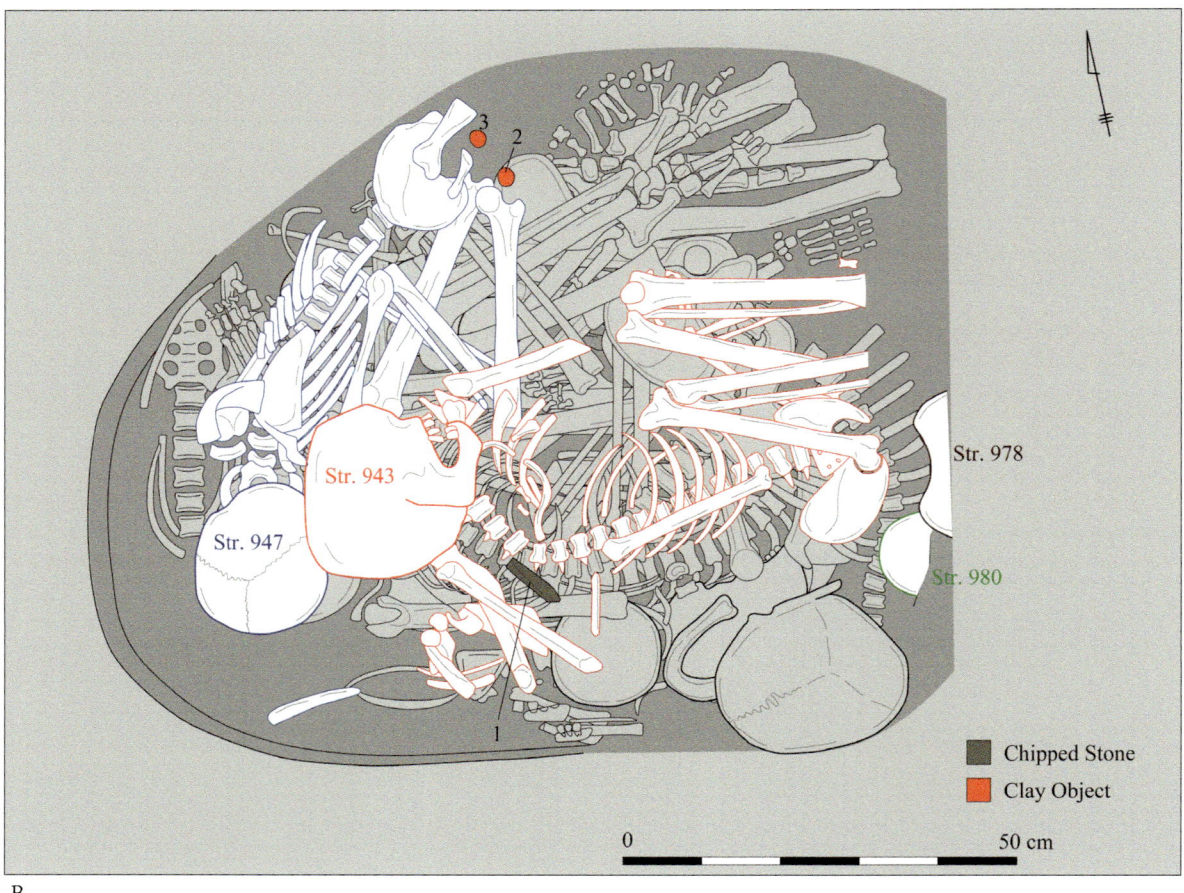

B

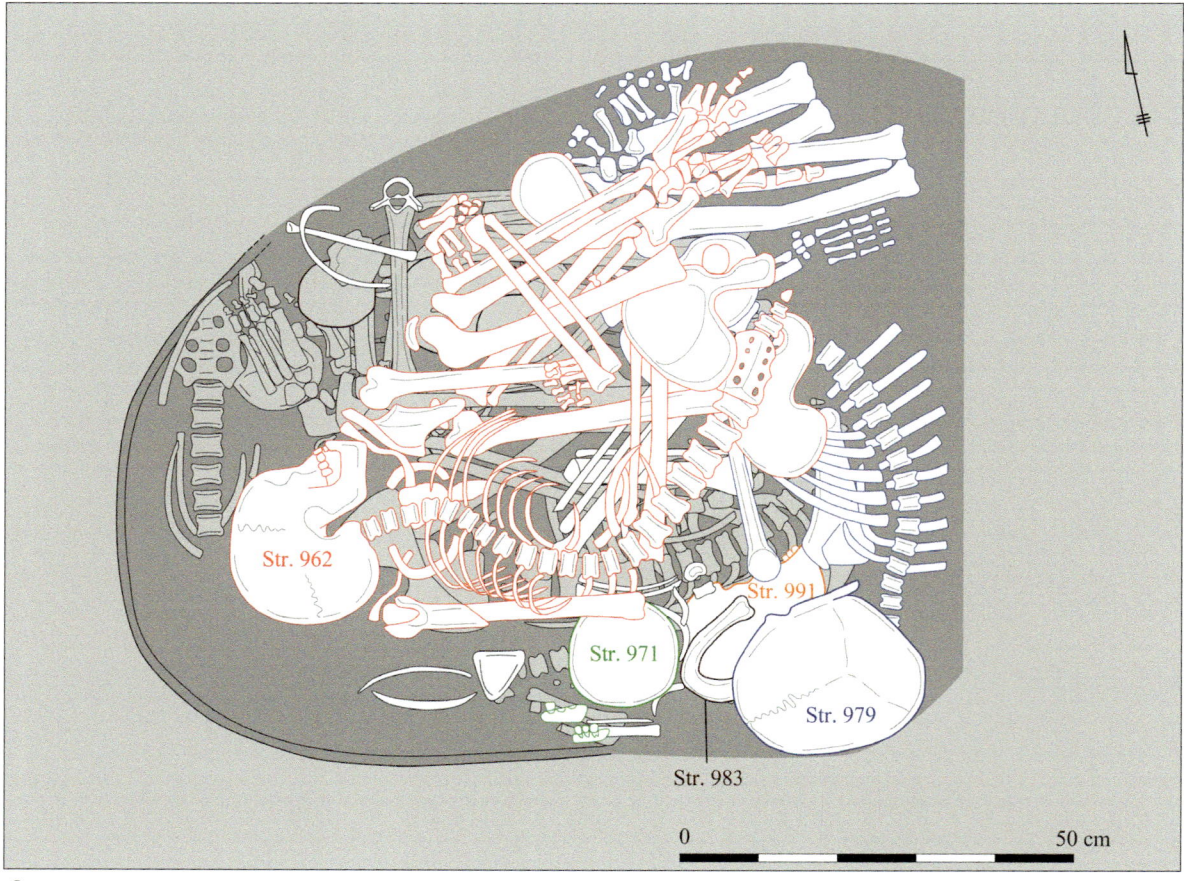

C

Figure 5-127b. Concentration 10 Burial: B. Uppermost level of C10 north; C. Upper level of C10 north.

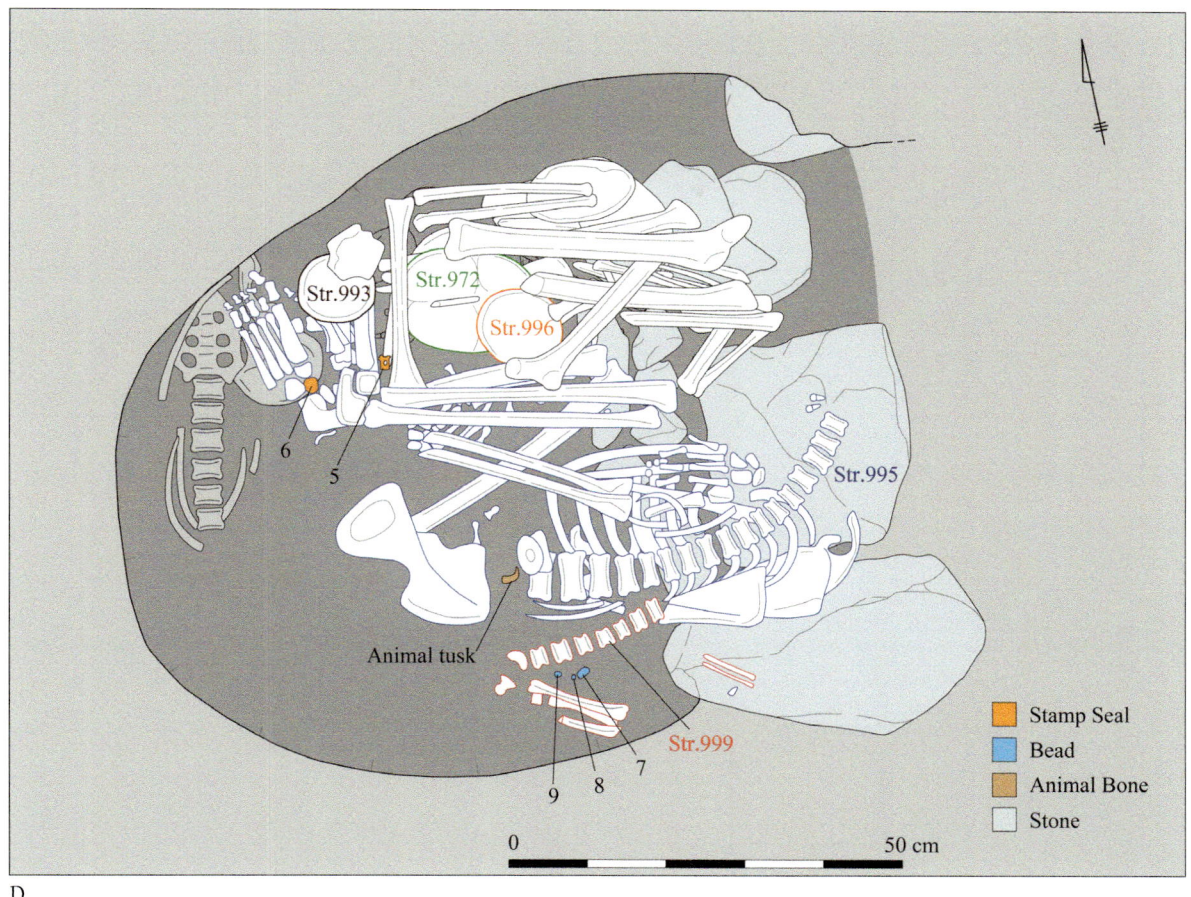

D

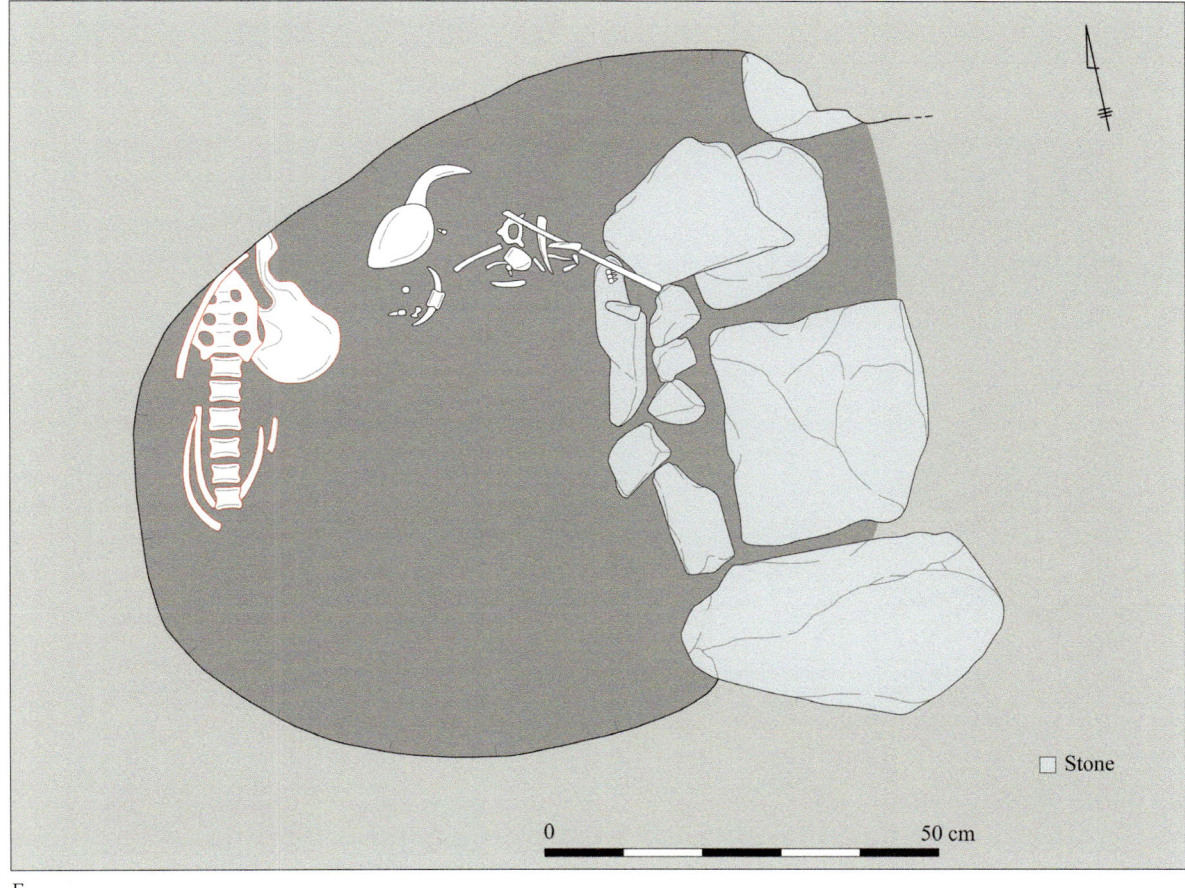

E

Figure 5-127c. Concentration 10 Burial: D. Middle level of C10 north; E. Lower level of C10 north.

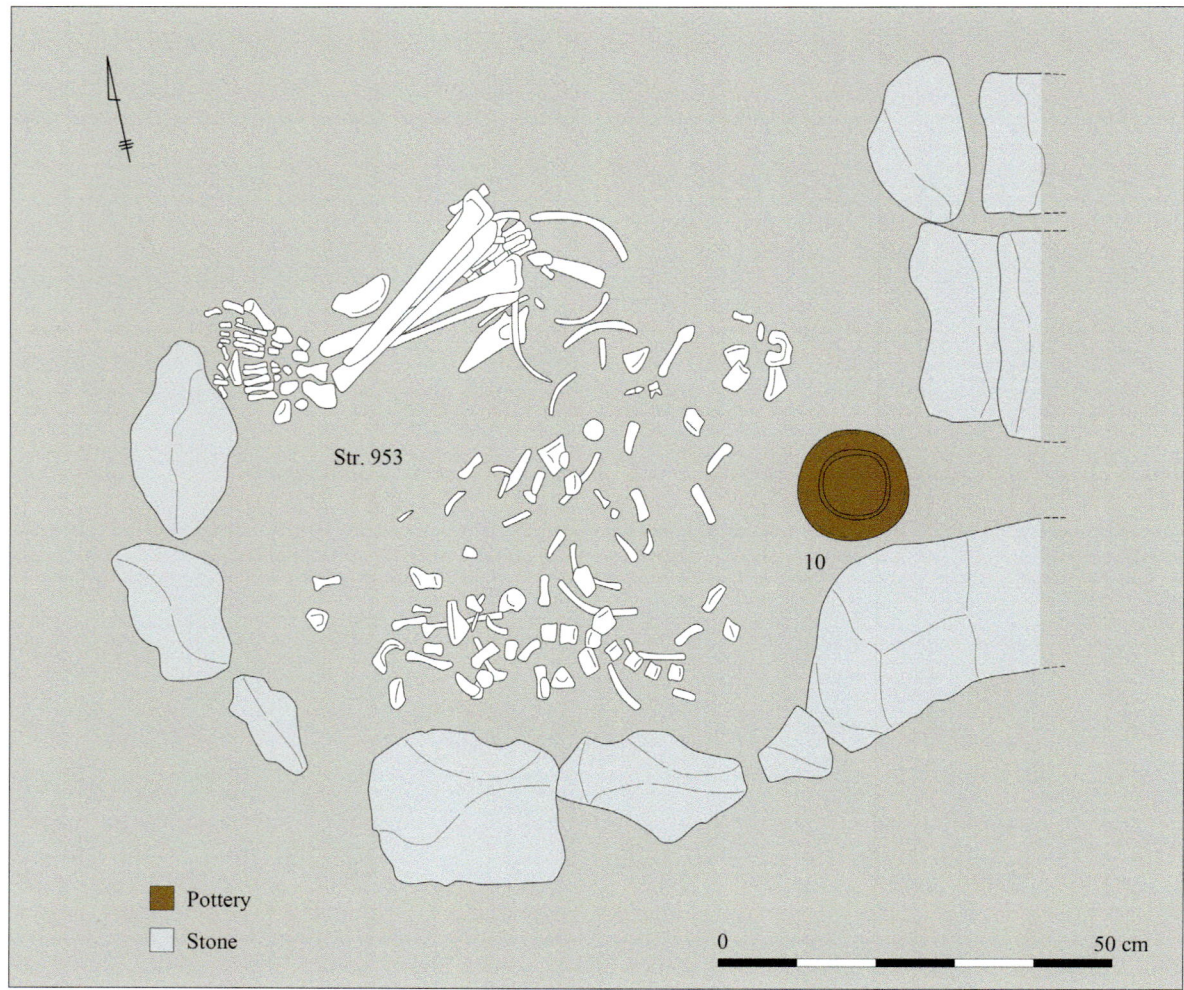

F

G   *from the west*

Figure 5-127d. Concentration 10 Burial: F. C10 south; G. C10 north and south.

H   *from the north*   I   *from the west*

J   *from the north*   K   *from the west*

L   *from the west*   M   *from the south*

Figure 5-127e. Concentration 10 Burial: H. Str. 962 (C10 north); I. Strs. 971, 979, 978, 980 and 983 (C10 north);
J. Str. 991 (C10 north); K. Strs. 972, 993, 995, 996 and 999 (C10 north); L. Str. 998 (C10 north);
M. Str. 953 (C10 south).

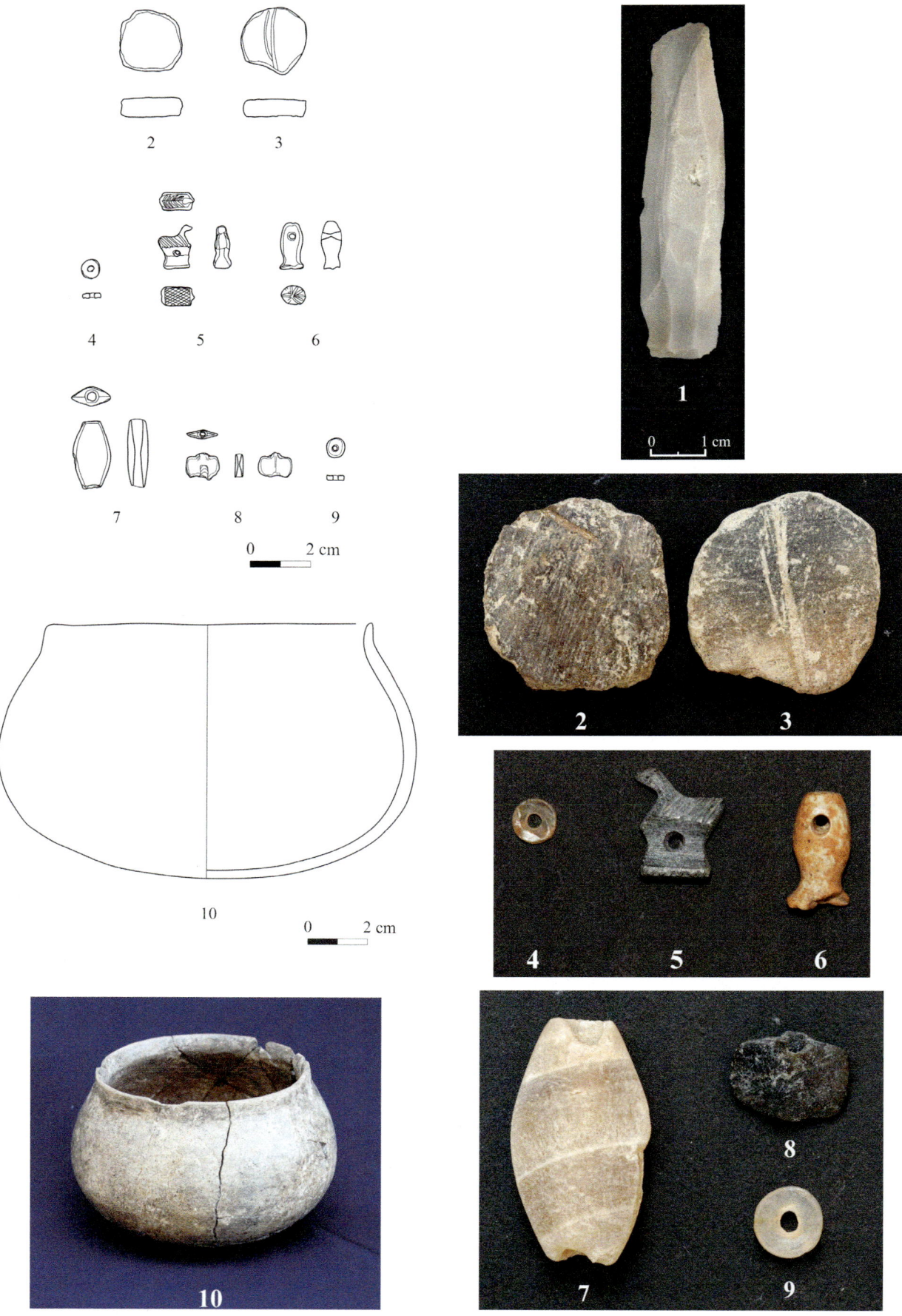

Figure 5-127f. Concentration 10 Grave goods: 1. Flint blade (Str. 943); 2–3. Disk type clay objects (Str. 947); 4. Stone bead (C10 north); 5. Stone stamp seal (Str. 995); 6. Bone stamp seal (Str. 995); 7. Stone barrel bead (Str. 999); 8. Stone butterfly bead (Str. 999); 9. Stone flat bead (Str. 999); 10. DFBW bowl (C10 south).

Chapter 6

The Human Remains of Tell el-Kerkh

Sean P. Dougherty

1. Introduction

The biological cost of the agricultural transition has been of considerable interest to researchers for several decades. In general, it has been found that sedentary populations subsisting on domesticated food resources often experienced increased population growth, but suffered higher incidences of sickness, malnutrition, and mortality (Cohen and Armelagos 2013; Cohen and Crane-Kramer 2007). Ironically, while the Near East is considered to be the region of the earliest farming societies, comparably little research exists that explores the health of these populations. Rather, most research concerning the health effects of the agricultural transition is derived from New World contexts.

In recent years, new research has shed some light on the Neolithic biological experience in western Asia. However, with the exception of Molleson's work at Abu Hureyra (2000), and the recent bioarchaeological work from Çatalhöyük (Molleson *et al.* 2005; Hillson *et al.* 2013; Larson *et al.* 2013; Larsen *et al.* 2015; Larsen *et al.* 2019), most studies are confined to skeletal samples dating to the Pre-pottery Neolithic period (Dahlberg 1960; Hershkovitz and Gopher 1988; Santana *et al.* 2012; Pearson *et al.* 2013), while others use multi-site comparisons to illuminate diachronic (and regional) trends in overall morbidity and mortality (Eshed *et al.* 2004a; Eshed *et al.* 2006; Smith and Horwitz 2007; Eshed *et al.* 2010). In contrast, very little is known about the Pottery Neolithic populations of the northwestern Levant. To that end, the cemetery sample excavated from the Pottery Neolithic site of Tell el-Kerkh provides a rare opportunity to examine the biological experience of a Neolithic village in northwest Syria.

From 2002 to 2010, excavations of a cemetery at Tell el-Kerkh have uncovered a minimum number of 244 individuals. These skeletal remains were subsequently analyzed during three seasons (2008-2010), and the observations from these analyses are reported here in what must ultimately be the 'final' report for the site, as the unfortunate events in Syria have prevented our return.

Although this report is necessarily final, it cannot be said to be *complete*. Based on previous work at Tell el-Kerkh in 2001, it was assumed that any new burials excavated would likely be relatively intact and undisturbed, and could be analyzed with few complications. Yet, as research began on the new material in 2008, it was quickly realized that these assumptions were incorrect. The great frequency of highly commingled, fragmentary burials and cremated remains forced an abrupt change in the course of the analysis.

For example, the cremains and the commingled burials needed meticulous attention to ascertain even basic data, such as the minimum number of individuals, and this came at the cost of time. The analysis became more of a data collection triage. Decisions had to be made as to what data would be collected, and what data would be saved for a study season planned after the completion of the cemetery excavation. The primary goal of each season, then, was simplified to ascertain the minimum number of individuals, basic demographic data, and record the more macroscopic, less observation-intensive, paleopathological indicators of disease and poor health.

Unfortunately, the planned study season never came. As a result, certain data, such as dental morphology and non-metric skeletal traits, are absent from this report, while others, like dental attrition, certain postcranial measurements, and odontometrics, are underrepresented. Likewise, the analyses of the commingled remains and cremains is arguably a bit more rudimentary than it should be, not having had the opportunity to apply more rigorous protocols and theoretical approaches that have appeared in recent publications (*e.g.* Adams and Byrd 2014; Osterholtz *et al.* 2014; Osterholtz 2016).

Nevertheless, while this analysis is admittedly not as complete as it should be, this report provides valuable insight concerning life and death during the Pottery Neolithic period in northern Syria.

2. Preservation

Any analysis of human skeletal remains is ultimately dependent upon the state of bone preservation. While primary burials, for example, may be intact and undisturbed *in situ*, the condition of those remains may deteriorate upon continued exposure during excavation, or during the process of removing the

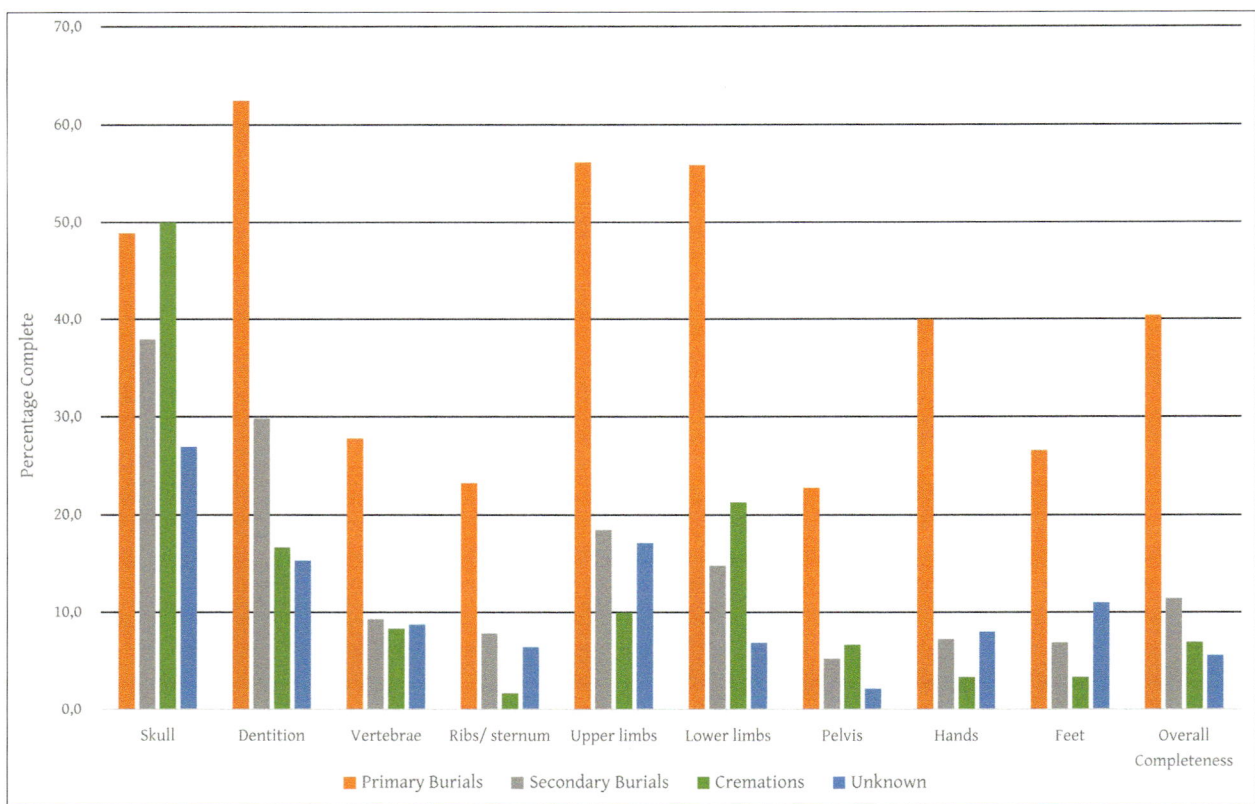

Figure 6-1. Regional variation in skeletal preservation.

remains from the ground, thus limiting the amount of data that can be obtained. Unfortunately, this was often the case for the skeletal remains from Tell el-Kerkh, where taphonomic changes to the human remains, both man-made and environmental, did not favor skeletal analysis.

Figure 6-1 illustrates the state of preservation for the skeletal remains of Tell el-Kerkh. As mortuary practices can greatly influence the condition of the human remains, it is not surprising that the primary burials were the most complete, whether by anatomical region, or overall. It should be noted, however, that this method of scoring preservation by skeleton, and by anatomical region, necessitates the observation of a clearly recognized individual skeleton. In cases where the skeletal remains were commingled, such as in cremation pits or in secondary burials, individuals were often identified and designated by the presence of a cranium, which was often not directly associated with postcranial bones. As a result, there is a clear disparity between the percentage of completeness for the crania and the postcranial remains for those burial types.

For example, the cremated skulls were observed to be on average around 40% complete, but the upper limbs were only around 10% complete, and the overall score was 6.6%. These lower scores, while they certainly reflect the poor preservation of the cremated remains, also reflect the inability to link commingled postcranial

remains to any particular cranium. Thus, the percentage of completeness for those human remains is likely underscored to a certain degree. However, given that the overall percentage of completeness for primary burials was only around 40%, the generally poor condition of even the best of the cemetery sample is made clear, so it is not too surprising that the secondary and cremated remains fared worse.

With respect to regional anatomy, in general, the heartier elements of the skeleton, such as the dentition, were the best preserved, while the more fragile elements, such as the vertebrae and bones of the pelvis were the least intact. This is particularly unfortunate as the bones of the pelvis, the *os coxae*, provide the most accurate indicators for the estimation of age and sex.

To provide a less generalized view of skeletal preservation, individual bones were observed and scored for completeness using variations of a three-point scale (1= 75%-100% complete; 2= 25%-75% complete; 3= <25% complete/extremely fragmentary). The system of inventory scoring was adapted from Buikstra and Ubelaker (1994), which is the inventory system commonly employed by most researchers in the last two decades, whether implicitly or explicitly.

The bones of the skull were inventoried and scored by side. Unpaired bones, such as the frontal, occipital, and mandible were divided into right and left halves along the midsagittal plane. For particular bones, the completion scores were determined by the presence or absence of certain features. For example, a complete occipital would necessarily receive a '1' score. If the occipital was found to lack only the basilar portion, it would receive a score of '2.'

The larger bones of the upper and lower extremities were subdivided into five segments for observation (proximal epiphysis, proximal third diaphysis, middle third diaphysis, distal third diaphysis, and distal epiphysis).

The bones of the hands and feet were scored similarly to those of the upper and lower limbs. However, following Buikstra and Ubelaker (1994), these smaller bones were not divided into sections, but scored in their entirety. Generally, for the metatarsals and metacarpals, a score of '1' signified that the bone was complete and intact; '2' indicated the loss of one articular surface, and '3' indicated the loss of both joint surfaces, or more than half of the entire bone.

The three-point scoring system was modified for vertebrae, including the bones of the sacrum. As determining what constitutes 60% of a vertebra is not straightforward, it was decided that the vertebrae would be scored with respect to retained features. For example, a generally complete vertebra was scored as a '1,' but a vertebra that retained only the body was a '2.'

A similar scoring system was applied to the scapulae. In this case, a '2' was scored if the scapula retained its major features (e.g. the glenoid fossa, lateral border, acromion), but lacked the thin regions of the infraspinous fossa. A '3' was given is the scapula was fragmented, and only one or two major features remained.

The ribs and sternum posed a particular problem for inventory. The sternum was scored as a unit using the three-point scale described above. However, it was initially intended that the ribs would be scored by side and number. However, due to general fragility, these bones were often in fragments no longer than two centimeters, if not in splinters, which made inventory very difficult, and rib number identification impossible. As a result, the ribs were scored *en masse*, with the score often reflecting the level of fragmentation.

In general, the poor preservation of the skeletal sample is clear (Tables 6-1 – 6-17). While just over two hundred individuals were included in the analysis, there were less than half of the expected number of bones present for observation. Intact, unbroken bones were extremely rare. Likewise, individual bones observed to be 75%, or more, complete were infrequent.

3. Mortuary Profile

Adult skeletal remains were evaluated for age and sex following the standard protocols utilizing the

Table 6-1. Preservation/fragmentation scores for the skull (n=201).

Score	Frontal		Parietal		Occipital		Temporal		Sphenoid		Zygomatic		Nasal		Maxilla		Palatine		Mandible	
	Left	Right	Left	Right	Left	Right	Left	Right	Left	Right	Left	Right	Left	Right	Left	Right	Left	Right	Left	Right
1	15	17	18	19	13	14	13	10	6	6	41	40	6	7	9	12	1	1	41	45
2	52	49	50	49	47	45	50	55	11	10	9	10	0	0	30	28	0	0	29	30
3	33	27	33	33	32	31	22	20	25	24	9	6	1	1	21	17	1	1	20	16
Not Present	101	108	100	100	109	111	116	116	159	161	142	145	194	193	141	144	199	199	111	110

Table 6-2. Preservation/fragmentation score
frequencies for the cervical vertebrae (n=201).

Score	C1	C2	C3	C4	C5	C6	C7
1	27	20	14	14	14	9	4
2	9	9	8	8	8	8	8
3	9	10	11	11	11	11	12
Not Present	156	162	168	168	168	173	177

Table 6-3. Preservation/fragmentation score frequencies
for the thoracic vertebrae (n=201).

Score	T1	T2	T3	T4	T5	T6	T7	T8	T9	T10	T11	T12
1	8	6	5	6	6	7	6	6	6	4	4	5
2	8	8	8	8	8	8	8	8	8	8	8	8
3	12	11	12	11	11	11	11	11	11	11	11	11
Not Present	173	176	176	176	176	175	176	176	176	178	178	177

Table 6-4. Preservation/fragmentation score frequencies for the lumbar vertebrae (n=201).

Score	L1	L2	L3	L4	L5
1	6	7	7	8	5
2	8	8	8	8	8
3	11	11	12	12	12
Not Present	176	175	174	173	176

Table 6-5. Preservation/fragmentation score frequencies for the sacrum (n=201).

Score	S1	S2	S3	S4	S5
1	7	3	2	2	1
2	8	7	5	4	2
3	9	7	5	5	4
Not Present	177	184	189	190	194

Table 6-6. Preservation/fragmentation score frequencies for the ribs and sternum (n=201).

Score	Left	Right	Sternum
1	0	0	1
2	6	6	3
3	34	34	5
Not Present	161	161	192

Table 6-7. Preservation/fragmentation score frequencies for the clavicle (n=201).

Score	Proximal Epiphysis		Proximal Third		Middle Third		Distal Third		Distal Epiphysis		Intact	
	Left	Right	Left	Right	Left	Right	Left	Right	Left	Right	Left	Right
1	15	13	33	26	37	29	36	29	16	19		
2	0	0	2	0	1	1	3	1	6	0		
3	1	0	2	4	2	4	1	2	0	1	0	1
Not Present	185	188	164	171	161	167	161	169	179	181		

Table 6-8. Preservation/ fragmentation score frequencies for the scapula (n=201).

Score	Left	Right
1	8	10
2	11	6
3	29	37
Intact	0	0
Not present	153	148

Table 6-9. Preservation/fragmentation score frequencies for the humerus (n=201).

Score	Proximal Epiphysis		Proximal Third		Middle Third		Distal Third		Distal Epiphysis		Intact	
	Left	Right	Left	Right	Left	Right	Left	Right	Left	Right	Left	Right
1	9	8	44	50	54	67	54	63	17	23		
2	8	4	7	8	3	1	5	5	3	3		
3	10	12	6	7	5	4	4	0	7	7	4	3
Not Present	174	177	144	136	139	129	138	133	174	168		

Table 6-10. Preservation/fragmentation score frequencies for the radius (n=201).

Score	Proximal Epiphysis		Proximal Third		Middle Third		Distal Third		Distal Epiphysis		Intact	
	Left	Right	Left	Right	Left	Right	Left	Right	Left	Right	Left	Right
1	31	26	46	56	52	55	37	55	18	22		
2	1	2	4	1	4	2	8	3	2	1	1	6
3	1	1	5	0	3	1	6	3	2	2		
Not Present	168	172	146	144	142	143	150	140	179	176		

Table 6-11. Preservation/fragmentation score frequencies for the ulna (n=201).

Score	Proximal Epiphysis		Proximal Third		Middle Third		Distal Third		Distal Epiphysis		Intact	
	Left	Right	Left	Right	Left	Right	Left	Right	Left	Right	Left	Right
1	32	28	57	56	58	54	49	46	18	20		
2	4	4	2	2	4	4	3	2	2	2	2	2
3	1	2	5	2	4	2	6	4	1	2		
Not Present	164	167	137	141	135	141	143	149	180	177		

Table 6.12a: Preservation/fragmentation score frequencies for the long bones of the hand (n=201).

Score	Mc 1		Mc 2		Mc 3		Mc 4		Mc 5		Total Phalanges	
	Lft	Rt	Lft	Rt	Lft	Rt	Lft	Rt	Lft	Rt	Lft	Rt
1	23	30	23	25	23	27	27	21	23	21		
2	5	2	12	10	9	9	11	12	7	16	486	400
3	5	1	3	3	7	6	7	4	5	2		
Not Present	168	168	163	163	162	159	156	164	166	162	155	160

Table 6.12b: Preservation/fragmentation score srequencies for the carpals of the hand (n=201).

Score	Scaphoid		Capitate		Hamate		Lunate		Triquetrum		Trapezium		Trapezoid		Pisiform	
	Lft	Rt	Lft	Rt	Lft	Rt	Lft	Rt	Lft	Rt	Lft	Rt	Lft	Rt	Lft	Rt
1	36	32	38	37	36	37	35	37	24	35	32	28	34	25	16	21
2	1	0	0	1	0	0	0	0	0	0	1	1	0	0	0	0
3	0	0	1	0	1	0	0	0	0	0	0	1	0	0	1	0
Not Present	164	169	162	163	164	164	166	164	177	166	168	171	167	176	184	180

Table 6-13. Preservation/fragmentation score
frequencies for the os coxa (n=201).

Score	Ilium		Ishium		Pubis	
	Left	Right	Left	Right	Left	Right
1	19	23	20	21	6	9
2	6	4	4	5	2	2
3	17	17	8	8	6	7
Not Present	159	157	167	167	187	183

Table 6-14. Preservation/fragmentation score frequencies for the femur (n=201).

Score	Proximal Epiphysis		Proximal Third		Middle Third		Distal Third		Distal Epiphysis		Intact	
	Left	Right	Left	Right	Left	Right	Left	Right	Left	Right	Left	Right
1	23	21	50	48	51	55	38	40	8	6		
2	7	5	3	7	4	2	4	10	10	6	2	4
3	4	3	7	5	10	8	11	6	7	10		
Not Present	167	172	141	141	136	136	148	145	176	179		

Table 6-15. Preservation/fragmentation score frequencies for the tibia (n=201).

Score	Proximal Epiphysis		Proximal Third		Middle Third		Distal Third		Distal Epiphysis		Intact	
	Left	Right	Left	Right	Left	Right	Left	Right	Left	Right	Left	Right
1	6	5	29	32	52	51	27	31	12	10		
2	1	2	8	6	2	2	7	6	3	1	5	6
3	17	15	20	14	13	15	19	14	8	11		
Not Present	177	179	144	149	134	133	148	150	178	179		

Table 6-16. Preservation/fragmentation score
frequencies for the fibula (n=201).

Score	Proximal Epiphysis		Proximal Third		Middle Third		Distal Third		Distal Epiphysis		Intact	
	Left	Right	Left	Right	Left	Right	Left	Right	Left	Right	Left	Right
1	6	2	50	46	56	57	48	50	21	22	4	1
2	0	1	9	12	5	1	10	9	1	2		
3	3	2	2	1	2	1	1	1	1	0		
Not Present	192	196	140	142	138	142	142	141	178	177		

Table 6-17a: Preservation/fragmentation score frequencies for the long bones of the foot (n=201).

Score	Mt 1		Mt 2		Mt 3		Mt 4		Mt 5		Total Phalanges	
	Lft	Rt	Lft	Rt	Lft	Rt	Lft	Rt	Lft	Rt	Lft	Rt
1	22	27	19	20	16	17	18	17	19	23		
2	3	4	9	12	6	10	8	8	9	9	207	205
3	3	3	4	2	7	3	3	2	0	2		
Not Present	173	167	168	167	172	171	172	174	173	167	171	172

Table 6-17b: Preservation/fragmentation score frequencies for the tarsals of the foot (n=201).

Score	Talus		Calcaneus		Navicular		Cuboid		1st Cuneiform		2nd Cuneiform		3rd Cuneiform	
	Lft	Rt	Lft	Rt	Lft	Rt	Lft	Rt	Lft	Rt	Lft	Rt	Lft	Rt
1	29	28	10	11	18	21	18	17	29	30	28	26	23	26
2	3	0	1	2	8	9	4	3	1	1	3	0	4	4
3	2	0	13	12	1	2	0	1	0	0	1	0	1	0
Not Present	167	173	177	176	174	169	179	180	171	170	169	175	173	171

morphological characteristics of the skull and os coxae (Buikstra and Ubelaker 1994). Reliable, accurate estimations of sex and age were not always possible due to the poor preservation of the necessary skeletal elements. The assessment of sex and age is dependent upon observations of multiple skeletal characteristics present on the os coxae, cranium, and mandible. The reliability of this assessment declines when the number of observable features is reduced. For most adults present within this sample, the assignment of sex and age was dependent upon such limited observations.

Due to the friable condition of the remains, the os coxae were often poorly preserved. The estimation of sex was typically limited to observations of cranial morphology. If the cranium could not be initially examined during recovery, sex estimation was often limited to the heartier areas of the skull, as the skeletal material rarely survived excavation and removal intact. As such, observations of general skeletal morphology (robust/gracile), as well as estimations based on osteometric data, such as femoral head diameter, or second metacarpal dimensions, were employed as secondary indicators (Ubelaker 1978; Stewart 1979; Bass 1987; White 2012; Wilbur 1998; Manolis *et al.* 2009). In those cases where the os coxae were not available for study, which was more often than not, the individuals were designated as 'probable' males or females, as described by Buikstra and Ubelaker (1994). However, for convenience, sex will simply be referred to as male or female in this text.

Adult age estimation relied upon the established methodologies utilizing the degenerative changes of the pubic symphyses and auricular surfaces of the os coxae (Todd 1920; Katz and Suchey 1986; Lovejoy *et al.*, 1985). Additional age data were acquired through observations of ectocranial suture closure (Meindl and Lovejoy 1985), and postcranial development.

Because the os coxae were often poorly preserved, and the crania were frequently incomplete, dental attrition was also employed for age estimation (Brothwell 1963; Lovejoy 1985). In these instances, individual attrition scores were compared with modal scores for known age categories, and the individual was assigned accordingly.

When possible, juvenile and subadult ages were estimated using both dental development (Gustafson and Koch 1974) and postcranial measurements (Scheuer and Black 2000). It should be noted, however, that skeletal development is more susceptible to growth disruption due to physiological stressors, such as poor nutrition (Ribot and Roberts 1996; Cardoso 2007). Because long bone measurements were used to estimate age for many nonadult individuals, it is possible that the estimated skeletal age reflects stunted skeletal growth rather than true skeletal age. Consequently, several ages could be underestimated.

An additional caveat is required. The cemetery sample from Tell el-Kerkh consists of a minimum number of 244 individuals. However, only 201 of these were examined directly. Fourteen were not examined, and thus categorized as individuals of unknown sex and age. The remaining 29 individuals were examined using high-resolution photographs taken during excavations, while the skeleton was *in situ* (for specific burial numbers, see Appendix 6.1). Those skeletons for whom age and/or sex could be estimated with some confidence were recorded accordingly. Those individuals for whom sex or age determination was less certain, or ambiguous, were recorded as 'unknown.' While making such assessments using photographs is never ideal, it was felt that even rudimentary data, such as general age estimation (adult, infant, etc.), for example, should not be lost, particularly since the skeletal remains are no longer available for study.

Individuals were assigned into the following age categories: fetal, perinatal, infant (B-1 year), juvenile (1-12 years), subadult (12-19 years), young adult (20-34 years), middle adult (35-49 years), and old adult (+50 years). The category of subadult is based, perhaps loosely, on the period between the eruption of the second permanent molar and the completion of the adult dentition. The adult age categories are the standard age categories of Buikstra and Ubelaker (1994).

It should be noted that the age categories of fetal and perinatal were utilized as field notations based upon both metric and non-metric observations of size, and tooth development, when available. In technical use, the fetal age refers to the period of two months *in utero* to birth, while the perinatal period refers to the period of 24 weeks *in utero* to seven days after birth (Saunders and Barrans 1999; Scheuer and Black 2000; Lewis 2007). However, in the case of the Tell el-Kerkh material, for which it was not possible to determine if the individual was live born or stillborn, it was considered more useful to use a system that allowed for the separation of those cases that may have been born within the last 36-40 weeks of gestation (and died shortly thereafter), and those for whom, given the observed state of development, the timing and condition of birth was more ambiguous.

The majority of skeletal remains (43%, n=105) are derived from primary burial contexts (Table 6-18). Nonadults represent 43% of the primary burial sample. Interestingly, there is a paucity of infant remains relative to the number of juveniles and fetal/perinatal burials among this burial group. Of the adults for which sex could be determined (n=50), there are slightly more males (54%) than females (46%), although this may be an artifact caused by the absence of data for 12 individuals. Notably, the majority of adults within primary burial contexts appear to have died within the young adult age range, with nearly equal numbers of males and females.

Fifty-nine individuals were uncovered from secondary burial contexts (Table 6-19). In contrast to the primary burials, the majority of individuals for whom age could be estimated were nonadults (53%), with juveniles accounting for the majority of the nonadults. Sex determination was possible for only 19 adults, and the ratio of males to females was nearly equal.

Forty-six individuals exhibited evidence of burning, or, at least, exposure to fire (Table 6-20). Eighteen nonadults and 28 adults were identified. As with secondary burials,

the majority of nonadults were juveniles, although this may be an artifact of preservation, as infant and fetal remains would be less likely to withstand the destructive forces of cremation.

Table 6-21 displays the sex and age distribution of skeletons recovered from unknown burial contexts. Over half (52%) of the individuals were nonadults. Unfortunately, very little data was available for the adults of the unknown burial sample, although one male and one female were identified.

The general trends observed among the separate burial types are continued when the cemetery sample is viewed in the aggregate, and this generally remains consistent whether the cemetery is viewed with respect to the totality of excavated remains (Table 6-22), or just those that were directly examined (Table 6-23). For the sake of simplicity and clarity, the discussion that follows

Table 6-18. Sex and age distribution* of the Tell el-Kerkh Cemetery: Primary burials.

Sex	Fetal	Perinatal	Infant	Juvenile	Subadult	Adult	Young Adult	Middle Adult	Old Adult	Unknown	Total
Male							2	4			6
Probable Male						5 (3)	10 (9)	6 (5)			21 (17)
Female						1	2	3			6
Probable Female						4 (2)	9 (6)	4			17 (12)
Unknown	6	6 (4)	5 (4)	19 (15)	7	9 (6)	1 (0)		1 (0)	1 (0)	55 (42)
Total	6	6 (4)	5 (4)	19 (15)	7	19 (12)	24 (19)	17 (16)	1 (0)	1 (0)	105 (83)

*Numbers in parentheses indicate the total directly observed.

Table 6-19. Sex and age distribution* of the Tell el-Kerkh Cemetery: Secondary burials.

Sex	Fetal	Perinatal	Infant	Juvenile	Subadult	Adult	Young Adult	Middle Adult	Old Adult	Unknown	Total
Male											
Probable Male						3	2	2	3		10
Female											
Probable Female						3 (2)	4	1	1		9 (8)
Unknown	1	3	4	16	3	3	1		1 (0)	8 (0)	40 (31)
Total	1	3	4	16	3	9 (8)	7	3	5 (4)	8 (0)	59 (49)

*Numbers in parentheses indicate the total directly observed.

Table 6-20. Sex and age distribution* of the Tell el-Kerkh Cemetery: Cremated remains.

Sex	Fetal	Perinatal	Infant	Juvenile	Subadult	Adult	Young Adult	Middle Adult	Old Adult	Unknown	Total
Male											
Probable Male						4	2	2			8
Female											
Probable Female					1	6					7
Unknown		1	1	11	4	12			1	1(0)	31(30)
Total		1	1	11	5	22	2	2	1	1(0)	46(45)

*Numbers in parentheses indicate the total directly observed.

Table 6-21. Sex and age distribution of the Tell el-Kerkh Cemetery: Burial type unknown.

Sex	Fetal	Perinatal	Infant	Juvenile	Subadult	Adult	Young Adult	Middle Adult	Old Adult	Unknown	Total
Male											
Probable Male						1					1
Female											
Probable Female							1				1
Unknown		2	4 (3)	11 (10)	1 (0)	9 (6)			1	4 (0)	32 (22)
Total		2	4 (3)	11 (10)	1 (0)	10 (7)	1		1	4 (0)	34 (24)

*Numbers in parentheses indicate the total directly observed.

Table 6-22. Sex and age distribution of the Tell el-Kerkh Cemetery, all burials included.

Sex	Fetal	Perinatal	Infant	Juvenile	Subadult	Adult	Young Adult	Middle Adult	Old Adult	Unknown	Total
Male							2	4			6
Probable Male							13	14	10	3		40
Female							1	2	3			6
Probable Female						1	13	14	5	1		34
Unknown	7	12	14	57	15	33	2		4	14	158
Total	7	12	14	57	16	60	34	22	8	14	244

Table 6-23. Sex and age distribution of the Tell el-Kerkh Cemetery, directly observed burials only.

Sex	Fetal	Perinatal	Infant	Juvenile	Subadult	Adult	Young Adult	Middle Adult	Old Adult	Unknown	Total
Male							2	4			6
Probable Male							11	13	9	3		36
Female							1	2	3			6
Probable Female						1	10	11	5	1		28
Unknown	7	10	12	52	14	27	1	0	2		125
Total	7	10	12	52	15	49	29	21	6		201

will primarily refer to the complete cemetery sample, and will reference the reduced cemetery sample as necessary.

Of the 244 individuals excavated from the cemetery, only 230 were of sufficient preservation to allow for age and sex determination. One hundred and six (46%) nonadults, and 124 adults (54%) were identified. Unfortunately, sex determination was only possible for 86 of the 124 adults. Forty-six males (53%) and forty females (47%) were observed, which does suggest that the males of Tell el-Kerkh had a greater risk of mortality than females. However, the age distribution for the respective sexes reveals an interesting contrast. For males, peak age of mortality falls within the young adult age range (35%), with only a slight reduction in frequency for the middle adult age group (30%). However, while females also appeared to experience

peak mortality during the young adult period, they did so at a greater proportion of the total number of female deaths (40%). In addition, among the females, there is a stark underrepresentation of middle adult deaths within the sample (20%).

For the Pre-pottery Neolithic, higher mortality rates and lower estimated life expectancies for females have been attributed to the risks of pregnancy and childbirth (Eshed et al. 2004a). To examine this further at Tell el-Kerkh, the estimated maternal mortality rate was calculated using the ratio of directly examined young adult females to young adult males (.87). The estimated maternal mortality is 214 deaths per 100,000 live births (following the work of McFadden and Oxenham 2019). This suggests that the greater number of young adult female deaths at Tell el-Kerkh may have been due, at least in part, to the hazards of childbirth.

In general, nonadult mortality was high, with 57 of 106 (53%) individuals dying during the juvenile years, and 33 (31%) expiring before the end of the first postnatal year. Eighteen percent are estimated to have died prior to 40 gestational weeks. Since infant age estimation was derived from standards of postcranial growth, it is possible that the high number of perinatal deaths, here representing deaths occurring between 36-40 gestational weeks, reflects growth disruption, rather than actual age. It is also cannot be determined if the individuals were premature, stillborn, or died during the neonatal period. Thus, it may not be possible to truly separate neonatal from perinatal deaths, and, by extension, accurately access endogenous or exogenous mortality. However, as low birth weight is associated with early infant mortality, as well as reduced size-for-age, it is likely that these results, whether reflecting accurate age estimation or stunted infant growth, reflect a common cause, and may provide some insight into Neolithic maternal health (Dougherty and Tsuneki 2015).

The general category of 'juvenile,' being broad, can obscure the greater nuances in mortality present within the cohort. With reference to 86 nonadults for whom age could be determined, a more precise pattern of nonadult mortality is visible (Figure 6-2). It appears that at Tell el-Kerkh, the peak risk of mortality for nonadults occurred within the first four years of life, particularly between the ages of one and three years, a period of rapid growth in which metabolic needs are high, and susceptibility to malnutrition and infection is increased (Saunders and Barrans 1999). Notably, there is a steady increase in mortality from the prenatal period to the third postnatal year, followed by a swift decline thereafter. That nonadult mortality decreased rapidly after age three suggests that those who survived early childhood were less likely to succumb to ill health during later adolescence. A similar mortality trend was observed by Eshed and co-workers (2004a), who found that, in the aggregate, juvenile mortality was highest for children in the first five years of life during the Pre-pottery Neolithic.

The overall mortality trend at Tell el-Kerkh reveals that mortality is highest for both young children and young adults. Because of the inherent imprecision of estimating age for adults, it is not possible to precisely compute mean age-at-death, or life expectancy. However, the overall mortality trend (Figure 6-2; Tables 6-22, 6-23), with the greatest proportion of deaths occurring below age 35, seems to imply that mean age-at-death is low. Following the work of Sattenspiel and Harpending (1983), who have shown that low mean age-at-death is less a reflection of the mortality rate than the fertility rate, this suggests that birth rates were high at Tell el-Kerkh.

To explore this further, the juvenility index was calculated for the cemetery sample. The juvenility index is the ratio of nonadult to adult individuals, with higher outcomes indicative of higher fertility. Initially introduced by Bocquet-Appel and Masset (1982), and later modified by others (Buikstra *et al.* 1986; Bocquet-

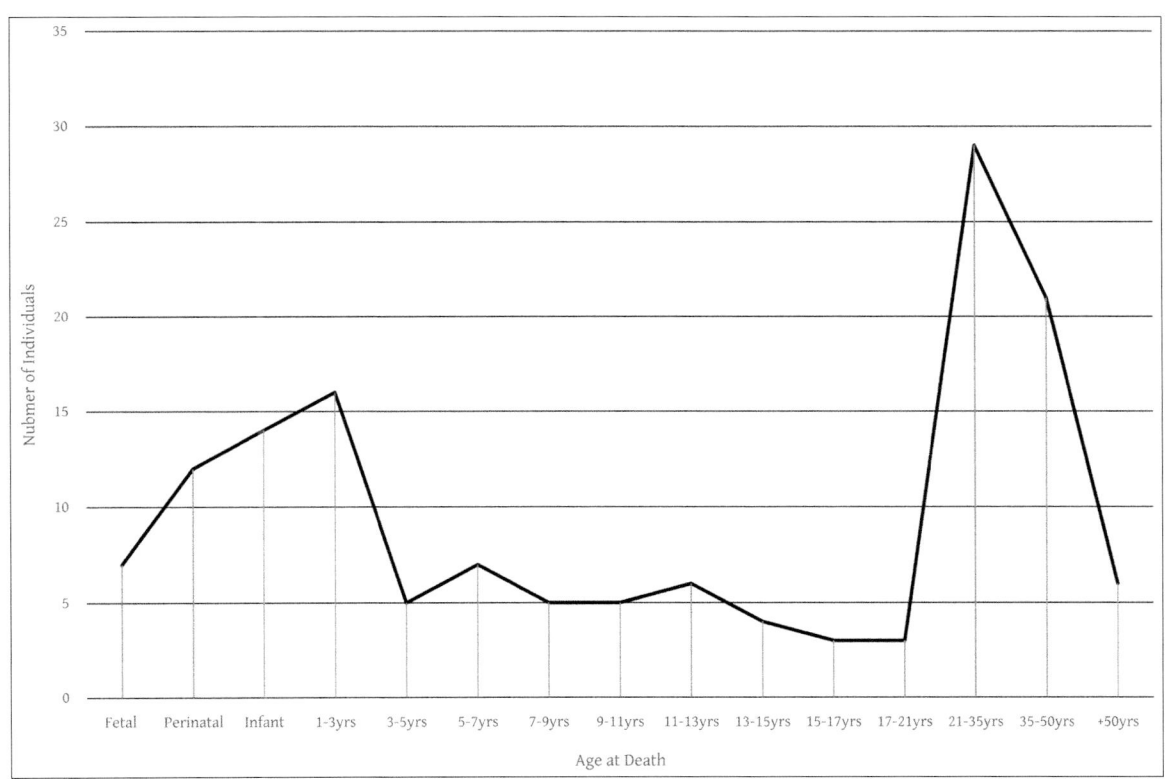

Figure 6-2. Mortality profile of individuals with known ages.

Appel 2002), the index was calculated as the ratio of juveniles to adults (D_{5-14}/D_{20+}). However, because these initial versions of the juvenility index did not include infants and young juveniles present within mortuary samples, the juvenility index (D_{0-14}/D_{total}) offered by McFadden and Oxenham (2017) is more appropriate for the Tell el-Kerkh sample, given that the majority of nonadult deaths fall below three years. Using this ratio, the juvenility index for the directly examined sample of burials at Tell el-Kerkh is .44, and the fertility rate is 5.62 births per female. Given these estimates, Tell el-Kerkh appears to have experienced high fertility during the Pottery Neolithic.

4. Postcranial Measurements

The analysis of postcranial measurements can provide information on growth, development, stature, and robusticity. Because skeletal growth and maintenance are greatly influenced by factors such as illness, nutrition, or activity, the metric analysis of long bones can reveal intrapopulation variation that may reveal that certain individuals suffered from poor health during development, or intensive labor activities as adults (Larsen 1997).

The postcranial measurements for adults and nonadults utilized for this analysis are described by Buikstra and Ubelaker (1994). Adult stature was estimated using the formulae developed for ancient Egyptians by Raxter and colleagues (2008). When the required skeletal material was not available, the formulae of Trotter and Gleser (1952), Meadows and Jantz (1992) and Holland (1995) for Black populations were employed. The use of these reference samples to estimate stature for Neolithic skeletal remains in western Asia has precedent in the work of both Hillson and colleagues (2013) and Molleson and coworkers (2005) at Çatalhöyük, as well as Molleson (2000) for Abu Hureyra.

For the nonadults, stature was estimated using the equations of Ruff (2007). Because Ruff's formulae were not developed for individuals below one year of age, estimates of fetal length were calculated from femur length using the regression formula developed by Fazekas and Kósa (1978).

Table 6-24. Postcranial measurement means for adult males, females, and individuals of unknown sex.

Bone	Measurement (mm)	Male					Female					Unknown				
		n	Min.	Max.	Mean	Standard Deviation	n	Min.	Max.	Mean	Standard Deviation	n	Min.	Max.	Mean	Standard Deviation
Clavicle	Max. Length	1	–	–	163	–	–	–	–	–	–	–	–	–	–	–
	Anterior-Posterior Diameter	1	–	–	10.10	–	–	–	–	–	–	–	–	–	–	–
	Superior-inferior Diameter	1	–	–	12.20	–	–	–	–	–	–	–	–	–	–	–
Humerus	Max. Length	–	–	–	–	–	–	–	–	–	–	–	–	–	–	–
	Epicondylar Breadth	7	57	63.7	60.49	2.62	2	52.65	56.1	54.38	2.44	–	–	–	–	–
	Vertical Head Diameter	–	–	–	–	–	–	–	–	–	–	–	–	–	–	–
	Max. diameter at midshaft	4	19.45	22.05	20.83	1.17	1	–	–	19.5	–	–	–	–	–	–
	Min. diameter at midshaft	4	15.1	17.9	16.45	1.15	1	–	–	14.65	–	–	–	–	–	–
Radius	Max. Length	3	233	261	243.33	15.37	–	–	–	–	–	1	–	–	214	–
	Anterior-posterior midshaft diameter	5	10.05	13	11.59	1.06	1	–	–	11	–	1	–	–	11.9	–
	Medial-lateral midshaft diameter	5	13.4	15.3	14.45	.84	1	–	–	13.9	–	1	–	–	13.35	–
Ulna	Max. Length	1	–	–	254	–	2	232	237	234.5	3.54	1	–	–	235	–
	Anterior-posterior midshaft diameter	3	12.2	12.7	12.52	.28	2	11.8	13.35	12.58	1.10	1	–	–	11.7	–
	Medial-lateral midshaft diameter	3	14.4	17.5	15.75	1.59	2	14.65	14.8	14.73	.11	1	–	–	14.7	–
	Physiological length	–	–	–	–	–	1	–	–	204	–	–	–	–	–	–
Second Metacarpal	Length	6	62.5	69.2	65.78	2.15	5	59.8	69.15	65.48	3.69	–	–	–	–	–
Femur	Max. Length	2	440	458	449	12.73	1	–	–	394	–	–	–	–	–	–
	Max. Head Diameter	9	39.9	49	44.83	2.88	8	36.75	41.45	39.36	1.5	–	–	–	–	–
	Anterior-posterior Subtrochanteric Diameter	1	–	–	24.40	–	3	19.5	20.5	20	.5	–	–	–	–	–
	Medial-lateral Subtrochanteric Diameter	1	–	–	29.40	–	3	26.6	27.8	26.98	1.2	–	–	–	–	–
	Anterior-posterior Midshaft Diameter	1	–	–	29.75	–	2	22.6	25.05	23.83	1.73	–	–	–	–	–
	Medial-lateral Midshaft Diameter	1	–	–	23.30	–	2	20.4	24.5	22.45	2.9	–	–	–	–	–
Tibia	Max. Length	–	–	–	–	–	–	–	–	–	–	–	–	–	–	–
Fibula	Max. Length	–	–	–	–	–	–	–	–	–	–	–	–	–	–	–
Calcaneus	Max. Length	2	70.25	75.25	72.75	3.54	1	–	–	62.5	–	–	–	–	–	–
	Middle Breadth	2	45.8	46.7	46.25	.64	1	–	–	35.9	–	–	–	–	–	–

Estimates of body mass were based upon measurements of maximum femoral head diameter for adults, and distal femoral metaphyseal breadth for nonadults (Auerbach and Ruff 2004; Ruff 2007; Ruff *et al.* 2012).

Table 6-24 displays the male and female means for each postcranial measurement. While the sample size per bone is small, generally, one does see an overall trend of sexual dimorphism, with male bone measurements being greater than female measurements. For the femoral head diameter, a measurement often used as tool for sex estimation, the difference between mean diameters for males and females is 5.47mm. This suggests, however rudimentarily, that for the population of Tell el-Kerkh, femoral head diameter is a fairly useful variable for assigning sex. However, given that the female range for the measurement is 36.75-41.45mm, and the male range is 39.9-49mm., caution must still be exercised in those cases when forced to rely the femoral head diameter as the only sex indicator.

Estimates of adult stature and body mass are shown in Table 6-25. The average height for males is 1.66m (5ft 4in), with an average body mass of 58.82kg. The average height for females is about 8.9cm less (3.5in), and the mean body weight is 8kg less. In these results, the sexual dimorphism apparent in the individual long bone measurements is carried over into both stature and body mass. However, these differences are not completely distinct, as the highest values for female stature do overlap with lowest values for males.

Nonadult stature (or body length for fetal individuals) and body mass are shown in Table 6-26. In practice, nonadult stature and body mass can provide useful information on growth, development, and physiological stress given that childhood growth is particularly sensitive to disruptions caused by malnutrition or illness (Bogin 1999; King and Ulijaszek 1999; Temple 2008). It may also reveal periods of rapid growth or stunting among the sample. Unfortunately, generating a growth curve for the nonadults requires a representative and inclusive sample. While the Tell el-Kerkh nonadult

Table 6-25. Estimations of stature and body mass.

	Burial	Age	Bone used for Stature Estimation	Estimated Stature (cm)	Estimated Body Mass (kg)
Females	533	Middle adult	–	–	50.52 (±4.44)
	712	Middle adult	–	–	44.31 (±4.44)
	725	Young adult	–	–	48.99 (±4.44)
	752	Adult	–	–	51.39 (±4.44)
	803	Young adult	Second Metacarpal[c]	162.3 (±5.15)	–
	909	Young adult	–	–	–
	924	Young adult	–	–	50.08 (±4.44)
	926	Adult	Ulna[b]	153.8 (±4.783)	–
	927.3	Young adult	Femur[a]	149.2 (±2.517)	47.03 (±4.44)
	941	Middle adult	Second Metacarpal[c]	157.7 (±5.15)	54.55 (±4.44)
	988	Middle adult	Ulna[b]	152.2 (±4.83)	53.13 (±4.44)
	1057	Adult	Second Metacarpal[c]	164.0 (±5.10)	–
	Mean			157.1	50.00
Males	748.1	Young adult	–	–	59.02 (±6.84)
	807	Middle adult	–	–	58.18 (±6.84)
	830	Adult	–	–	52.16 (±6.84)
	836	Middle adult	–	–	70.5 (±6.84)
	904	Young adult	Calcaneus[d]	168.2 (±4.88)	56.5 (±6.84)
	921	Young adult	Calcaneus[d]	171.7 (±4.88)	56.78 (±6.84)
	943	Adult	Second Metacarpal[c]	165.3 (±5.15)	–
	984	Young adult	Radius[a]	169.8 (±3.731)	60.7 (±6.84)
	1045	Adult	Femur[a]	163.2 (±3.218)	70.5 (±6.84)
	1047	Young adult	Femur[a]	167.3 (±3.218)	–
	1050	Young adult	Ulna[b]	164.1 (±4.74)	–
	1058	Middle adult	Radius[a]	160.2 (±3.731)	–
	1064	Young adult	Second Metacarpal[c]	164.1 (±5.10)	45.05 (±6.84)
	Mean			165.99	58.82
Unknown Sex	995	Adult	Radius[a]	m: 157.4 (±3.731) f: 150.7 (±4.057)	–
	Mean			m: 157.4 f: 150.7	–

[a]Raxter *et al.* 2008.; [b]Trotter and Gleser 1952; [c]Meadows and Janz 1992; [d]Holland 1995.

263

Table 6-26. Estimations of nonadult stature (body length), and body mass, by age.

Burial	Age Category	Age Range	Bone used for Stature Estimation	Estimated Stature (cm)	Estimated Body Mass (kg)
828	Fetal/Perinatal	28-32wks ges.	Femur	36.87	–
925	Fetal/Perinatal	34-38wks ges.	Femur	49.46	–
519	Fetal/Perinatal	37-41wks ges.	Femur	54.74	–
946	Fetal/Perinatal	36-40 wks ges.	Femur	52.87	–
913	Juvenile	1-2 yrs	Femur & Tibia	72.52 (±3.22)	8.6 (±1.43)
730	Juvenile	2-3 yrs	Humerus	94.41(±4.97)	–
829	Juvenile	2-3 yrs	Tibia	80.32 (±3.46)	–
1066	Juvenile	2-3 yrs	Femur	91.71 (±5.28)	–
927.2	Juvenile	4-5 yrs	Femur	98.18 (±4.12)	14.83 (±2.36)
713	Juvenile	10-12 yrs	Tibia	125.5 (±4.61)	–

sample numbers 105, there were only nine individuals for whom stature could be estimated, and only two for body mass. Although the nonadult sample includes 14 infants, none could be included here. Likewise, the majority of juveniles within the late childhood period of development are also absent. Nevertheless, while the nonadult sample cannot be called representative, it does appear that from the earliest ages on, growth is fairly steady, with, potentially, a rapid increase in growth between the first and third years.

5. Non-Specific Indicators of Morbidity and Malnutrition

To further explore the factors that may have influenced nonadult and adult mortality, the skeletal remains were examined for four non-specific indicators of morbidity: 1) Linear enamel hypoplasia; 2) porotic hyperostosis; 3) cribra orbitalia; and 4) periostitis.

1) Linear Enamel Hypoplasia

Linear enamel hypoplasias (LEH) are defects in dental enamel caused by a 'cessation of ameloblastic activity' (Sarnat and Schour 1941:1989). This decrease in 'ameloblastic activity,' which refers to the activity of enamel-producing cells, results in a reduction of enamel thickness, giving rise to hypoplastic zones of enamel, which manifest in both pitted and linear surface disturbances. Because enamel is a permanent and non-renewable substance, enamel hypoplasias serve as records of childhood morbidity. They have been linked to a wide variety of causes, such as periods of illness, weaning stress, malnutrition, starvation, metabolic disease, infection, or even poisoning, experienced during the childhood years (Neiburger 1990; Goodman et al. 1991; Guatelli-Steinberg 2016; Bereczki et al. 2019). However, since enamel defects cannot be linked specifically to any one particular cause, they are cemterpreted as general indicators of great physiological stress taking place during tooth development (Goodman, et al. 1980; Goodman and Rose 1990).

Age of incidence was established using the method presented by Goodman and Rose (1990: 98). This method employs an algorithm to identify the age of defect onset, and yields presumably more precise estimations that fall below the six to twelve month intervals provided by other methods. Because the equations were generated through regression techniques, the method is based upon the underlying assumption that teeth develop at equal and constant increments (Goodman and Rose 1990: 90).

A total of 1490 permanent teeth from 88 individuals were examined. Three hundred twenty-four linear enamel hypoplastic defects were found on 172 teeth (11.5% of 1490). The defects were most frequently observed on the right mandibular canine, while the first mandibular molars, and the third maxillary and mandibular molars, did not display any defects (Figure 6-3). The maximum number of LEH was observed on the teeth of an older juvenile (10-12 years), who was found to have 37 enamel defects. This individual does appear to be an outlier, as most individuals typically had between two to five hypoplastic defects (Figure 6-4).

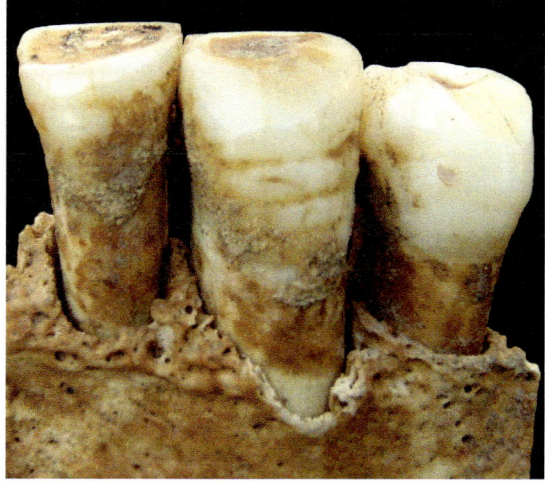

Figure 6-3. Three linear enamel hypoplastic defects are visible on the right mandibular canine of Str. 921. Periodontal resorption is also evident.

Thirty-six individuals (40.9%) were found to display at least one linear enamel hypoplastic defect (Table 6-27). Of these, 13 were nonadults (36.1%). Males accounted for well over half of the adults with LEH (56.5%), while only eight females exhibited the condition (Table 6-28).

The ages of LEH formation for the left mandibular canine and the left first maxillary incisor are shown in Figure 6-5. These teeth were selected as they are generally considered to be the most vulnerable to disruptions in enamel formation (Goodman and Armelagos 1985).

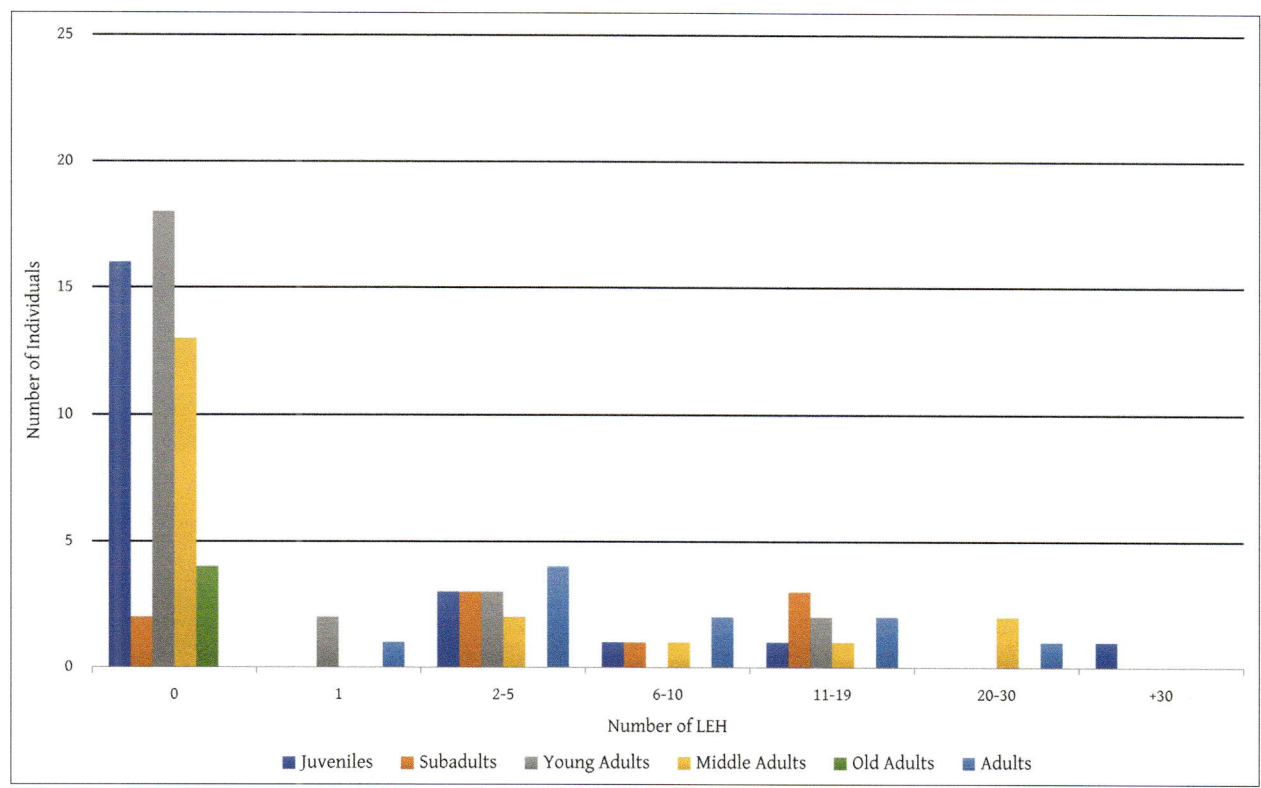

Figure 6-4. Modal distribution of linear enamel hypoplasia.

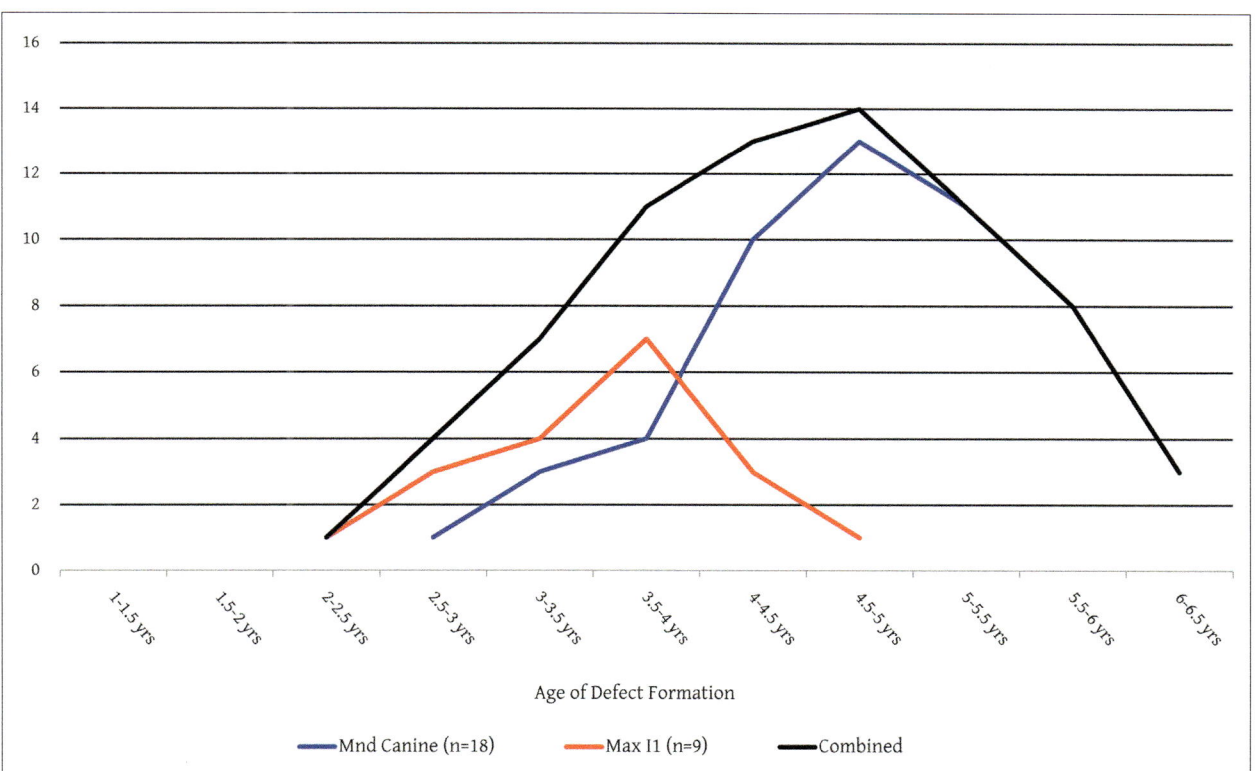

Figure 6-5. Age of enamel defect formation.

Table 6-27. Individuals exhibiting linear enamel hypoplastic defects.

Burial	Sex	Age	Number of Linear Enamel Hypoplasias	Number of Teeth Affected	Number of Observable Teeth	Percentage of Teeth Affected
507	Unknown	Juvenile	3	2	19	10.5
521	Unknown	Subadult	3	3	24	12.5
524	Probable female	Middle adult	10	7	20	35
533	Female	Middle adult	4	2	25	8
711	Unknown	Subadult	5	4	18	22.2
712	Probable female	Middle adult	27	10	23	43.4
713	Unknown	Juvenile	37	14	28	50
714	Probable male	Adult	2	1	16	6.2
716	Probable male	Adult	16	9	28	32.1
718.1	Probable male	Young adult	4	3	13	23
725	Probable female	Young adult	1	1	24	4.1
729	Probable female	Young adult	3	3	30	10
731	Probable male	Adult	14	6	28	21.4
732	Unknown	Subadult	17	13	31	42
741.1	Unknown	Juvenile	2	1	10	10
751	Unknown	Juvenile	2	1	1	100
757	Unknown	Juvenile	16	7	21	33.3
826	Unknown	Subadult	13	10	32	31.2
860	Unknown	Adult	4	3	6	50
861	Probable female	Young adult	11	4	20	20
863	Probable female	Adult	4	3	19	15.7
908	Unknown	Subadult	16	6	28	21.4
921	Male	Young adult	12	5	27	18.5
926	Probable Female	Adult	3	2	17	11.7
943	Probable male	Adult	8	3	32	9.3
962	Male	Middle adult	2	1	22	4.5
979	Unknown	Subadult	10	7	28	25
984	Probable male	Adult	20	11	30	36.6
985	Unknown	Juvenile	6	4	15	40
988	Probable female	Middle adult	11	5	31	16.1
1044	Probable male	Middle adult	24	12	29	41.3
1047	Probable male	Adult	6	3	31	9.6
1050	Probable male	Young adult	1	1	11	9
1052	Unknown	Subadult	4	2	20	10
1053	Probable male	Adult	1	1	15	6.6
1056	Probable male	Young adult	2	2	30	6.7

Table 6-28. Summary of individuals with linear enamel hypoplastic defects.

	Juvenile	Subadult	Adult	Young Adult	Middle Adult	Total
Male			7	4	2	13
Female			2	3	4	8
Unknown	6	7	1			15
Total	6	7	10	7	6	36

There is a steady increase in defect formation beginning at age two. The peak age of formation for the maxillary incisor is between 3.5-4 years, and the peak age for the mandibular canine is 4.5-5 years of age. For both teeth, however, there is marked increase in defect formation during the third year.

Because LEH is a non-specific indicator of physiological stress, it is difficult to identify the exact cause of these growth disruptions, and even more difficult to ascertain why certain individuals at Tell el-Kerkh experienced repeated physiological disruptions well into adolescence, while others did not. For those individuals with LEH more frequently occurring in the earlier years of life, it is notable that porotic hyperostosis and cribra orbitalia (discussed below) were also most prevalent among individuals of similar age. This suggests that the children of Tell el-Kerkh, perhaps recently weaned, were exposed to pathogenic hazards, or forced to endure nutritional deficiencies, that resulted in illness and severe physiological stress.

2) Porotic Hyperostosis and Cribra Orbitalia

Cribra orbitalia and porotic hyperostosis are cranial lesions created by the proliferation of spongy bone in response to the increased production of erythrocytes (red blood cells) within bone marrow (Hengen 1971; Stuart-Macadam 1987, 1989; Aufderheide and Rodriguez-Martin 1998). Porotic hyperostosis is visible as areas of porosity or fine pitting on the cranial surface, most often on the parietal bones, and is also associated with thickened diploie, and a thinning of the external cortical layer of bone. Cribra orbitalia, while similar in development to porotic hyperostosis, is visible as porosity of the superior orbital plate. Both conditions can manifest as areas of porosity that are level with the natural surface of bone, or as coral-like surface expansions.

Historically, the bony changes, particularly porotic hyperostosis, were associated with hereditary anemias, such as sickle cell disease, or thalassemia (Cooley et al. 1927; Caffey 1937). Later researchers also observed that the conditions could be linked to malaria, chronic blood loss due to parasitic infection, and iron-deficiency anemia (Eng 1958; Layrisse and Roche 1964; Angel 1966; Stuart-Macadam 1992).

Among biological anthropologists, iron-deficiency anemia was the favored explanation for porotic hyperostosis and cribra orbitalia for decades. However, more recently, several researchers have begun to question this once certain relationship, and have proposed that deficiencies in micronutrients like folic acid (Vitamin B$_{12}$) or Vitamin C (scurvy), are more likely causes (Ortner and Ericksen 1997; Rothschild 2002; Sullivan 2005; Walker et al. 2009; Snoddy et al. 2018; but

see Oxenham and Cavill 2010). While these etiologies do seem unrelated, the underlying thread that binds them is that, in want of healthy red blood cells, the body is forced to produce, or attempt to produce, more, which leads to the hyperplastic expansion of bone marrow within the cranium.

In short, porotic hyperostosis and cribra orbitalia are not necessarily pathognomonic for any particular disease. Both conditions can be linked to hemolytic anemias, vitamin deficiencies, malaria, parasite-induced chronic blood loss, and even chronic diarrhea. Thus, in the absence of other skeletal changes that would reveal a more diagnostic constellation of pathology, it is best to consider the conditions as non-specific indicators of morbidity or physiological stress.

Ninety-seven crania (48 nonadults, 49 adults) were adequately preserved for examination. The superior orbital plates of 68 individuals were examined for evidence of cribra orbitalia. Eighty-nine individuals could be examined for porotic hyperostosis.

Of the 97 crania, twenty exhibited cribra orbitalia, porotic hyperostosis, or both (Table 6-29). The two conditions were rarely concurrent, appearing together on only four crania. The majority of the pathological cases were nonadults (60%), with over half dying at, or below, age six (Table 6-30). Eight adults, six of which were male, displayed only healed lesions.

In all nonadult cases, the lesions appeared active at the time of death (Figures 6-6, 6-7). Notably, of the nine nonadults for whom teeth could be examined, all had 3 to 37 linear enamel hypoplastic defects. In contrast, the dental pathology was not present on any of the adults, all of whom exhibited healed lesions. This might suggest, then, that these children, having endured some manner of physiological stress in early development, were left less prepared to survive subsequent morbid insults later on.

As discussed above, it is generally difficult, if not impossible, to link cribria orbitalia or porotic hyperostosis to any one particular cause, at least without other diagnostic evidence from elsewhere in the skeleton (Lewis 2012; Brickley 2018). However, in one case, Str. 985, a juvenile (6-7 years), the presence of cribra orbitalia may be the result of Vitamin C deficiency. In addition to the porosity visible on the superior orbital plates, fragments of the greater wing of the sphenoid bone also exhibited unusual porosity. Such porosity, linked to vascular hemorrhaging in soft tissue overlaying the region, has been argued to be a diagnostic feature of scurvy (Ortner and Erickson 1997; Snoddy et al. 2018). Unfortunately, other diagnostic features of scurvy, such as severe porosity of the maxilla, or other skeletal elements, were not observed.

Table 6-29. Individuals exhibiting porotic hyperostosis and/or cribra orbitalia.

Burial	Sex	Age	Cribra Orbitalia	Porotic Hyperostosis	Condition
502	Unknown	Juvenile	+		Active
521	Unknown	Subadult	+		Active
713	Unknown	Juvenile	+		Active
717	Unknown	Infant		+	Active
731	Probable male	Adult		+	Healed
739	Probable male	Middle adult		+	Healed
741.1	Unknown	Juvenile	+		Active
746.1	Unknown	Juvenile	+	+	Active
835.2	Unknown	Juvenile	+		Active
835.4	Unknown	Subadult	+		Active
851.1	Unknown	Infant	+	+	Active
904	Probable male	Young adult	+	+	Healed
908	Unknown	Subabult		+	Active
910.3	Unknown	Infant		+	Active
921	Male	Young adult	+	+	Healed
962	Male	Middle adult		+	Healed
978	Probable female	Adult		+	Healed
985	Unknown	Juvenile	+		Active
1047	Probable male	Adult		+	Healed
1051	Female	Middle adult		+	Healed

Table 6-30. Summary of individuals with cribra orbitalia
and/or porotic hyperostosis.

	Cribra Orbitalia (n=68)	Porotic Hyperostosis (n=89)	Both Lesions (n=60)	Total
Fetal/Perinatal (n=12)	–	–	–	–
Infant (n=7)	–	1	1	2
Juvenile (n=21)	5	1	1	7
Subadult (n=8)	2	1	–	3
Adult (n=20)	–	3 (2m, 1f)	–	3
Young Adult (n=15)	–	–	2 (2m)	2
Middle Adult (n=14)	–	3 (2m; 1f)	–	3
Total (n=97)	7	9	4	20

Figure 6-6. A fragment of parietal bone exhibiting active porotic hyperostosis, Str. 717.

Figure 6-7. Cribra orbitalia affecting the superior orbital plate of Str. 521.

Thus, while scurvy remains a strong possibility here, it cannot be diagnosed with complete certainty.

3) Periostitis

Periostitis (also termed subperiosteal new bone formation, or periosteal reaction) refers to the condition of proliferative new bone formation visible as a plaque on the outer cortex of bone. In its more active stage, periostitis appears as an area of woven bone adhered to the cortical surface. This newly formed bone then remodels into a more smooth, dense, sclerotic zone of compact bone, which is considered to be the 'healed' form of the condition. As with the pathological disorders described above, periostitis is not indicative of any one particular illness or disease, but appears to exist as a more generalized, inflammatory response to a wide variety of conditions, including localized bone trauma (so-called bone bruises), tendon injuries, tuberculosis, and treponemal infections, to name a few (Ortner and Putschar 1985; Weston 2008). However, in want of other diagnostic criteria, periosteal reactions are typically taken as non-specific indicators of disease, whatever the cause (Larsen 1997; DeWitte and Bekvalac 2011; Marques *et al.* 2019).

While periostitis is a commonly found pathology among archaeological skeletal samples, this is not the case at Tell el-Kerkh. Only three individuals, both middle adult females, were discovered to have the lesions, providing a prevalence of 5% (n=60) among individuals with sufficiently preserved femora, tibia, and fibulae.

Sclerotic areas of periosteal bone formation were observed on the lower extremities of Str. 921, a young adult male. The patches of new bone formation coated the distal right fibula, and the distal diaphyses of both tibiae.

The second, Str. 941, was observed to have an area of proliferative new bone formation present on the medial aspect of the distal right fibula. As this is an area associated with soft tissue connections, such as the interosseous ligament, it is unknown if this periosteal reaction is related to a greater somatic inflammatory response, or if it is a more localized response to some disorder, such as an injury, that affected the right ankle.

The third, and far more extensive, case of periostitis comes from Str. 988 (Figure 6-8). Both femora exhibit a plaque of new bone formation suggestive of an ongoing inflammatory process. The right femur has 67mm length of periosteal reaction on the proximolateral shaft, just opposite of the gluteal tuberosity. There are several patches of both woven and remodeled bone on the anteromedial diaphysis. The left femur exhibits subperiosteal bone formation along the anteromedial

Figure 6-8. Periostitis of the left proximal femur, Str. 988.

length of the diaphysis, but the appearance is more sclerotic, with vessel impressions, covering a 121mm area.

6. Infectious Disease

With the increase in sedentism and population size brought by the transition to agricultural during the Neolithic came new opportunities for infectious disease (Larsen 1995). These diseases may be viral, such as smallpox or polio, or bacterial, such as leprosy, tuberculosis, or some manner of treponemal infection. To be viewed archaeologically, such infections must necessarily be chronic, as the individual must endure the infection long enough for bony changes to manifest.

It is often the case that illness can produce non-specific skeletal lesions, discussed above as periosteal reactions. However, certain diseases, such as venereal syphilis, leprosy, and tuberculosis, can produce diagnostic constellations of skeletal lesions that leave little doubt as to the etiology (Ortner and Putschar 1985), provided that the skeleton is reasonably intact to allow for a thorough examination.

From Tell el-Kerkh, there is the curious case of Str. 748, a young adult male. This individual exhibits an extraordinarily pathological second lumbar vertebra (Figure 6-9). This vertebra displays a large, concave lesion affecting the superior surface of the body, with associated anterior wedging. There is no sign of active bone formation at the site of the concavity, although osteophytic growth is present along the margins of the body, and sclerotic, vertical pillars of bone are present along the sides. This apparently erosive lesion has removed most of the superior endplate of the body, with only the posterior and left lateral edges remaining. The trabeculae within the concavity of the body are exposed, and some appear sclerotic. Sharp margins define the edges of the concavity.

The list of potential causes of similar vertebral pathology is lengthy (Buikstra 1976; Mann and Hunt

Figure 6-9. The second lumbar vertebra of Str. 748. The unusual erosive cavitation of the vertebral body is suggestive of tuberculosis.

2005). However, many diseases that affect the vertebrae, such as brucellosis, are typically multifocal, do not result in vertebral collapse, or are environmentally specific with respect to pathogen of origin.

The most conservative diagnosis of the condition of this vertebra is a compression fracture, or vertebral endplate collapse. The diminished superior/inferior height, and anterior wedging are indicative of such a fracture. However, the characteristics of the bone, such the sharp margins around the central concavity, the discontinuous superior surface of the vertebral body, and the apparent lytic destruction do not align with the expected appearance of a normal compression fracture. Moreover, vertebral compression fractures are most commonly associated with age-related bone loss, particularly among post-menopausal females, which would seem to disqualify this young adult male.

Tuberculosis, when affecting the vertebrae, most frequently affects the lumbar spine. The disease process typically results in lytic lesions (also described as resorptive or erosive) often associated with marrow spaces, such as the spongy bone of the vertebral body, but is unassociated with proliferative bone formation (Steinbock 1976; Aufderheide and Rodriguez-Martin 1998). Moreover, the concavity observed here, with the associated sharp margins of the remaining superior end plate can be accounted for by progression of a tubercular abscess, which, owning to vascularity, forms near the anterior aspect of the vertebra body, and progresses dorsally into the intervertebral space (Aufderheide and Rodriguez-Martin 1998). In addition, the chronic nature of the infection affords periods of healing, which, in bone, can reveal itself as sclerotic trabeculae. This would account for the general appearance of the exposed trabeculae.

However, a few details are cause for caution. In particular, tuberculosis is often characterized by lesions

affecting adjacent vertebrae, and can also affect other areas of the skeleton, such as the ribs (Buikstra 1976; Steinbock 1976; Ortner and Putschar 1985; Roberts and Buikstra 2003). In the case of this individual, however, other skeletal evidence was absent. Notably, the lower thoracic vertebrae, though in poor condition, showed no sign of pathology.

In addition, tuberculosis is noted as being a disease of poverty and population density (Roberts and Buikstra 2003), a description that alludes to tuberculosis as it existed in the more recent, historical past. While poverty is less likely to be a factor at Tell el-Kerkh, it is a question of whether or not the population density of the settlement was adequate to sustain the presence of a communicable disease. At Çatalhöyük, for example, Larsen and colleagues (2019) note the absence of specific density-dependent infectious diseases, like tuberculosis, which seems to imply that a society with a theoretical peak population size of 8000 or less could not adequately sustain the disease.

However, while population density is certainly a factor in the opportunistic transmission of the disease, it need not be the only variable with respect to contact and infection. Tuberculosis is a zoonotic disease that can be contracted from animal vectors such as cows (*Mycobacterium bovis*), and goats (*Mycobacterium caprae*). Both animals are common domesticates found in Neolithic settlements, including Tell el-Kerkh (Tsuneki *et al.* 1999). Thus, at Tell el-Kerkh, the interaction between humans and livestock could have provided the opportunity for exposure.

Diagnosing any disease on the basis of one bone is fraught with hazards. Yet, in this particular case, the pathological changes, the location within the vertebral column, and the presence of potential animal vectors within the settlement, provide potential evidence for the presence of tuberculosis at Tell el-Kerkh.

7. Dental Pathology

A total of 1543 permanent teeth from 93 individuals were available for observation. In addition, 269 deciduous teeth from 28 nonadults were also examined. The teeth were inventoried, measured, and analyzed following the standards presented by Buikstra and Ubelaker (1994), unless otherwise noted. The measurements were taken using Mitutoyo dial calipers accurate to .05mm, and are presented in Appendix 6.6.

The dental inventories for the permanent and deciduous dentitions are shown in Figure 6-10 and Figure 6-11, respectively. Generally, the teeth were fairly well preserved, certainly more so than the skeletal elements, which is not surprising given the durable

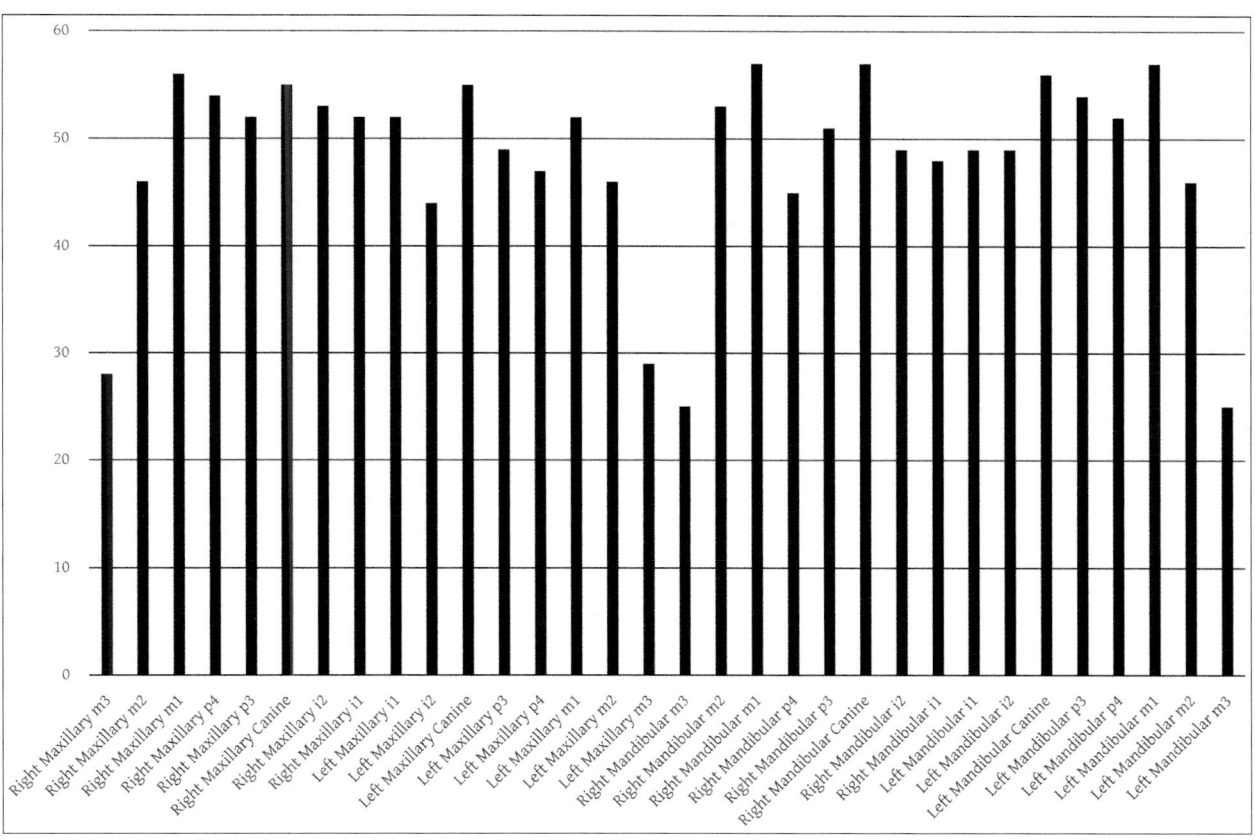

Figure 6-10. Inventory of permanent teeth.

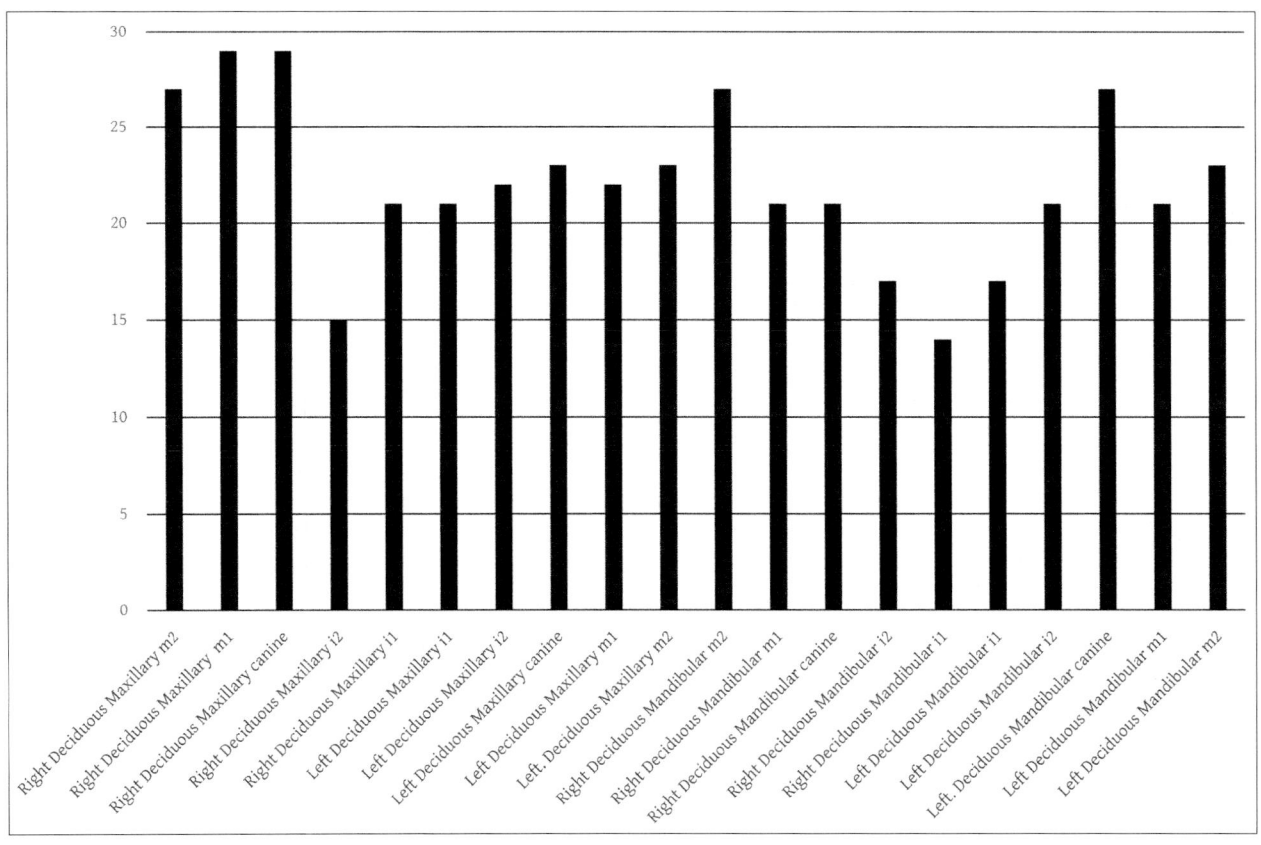

Figure 6-11. Inventory of deciduous teeth.

structure of teeth. For both juveniles and adults, the larger, posterior teeth were present in greater numbers, but the differences were negligible. There were eleven cases of third molar agenesis among five individuals (males=3; females=2).

The teeth, maxillae, and mandibles were examined for evidence of dental disease and dental wear. Over forty individuals (33%, n=121) were found to have suffered from dental caries, or other dental pathology (Table 6-31). The summarized frequencies of observed dental pathology are provided in Table 6-32.

1) Dental Caries

Dental caries refers to the progressive, focal destruction of tooth enamel, as well as the underlying tissue, caused by the acidic metabolic by-products of oral bacteria, such as *Streptococcus mutans* (Hillson 1996; Larsen 1997; Temple 2016). Because these oral bacteria tend to thrive, in particular, on carbohydrates, such as sucrose, there is a strong link between diets rich in carbohydrates and the incidence of dental caries (Keenleyside 2008; Buzon and Bombak 2010; Klaus and Tam 2010).

Carious deciduous molars were observed in two subadults (7.14%, n=28). In these cases, the affected teeth were remnant deciduous molars that had yet to be replaced.

The frequency of carious permanent teeth is low, with only 44 of 1543 (2.85%) affected. Likewise, the number of deciduous teeth found to have dental caries is similarly low, with only 1.11% of the observed teeth exhibiting the lesions.

Of the 55 dental caries observed, just over half (50.9%) were interproximal. This suggests that oral hygiene, however it manifested in the Late Neolithic, did not include any form of flossing. Occlusal caries accounted for 36.3% of the observed caries. Cervical caries, which affect the area around the cemento-enamel junction, were the least common.

Fifty-five caries were observed among 23 individuals with permanent teeth, representing 19% of the dental sample (Figure 6-12). Twenty-one were adults (22.5%, n=93). More males than females had carious teeth. However, with respect to sex-specific sample size, a slightly greater percentage of females (33%, n=24) than males (32%, n=31) had dental caries.

While, in general, the number of males relative to females with dental caries is very similar, the age at death for those individuals seems to reveal a disparity in caries onset. For males, carious teeth were most frequently observed among individuals who died at

older ages, rather than at younger ages. In contrast, for females, dental caries was most commonly found affecting the teeth of young adults. This suggests, however remotely, that females at Tell el-Kerkh were developing carious lesions at a younger age than males. This could mean that women at Tell el-Kerkh had greater access to cariogenic foods than males, and may also reflect gendered divisions of occupation or food access. In addition, poor oral health among females has been linked to physiological changes associated with high fertility (Lukacs and Largaespada 2006; Lukacs 2008), and this may also contribute to the divergent age-related pattern of oral health among young adult males and females at Tell el-Kerkh.

2) Periodontal Disease

While oral bacteria are often held in check by the immune system's responses, an accumulation of bacteria within dental plaque can trigger an inflammatory response that deleteriously affects the surrounding tissue. In the early stages, this is visible as gingivitis, a condition in which the gum tissue appears swollen and red. If left untreated, the disease will progress into periodontitis. In this, the inflammatory response will begin to affect the underlying alveolar bone, leading to alveolar recession (horizontal bone loss), and increasing tooth root exposure (Clarke *et al.* 1986; Hillson 1996).

However, while tooth root exposure (the amount of root visible between the cemento-enamel junction and the alveolar rim) can indicate periodontal disease, care must be taken to distinguish between root exposure due to periodontitis, and that which is caused by continuous dental eruption, particularly when heavy dental wear is present (Whittaker *et al.* 1990; Glass 1991). For this reason, periodontitis was scored as present only in less ambiguous cases, such as those that demonstrated a clear loss of alveolar crest height or showed clear signs of alveolar destruction. As a result, the actual prevalence of periodontal disease at Tell el-Kerkh may be underrepresented.

At Tell el-Kerkh, twenty-two individuals (males=14; females=7; unknown=1) were observed with alveolar recession indicative of periodontitis, often with several millimeters of root exposure. Although more males than females were observed with this dental pathology, the age-specific proportions suggest that for females, periodontal disease was more frequently endured during the young adult period, whereas for males, it had a higher prevalence during the middle adult years.

3) Antemortem Tooth Loss

Antemortem tooth loss refers to the loss of a tooth, or teeth, during life, with subsequent healing of the

Table 6-31. Individuals with selected dental pathology.

Burial	Sex	Age	Caries					Other Dental Pathology	
			Carious Teeth	Occlusal	Inter-proximal	Cervical	Total Caries	Antemortem Tooth Loss	Periapical Abscess
521	Unknown	Subadult	2 (Deciduous)	2	–	–	2	–	–
524	Probable female	Middle adult	–	–	–	–	–	3	–
533	Probable female	Middle adult	–	–	–	–	–	1	–
710	Probable male	Old adult	–	–	–	–	–	10	–
712	Probable female	Middle adult	–	–	–	–	–	2	–
714	Probable male	Adult	1	–	1	–	1	–	–
715	Probable male	Adult	3	–	4	–	4	–	–
718.1	Probable male	Young Adult	–	–	–	–	–	1	1
720.1	Probable male	Old adult	–	–	–	–	–	3	–
722	Probable female	Middle adult	–	–	–	–	–	1	–
729	Probable female	Young adult	1	1	–	–	1	–	–
731	Probable male	Young adult	–	–	–	–	–	1	–
737	Probable male	Adult	3	1	1	2	4	1	–
739	Probable male	Middle adult	–	–	–	–	–	1	–
743	Probable male	Middle adult	–	–	–	–	–	1	–
757	Unknown	Juvenile	1 (Deciduous)	1	–	–	1	–	–
803	Probable female	Adult	3	2	1	–	3	3	–
826	Unknown	Subadult	1	2	–	–	2	–	–
830	Probable male	Adult	1	1	2	–	3	2	–
832.5	Unknown	Adult	1	–	1	–	1	–	–
847.2	Probable male	Old adult	–	–	–	–	–	3	–
860	Unknown	Adult	1	–	1	–	1	–	–
862	Probable female	Adult	1	–	1	–	1	–	–
863	Probable female	Middle adult	–	–	–	–	–	3	–
921	Male	Young adult	2	–	2	–	2	2	–
926	Probable female	Adult	2	2	–	–	2	–	2
930.1	Probable female	Young adult	1	1	–	1	2	–	–
930.2	Probable female	Young adult	–	–	–	–	–	2	–
931	Unknown	Adult	1	1	–	–	1	–	–
941	Probable female	Middle adult	6	2	1	4	7	3	–
947	Probable male	Middle adult	1	–	1	–	1	1	–
962	Probable male	Middle adult	3	–	4	–	4	6	2
978	Probable female	Young adult	3	1	2	–	3	2	–
979	Unknown	Subadult	1	1	–	–	1	–	–
983	Probable female	Adult	2	–	2	–	2	–	–
984	Probable male	Young adult	3	–	3	–	3	–	–
1044	Probable male	Middle adult	–	–	–	–	–	1	–
1045	Probable male	Adult	2	2	–	–	2	–	–
1058	Male	Middle adult	1	–	1	–	1	2	–
1080	Probable female	Old adult	–	–	–	–	–	2	–
Total			47	20	28	7	55	53	5

Table 6-32. Summary of individuals with various dental pathology.

	Age	Caries	Antemortem tooth loss	Periapical Abscess	Periodontal disease	Calculus		
						Light	Moderate	Heavy
Male (n=31)	Young adult	2	3	1	4	5		1
	Middle adult	3	8	1	8		2	1
	Old adult		3				1	
	Adult	5			2	2	1	3
	Total	10	14	2	14	7	4	5
Female (n=24)	Young adult	3	3		3	3	2	
	Middle adult	1	6		1	2	1	1
	Old adult		1		1			1
	Adult	4		1	2	1	1	
	Total	8	10	1	7	6	4	2
Unknown (n=38)	Juvenile					2		
	Subadult	2				2		
	Young adult				1			
	Middle adult							
	Old adult							
	Adult	3				1		1
	Total	5			1	5		1
Total		23	24	3	22	18	8	8

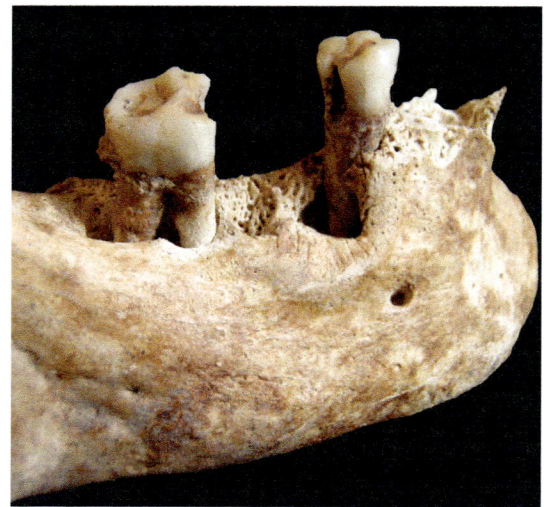

Figure 6-12. Interproximal dental caries of the left second premolar with associated antemortem tooth loss of M1, and alveolar resorption, Str. 962.

surrounding bone. The causes of tooth loss are varied, and can include periodontitis, dental caries, dental wear, and trauma. Due to the association of tooth loss and periodontitis, in particular, antemortem tooth loss is considered to be indicative of poor oral health.

The mandibles and maxillae of seventy-five individuals were examined for evidence of antemortem tooth loss. Of these, 32% were observed to have suffered the loss of at least one tooth. As with caries and

periodontitis, antemortem tooth loss more frequently affected males. This is, perhaps, not surprising given that both caries and periodontal disease are factors that can contribute to eventual tooth loss. For both males and female, the highest frequency of tooth loss was found among the middle adult age cohort, which likely reflects the age-progressive nature of dental disease.

4) Periapical Abscess

Abscesses are lesions of the alveolar bone surrounding the apex of the tooth root. They are the result of a bacterial invasion of the pulp cavity that eventually proceeds into the alveolar bone adjacent to the root apex. As the infection spreads from the tooth root to bone, the subsequent immune response, which includes seeping pus, leads to the formation of a granuloma. Subsequently, the bordering alveolar bone is resorbed, and a pus-filled fistula is formed (Hillson 1996; Nelson 2016).

Periapical abscesses were very rare among the dentitia of Tell el-Kerkh, affecting the maxillae or mandibles of only three individuals (4%, n=75), two of which were males. While the abscesses more commonly affected the posterior teeth of the males, the only female in the group (Str. 926) exhibited evidence for periapical abscess of the right mandibular central and lateral incisors. This is of particular interest because these teeth showed very severe non-masticatory tooth wear (discussed below).

5) Calculus

As plaque mineralizes over time, it forms hard deposits known as calculus. Although the mechanism by which mineralization is not well understood, the presence of calculus has been associated with both carbohydrate-rich diets, as well as poor oral hygiene (Hillson 1996; Keenleyside 2008; Klaus and Tam 2010). Although, a calculus-per-tooth methodology is ideal, at Tell el-Kerkh, it was observed that extant calculus often exfoliated from the tooth surface, making it difficult to assess from which tooth the calculus originated, and also calling into question which teeth were free of calculus versus those which had simply lost it. Thinking that individual tooth counts might underestimate the actual prevalence of calculus, it was thought best to simply generalize the degree of calculus (light, moderate, heavy) for each individual.

Thirty-four individuals (36.5%) were found to have teeth with accumulated calculus deposits, with males more frequently affected. For both males and females, calculus was visible on the teeth of over half of the respective dental samples.

In general, light calculus was most common, representing 53% of the calculus examples. Males, however, did more frequently have what were considered to be heavy calculus deposits, particularly on the posterior teeth, and they did so at younger ages than the females. However, in contrast, more young adult females than males were observed with moderate accumulations of calculus. Unfortunately, because the sample is small, and because several individuals could not be properly placed into an age cohort, it is not clear if this pattern of calculus accumulation reflects a normal continuum that is simply missing data, or if there are factors of diet, behavior, or even physiology, that would favor the development of heavy calculus among some males of a younger age.

6) Dental Wear

Enamel, the hard tissue that forms the tooth's crown, is a non-renewable substance. As such, whether due to normal masticatory use, or more idiosyncratic, non-masticatory behaviors, such as bruxism or tool use, the crown enamel can be progressively worn away, diminishing crown height, and potentially exposing the internal tooth structures. Dental wear is a progressive condition that advances with age at what is generally assumed to be a regular rate, making age estimation via tooth wear possible (Lovejoy 1985; Gilmore and Grote 2012). However, abrasive elements in food can increase the rate of wear, and thus provide insight into diet, as well as food processing (Smith 1972; Smith 1984; Larsen 1997).

Dental wear was scored following the recommendations Buikstra and Ubelaker (1994), who advocate using two different methodologies for scoring tooth wear. The Smith (1984) system is employed for the incisors, canines, and premolars. It utilizes an eight-point scale to score tooth wear severity. For the molars, the Scott (1979) system is used. This method employs what amounts to a 40-point scale, as each molar quadrant can receive a maximum wear score of ten, with a total score of 40 indicating complete tooth crown obliteration.

The average tooth wear scores by age for the maxillary and mandibular dentitions are shown in Figures 6-13 and 6-14. Due to the differences in scale between each system, this has the unfortunate effect of creating the appearance of an extreme increase in tooth wear severity from the anterior to the posterior teeth. Thus, it is better to view these results with respect to tooth class, rather than the dentition as a whole. Nevertheless, despite the scaling issues, there is an age-wise progression in tooth wear, with the older age cohorts expressing greater severity of tooth wear. But for the occasional outlier, tooth wear, on average, appears relatively moderate, with most tooth scores averaging around the median of the Scott (1979) or Smith (1984) scales.

The mandibular and maxillary dental wear for males and females is compared in Figures 6-15 and 6-16. For the most part, males displayed greater dental attrition than females. However, a closer look at the pattern of wear for the maxillary dentition reveals an inverse of this pattern. The female anterior teeth, particularly the incisors, exhibit a marginal increase in wear compared to those of their male counterparts. Though subtle, this divergence in dental wear patterning is suggestive of non-masticatory behavior, rather than normal dental attrition.

7) Extramasticatory Dental Wear

Teeth, of course, are typically used for chewing food. However, on occasion, teeth are employed for non-masticatory purposes, sometimes providing the individual with a 'third hand,' or a spontaneous tool. In those cases, repeated non-masticatory use can produce unusual, idiosyncratic patterns of wear that deviate from the expected trends of normal dental attrition (Molnar 1972; Merbs 1983; Turner and Machado 1983; Turner and Anderson 2003).

At Tell el-Kerkh, nine individuals were observed to have unusual dental wear patterns that are suggestive of extramasticatory use (Table 6-33). Of these, 66.7% were female, most commonly of middle adult age. Two of the three males within this group were young adults.

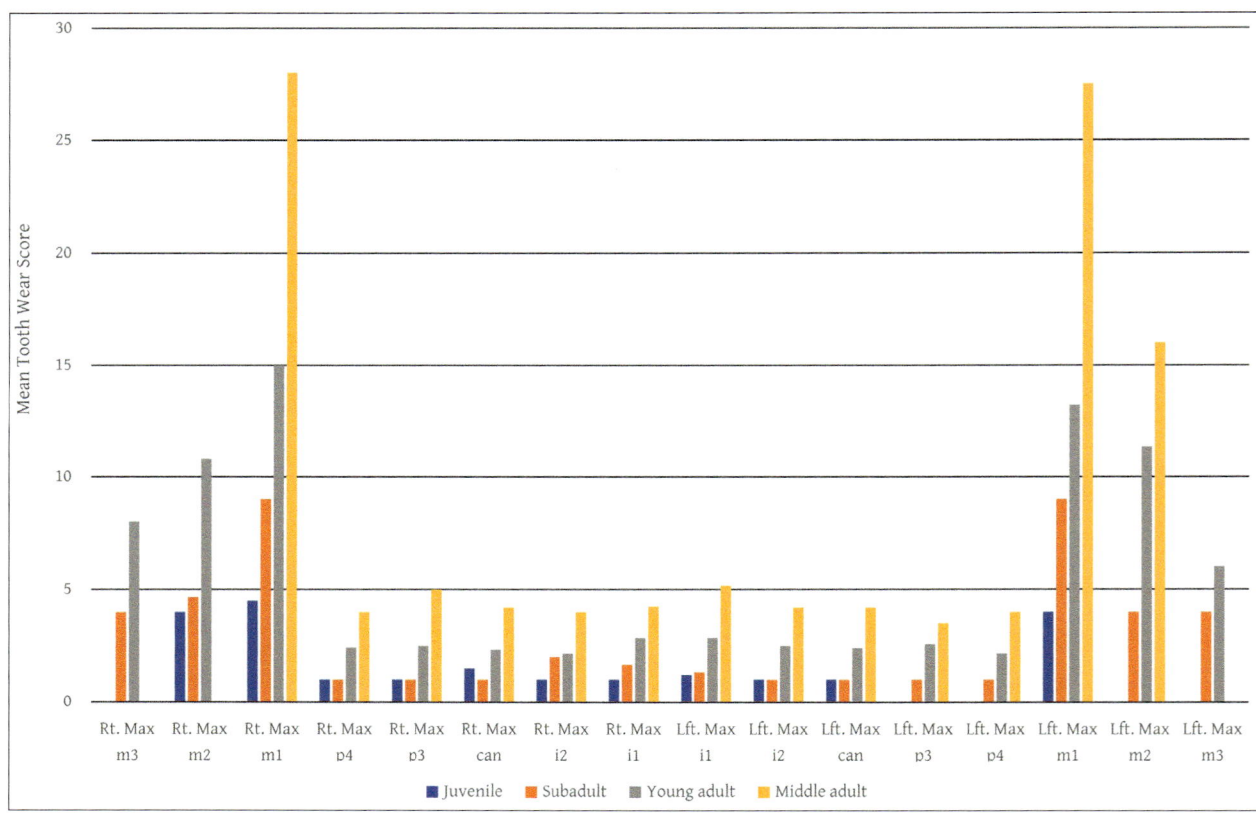

Figure 6-13. Comparison of age-specific tooth wear scores for the maxillary dentition.

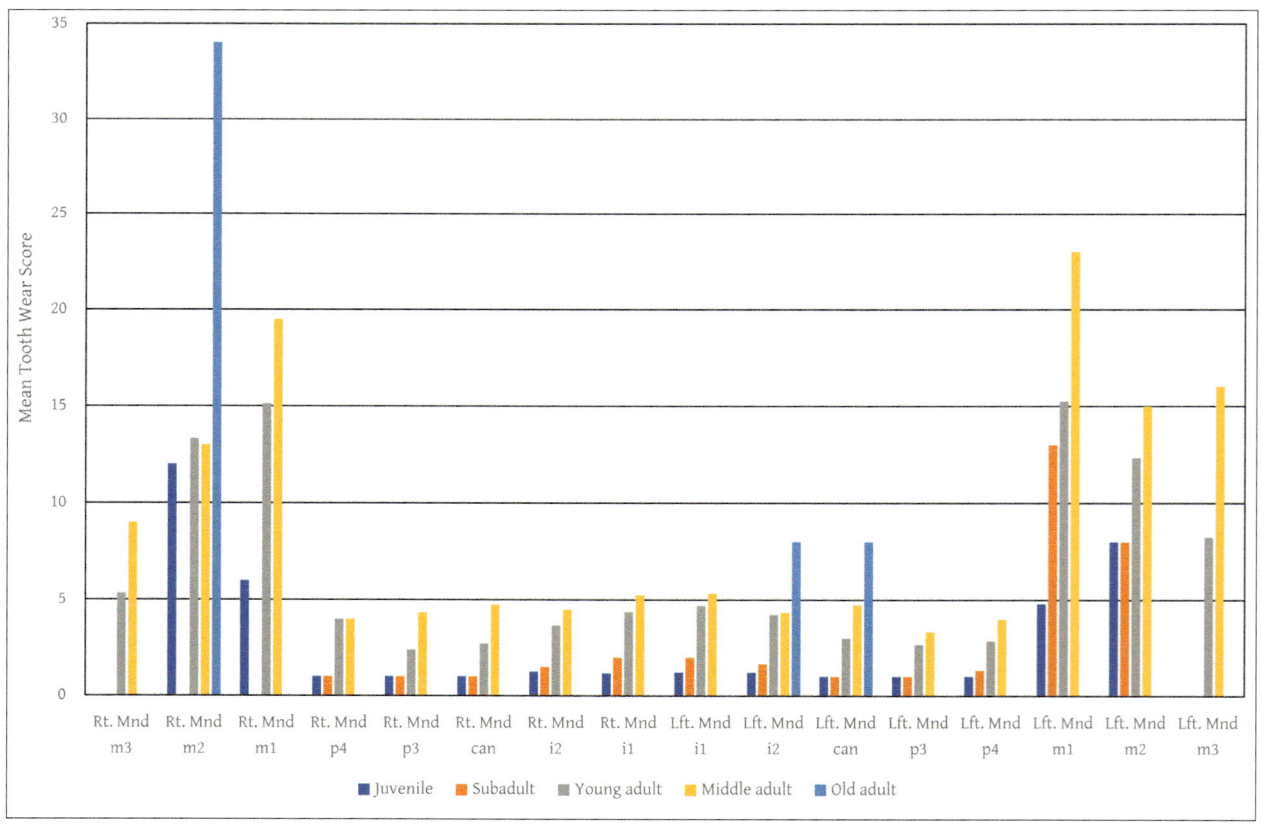

Figure 6-14. Comparison of age-specific tooth wear scores for the mandibular dentition.

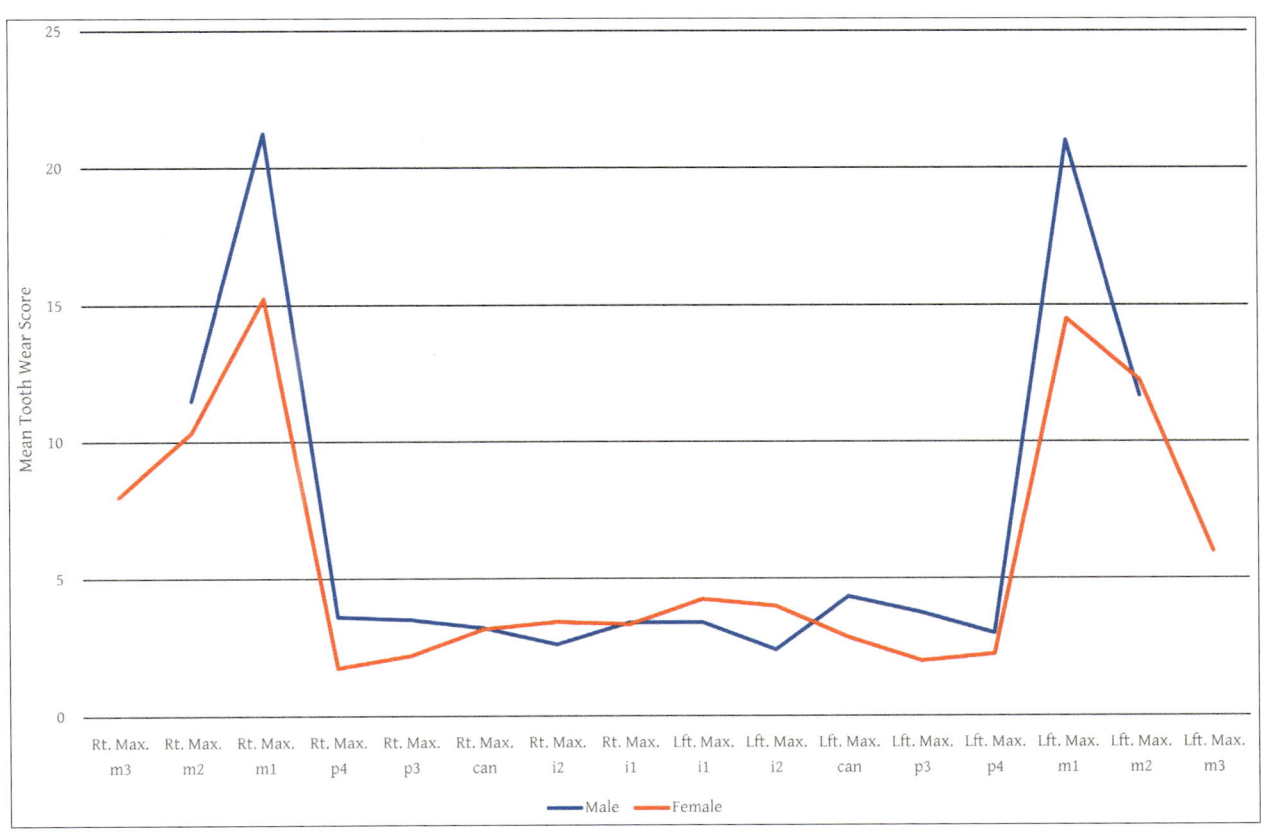

Figure 6-15. Comparison of adult male and female maxillary dental wear scores.

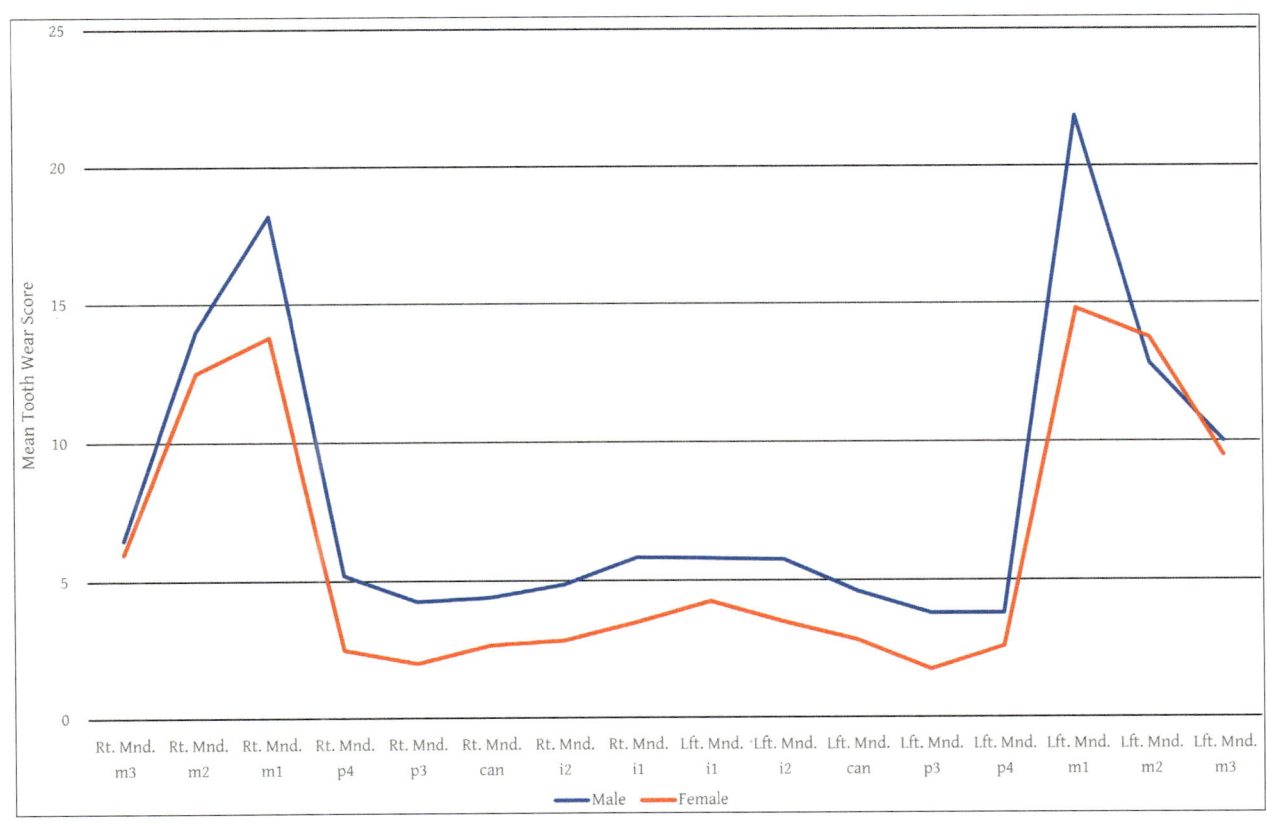

Figure 6-16. Comparison of adult male and female mandibular dental wear scores.

Table 6-33. Individuals with extramasticatory dental wear.

Burial	Sex	Age	Description
524	Probable female	Middle adult	Lingual surface attrition of the maxillary anterior teeth.
712	Probable female	Middle adult	Lingual surface attrition of the maxillary anterior teeth.
722	Probable female	Middle adult	Lingual surface attrition of the maxillary anterior teeth.
737	Probable male	Adult	Lingual surface attrition of the maxillary anterior teeth.
921	Male	Young adult	Lingual surface attrition of the maxillary anterior teeth.
926	Probable female	Adult	Asymmetrical mandibular wear favoring the left side; severe, angulated labial surface wear of the mandibular central incisors.
941	Probable female	Middle adult	Lingual surface attrition of the maxillary anterior teeth; scalloping of the distal aspect of the right maxillary canine crown.
978	Probable female	Young adult	The buccal aspect of the left second mandibular premolar has been chipped, or worn, away.
1056	Probable male	Young adult	Eight parallel grooves decorate the distal-buccal surface of the right maxillary canine.

The most common form of non-masticatory wear at Tell el-Kerkh can best be described as lingual surface attrition of the maxillary anterior teeth (LSAMAT). This pattern of dental wear, initially identified by Turner and Machado (1983), has been associated with a number of occupational behaviors, most of which are culturally specific (Irish and Turner 1987; Lukacs and Pastor 1988). In general, LSAMAT is thought to be caused by the practice of gripping some manner of fibrous material (plant-based, or animal tissue), with the teeth, then pulling it in a downward direction as the tongue presses the material against the lingual surfaces of the anterior teeth.

At Tell el-Kerkh, four females and two males were observed with LSAMAT. It is, of course, difficult to assign a specific occupational behavior to this observed pattern of tooth wear. However, because more females than males displayed the dental wear pattern, it may be worth considering if there was some sort of social division of labor at hand, or if the similarities in tooth wear among these few males and females may be the result of similar actions, but for different purposes.

A far more unusual form of dental wear was observed on the mandibular dentition of Str. 926. An apparent target of post-mortem cranial removal, this adult female lacked a maxillary dentition. However, the remaining mandibular dentition exhibits a pattern of wear that suggests both occupational use, and asymmetrical biting preference. Tooth wear is well

advanced from the left mandibular canine to the right mandibular second incisor. Dental wear is most pronounced on the central incisors, which exhibited a well-polished surface of dentin that is worn at an oblique angle with the downward slope on the labial aspect (Figure 6-17). This suggests that the right, anterior teeth were utilized as a gripping tool, and that there was a downward action that abraded the labial surfaces of the mandibular incisors.

In addition, the left first and second mandibular molars of Str. 926, the only extant left posterior teeth, also show an extraordinary pattern of wear (Figure 6-18). The first molar is worn distally, and the second

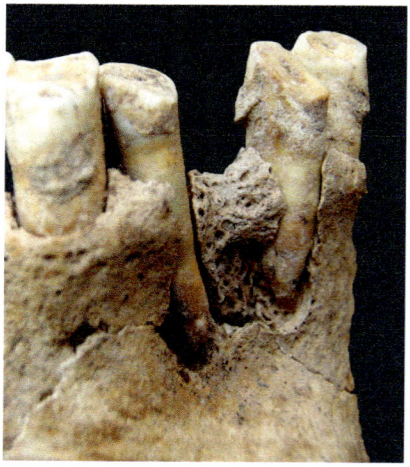

Figure 6-17. Severe dental wear of the anterior mandibular teeth, Str. 926. Note the oblique labial wear of the remaining central incisor.

Figure 6-18. The left mandibular first and second molars of Str. 926 share a severe, concave pattern of dental wear. Note the non-carious pulp chamber exposure exhibited by the second molar.

molar is worn mesially, creating a shared concave occlusal surface. In stark contrast, the right posterior dentition is not as dramatically worn. However, there is significant crowding of the first and second molar in which the distal aspect of the first molar crown has been overlapped by the crown of the second molar. It may be that the impacted molars caused a certain amount of discomfort that forced the individual to favor the opposite side, which then resulted in asymmetrical dental attrition.

Another unusual case of dental wear is found in Str. 1056, a young adult male. While the overall pattern of tooth wear is otherwise unremarkable, the right maxillary canine exhibits a curious configuration of up to 12 grooves on the buccal surface (Figure 6-19). The grooves, likely the product of some abrasive element, are regularly spaced, with eight prominent grooves along the upper midsection of the crown. While the causative agent is unknown, the direction of the grooves along the crown surface suggests the forceful, perhaps repeated, anterior-posterior movement of an abrasive, potentially striated, object.

Figure 6-19. The right maxillary canine of Str. 1056 displays multiple abrasive stria.

8. Trauma

Fourteen individuals, all adults (males= 11; females= 3), were found to have experienced at least one traumatic injury (Table 6-34). Among these 14 individuals, 35 fractures were observed, as well as three ossified soft tissue injuries (myositis ossificans), and three traumatic tooth crown removals. Notably, only three females (21%) were present among the 14 individuals with fractures (Table 6-35), but they possessed 32% of the total number of observed fractures.

1) Antemortem Fractures

Fractures were present within all anatomical regions, although the absence of leg fractures is unexpected (Figure 6-20). Males primarily experienced postcranial fractures, with 48% affecting the bones of the hand. For females, rib fractures were most frequent (38.4%), followed by fractures of the distal ulna (23%), and cranium (23%).

Seven individuals (male= 5; female= 2) had multiple fractures, which accounted for 81% of the total number of fractures (Table 6-36). Because 50% of the multiple fractures were those affecting the ribs or the hands, many likely represent single traumatic events, rather than repeated incidents. This appears to be the case for the males, for whom multiple traumata were often located within the postcranial skeleton, and most frequently affected the bones of the hand. One male, Str. 921, exhibited healed fractures of the left clavicle and radius, injuries that suggest a fall with an outstretched hand. Given that this individual also had a fractured toe, it is tempting to speculate that this toe, having been stubbed against an unseen object, may have been the initial cause of the fall.

In contrast, the fracture pattern for females with multiple traumata was more dispersed, and may be indicative of both intentional and unintentional injuries. For example, the greatest number of fractures was observed on a young adult female (Str. 909) with seven healed injuries: Five rib fractures, a fractured left second metatarsal, and a fractured distal ulna. A second young adult female (Str. 803) exhibited two fractures to the left ulna, and a fractured right clavicle (Figure 6-21). In addition, this individual suffered the traumatic destruction of the crown of the right maxillary lateral incisor.

Given that the fractures found in both females are all well-healed, it is difficult to determine the timing of the injuries. However, the overall constellation of injuries is curious, and appears to be a combination of both unintentional and intentional injuries. For example, it is likely that the aforementioned fractured metatarsal of Str. 909 and the fractured clavicle of Str. 808 are the

Table 6-34. Individuals with fractures, or other traumatic injuries.

Burial	Sex	Age	Number of Bone Fractures	Description
715	Probable male	Young adult	1	Healed fracture of the right radius at midshaft.
719.1	Unknown (Probable male?)	Adult	1	Healed fracture of the left fourth metacarpal.
720.1	Probable male	Old adult	1	Healed fracture of the left first metacarpal, tentatively attributed to individual 720.1.
731	Probable male	Young adult	3	Healed fracture of the left first metacarpal proximal articular surface; fractures of right capitate, right trapezoid.
803	Probable female	Young adult	3	Traumatic loss of the right lateral maxillary incisor; healed fracture of the right clavicle; two healed fractures of the left ulna.
807	Male	Middle adult	2	Perimortem penetrating fracture and linear fracture of the right frontal bone, and comminuted fracture of right mandible.
836	Male	Middle adult	1	Healed fracture of a right, mid-thoracic rib.
909	Probable female	Young adult	7	Healed fractures of the five right ribs; healed fracture of the left distal ulna; healed fracture of the left second metatarsal; traumatic loss of the right mandibular central incisor.
921	Male	Young adult	6	Healed fractures of the right second, third, and fifth metacarpals; remodeled fracture of the left radius distal radius; healed fracture of the left clavicle; healed fracture of the distal first foot phalanx, with associated degenerative joint changes; myositis ossificans along both linea aspera.
941	Probable female	Middle adult	–	Traumatic loss of the right lateral mandibular incisor.
962	Male	Middle adult	1	Healed fracture of an intermediate finger phalanx, side and number unknown.
1044	Probable male	Middle adult	3	Healed fracture of the left first metacarpal; healed depressed fracture located on the right posterior parietal; healed fracture of an unnumbered distal foot phalanx.
1047	Probable male	Young adult	5	Healed fracture of the right first metacarpal and trapezium; two healed rib fractures; healed fracture of the left fifth proximal toe phalanx; myositis ossificans extending from the left linea aspera.
1050	Probable male	Young adult	1	Actively healing comminuted (butterfly) fracture of the left femur at midshaft.

Table 6-35. Sex and age distribution of individuals with fractures.

	Adult	Young Adult	Middle Adult	Old Adult	Total
Male		5	4	1	10
Female		2	1		3
Unknown	1				1
Total	1	7	5	1	14

products of some manner of accident. Yet, it is notable that both females display fractures of the distal ulnae, injuries not found among the males. Fractures of the distal ulna are often associated with a defensive posture, and are the result of direct force, such as a blow from a blunt weapon (Galloway 1999; Judd 2008). For Str. 909, the fractured ulna was accompanied by several rib fractures. Rib fractures, though often associated with unintentional injury, can result from interpersonal violence (Judd 2006; Tung 2007; Steadman 2008). For Str. 803, the ulnar fractures were associated with the traumatic crown loss of an incisor. This evidence strongly suggests that these two individuals may have been targets of interpersonal violence.

2) Perimortem Fractures

The majority of the fractures observed at Tell el-Kerkh were antemortem. Two individuals, however, suffered from what appear to have been fatal injuries.

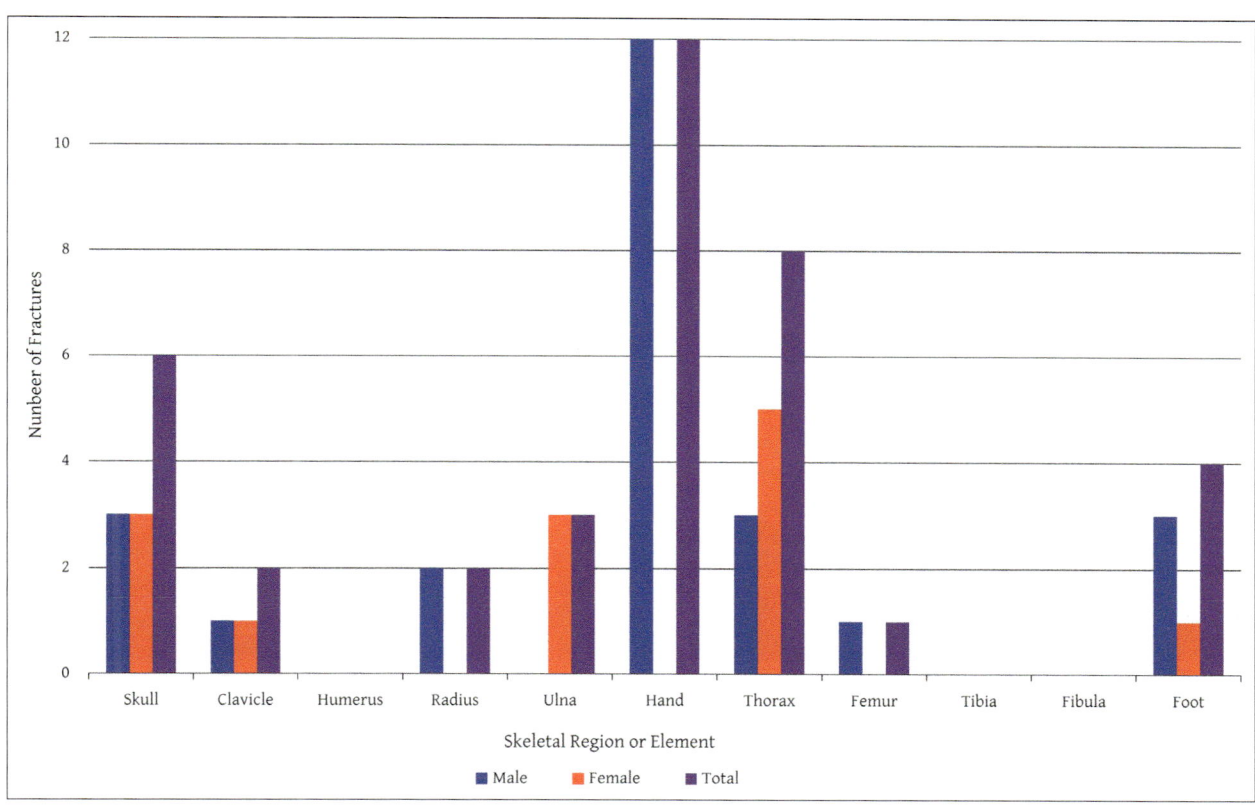

Figure 6-20. The anatomical distribution of observed fractures.

Table 6-36. Frequency of individuals with multiple fractures.

	Age	Multiple Cranial	Multiple Postcranial	Cranial and Postcranial
Male	Adult			
	Young Adult		3	
	Middle Adult	1		1
Female	Young Adult		1	1
	Middle Adult			
Total		1	4	2

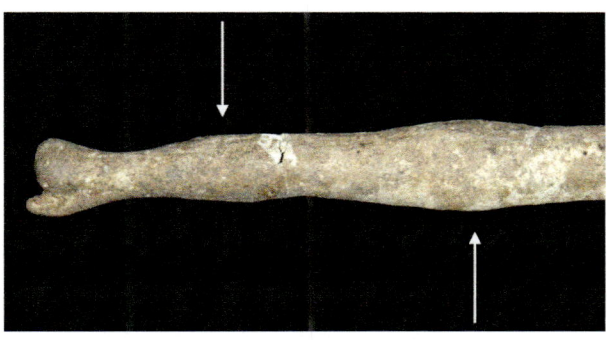

Figure 6-21. The left ulna of Str. 803 exhibits
two remodeled fractures.

The first is a young adult male (Str. 1050) who suffered a 'butterfly' fracture of the left femoral diaphysis (Figure 6-22). Coarse osteoclastic changes to the cortical bone, and the lack of clear callus formation, suggest that the individual survived the initial injury for one or two weeks, but succumbed shortly thereafter.

Owing to the strength of the bone, femoral diaphyseal fractures are generally uncommon. When they do occur, fractures of the shaft can be attributed to either direct or indirect violence (Geckeler 1943; Lovell 1997; Galloway 1999), but great force is typically required

Figure 6-22. Detail of the 'butterfly' fracture of the left femoral midshaft, Str. 1050. The coarse porosity is indicative of osteoclastic activity during the healing process.

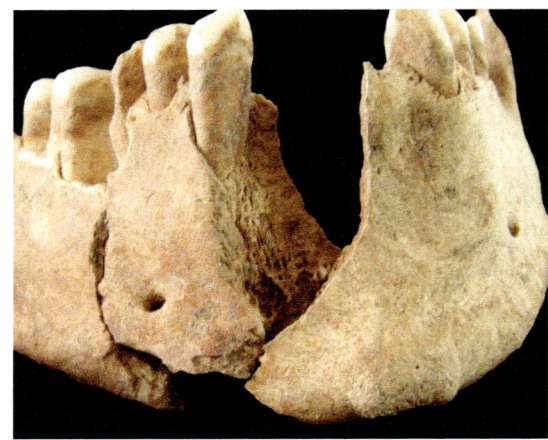

Figure 6-24. A comminuted perimortem fracture of the mandible, Str. 807.

in either case. In modern, clinical settings, fractured femoral shafts are most common among young adults, and are typically associated with vehicular accidents, or falls (Eliason 1921; Galloway 1999). Since it is unlikely that this individual was hit by a car, a fall from a great height is the most probable cause.

The second is a middle adult male (Str. 807) that had catastrophic perimortem fractures of the right mandibular body, and a penetrating fracture of the frontal bone, above the right orbit. The penetrating wound has an elliptical outline (Figure 6-23). Radiating fractures lead out from the impact site, and travel through the frontal squama and supraorbital arches. Intersecting with one of the radiating fractures is a curvilinear fracture that travels along the right side of the frontal. While this fracture could be related to the penetrating wound, it is more likely to be the result of a second traumatic event.

The mandibular body exhibits a comminuted fracture to the right of the mental eminence (Figure 6-24). The area of the fracture is defined by a curvilinear fracture line that extends from the alveolar bone of the left lateral incisor to the right first molar, which was longitudinally sheared in half.

The fatal injuries experienced by this individual are indicative of interpersonal violence. The severity of the fractures implies the use of some sort of heavy implement. Blows to the cranium or mandible by bare fists are unlikely to have caused the devastation seen here, and would certainly not be responsible for the penetrating fracture. It is likely that some manner of stone tool, or even a hand-held rock, was employed. Interestingly, observing both depressed fractures and similar penetrating cranial fractures at Çatahöyük, Knüsel and Glencross (2017) have suggested that sling stones, in addition to hand-held weapons, were the cause of such cranial injuries. It is not clear, however, if slings were used, or even present, at Tell el-Kerkh.

3) Soft Tissue Injuries

In addition to bone trauma, evidence of soft tissue trauma was also observed at Tell el-Kerkh. Myositis ossificans (traumatica) is a condition that arises subsequent to an avulsion injury to a tendon or ligament (Aufderheide and Rodriguez-Martin 1998). The subsequent subperiosteal hematoma becomes ossified, leading to an irregular mass of hard tissue projecting from the bone. The condition can be associated with a fracture, or a minor muscle injury, such as a sprain, or muscle pull.

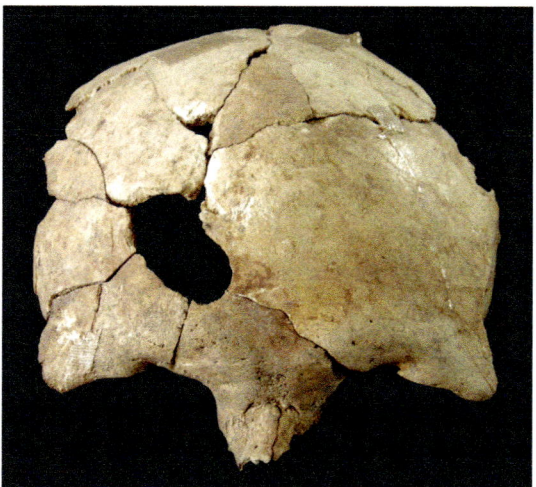

Figure 6-23. A fatal penetrating fracture of the right frontal bone, Str. 807.

Two individuals (Str. 921, Str. 1047), both young adult males, exhibited myositis ossificans. In both cases, the ossified soft tissue was present along the linea aspera of the femora. This likely indicates injuries associated with the biceps femoris muscle. Str. 1047 also has an ossified acromioclavicular ligament, and the patellae show signs of an ossified patellar tendon. Because both individuals are skeletally robust, it is likely the soft tissue injuries are related to habitually performed (and rigorous) occupational activities.

9. Osteoarthritis and Other Degenerative Joint Changes

Osteoarthritis refers to the progressive destruction of articular cartilage in synovial joints, and the resulting bony changes, such as eburnation or macroporosity. Here, 'degenerative joint changes,' or, elsewhere, 'degenerative joint disease' refers to the progressive destruction of cartilaginous joints, such as intervertebral joints, and serves as an umbrella term for intervertebral disk disease, and Schmorl's nodes. This follows the distinction made by several researchers who opt for a more clinical distinction in terminology (Waldron 2009, 2012; Jurmain et al. 2012), although more often than not, degenerative changes in the vertebrae, such as osteophytosis, are treated as a form of osteoarthritis (see Larsen 1997; Williams et al. 2019), and degenerative joint disease is used synonymously with osteoarthritis.

Attempting to associate osteoarthritis or degenerative vertebral changes with particular activities has been a recurring practice among bioarchaeologists (Molleson 2007; Jurmain et al. 2012). However, the inconvenient reality is that osteoarthritis and other degenerative joint changes are influenced by both age and activity, so linking joint changes to particular activities is generally not possible. However, given that osteoarthritis, for example, is an age-progressive condition, the presence of joint surface changes at earlier ages can provide insight into activity load.

Osteoarthritis and other degenerative joint changes are often described as the most commonly observed skeletal pathologies among archaeological populations (Waldron 2012). This does not seem to be the case at Tell el-Kerkh, however. Only ten individuals were found to have evidence of osteoarthritis or other degenerative conditions (Table 6-37). Of these, only one was female (Str. 533), although sex could not be determined for one individual.

In general, the majority of individuals with various degenerative changes were of middle adult age, which points to the progressive aspect of the condition. However, four young adults were also present in this group, which does suggest that certain conditions, such as vertebral osteophytosis of the lower spine, may be initiated at earlier ages as a result of activity. That one young adult (Str. 904) exhibited osteoarthritic changes at the elbows, wrist, and hands, also implies some behavioral catalyst to the joint pathologies of the young adults, whether in terms repetitive actions, mechanical strain, or injury. Notably, this individual

Table 6-37. Individuals with osteoarthritis, or other degenerative bone conditions.

Burial	Sex	Age	Description
533	Female	Middle adult	Eburnation visible on the distal articular surface of the right first metacarpal; Schmorl's node and osteophytes present on the second lumbar vertebra.
715	Male	Young adult	Temporomandibular joint disorder affecting the right mandibular condyle and mandibular fossa.
748	Probable male	Young adult	Partial fusion of the 11th and 12th thoracic vertebrae due to osteophytic formation, likely related to other pathological condition affect the 2nd lumbar.
807	Male	Middle adult	Osteophytic development along the superior margin of the 4th lumbar body.
904	Probable male	Young adult	Minor lipping along the margins of the right and left ulnar trochlear notches, with right side being more pronounced; minor lipping present on the proximal articular surfaces of the metacarpals; minor lipping present on the carpal articular surfaces.
921	Male	Young adult	Osteophytes present on the inferior margin of the 5th lumber body; degenerative changes of the proximal articular surface of the distal first toe phalanx associated with traumatic injury.
962	Male	Middle adult	Minor lipping along the margins of both glenoid fossae; Asymmetrical osteoarthritis (lipping, eburnation, macroporosity) affecting the left articular facets of three cervical vertebrae, possibly C_{3-6}.
995	Unknown	Adult	Eburnation present on the posterior subtalar facet of the left talus, and the posterior talar facet of the left calcaneus; osteophytes present along the superior margin of a lumbar body (4th or 5th).
1044	Probable male	Middle adult	Porosity and osteophytes present on the bodies of C_{2-7}; osteophytes are present on the superior margin of the first sacral body; present finger phalanges have prominent flexor crests; lipping and eburnation is present on the articular surfaces of the left and right pisiforms and triquetrum; minor lipping is present along the rim of both patellar articular surfaces.
1058	Male	Middle adult	Highly fragmented vertebral fragments exhibit degenerative changes (porosity, osteophytes).

Table 6-38. Anatomical distribution of osteoarthritis and other degenerative changes.

		Cranio-facial	Major joints of the upper limb	Hands	Spine				Major joints of the lower limb	Feet
					Cervical	Thoracic	Lumbar	Sacral		
Male	Young adult	1	1	1		1	1			1
	Middle adult		1	1	2		2	1	1	
Female	Middle adult			1			1			
Unknown	Adult						1			1
Total		1	2	3	2	1	5	1	1	2

also had prominent muscle insertion sites, as well as femoral robusticity indices indicative of habitual biomechanical stress (see below), which further seem to support the notion of activity-induced pathological changes.

Degenerative joint changes were most frequently located in the spine, with lumbar vertebrae being the most affected (Table 6-38). Osteophytic development (osteophytosis, intervertebral disc disease) was most common. One individual (Str. 962), however, did exhibit severe osteoarthritis of the superior and inferior articular facets of three lower cervical vertebrae. To varying degrees, the facets each exhibit macroporosity, eburnation, and osteophytic lipping along the margins. Remarkably, the osteoarthritic changes are exclusive to the left side.

A vertebral burst fracture (Schmorl's node) of the second lumbar vertebrae was observed in one female (Str. 533). This type of fracture results from a compressed herniation of the intervertebral disc, creating a depressed area on the superior surface of the vertebral body. Schmorl's nodes are typically associated with heavy loading or bending stresses on the spine.

A case of temporomandibular joint disorder was observed on the skull of a young adult male (Str. 715). In this individual, the right mandibular fossa was wide and shallow, and the associated right mandibular condylar surface had sclerotic accretions, some porosity, and had been rendered flat, with a slight anterior angulation. Perhaps related, dental wear is slightly more advanced on the right side. This condition is associated with non-masticatory tooth use, dental attrition, and bruxism, but trauma can also be a cause.

As a final point concerning osteoarthritis and degenerative joint changes at Tell el-Kerkh, it is troubling that such low frequencies were observed. There is no doubt, given its prevalence in other archaeological material, as well as living populations, that degenerative joint changes are underrepresented here. One explanation for this is that since the adult sample from Tell el-Kerkh skews younger, it could be that these individuals simply died before the bony changes could manifest, even if soft tissue symptoms were present. Since osteoarthritis is age-progressive, it is possible that most young adult individuals at Tell el-Kerkh were just simply unaffected at the time of death. However, given that four young adults were observed to have degenerative joint changes, it strains credulity to think that these four were simply outliers.

It is more likely that the low prevalence of osteoarthritis and other degenerative joint changes is less a reflection of the sample's health than of poor skeletal preservation. A proper examination of joint disorders necessarily requires good preservation of articular surfaces, vertebral bodies, and so forth. Unfortunately, such material was not plentiful at Tell el-Kerkh. For example, at its best, the vertebral column averaged only 30% completion (see above). Likewise, the articular surfaces of the long bones were among the most poorly preserved elements of the skeleton. Thus, the rare observations of osteoarthritis and degenerative joint disease at Tell el-Kerkh are likely due to missing skeletal data, rather than actual low frequencies.

10. Osteometric Indicators of Activity

The analysis of grave goods from the cemetery points to the potential existence of a gendered division of labor at Tell el-Kerkh (Tsuneki 2011). To examine this further, indices of skeletal robusticity were calculated from available postcranial metric data (Table 6-39). These indices attempt to quantify directional changes in the external dimensions of long bones, and can be used to infer the levels of activity-induced biomechanical stress undertaken by members of a population. Granted, other methods, such as those that analyze either cross-sectional geometry (Ruff 2000) or estimates of total subperiosteal area may be more precise (Steckel et al. 2002), but the various indices of robusticity do not require imaging technology, or perfectly preserved bones. Moreover, most indices, as noted by Phillips (2003), utilize measurements taken from areas in which

Table 6-39. Indices of robusticity.

	Burial	Age	Ulnar Interosseous Crest Robusticity	Platymeric Index	Pilastric Index	Femoral Robusticity Relative to Body Mass
Female	909	Young Adult	–	.74	1.02	–
	924	Young Adult	–	.70	–	–
	926	Adult	6.18	–	–	–
	927.3	Young Adult	–	.78	1.107	5.65
	988	Middle Adult	6.37	–	–	–
	Mean		6.28	.74	1.06	5.65
Male	904	Young Adult	–	.83	1.27	5.98
	1050	Young Adult	5.66	–	–	–
	Mean		5.66	.83	1.27	5.98
Unknown	995	Adult	6.26	–	–	–
	Mean		6.26	–	–	–

muscle origin or insertion points are located, so they can, in effect, quantify bone development in response to muscular activity.

As with most measures of robusticity, whether metric or nonmetric (such as musculoskeletal markers), it is not possible to determine the absolute cause of bone robusticity. However, researchers have linked long bone dimensions to more generalized activities. For example, Larsen (1997) and Ruff (2019) have reported greater femoral diaphyseal circularity among more sedentary populations when compared to non-sedentary groups, such as hunter-gathers or pastoralists. In addition, differences in femoral dimensions between males and females have been interpreted to indicate divisions of labor (Cole 1994; Ruff 1987, 1994), or a lack thereof in the case of Çatalhöyük (Larsen *et al.* 2013). Thus, the analysis of bone robusticity can provide some insight into the general activity patterns of ancient populations.

For the upper limb, only the interosseous crest index of the ulna could be calculated for Tell el-Kerkh. The interosseous crest index provides a score of ulnar mediolateral midshaft width relative to bone length, and in so doing, provides an indirect measure of the development the flexor digitorum profundus muscle, which originates along that region (Phillips 2003). In effect, the index may provide insight into habitual activity associated with finger use.

At Tell el-Kerkh, the interosseous crest index was calculated for two females, one male, and one adult of unknown sex. The average interosseous crest index was 6.28 for females, while the one male for whom the index could be calculated had an index of 5.66.

For the lower limb, platymeric, pilasteric, and femoral robusticity indices were calculated. The platymeric index is the ratio of femoral anterioposterior subtrochanteric diameter to mediolateral subtrochanteric diameter (Bass 1987). It reveals the degree of anterioposterior flattening, or lack thereof, present in the proximal femur, with a higher value indicating greater circularity. The degree of mediolateral flattening, or circularity, at the femoral midshaft is calculated using the pilasteric index, which is the ratio of anterioposterior midshaft to mediolateral midshaft diameters. A pilasteric index value of one reflects a generally circular femoral midshaft, while a value greater than one indicates greater mediolateral flattening, and a longer anteroposterior diameter. In both cases, the indices are thought to represent particular biomechanical loading stresses present on the femur that are related to some manner of strenuous activity, or, as Angel (1946: 77) described it, the result of a 'dynamic posture.' It should be noted that the pilasteric index is often calculated as anteroposterior diameter divided by the mediolateral diameter (Angel 1946; Phillips 2003; Frohlich *et al.* 2008; Pomeroy and Zakrewski 2009), but other researchers may flip the equation (Larsen 1997; Larsen *et al.* 2013).

The platymeric index for the only male for whom the value could be calculated is .83. The average female platymeric index is .74. For both males and females, the platymeric indices indicate the presence of anterioposterior flattening, with associated broadening along the mediolateral plane, in the subtrochanteric region of the femoral. This region of the proximal femur is affected by the muscles that flex, extend, and abduct the hip.

The pilasteric index is 1.27 for the solitary male, and the average pilasteric index for only two females is 1.06. The pilasteric values reveal a greater anterioposterior femoral midshaft diameter compared to the transverse diameter, suggesting the development of increased bending strength in response to biomechanical stress. The anteroposterior diameter is greatly affected by the prominence of the linea aspera, an attachment point for muscle groups used in both hip and knee movements.

The femoral robusticity index is a measure of the size of the femoral diaphysis relative to its length. Often, this index is calculated using the femoral bicondylar length as the divisor (Bass 1987), a measurement that was not attainable for the Tell el-Kerkh sample due to the poor preservation of the femoral condyles, if not the femur entirely. However, Ruff (2000:78) provides a version of the femoral robusticity index that replaces femoral length with femoral head diameter, which could be applied to two individuals within the Kerkh sample. The added benefit of the Ruff femoral robusticity index is that the index takes into account the effect of body mass on bone geometry.

Unfortunately, the index of femoral robusticity could only be calculated for two individuals, a male and a female. The male, Str. 1050, yielded an index of 5.98. For the young adult female, Str. 927.3, the index was 5.65. However, while it is tempting to infer that the difference seen here is indicative of distinct disparities in biomechanical stress endured by males and females, it remains a question as to what extent these two individuals are truly representative of the inhabitants of Tell el-Kerkh.

Although the data are limited, the few indices of robusticity that could be acquired suggest that the male and female inhabitants of Tell el-Kerkh partook in habitual activities that affected their bones in different ways. For the interosseous crest index, while a sample of three individuals provides little solid ground for any sort of conclusion, the greater mean index for the females may suggest a division of labor at Tell el-Kerkh that requires greater daily manual dexterity among the women. Though perhaps coincidental, it is notable that Str. 926, an adult female with an index of 6.18, was also found to have unusual, non-masticatory tooth wear suggestive of repetitive, occupational use, so it is conceivable that the habitual activities associated with the abnormal tooth wear were also associated with repetitive finger use.

Further evidence of such a division in labor may also be seen in the platymeric and pilasteric indices, which are likely affected by walking, running, or even repeated postural changes, such as standing from a squatting position. As with the interosseous crest index, there are apparent differences in the femoral indices for males and females. It notable, however, that the female values are the inverse of the male values, with, for example, the female pilasteric index being more circular, while the only male value indicates a greater amount of mediolateral flattening. This suggests that female activities place more biomechanical emphasis on hip movement, while biomechanical stress on the femoral shaft was greater for males. When this is considered with the evidence from the forearm, it does seem to suggest that women at Tell el-Kerkh were employed in more sedentary, and potentially more dexterous, occupational behaviors. However, given the very small sample for which robusticity could be quantified, an interpretation such as this must be taken with caution.

11. Summary and Conclusions

The biological cost of the Neolithic transition is well documented. The Neolithic is characterized by social and technological innovations, the establishment of sedentary societies, and increasing reliance upon animal domesticates and agriculture for nutritional resources. These changes came at a biological cost (recently reviewed by Scott 2017). As permanent habitation sites were established, increased sedentism was associated with increased fertility, which led to changes in population density. As populations increased, new opportunities arose for the spread of infectious disease either through interpersonal contact, poor sanitation, or other vectors, such as insects. The reliance on agriculture and crop specialization exposed these societies to nutritionally deficient diets, as well as seasonal resource scarcity, leading to higher incidences of malnutrition, and associated health problems. Repeated close interaction with livestock, and their associated pests, likely provided new opportunities for the spread of novel infectious disease, as well. But to what degree is this Neolithic experience illustrated at Tell el-Kerkh?

At Tell el-Kerkh, the results are generally consistent with other research on Neolithic populations. In summary, a selection of the relevant findings are as follows:

1. The cemetery sample consisted of 244 individuals, with nearly equal proportions of males and females. The modal age at death for both sexes was during the young adult period, although a greater proportion of females died as young adults.
2. Estimated maternal mortality based on the ratio of young adult females to males (.87) is 214 per 100,000 live births, which suggests that the greater proportion of young adult female deaths may have been related to the dangers of childbirth.

3. Forty-six percent of the burials were nonadult, with 53% of 106 nonadults dying within the juvenile period, and 33% dying before the end of the first year. Peak mortality occurred between ages 1-3. The juvenility index is .44. The estimated fertility rate is 5.62 births per female of reproductive age. This indicates a moderately high fertility at Tell el-Kerkh.

4. That non-adult mortality decreased rapidly after age three suggests that those who survived early childhood were less likely to succumb to ill health during later adolescence. However, that adults showed fewer indicators of poor health at the time of death does not mean that they were unaffected by the hazards of the Neolithic communal environment, only that they did not accumulate the scars from them (Wood *et al.* 1992). Therefore, it is very telling that 40% of the females within the sample died during the young adult years. Although few bore direct evidence of chronic conditions, the young age at death implies acute health risks, and the biological inability to overcome them.

5. Evidence for non-specific illness, or physiological stress was common. The crude prevalence rate of linear enamel hypoplasia was 40.9. The peak age of physiological stress appears to have fallen between 3-5 years of age.

6. Active lesions of cribria orbitalia and porotic hyperostosis were most frequently observed among individuals between 1-3 years, which is the period of peak mortality risk for juveniles. This is also the period during which the frequency of linear enamel hypoplasias also began to increase. This suggests that young juveniles were exposed to environmental factors that produced some amount of physiological stress. Although it needs further investigation, the evidence of juvenile morbidity and mortality observed at Tell el-Kerkh could be related to weaning, and the subsequent exposure to insufficient dietary resources and new gastro-intestinal pathogens.

7. Although caution is necessary with a diagnosis based upon limited skeletal evidence, it appears that there may have been a risk of tuberculosis infection at Tell el-Kerkh, with domesticated animals as likely vectors.

8. A decline in oral health is associated with the adoption of an agricultural subsistence strategy due to the increased reliance upon cariogenic foods (Larsen 1995; Temple 2016). However, this seems not to have been the case at Tell el-Kerkh. For example, the prevalence of dental caries was low, affecting 21 adults. Only 2.8% of 1583 permanent teeth were found with such lesions. These results are consistent with those of Eshed and colleagues (2006) who found low caries rates among a combined sample from several Pre-pottery Neolithic sites in the southern Levant. As Neolithic populations are often assumed to rely heavily upon a carbohydrate-rich diet, the low caries rate is unexpected, and may indicate a more varied diet, or less reliance on carbohydrate-rich foods.

9. While caries rates were low, and more males with observed to have dental caries, a slightly greater proportion of young adult females were found with the pathology. In clinical studies, a decline in female oral health has been linked to the hormonal and physiological changes associated with puberty and pregnancy (Lukacs and Largaespada 2006; Lukacs 2008; Temple 2016; Lukacs 2017). Given the estimated high fertility at Tell el-Kerkh, it is possible that the pattern of caries seen here is linked to such physiological alterations. However, given that this pattern of poorer oral health among young adult women was not consistent with respect to other dental pathologies, the contribution of fertility to female dental health is unclear.

10. In studies of Pre-Pottery Neolithic skeletal material, patterns of musculoskeletal markers and joint pathologies have been interpreted to indicate gendered divisions of labor (Molleson 2000; Eshed *et al.* 2004b). Unfortunately, a thorough study of musculoskeletal markers was not possible for the skeletal sample from Tell el-Kerkh. However, observations of postcranial robusticity, osteoarthritis, and extramasticatory tooth wear allude to the presence of similar divisions of labor at Tell el-Kerkh, and this would seem to be supported by the archaeological evidence as reported by Tsuneki (2011).

11. Trauma was uncommon, affecting only 14 of 105 observed individuals, or 5.73% of the total sample. The majority of fractures suffered by males affected the postcranial skeleton. This suggests that the males of this population were at an increased risk of accidental injuries, likely from falls or the hazards of activity or labor occupations. However, that two males experienced blunt force cranial trauma does illustrate the presence of conflict within this society, but the paucity of further evidence obscures the true extent of violence among males. For the females, the limited skeletal evidence suggests a different experience. Two of the females exhibited craniofacial injuries and fractured distal ulnae. While such injuries can be linked to unintentional events, such as falls, these injuries are typically indicative of interpersonal violence. It is notable, then, that ulna fractures are absent from the male cohort. From this evidence, it can be hypothesized that women in this society may have been at a

heightened risk of injury from assault, rather than from occupational pursuits. However, it is not known if these injuries represent occasional violent encounters, or more systemic violence against women.

To conclude, there is a long history of human habitation within the Rouj basin in which Tell el-Kerkh is found. Evidence for occupation dates to the Pre-Pottery Neolithic B period. By the Late Pre-pottery Neolithic B, the settlement size had greatly expanded, and may have been as large as 16 hectares (Tsuneki 2012). But by the Pottery Neolithic, the period during which the cemetery at Tell el-Kerkh was in use, many centuries had passed, and the site had contracted to as little as 6 hectares. In effect, this cemetery sample reflects not so much a population experiencing the Neolithic transition, but a population in the midst of its conclusion. The once innovative practices of agricultural production, domesticated livestock, and permanent dwellings had been long established, and the biological costs of those cultural changes were likely just considered to be normal features of everyday life. In the skeletons of Tell el-Kerkh, the biological legacy of the Neolithic is seen. Agricultural intensification, and the population changes that followed, were accompanied by penalties to health, and the frailest of the community were often at the greatest risk.

Appendix 6-1: Catalogue of Human Remains

Str. 502:
Sex: Indeterminate
Age: Juvenile, 2-3yrs.
   This individual exhibited active cribra orbitalia affecting the right orbit. The left was not preserved.

Str. 504:
Sex: Indeterminate
Age: Perinatal

Str. 507:
Sex: Indeterminate
Age: Juvenile, 8-10yrs.
   Three linear hypoplastic enamel defects were visible on the available dentition. Two were present on the left maxillary canine, and the third was located on the right mandibular canine.

Str. 513:
Sex: Indeterminate
Age: Perinatal

Str. 519:
Sex: Indeterminate
Age: Fetal

Str. 521:
Sex: Indeterminate
Age: Subadult, 12-15yrs.
   This individual exhibited bilateral cribra orbitalia, dental caries, and linear enamel hypoplasia. The three enamel defects were located on both maxillary canines, and the right mandibular canine.

Str. 524:
Sex: Probable female
Age: Middle adult
   This individual exhibited moderate-to-heavy dental attrition. Lingual surface anterior maxillary attrition was evident. Antemortem tooth loss of the right mandibular P4-M2 was observed. Ten linear enamel hypoplastic defects were distributed among seven teeth.

Str. 527:
Sex: Indeterminate
Age: Infant (B-3mos).

Str. 528:
Sex: Indeterminate
Age: Juvenile, 1-3yrs.

Str. 533:
Sex: Female
Age: Middle adult, 40-50yrs.

This individual exhibited two hypoplastic defects on each of the mandibular canines. The left maxillary P3 had been lost prior to death. Well-defined linea aspera were observed. The available fragments of femora appeared platymeric, although metric assessments could not be performed due to fragmentation.

Str. 710:
Sex: Probable male.
Age: Old adult.
   Unfortunately, the majority of the dentition was not preserved, and only the right maxilla was present. But for a heavily worn right maxillary second molar, the individual was edentulous. It should be noted that age estimation relied primarily on the condition of the dentition, as other more reliable age indicators were not present.

Str. 712:
Sex: Probable female
Age: Middle adult
   Lingual surface attrition of the anterior maxillary dentition was observed. Antemortem tooth loss of the left maxillary second premolar and first molar was evident. Twenty-seven linear enamel hypoplasias were observed among maxillary and mandibular teeth. Exposed cross-sections of the cranial vault revealed unusually thick diploie. No porotic hyperostosis was evident, either healed or unhealed. It may be linked to a possible healed endocranial reaction that is suggested by the uneven, swollen appearance of the inner table, particularly around the area of the cruciform eminence.

Str. 713:
Sex: Indeterminate.
Age: Juvenile, 10-12yrs.
   Cribra orbitalia was present in both orbits. Thirty-seven linear enamel hypoplastic defects were observed, 26 of which were distributed among all four canines.

Str. 715:
Sex: Probable male
Age: Young adult
   The light to moderate dental attrition suggests a young adult age. However, other reliable indicators of age were not available.
   Four dental caries are present among the maxillary molars.
   A healed fracture of the mid-proximal right radius was present. The healed fracture is located at midshaft. The callus protrudes medially. Post-mortem breakage of the bone exposed the internal structure of the fracture. The marrow cavity has narrowly reopened toward the proximal end of the

fracture. Though not entirely comprised of woven bone, the callus is active in appearance with a fairly rugose surface, with sclerotic islands, and pillars. It could be categorized as being in the stage of consolidation. The ulna also exhibits bony changes with a swollen area that articulates with the radial callus. It is likely bone formation triggered by the fracture and associated inflammation.

Degenerative changes to the right temporal-mandibular joint are also evident. The mandibular fossa is wide and shallow. The condylar surface has thick, sclerotic accretions, some porosity, and is flattened with anterior angulation.

Str. 716:
Sex: Probable male
Age: Middle adult
   The dental attrition suggests a middle adult, perhaps earlier in the age range. Sixteen linear enamel hypoplastic defects were observed, most commonly on the mandibular canines.
   The major muscle insertion sites of the appendicular skeleton were robust.

Str. 717:
Sex: Indeterminate
Age: Juvenile, 1-2yrs.
   Active porotic hyperostosis was present on the left and right posterior parietals.

Str. 725:
Sex: Probable female
Age: Young adult
   This is a fairly gracile individual with one hypoplastic defect on the mandibular right second premolar, and light calculus deposits on the anterior dentition.

Str. 726:
Sex: Indeterminate
Age: Infant, 9-18mos.

Str. 729:
Sex: Probable female
Age: Young adult
   One dental caries was observed on the right mandibular first molar. Three linear enamel hypoplastic defects were recorded on the first and second maxillary molars, and the right second maxillary molar.

Str. 730:
Sex: Indeterminate
Age: Juvenile, 2-3yrs.

Str. 738:
Sex: Indeterminate
Age: Infant, B-3mos.

Str. 739:
Sex: Probable male
Age: Middle adult
   This individual exhibits healed porotic hyperostosis, and the antemortem loss of the left mandibular first molar.

Str. 746:
   This burial contained the commingled remains of two juveniles.
   1. Juvenile, 1-2yrs., with active cribra orbitalia and porotic hyperostosis.
   2. Juvenile, 6-8yrs.

Str. 748:
   This is a commingled deposit with the remains three individuals.
   1. A young adult, probable male. This individual exhibited osteophytic lipping of the inferior margins of the eleventh thoracic vertebra, with partial fusion to the twelfth. This is may be due to a pathological second lumbar vertebra, which displays a large, concave, erosive lesion affecting the superior surface of the body, with associated anterior wedging. There is no sign of active bone formation at the site of the concavity, although osteophytic growth is present along the margins of the body, and sclerotic pillars of bone are present along the sides. This apparently erosive lesion has removed most of the superior surface of the body, with only the posterior and left lateral annular ring remaining. Sharp margins define the edges of the concavity. The trabeculae of the body are exposed and appear sclerotic. The lesion is suggestive of tuberculosis, but the lack of other skeletal evidence makes this diagnosis tenuous.
   2. A juvenile, 2-3yrs.
   3. An infant.

Str. 750:
Sex: Indeterminate
Age: Juvenile, 5-6yrs.
   An example of post-mortem cranial removal, the cranium of this individual was absent, although the cervical vertebrae were present, and articulated. The mandible was present, and remained in anatomical position in situ. Disarticulated maxillary teeth were present.

Str. 752
Sex: Probable female
Age: Adult
   The skull of this individual was absent, although the postcranial skeleton remained articulated. The skeletal remains were fragile, very fragmented, provided little information. In the absence of cranial and pelvic morphological indicators, a

measurement of the femoral head diameter (40mm) was used to estimate sex.

Str. 756:
Sex: Indeterminate
Age: Juvenile
This individual is represented only by cranial vault fragments.

Str. 757:
Sex: Indeterminate
Age: Juvenile, 7-8yrs.
This individual had 16 linear enamel hypoplastic defects, as well as dental caries affecting the remaining deciduous molars.

Str. 759 (Not observed):
Sex: Indeterminate
Age: Adult
This individual is represented by disarticulated left and right feet.

Str. 803:
Sex: Probable female
Age: Young adult
This individual exhibited a healed fracture of the right clavicle located in the middle third of the diaphysis. Two healed fractures of the left ulna within the distal third of the shaft were also present. As no shape or rotational alterations are evident, both fractures were likely transverse. In addition, the right central maxillary incisor tooth has been fractured, the crown lost, and the remaining root and dentin are polished.
Antemortem tooth loss of the right maxillary first molar and the right mandibular second molar was observed. Dental caries were also present on the right maxillary second and third molars, as well as the left mandibular second molar. Anterior maxillary alveolar bone loss was also evident.

Str. 807:
Sex: Male
Age: Middle adult male, 35-40yrs.
This individual exhibited perimortem fractures of the right frontal bone and mandible. A penetrating wound is present to the right of glabella, superior to the right orbit. Radiating fractures progress through the supraorbital ridge, and the frontal squama. A curvilinear fracture is present on the right side of the frontal bone. Multiple fractures have separated the body and eminence of the right mandible.
In addition, small osteophytes are present on the superior margin of the fourth lumbar vertebra.

Str. 822:
Sex: Indeterminate
Age: Juvenile, 10-12yrs.

Str. 823:
Sex: Indeterminate
Age: Subadult, 14-16yrs.

Str. 825:
Sex: Indeterminate
Age: Juvenile, 10-12yrs.

Str. 826:
Sex: Indeterminate
Age: Subadult, 14-15 yrs.
Thirteen linear enamel hypoplastic defects were present.

Str. 828:
Sex: Indeterminate
Age: Fetal

Str. 829:
Sex: Indeterminate
Age: Juvenile, 2-3yrs.

Str. 830:
Sex: Probable male
Age: Middle adult
This individual has antemortem tooth loss of the right maxillary first incisor, and the right mandibular first molar. Three dental caries were present on the left mandibular first molar.

Str. 832:
A burial deposit containing the commingled remains of at least five individuals.
1. A likely perinate, sex indeterminate.
2. A juvenile, sex indeterminate.
3. A juvenile, sex indeterminate.
4. An adult, sex indeterminate.
5. An adult, sex indeterminate.

Str. 834:
Sex: Indeterminate
Age: Juvenile, 2-3yrs.

Str. 836:
Sex: Male
Age: Middle adult
This individual has a healed fracture of a right, mid-thoracic rib. Alveolar bone changes likely due to periodontal disease were present, as were light calculus accumulations.

Str. 838:
Sex: Indeterminate
Age: Perinatal

Str. 841:
Sex: Indeterminate
Age: Perinatal

Str. 851:

This deposit contained the commingled remains of two individuals.

1. An infant (10-12mos.), sex indeterminate. Fragments of the infant's cranial vault exhibited active porotic hyperostosis.
2. An adult, sex indeterminate.

Str. 852:

This burial deposit contained the commingled remains of two individuals.

1. A probable male, adult
2. A juvenile (1-2yrs.), sex indeterminate.

Str. 902:

Sex: Indeterminate
Age: Juvenile, 1-2yrs.

Str. 904:

Sex: Probable male
Age: Young adult

Healed cribra orbitalia and porotic hyperostosis are evident. Probable agenesis of both maxillary third molars, and the right mandibular third molar. Moderate calculus accumulation on the anterior maxillary teeth.

Minor lipping is present along the margins of both ulnar trochlear notches, as well as the articular surfaces of the metacarpals, and carpals.

Both humerii have septal apertures.

Str. 908:

Sex: Indeterminate
Age: Subadult, 11-13yrs.

Linear enamel hypoplastic defects are present on several teeth. A small patch of active porotic hyperostosis is present on a fragment of posterior left parietal, near lambda.

Str. 909:

Sex: Probable female
Age: Young adult

The few remaining cranial indicators of sex are, unfortunately, ambiguous. However, general skeletal gracility would seem to suggest that this individual is a young adult female.

There is evidence of several antemortem injuries to the forearm, foot, and thorax. This individual has healed and remodeled fractures of the left distal ulna, the distal left second metatarsal, and six fractures affecting five mid-thoracic, probably left, ribs.

Dental attrition varies by location in the dental arcade. Anterior tooth wear is more advanced than posterior tooth wear.

Str. 910:

This burial contains the fragmentary remains of at least three individuals.

1. Adult, sex indeterminate.
2. Old Adult, sex indeterminate. The presence of ossified thyroid cartilage suggests an older age estimation.
3. Infant (6mos.-1yr.), with active porotic hyperostosis.

Str. 911:

Sex: Indeterminate
Age: Perinatal

Str. 912:

Sex: Indeterminate
Age: Infant

Str. 913:

Sex: Indeterminate
Age: Juvenile, 1-2yrs.

Str. 914:

Sex: Indeterminate
Age: Juvenile, 3-4yrs.

Str. 918:

Sex: Indeterminate
Age: Infant, 4-6mos.

Str. 920:

Sex: Indeterminate
Age: Juvenile, 3-4yrs.

Str. 921:

Sex: Male
Age: Young adult

This skeleton exhibits healed fractures of the left radius and clavicle, and the right second, third, and fifth metacarpals. The fractures are well within the stage of remodeling, with little trace of the original fracture line. Additionally, a distal first toe phalanx shows signs of traumatic injury with subsequent degenerative changes.

Healed areas of periostitis were present on the distal right fibula, and both tibiae.

Both femora exhibited prominent, rough linea aspera, with apparent myositis ossificans present at midshaft.

The maxillary dentition displays anterior lingual surface attrition, and light calculus deposits. Twelve linear enamel hypoplastic defects were observed. Three teeth were lost prior to death. Periodontal disease was visible. Agenesis of the left maxillary third molar was evident.

Small osteophytes were present on the margins the body of the fifth lumbar vertebra.

Str. 922:

Sex: Indeterminate
Age: Adult

This individual is represented only by bones from the hands and feet.

Str. 924:
Sex: Female
Age: Young adult

Str. 925:
Sex: Indeterminate
Age: Fetal

There is an unusual plaque of new bone formation present on the greater wing of the sphenoid.

Str. 926:
Sex: Probable female
Age: Adult

There was no cranium in situ. It appears to have been removed after the soft tissue had decomposed, as no cut marks are present on the cervical vertebrae, and the mandible was still present. The mandible provides a sex estimation of probable female.

This individual had highly unusual mandibular tooth wear that is suggestive of the use of the dentition as a gripping tool. Tooth wear is heavy from the left mandibular canine to the right mandibular second incisor. Both central incisors are worn at an oblique angle with the downward slope on the labial aspect. This suggests a favored direction of use/movement/grip.

The left first and second molars, the only present left posterior teeth, also show heavy, asymmetrical wear. They show angular wear in which the first molar is worn distally, and the second molar is worn mesially, which creates a shared concave occlusal surface. The distal occlusal surface of first molar is worn to the root. The mesiobuccal occlusal surface of second molar exhibits non-carious pulp exposure.

The right posterior dentition is not as dramatically worn. However, there is severe crowding of the first and second molar in which the distal aspect of the first molar crown has been overlapped by the crown of the second molar. It may be that the impacted molars caused a certain amount of discomfort that forced the individual to favor the opposite side, which then resulted in asymmetrical dental attrition.

Advanced periodontal disease affects the entire right mandibular dentition, and it appears that the right central incisor was held in place more by the gingiva than alveolar bone. A periapical abscess is present at the right mandibular incisor, and another may have been present for the adjacent central incisor, although post-mortem damage of the alveolar bone precludes certainty. Three linear enamel hypoplastic defects are visible. Two dental caries are also present.

Str. 927:
Three individuals were identified within this burial deposit.
1. A young adult female, with no skull found in situ. The long bones of this individual are notably gracile, more so than is common among this sample. The available fragment of the left ilium has an irregular auricular surface with bone deposits that suggest fusion to the sacrum. Unfortunately, the sacrum was too fragmented to make further observations with respect to the possibility of abnormal sacro-iliac fusion.
2. A perinate, sex indeterminate.
3. A juvenile (4-5yrs.), sex indeterminate.

Str. 930:
This secondary deposit contained the commingled remains of at least three individuals, although the third is represented by only one bone. The other two are represented by crania, mandibles, and several postcranial elements.
1. A probable female, young adult, with two caries in the right second maxillary molar. There are moderate calculus deposits on the buccal surfaces of most teeth.
2. A probable female, young adult. This is a curious individual with a smaller than average mandibular size. Unfortunately, the mandible was fragmented at the root of the ascending rami, so measurements of mandibular length, etc., were not possible. However, the mandible and the maxilla are visibly small compared to others within the sample. It is also evident that the teeth of both dentitions are widely spaced. The second and third mandibular molars are absent, and there is little indication, given the reduced space, that they had ever developed. The maxilla suffered post-depositional damage at the level of the first molar, so it is unknown if the absence of the more posterior molars noticed in the mandible was mirrored in the maxilla. However, this does seem likely given the size of both jaws. In addition, intra-orbital breadth appeared to be wide. Unfortunately, the condition of the skeleton was poor, so a more thorough investigation of what could be a pathological condition was prevented. It should also be noted that given that the sex was assigned based solely upon cranial characteristics, this potentially pathological morphology may have diminished the accuracy of the estimation.
3. A single adult occipital bone with a nuchal crest within the female range. The occipital bone exhibits a pathological endocranial surface. The internal table has been eroded, and the underlying spongy bone has become swollen and sclerotic. This surface change is present within the visible cerebellar and cerebral fossae, as well as within

the transverse sinus. A meningeal infection is a possible cause.

Str. 931:
Sex: Indeterminate
Age: Adult

This individual was represented by an incomplete maxillary dentition and vault fragments. The maxillary teeth had heavy calculus accumulations. The right maxillary first premolar was carious.

Str. 933:
Sex: Indeterminate
Age: Fetal

Str. 941:
Sex: Probable female
Age: Middle adult

Seven dental caries were found among six teeth. Three teeth were lost antemortem. Non-carious pulp exposure is present on the right second mandibular incisor, and the polished appearance of the root surface, as well as the lack of severe attrition on the surrounding teeth, suggests traumatic crown loss.

Lingual maxillary surface attrition is visible. The right maxillary canine exhibits an unusual scalloped pattern of wear on the distal aspect of the crown.

Additionally, new bone formation is present on the medial aspect of the distal right fibula, just proximal to the epiphysis.

It was also noted that the deltoid tuberosities of both humerii, and the attachment sites for the pronator quadratus muscles, showed pronounced development, which suggests arm-intensive habitual movements involving pronation, abduction, and flexion.

Str. 942:
Sex: Indeterminate
Age: Adult

An isolated adult skull.

Str. 946:
Sex: Indeterminate
Age: Perinatal

Str. 977:
Sex: Indeterminate
Age: Fetal

Str. 981:
Sex: Indeterminate
Age: Fetal

Str. 1040

Two individuals are represented by very few skeletal elements.

1. An adult, sex indeterminate. This individual is represented by the bones of the right upper limb.
2. A juvenile (5-6 yrs.), represented by a right mandible.

Str. 1044:
Sex: Probable male
Age: Middle adult

The advanced degenerative changes in the cervical vertebrae with notable macroporosity on the joints of the fifth cervical bone do suggest an older age, although they may be activity induced, rather than age-related.

The carpals exhibit advanced degenerative changes that are unique to this sample. The right pisiform has marginal lipping and 50% of the articular surface shows eburnation. The bone is oddly squat. The left pisiform has slight thickening of the margins, and eburnation. The right triquetral has sharp lipping around the pisiform articulation, and eburnation of the facet. This is an unexpected area for degenerative changes, particularly in light of the fact that the other carpals appear unaffected. It is possible that the condition is traumatic in origin, or it may be linked to habitual activity.

Eburnation (2mm area) is present on distal left first metacarpal, which also has a healed fracture in the proximal third of the diaphysis. Sharp flexor crests are present on the finger phalanges, so hand-intensive labor is suggested. Also, there are robust muscle attachments for the gluteal muscles on what appears to be platymeric femora.

There is a healed depressed fracture of the posterior right parietal (17.1mm x 9.85mm), and a distal toe phalanx was also fractured.

Dental attrition is heavy. Twenty-four linear enamel hypoplastic defects were counted. Only the right maxillary second molar was lost antemortem, although advanced alveolar resorption of the surrounding area has left little support for the third, which was mostly likely held in place by the gingiva.

Str. 1045:
Sex: Probable male
Age: Adult

This individual had two caries affecting the right maxillary second premolar, and the left second mandibular molar.

Str. 1047:
Sex: Probable male
Age: Young adult

This individual displays well-developed muscle attachments, and sharp flexor crests on the proximal finger phalanges. The acromio-clavicular ligament was ossified. There is a small myositis ossificans extending from the left linea aspera. The patellae exhibited ossification of the patellar ligaments. Both ulnae had enthesopathies of the triceps insertion. Enthesopathies of the calcaneal tendon were also evident.

Several small, healed fractures were present: a healed fracture of the right first metacarpal and trapezium, which had flattened, two healed rib fractures, and a fractured distal toe phalanx.

The parietals exhibited healed porotic hyperostosis. There were six linear enamel hypoplastic defects.

Str. 1048:
Sex: Indeterminate
Age: Perinatal

Str. 1050:
Sex: Probable male
Age: Young adult
This individual had a healing comminuted (butterfly) fracture of the left femur, and possibly the left distal fibula. The fracture is located within the middle third of the diaphysis. Osteoclastic and osteoblastic changes are present. The individual survived the fracture event for at least one week before succumbing to the injury, which was likely a compound fracture. If the burial position is any indication, it does not appear that the femur could be reset properly, as the thigh was in a rotated position.

One enamel defect was observed on the left maxillary canine.

Str. 1051:
Sex: Female
Age: Middle adult
Healed porotic hyperostosis is present, and the associated diploic space is thick. Agenesis of the right mandibular third molar is probable.

Str. 1052:
Sex: Unknown
Age: Subadult, 12-13 yrs.
Four hypoplastic enamel defects were present on the right maxillary premolars.

Str. 1053:
Sex: Probable male
Age: Adult
One linear enamel hypoplastic defect was observed on the right mandibular canine.

Str. 1056:
Sex: Probable male
Age: Young adult
In general, the extant long bones were robust. Two linear enamel hypoplastic defects were present on the left and right second maxillary premolar. The right mandibular canine has 12 lines of abrasion, eight of which are fairly prominent, across buccal

surface of the crown's distal aspect. The occlusal surface is only lightly worn. Agenesis of the right mandibular third molar was evident.

Str. 1057:
Sex: Female
Age: Adult
No skull was present. The long bones were thin and gracile.

Str. 1058:
Sex: Male
Age: Middle adult
The right maxillary first molar and second premolar were lost antemortem.

Str. 1059
The remains of two individuals were present within this secondary burial deposit.
1. Subadult (possibly in the mid-to late teenaged years, perhaps 15-17 years), sex indeterminate.
2. Juvenile, sex indeterminate

Str. 1062 (not observed):
Sex: Unknown
Age: Unknown

Str. 1064:
Sex: Male
Age: Young adult
Alveolar bone loss is present around the mandibular incisors.

Str. 1066:
Sex: Indeterminate
Age: 2-3 yrs.

Str. 1067:
Two individuals are present, but represented only by left feet.
1. Juvenile, sex indeterminate. This individual was represented by a juvenile left foot.
2. Adult, sex indeterminate. This individual was represented by an adult left foot.

Str. 1068 (not observed):
Sex: Unknown
Age: Infant

Str. 1070 (not observed):
Sex: Unknown
Age: Unknown

Str. 1072:
Sex: Indeterminate
Age: Juvenile, 11-12 yrs.
The skull of this individual was not present in situ, and the first and second vertebrae were also

missing, which suggests that the head was removed while the soft tissue was still intact. No cutmarks were visible on the remaining articulated cervical vertebrae, but their poor condition may have obscured such evidence. Although the axial skeleton was articulated and intact, both lower limbs and the left upper limb, but for a few hand bones, were not present.

Str. 1073:
Sex: Indeterminate
Age: Juvenile, 1-2 yrs.

Concentration 1

Str. 718:
This burial contained the remains of two individuals.
1. A probable young adult male with a periapical lesion of the right maxillary first molar. Generally, robust long bones.
2. An infant represented only by a right petrous and a developing mandibular first molar.

Str. 719:
This burial contained the commingled remains of two individuals.
1. An adult, sex indeterminate, with a healed fracture of a left fourth metacarpal. The general appearance of the post-cranial remains does suggest that the individual is likely male.
2. A young juvenile, 1-2yrs.

Str. 720:
This burial contained the commingled remains of at least three individuals as evident from repeated skeletal elements. There was a left first metacarpal with a healed fracture found among the remains, but it cannot be attributed to any one individual.
1. A probable old adult male.
2. An adult, sex indeterminate.
3. An adult, sex indeterminate, with light dental attrition, suggesting a young adult age.

Str. 721:
Sex: Indeterminate
Age: Subadult, 11-13yrs.

Str. 722:
Sex: Probable female
Age: Middle adult.
A small auditory exostosis is associated with the right external acoustic meatus. There is antemortem loss of the left mandibular canine.
Lingual surface maxillary attrition of the anterior teeth is evident.

Str. 740:
Sex: Indeterminate
Age: Juvenile, 10-12yrs.
Str. 741:
Sex: Indeterminate
Age: Juvenile, 5-7yrs.

Str. 742:
Sex: Indeterminate
Age: Juvenile, 6-8yrs.

Str. 743:
Sex: Probable male
Age: Middle adult
Antemortem tooth loss of the left first mandibular molar.

Concentration 2

Str. 711:
Sex: Indeterminate
Age: Subadult, 15-18yrs.
Five hypoplastic defects were observed on the both pairs of mandibular premolars.

Str. 714:
Sex: Probable male
Age: Adult
This individual was poorly preserved, and highly fragmented. Fragments of the femora were visible robust, and the linea asperae were thick and well-defined. A carious lesion was present on the right maxillary second premolar. Two enamel hypoplastic defects were present on the right mandibular canine.

Str. 731:
Sex: Probable male
Age: Young adult
The tooth wear of this individual suggests a young adult age. In addition to 14 linear enamel hypoplasias, this individual also experienced the antemortem loss of the left mandibular first incisor, likely traumatic in origin. Available parietal fragments exhibit healed porotic hyperostosis.
This robust individual also appears to have suffered a traumatic injury to both hands. On the left hand, there is a healed crush fracture of the left first metacarpal. On the right, two carpals, the right capitate and trapezoid, exhibit bony, degenerative changes suggestive of an associated traumatic event. The right second metacarpal may have also been fractured, but it is unclear given the state of preservation.

Str. 732:
Sex: Indeterminate
Age: Subadult, 12-15yrs.
Seventeen hypoplastic defects are distributed among the nearly complete dentition.

Str. 737:
Sex: Probable male
Age: Middle adult
Minor dental disease is evident in this individual who displays the antemortem loss of the right first mandibular molar, and four carious lesions. Lingual surface attrition of the anterior maxillary dentition is present.
Viewed in cross-section, the cranial diploie is thick, but there is no outward indication of any underlying pathological cause.

Str. 751:
Sex: Indeterminate
Age: Juvenile, 5-6yrs.
Two hypoplastic defects were observed on the left maxillary second incisor.

Concentration 3

In addition to the structure numbers listed below, this burial concentration also includes nine individuals (one cremation, eight secondary burials) that were not available for analysis.

Str. 831:
This is a cremation deposit contained the commingled remains of at least six individuals.
1. A probable adult female.
2. A probable adult female.
3. A probable adult male.
4. A juvenile, sex indeterminate.
5. An adult, sex indeterminate.
6. An adult, sex indeterminate.

Str. 847/848/850:
This secondary burial deposit contained the commingled remains of at least five individuals.
1. A probable male, adult.
2. A probable male, old adult. The age estimation of this individual is based upon advanced dental attrition of the mandibular and maxillary teeth, and the antemortem loss of the second and third right mandibular molars.
3. A probable male, adult.
4. An infant, sex indeterminate.
5. A probable female, adult.

Str. 854:
Sex: Indeterminate
Age: Juvenile, 5-7yrs.

Concentration 4

Str. 833:
Sex: Probable male
Age: Young adult

Str. 839:
Two burned, commingled individuals were associated with this burial.
1. A probable male, middle adult.
2. A probable male, adult.

Str. 845:
Sex: Probable male
Age: Adult

Str. 846:
Sex: Probable female
Age: Young adult

Str. 853:
Sex: Probable female
Age: Adult

Str. 859:
Sex: Probable female
Age: Old adult

Concentration 5

Str. 842:
Sex: Probable male
Age: Middle adult

Str. 855:
Sex: Probable male
Age: Young adult

Str. 856:
Sex: Probable female
Age: Adult

Str. 857:
Sex: Probable male
Age: Young adult

Str. 858:
Sex: Probable female
Age: subadult

Concentration 6

Str. 865:
This burial designation includes the commingled remains of at least two individuals.
1. A probable female, adult.
2. A probable female, adult.

Str. 866:
Sex: Indeterminate
Age: Adult

Str. 867:
This burial designation included the commingled remains of at least two individuals.

1. Juvenile, sex indeterminate.
2. Juvenile, sex indeterminate.

Str. 868:
This burial designation includes the commingled remains of two individuals.
1. Juvenile, sex indeterminate.
2. Juvenile, sex indeterminate.

Concentration 7-1

Str. 860:
Sex: Indeterminate
Age: Adult
An adult represented by the bones of the left upper limb and six teeth. Linear enamel hypoplastic defects are present on three teeth.

Str. 861:
Sex: Probable female
Age: Young adult
Eleven linear enamel hypoplastic defects were observed among several teeth.

Str. 862:
Sex: Probable female
Age: Young adult
One dental caries was present, as was light calculus accumulation.

Str. 863:
Sex: Probable female
Age: Middle adult
Antemortem tooth loss of three posterior mandibular teeth, in addition to three hypoplastic defects, was observed. The occlusal surfaces showed moderate attrition. Heavy calculus was present on the labio-buccal surfaces of the dentition.
Observable muscle attachment sites (deltoid tuberosities, supracondylar crests, both linea aspera, gluteal tuberosities) are well developed. Both patellae have vastus notches.

Concentration 7-2

Str. 932:
A commingled deposit containing cremated and unburnt remains. At least six individuals are present.
1. A probable male, adult.
2. A subadult, sex indeterminate.
3. A juvenile, sex indeterminate.
4. A fetus, sex indeterminate.
5. A juvenile, sex indeterminate.
6. Juvenile (1-2yrs.), sex indeterminate.

Str. 984:
Sex: Probable male

Age: Young adult
Three dental caries, and 20 linear enamel hypoplasias, are present in the dentition of this robust individual.

Str. 985:
Sex: Indeterminate
Age: Juvenile, 6-7 yrs.
Cribra orbitalia is present on both supraorbital plates. A fragment of sphenoid also exhibits porosity. The combination of lesions may indicate a Vitamin C deficiency rather than anemia.
The right hypoglossal canal is bridged.

Str. 988:
Sex: Female
Age: Middle adult
Both femora exhibit a plaque of new bone formation suggestive of an ongoing inflammatory process. The right femur has 67mm length of periosteal reaction at the proximolateral shaft, just opposite the gluteal tuberosity. There are several patches of new bone formation on the anteromedial diaphysis, with a mixture of woven and sclerotic bone. The left femur is similar, but new bone deposits are more sclerotic with vessel impressions, covering a 121mm area.
Eleven linear enamel hypoplasias are also present.
The right humerus has a septal aperture.

Concentration 8

This is a cremation deposit containing the commingled fragments of at least nine individuals. Two fragmented adult crania, both of which lacked any diagnostic features useful for sex estimation, were grayish-white in color, and displayed the morphological changes, such as shrinking and warping, that are associated with high temperature fire exposure.

Str. 835.1:
Sex: Indeterminate
Age: Infant, B-3mos.

Str. 835.2:
Sex: Indeterminate
Age: Juvenile

Str. 835.3:
Sex: Indeterminate
Age: Juvenile, 4-6yrs.
The age estimation for this individual relied upon the visible mandibular dental development. A right superior orbital plate and arch, thought to be associated with this individual, displays active cribra orbitalia.

Str. 835.4:
Sex: Indeterminate

Age: Subadult
 Active cribra orbitalia was visible in the right orbit of this individual.

Str. 835.5:
Sex: Indeterminate
Age: Old adult
 An edentulous mandible, and nearly edentulous right maxilla provide the age estimation for this individual. However, the mental region of the mandible was not present, so sex could not be determined.

Str. 835.6:
Sex: Indeterminate
Age: Adult

Str. 835.7:
Sex: Indeterminate
Age: Adult

Str. 835.8:
Sex: Probable male
Age: Adult

Concentration 9

Str. 919:
 This burial contains the commingled remains of at least five individuals. Some elements have clearly been exposed to high temperature firing. Others show red/brownish darkening also indicating exposure to fire, but at lower temperatures.
 1. A subadult (<16yrs.), sex indeterminate.
 2. A juvenile, sex indeterminate.
 3. An adult, sex indeterminate.
 4. An adult, sex indeterminate.
 5. An adult, sex indeterminate. This individual is represented by the grayish-white cremated cranial and post-cranial remains. The fragments display color changes and drastic morphological modification that is indicative of high temperature exposure while the bone was still fresh, or soft tissue was still present.

Concentration 10

Str. 943:
Sex: Probable male
Age: Young adult.
 Seven hypoplastic bands were present on the mandibular canines.

Str. 947:
Sex: Probable male
Age: Middle adult.
 Both mandibular first molars have completely exposed mesial-buccal roots, which suggests

pronounced periodontal disease. Antemortem loss of the right maxillary second molar was also observed. The left maxillary third molar was carious. Agenesis of the left mandibular third molar was evident.

Str. 953.1 (Concentration 10, South):
Sex: Indeterminate
Age: Adult
 An adult of Indeterminate sex represented by left and right tibia and fibulae.

Str. 953.2 (Concentration 10, South)
Sex: Indeterminate
Age: Adult

Str. 953.3 (Concentration 10, South)
Sex: Indeterminate
Age: Adult

Str. 953.4 (Concentration 10, South)
Sex: Indeterminate
Age: Adult

Str. 953.5 (Concentration 10, South)
Sex: Indeterminate
Age: Adult

Str. 953.6 (Concentration 10, South)
Sex: indeterminate
Age: Perinatal

Str. 953.7 (Concentration 10, South)
Sex: Indeterminate
Age: Subadult, 10-14yrs.

Str. 962:
Sex: Male
Age: Middle adult.
 This individual has severe degenerative changes of the left superior and inferior articular facets of the lower cervical vertebrae. Unfortunately, the highly fragmentary condition of the vertebrae prevents an exact assignment of number. It is most likely that these pathological fragments are C5-7, perhaps C4-6. To varying degrees, the facets each exhibit macroporosity, eburnation, and osteophytic lipping along the margins.
 The right mandibular second molar and second premolar each have interproximal caries that would have been adjacent with the first molar. The presence of these lesions is likely related to the antemortem loss of the first molar, and the healing periapical abscess that remains. Five addition teeth were also lost prior to death. Two interproximal caries are also present on the left maxillary third molar.
 Two hypoplastic bands were also visible.

A mandibular torus is present on the body of the right mandible in the area of the third molar.
An unsided intermediate finger phalanx exhibited a healed compression fracture.
Vault fragments showed evidence of healed porotic hyperostosis.

Str. 971:
Sex: Indeterminate
Age: Juvenile, 3-4yrs.

Str. 972:
Sex: Indeterminate
Age: Juvenile, 11-12 yrs.

Str. 978:
Sex: Probable female
Age: Young adult
This individual had three carious posterior maxillary teeth, and antemortem tooth loss of the left second and third mandibular molars. The buccal surface of the left second premolar is worn, or chipped, away. No other teeth exhibit similar dental wear.
Healed porotic hyperostosis was also present.

Str. 979:
Sex: Indeterminate
Age: Subadult, 12-13yrs.
Ten hypoplastic enamel defects were distributed among both dentitions. Light calculus is present on the labial and buccal surfaces of most teeth.

Str 980 (Concentration 10, not observed):
Sex: Unknown
Age: Unknown

Str. 983:
Sex: Probable female
Age: Young adult
This individual is represented by an isolated mandible with interproximal dental caries of the left first and second molars.

Str. 991:
Sex: Indeterminate
Age: Juvenile, 5-6 yrs.

Str. 993:
Sex: Indeterminate
Age: Infant, 9-12mos.
This individual is primarily represented by cranial fragments and a mandible. The mandible contained an unerupted deciduous first molar that had yet to form roots.

Str. 995:
Sex: Indeterminate
Age: Adult

This individual was represented by fragmentary post-cranial remains.
Osteophyte formation was present along the superior edge of a lower lumbar vertebral body (L4 or L5).
Eburnation and lipping was observed along the margins of the articular surfaces for the talar-calcaneal joint.

Str. 996:
Sex: Indeterminate
Age: Juvenile, 4-5 yrs.

Str. 998:
Sex: Indeterminate.
Age: Adult
An isolated, poorly preserved adult pelvis.

Str. 999 (Concentration 10, not observed):
Sex: Unknown
Age: Unknown
Burials Reviewed by Photograph

Str. 1074
Sex: Indeterminate
Age: Infant

Str. 1075
Sex: Indeterminate
Age: Young adult
Open sutures may indicate a younger age.

Str. 1076
Sex: Indeterminate
Age: Unknown

Str. 1077
Sex: Probable female
Age: Young adult

Str. 1078
Sex: Indeterminate
Age: Perinatal

Str. 1079
Sex: Probable male
Age: Young adult
The visible teeth of this individual appear to have minimal wear, which does suggest a young adult age.
Both linea aspera of the femora are well-developed.

Str. 1080
Sex: Indeterminate
Age: Old adult
From what can be viewed from the image, the left second and third mandibular molars were lost antemortem. Moderate to heavy calculus is visible

on the extant dentition. Alveolar bone loss does seem evident, as well. Heavy attrition is visible on the both the mandibular and maxillary first molar, which does suggest an older individual. The gonial angle and rounded mental eminence suggest that this may be female.

Str. 1081
Sex: Probable female
Age: Adult
The condition of the remains limited sex estimation. However, the general appearance and gracility of the visible skeletal elements suggest that this individual was female. Sacral fusion suggests an age about 25 years. From what is visible in the photograph, the right lateral supracondylar crest is sharp, and well-defined.

Str. 1082
Sex: Indeterminate
Age: Old adult
Osteophytes are visible on the inferior margin of the third lumber vertebra. This is the only visible potential indicator of age.

Str. 1083
Sex: Indeterminate
Age: Adult

Str. 1084
Sex: Probable female
Age: Adult

Str. 1085
Sex: Probable female
Age: Young adult
Alveolar bone loss is visible for the left maxillary and mandibular first molars. Both the left maxillary and mandibular first molars are heavily worn, although the anterior teeth are not. The left first molar has been worn to the root, and the distal root pairs may have been lost antemortem.

Str. 1086
Sex: Probable male
Age: Adult

Str. 1087
Sex: Probable female
Age: Young adult
Incomplete fusion of the posterior iliac crest, as well as minimal attrition visible on the complete adult dental arcade, suggests an age between 18-22 years. Light calculus accumulation is visible, and the teeth are only lightly worn.

Str. 1088
There are three individuals present in the deposit.

1. A probable adult male represented by a complete skull and right upper limb.
2. An adult, sex indeterminate, represented by the lower limbs, the right upper limb, and the left hand and forearm, which was associated with a stamp seal.
3. A juvenile represented by an ulna and toe phalanges.

Str. 1089
Sex: Indeterminate
Age: Juvenile
The age of this individual was estimated using the visible maxillary dentition. The second molar is not erupted, but the permanent incisors appear to be in occlusion. It is not clear if both deciduous molars are present, or have been replaced by the adult premolars, because dirt obscures the crowns of these teeth. The shape of the visible cusps does suggest that at least the first premolar is present. Though uncertain, an age range of 8-12 years is likely.

Str. 1090
Sex: Probable male
Age: Middle adult
The mandibular third molars have lost their cups, and there is dentin exposure. Alveolar bone loss is visible.

Str. 1091
Sex: Indeterminate
Age: Subadult, 16-20yrs.
Incomplete epiphyseal fusion of the sternal end of the clavicle, as well as the lack of annular rings on the vertebrae, are the indicators of age.

Str. 1092
Sex: Indeterminate
Age: Juvenile, <12yrs.

Str. 1093
Sex: Indeterminate
Age: Juvenile, 2-3yrs.
The complete juvenile dentition is present, and in occlusion. The crown of the first maxillary adult molar is not complete.

Str. 1094
Sex: Indeterminate
Age: Juvenile
No skull was present in situ. What appears to be an isolated maxillary lateral incisor is visible in the photo, as is the incomplete root of another unidentifiable tooth.

Str. 1095
Sex: Indeterminate
Age: Adult

Str. 1096
Sex: Indeterminate
Age: Adult

Str. 1097
Sex: Probable female
Age: Adult

Str. 1098
Sex: Indeterminate
Age: Perinatal

Str. 1099
Sex: Indeterminate
Age: Adult

Burials Unassociated with the Cemetery

Str. 522:
Sex: Indeterminate
Age: Infant

Str. 656:
Sex: Indeterminate.
Age: Juvenile, 10-12yrs.

Str. 810:
Sex: Probable male
Age: Subadult, 14-16yrs.
    An isolated skull recovered from east wall of excavation area.

Str. 901:
Sex: Indeterminate
Age: Perinatal

Str. 1009:
Sex: Probable male
Age: Young adult
    A later period burial (el-Rouj 2d).

Appendix 6-2: Sex Determination

Burial	Sex	Age	Pelvic Features					Cranial Features					Notes
			Ventral Arc	Subpubic concavity	Ischiopubic ramus	Sciatic Notch	Preauricular Sulcus	Nuchal crest	Mastoid Process	Supraorbital ridge	Glabella	Mental Eminance	
502	Unknown	Juvenile											
504	Unknown	Perinatal											
507	Unknown	Juvenile											
513	Unknown	Perinatal											
519	Unknown	Fetal											
521	Unknown	Subadult											
524	Probable female	Middle adult							Probable Female	Probable Female			
527	Unknown	infant											
528	Unknown	Juvenile											
533	Female	Middle adult	Female		Female			Female					
710	Probable male	Old adult						Probable male			Male		
711	Unknown	Subadult											
712	Probable female	Middle adult				Female	Probable Female	Ambiguous		Male			
713	Unknown	Juvenile											
714	Probable male	Adult										Probable male	
715	Probable male	Young adult						Probable male	Probable male	Male		Male	
716	Probable male	Middle adult						Male	Probable male	Male			
717	Unknown	Juvenile											
718	Probable male	Young adult							Probable male	2,5	Probable male		
718,2	Unknown	infant											
719,1	Unknown	Juvenile											
719,2	Unknown	Adult											
720,1	Probable male	Old adult										Probable male	Robust
720,2	Unknown	Adult											
720,3	Unknown	Young adult											
721	Unknown	Subadult											
722	Probable female	Middle adult							Ambiguous		Probable Female		
725	Probable female	Young adult						Probable male	Probable Female			Probable Female	
726	Unknown	Infant											
729	Probable female	Young adult							Ambiguous	Probable Female	Female		
730	Unknown	Juvenile											
731	Probable male	Young adult										Male	
732	Unknown	Subadult											
737	Probable male	Middle adult							Male			Probable male	
738	Unknown	infant											
739	Probable male	Middle adult							Male	Probable male	Male	Male	
740,1	Unknown	Juvenile											
741,1	Unknown	Juvenile											
742,1	Unknown	Juvenile											
743	Probable male	Middle adult						Probable male	Ambiguous		Probable male	Probable male	
746,1	Unknown	Juvenile											
746,2	Unknown	Juvenile											
748,1	Probable male	Young adult						Probable Female	Male	Probable male	Male		
748,2	Unknown	Juvenile											
748,3	Unknown	infant											
750	Unknown	Juvenile											
751	Unknown	Juvenile											

Burial	Sex	Age	Pelvic Features					Cranial Features					Notes
			Ventral Arc	Subpubic concavity	Ischiopubic ramus	Sciatic Notch	Preauricular Sulcus	Nuchal crest	Mastoid Process	Supraorbital ridge	Glabella	Mental Eminance	
752	Probable female	Adult											Femoral Head Diam.: 40mm & 41.5mm
756	Unknown	Juvenile											
757	Unknown	Juvenile											
759	*Unknown*	*Adult*											*Not Examined*
803	Probable female	Young adult							Ambiguous			Ambiguous	MC estimation predicts female.
807	Male	Middle adult	Male	Male	Male					Male	Male	Ambiguous	
822,1	Unknown	Juvenile											
823	Unknown	Subadult											
825	Unknown	Juvenile											
826	Unknown	Subadult											
828	Unknown	Fetal											
829	Unknown	Juvenile											
830	Probable male	Middle adult							Male	Probable male		Male	
831,1	Probable female	Adult							Probable Female				
831,2	Probable female	Adult							Probable Female				
831,3	Probable male	Adult						Probable male	Probable male				
831,4	Unknown	Juvenile											
831,5	Unknown	Adult											
831,6	Unknown	Adult											
832,1	Unknown	Perinatal											
832,2	Unknown	Juvenile											
832,3	Unknown	Juvenile											
832,4	Unknown	Adult											
832,5	Unknown	Adult											
833	Probable male	Young adult							Male	Male			
834	Unknown	Juvenile											
835,1	Unknown	infant											
835,2	Unknown	Juvenile											
835,3	Unknown	Juvenile											
835,4	Unknown	Subadult											
835,5	Unknown	Old adult											
835,6	Unknown	Adult											
835,7	Unknown	Adult											
835,8	Probable male	Adult										Probable male	
836	Male	Middle adult	Male	Male	Male				Ambiguous	Male	Male	Male	
838	Unknown	Perinatal											
839,1	Probable male	Middle adult			Male							Probable male	
839,2	Probable male	Adult										Probable male	
841	Unknown	Perinatal											
842	Probable male	Middle adult							Male	Male	Male	Male	Robust
845	Probable male	Adult										Probable male	
846	Probable female	Young adult										Probable Female	
847,1	Probable male	Adult										Probable male	
847,2	Probable male	Old adult										Probable male	
847,3	Probable male	Adult						Male	Male			Male	
847,4	Unknown	infant											
847,5	Probable female	Adult								Probable Female	Probable Female		

Burial	Sex	Age	Pelvic Features					Cranial Features					Notes
			Ventral Arc	Subpubic concavity	Ischiopubic ramus	Sciatic Notch	Preauricular Sulcus	Nuchal crest	Mastoid Process	Supraorbital ridge	Glabella	Mental Eminance	
851,1	Unknown	infant											
851,2	Unknown	Adult											
852,1	Probable male	Adult										Probable male	Robust
852,2	Unknown	Juvenile											
853	Probable female	Adult						Female				Female	
854	Unknown	Juvenile											
855	Probable male	Young adult						Probable male	Probable male	Probable male	Probable male	Probable male	
856	Probable female	Adult						Probable Female	Ambiguous	Probable Female	Female	Probable male	
857	Probable male	Young adult						Probable male	Probable male	Probable male	Probable male		
858	Probable female	Subadult								Probable Female			
859	Probable female	Old adult										Female	
860	Unknown	Adult											
861	Probable female	Young adult								Female	Probable Female		
862	Probable female	Young adult							Ambiguous		Female		
863	Probable female	Middle adult							Probable male	Probable Female	Female		
865,1	Female	Adult						Female	Female	Female	Female	Female	Gracile
865,2	Probable female	Adult							Probable Female		Probable Female		
866	Unknown	Adult											
867,1	Unknown	Juvenile											
867,2	Unknown	Juvenile											
868,1	Unknown	Juvenile											
868,2	Unknown	Juvenile											
902	Unknown	Juvenile											
904	Probable male	Young adult				Female	Ambiguous	Probable male	Male	Male	Probable male		
908	Unknown	Subadult											
909	Probable female	Young adult							Ambiguous		Ambiguous		
910,1	Unknown	Adult											
910,2	Unknown	Old adult											
910,3	Unknown	Infant											
911	Unknown	Perinatal											
912	Unknown	infant											
913	Unknown	Juvenile											
914	Unknown	Juvenile											
918	Unknown	infant											
919,1	Unknown	Subadult											
919,2	Unknown	Juvenile											
919,3	Unknown	Adult											
919,4	Unknown	Adult											
919,5	Unknown	Adult											
920	Unknown	Juvenile											
921	Male	Young adult				Male		Ambiguous	Male	Probable male	Probable male	Male	
922	Unknown	Adult											
924	Female	Young adult				Female	Probable Female	Ambiguous	Probable Female	Probable Female		Probable Female	
925	Unknown	Fetal											
926	Probable female	Adult										Female	
927,1	Female	Young adult	Female	Female	Female	Female	Female						
927,2	Unknown	Perinatal											
927,3	Unknown	Juvenile											

Burial	Sex	Age	Pelvic Features					Cranial Features					Notes
			Ventral Arc	Subpubic concavity	Ischiopubic ramus	Sciatic Notch	Preauricular Sulcus	Nuchal crest	Mastoid Process	Supraorbital ridge	Glabella	Mental Eminance	
930,1	Probable female	Young adult							Probable Female	Probable Female	Probable Female	Probable Female	
930,2	Probable female	Young adult						Female		Female	Female	Female	
930,3	Probable female	Adult						Probable Female					Occipital fragment only
931	Unknown	Adult											
932,1	Probable male	Adult										Probable male	Robust
932,2	Unknown	Subadult											
932,3	Unknown	juvenile											
932,4	Unknown	Fetal											
932,5	Unknown	Juvenile											
932,6	Unknown	Juvenile											
933	Unknown	Fetal											
941	Probable female	Middle adult				Female	Female		Probable Female	Probable Female	Probable Female	Female	
942	Unknown	Adult								Ambiguous			
943	Probable male	Young adult								Probable Female	Male		
946	Unknown	Perinatal											
947	Probable male	Middle adult						Ambiguous	Male	Female		Probable male	
953,1	Unknown	Adult											
953,2	Unknown	Adult											
953,3	Unknown	Adult											
953,4	Unknown	Adult											
953,5	Unknown	Adult											
953,6	Unknown	Perinatal											
953,7	Unknown	Subadult											
962	Male	Middle adult						Male	Male	Probable male	Male		
971	Unknown	Juvenile											
972	Unknown	Juvenile											Se
977	Unknown	Fetal											
978	Probable female	Young adult						Ambiguous		Probable Female		Probable Female	
979	Unknown	Subadult								Probable Female		Probable Female	
980	Unknown	Unknown											Not examined
981	Unknown	Fetal											
983	Probable female	Young adult										Probable Female	
984	Probable male	Young adult								Ambiguous		Male	Robust
985	Unknown	Juvenile											
988	Female	Middle adult				Female	Female	Probable Female	Female	Female		Probable Female	
991	Unknown	Juvenile											
993	Unknown	Infant											
995	Unknown	Adult											
996	Unknown	Juvenile											
998	Unknown	Adult											
999	Unknown	Unknown											Not examined
1040,1	Unknown	Adult											
1040,2	Unknown	Juvenile											
1044	Probable male	Middle adult							Probable male	Probable Female	Male	Male	
1045	Probable male	Adult				Probable male							
1047	Probable male	Young adult				Probable male		Probable male	Male	Probable male		Male	
1048	Unknown	Perinatal											
1050	Probable male	Young adult											Robust

306

Burial	Sex	Age	Pelvic Features					Cranial Features					Notes
			Ventral Arc	Subpubic concavity	Ischiopubic ramus	Sciatic Notch	Preauricular Sulcus	Nuchal crest	Mastoid Process	Supraorbital ridge	Glabella	Mental Eminance	
1051	Female	Middle adult				Female		Female	1,5	Probable Female	Female	Female	
1052	Unknown	Subadult											
1053	Probable male	Adult							Probable male	Ambiguous	Ambiguous	Probable male	
1056	Probable male	Young adult							Male	Ambiguous			
1057	Female	Adult	Female	Female	Female	Female							Headless burial
1058	Male	Middle adult							Probable male			Male	
1059,1	Unknown	Subadult				Probable Female							
1059,2	Unknown	Juvenile											
1062	Unknown	Unknown											*Not Examined*
1064	Male	Young adult	Male	Male	Male				Female			Probable male	
1066	Unknown	Juvenile											
1067,1	Unknown	Juvenile											
1067,2	Unknown	Adult											
1068	Unknown	Infant											
1070	Unknown	Unknown											
1072	Unknown	Juvenile											
1073	Unknown	Juvenile											
1074	Unknown	Infant											*Photo*
1075	Unknown	Young adult											*Photo*
1076	Unknown	Unknown											*Photo*
1077	Probable female	Young adult							Probable Female			Probable Female	*Photo*
1078	Unknown	Perinatal											*Photo*
1079	Probable male	Young adult		Male				Probable male	Probable male				*Photo*
1080	Unknown	Old adult											*Photo*
1081	Probable female	Adult											*Photo. Gracile, female-associated grave goods.*
1082	Unknown	Old adult											*Photo. Os coxa outline looks male,r.*
1083	Unknown	Adult											*Photo*
1084	Probable female	Adult								Female	Female		*Photo*
1085	Probable female	Young adult				Female		Female	Probable Female		Female	Probable Female	*Photo*
1086	Probable male	Adult							Male				*Photo*
1087	Probable female	Young adult							Female	Female	Female	Female	*photo*
1088,1	Probable male	Adult											*Photo. Femoral head diam. ~45mm*
1088,2	Unknown	Adult											*Photo*
1088,3	Unknown	Juvenile											*Photo*
1089	Unknown	Juvenile											*Photo*
1090	Probable male	Middle adult							Male				*Photo*
1091	Unknown	Subadult											*Photo.*
1092	Unknown	Juvenile											*Photo.*
1093	Unknown	Juvenile											*Photo.*
1094	Unknown	Juvenile											*Photo.*
1095	Unknown	Adult											*Photo.*
1096	Unknown	Adult											*Photo.*
1097	Probable female	Adult											*Photo.*
1098	Unknown	Perinatal											*Photo.*
1099	Unknown	Adult											*Photo.*
E271B	Unknown	Unknown											*Not examined.*
E271B	Unknown	Eight unknown											*Not examined*

Appendix 6-3: Age Determination

Burial	Sex	Age	Range	Pubic Symphysis		Auricular Surface Score	Cranial Suture Closure		Notes
				Todd Score	Suchey-Brooks Score		Vault Score	Lateral Score	
502	Unknown	Juvenile	2-3yrs						Complete deciduous dentition
504	Unknown	Perinatal	36-40wk ges						Incomplete deciduous incisor crowns, unfused mandibular symphysis
507	Unknown	Juvenile	8-10yrs						Mixed permanent/deciduous dentition, unfused long bone epiphyses
513	Unknown	Perinatal							
519	Unknown	Fetal							Deciduous m1 crown coalesced, unfused mandibualr symphysis
521	Unknown	Subadult	12-15yrs						Unfused femoral epiphyses, etc.
524	Probable female	Middle adult							Moderate to heavy tooth wear
527	Unknown	Infant	B-3mos						Incomplete deciduous incisor crowns, unfused mandibular symphysis
528	Unknown	Juvenile	1-3yrs						
533	Female	Middle adult	40-50yrs	9	5,5	5,5			
710	Probable male	Old adult	50+						Edentulous max, heavy mandibular wear
711	Unknown	Subadult	15-18yrs						M3 crown complete
712	Probable female	Middle adult				4			Epiphyseal line visible on sternal end of clavicle
713	Unknown	Juvenile	10-12yrs						Unfused os coxa, etc.
714	Probable male	Adult							Moderate wear
715	Probable male	Young adult							Light to moderate wear
716	Probable male	Middle adult							Moderate wear
717	Unknown	Juvenile	1-2yrs						
718	Probable male	Young adult	25-30yrs			2,5	1		
718,2	Unknown	Infant							
719,1	Unknown	Juvenile	1-2yrs						Dm2 root 50% complete
719,2	Unknown	Adult							
720,1	Probable male	Old adult							Heavily worn teeth
720,2	Unknown	Adult							
720,3	Unknown	Young adult							
721	Unknown	Subadult	11-13yrs						M3 crown incomplete
722	Probable female	Middle adult							Moderate wear
725	Probable female	Young adult							Light wear
726	Unknown	Infant	9-18mos						
729	Probable female	Young adult					3		Light wear
730	Unknown	Juvenile	2-3yrs						
731	Probable male	Young adult							
732	Unknown	Subadult	12-15yrs						M2 roots complete
737	Probable male	Middle adult							
738	Unknown	Infant	B-3mos						Unfused mandibular symphysis
739	Probable male	Middle adult				5	10		
740,1	Unknown	Juvenile	10-12yrs						
741,1	Unknown	Juvenile	5-7yrs						
742,1	Unknown	Juvenile	6-8yrs						
743	Probable male	Middle adult					9		
746,1	Unknown	Juvenile	1-2yrs						
746,2	Unknown	Juvenile	6-8yrs						
748,1	Probable male	Young adult				3	0		Light wear
748,2	Unknown	Juvenile	2-3yrs						
748,3	Unknown	Infant							
750	Unknown	Juvenile	5-6yrs						
751	Unknown	Juvenile	5-6yrs						
752	Probable female	Adult							
756	Unknown	Juvenile							
757	Unknown	Juvenile	7-8yrs						
759	Unknown	Adult							
803	Probable female	Young adult							Light tooth wear
807	Male	Middle adult	35-40yrs	6	4	4			

Burial	Sex	Age	Range	Pubic Symphysis		Auricular Surface Score	Cranial Suture Closure		Notes
				Todd Score	Suchey-Brooks Score		Vault Score	Lateral Score	
822,1	Unknown	Juvenile	10-12yrs						
823	Unknown	Subadult	14-16yrs						
825	Unknown	Juvenile	10-12yrs						
826	Unknown	Subadult	14-15yrs						
828	Unknown	Fetal	28-32wks ges						
829	Unknown	Juvenile	2-3yrs						Complete deciduous dentition
830	Probable male	Middle adult					0		
831,1	Probable female	Adult							
831,2	Probable female	Adult							
831,3	Probable male	Adult							
831,4	unknown	Juvenile							
831,5	unknown	Adult							
831,6	unknown	Adult							
832,1	Unknown	perinatal							
832,2	Unknown	Juvenile	10-12yrs						
832,3	Unknown	Juvenile							
832,4	Unknown	Adult							
832,5	Unknown	Adult							
833	Probable male	Young adult					0		
834	Unknown	Juvenile	2-3yrs						Complete deciduous dentition
835,1	Unknown	Infant	B-3mos						
835,2	Unknown	Juvenile							
835,3	Unknown	Juvenile							
835,4	Unknown	Subadult							
835,5	Unknown	Old adult							
835,6	Unknown	Adult							
835,7	Unknown	Adult							
835,8	Probable male	Adult							
836	Male	Middle adult		9	4				
838	Unknown	Perinatal							Deciduous crowns less than 25%complete; unfused mandibular symphysis
839	Probable male	Middle adult		9	5				
839,2	Probable male	Adult							
841	Unknown	Perinatal	37-41wks ges						
842	Probable male	Middle adult							
845	Probable male	Adult							
846	Probable female	Young adult							Light tooth wear
847,1	Probable male	Adult							
847,2	Probable male	Old adult							
847,3	Probable male	Adult							Heavy tooth wear
847,4	unknown	Infant							
847,5	Probable female	Adult							
851,1	unknown	Infant	10-12mos						
851,2	unknown	Adult							
852,1	Probable male	Adult							
852,2	unknown	Juvenile	1-2yrs						
853,839	Probable female	Adult							
854	Unknown	Juvenile	5-7yrs						
855	Probable male	Young adult							
856	Probable female	Adult							
857	Probable male	Young adult							
858	Probable female	Subadult							
859	Probable female	Old adult							Heavy tooth wear
860	Unknown	Adult							
861	Probable female	Young adult							Light tooth wear
862	Probable female	Young adult							
863	Probable female	Middle adult							Moderate tooth wear
865	Probable female	Adult							

Burial	Sex	Age	Range	Pubic Symphysis		Auricular Surface Score	Cranial Suture Closure		Notes
				Todd Score	Suchey-Brooks Score		Vault Score	Lateral Score	
865,2	Probable female	Adult							
866	Unknown	Adult							
867	Unknown	Juvenile							
867,2	Unknown	Juvenile							
868	Unknown	Juvenile							
868,2	Unknown	Juvenile							
902	Unknown	Juvenile	1-2yrs						
904	Probable male	Young adult	30-35yrs			4	0		
908	Unknown	Subadult	11-13yrs						Permenant M2 roots near completion
909	Probable female	Young adult				4			
910,1	unknown	Adult							
910,2	unknown	Old adult							Ossified thyroid cartilage
910,3	unknown	Infant	6m-1yr						
911	Unknown	perinatal	B-1mos						Unfused mandibular symphysis
912	Unknown	Infant							
913	Unknown	Juvenile	1-2yrs						Dm2 crowns nearly complete
914	Unknown	Juvenile	3-4yrs						Permenant M1 crown complete
918	Unknown	Infant	4-6mos						
919,1	unknown	Subadult	13-16y						
919,2	unknown	Juvenile							
919,3	unknown	Adult							
919,4	unknown	Adult							
919,5	Unknown	Adult							
920	Unknown	Juvenile	3-4yrs						
921	Male	Young adult	30-35yrs	6	4	4			
922	Unknown	Adult							
924	Female	Young adult							Light tooth wear
925	Unknown	Fetal	34-38wks ges						
926	Probable female	Adult							
927,1	Unknown	Perinatal	38-40wks ges						No crowns complete
927,2	Unknown	Juvenile	4-5yrs.						
927,3	Female	Young adult	30-40	5	3	5			
930,1	Probable female	Young adult							
930,2	Probable female	Young adult							Limited visible sutures are open
930,3	Probable female	Adult							
931	Unknown	Adult							
932,1	Probable male	Adult							
932,2	Unknown	Subadult							
932,3	Unknown	juvenile							
932,4	Unknown	fetus							
932,5	Unknown	Juvenile							
932,6	Unknown	Juvenile	1-2yrs						
933	unknown	Fetal							
941	Probable female	Middle adult				4,5			
942	Unknown	Adult							
943	Probable male	Young adult							
946	Unknown	Perinatal	36-40wks ges						
947	Probable male	Middle adult							Moderate to heavy tooth wear
953,1	Unknown	Adult							
953,2	Unknown	Adult							
953,3	Unknown	Adult							
953,4	Unknown	Adult							
953,5	Unknown	Adult							
953,6	Unknown	perinatal							
953,7	Unknown	Subadult							
962	Male	Middle adult					6		Vertebral degenerative joint disease
971	Unknown	Juvenile	3-4yrs						
972	Unknown	Juvenile	11-12yrs						

Burial	Sex	Age	Range	Pubic Symphysis		Auricular Surface Score	Cranial Suture Closure		Notes
				Todd Score	Suchey-Brooks Score		Vault Score	Lateral Score	
977	Unknown	Fetal							
978	Probable female	Young adult							No tooth wear on M3
979	Unknown	Subadult	12-13yrs						
980	Unknown	Unknown							
981	Unknown	Fetal							Unfused tympanic rings
983	Probable female	Young adult							
984	Probable male	Young adult							
985	Unknown	Juvenile	6-7yrs						
988	Female	Middle adult				5			
991	Unknown	Juvenile	5-6yrs.						
993	Unknown	Infant	9-12mos.						Complere dm1 crown, developing M1 crown
995	Unknown	Adult							
996,1	Unknown	Juvenile	4-5yrs						
998	Unknown	Adult							
999	Unknown	Unknown							
1040	Unknown	Adult							
1040,2	Unknown	Juvenile	5-6yrs						
1044	Probable male	Middle adult							Heavy wear
1045	Probable male	Adult							
1047	Probable male	Young adult							Little to no tooth wear on M3
1048	Unknown	Perinatal							Uunfused mandible, tympanic rings
1050	Probable male	Young adult	30-35			4			
1051	Female	Middle adult							
1052	Unknown	Subadult	12-13yrs						
1053	Probable male	Adult							
1056	Probable male	Young adult					0		Little to no tooth wear on M3
1057	Female	Adult							
1058	Male	Middle adult							
1059,1	Unknown	Subadult	15-17yrs?						
1059,2	Unknown	Juvenile							
1062	Unknown	Unknown							
1064	Male	Young adult	18-20yrs	2	1				
1066	Unknown	Juvenile	2-3yrs						
1067,1	Unknown	Juvenile							
1067,2	Unknown	Adult							
1068	Uknown	Infant	B-2mos						
1070	Unknown	Unknown							
1072	Unknown	Juvenile	11-12yrs						
1073	Unknown	Juvenile	1-2yrs						
1074	Unknown	Infant							
1075	Unknown	Young adult	21-30yrs						Light to moderate tooth weae
1076	Unknown	Unknown							
1077	Probable female	Young adult							
1078	Unknown	perinatal							
1079	Probable male	Young adult							Minimal visible visible tooth wear
1080	Unknown	Old adult							Heavy m1 wear
1081	Probable female	Adult							
1082	Unknown	Old adult							
1083	Unknown	Adult							
1084	Probable female	Adult							
1085	Probable female	Young adult							Mininal visible tooth wear
1086	Probable male	Adult							
1087	Probable female	Young adult	18-22yrs						Incomplete fusion of the posterior iliac crest
1088,1	Probable male	Adult							
1088,2	Unknown	Juvenile							
1088,3	Unknown	Adult							
1089	Unknown	Juvenile	8-12yrs						M2 not erupted, but other adult teeth appear present.

Burial	Sex	Age	Range	Pubic Symphysis		Auricular Surface Score	Cranial Suture Closure		Notes
				Todd Score	Suchey-Brooks Score		Vault Score	Lateral Score	
1090	Probable male	Middle adult							Moderate tooth wear; dentin exposure on most mandibular teeth
1091	Unknown	Subadult	16-20yrs						Unfused sternal end of clavicle, annular rings
1092	Unknown	Juvenile							
1093	Unknown	Juvenile	2-3yrs						Deciduous dentition complete, M1 forming
1094	Unknown	Juvenile							
1095	Unknown	Adult							
1096	Unknown	Adult							
1097	Probable female	Adult							
1098	Unknown	perinatal							
1099	Unknown	Adult							
E271B	Unknown	Unknown							
E271B	Unknown	Eight Unknown							

Appendix 6-4: Adult Postcranial Osteometric Data

Burial	Sex	Age	Clavicle Max Length	Clavicle Ant-Post Diameter	Clavicle Sup-Inf Diameter	Humerus Max Length	Humerus Epicondylar Breadth	Humerus Vertical Diameter Head	Humerus Max Midshaft Diameter	Humerus Min Midshaft Diameter	Radius Max Length	Radius Ant-Post Midshaft Diameter	Radius Med-Lat Midshaft Diameter	Ulna Max Length	Ulna Ant-Post Midshaft Diameter	Ulna Med-Lat Midshaft Diameter	Ulna Physiological Length	2nd Metacarpal Min Circumference	2nd Metacarpal Mid Length	Femur Max Length	Femur Bicondylar Length	Femur Epicondylar Breadth	Femur Max Diameter Head	Femur Ant-Post Subtrochanteric Diameter	Femur Med-Lat Subtrochanteric Diameter	Femur A-P Midshaft Diameter	Femur M-L Midshaft Diameter	Femur Mid Circumference	Tibia Length	Tibia Max Length	Tibia Max Prox Epi Breadth	Tibia Max Dist Epi Breadth	Tibia Max Diameter Nutrient Foramen	Tibia M-L Diameter Nutrient Foramen	Tibia Circumference Nutrient Foramen	Fibula Max Length	Fibula Max Diameter Midshaft	Calcaneus Max Length	Calcaneus Middle Breadth
533	Female	Middle adult																					39,6																
712	Probable female	Middle adult																					36,75																
725	Probable female	Young adult																					38,9																
748,1	Probale male	Young adult																					44,9																
752	Probable female	Adult																					40																
803	Probable female	Young adult					56,1												68,35																				
807	Male	Middle adult																					44,6																
830	Probale male	Adult																					42,45																
836	Male	Middle adult																					49																
904	Probable male	Young adult					57		19,45	15,1	233	10,05	14,7						65,45				44	24,4	29,4	29,75	23,3											70,25	45,8
909	Probable female	Young adult																						20,5	27,55	25,05	24,5												
921	Male	Young adult					58,7		21,5	16,45		11,5	15,1						62,5				44,1															75,25	46,7
924	Female	Young adult																					39,4	19,5	27,8														
926	Probable female	Adult	163	10,1	12,2									237	13,35	14,65	204		65,4																				
927,1	Female	Young adult																	59,8	394			38	20	25,6	22,6	20,4											62,5	35,9
941	Probable female	Middle adult																	64,7				41,45																
943	m?	Adult													12,65	15,35			66,4																				
984	m?	Young adult					63,7		20,3	16,35	261	12,1	13,4										45,5																
988	Female	Middle adult					52,65		19,5	14,65		11	13,9	232	11,8	14,8							40,8																
995	Unknown	Adult									214	11,9	13,95	235	11,7	14,7																						
1045	Probable male	Adult																		440			49																
1047	Probable male	Young adult					61,9		22,05	17,9		13	15,3		12,7	17,5			69,2	458																			
1050	Probable Male	Young adult					63,25							254	12,2	14,4																							
1057	Female	Adult																	69,15																				
1058	Male	Middle adult					60,8				236	11,3	13,75						65,5				39,9																
1064	Male	Young adult					58,1												65,65																				

Appendix 6-5: Nonadult Postcranial Osteometric Data

Burial	Sex	Age	Clav. L Length	Clav. R Length	Clav. L MSD	Clav. R MSD	Hum. L Length	Hum. R Length	Hum. L Width	Hum. R Width	Hum. L MSD	Hum. R MSD	Ulna L Length	Ulna R Length	Ulna L MSD	Ulna R MSD	Rad. L Length	Rad. R Length	Rad. L MSD	Rad. R MSD	Ill. L Length	Ill. R Length	Ill. L Width	Ill. R Width	Isch. L Length	Isch. R Length	Isch. L Width	Isch. R Width	Pub. L Length	Pub. R Length	Fem. L Length	Fem. R Length	Fem. L Width	Fem. R Width	Fem. L MSD	Fem. R MSD	Tib. L Length	Tib. R Length	Tib. L MSD	Tib. R MSD	Fib. L Length	Fib. R Length	Fib. L MSD	Fib. R MSD
504	Unknown	Perinatal															51,9									17,85		12,05																
519	Unknown	Fetal					67,05		11,1		5,55																				77,6	78	19,45	20,1	6,75	7,05		69,1		7,2		66		
713	Unknown	Juvenile																																				235						
730	Unknown	Juvenile					147,4				10,85																																		
757	Unknown	Juvenile																			77,65		71,55																					
828	Unknown	Fetal					47,15	47					40,25	40				38,45														50,25												
829	Unknown	Juvenile											94,4																															
841	Unknown	Perinatal					66,4																															123,2						
913	Unknown	Juvenile		60,35		5,7	93,25		8,6		23,9		80,55	80,2	6,35	6,25	70,8	70,9	6	5,8		51,4		45,45	18,2				25	25,7	70,8	116,5		31,9		9,9	60,65	96,8	7,4	9,3		91,95		5,1
925	Unknown	Fetal										16,5									19,45	17,6	12,45					69,8	7,2	7,3	18,55	18,8	69,4	62,2	7,2	7,7										
927,1	Unknown	Perinatal																3,5	4,05																			69,55		7,16	65,6			
927,2	Unknown	Juvenile							14,3	15,1				124,8		8,2						78,9		67,3	17,3	17,3	11,2	11,6			205		47,35		13,75									
933	Unknown	Fetal				3,7											51,3																				62,8	62,9	6,65	6,5	59,5		4,05	
946	Unknown	Perinatal		43,8			62,2	62,8	15,1	15,25	5,35	5,35										31,9		27,8	17,3	17,55	11,3	11,5	14,4	14,5	75,1		19,4	17,7	6,55			66,25		6,1				
977	Unknown	Perinatal												56,8		4,55		49															19,3	18,25			61,6		6,5		58,55		3,75	
981	Unknown	Perinatal																49,4		4,1					24,4		11,8										62,5	62,8	6,9	6,8	58			
1048	Unknown	Perinatal																														190,5				14,5						73,1		4,6
1066	Unknown	Juvenile																																										

Appendix 6-6a: Odontometrics of the Permenant Teeth

Burial	Sex	Age	Left Maxillary m3			Right Maxillary m3			Left Maxillary m2			Right Maxillary m2			Left Maxillary m1			Right Maxillary m1			Left Maxillary p4			Right Maxillary p4			Left Maxillary p3			Right Maxillary p3			Left Maxillary Canine			Right Maxillary Canine			Left Maxillary i2			Right Maxillary i2			Left Maxillary i1			Right Maxillary i1		
			MD	BL	CH	MD	BL	CH	MD	BL	CH	MD	BL	CH	MD	BL	CH	MD	BL	CH	MD	BL	CH	MD	BL	CH	MD	BL	CH	MD	BL	CH	MD	BL	CH	MD	BL	CH	MD	BL	CH	MD	BL	CH	MD	BL	CH	MD	BL	CH
507	Unknown	Juvenile																							7.75			8.2						7.5		10.35																
521	Unknown	Subadult																										7						7.85	12																
711	Unknown	Subadult																			6.1 8.15 6.15						6 8.65						7.5 7.85 9.1					6.3 5.8 9.65						8.5 7 10.15					
712	Probable female	Middle adult							9.95 10.55 7.8												6.35 9.05 6.9											7.05 7.6						6 5.9 8.4						8.7 6.8 8.95					
713	Unknown	Juvenile	9.8								7.3			7.65					7.9																								12.1					
714	Probable male	Adult	10.05 7.3						9.8								11.35											11.95																				
732	Unknown	Subadult							9.3																																							
741,1	Unknown	Juvenile																																													
757	Unknown	Juvenile																									9.7										9.35			9.3								
860	Unknown	Adult				9.45	9.6 6.5		11.5 10.4 7.7		10.5 12.1 7.6								10.1			6.15 7.9			6.15 7.9		7.5 7.35	5.6 6.1		8.2 6.15			5.5												
861	Probable female	Young adult		9.5					9.5 10.3 7.4									10.1 11			6.9 9.1 8.1			7.05 8.9 8.25			8.6					9.7 8.85			5.5 5.85			6.9 7.5			8.8 7.1					
862	Probable female	Adult	8.1 10.2						8.7 9.6									9.35 10.4			6.5 8.9			6.2 8.6			7.35 8		7.3			8 7.5			6.5 7.5			8.65 7			8.05 7.95					
863	Probable female	Adult	10.4					11.75	9.8 11.35		9.5 11.15		9.9 10.6 7.95		10.2 10.75			6.5 9.05 7.4			6.5 9.45			7 9.1			7.35 7.7			7.8			6.05 5.35			9.25 7.75			9.6 6.95				
908	Unknown	Subadult	10.5			8.9 11.75		10 11.7 8		9.5 11.15		9.8 10.95 6.65			6.3 8.2			6.5 8.75 7.6			7.55 7.8			8.15			5.8					8.15 6.9					
924	Female	Young adult	8.4 10.05 7.3						10.25 11.25 7.85		9.75 9.95		11.05 11.15 7.45		10.15 10.7 7.55			6.45 8.55 7.35			6.6 8.95			7.05 8.4 7.9			7.74 8.4 9.9			7.55 8.7			6.4 6.8 9.85			8.85 7.45 12.15			8.75 7.25 11		
927,3	Unknown	Juvenile															10.35 9.7 7.6		10.35 10.1 6.85												8			6.75 7.15										
943	Probable male	Adult	9.6	9.35 10.6		9.5 11.2 7.35		10.5 11.55		10.5 11.55		6.75 9.3 7.2		6.7 9.45 7.45		6.6 8.75 7.5		6.2 8.6 7.25		7.9 8.85 9.7		7.55 8.8 11.1		6.3 6.75 9.7		6.9 6.25 10.2		9.1 7.5		8.8 7.5					
962	Male	Middle adult	8.1 10.2						9.5 10.3		9 10.6		9.35 10.4		10.4 11			6.65 8.9		6.2 8.6		6.75 8.9		7.35 8 11.5		7.3		7.7 8 11.11 7.25		8.5 11.25		6.65 6.25		6.35 5.95		8.65 7		8.05 7.5		
972	Unknown	Juvenile															7.95 8.05			6.5 9.45			6.5 9.45			6.5 9.05			7.9 9.05			7.25 8 11.5						9.25 7.75					
978	Probable female	Young adult	10.5						9.8 11.35		9.5 11.15		11.9 11.85		10.2 11.9 7.95			6.45 9.35		6.6 8.95		6.85 8.2 7.4		7 9.1 7.9		7.9 8.55 8.7		7.95 8.7		6.4 6.65 9.35			8.2 7.8			8.65 7.5		
979	Unknown	Subadult	8.6 9.4 7						9.3 9.65 6.85		9.75 9.95 7.7		9.75 10.6 7.55		10.15 10.7 7.4			6.7 9 7.6		6.6 8.95 7.75		6.5 8.4 7.25		6.95 8.75 8.8		7.75 7.85 10.95		8 7.55 11.1		6.75 6.2 9.9		8.6 7 12.05		8.75 7.25 11		
983	Probable female	Adult															11.05 11.15 7.45		10.35 10.1											8.8																
984	Probable male	Young adult	9	9.35 10.6		8.95 10.3		9		9.75 10.25		9.6 11.05		6.35 8.95		6.65 8.9		6.65 8.9		7.8 8.75 9.7		7.75 8.8		6.65 6.25		6.5 6.25		8.2 6.8		8.25 7.15				
985	Unknown	Juvenile															10.15 10.75 7.25		10 10.3 7.1		7.05 9.45		7.05 9.45		7.7 8.5 11.1		7.65 8.5 11.25		8.2 7.1 11.4		8.35 7.2 11.75		
988	Female	Middle adult	9.8	8.9 10.4		8.4 9.9		8.2 11.05		10.15 11.1		10.4 11		6.3 9.1		6.8 8.8		6.75 8.9		7.9 8.25		7.65 8.55		6.3 6.25		6.4 6.2		8.2 7.15		8.3 7.3		
996,1	Unknown	Juvenile																				8.8			8.65																						
1052	Unknown	Subadult				10.7			10.55		10.3 11.1		10.2 11.1 8.4		11.8 10.7			7.05 9.45 8.65		6.5 8.8		6.4 8.65 8.9		6.6 8.85		7.2 7.55 10.55 12		7.7 8 11.75		6.75 6					8.2 7.8		
1056	Probable male	Young adult							11.5 9.2		11.5 9.6		10.65 11.4		11.8 10.7			6.65 9.05		6.5 8.8		6.8 8.9		6.75 8.35		7.2 8.35 12		10.1 7 11.75		6					9.1 7.5		9.2 7.2
1072	Unknown	Juvenile															9.2 9.7 6.65		10.1 6.85 7.25		6.1 8.15		6.15 7.45		6 8.2		5.6 8.1		9.1 9.7		9.7		5.8 5.8 8.4		5.5 5.35		6.65 8.95 11.8		8.9 6.9 11
		N	7	7	2	5	5	1	11	11	6	9	9	6	13	13	8	13	13	5	13	13	9	10	10	5	12	12	9	7	7	2	15	15	11	12	12	6	11	11	7	7	7	3	14	14	7	12	13	4
		Mean	8.1	9.4	7	8.9	8.7	6.5	9.2	9.2	6.85	9.6	9.6	7.3	9.2	9.7	6.65	10.1	6.85	7.25	6.1	8.15	7.9	7.45	5.6	8.1	7.25	8.2	7	7.05	6.15	9.1	7.55	9.1	5.8	5.35	9	6.65	6.9	8.05	8.9	6.9	11
		Standard Deviation	0.48	0.40	0.21	0.74	1.14	–	0.88	0.85	0.41	0.94	0.74	0.40	0.68	0.58	0.44	0.49	0.65	0.36	0.27	0.28	0.64	0.35	0.48	0.44	0.54	0.27	0.44	0.76	0.80	0.34	0.51	0.62	0.66	0.47	0.40	0.58	0.34	0.30	0.30	0.83
		Maximum	9.6	10.5	7.3	10.7	11.75	6.5	11.5	11.7	8	11.5	12.1	8.4	11.9	11.85	7.95	11.9	11.9	8.4	7.05	9.45	8.65	7.9	7	9.1	8.8	10.1	8.8	11.75	9.7	9.9	7.5	12	6.75	5.8	8.4	6.9	7.9	12.15	9.6	7.95	13
		Minimum	7.3	7	5	8.7	9.6	6.5	8.4	9.2	6.85	8.2	9.6	7.3	6.1	8.15	6.15	6.85	9.35	10.1	5.6	8.1	7.25	6	8.2	5.8	5.5	5.35	8.4	6.65	6.9	11

Appendix 6-6b: Odontometrics of the Permanent Teeth

Measurement abbreviations: MD = Mesiodistal Diameter, BL = Buccolingual Diameter, CH = Crown Height.

Burial	Sex	Age	L m3 MD	L m3 BL	L m3 CH	R m3 MD	R m3 BL	R m3 CH	L m2 MD	L m2 BL	L m2 CH	R m2 MD	R m2 BL	R m2 CH	L m1 MD	L m1 BL	L m1 CH	R m1 MD	R m1 BL	R m1 CH	L p4 MD	L p4 BL	L p4 CH	R p4 MD	R p4 BL	R p4 CH	L p3 MD	L p3 BL	L p3 CH	R p3 MD	R p3 BL	R p3 CH	L C MD	L C BL	L C CH	R C MD	R C BL	R C CH	L i2 MD	L i2 BL	L i2 CH	R i2 MD	R i2 BL	R i2 CH	L i1 MD	L i1 BL	L i1 CH	R i1 MD	R i1 BL	R i1 CH
507	Unknown	Juvenile												7.9			7.3			6.9												8.3												9.3						
521	Unknown	Subadult									12.7																		9				12.25	12	11.2						9.5									
711	Unknown	Subadult							10.3	8.9	6.1				9.7	9.4	5.8				6.6	6.8					6.1	7.2					6.1	7.45	10.1				6.1	5.6					4.95	5.95	7.9			
712	Probable female	Middle adult							10.1	10.3	5.4				10.85	10.6	5.9				6.55	7.45	7.2				6.55	7.65	8				6.85	6.4	9.2				5.95	5.65	7.6				5.4	4.75	6.25			
713	Unknown	Juvenile												8.25																					12.35			12.35			9.75			10			9.75			
714	Probable male	Adult							10.4	9.8																7																								
732	Unknown	Subadult																														7.25									9.15									
741.1	Unknown	Juvenile																																																
757	Unknown	Juvenile										9.05	8.3																						10.5			10.15			9.05			9.1			8.5			8.9
860	Unknown	Adult	8.9			8.9	9.15														6.6	7.3	7.8	6.5	7.3	7.8	6.4	6.8	8.3	6.35	7	8.3							5.7	6.1	8.7			9.1						8.9
861	Probable female	Young adult																																										9.1						
862	Probable female	Adult				9.2	8.7	5.95				9.45	9	7.45																												5.7	6.05							
863	Probable female	Adult													10.8	10.2				7.8	6.8	7.9					6.6	7.4					6.25	6.85		5.85	6.85					6.01	6							
908	Unknown	Subadult							10.4	9.7	7.1	10.16	9.8	7.8	10.45	10.2	7	10.6	10.15		6.7	7.65	8.1	6.8	7.7	7.85	6.4	7.8	8.2	6.5	7.5	8.35	6.1	7.2	9.1	5.85	7.05	10.35	5.9	6.2	8.7	5.95	6.2	8.5	5.3	5.56	8	5.15	5.5	7.15
924	Female	Young adult							9.95	10.1	6.8				10.2	10.2	5.8				6.65	7.6	7.25				6.9	7.9	8	6.6	7.9	8	6.45	7.8	10.15				6.3	6.7	8.9				5.35	6.1	8.5			
927.3	Unknown	Juvenile													9.95	11.2	7.6	9.9	11.25	7.8																														
943	Probable male	Adult	10	9		10.05	9.2		10.3	9.6		10.35	9.65		11	10		10.05	10.25		7.1	8.1		7.9	8.7		6.6	7.75		6.65	7.8	7.9	6.7	8.1		7.1	8.05		6	6.35		5.9	6.25		5.2	6.3		5	6.65	
962	Male	Middle adult			6.3										9.45	9.2			9.1		6.85	7.6		6.8	8		7.8	6.7		6.7	7.65		6.7	7.55	10.5	6.7	7.05	10.25	5.2	6.05		5.55	5.8			5.9	9.5	5.05	5.5	
972	Unknown	Juvenile							10.2	9.15		10.2	9.4	7.7	10.3	9.8	7.5	10.35	9.85	8.35	7	7.55	8.7				8.7	7.2	9.5	6.8	7	9	6.55	7.7	10.31	6.9	7.95		5.35	6.4		5.25	6.3		4.65	5.95		4.9	5.95	
978	Probable female	Young adult				5.75		9.95	10	9.05	6.65	10.25	10.05		10.65	11.1		11.9	11.15		7.75	9.25		7.75	8.75		6.5	8.1		6.8	8.3		6.5	8.2					5.9	6	10.1	5.9	6.15	9.95						
979	Unknown	Subadult										10.3	9	6.55	10.6	9.9	6.3	10.4	9.8	6.85	7.4	7.8	7.8	7.25	7.6	7.5	6.65	7.05	8.7	6.85	7	8.8	7.1	7.1	12.25	6.85	7.75	12.1						10	5.7	5.7	8.7	5.7	5.7	8.4
983	Probable female	Adult							10.6	10.35		10.7	10.2		10.75	10.35		10.6	10.2		6.9	8.1		7.1	8.2		6.7	7.7		7						7	8.5													
984	Probable male	Young adult	11.25	10.11		10.35	9.35		10.6	9.75					10.65	10.4		10.2	10.2		7	8.6		7.3	8.25					7.1	7.9		7.1	8		7	8		5.15	6.35		5.7	6.5		5	6.3		4.85	5.8	
985	Unknown	Juvenile							10.55	9.55		10.4	9.7		10.65	9.8	7.2	10.6	9.85	7.35							6.55	7.55		6.9	7.9		7	7.6	11.75	6.9	7.9	11.75							6			5.65	5.7	9.95
988	Female	Middle adult	10.8	9.8		10.7	9.3								10.7	10.55		10.6	10.55		7	8.05		6.75	8.05		6.75	7.5		6.85	8		7	7.9		6.85	8					5.8	6.3	8.25				5.6	5.8	10.8
996.1	Unknown	Juvenile																																																
1052	Unknown	Subadult							10.5	9.55	8.6	10.6	9.5	9	11	10.25	7.6	11.15	10.2	8.05	7.35	8.1		7.4	8.05	9.1	6.75	7.5	9.3	6.6	7.7	9.1	6.65	7.2	11.9	6.5	7.2	12.1	5.85	6.8		6.1	5.5	9.5	5.75	6	10.9	5.55	5.95	8.9
1056	Probable male	Young adult				10.5	10.5		11	10.9		10.25	10.85		10.95	11.1		11.1	11.05		7.1	8.05		7.35	7.8		6.55	7.2		7.05	7.5		6.75	8		6.55	7.8					6.05	6.6		5.15	6.9		4.9	6.6	
1072	Unknown	Juvenile																																														10	10	6
N			5	4	1	7	7	1	14	14	8	11	11	7	17	17	10	12	13	7	17	17	7	11	11	6	16	16	8	11	11	8	17	17	13	13	13	8	12	12	10	11	11	8	11	11	8	9	9	7
Mean			10.14	9.60	6.30	9.35	9.45	5.95	10.34	9.69	7.54	10.16	9.59	7.81	10.51	10.25	6.80	10.62	10.28	7.40	6.94	7.85	7.74	7.17	8.04	8.04	6.78	7.44	8.46	6.68	7.50	8.38	6.99	7.83	11.07	6.69	7.66	11.21	5.80	6.19	8.95	5.81	6.15	9.21	5.63	5.95	8.56	5.24	5.92	9.02
Standard Deviation			0.92	0.47	-	1.72	0.59	-	0.30	0.59	2.27	0.49	0.68	0.75	0.45	0.56	0.77	0.55	0.61	0.69	0.33	0.54	0.55	0.43	0.44	0.84	0.62	0.39	0.65	0.27	0.40	0.61	1.39	1.18	1.07	0.35	0.49	0.95	0.38	0.36	0.76	0.25	0.31	0.62	1.32	0.53	1.36	0.35	0.40	1.26
Maximum			11.25	10.11	6.3	10.7	10.5	5.95	11	10.9	12.7	10.7	10.85	9	11	11.2	7.6	11.9	11.25	8.35	7.75	9.25	8.7	7.9	8.75	9.1	8.7	8.1	9.5	7.1	8.3	9.1	12.25	12	12.35	7.1	8.5	12.35	6.3	6.8	10.1	6.1	6.6	10	6	6.9	10.9	10	10	10.8
Minimum			8.9	9	6.3	5.75	8.7	5.95	9.9	8.9	5.4	9.05	8.3	6.55	9.45	9.2	5.8	9.9	9.1	6.5	6.55	6.8	7.2	6.5	7.3	7	6.1	6.7	7.7	6.1	7	7.25	6.1	6.4	9.1	5.85	6.85	10.15	5.15	5.6	7.6	5.25	5.5	8.25	4.75	4.85	6.25	4.85	5.5	6

Chapter 7

Radiocarbon Dating at Tell el-Kerkh

Yu Itahashi and Minoru Yoneda

In this chapter, we report radiocarbon dating for human bones and also present a summary of radiocarbon dating for charcoals on previously unpublished. Regarding human bones, we report mainly on human bones excavated from the cemetery.

1. Materials

A total of twenty-six charcoal and carbonized samples were measured radiocarbon dating (Table 7-1 and Figure 7-1). Among the excavated human bones from Tell el-Kerkh, fifty samples are dated (Table 7-2 and Figure 7-2). In the human samples, seven bones of child found from the occupation layers considered as Pre-Pottery Neolithic B are reported the radiocarbon date. Other individuals have been found in cultural layers associated with the Pottery Neolithic period (PN), and some have been excavated from the cemetery in the Central area.

2. Methods

For the ^{14}C measurements of human bones, the preparation and graphitization methods of collagen followed those described by Yoneda et al. (2002). Briefly, 2.5 mg of collagen (containing ~1 mg of carbon) was purified by chemical treatment, and carbon dioxide was produced by combustion at 850°C in an evacuated and sealed quartz tube; the CO_2 was then cryogenically purified in a vacuum system (Minagawa and Wada 1984). Then, graphite was produced by the catalytic reduction of CO_2 with iron powder (Kitagawa et al. 1993). The radiocarbon content of the human bones was measured using accelerator mass spectrometers (AMSs) at the National Institute for Environmental Studies-Tandem accelerator for Environmental Research and Radiocarbon Analysis (NIES-TERRA) (Tanaka et al. 2000), the Micro-Analysis Laboratory Tandem accelerator (MALT) (Matsuzaki et al. 2007) and the laboratory for

Table 7-1. Results of the radiocarbon dating for charcoal and carbonized samples from Tell el-Kerkh.

Sample No.	Area	Square	Structure	Period	Samble material	Lab. No.	^{14}C age (BP)	calibrated BC (1σ)	calibrated BC (2σ)
no. 1	East Trench	E273		Rouj 2d	charcoal	UCIAMS-21690	6815±20	5725–5669	5736–5655
no. 2	Central Area	E271		Rouj 2d	charcoal	NUTA2-2105	6950±50	5887–5752	5975–5730
no. 3	East Trench	E273		Rouj 2d	charcoal	UCIAMS-21691	6985±25	5968–5835	5980–5782
no. 4	East Trench	E272		Rouj 2d	charcoal	UCIAMS-21687	6980±30	5967–5804	5978–5757
no. 5	East Trench	E272		Rouj 2d	charcoal	UCIAMS-21688	6990±25	5969–5839	5980–5791
no. 6	East Trench	E272		Rouj 2d	charcoal	UCIAMS-21685	7460±25	6390–6260	6400–6241
no. 7	Central Area	E271	Str. 240	Rouj 2c	carbonized grain	NUTA2-2104	7230±40	6214–6023	6221–6016
no. 8	East Trench	E272		Rouj 2c	charcoal	UCIAMS-21689	7125±25	6024–5932	6061–5923
no. 9	East Trench	E273		Rouj 2c	charcoal	UCIAMS-21692	7005±25	5972–5845	5983–5803
no. 10	East Trench	E273		Rouj 2c	charcoal	UCIAMS-21695	7450±25	6380–6255	6393–6242
no. 11	East Trench	E273		Rouj 2c	charcoal	UCIAMS-21696	7255±25	6216–6066	6222–6058
no. 12	East Trench	E273		Rouj 2c	charcoal	USIAMS-21697	7450±25	6380–6255	6393–6242
no. 13	Central Area	E270-E290		Rouj 2c	charcoal	NUTA2-2089	7420±45	6372–6236	6415–6101
no. 14	Central Area	E310	Str. 167	Rouj 2c	carbonized grain	NUTA2-2023	7670±45	6570–6457	6597–6434
no. 15	Central Area	E310	Str. 167	Rouj 2c	carbonized grain	NUTA2-2024	7730±80	6638–6476	6768–6423
no. 16	Central Area	E310	Str. 167	Rouj 2c		Lyon-12086	7830±50	6748–6593	7018–6504
no. 17	Northwest Area	D6		Rouj 1c	charcoal	NUTA2-2106	8660±100	7932–7585	8170–7528
no. 18	Northwest Area	D6	Str. 217	Rouj 1c	charcoal	NUTA2-2109	8390±50	7532–7370	7578–7337
no. 19	Northwest Area	D6b 3		Rouj 1c		Lyon 2554	8235±40	7336–7090	7455–7078
no. 20	Northwest Area	D6b	Str. 414 pit	Rouj 1c	charcoal	GrA-22266	8230±45	7334–7087	7454–7077
no. 21	Northwest Area	D6b	Str. 415 shallow pit	Rouj 1c	charcoal	GrA-22275	8380±50	7527–7366	7578–7327
no. 22	Northwest Area	D6	D6b-18	Rouj 1a		Lyon-2555	9250±40	8553–8354	8613–8315
no. 23	Northwest Area	D6	D6b-29	Rouj 1a		Lyon-2556	9165±40	8426–8295	8538–8288
no. 24	Northwest Area	D6Bb-31	D6b-31	Rouj 1a		Lyon-12087	9205±60	8534–8310	8603–8291
no. 25	Northwest Area	D6b	D6b-44	Rouj 1a	charcoal	GrA-22276	9240±50	8550–8348	8612–8303
no. 26	Northwest Area	D6b	D6b-45	Rouj 1a	charcoal	GrA-22276	9350±90	8749–8470	9111–8304

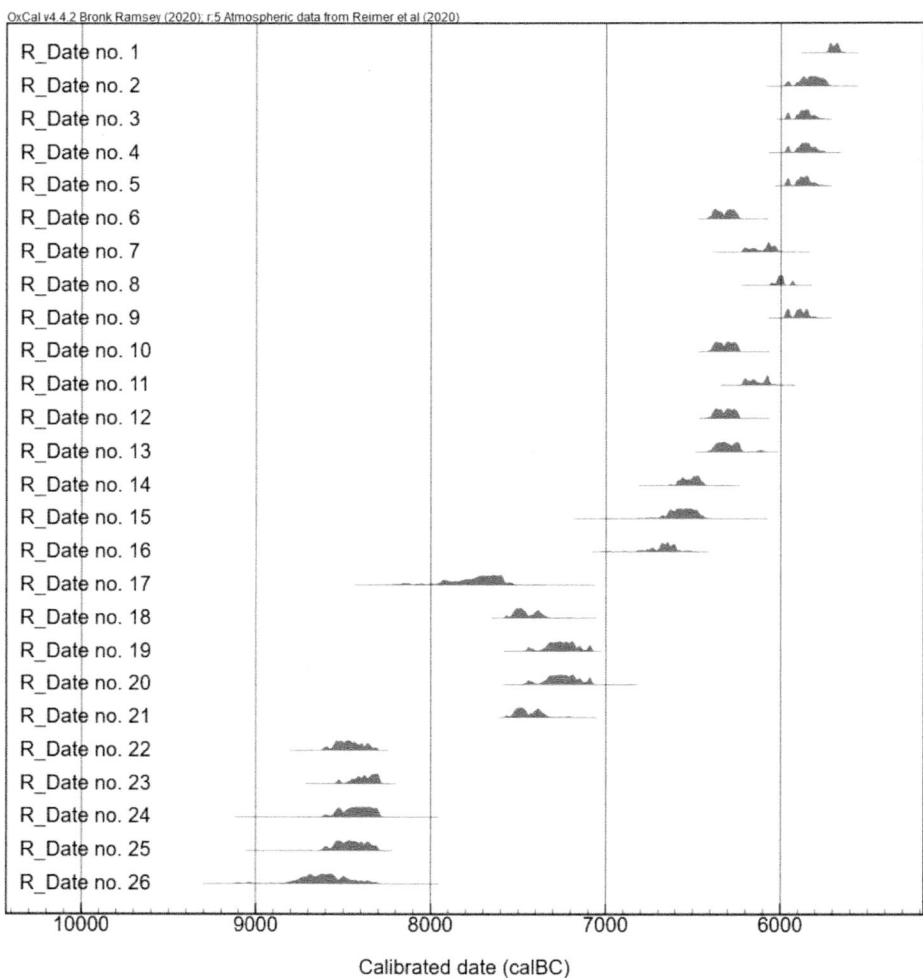

Figure 7-1. Calibrated dates for charcoal and carbonized samples from Tell el-Kerkh.

Table 7-2. Results of the radiocarbon dating for human bones from the PPNB layer.

Sample-No.	Square	C/N	%C	%N	Layer	Period	Lab. code #	^{14}C age (BP)	calibrated BC (1σ)	calibrated BC (2σ)
STR162	D6d	3.2	41.7	15.0	3	PPNB	TERRA-102804c26	8090 ±55	7177–6863	7316–6824
STR179	D6d	3.2	41.7	14.7	4	PPNB	TERRA-102804c05	8190 ±50	7312–7077	7344–7061
STR216	D6d	3.4	40.8	13.6	5	PPNB	TERRA-102804c19	8390 ±85	7574–7348	7588–7190
STR220	D6d	3.5	38.1	12.6	4	PPNB	TERRA-110404c06	8315 ±60	7484–7200	7525–7178
STR232	D6d	3.2	42.2	15.3	4	PPNB	TERRA-102804c07	8315 ±55	7481–7203	7518–7184
STR242	D6d	3.4	41.9	14.7	4	PPNB	TERRA-102804c35	8420 ±60	7578–7380	7586–7345
STR411	D6d	3.6	39.6	12.0	5	PPNB	TERRA-102804c28	8370 ±55	7523–7358	7578–7197

radiocarbon dating at the University of Tokyo and Paleo Labo Co., Japan (Kobayashi *et al.* 2007). In the AMS analyses, the new oxalic acid standard (NBS RM-4990C) and ANU sucrose (IAEA-C6) were usually loaded concurrently with unknown samples. The radiocarbon dates were statistically analyzed and calibrated using OxCal (Bronk Ramsey 1995, 2009, 2017) and IntCal20 calibration data (Reimer *et al.* 2020).

3. Results of Charcoal and Carbonized Samples

The results of the radiocarbon dating for charcoal and carbonized samples are shown in Table 7-1 and Figure

7-1. The lowest layer, Rouj 1 is thought of an occupation period corresponding to the Pre-Pottery Neolithic B (PPNB) in the Levantine chronology. The samples from the Northwest Area at Rouj 1a, were dated at 8750-8300 cal BC. The Rouj 1a is considered as the Early PPNB on the basis of characteristic tool-types such as the Aswad points and the large blades with fine retouch on one lateral edge (Tsuneki 2012, Arimura 2020). Then, the samples from the Rouj 1c corresponding to Late PPNB, were dated at 7550-7090 cal BC. The samples from the occupation layer corresponding to Rouj 2c shows the time difference depending on the locations. Samples from Square E310 of the Central Area represented the

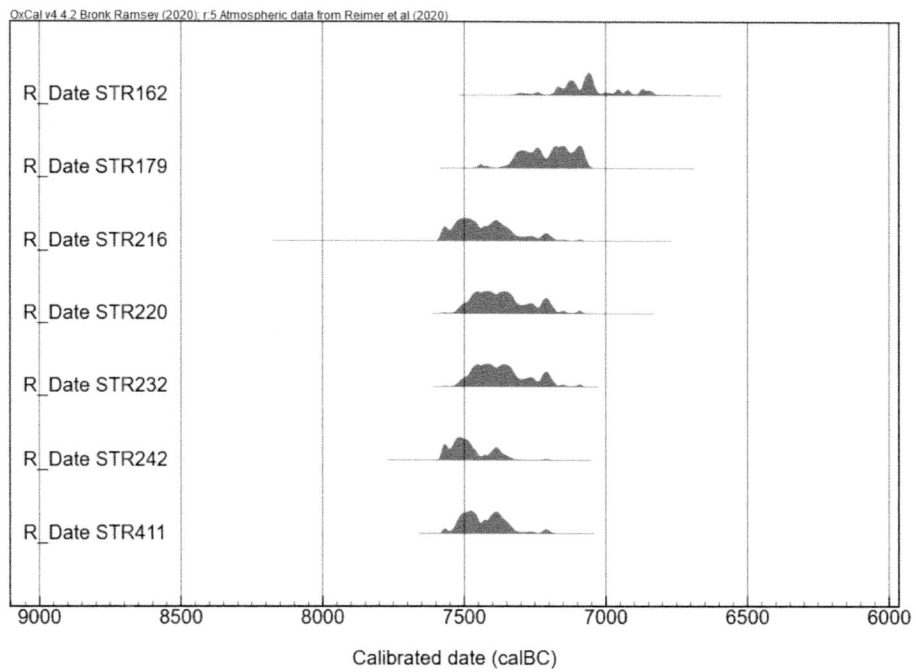

OxCal v4 4.2 Bronk Ramsey (2020); r:5 Atmospheric data from Reimer et al (2020)

Calibrated date (calBC)

Figure 7-2. Calibrated dates for human bones from the PPNB layer.

oldest date, 6750-6450 cal BC. A sample excavated from Squares E270-E290 of the Central Area indicated 6370-6240 cal BC, later than that from E310. Furthermore, samples excavated from Squares E272-E273 of the East trench were dated 6380-5850 cal BC. Although one of the samples from the occupation layer corresponding to Rouj 2d was dated similarly to Rouj 2c, another five samples were dated to 5970-5670 cal BC.

4. Results of Human Samples

The results of the radiocarbon dating for human bones from PPNB layers are shown in Table 7-2 and Figure 7-2. The PPNB human bones were dated at 7580-6860 cal BC, which is in close agreement with previous charcoal dates from the Rouj 1c, Late PPNB. However, two individuals, STR162 (Layer 3, 7180-6860 cal BC) and STR179 (7310-7080 cal BC) show later date than others (Layers 4–5, 7580-7350 cal BC).

Individuals found outside the cemetery corresponding to the Layers 4-6 of the Central Area (Rouj 2c period) were dated at 6380-5900 cal BC. This result indicates that the dead were buried outside the cemetery when the communal cemetery was in operation. The human bones buried in the transitional period of Layer 3 showed a wide range of ages at 6330-5640 cal BC. In the humans from the layers corresponding to the Rouj 2d period individuals were dated at 6060-5680 cal BC (Table 7-3 and Figure 7-3).

The ^{14}C age of individuals in the cemetery (Table 7-4 and Figure 7-4) did not show significant differences between the Layers 4, 5 and 6, showed overlapping dates. Because a burial of each individual was dug from the original floor, there is the potential for that the differences of found depth did not reflect the differences of dates. Excluding some individuals with large measurement errors, it is interpreted from the ^{14}C age of individuals that the cemetery was used 6410-6080 cal BC. Thus, this cemetery is considered to have been used for several generations. These ^{14}C dates of human bones in the cemetery match those of carbonized samples from the same Central Area.

Table 7-3. Results of the radiocarbon dating for human bones found outside the cemetery in the PN layer.

Sample-No.	Square	C/N	%C	%N	Layer	Period	Lab. code #	^{14}C age (BP)	calibrated BC (1σ)	calibrated BC (2σ)
STR16	E290d	3.4	41.4	14.9	3	2c	TERRA-102804c23	7330 ±85	6331–6074	6388–6030
STR19	E270d	3.3	41.4	15.0	2	2d	TERRA-102804c29	7075 ±50	6012–5899	6060–5841
STR29	E290d	3.3	42.4	15.2	4a	2c	TERRA-110404c09	7410 ±50	6373–6231	6415–6090
STR44	E290d	3.4	40.8	14.1	4a	2c	TERRA-102804c34	7390 ±60	6376–6103	6394–6086
STR45	E290d	3.5	41.9	14.7	4a	2c	TERRA-102804c37	7250 ±80	6221–6030	6340–5925
STR48	E290d	3.3	41.3	14.4	3	2c	TERRA-102804c17	7155 ±50	6063–5991	6210–5901
STR223	E271c	3.2	41.8	15.1	1	2d	TERRA-102804c38	6875 ±60	5836–5676	5890–5640
STR246	E271c	3.3	41.9	14.5	3	2c	TERRA-102804c08	6795 ±50	5724–5644	5778–5573
STR301	E270-290	3.2	42.2	15.4	4	2c	TERRA-102804c09	7310 ±50	6223–6090	6336–6060
STR307	E291c	3.6	40.7	13.0	2	2d	TERRA-102804c14	7100 ±70	6057–5898	6081–5802
STR309	E291a	3.3	42.3	14.8	2	2d	TERRA-102804c10	6930 ±50	5877–5741	5971–5722
STR331	E311b	3.3	41.8	14.6	3	2c	TERRA-102804c15	7010 ±80	5984–5803	6021–5731
STR337	E291d	3.2	40.9	14.4	3	2c	TERRA-102804c18	7120 ±55	6059–5921	6076–5851
STR402	E311d	3.5	39.4	13.7	4a	2c	TERRA-102804c36	7160 ±50	6065–5991	6214–5911
STR426	E291c	3.2	41.9	15.0	4a	2c	TERRA-102804c16	7320 ±85	6244–6070	6379–6026
STR433	E271c	3.3	40.4	13.9	4a	2c	TERRA-110404c04	7200 ±90	6217–5987	6243–5851
STR436	E271c	3.3	39.6	14.1	4a	2c	TERRA-110404c08	7330 ±50	6232–6089	6361–6068

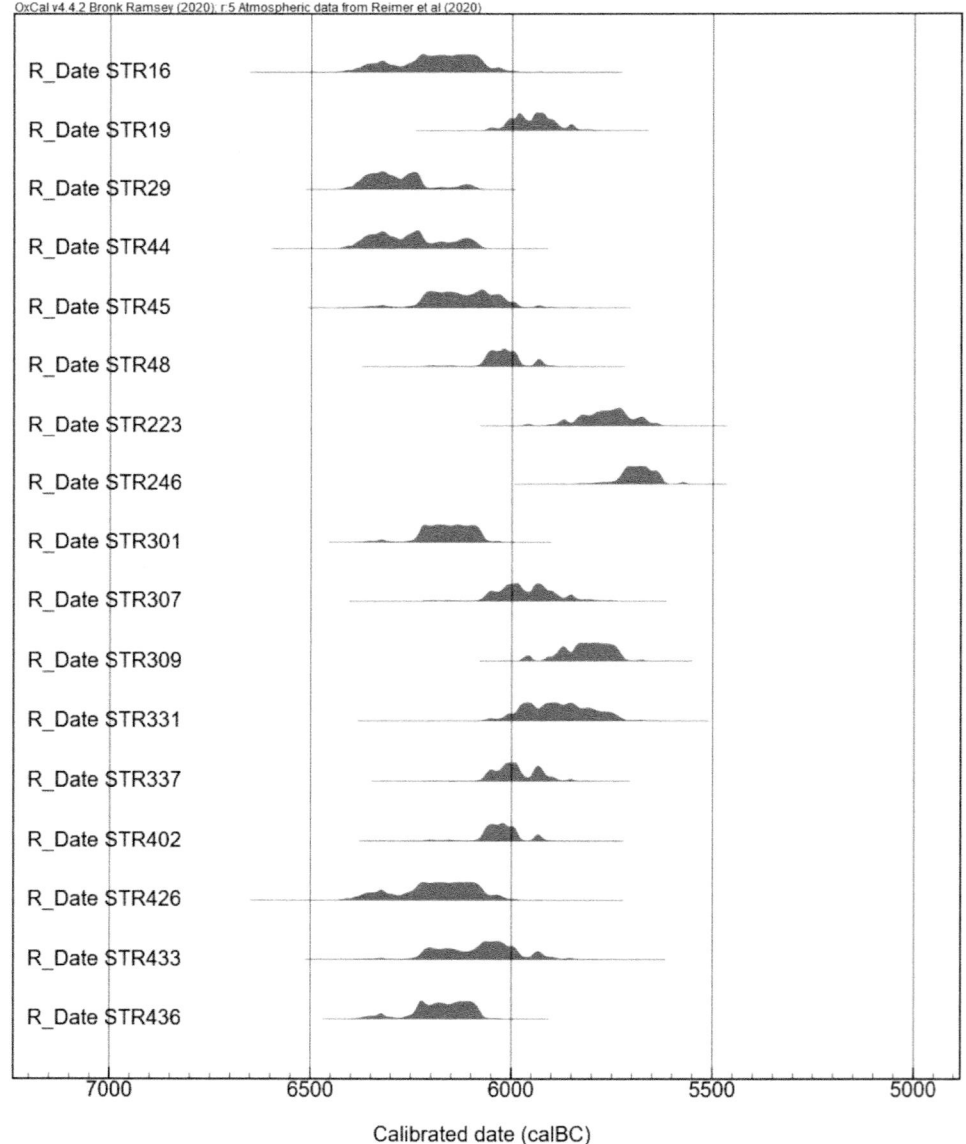

Figure 7-3. Calibrated dates for human bones found outside the cemetery in the PN layer.

Table 7-4. Results of the radiocarbon dating for human bones found in the cemetery of the PN layer.

Sample-No.	Square	C/N	%C	%N	Layer	Period	Lab. code #	^{14}C age (BP)	calibrated BC (1σ)	calibrated BC (2σ)
STR502	E271c	3.5	41.0	13.7	4	PN	PLD-25745	7375 ±25	6339–6100	6371–6087
STR504	E271c	3.3	46.1	16.2	4	PN	PLD-26004	7480 ±30	6413–6263	6422–6246
STR507	E271a	3.4	45.4	15.7	4	PN	PLD-25746	7380 ±30	6360–6104	6376–6088
STR519	E271a	3.4	45.5	15.4	4	PN	MTC-15234	7115 ±70	6064–5914	6211–5805
STR533	E271c	3.5	43.5	14.4	4	PN	TKA-17987	7400 ± 25	6359–6230	6379–6111
STR710	E271d	3.2	40.5	14.6	4	PN	PLD-25747	7455 ±25	6382–6260	6396–6241
STR712	E271d	3.4	41.3	14.0	4	PN	TKA-17994	7360 ± 30	6331–6090	6361–6082
STR714	E271b	3.5	41.8	14.1	4	PN	TKA-17989	7370 ± 25	6336–6095	6367–6085
STR715	E271d	3.5	41.9	14.0	4	PN	TKA-17988	7445 ± 25	6377–6251	6390–6240
STR716	E271b	3.4	41.6	14.2	4	PN	TKA-17990	7435 ± 25	6372–6246	6386–6236
STR718	E271b	3.5	41.7	14.1	4	PN	TKA-17991	7280 ± 30	6218–6077	6223–6072
STR726	E271d	3.2	41.2	14.9	4	PN	PLD-25748	7350 ±25	6240–6091	6331–6082
STR739	E271b	3.4	41.3	14.0	4	PN	TKA-17992	7370 ± 25	6336–6095	6367–6085
STR748	E271b	3.4	41.2	14.0	5	PN	TKA-17993	7385 ± 25	6360–6223	6376–6091
STR752	E271b	3.3	41.1	14.7	4	PN	PLD-25749	7350 ±25	6240–6091	6331–6082
STR825	E271b	3.4	49.7	17.1	5	PN	MTC-13169	7465 ±80	6406–6246	6463–6090
STR830	E271b	3.3	48.8	17.5	5	PN	MTC-13170	7550 ±80	6471–6262	6570–6234
STR909	E271a	3.2	42.0	15.2	5	PN	MTC-15235	7255 ±440	6591–5676	7311–5364
STR926	E270a	3.2	41.0	15.1	6	PN	PLD-26006	7375 ±25	6339–6100	6371–6087
STR927j	E270b	3.3	40.1	14.3	6	PN	PLD-26005	7475 ±25	6400–6261	6419–6246
STR927y	E270b	3.2	42.1	15.4	6	PN	PLD-25750	7345 ±30	6237–6091	6331–6080
STR930	E270b	3.3	41.1	14.4	6	PN	PLD-25751	7315 ±25	6224–6091	6228–6084
STR1044	E251c	3.4	47.5	16.4	4	PN	TKA-17984	7430 ± 30	6371–6242	6387–6234
STR1047	E251c	3.3	47.2	16.9	4	PN	TKA-17985	7450 ± 35	6380–6254	6401–6235
STR1050	E251c	3.3	47.7	17.2	4	PN	TKA-17986	7370 ± 25	6336–6095	6367–6085

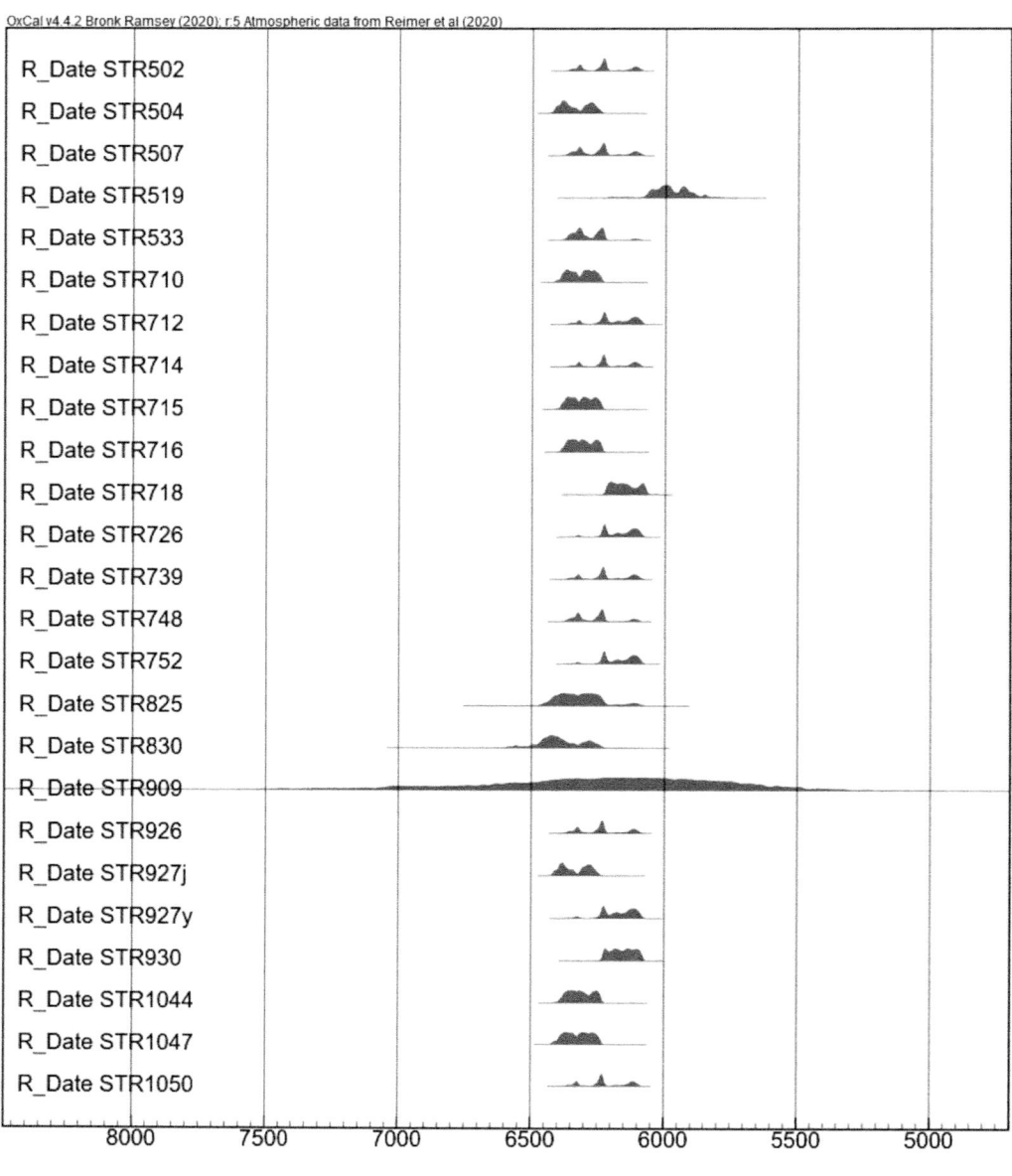

Figure 7-4. Calibrated dates for human bones found in the cemetery of the PN layer.

Chapter 8 (Discussion 1)

Body Transformation:
Skull Retrieval, Manipulation and Circulation of Human Remains at Kerkh Cemetery

Sari Jammo

1. Introduction

Excavations at Tell el-Kerkh since 1997 to 2010 yielded 244 individuals uncovered from an outdoor communal cemetery located adjacent to the residential area. Deceased were interred in different ways, and various and complex funeral were uncovered. This chapter intends to shed the light on some aspects of the burial customs and funerary practices including skull removal and manipulation of human remains from different burial types. Ten headless individuals have revealed from the primary burials belong mainly to young adult females and small children. Moreover, a number of individuals were identified by detached skulls/crania accompanied with or without long bones. The skulls/crania were even solo discovered on the cemetery ground, or found beside individuals in the primary burials, or accompanied with/without long bones and discovered in the collective burials and crematorium pits. Investigations illustrated a remarkable number of individuals were subjected to multi-stage treatments before ultimately interred in the final deposit. Further, some bodily remains seem to have been retrieved from its original interment context and transfer to another which indicates to circulation of bodily parts.

2. The Pottery Neolithic and Funerary Practices

The study of burial customs and funerary practices in the Neolithic societies introduced multiple perspectives about death, life and development of spiritual and symbolic thoughts in human society. Funerary practices provide us with plenty of information about many aspects of society, such as social structure, social ranking, hierarchy system, and gender division. Ritual practices in ancient societies played an important role in understanding the cycle of life. These practices revolving around traditional ceremonies that were performed repeatedly to sustain the collective memory and identity (Kujit 2001). The members of the societies performed a number of multi-stage rituals that anthropologists call 'rites of passage' (Hertz 1960; Van Gennep 1960). The rites represent the transition of an individual or group from one social state to another, such as in birth, death, marriage, and other life transitions that require celebration. The death in many instances was followed by ritual and ceremonial performances toward the deceased. Some of the rituals took place immediately following death; however, subsequent rituals occurred after an interval period of death. Hence, the relationship between the living and dead does not end at the time of the dead but rather is inextricably linked where the perception of the death and the treatment of the deceased is the perspective of the living (Pearson 2016).

Burial data from many Neolithic sites in the Near East used in order to understand the relationship between the burial custom, funerary practices of the dead, grave goods deposition, and constructing the views on identity, social and economic status. Archaeological investigations in the Neolithic Period, especially in the Pre-Pottery Neolithic A (PPNA) and Pre-pottery Neolithic B (PPNB), were remarkable. Excavations were widely undertaken on many sites, and hundreds of papers covering various topics were published.

The transformation from the Pre-Pottery Neolithic to the Pottery Neolithic (PN) period occurred around the 7th millennium BC. in the northern Levant and slightly later in the southern Levant (Akkermans and Schwartz 2003: 99). During this period, the development process and shift from hunting-gathering subsistence to a farming way of life was complete, and the society gradually became reliant on agriculture and herding. These developments were reflected in the ability to produce food, more developed tools for daily life, and various kinds of adorned artifacts. Various kinds of grains were cultivated, and animals were domesticated (Tanno and Willcox 2006b). This was a period of complex human technological development in prehistory, and much progress emerged, indicating a growth in the awareness and ability to live independently. However, the excavation evidence from the PN sites was for a long time poor and did not reveal sufficient information to understand the social structure and mortuary treatment in PN societies. Even though surveys undertaken in different regions and uncovered remarkable number of PN sites (e.g., Nieuwenhuyse and Akkermans 2019; Tsuneki 2012; Nishiaki 2013; Mière 2013), the number of excavated sites were relatively low. Therefore, it was difficult to define a common conclusion for the region in relation to social structure and mortuary treatment. Initial excavations in the PN sites uncovered a handful of burials and thus there were prevailing beliefs that the PN people buried their dead in off-site cemeteries (Tsuneki 2013). However, the increasing number of burials in recent decades from a handful of sites has refuted these beliefs. It seems to prove that people of the PN period generally continued to bury their dead within the confines of their settlements, as per prior custom, beneath the floors or between residential structures. However, at a few sites, special locations designated as burial grounds or 'cemeteries' appear to have emerged for the first time during this period in sites such as Tell el-Kerkh (Tsuneki 2010a, 2011, 2013; Jammo and Tsuneki 2020) and Tell Sabi Abyad (Akkermans 2008; Akkermans *et al.* 2014; Plug, Plicht and Akkermans 2014).

Initially, it is necessary to understand the general characteristics, social structure, and funerary practices in PN societies and its complexity. Investigations clarified that the PN societies were characterized by significant diversity of regional cultures (Jammo 2018; Odaka 2013; Gibbs and Banning 2013; Akkermans 2008). The settlement pattern and occupation period of the settlement is a considerable matter of debate. Evidence of a few generations successively inhabiting a settlement or for inhabiting it for a long time has been accumulated.

Investigation in PN sites, in general, exhibited two basic features:

1. The first is inherited from the PPN period. The general characteristics of the site, settlement pattern, funeral practices, and burial ground attested a form of continuation from previous periods. However, some variation could be noticed from site to site throughout the regions.
2. The second type of PN sites represented the transformation process. The general layout of the settlement, the appearance of new funeral practices, and interring the deceased within a cemetery attested the shift to a new stage of social development.

The PN period is characterized by emerging social complexity of various aspects related to funeral rituals, social organization and social stratification. Investigations have revealed a prominent variation compared with the previous PPN period. Most of the sites in PPN period in the Levant shared common rituals and features with neighboring sites, and Levantine

and Anatolian sites have uncovered astonishing ritual practices. The ritual buildings, skull decoration, plastering and caching skulls were clearly observed in the PPN period. However, the picture dramatically changed between the PPN and PN periods.

Rich evidence about the treatment of human skulls was uncovered from the Neolithic period especially during the PPNA and PPNB periods. The Skull was separated from the rest of the body using different methods and later subjected to a specific treatment. Skull removal practices and the subsequent treatments of the skulls such as decorating, plastering and caching flourished during the PPN periods and dominated the funeral rituals in society. The treatment of the skull reflected the importance of the skull in Neolithic societies. The skull had a relationship with the life and identity of the dead, and created linkage between the living and dead. Excavation evidence illustrates two methods of detaching skulls:

1. Skull removal refers to the removal of the entire skull (cranium and mandible) from the rest of the body after the completion of flesh decomposition following a span of time of the interment.
2. Skull decapitation refers to separating the skull from the rest of the body immediately after death or when the flesh was still fresh using a sharp flint tool. In this case, traces of cut marks were observed on the cervical vertebrae.

The first method was more common and widely practiced, whereas the second pattern was limited and attested in some sites and connected with secondary burials custom such as Tell Qaramel (Kanjou *et al.* 2015) and Körtik Tepe (Erdal 2015) in PPNA, Tell Qarassa (Santana *et al.* 2012) in PPNB, and Çatalhöyük (Boz and Hager 2013) in PN. Kuijt (2008) suggests that secondary mortuary practices are prearranged. These practices are subject to a sequence of steps and ceremonies bearing spiritual and symbolic meanings and require the participation of several households.

The skull removal and skull decoration practices underwent remarkable changes and sharply decreased in the late PPN and PN periods. Therefore, it is suggested that these practices were abandoned in the PN period. However, a few specimens were uncovered in the Late PPN in some sites such in Abu Hureyra (2C) (Moore and Molleson 2000), Ba`ja (Gebel and Hermansen 2000, 2001), and Ain Ghazal (Rollefson, Simmons and Kafafi 1992) and in the PN sites such as Tell el-Kerkh (Jammo 2014, 2018), Tell Sabi Abyad (Akkermans 2013), Hakemi Use (Tekin 2010, 2011; Erdal 2013). Further, the common practice of plastered, decorated, and cached skulls in the PPNB also disappeared in the Levant during the PN. However, plaster specimens were uncovered for the first time in the PN Anatolian sites such as Çatalhöyük (Hodder 2004, 2009; Boz and Hager 2013, 2014; Haddow and Knüsel 2017) and Köşk Höyük (Özbek 2009; Öztan 2011).

Increased details were gained from the examination of the mortuary practices in PN, which clarified the similarities and differences in various aspects in different regions. While some of the common PPN ritual practices absent or sharply decreased in the PN period, the types of burials and funeral practices in this period showed substantial variety. Moreover, the absence of the PPN common ritual practices or the undertaking of it on a limited scale in the PN, may indicate a major change related to the degree of development of the society between these periods. The PN societies showed wide variety in handling deceased, and some of these treatments continued and echoed during the subsequent periods. Pottery was a remarkable invention in this period, and it was invested widely in the ritual practices. For instances, small children and infants were buried for the first time in pottery vessels in this period (Plug and Nieuwenhuyse 2018; Tsuneki *et al.* 2011; Orrelle 2008). Further, children in the PN societies were in some instances treated carefully and separated from adult burials (Akkermans 2008; Miyake *et al.* 2009). Moreover, children were associated with different types of grave goods and some others were accompanied with a remarkable number. The variety in the mortuary treatment of children, undoubtedly meaningful, probably indicate to conspicuous ideology toward children's burials in the PN period.

Cremation is unusual practices in the Neolithic period, however, the exploitation of fire and the intentional investment in PN ritual practices were clearly documented at a few sites. The cremation ritual took different forms from one site to another. At Tell el-Kerkh, the use of the fire was manifested by the discovery of crematorium pits where a number of deceased were cremated. At Tell Sabi Abyad, the fire was used in the so-called 'burnt heart' ritual which applied to adults (Plug and Nieuwenhuyse 2018). Also, some of the buildings in Tell Sabi Abyad and Tell Bouqras were purposely set on fire and a number of deceased exposed to cremation were found in these buildings. It suggests that these buildings were ritual places and the deceased were cremated in fulfillment of rituals related to fire and death (Akkermans *et al.* 2012; Verhoeven 2000; Merrett and Meiklejohn 2007). Cremation rituals were documented from a few PN sites in the region; however, the place of the cremation, preparation, and the number of cremated individuals was significantly different. Undoubtedly, the use of fire in the ritual is one of the significant funerary practices in the PN period and it was applied

to a number of deceased, however, those who have benefited from this ritual still a subject of debate.

The PN societies have experienced an explicit regional diversity from the perspective of material culture such as pottery and its stylistic development scale, grave goods, and other aspects related to the funerary practices and social organization. The diversity and complexity in funerary practices during the PN period demonstrate a distinct local-based culture or regional culture distinguishing sites and regions in this period. Hence, it is difficult to unite the region in a common feature or type of mortuary practices. The common point between most if not all PN sites, undoubtedly, is that these sites have shown signs of less attention to the funerary practices that prevailed in the PPN period.

3. Status of Burial Disturbance at Kerkh Cemetery

Excavations at Kerkh cemetery have uncovered a wide variety of funerary practices in each burial type. The deceased were buried in primary, secondary, cremation, collective, urn burials and some were found in a complex pattern classified as unknown. Burials unearthed from each burial type illustrate simple and complex patterns. The dead were in some instances buried intact, however, articulated, dismembered, and partly represented human remains in the burials were also found. Some deposits revealed a mixture between two burial types in the same burial context, such as cremated remains in the collective burials or detached skulls beside intact burials, which indicate complex patterns of inhumation in the cemetery. Chapter 5 provides descriptions of each burial in the cemetery. Given the interment condition, a considerable number of deceased were disturbed, lacking parts of bodily remains, partly represented in the grave, manipulated, and/or that were probably removed from its original interment context into another.

As mention before, Kerkh cemetery contained remains of 244 individuals. Regarding the primary burials, 104 individuals came from this context and they were mainly uncovered on the cemetery ground in burial context and in the collective burial pits. Remains of 84 individuals came from burial deposits in the cemetery ground, and 20 from the collective pits (Table 8-1). The number of intact individuals from the burial deposits is 70, and 16 disturbed, whereas, 8 intact and 12 disturbed from the collective burials. Most deceased in this burial context were intact which indicates that no subsequent opening to the grave has occurred. However, a few individuals were lacking bodily parts or buried in an unusual position. Given the total of 244 individuals uncovered from the cemetery, the number of intact or untouched deceased (84 individuals) is relatively small.

The cemetery presented evidence of intentional acts upon skulls in primary burials. In total, 10 headless individuals were uncovered. Some individuals' skulls were completely missing, but occasionally only the cranium was removed in fulfillment of the funeral practice of skull removal (details below). In addition, the head of one individual Str. 834 was manipulated and found in an upside-down position. On the other hand, some individuals were buried in an unusual position. They were even lacked limbs, or interred in a severely complex position. For instances, Str. 712 is a middle adult individual, probable female, who was buried in a flexed position on her right side. The most outstanding element of this burial is the twisted treatment of the head. The skull was twisted, and it faces downward. Also, Str. 941 is another middle adult, probably female buried in a flexed position in a burial pit. Notably, her head was severely bent and oriented in a counterclockwise direction. In addition, Str. 1075 is a young adult was buried in a prone position; however, the lower limbs were completely missing from the burial, which raises questions about the characteristics of this type of inhumation. Also, a number of individuals were buried with an unusual head position, which was bent or twisted sharply relative to the body axil. Str. 1077 was a young adult, probable female buried in a tightly flexed and compact position on her back. The spine formed an arch shape, and her skull was twisted strongly, forming 90 degrees with her body axil.

In the primary burials, long bones, skulls/crania were sometimes discovered missing from the burials. However, number of detached skulls/crania were subsequently discovered beside primary burials, or found solo on the ground of the cemetery in the secondary dispositional context. This probably indicates that the bodily parts were retrieved from the primary burials and reburied in a different context.

Secondary burials also contain deceased interred in various ways. Few of the burials in this context retained all the skeletal elements, whereas, the majority were manipulated, disturbed and dismembered or lacked bodily parts. Burials in this context were even single inhumation in burial deposit or in the collective burials, however, the majority from the latter. Remains of 17 individuals came from burial deposits, and 41 from the collective burials (Table 8-1). A number of individuals in this burial context were represented partly by a separated skull/cranium or portion of skulls. These skull/crania seem to have been removed from its original context and relocated beside individuals in the primary burials (e.g. Str. 912) or solo discovered on the cemetery ground (e.g. Str. 1080). Further, some individuals seem to have been interred where they were discovered, but many bodily parts were missing (e.g. Str. 710). On the other hand, three dismembered individuals in Str. 930 were

uncovered in a context contains animal bones, pottery sherds and stones. It is difficult to speculate the reason beyond burying disarticulated human within this accumulation. In addition, Str. 1052 is a secondary burial interred in a unique pattern. The remains of this individual manifested arrangement for its bodily parts in a specific order especially the long bones and skull. The deliberate arrangement of its bones indicates that this individual underwent multi-stage treatment post mortem before interring in its ultimate location.

Evidence for separated skulls and missing body parts, including long bones, were clearly identified in the collective burials. In many instances, burials were represented by solo skulls or skulls/crania accompanied by long bones. However, complete or nearly complete skeletons with bodily parts missing, were documented. Given the number of individuals interred in these contexts, the skeletons were in some instances imposed over each other and overlapped.

The cremated individuals uncovered from the crematorium pits and other burial deposits in the cemetery displayed more complex characteristics. Remains of at least 46 cremated individuals were uncovered in the cemetery (Hironaga in Chapter 9). Cremated remains were uncovered from two main contexts: (1) From the crematorium pits (2) From collective burials or burials contain intact remains (Table 8-1). Many cremated individuals were represented or identified by the skull and long bones; however, small bones were also identified. Remains of a number of cremated individuals were left in the crematorium pit after the end of cremation. Given the small size of the pit, the deceased was not cremated when the flesh was still fresh, but rather after or nearly decomposed. Hence, the skeletal remains were retrieved from the original interment context to the crematorium pit. Furthermore, some cremated remains were discovered in burials contain intact burials, which indicate relocating the cremated remains to another burial context. The characteristics of these deposits suggest that the retrieval and transfer of bodily remains from one interment context to another, and *vice versa*, might have taken place in the cemetery.

Further complex inhumation patterns uncovered in the unknown burials. Remains of 34 individuals were uncovered and all of them were heavily disturbed, dismembered, and lacking many bodily parts. Only two burials were uncovered from a collective burial pit and the rest were from burial deposits in the cemetery (Table 8-1). The deceased were represented by parts of fragmented skulls, fragmented long and small bones, phalanges and notably some of them were accompanied by grave goods. Few of these burials seem to have been buried where they were discovered, but most of the body parts were missing. Other burials contain body

Table 8-1. Status of burial disturbance at Kerkh Cemetery.

Burial Type	Status	Burial deposit	Collective burial	Crematorium pit	Total
Primary burials	Intact	70	8	–	104
	Disturbed	14	12		
Secondary burials	Single inhumation	17	–	–	58
	Collective	–	41		
Cremation burials	Primary cremation	–	–	17	46
	Secondary cremation	5	24	–	
Urn burials	In pottery vessel	2	–	–	2
Unknown burials	Dismembered	32	2	–	34
Total		140	87	17	244

parts such as limb bones, or phalanges. The status of the human remains in this burial context may indicate to retrieve body parts and relocate them in another burial context.

The dead at Kerkh cemetery were subjected to a simple and complex treatment postmortem. Some of the burials seem to have been left intact after the grave was closed, however, many were subjected to multi-stage treatments and some bodily parts were retrieved from its original grave and subsequently relocated. Given the fact that cutting traces were not observed on the human skeletons due to the preservation condition of the human bones, the retrieval of the bodily parts may have occurred after the flesh had decomposed. Evidently, particular attention has been paid to some parts of the body. The disturbed and partly represented individuals in all burial types demonstrate that skulls/crania and long bones were the most targeted bones. The remarkable evidence in handling the human remains in different ways at Kerkh cemetery provides new insight into the complexity and variability of funerary practices in this period.

4. Detached Skulls

The state of representation of the deceased in the burials at the cemetery was varied. Some individuals were buried completely intact, whereas others were represented by some skeletal remains. In some instances, the skull and the long bones were present in the grave, but other skeletal elements were missing. However, in other instances, only detached skulls/crania were uncovered. A minimum number of forty-one detached skull/cranium, or detached skull/cranium accompanied with long bones have been derived from different burial types in the cemetery. Some of these skulls/crania were intact; however, others were fragmented or partly represented. Separated mandibles were sometimes uncovered on the cemetery ground.

Detached skulls and crania were not found in caches or any similar context, but they were discovered on the

cemetery ground (Figure 8-1). In total, ten detached and separated skulls/crania were uncovered. Four came from Layer 4, four from Layer 5, and two from Layer 6. Some of these skulls were detached intact, or in some specimens the mandible was missing while the cranium was present, or they were represented partly by some skull fragments.

Detached skulls and crania in the cemetery were derived from three main depositional contexts:

4-1. Detached Skulls and Crania Associated with Primary Burials

The total number of skulls and crania derived from this depositional context is limited. Only four specimens were uncovered (Table 8-2) (Figure 8-1). Only one complete cranium (Str. 1084) was uncovered on the knee of an adult probable male (Str. 1086) on the top of the group of burials (G1) in layer 5. The other three specimens were portions of isolated skulls. Two specimens were discovered with a young adult male burial (Str. 904). The first one is perinatal (Str. 513) was discovered in front of the young adult male's head, and the second specimen (Str. 912) was an infant discovered near his foot. The last specimen (Str. 1048) included portions of an isolated skull discovered just in front of a young adult male face (Str. 1047) within the burial group (G2) in layer 4.

4-2. Solo Detached Skulls and Crania Discovered on the Cemetery Ground

Skulls and crania of this depositional context were uncovered from different parts of the cemetery. In total, six specimens were identified (Table 8-3). They were two juveniles, three adults and one its age is indeterminate. One adult was represented by an isolated cranium and the other adults by isolated skulls, and the unknown one by portions of an isolated skull. Also, one juvenile was represented by an isolated skull and the other with a half skull discovered below the stone row of collective burials C2. In this context, the

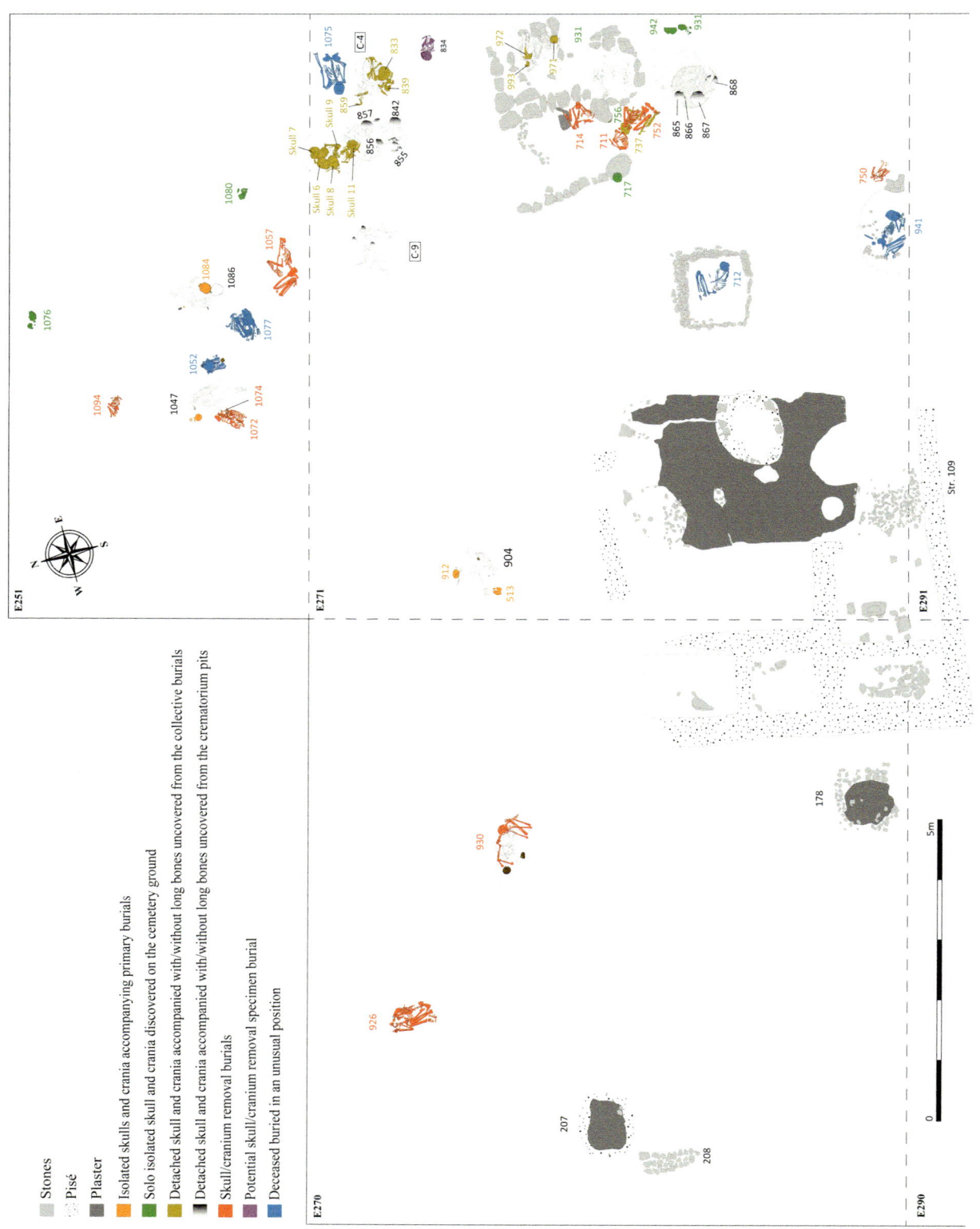

Figure 8-1. Location of individuals mentioned in the text.

Stones
Pisé
Plaster
Isolated skulls and crania accompanying primary burials
Solo isolated skull and crania discovered on the cemetery ground
Detached skull and crania accompanied with/without long bones uncovered from the collective burials
Detached skull and crania accompanied with/without long bones uncovered from the crematorium pits
Skull/cranium removal burials
Potential skull/cranium removal specimen burial
Deceased buried in an unusual position

Table 8-2. Isolated skulls and crania accompanying primary burials.

Layer	Str. no.	Age	Sex	Burial type	Face direction	Description	Grave goods
4	513	Perinatal	–	Secondary	–	Portions of an isolated skull discovered in front of Str. 904 head.	Animal-shaped stone pendant: 1
	1048	Perinatal	–	Secondary	–	Portions of an isolated skull discovered in front of Str. 1047.	–
5	912	Infant	–	Secondary	–	Portions of an isolated skull discovered at the left foot of Str. 904.	–
	1084	Adult	Probable female	Secondary	Upward	Isolated cranium discovered obove Str. 1086 knee.	–

Table 8-3. Solo isolated skull and crania discovered on the cemetery ground.

Layer	Str. no.	Age	Sex	Burial type	Face direction	Gave goods	Description
4	717	Juvenile, 1–2 yrs.	–	Secondary	–	–	Isolated skull
	756	Juvenile	–	Secondary	–	–	Half skull
5	1076	–	–	Unknown	–	–	–
	1080	Old adult	–	Secondary	S	–	Isolated skull
6	931	Adult	–	Secondary	–	–	Isolated cranium
	942	Adult	–	Unknown	–	–	Isolated skull

skulls and crania were, in most instances, separated from the adjacent burials or buried individually on the edge of the excavated area in the cemetery or beside the group burials.

4-3. Detached Skulls and Crania Accompanied with and without Long Bones Found in the Collective Burials and Crematorium Pits

The majority of the skulls and crania were derived from this depositional context. In total, thirty-one individuals were identified via the crania and skull that were uncovered from the collective burials and crematorium pits (Tables 8-4 and 5). The skulls/crania

uncovered from the collective burials and crematorium pits were represented in complex patterns. The large number of human remains and fragmented bones in the collective burials and crematorium pits make it difficult in some instances to match the skulls with the rest of the body.

Detached skulls or crania, and detached skulls/crania accompanied with long bones were widely uncovered in these contexts. Most of the skulls might have been buried intact in these contexts. Some of them were fragmented after exposure to air during excavation or exposure to high temperatures in the crematorium pits. Given the small size of the collective burials and

Table 8-4. Detached skull and crania accompanied with/without long bones uncovered from the collective burials.

Layer	C. no.	Str. no.	Age	Sex	Burial type	Face direction	Gave goods	Description
4	C-2	737	Middle adult	Probable male	Secondary	W	–	Skull and long bones
5	C-3	847						Adult cranium 2 Nonadult crania 2 Skulls 5
		848						
		850						
		North						
	C-4	833	Young adult	Probable male	Secondary	–	–	Skull and long bones
		839,1	Middle adult	Probable male	Cremation	–	–	Skull and long bones
		839,2	Adult	Probable male	Cremation			Skull and long bones
		845	Adult	Probable male	Secondary	–	Stone beads: 3 Shell beads: 2	Skull and long bones
6	C-10	971	Juvenile, 3-4 yrs.	–	Secondary	–	–	Skull
		972	Juvenile, 11-12 yrs.		Secondary			Skull
		980	–	–	Unknown	–	–	Skull
		993	Infant, 9-12 mths.		Secondary	–	–	Skull

Table 8-5. Detached skull and crania accompanied with/without
long bones uncovered from the crematorium pits.

Layer	C. no.	Str. no.	Age	Sex	Burial type	Face direction	Gave goods	Description
6	C-5	842	Middle adult	Probable male	Cremation	S	DFBW jar: 2 Bone stamp seal: 1	Cremated skull
		855	Young adult	Probable male		–		Cremated skull
		856	Adult	Probable female				Cremated skull
		857	Young adult	Probable male				Cremated skull
		858	Subadult	Probable female				Cremated skull
	C-6	865	1. Adult	Probable female	Cremation	–	DFBW: 1 wheat	Cremated skull
			2. Adult	Probable female				
		866	Adult					Cremated skull
		867	1. Juvenile	–				Cremated skull
			2. Juvenile					
		868	1. Juvenile					Cremated skull
			2. Juvenile					
	C-9	919	Adult	–	Cremation	–	–	Cremated cranium

crematorium pits, it is difficult to fit a large number of intact corpses. Further, the presence of more dismembered and less intact skeletons indicates a high probability that the deceased was not necessarily represented as an intact body in most instances, but rather partially.

5. Headless Individuals at Kerkh Cemetery

Up to the 2010 excavation season, the cemetery revealed number of headless individuals. They were derived even from the primary context or from the collective burials. The skulls and the crania seem to have been removed from the grave to fulfill the practice of skull removal. Some of these specimens were intensively studied during the excavations, and full details were provided. However, other specimens underwent studies depending on the field reports, drawings, and photos, hence the bones were not analyzed accurately due to current situations in Syria.

Based on the final analyses and studies done until the completion of this report, ten headless individuals were uncovered (Table 8-6). They were five adults, and notably, four were females (Strs. 752, 926, 927, 1057) and one male (Str. 714), one sub-adult (Str. 711), three juveniles one of them is very young (Str. 750, 1072, 1094) and an infant (Str. 1047).

5-1. Str. 711

Str. 711 is a primary disturbed burial for a sub-adult 15-18 yrs. old, discovered in C2 (Figure 8-2). The sex is indeterminate. It was buried in a flexed position, lying on its right side. The body axis direction is east-west,

Figure 8-2. Str. 711, a 15–18-year-old sub-adult
with most parts of the cranium missing.

and the head seems to be pointed to the northeast. Most of the skeletal remains were recovered, but most parts of the cranium were missing. However, part of the mandible was present in its proper anatomical position *in situ*. The presence of several individuals in the collective context makes it difficult to assert whether the cranium was removed prior to interment or after. In addition, it could have been removed accidentally when new interments occurred in the burial site. However, this individual was buried on the top of the burial stone structure, which may indicate that it was one of those buried at the latest stage and where no further deceased were interred after that. On the other hand, no separated cranium was uncovered in the burial too, which ruled out the accidental removal of the cranium. Thus, this individual might have fulfilled cranium removal.

Table 8-6. Skull/cranium removal specimens uncovered at Kerkh Cemetery.

Str. no.	Age	Sex	Burial type	Position	Body axis direction	Gave goods	Notice	Layer	C. no
711	Subadult, 15-18 yrs.	–	Primary (disturbed)	R	E-W	–	Cranial removal	4	–
714	Adult	Probable male	Primary (disturbed)	L	SW-NE	Shell bead: 2	Cranial removal		
750	Juvenile, 5-6 yrs.	–	Primary	P	NW-SE	–	Cranial removal	5	
752	Adult	Probable female	Primary	R	NW-SE	–	Skull removal	4	
926	Adult	Probable female	Primary	R	N-S	Stone bead: 1 Shell beads: 4 Bone beads: 2	Cranial removal	6	
927	1. Young adult, 30-40 yrs.	Female	Primary	R	W-E	DFBW bowl: 1 DFBW sherd: 1 Stone beads: 3 Shell beads: 2 Bone bead: 1 Shell: 1	Skull removal		–
	2. Perinatal, 38-40 wks.		Secondary	–	–		–		
	3. Juvenile, 4-5 yrs.								
1057	Adult	Female	Primary	R	E-W	–	Skull removal	5	
1072	Juvenile, 11-12 yrs.	–	Primary (disturbed)	S	SW-NE	–	Skull removal		
1074	Infant	–	Primary (disturbed)	P	S-N	–	Skull removal		
1094	Juvenile	–	Primary	R	SE-NW	–	Skull removal		
834	Juvenile, 2-3 yrs.	–	Primary	L	NW-SE	–	Potential skull removal. The skull must had been separated and re-placed on upside down position facing north direction.		

5-2. Str. 714

Str. 714 is a primary disturbed burial of an adult, probably male discovered just to the northeast of burial Str. 711 (Figure 8-3). This individual was highly fragmented and poorly preserved. It was buried in a flexed position lying on its left side. The direction of the body axis is southwest–northeast. Notably, the cranium was also missing in this specimen, but the mandible was almost completely preserved. The maxilla was missing, however, the right maxillary second premolar was found with a pile of teeth placed on the tibia (likely done by the excavator during skeleton cleaning). Thus, it is not precisely clear whether this tooth belongs to the Str. 714 or not. If so, the tooth must have fallen from the cranium at the time of removal and the cranium was relocated in a different context.

5-3. Str. 750

Str. 750 is a primary burial of a juvenile 5-6 years old, lacking its cranium (Figure 8-4a). The location of the mandible and the visibility of the posterior skeletal elements of the torso suggest that it was buried in a flexed, but prone, position. The second cervical vertebra and three maxillary deciduous teeth were present in their proper anatomical position *in situ*

Figure 8-3. Str. 714, an adult, probably male with missing cranium.

(Figure 8-4b). Hence, the cranium could have been removed after flesh decomposition. Notably, three

Figure 8-4a. Str. 750, a 5–6-year-old juvenile with missing cranium.

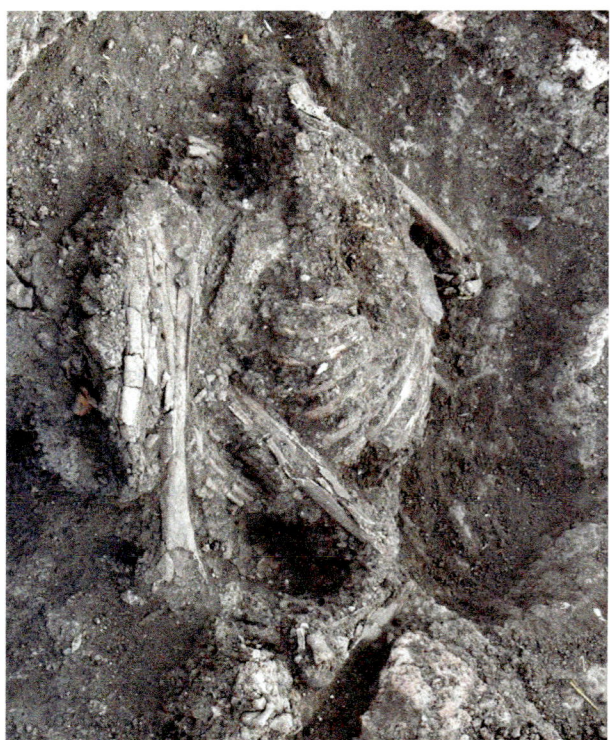

Figure 8-5. Str. 752, a 20-year-old adult, probably female with missing skull.

had also decomposed before the cranium was removed, sparing the actor from having to cut through the tissue. If the child had been decapitated, meaning, with cuts through the soft tissue, there would be far more disruption to the head and neck region.

5-4. Str. 752

Str. 752 is a primary burial belonging to an adult, probably female (Figure 8-5). The skeleton was highly fragmented after exposure to air during excavations; thus, precise details were not obtained. However, she was buried on her right side down and body axis oriented northwest-southeast. Cranial elements were missing. Remarkably, her skull was completely removed from the grave, and the cervical vertebrae were also missing.

5-5. Str. 926

Figure 8-4b. Str. 750. 1. mandible; 2. second cervical vertebrae; 3. maxillary teeth.

maxillary teeth were still in the ground, suggesting that if the cranium had been removed, the soft tissue that would support those teeth had decomposed, and the teeth fell out. In addition, since the mandible is in its proper anatomical location, this also suggests that the soft tissue connections, such as muscle and ligaments,

Str. 926 is a primary burial of an adult, probably female (Figure 8-6a). She was buried in a flexed position on her right side down. Notably, her cranium was missing, but the mandible was present in its natural anatomical position, which was intact. No cut marks were noticed on the mandible and cervical vertebrae, indicating that her cranium was removed after the flesh was completely decomposed. She had unusual mandibular teeth, suggesting the use of dentition as a gripping tool. The left side mandible shows heavy wear on the first and second molars, which includes

Figure 8-6a. Str. 926, an adult female with missing cranium.

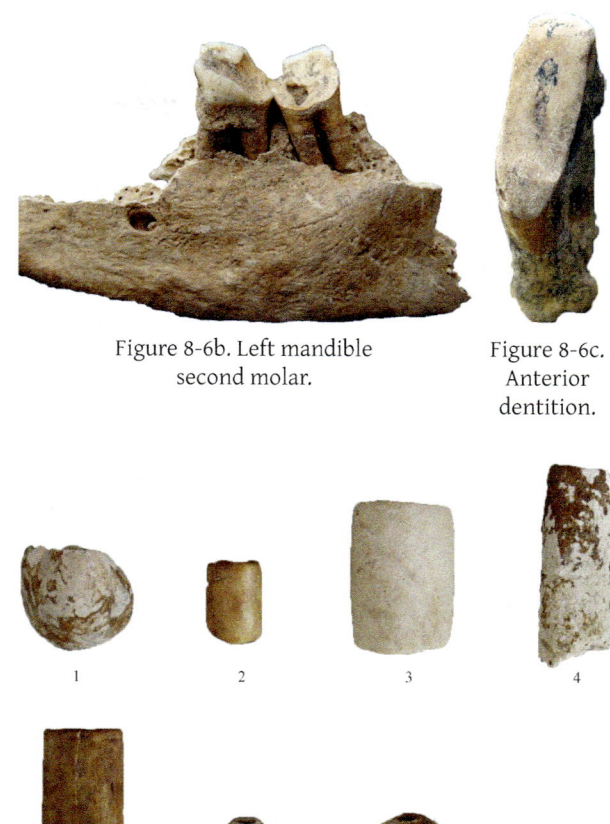

Figure 8-6b. Left mandible second molar.

Figure 8-6c. Anterior dentition.

Figure 8-6d. Grave goods. 1. shell bead; 2. bone bead; 3. limestone bead; 4. tusk shell bead; 5. bone bead; 6-7. conch shell beads.

non-carious pulp exposure (Figure 8-6b). Additionally, on the anterior dentition, oblique wear on the labial surface of the right central incisor can be observed, suggesting that she favored the anterior dentition and the left side of the jaw (Figure 8-6c). These traces are usually related to non-masticatory behavior that suggests the use of the dentition as a gripping tool.

This individual was adorned with seven beads distributed in various locations along her body within the grave (Figure 8-6d). Two beads made of shells and bones were found under her left arm, three beads made of tusk shell, limestone, and bone near the lower spine, and two-conch shells around her neck.

5-6. Str. 927

Str. 927 is a triple burial that contained the remains of three individuals (Figure 8-7a). The remains were disturbed and buried together in the same grave. The main individual is a young adult female, and the other individuals are perinatal and juvenile. The body axis of the female was oriented west-east, while the perinatal and juvenile positions could not be identified. The female was buried in a flexed position on her right side down (Figure 8-7b). The lower part of her body was

articulated, and the upper part was disturbed. Notably, her skull was completely removed, but the first cervical vertebra was present. It is most likely that the skull was removed after the flesh was completely decomposed.

Interestingly, a small Dark Faced Burnished Ware (DFBW) bowl was placed near the skull that already existed (Figure 8-7c). The skull of the juvenile was identified on the back of the adult female, while the perinatal mandible was discovered at the abdomen of the female, suggesting that this female may have been pregnant when she died. It seems they were buried together at the same time. The disturbed status of the grave was most likely the result of human interference in the context of rituals when the skull was removed after a period of interment.

This assemblage was supplied with various grave goods, including a small DFBW bowl placed near the adult female's missing skull, and a large pottery fragment close to the bowl (Figure 8-7d). Five beads made of agate, limestone, blue stone, and shell were found near the female's abdomen and under the perinatal

Figure 8-7a. Str. 927, a triple burial.

Figure 8-7b. Young adult female of Str. 927.

Figure 8-7c. DFBW.

Figure 8-7d. Large pottery fragment.

1

2   3   4   5   6

Figure 8-7e. Beads. 1. bone bead; 2-3. shell beads; 4. turquoise bead;
5. stone bead; 6. agate bead.

Figure 8-7f. Shell.

(Figure 8-7e, f), and another incised bone bead near the female's pelvis.

In Kerkh cemetery, it was notable that a number of deceased were accompanied by (DFBW) or limestone bowls stood in front of or behind the head as in the case of Strs. 715, 927, and 1058. Both Str. 715 and 1085 retained their skull intact, but the skull of Str. 927 was missing. In case of placing a bowl in front of or behind the head of the dead is a burial custom at Tell el-Kerkh, Str. 927 undoubtedly retained her skull when she buried. According to the female body position and axis direction, the (DFBW) bowl must have been placed in front of the skull. Eventually, the skull ended removed and the bowl retained in its original place. Placing the pottery bowl in front of the head probably helped to marking the place of the skull, and on the other hand, facilitated its removal.

5-7. Str. 1057

Str. 1057 is a primary burial of an adult probable female buried on her right side in a flexed position (Figure 8-8). Her body axis direction was east-west. The lower limbs were tightly folded. The skull was completely missing, but some cervical vertebrae were present *in situ*. Notably, her long bones were thin and gracile.

5-8. Str. 1072

Str. 1072 is a disturbed primary burial for a juvenile, 11-12 yrs. old; however, the sex was indeterminate

(Figure 8-9). It was buried in a supine position lying on its back and its body oriented toward the southwest-northeast direction. The skull, the first and second cervical vertebrae were missing from the burial, which suggests that the head was removed while the soft tissue was still intact. The remaining cervical vertebrae were articulated and in a poor condition to observe if cutmarks were visible or not. This individual was buried over other individual (Str. 1074) and it was covered most of its body parts. Interestingly, both individuals' skulls were missing. Notably, both the lower limbs and the left upper limb, but for a few hand bones, were not present. The left part of the hip pone (ilium) was present, but the right side is missing.

5-9. Str. 1074

Str. 1074 is a primary disturbed burial of an infant whose sex is indeterminate (Figure 8-10). The skeleton was disturbed, and it was difficult to determine the burial position. Likely, it was buried in a flexed position in a prone position and the body axis direction was south-north. Notably, the skull was missing from the burial. It was buried beneath the juvenile (Str. 1072), and a large part of its body was covered by the former burial. Curiously enough, both individuals who were over each other's skulls were entirely removed.

Upon on the condition of these two individuals, the removal of their skulls could be contemporaneous. Further, disturbance of the juvenile (Str. 1072) may be

Figure 8-8. Str. 1057, an adult, probably female with missing skull.

Figure 8-9. Str. 1072, a 11–12-year-old juvenile
with missing skull.

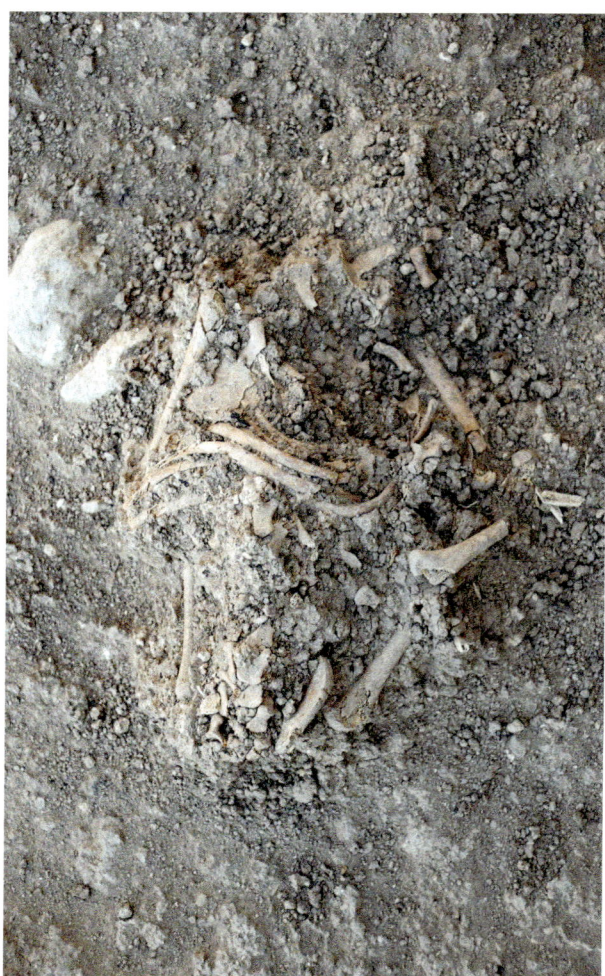

Figure 8-10. Str. 1074, an infant
with missing skull.

related to the removal of the infant skull (Str. 1074). If the juvenile's lower limbs were flexed over the chest, the skeletal remains restrict reach the infant skull. Hence, the lower limbs and the right part of the hipbone have covered the small body of the infant. Therefore, these bones were removed in order to retrieve the skull of the infant. However, the poor condition of the bones didn't help determine whether the skulls and the long bones were removed when the flesh was decayed or not. Then the long bones and skulls must have been moved from the original context to another.

5-10. Str. 1094

Str. 1094 is a primary burial for a juvenile lying on its right side down in a flexed position (Figure 8-11). The body axis oriented southeast-northwest, and the lower limbs were tightly folded. The skull of this individual was completely missing from the burial. An isolated maxillary lateral incisor is visible in the photo, as is the incomplete root of another unidentifiable tooth. A small flint flake was uncovered near its feet.

* Potential headless individual

In addition to the ten headless individuals, one individual attested a manipulation of its head. This individual was uncovered on the eastern side of the cemetery. Precise bone analysis has not been accomplished to classifying it as skull removal specimens, and further details are required. Thus, this burial will tentatively be classified as a potential headless individual.

5-11. Str. 834

Str. 834 is a primary burial of a juvenile (2-3 years) buried in a flexed position, lying on its left side (Figure 8-12). The body axis direction is west-east, and it faces the north. Curiously, the skull of this individual is upside down and seems to have been intentionally manipulated. Therefore, the skull of this individual must have been separated from the rest of the body and was subsequently placed in this position. Because the condition of the cervical vertebrae was not confirmed, it is difficult to determine whether the skull was separated prior to

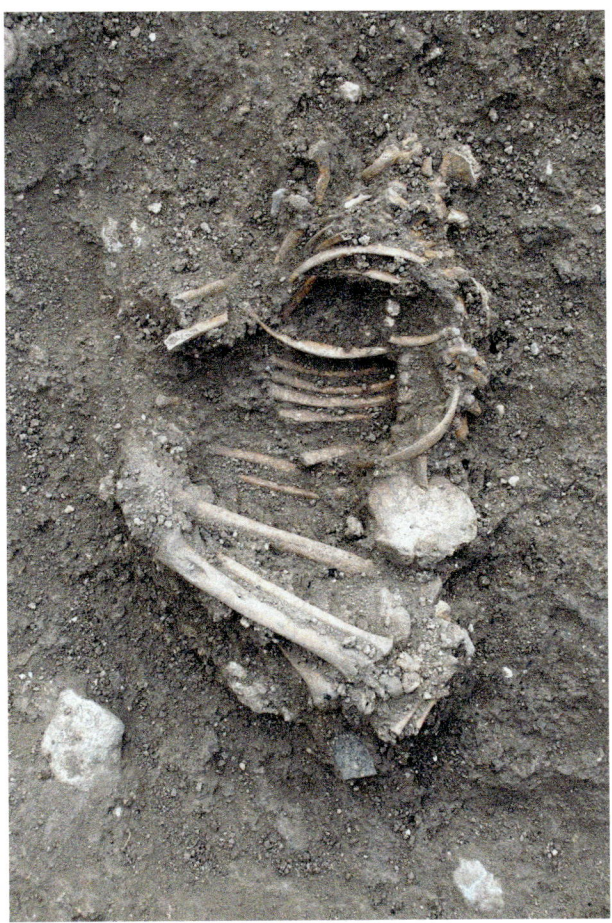

Figure 8-11. Str. 1094, a juvenile with missing skull.

6. Scope of Practicing Skull Removal in PN and Subsequent Periods

To date, northern Syria, central and southeastern Anatolia have been considered promising regions to investigate PN societies and gather information related to lifestyle during this period. In the last few decades, a handful of sites have been excavated and revealed extensive information enriched our understanding about the development of the PN societies including settlement organization, social structure and funerary practices and its complexity. Excavations have illustrated that the types of burials and funeral practices in the PN period varied substantially. The burial practices in the PN period attested dramatic changes and high degree of complexity compared to the PPN period (e.g., Verhoeven 2002).

As mentioned earlier, skull removal was practiced widely in the PPN periods. However, based on the limited specimens uncovered so far, this practice sharply decreased during the PN and the subsequent periods. Excavations in the PN sites in northern Levant and central and southeastern Anatolian attested evidence of skull removal practice. Further, fewer specimens were uncovered in some Mesopotamian sites in the later periods. Although some PN sites uncovered a reasonable number of burials, the headless burial and detached skull were limited. For example, considering the headless and potential headless individuals at Tell el-Kerkh, only 10 specimens out of the 244 were uncovered. In the Balikh valley in Tell Sabi Abyad, Operation III yielded the largest number of deceased, and 192 graves were uncovered until the 2009 season (Plug and Nieuwenhuyse 2018). However, only two specimens belonging to adults were reported.

or after the flesh had decomposed. However, in both cases, it is evident that this individual was subjected to postmortem treatment, maybe to fulfill the practice of skull removal.

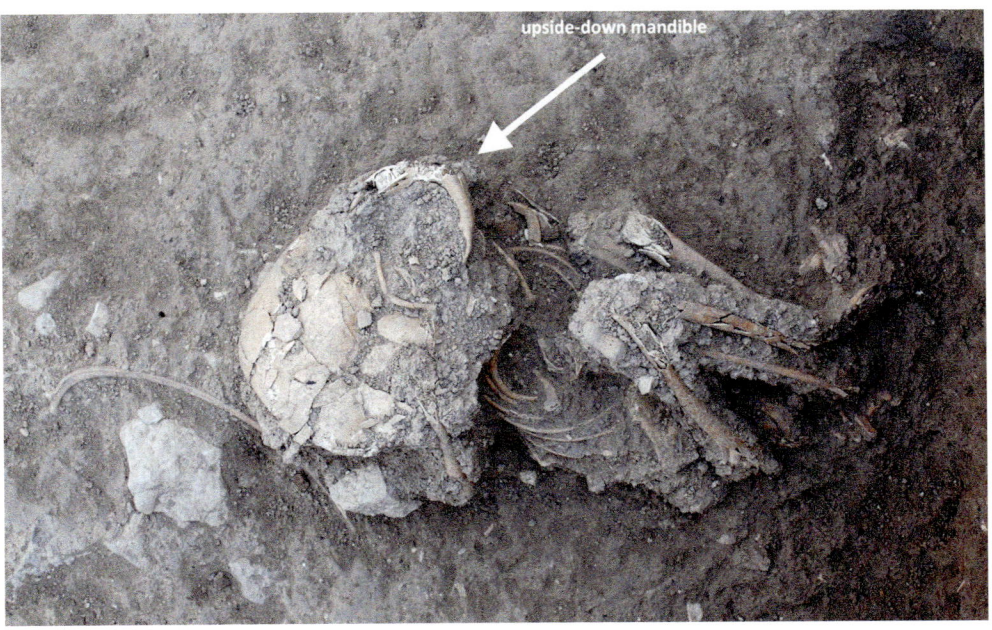

Figure 8-12. Str. 834, a 2–3-year-old juvenile with a skull in an upside-down position.

One with the cranium removed and the other with a separated skull, which was re-deposited in the grave (Akkermans 2008). From Çatalhöyük in Central Anatolia, several headless burials, along with isolated and plastered skulls were reported. Of those headless individuals, two with cut marks were uncovered (Boz and Hager 2013, 2014). Fifteen headless individuals were uncovered from the primary burials. The skull was completely removed from 12 of them, and the cranium was removed from three. Furthermore, 10 crania and 6 skulls were uncovered in the secondary deposits associated with primary burials. One of the skulls was plastered, which is the first of its kind found at Çatalhöyük during this period (Haddow and Knüsel 2017). Excavations at Central Anatolia in Köşk Höyük revealed 88 burials containing 82 complete skeletons (Bonogofsky 2005). A total of nineteen skulls and two headless burials were uncovered. Among the skulls, 13 were plastered and some were covered with red ocher and 6 were untreated skulls. The two headless burials are children 15-16 years old, and the second is an adult female 50-55 years old and both are buried beneath the floor (Özbek 2009). Furthermore, the excavation in Hakemi Use in the Upper Tigris region has unearthed the remains of 95 individuals from 89 graves. Three isolated skulls were uncovered in the corner of the room in a house. It is suggested that the interment of the skulls in this house is associated with the building (Erdal 2013).

In the subsequent Halaf period in Iraq, evidence for detached skulls were uncovered from Tell Arpachiyah. Two graves containing five skulls were uncovered. One skull was found in a jar in grave 1, and four separated skulls were uncovered in a collective burial. Three skulls were buried in bowls, and the fourth one was buried inside a squat jar. It is suggested that the skulls apparently belong to special people who occupied a high rank in society (Hijara 1978). Three burials from Yarim Tepe II uncovered five skulls. Two skulls came from two burials, and the third burial comprised three skulls laid on their left side (Merpert, Munchaev and Bader 1978). Further, a number of headless human burials were found in the tholos at Tell Azzo I in the Upper Tigris region in northern Iraq (Killick and Roaf 1983).

Some remarkable features such as the ritual building and the practices of skull manipulation that were prevalent in the PPN period were drastically decreased or disappeared during the PN period. Although the PN societies displayed a wide variety in handling deceased individuals (simple primary inhumation, single, double, and collective burials, cremation burials, pits, and urn burials). Some PN sites uncovered a reasonable number of burials, and human remains during this period were relatively scarce at some sites. In both cases, as shown in the narrative earlier, the funeral practice of skull removal and skull decoration continued into the PN period, however it also pointed to a sharp decline.

7. The Criteria for Selecting Individuals for Postmortem Treatment

The transformation to the PN period was accompanied by considerable changes in the subsistence economy, which may affect social behavior and the way they thought and dealt with the dead. The limited evidence of skull removal derived from the PN sites in various regions emphasizes a sharp decline of interest in the postmortem treatment of the skull. Although it is difficult to define the exact reason beyond the decline in the practice of skull removal in the PN period, on a limited basis it was confined to a number of the deceased. However, following the historical sequence of this practice, the available evidence could be significantly helpful to understand the reason.

The criteria for selecting individuals for skull/crania removal practices and subsequent treatment such as plastering in the PPNB period has been largely debated. For a prolonged period, discussing the social position in the Neolithic community was confined to the extraordinary practice of plastering and decorating skulls, which flourished in the PPNB period and was traditionally interpreted for worshiping ancestors even though children benefit from this practice. Further, researchers (e.g., Akkermans 1989, 2008; Campbell 1995; Verhoeven 2002) argued that no clear evidence for social hierarchy or leadership has been documented in the PPNB and PN societies. However, recent investigations on burial rituals based on the late PPNB (LPPNB) and PN periods excavation evidence has encouraged a number of researchers (including myself) to raise questions about the underlying reason behind the diverse ritual contexts and deceased treatments. The deceased were interred in different ways individually, collectively, cremated, and in pottery vessels, and in some instances, the grave was accurately prepared. Further, post-mortem treatments have been widely observed, such as skull/cranium removal, skull deformation, skull decoration, exploitation of fire in ritual practices, age-based cemetery, etc. In addition to the grave goods inclusion, which may reflect the status of property (especially stamps holders), or labor for some individuals.

Considering the majority of intact deceased in the Neolithic sites, those who underwent multi-step treatments or those whose skulls were retrieved and plastered were relatively smaller. Even though it cannot be stated for certain, there is an increased emphasis on the existence of criteria for determining the deceased for a specific treatment or preparing an interment context.

The diversity in ritual treatments and the criteria for determining the deceased for subsequent treatments postmortem become significant themes. It has been argued that the diversity in treatment and deceased selection is attributed to various concepts related to the decedent's social position and role or cultural identity in society (Erdal 2013; Bocquentin, Kodas and Ortiz 2016; Haddow and Knüsel 2017; Benz *et al.* 2019). The social status and ranking in the Neolithic period were expressed and interpreted in various forms. Evidence for the emergence of social hierarchy at 'Ain Ghazal attributed to the discovery of special building structures devoted to cult activity (Rollefson 2000), which suggest the emergence of social hierarchy 'based on religious control' (Rollefson 2010: 150). These buildings were even confined to kinship bases and overseen by specific people like a 'shaman or priest' which suggested that the veneration of a person had social status in society (Rollefson and Kafafi 2013: 19). The recent extraordinary evidence uncovered from the LPPNB Ba'ja in the southern Levant has illustrated a deliberate preparation of the internment context that seemingly related to the deceased's personal and social identity. The construction of the grave and the 'exceptional' grave goods uncovered in the grave, dedicated to the young adult male have (Benz *et al.* 2019: 1) prompted—for the first time—to the emergence of hierarchy and leadership in the LPPNB period.

Excavation evidence at the Neolithic sites revealed that small children and infants experienced sometimes a different than adults after death. The skull of children was sometimes removed and interred with adults and occasionally plastered. Moreover, the infant and juvenile remains were utilized in some instances for sacrifice as was the case at 'Ain Ghazal (Rollefson 1983) or the foundation deposit in Jericho and 'Ain Ghazal (Kenyon 1981; Rollefson 2000). In some instances, they were recognized with adult skulls at several sites (Benz 2012).

Excavation remains from the PN sites also suggest high child and infant mortality, and the interest in their burials is unequivocally clear (e.g., Campbell 1995; Moses 2004; Molleson, Andrews and Boz 2005; Akkermans 2008; Miyake *et al.* 2009; Erdal 2013; Helwing 2016). The ritual of foundation deposits, which were prevalent in the PPN period, continued into the PN period; however, few specimens were uncovered, such as in Tell el-Kerkh (Tsuneki 2002). Further, small children and fetuses were selected and interred inside different-shaped pottery vessels used as a body container. This depositional context and manner of interment are appeared for the first time in the PN period in the northern Levant and considered a fundamental characteristic of this period, which started with the invention of the pottery and invested it in funeral practices. This custom continued

into later periods, and several specimens have been uncovered (Orrelle 2008).

Evidence for the segregation of the burial location based on age was observed in a number of sites in this period, and children were selected to be buried separately. Excavations at Tell el-Kerkh in the Late Neolithic layers illustrated over-representation of small children and infants which raises questions about the spatial distribution of child burials these layers. Also, children at Sabi Abyad were buried separately from adults in Operation I, which not only indicates to the separation of the deceased based on age, but rather suggests changes in children's social status and social roles in society (Akkermans 2008). Excavations at Salat Cami Yanı in the Upper Tigris regions revealed a limited number of deceased, but notably, they were all infants. A similar pattern of infant burials was also detected from two other buildings. It seems that the burial of infants indoors was widely performed (Miyake *et al.* 2009).

Small children were also benefited from the funeral practice of skull removal, and their skulls were sometimes plastered. The evidence for the removal of the skull for infants and children at Tell el-Kerkh and plastering at Köşk Höyük indicates that children were not eliminated from this practice, but rather refers to a deliberate attention to children.

The diversity in the treatment of children and infants like adults and more in the PN period indicates a privileging interest. Moreover, interring children sometimes separately suggests that the age at death is a considerable issue. Hence, the treatment of the children suggests that socially, to a certain degree, they were recognized as individuals who have a role in society. Moreover, interring children in various contexts, sometimes with other members or in a separate context, would seem to suggest that children and infants had a status that was socially different from adults, which may perhaps indicate changes in social status.

The interest in children's mortuary treatment during the PN period has been widely affirmed in different regions (Gopher and Orrelle 1995; Orrelle and Gopher 2000; Eshed and Nadel 2015), which may promote the suggestion of interest in children's inhumation during the PN period. The variability of interment patterns may indicate special care, new ideology, and change in the belief system for dealing with the deceased, focusing on children is meaningful.

8. Whose Skull Was Removed?

Investigation at Tell el-Kekrh ritual practices indicates that the community members have employed mortuary practices on different age groups: adults, non-adults, and even small children. Some individuals underwent single-stage mortuary practices confined to primary internment after death; however, secondary multi-stage ritual practices were employed. Thus, the interaction between the living and dead is revived through participation in ritual practices that are probably arranged in advance.

Further investigation on human remains revealed a remarkable number of small children and young adult burials (around 20 years old). The high mortality of the males occurred during the young adult age and less during the middle adult age, whereas a large number of females experienced mortality during the young adult age. Examining the ratio of young adult male and female mortality indicates that maternal mortality was high, which suggests that the majority of young adult female mortality may have been due to risks of childbirth (Dougherty in Chapter 6). Furthermore, non-adult mortality was high and the number of fetal, perinatal, infant and juvenile's burials were remarkable. A large number of the population died below the age of three. The remarkable child mortality and childbirth risk mortality indicate the rough reality of life in Kerkh Neolithic society. In contrast, very few people survived beyond the age of fifty. Further, bioanthropological analysis revealed a high frequency of death between 1 and 3 years of age. The high frequency of juvenile death occurred due to poor health conditions (Dougherty 2011), which ultimately affected the health of the youngest within Neolithic society. Additionally, the presence of fetal, perinatal, and first-year infants within the skeletal sample suggests the existence of conditions that may have jeopardized maternal health.

Even though the Kerkh society appears to have experienced high fertility during the Pottery Neolithic (Dougherty in Chapter 6), the mortality rate was relatively high. It can be concluded that young adult females and small children have experienced a high mortality ratio, and their death was a frequent event that happens occasionally. The frequent death may require a commitment from the living toward their dead since death seems to be a recurrent event in the society. Hence, people were expressing their commitment to the dead through mortuary practices, which provided opportunities for community members to participate in the funerary after death or ritual ceremony that took place after months or years of death. Given the fact that many deceased at the cemetery underwent treatment after death, indicates that the selection was a significant matter. There must have been criteria for selecting the deceased for treatment postmortem, which might concern age, sex, the role of the deceased in the society or social status.

Pregnancy, childbirth, and death frequently occurred at Tell el-Kerkh. Investigations indicate that the

fertility rate in Kerch society was 5.62 births per female (Dougherty in Chapter 6), which is relatively high compared to the rates in modern societies. The frequent death of fetal/perinatal and children below three years in Kerkh society may have a major impact on the increased fertility to compensate for the birth deficiency, which, on the other hand, is a fundamental factor for high maternal mortality. Consequently, childbirth has been a major factor for young female mortality in Kerkh society. Thus, women played an important role in regenerating the society and bringing new members. Given that four of the adult skull removal specimens are females indicate attention to their death, which may reflect the important role they played in their households and in the society. Moreover, considering the possibility of pregnancy in young adult females (Str. 927) 'when' she died suggests that the criteria for selecting females for skull/cranium removal are probably related to maternal mortality.

On the other hand, the spatial analyses of the skull removal specimens in the cemetery illustrate the scale of practicing this custom. As mentioned formerly in Chapter 4, the common feature of aggregating the burials in the cemetery have illustrated the social structure of Kerkh society which consisted of a number of extended households buried in burial groups. The cemetery revealed at least 24 group burials including the collective burials and crematorium pits. Samples from seven groups within the cemetery were selected to compare the isotope values of collagen, glutamic acid, and phenylalanine (Itahashi *et al.* 2018). The results of the analysis indicated that the values varied with respect to each burial group. Variation in values indicate that individuals buried within each group consumed slightly different meat, even within the limited isotope range for this inland environment. It also suggests that they lived in close relationships, and ate together regardless of sex, age, and property. Thus, the results support the view that individuals at Tell el-Kerkh were buried along with those with whom they shared common dietary sources and were probably related and/or household members. Grouping the burials in the cemetery indicate that inhabitants have selected a part of the cemetery to bury their dead. Also, the dead were buried in designated places in the cemetery, and in some instances, the grave was surrounded by rows of limestones to identify the household burial. The assemblage of the burials and determining the location of the burial in the cemetery is meaningful indicates marking the burial place of the extended household.

Notably, eight headless individuals were uncovered from four household burials, whereas the other two burials were buried individually. Three groups contain more than one headless individual, which may indicate a prevalent burial custom among these groups. Group 4 in layer 4 uncovered three headless individuals (Str. 711, 714, 752). One individual (Str. 714) was discovered at the bottom of the concentration which seems to be the first whose cranium was removed and this individual was included in the isotope analyses. The other two individuals (Strs. 711 and 752) were at a higher level at the entrance of C2 and their skulls seem to have been removed later in different occasions. Group 2 in layer 5 uncovered two small children Strs. 1072 and 1074 (juvenile and infant) lacking their skulls. They were buried over each other and the skulls for both individuals were missing. It is unknown if they were buried together, but the skulls for both individuals seem to have been removed at the same time. Group 1 in layer 6 uncovered two headless females (Strs. 927 and 930(f.)), one had her skull removed, and the other her cranium. Further, both individuals were included in the isotope analyses, which indicates that living in close relationships (households). All headless specimens among the burial groups were intact, and no evidence for burial disturbance when the skulls/crania were retrieved. However, those who were buried or overlapped with other individuals in the same burial such as Strs. 927, 1072 and 1074 show evidence of disturbance. Probably, there were no intention to disturb the grave when the skull/cranium was retrieved except when necessary. It suggests that those who had retrieved the skulls were aware of the location of the burial or probably took part in the funerary ceremony.

Obviously, the practice of skull removal at Kerkh society was confined to a number of households. These households treated their deceased in different ways regardless of age and sex, which indicates the promotion of household autonomy. Hence, we argue that the skull removal practices in Tell el-Kerkh were subjected to changes in society's social structure in the PN period. This social change would be expressed through differences and variety in the treatment of certain individuals and material representation in burial contexts. Thus, this practice was undertaken on a limited basis that was confined to a few households who applied it to some of their deceased who may experience a special status at the household scale.

9. Manipulation and Circulation of Human Remains

Excavations at Tell el-Kerkh have illuminated the increasing diversity of ways that the remains of the dead were manipulated. As mentioned earlier, a large number of individuals in the cemetery seems to have been subjected to multi-stage treatments after death, which indicates that the burials were opened and closed periodically on numerous occasions. Initially, the deceased seems to have been buried intact, and after a span of time, some skeletal parts were retrieved,

cremated, relocated, and interred in the ultimate place (Figure 8-13). Given the multiple interment patterns and stages of funeral practices in Kerkh cemetery, the deceased seems to have been subjected to different scenarios that went through multiple stages of treatment.

The lack of visible cut marks on the analyzed skeletal remains infers that the deceased were initially buried intact and the remains were removed from the burial for subsequent treatment after the flesh completely or nearly skeletonized. The retrieved bodily parts might be buried even in the cemetery ground, as in the case of the detached skulls/crania, or they may have been buried in collective burials. Another scenario is that the retrieved parts were moved to the crematorium pit for cremation, and subsequently the cremated remnants were relocated from the pit to another locus. Unlike single-event primary interments, those whose skulls were removed, their remains were cremated, or those partially interred in the collective burials were subjected to multiple steps of treatment, and these activities have been recurrent in the cemetery. Hence, the diversity and different practices in the cemetery produced different experiences of dealing with the deceased after death.

A number of evidences from different burial types will be highlighted to illustrate the multiple stages of treatment that the deceased went through.

Re-considering that the secondary burials Str. 1052 was mentioned at the beginning of this chapter, it is obvious that this individual was exposed to different methods of aggregation or dispersal (Figure 8-14). The arrangement of the long bones, ribs, and the skull on the top of this heap suggest the impossibility of burying the body in this way immediately after death when the flesh was still fresh. The absence of several small bones, such as phalanges and vertebrae, indicates that this individual was probably interred somewhere in the cemetery. Then after decomposition, the burial was re-opened and specific parts of the skeleton were retrieved and relocated. The remains were deliberately arranged and ultimately buried in its final deposit within a group of burials. The small coarse pottery may be a personal belonging or had been used during the funeral ceremony, and then later placed there before burial closure. This individual was ultimately discovered within a cluster of five burials (including Str. 1052). Interring the deceased in the burial group might indicate a kin-relationship between the members who have been buried in this place.

On the other hand, the missing skulls/crania of the headless individuals and detached skull uncovered in different parts of the cemetery raises the question

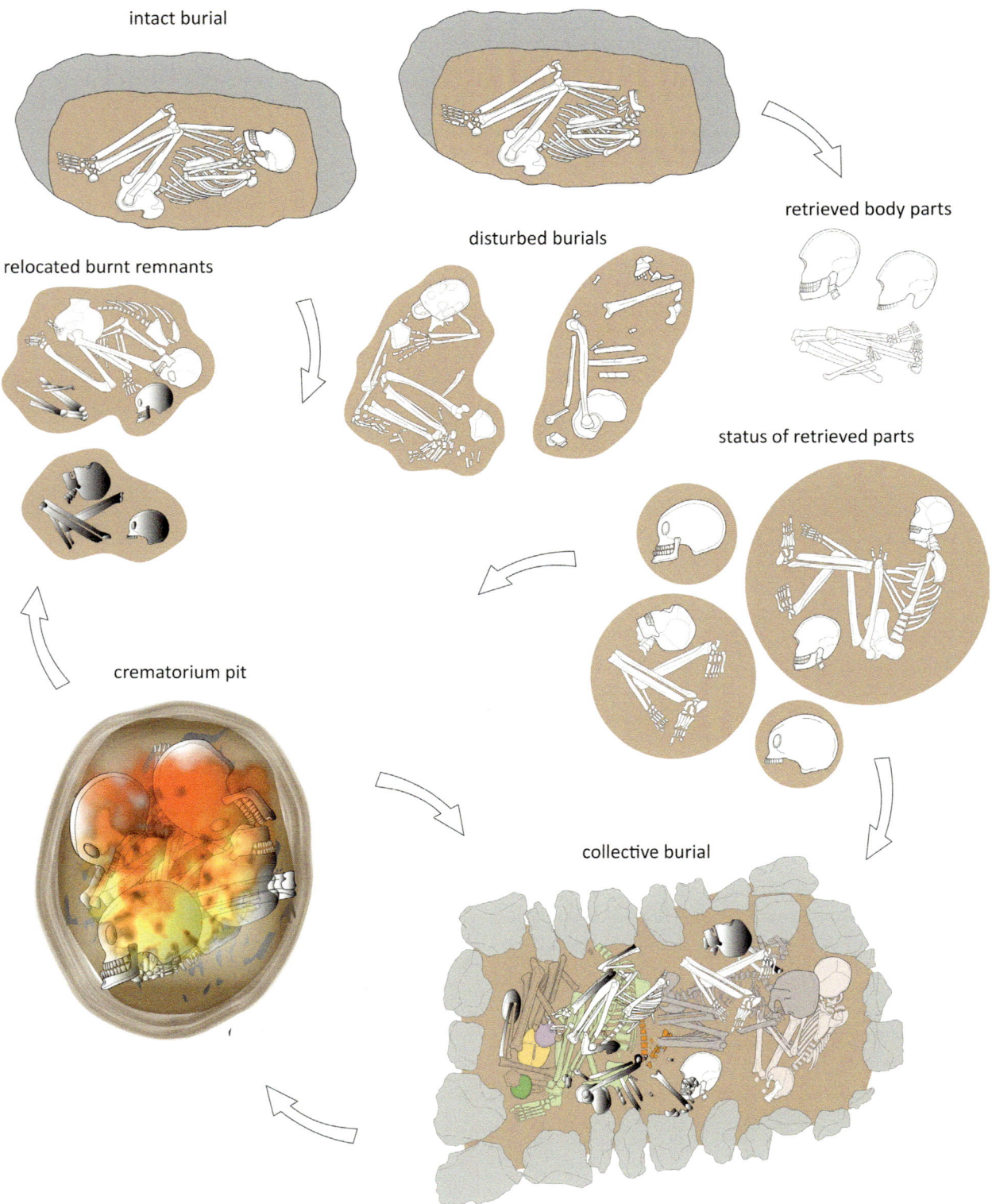

intact burial

retrieved body parts

relocated burnt remnants

disturbed burials

status of retrieved parts

crematorium pit

collective burial

Figure 8-13. Retrieval, manipulation, and circulation of human remains at Kerkh Cemetery.

where are the remnants of these skeletons? and why were they found in this status? So far, no skull cache has been uncovered in the cemetery. The presence of headless individuals and detached skulls in the cemetery creates the speculation that the headless skeletons and detached skulls could be matched. However, this speculation was elusive because the sex and age category of the headless individuals did not correspond with the detached skulls. Hence, the predominant scenario is that the detached skulls were retrieved from the original burial and eventually aggregated in a different context, which might be somewhere in the cemetery, in one of the collective burials, or crematorium pits.

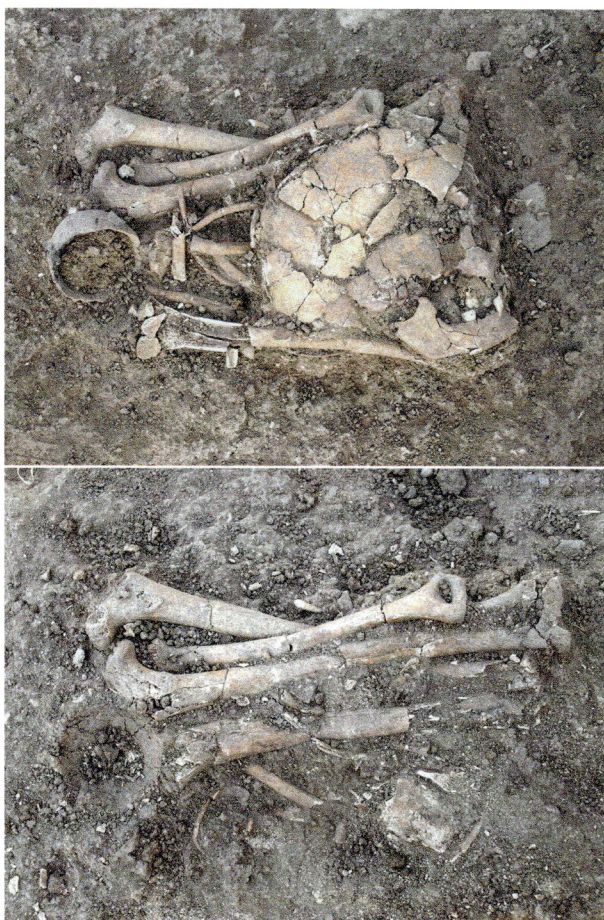

Figure 8-14. Str. 1052, a 12–13-years-old subadult.

The characteristics of collective burials and the disturbed status of the deceased in each context varied. (See Chapter 4: Collective Burial). Some of the deceased in collective burials were buried intact, whereas others lacked some body parts or were represented partly. Furthermore, isolated skulls/crania in some instances were also uncovered. The presence of small bones from the extremities suggests that some of these corpses were probably intact when interred, and might be later disturbed by successive interments or due to exhumed body parts from the grave. Therefore, some individuals may have been represented partly in the grave pit. Hence, the rest of their body parts may have been removed and buried in another context or *vice versa*. The detached body parts of some individuals may indicate that these parts were probably removed from their original grave and ultimately ended here.

The scenario becomes more complex when considering the cremation context. The cremated remains uncovered in different parts of the cemetery, suggests that the deceased were subjected to a multi-stage treatment. Hironaga in Chapter 9 in this volume classified the cremation burials in the cemetery into two types: primary and secondary cremation. The first type refers to the cremated and charred human

remains in the crematorium pit, whereas the second type refers to the re-located remains after the end of cremation. The skeletal remains in the crematorium pits 5 and 6 illustrate the fact that some human remains were still in articulation after the end of cremation. A mandible in the C5 is still in articulation with the cranium suggests that they were not decomposed, or at least, totally decomposed when cremated. Some of the bones seem to have been burned with soft tissue, which indicates that the bones were burned when they were not completely skeletonized. Furthermore, there were many small bones in the crematorium pits. Thus, one of the scenarios suggests that the bones were probably burned where they were excavated. This means that some deceased were buried directly in the crematorium pit because if the bones were retrieved from the original interment deposit after skeletonization and moved to the pit, smaller bones tended to get left *in situ*, and body parts were disconnected. Another scenario is that the time of death could have synchronized cremation practice. The corpse was cremated directly or after a short span of time of death before decomposition took place. Hence, the bones were still articulated when cremated. Given the small size of the crematorium pit, several complete bodies are difficult to accommodate. Therefore, the predominant scenario of the cremation process is that the bodies were at the beginning inhumated, then the burial dug up, bodily parts were retrieved, and then intentionally manipulated using fire and eventually relocated to its final deposit. In some cases, the presence of the soft tissue and articulated remains indicate that the retrieval took place prior to complete decomposition. Therefore, the body might have been dismembered prior to decomposition in some way, such as using sharp tools, but the condition of the cremated bones restricted the evidence.

Evidence for secondary cremation was observed in different places in the cemetery. Cremated human remains were uncovered besides unburned human remains in the collective burials or in other individuals' burials. The lack of traces of heat or changes in the soil color where these cremated remains were uncovered indicates that these remains were not cremated where they discovered (Hironaga in Chapter 9). Thus, the prevalent scenario suggests that, at the end of cremation, the remnant of burnt bones was removed from the crematorium pit and re-buried in various locations in the cemetery with another member's remains. Nevertheless, it is not clear whether these cremated remains were returned to the original burial from which they were initially retrieved.

10. Conclusion

The deceased at Kerkh cemetery was treated in different ways, and their bodies were transformed from one status to another at different rates before they were finally interred. The number of completely intact or untouched deceased after inhumation was small compared to those subjected to different rates and forms of manipulation. This suggests that postmortem treatment might be a prevailing custom in Tell el-Kerkh society. Based on these evidences, I tend to argue that interring the deceased right after death at Tell el-Kerkh might have been an interim step waiting for subsequent intervention, probably when the flesh nearly or completely decomposed, or when the ritual ceremony was determined. Hence, decomposition is a middle-stage procedure between the time of death and the reopening of the grave. This stage is necessary to facilitate the retrieval and relocation of body parts after flesh decomposed. If this suggestion is true, a question arises here: Is it possible in any case that cremation has been implemented to facilitate and accelerate flesh decomposition by fire? I would rather leave this discussion at that level for the moment because we do need further investigation and a deeper understanding of cremation and the role of fire in ritual activities in the PN period. However, we can elaborate that the postmortem treatments at Tell el-Kerkh may have aimed at enhancing social cooperation and strengthening ties between society members through participation in frequent ritual ceremonies. The diversity in mortuary practices and bodily treatment revealed from Kerkh cemetery provides us plenty of information that facilitates some degree of proposing interpretations of the way of life in the Neolithic period, beliefs about bodies, personality, and the relationship between the living and dead. The relationship between living and dead did not end at the moment of grave closure. In many instances, multi-stage funerary practices following death involved ceremonial performances to build social memory. Thus, it is argued that these behaviors were put forward to create social, collective memory, and community identity (Watkins 2015; Kuijt 2001).

In this paper, I opine that those who have selected the deceased for funerary practices and determined the burial place, and those who have performed and participated in the ritual ceremony after weeks or years postmortem are probably different. The selection of the deceased and the type of treatment might have related concepts perceived and performed on a household member's scope. However, other households and community members widely participated in ritual ceremonies. Ethnographic studies on mortuary practices and rituals (e.g., Metcalf and Huntington 1991; van Gennep 1960; Hertz 1960) provide important information for studying the rites of passage, interactions between living and dead, and the forms of corpse transformation. Therefore, I have clearly proposed in this study that the mortuary practice of skull removal, for instances, in the PN period (Tell el-Kerkh as a case study) reflected the impact of changes

in the social structure. The rituals were managed and controlled by household, and participation was a communal event. Therefore, the social structure might have played a role in decreasing the practicing of skull removal, and this funerary practice became a selective and private decision confined to a number of people. Perhaps those who were chosen have experienced a social status within a household-scale or experienced an important role or status in society.

The multi-households constituting Kerkh society might have created a form of a social system that eventually aimed to manage and maintain society and the social ties between its members. The social system might stimulate social ties and social cohesion between community members. Hence, participating in the ritual events, circulating and mixing the remains of the deceased in different burial contexts ultimately demonstrates the promotion of social unity and communal cohesion between all community members.

The diversity of funerary practices at Kerkh cemetery illustrates that the bodily remains were meaningful to the living and they demonstrate the commitment to the dead through funerals that might commemorate the deceased. Retrieving body parts including skulls, secondary treatment, and ultimately interred in a different context either within the collective burials, crematorium pits, or aggregating in groups within the cemetery seems to have been the predominant feature of the Kerkh cemetery. The bodies were interred with other individuals who had probably died before them in the same burial pit or in close proximity. The proximity of the graves and deceased bodies in the same inhumation space in the cemetery suggests that these people were defined as sharing close relationships and reflecting social groups of households living together and forming a community. Determining the location of the cemetery beside the habitation area where the daily activities take place and the living probably moved around, may evoke memories and sense of remembering the community's ancestry.

Parts of the body such as skulls and long bones were in some cases circulated in a range of interactions between people and the community's households. The collective and aggregate nature of the burials indicates a concern with relations between the dead, which probably reflects the nature of the relations between the living in return. Eventually, the retrieval, manipulation, and circulation of human remains were focused on the remains of the dead as part of a prevalent funerary custom in Tell el-Kerkh society. These practices ultimately led to the reinforcement of community members' relations by retrieving and aggregating the remains of their dead together in different and meaningful contexts.

Chapter 9 (Discussion 2)
The Meaning of Cremation

Naoko Hironaga

1. Introduction

Burnt human bones are sometimes found in graves, either inside or outside at Neolithic sites in West Asia. The remains were frequently burnt by accident because evidence for intentional cremation is scarce. However, burials including burnt bones were discovered at some sites dating to the Late Neolithic in recent decades, and evidence suggests that cremation practices were increasing. One of these sites is Tell el-Kerkh located in the northern part of Syria. Many burnt human bones were discovered from the cemetery in layers dating 6400-6100 cal BCE in the Central Area at Tell Ain el-Kerkh in Tell el-Kerkh.

This paper will classify the cremation burials discovered at Kerkh Cemetery into primary cremation type and secondary cremation type. Similarly, it will also classify cremations from the Pre-Pottery Neolithic to the Late Neolithic discovered from other sites. Later, this study will discuss the transition of the cremation types throughout the Neolithic in West Asia.

2. Ancient Cremations in West Asia

In West Asia, graves including intentionally incinerated human bones emerged in the Neolithic. Limited evidence of cremation was found from sites in various areas in West Asia (Figure 9-1). The mortuary practices of the Late Neolithic have various types: primary burial and secondary burial of single or multiple remains, urn burial, skull removal, and cremation (Akkermans and Schwartz 2003: 146-148). Even though cremation is recognized as one burial method, there has been limited discussion on this because the evidence for cremations is scarce. (e.g. Croucher 2012: 274-281; Sołtysiak and Fazeli Nashli 2016: 10; Lichter 2017: 119). Cremation in the prehistoric period is considered not only a disposal method for the deceased, but also included ritual elements (e.g. Croucher 2012; Kuijt 2000; Bienert 1991). Therefore, archaeological studies on cremation frequently focus on the social and ritual aspects, and a morphological classification for cremation is rarely undertaken.

Human bones with evidence of fire exposure that have been excavated from prehistoric sites are often referred to simply as 'burnt bones' because it is difficult to distinguish whether the temperature-induced changes were deliberately caused, or the result of accident. The act of intentionally burning bones and burying burnt bones is called cremation. Cremation is often used as a term to describe the entire burial practice involving burnt bones and its associated remains and structures. In addition, ritual and ceremonial practices were often implicit when considering the term, cremation.

Cremation practices can be classified into primary cremation and secondary cremation depending on the final burial place of the cremated bones (Quinn et al. 2014: 30). Primary cremation indicates a cremation whereby cremated bones were buried at the place of incineration, or in situ. Secondary cremation indicates a cremation where cremated bones were buried in a different place from the incineration location. In general, the terms 'primary burial' and 'secondary burial' indicate the stage of burial, whereas the terms 'primary cremation' and 'secondary cremation' indicate the difference between whether or not the burial place is the same as the incineration location. Depending on whether the cremated bones were deliberately moved may give a hint of the deceased's social information. (Quinn et al. 2014: 31; Cerezo-Román 2014: 162-166).

In general, the terms crematorium and pyre are often used to describe a place of incineration. When a pit is used for cremation in prehistoric West Asia, it is called a 'crematorium pit.' Furthermore, a burning place for cremation is also called a 'crematorium' and 'a cremation in situ', regardless of whether it is with or without a structure. (e.g. Merpert and Munchaev 1993: 212-215; Garstang 1953: 111). It is possible to distinguish a crematorium pit when a pit has an intense heat trace on its floor and inner wall, and also contains burnt human bones, ash, and carbonized materials. However, it should be considered as such even if there are few burnt bones, as most bones from the corpse may have been moved for secondary cremation.

Secondary cremation in prehistoric West Asia was frequently discovered in pits, in pottery and as a deposit within or without a structure (e.g. Merpert and Munchaev 1993; Kızıltan and Polat 2013). In many cases, the place of the secondary cremation was discovered

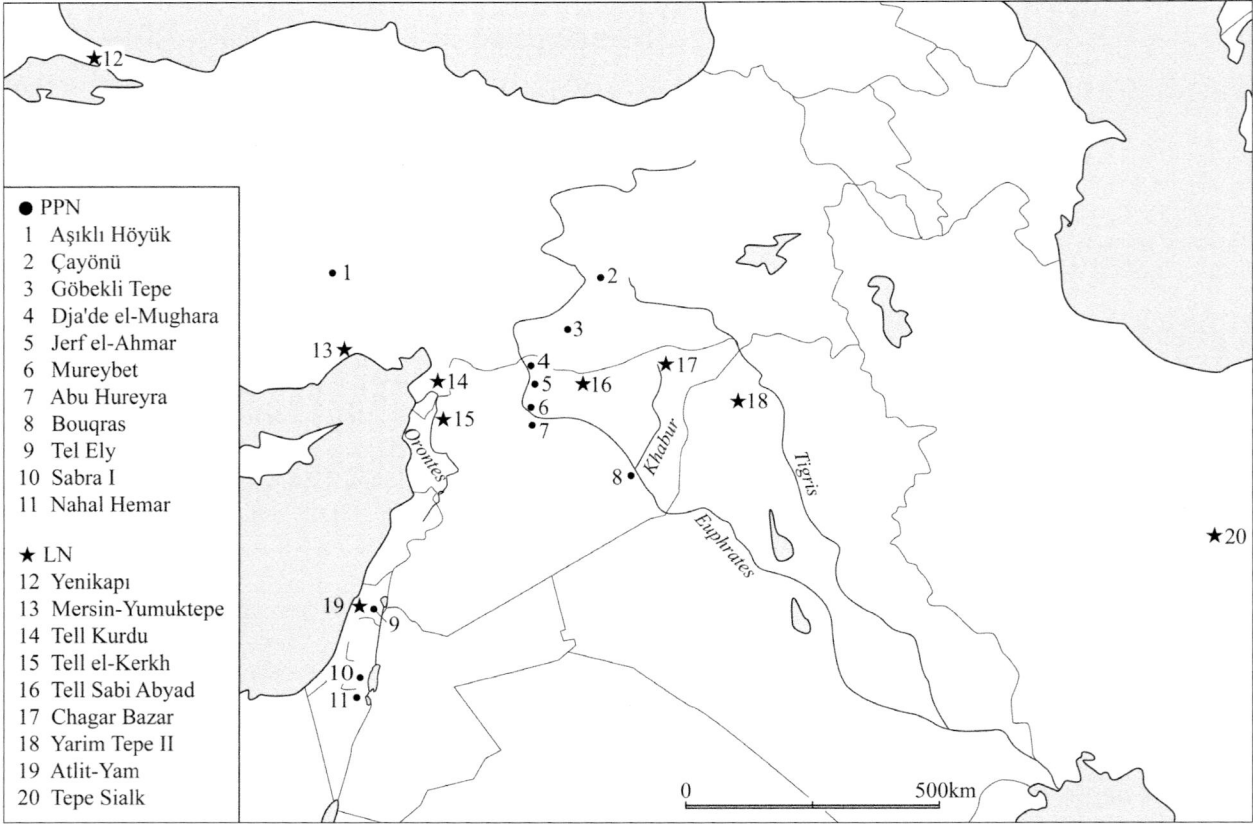

Figure 9-1. Map of the main sites discussed in this study.

and interpreted as the final burial place. However, it is possible these do not represent the final burial places because burnt bones might be abandoned or left behind during the middle stage of a secondary burial. Furthermore, they might be moved for disposal or burial to other places in cases when a structure or a pit was created after the cremated bones were buried. This might be judged as a secondary cremation.

Artifacts accompanying cremated bones can be classified as 'pyre goods' or 'grave goods'. The former are offerings to be burnt together with a corpse. The latter are offerings to be buried together with the cremated bones after cremation (Quinn *et al.* 2014: 29). Although the offerings are difficult to accurately categorize into pyre goods and grave goods, it may be possible to identify the type depending on the presence of heat exposure and the excavation context.

3. Cremation at Tell el-Kerkh

At least 46 individuals in 9 cremation burials were discovered from Kerkh Cemetery during excavations from the 2007 to 2010 seasons (Tsuneki *et al.* 2011). The cremation burials were discovered at the southeast section in the lower layers of Kerkh Cemetery (Figure 9-2).

Both the primary cremation and the secondary cremation were present in Kerkh Cemetery. At least 17

individuals from C5, C6 and C9 are classified as primary cremations (Table 9-1). All of these were discovered in crematorium pits (Figure 9-3). These pits contained burnt human bones, ashes and carbonized materials and carbonized pieces of wood. Furthermore, the inner walls and bottom of the pits were intensely burnt and had turned orange color. At C6, two floor surfaces were recognized. After the older pit was used for cremation, the newer pit was probably expanded to the east side, later used again as a crematorium. A few mud plaster traces remained on the wall of the northwestern section of the newer pit. At the bottom of C9, very thin black organic material was observed. Most of the burnt human bones in C5 and C6 had turned a white or bluish white color indicating that they were burnt at high temperatures. In addition, a lot of skulls and long bones kept their original shape. At C9, burnt bones that turned black and dark brown color from the end of the pit were also found which indicates incineration at a low temperature. In all of these cases, there was no evidence that cremated bones were moved from other places to these pits after cremation. This is because some of the remains were articulated in spite of mixing with the ash and carbides that filled the pit. However, some of the bones such as the skull and long bone of several skeletons were found together in the pit from C5 and C6 in particular. Probably, the corpses were disarticulated due to decay and skeletonization before cremation. They were probably then collected in a similar way to a secondary burial and placed in

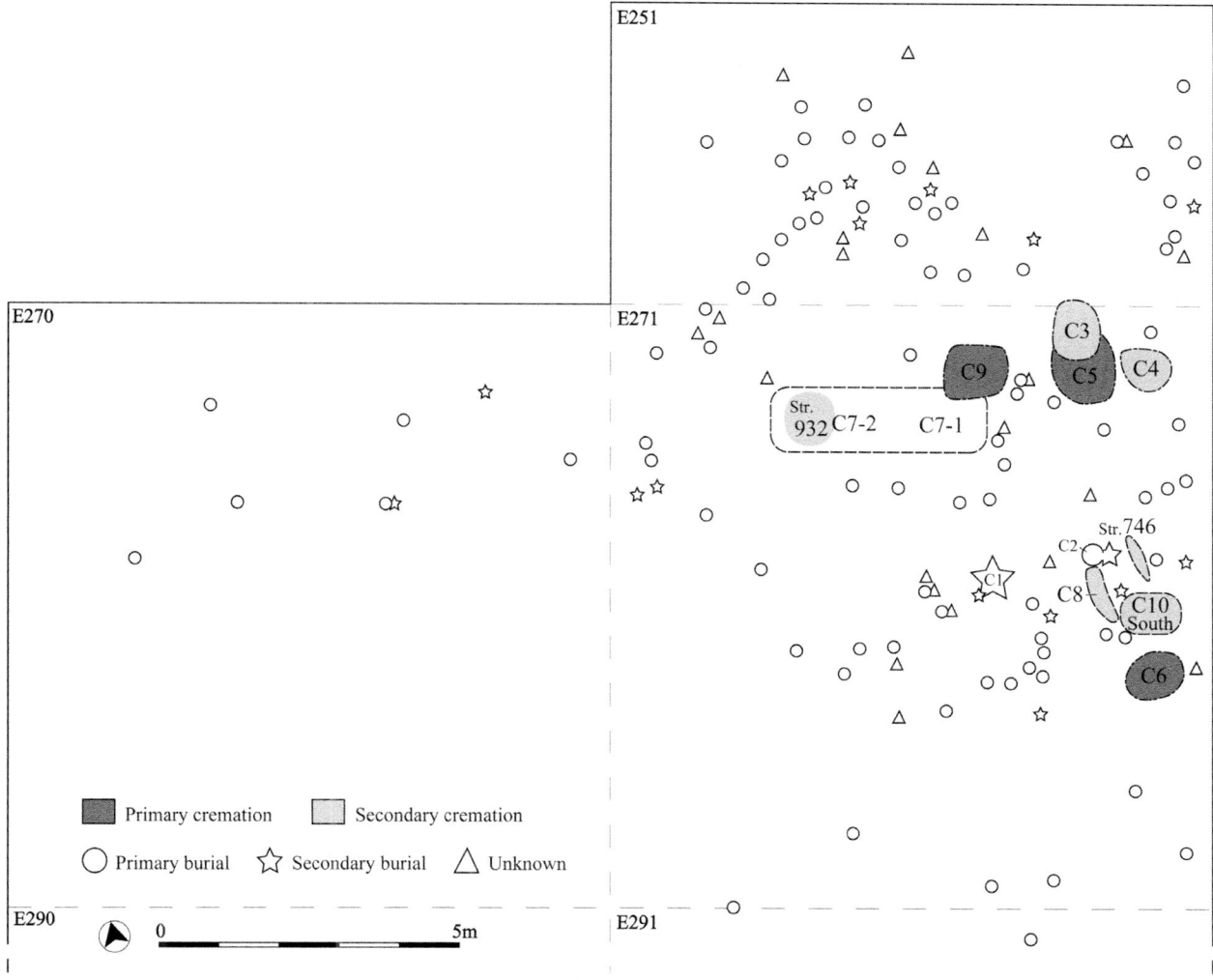

Figure 9-2. The Kerkh Cemetery.

the crematorium pit. The author inferred that several individual skeletons were cremated at the same time in one pit (Hironaga 2011).

In the primary cremation category, there are 17 individuals including 10 adults, 2 sub-adult and 5 juveniles (Table 9-2). There is no difference between sex in the adults, and burnt human bones under 1 year old and over 50 years old were not found. Around five individuals might have been cremated in one pit at the same time, though the number of individuals cremated in each pit in C6 was unknown. The burnt bones found from C6 could be a mixture of bones cremated in the older and newer pits. However, the bones cremated in the older pit could have been moved to other pits or locations as a secondary cremation site when the C6 pit was expanded.

Artifacts were found above every primary crematorium pit (Figure 9-4). A short necked dark faced burnished ware (DFBW), and a squat typed DFBW jar were recovered from C5. Furthermore, the former contained a bone stamp seal. A mass of carbonized wheat and a row of small stones were found in C6. Perhaps, the

carbonized wheat was burnt there after cremation. A stone ball was found in C9. It is a sphere with a diameter of about 14cm, and the surface is polished and it is made of limestone. It is inferred that they are grave good offerings or grave markers after cremation. On the other hand, a small necked DFBW jar was found at the bottom edge of the C6 pit, and two grains of carbonized emmer wheat were found inside. These probably represent the pyre goods burned during cremation. Perhaps, this might have been a vessel to contain an offering of wheat for the dead.

At least 29 individuals from 6 burials are classified as secondary cremation (Table 9-1). Among them, at least 19 individuals from 4 contexts were recovered from a pit. The excavated situation of C3 and C4 is very similar. At least 21 individuals including 7 burnt individuals and 14 non-burnt individuals were recovered from an oval shaped pit of around 1m × 0.7m in C3. At least 7 individuals including 3 burnt individuals and 4 non-burnt individuals were recovered from an oval shaped pit of around 0.8m × 0.7m in C4. In both cases, the burnt human bones and the non-burnt human bones were mixed and were piled up. On the other hand, at least 3

Table 9-1. Categorization of cremation burials from Kerkh Cemetery.

No.	Location	Layer	Primary cremation Crematorium pit	Secondary cremation Pit	Secondary cremation Deposit	Artifact and feature	Age and sex	Mixed unburnt bones
Str. 746	E271b	4			✓		Juvenile: 2	
C3	E251d, E271b	5		✓			Adult, female: 2 Adult, male: 1 Adult: 2 Juvenile: 1 Unknown: 1	✓
C4	E271b	5		✓			Middle adult, male*: 1 Adult, female*:1 Adult, male*: 1	✓
Str. 932	E271a	6		✓			Adult, male: 1 Subadult: 1 Juvenile: 1	✓
C5	E271b	6	✓			DFBW: 2 Stamp seal: 1 Oval pit (1.05m x 1.25m, Depth: 0.4m)	Middle adult, male*: 1 Young adult, male*: 2 Adult, female*: 1 Subadult, female*: 1	
C6 Upper	E271d	6	✓			Carbonized wheat A row of small stones Oval pit (1.0m x 0.8m, Depth: 0.2m)	Adult, female*: 2 Adult: 1 Juvenile: 4	
C6 Lower			✓			DFBW: 1 Circular pit (0.6m x 0.6m, Depth: 0.3m)		
C8	E271d	6			✓	Drill: 1 DFBW fragments	Old adult: 1 Adult, male*: 1 Adult: 2 Subadult: 1 Juvenile: 2 Infant (birth-3mos.): 1	
C9	E271b	6	✓			Stone ball: 1 Brack organic matter Rectangular pit (1.03m x 0.9m, Depth: 0.15m)	Adult: 3 Subadult: 1 Juvenile: 1	
C10 South	E271b	6		✓		DFBW: 1	Adult: 4 Subadult (10-14yrs.): 1 Perinatal: 1	

* probably

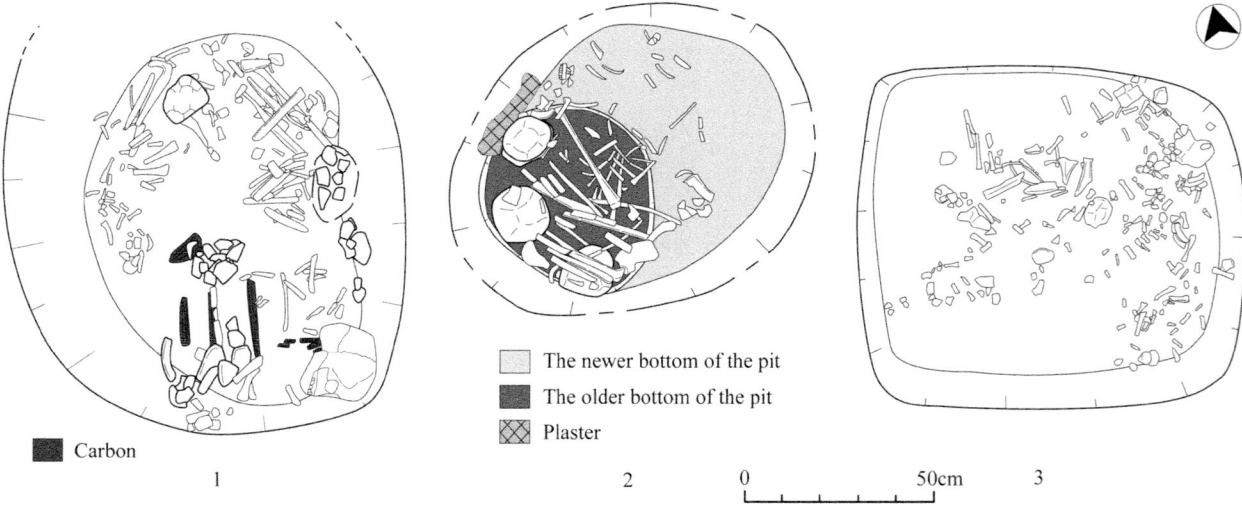

Carbon

The newer bottom of the pit

The older bottom of the pit

Plaster

1   2   0   50cm   3

Figure 9-3. Crematorium pits in Kerkh Cemetery: 1. C5; 2. C6; 3. C9.

burnt individuals and at least 4 non-burnt individuals were mixed and were scattered in the pit in Str. 932 (C7-2). The C10 south pit contained 6 only burnt individuals, and the burnt bones were broken into small pieces.

At least 10 individuals from 2 burials are classified as deposit type (Table 9-1). In Str. 746, part of the skull and long bones of mainly juveniles were found. Most of the burnt human bones in C8 were found in small fragments. Several pieces from DFBW bowls covered

Table 9-2. Age and sex of cremated individuals from Kerkh Cemetery.

		Fetal	Perinatal	Infant	Juvenile	Subadult	Adult	Young adult	Middle adult	Old adult	Unknown	Total
Primary cremation	Male											0
	Probable male							2	1			3
	Female						2					2
	Probable female				1		1					2
	Unknown				5	1	4					10
	Total	0	0	0	5	2	7	2	1	0	0	17
Secondary cremation	Male						2					2
	Probable male						2		1			3
	Female						2					2
	Probable female						1					1
	Unknown		1	1	6	3	8			1	1	21
	Total	0	1	1	6	3	15	0	1	1	1	29
Total		0	1	1	11	5	22	2	2	1	1	46

Figure 9-4. Offerings from the crematorium pits in Kerkh Cemetery: 1. C5; 2. C6; 3. C9; 4-a. A DFBW and a stamp seal from C5; b. A DFBW from C5; c. A DFBW from C6; d. A stone ball from C9.

the cranial bones of one individual. This is considered the same as the burial method of covering a corpse with fragments of pottery widely found in the Late Neolithic sites of West Asia (Akkermans 2008: 623-624; Gerritsen and Sholts 2004: 71). The deposit depth is approximately 1.5m × 0.5m. There was no heat mark within the soil. A burnt pit containing ash and carbide was excavated close by, however human bones were not found in the pit.

From these secondary cremation burials, most burnt human bones had turned a bluish and white color indicating that they were burnt at high temperature. Furthermore, heat-induced changes were not present inside the pit and in the deposit soil. Therefore, it is suggested that these remains were intentionally cremated, and then transferred there from a crematorium.

Grave goods accompanying the secondary cremations were only found in C8 and in the south of C10. A flint drill was found between the burnt human bones in C8. An upright DFBW bowl was recovered from the southeast bottom of the southern pit in C10. A few dozen grains of carbonized wheat were found from the inside of this bowl. This is similar to the carbonized wheat that was recovered from the jar at the bottom of the C6 pit. In secondary cremations, the artifacts accompanying burnt bones were found from burials in the low layer. The rate of offering found in secondary cremations is less than that in primary cremation.

4. Transition in Cremation Practices

4-1. Pre-Pottery Neolithic

Burnt human bones have been already found at a few sites, Kebara Cave (Turville-Petre 1932; Bar-Yosef and Sillen 1993) and Wadi Hammeh 27 (Webb and Edwards 2002) in the South Levant and Beldibi Cave in Anatolia (Bostanci 1959), towards the end of the Paleolithic in West Asia. It is unclear whether the heating of the burnt human bones found at the sites are intentional or accidental. As a result of research on Kebara cave, Bar-Yosef and Sillen indicated that, 'the skeletal parts may be not randomly tossed into the fire but that some systematic procedure was involved' (Bar-Yosef and Sillen 1993: 207).

In the Pre-Pottery Neolithic, burnt human bones have been found from the sites located in the middle Euphrates river basin, in addition to those from other periods and regions (Figure 9-1). Among these are ambiguous cases of intentional burning like some examples from Sabra I (Gebel 1988: 78), Nahal Hemar (Arensburg and Hershkovitz 1988: 50), Mureybet (Özbek 1976: 161), Abu Hureyra (Moore and Molleson 2000: 280) and Göbekli Tepe (Gresky, Haelm and Clare 2017: 7).

On the other hand, evidence that human bones were intentionally burnt was also found. At Aşıklı Höyük located in Anatolia, the human bones of 26 individuals with evidence of burning were found under the floor of the room with the hearth. These bones belonged to adults, children and infants. The relevance between the burial and the hearth is unknown, however burning on the bones could possibly be due to their being near the hearth (Le Mort et al. 2000: 46; Özbek 1998).

At Çayönü, 71 skulls and some post-cranial remains with signs of high temperature exposure were found from the upper layers of the Skull Building. A lot of burnt human bones have also been found in the lower layers. The building was intentionally burnt to destroy, and the corpses probably were burnt together during the destruction (Le Mort et al. 2000: 40; Özdoğan 1999). At Jerf el-Ahmar located in the middle Euphrates river basin, three human skulls with heat marks were deposited on a hearth covered by stone (Jammous and Stordeur 1996: 28; Stordeur, Helmer and Willcox 1997: 284; Stordeur and Abbès 2002: 583). Also, at Dja'de el-Mughara, two skulls with evidence of burning have been found from under the floor (Le Mort et al. 2000: 46). At Bouqras, burnt human bones were found in the building called the 'Charnel house' (Merrett and Meiklejohn 2007; Akkermans et al. 1983). Merrett and Meiklejohn indicated, 'Because there is no evidence for purposeful burial for any of the Bouqras individuals, the evidence suggests part of a process of ritual preparation of human remains for secondary ceremonial treatment.' (Merrett and Meiklejohn 2007: 136). At Tel Ely located in the southern Levant, burnt human bones were found along with parts of the animal bones and horns. It is suggested that they are ritually buried remains (Haas 1974: 36).

Except for cases where the detection is unclear in the Pre-Pottery Neolithic, two cremation cases were found from buildings, which appear to have been burnt intentionally, and four cremation cases were found from a context in which heat-induced soil changes were not recognized. The former is probably not a cremation for burial, although the act of the burning a building perhaps included a ritual act that incorporated human remains. The latter two cases were probably related to the skull cult.

As mentioned above, in the Pre-Pottery Neolithic, most intentional burnt human bones were found within buildings or under floors. Furthermore, most of them probably relate to some ritual or secondary burial. Secondary burial was a very common burial method in the Neolithic of West Asia.

At the sites mentioned above, the discovery of a headless skeleton on the floor of a building possibly inferred intentional destruction by fire (Jerf el-

Ahmar); skull removal (Tel Ely); a large number of under-floor burials (Athıklı Höyük); and 'Maison des Morts' (Dja'de el-Mughara) and the 'Skull Building' (Çayönü) are considered to be special buildings for burials. They are considered to indicate the existence of skull cult or some similar ritual. Furthermore, the acts of intentionally destroying a building by fire were occasionally seen at some sites dating to the Neolithic (Croucher 2012: 274-276). The cremation incorporating ritual acts were carried out in the Pre-Pottery Neolithic as a result of combining the act of using fire in rituals with the development of secondary burial techniques that often contain ritual elements.

4-2. Late Neolithic

In the Late Neolithic, cremated human bones were discovered from Yarim Tepe II (Merpert and Munchaev 1993) in northern Iraq, Tepe Sialk (Sołtysiak and Fazeli Nashli 2016) in the Iranian plateau, Yenikapı (Kızıltan and Polat 2013) in northwestern Anatolia, Mersin-Yumuktepe (Garstang 1953) in southwestern Anatolia, Tell Kurdu in the northern Levant (Özbal 2006; Yener et al. 2000), and Tell Sabi Abyad (Verhoeven 2000) in the Balikh river basin (Figure 9-1). In cases like Atlit-Yam and Chagar Bazar, it is unknown whether the human bones were burnt intentionally (Hershkovitz and Galili 1990: 325; Mallowan 1936: 44).

A total of four cases from Yenikapı, Mersin-Yumuktepe, and Tell Sabi Abyad were classified as primary cremations (Table 9-3). There are two crematorium pit types, one cremation accompanied by a destroyed building and a deposit type. The crematorium pits are all oval shaped, less than 1m in diameter, and had changed color due to the fire (Kızıltan and Polat 2013: 125). It is suggested that the cremation at Tell Sabi Abyad is a result of ritual, and not a normal burial as it was accompanied by the act of destroying the building intentionally by fire. Therefore, the excavator indicated that it seems that these two persons had a special social status (Verhoeven 2000: 56). The deposit at Mersin-Yumuktepe is a mass cremation in situ (Garstang 1953: 111). Artifacts accompanied all of the primary cremations. Perhaps, one pottery from Yenikapı is a pyre good because it was found below the burnt human bones (Kızıltan and Polat 2013: 125).

The 26 cases from Yenikapı, Tell Kurdu, Yarim Tepe II, and Tepe Sialk were classified as secondary cremations (Table 9-3). There are 5 pit types, 18 urn types and 3 deposit types (Kızıltan and Polat 2013; Ghirshman 1939; Yener et al. 2000; Merpert and Munchaev 1993). The pit type includes burials at Tell Kurdu and Yarim Tepe II. Most pits are oval shaped, though each size is different. The age of cremated individuals has been identified in some cases. They included both infants and adults, and were buried in single contexts. Artifacts were found

from 3 out of 5 pits. Furthermore, all contained pottery or pottery shards. Some of the pottery shards were deliberately smashed (Yener et al. 2000: 209; Merpert and Munchaev 1993: 212).

The urn type includes burials at Yenikapı, Tell Kurdu, Yarim Tepe II and Tepe Sialk. The excavators of Yarim Tepe II regarded burials 40 and 43 as primary cremations (Merpert and Munchaev 1993: 215-217). However, even though it can be inferred that the urn containing burnt human bones of the burial 40 was buried in the crematorium pit, it seems reasonable to classify the burnt human bones as a secondary cremation because they were moved to the urn. Similarly, Burial 43 was classified as a secondary cremation because cremated human bones were recovered from an urn.

Therefore, for the purpose of this paper these instances are classified as secondary cremations. All urns except the one from Tepe Sialk were found in close proximity with other urns at each site. Most of the urns were jar or vase shapes because it is probably easier for these shapes to accommodate human bones. Cremated human bones in the urns belong to infants, adolescents or adults. At Tell Kurdu, it is assumed that cremated human bones belonging to the same individual were divided into three urns, and were placed as a foundation deposit (Özbal 2006: 294).

Artifacts were found accompanying burial 40 in Yarim Tepe II. Some of the vessels were deliberately shattered (Merpert and Munchaev 1993: 215). In addition, some of the vessels were found from a pit assumed to be a crematorium near where the burial 43 was excavated. It is inferred that they were deliberately broken and thrown into the fire during the cremation ritual (Merpert, Munchaev and Bader 1977: 92). Therefore, they can be classified as pyre goods.

The deposit type in secondary cremation includes burials at Yenikapı, Yarim Tepe II and Tepe Sialk. The deposit from Tepe Sialk was found from the same place as the urns (Ghirshman 1939: 10). Vessel sherds that were probably smashed on purpose accompanied both deposits at Yenikapı and Yarim Tepe II. However, there are differences in the interpretation of the two deposits. Kızıltan and Polat described the Yenikapı deposit as 'it seemed as if the bones and pottery sherds scattered in the area are from one or more destroyed cremation vessels' (Kızıltan and Polat 2013: 125). Conversely, the Yarim Tepe II deposit was interpreted to be an instance where vessels were deliberately shattered and burned during or after the cremation event. Later the vessel fragments were moved with the cremated human bones to another area (Merpert and Munchaev 1993: 212).

In the summary, the same types of cremations were discovered from the same period layers at

Table 9-3. Categorization of cremation burials dating to the Late Neolithic.

Site	Period or level Excavation area	No.	Primary cremation			Secondary cremation			Artifact and feature	Age and sex
			Crematorium pit	Destroyed building	Deposit	Pit	Urn	Deposit		
Yenikapı	Yarimburgaz 4 style Marmaray sector						✓			
							✓			
							✓			
							✓			
							✓			
							✓			
							✓			
								✓		
		Cremation pit No.1	✓						Vessels Oval pit (0.95m x 0.84m)	
		Cremation pit No.2	✓						Beads and a vessel Oval pit (0.81m x 0.64m)	
Mersin-Yumuktepe	Level XIX Area 234	(vi)			✓				Vases and a few sherds	
Tell Kurdu	Amuq C Trench 7, North mound					✓			Jar	Adult, male: 1
	Later phase Area E, North mound	Burial 25:8					✓			Adult, female* (20-40yrs.): 1
							✓			
							✓			
Tell Sabi Abyad	Level 6 Burnt village, Operation I	Room 7, Building V		✓					Large clay objects	Adult, male: 1 Adult, female (30yrs-): 1
Yarim Tepe II	Level 7 Square no.23	Burial 40					✓		Beads (within urn), vessels, a cup, a plate, miniature vessels, a spindle whorl, shells, pendants and beads.	10-13yrs.: 1
		Burial 43					✓			ca.10yrs.: 1
	Level 8-9 Square no.23	Burial 50				✓			Vessels fragments Oval pit (0.7m x 0.3m)	Adult: 1
		Burial 51						✓	Vessels fragments Round area (0.9m-1.0m)	Adult: 1
		Burial 52				✓			Oval pit (0.25m x 0.35m)	Juvenile: 1
		Burial 53				✓			Oval pit (1.16m x 0.53m)	Juvenile: 1
		Burial 54				✓			Vessels fragments, a spindle whorl, a bone bit and a polished red stone fragment. Oval pit (1.25m x 0.43m)	
Tepe Sialk	Period I Trench II, North mound						✓			Infant (lower age): 1
								✓		Infant: 1
	Sialk I.4 (Late neolithic II) Trench V	C5091					✓			Infant: 1
		C5102					✓			ca.15yrs.: 1
		C5110					✓			Adult (25-30yrs.): 1
		C5112					✓			Adult, male* (30-50yrs.): 1
		C5113a,b					✓			Adult, female*: 1

* probably

many sites. This indicates that a specific type of cremation was mainly used at a certain period of the site. Almost all cremations were discovered inside or outside of a structure within a settlement. The primary cremations comprise only four out of thirty cases. Perhaps, in this period, there might have been more cremated human bones that were removed from a crematorium than those buried in situ after cremation. In secondary cremations, urn type burials account for more than half of the burials. The potteries, especially jars, were frequently used as coffins for primary or secondary skeletons since the Late Neolithic, when pottery emerged. Similarly, it is obvious that the pottery played the role of a coffin for cremated human bones. Furthermore, some cremations from Tell Sabi Abyad and Tell Kurdu probably included specific ritual acts related to a building. Artifacts were found from eight of thirty cremations. It is a noteworthy point that artifacts accompanied all primary cremations. In secondary cremations, the presence of artifacts is rare. Furthermore, all artifacts with secondary cremations were found in pit type burials.

5. Cremation as Burial and Ritual

The sites in which the burnt human bones were discovered were located in central Anatolia, the Euphrates valley and the south Levant in the Pre-Pottery Neolithic. In the Late Neolithic, the practice diffused to north-western Anatolia and the Plateau of Iran (Figure 9-1). Furthermore, some evidence of cremations were also reported in the sites located in the Balkans in the same period. This suggests that the cremation custom was not only widely carried out in West Asia, but also its neighboring region in the Late Neolithic (Gallis 1982; Bacvarov 2004).

The excavated states of cremated human bones have common features in each period throughout the Neolithic (Figure 9-5). In excavated cases the details were evident, burnt human bones were discovered indoors and showed relationships with a hearth until the 9th – 8th millennium BCE. Then, burnt human bones began to be discovered within special buildings for burials since the 8th – 7th millennium BCE. In the Pre-Pottery Neolithic, the burnt skeletons were buried in a

Figure 9-5. Transition of types of cremation throughout the Neolithic.

similar location as non-burnt skeletons (e.g. Akkermans and Schwartz 2003: 145-149; Koutsadelis 2007). In 7th – 6th millennium BCE, the number of burnt human bones increased. Furthermore, the burnt human bones were found not only indoors but also outdoors. Evidence of crematorium pits were uncovered from layers of the second half of the 7th millennium BCE at Tel el-Kerkh for the first time in West Asia. The urn type of secondary cremation was not found in Kerkh Cemetery within the early layers of the Late Neolithic, although covering cremated skeleton by fragments of pottery was performed at Kerkh Cemetery. Urns for cremation became widely used in each site from 6th millennium BCE. On the other hand, the act of deliberately burning a building with deceased continued since the Late Neolithic.

Secondary cremation was continuously carried out in West Asia throughout the Neolithic. It is difficult to know the condition and location of the burnt human bones between being cremated and later buried in secondary cremation. However, it is assumed that burnt human bones might have been used in some ritual from the discovery of burnt skeletons, for example, those related to the Skull Cult and associated with animal bones and horns. Perhaps the act in itself to burn human bones was even a ritual. This implies that secondary cremation had a temporal and spatial distance between cremation and the final burial because the burnt human bones might finally have been buried after their use in some ritual and completing their role.

Some primary cremations obviously show a relationship between the act of destroying a building and the act of burning a dead body in the Neolithic. It is assumed that these practices are cremations as rituals. On the other hand, primary cremations were found in the crematorium pit with no relation to a building like the cases at Tell el-Kerkh and Yenikapi. In these instances, the burnt human bones do not appear to be associated with ritual practice, such as those for ancestors or destroying buildings. In other words, cremation exclusively for a funerary purpose appeared for the first time in the Late Neolithic. Crematorium pits found from Kerkh Cemetery probably represent the oldest evidence of such primary cremation discovered so far. Furthermore, primary cremations from Kerkh Cemetery were probably closely related to secondary burial, since there were cases with disarticulated skeletons that were decaying and going through skeletonization before cremation.

In the Neolithic of West Asia, the practice of cremation might have emerged as a from a combination of secondary burial, rituals, and fire. Therefore, it can be inferred that a process of cremation practices included not only a funeral but also other rituals unrelated to burial. The succession of secondary cremation and the emergence of primary cremation in the Late Neolithic probably represent gradual changes in rituals in addition to a transition in burial practices.

6. Conclusion

The burnt human bones were treated as secondary burials throughout the Pre-Pottery Neolithic. In the Late Neolithic, the previous period's cremation methods continued to be practiced. At the same time, pottery emerged in this period and was often used as urns and for ritual breakage in a cremation. Furthermore, primary cremation unequivocally unrelated to the act of destroying a building appeared. It was revealed that the cremation had various forms, and the form changed over time. It is suggested that various forms may represent some different rituals because cremation is not only related to a funeral but also a ritual with fire. It is inferred that the cremation form gradually changed due to social background including rituals and the development of pyro-technology from the Pre-Pottery Neolithic to the Late Neolithic. In the transition, both forms of primary cremation and secondary cremation probably existed in some sites during the same period. Perhaps the existence of primary and secondary cremations during the same period at Kerkh Cemetery meant a coexistence of two different concepts toward cremation among the Kerkh people.

Chapter 10 (Discussion 3)

Stable Isotope Analyses of Human and Animal Bones at Tell el-Kerkh

Yu Itahashi and Minoru Yoneda

1. Introduction

The Northern Levant region was a locus of 'Neolithization', and changes in subsistence that occurred in the region were presumably reflected in the content and/or quantity of food consumed by Neolithic populations. Thus, in this study, in an attempt to analyze the human diets of Neolithic communities in the Northern Levant, we employed stable carbon and nitrogen isotope analysis of bone collagen and nitrogen isotope analysis individual amino acids to detect dietary changes occurring between PPNB and PN periods. Palaeodietary reconstructions based on stable isotopes in bone collagen have been used in previous archaeological studies to provide direct information on past human activity (Schoeninger and DeNiro, 1984). In the Near East, a number of studies have been conducted on isotopic compositions of remains of Neolithic populations, such as at Çatalhöyük (Richards *et al.* 2003; Styring *et al.* 2015), Nevalı Çori (Lösch *et al.* 2006), Aşıklı Höyük (Pearson *et al.* 2010), Çayönü Tepesi (Pearson *et al.* 2010, 2013), Hasankeyf Höyük (Itahashi *et al.* 2017), Hakemi Use (Itahashi *et al.* 2019) and Aktopraklık (Budd *et al.* 2013).

In addition to determining the carbon and nitrogen isotope ratios of bulk collagen, we determined the nitrogen isotope values of individual amino acids in collagen. The method has recently been applied in studies of ancient animal and human remains (e.g., Naito *et al.* 2010, 2013; Styring *et al.* 2010, 2015; Itahashi *et al.* 2014; 2017; 2019). Because this approach is based on a difference in the trophic isotope discrimination of two common amino acids (glutamic acid and phenylalanine), the trophic position (TP) of an organism can be estimated independent on the isotope values of food resources (Chikaraishi *et al.* 2014). Therefore, analysis of the nitrogen isotope values of individual amino acids enables assessment of the trophic position of humans without being affected by variations in the isotope values of bulk protein among animals, provided the humans consumed only terrestrial herbivores as animal protein.

In order to detect an immigrant to a community from other region, strontium isotope analysis is useful in the archaeological studies (Sillen 1986; Hoppe *et al.* 2003; Kusaka *et al.* 2011). Because strontium equilibrates between animal and plant body tissue and drinking water originated from a surface water, strontium isotope value of animal and plant is similar to that of water in the habitat. Because tooth enamel is not replaced after the formation in childhood, strontium isotope value of tooth enamel shows a value in a region living in childhood even if the individual migrated to the other region.

In the present study, we measured isotope analyses of bulk collagen, individual amino acids and tooth enamel in Neolithic samples from Tell el-Kerkh. Based on these data, we obtained information about the diets of the populations in these areas, which allowed us to interpret temporal changes in human diets and social structure in the Northern Levant throughout the entire Neolithic period, thus allowing a comparison of the isotope signatures of human remains during Neolithic period.

2. Materials

In this study, we extracted collagen for carbon and nitrogen isotope analyses from the Tell el-Kerkh samples, including from 7 human skeletons and 26 animal bones from the PPNB layer, 99 human skeletons and 21 animal bones from the PN layer. Animal bones were including cattle or aurochs (*Bos* sp.), pig (*Sus scrofa*), sheep (*Ovis* sp.), goat (*Capra* sp.), gazelle (*Gazella* sp.), hare (*Lepus* sp.), dog (*Canis lupus*), fox (*Vulpes* sp.) and freshwater fishes (Cyprinidae). In addition, we carried out the same collagen and amino acid isotope analyses on 18 human bones and 12 animal bones, including those from cattle, pigs, sheep, goats, and freshwater fishes (Cyprinidae) of PN layer and 4 human bones of PPNB layer.

Cereal remains collected from square E271 of PN layer 6 at Tell el-Kerkh have predominantly been identified as Emmer (*Triticum turgidum* ssp. *dicoccum*) (Tanno and Willcox 2006b); we analyzed the carbon and nitrogen isotope values for 10 grains of Emmer wheat to provide a baseline for analysis of vegetable diets consumed by humans at Tell el-Kerkh.

And for strontium isotope analysis, we prepared 14 enamels of human molar and 7 enamels of rodent incisor, probably mouth, from the PN layer.

3. Methods

Charred kernels were prepared by non-based pretreatment, using a method based on previous research (Kanstrup *et al.* 2014). The charred kernels were cleaned by ultra-sonication in Milli-Q water for 10 min at room temperature, washed by soaking in 0.1M HCl for 10 min at room temperature to remove attached carbonate, rinsed repeatedly with Milli-Q water, freeze-dried, and then milled to a fine powder. The percent carbon (%C) and nitrogen (%N) and the stable isotope compositions of carbon (δ^{13}C) and nitrogen (δ^{15}N) were measured.

Collagen samples (i.e., gelatin consisting mainly of collagen) were extracted from bones by gelatinization, based on improvements of the methods used in previous research (Longin 1971; Yoneda *et al.* 2002). First, the bone fragments were cleaned by brushing and ultrasonic cleaning. Then the bone fragments were cleaned by Milli-Q water and ultrasonic cleaning in Milli-Q water. Then bones setting in small cellulose tube put in 0.4M HCl to remove hydroxyapatite two nights at 4°C. To remove humic acid and fulvic acid, bone fragments are soaked in 0.1M NaOH and centrifuged for 5 minutes three times followed by removing supernatant fluids. Then the samples were then washed with Milli-Q water. The remains were heated in pH 4 HCl water at 90°C for two nights to extract the gelatin, and the dissolved gelatin was then filtrated and freeze-dried to obtain collagen samples.

The stable isotope values of the collagen and charred kernel samples were determined by an elemental analyzer–isotope ratio mass spectrometer (EA–IRMS) (Flash 2000 EA coupled to a MAT 253 IRMS; Thermo Fisher Scientific) at the National Museum of Nature and Science in Japan and (Flash 2000 EA coupled to a Delta V Advantage IRMS) at the University museum of the University of Tokyo. Analytical errors (1σ) for nitrogen and carbon were < 0.2‰ based on USGS-40 and also were checked in each measurement by ten replicate analyses of reference alanine and histidine after analysis of every six unknown samples (SI Science Co., Ltd). The purity of the collagen samples was evaluated on the basis of the carbon (%C) and nitrogen (%N) content in the extracted collagen samples. The atomic C/N ratio was expected to be in the range of 2.9–3.6 (DeNiro 1985), and extracted gelatin yields were expected to be >1% (Ambrose 1991); otherwise, data were eliminated from discussion.

The δ^{13}C is represented as proportion of sample to standard limestone (belemnite) from the Pee Dee

Formation in South Carolina, called PDB and the values are usually presented by per mil.

$$\delta^{13}C\ (‰) = [(^{13}C/^{12}C)_{sample} - (^{13}C/^{12}C)_{PDB}] / [(^{13}C/^{12}C)_{PDB}] \times 1000$$

Similarly, δ^{15}N is represented as proportion of sample to atmospheric N_2 and the values are usually presented by per mil.

$$\delta^{15}N\ (‰) = [(^{15}N/^{14}N)_{sample} - (^{15}N/^{14}N)_{AIR}] / [(^{15}N/^{14}N)_{AIR}] \times 1000$$

The isotope value of body tissues is more positive than that of dietary materials, by 0.5‰ for the δ^{13}C value of collagen ($\delta^{13}C_{col}$) (Ambrose 1991). Furthermore, the difference in the δ^{15}N value of collagen ($\delta^{15}N_{col}$) between prey and predators was initially considered to be 3.4‰, but has recently been found to be up to 5‰ (Minagawa and Wada 1984, McCutchan *et al.* 2003; Hedges and Reynard 2007). Consequently, the values for foods were calculated by applying these corrections to the bone collagen composition.

For bone samples, amino acids were extracted from approximately 2mg by hydrolysis of the collagen sample with 12M HCl at 110°C for 12h, after which they were derivatized for isotope analysis following the method of Chikaraishi *et al.* (2010). The hydrolyzed samples were reacted with 1:4 (v/v) thionyl chloride:2-propanol at 110°C for 2h, followed by treatment with 1:4 (v/v) pivaloyl chloride:dichloromethane at 110 °C for 2h. The amino acid derivatives were extracted by liquid-liquid extraction using 3:2 (v/v) n-hexane:dichloromethane and distilled water.

The δ^{15}N values of the amino acids were determined by gas-chromatography–combustion–isotope-ratio mass spectrometer (GC–C–IRMS) (Agilent 6890GC, coupled to a ThermoFinnigan DeltaplusXP IRMS via a Combustion III interface to oxidize the derivatives at 950°C and reduce the NO_x produced in a furnace at 550°C) using a programmable temperature vaporizing (PTV) injector (Gerstel) at the Japan Agency for Marine–Earth Science and Technology (JAMSTEC) and GC–C–IRMS (TRACE1310GC, coupled to a Thermo Finnigan Delta V Advantage IRMS via a GC Isolink II interface for oxidation at 950°C and reduction at 550°C) using a PTV injector at the University museum of the University of Tokyo. The amino acid derivatives were injected onto an HP Ultra–2 capillary column (50m; i.d. 0.32mm; film thickness 0.52μm; Agilent Technologies). The carrier gas (He) flow rate was controlled to be 1.4mL min⁻¹ in constant flow mode. Standard mixtures of ten amino acids (alanine, glycine, valine, leucine, norleucine, aspartic acid, methionine, glutamic acid, phenylalanine, and hydroxyproline; SI Science Co., Ltd), with known δ^{15}N values, were analyzed every five runs. The analytical precision (1σ) for replicate analyses of the reference amino acids was < 0.5‰ for samples containing amino acids with more than 2nmol N. The error in the estimated trophic position was 0.20 (1σ; Chikaraishi *et al.* 2010), 0.13 (Chikaraishi *et al.* 2009) and 0.14 (Chikaraishi *et al.* 2014) determined by the ratio of estimated TPs to the theoretical values in controlled feeding experiments using different terrestrial plants and animal species that have a variety of feeding habits. Furthermore, the TPs of aquatic ecosystems are calculated differently to those of terrestrial ecosystems based on difference of the margin of $\delta^{15}N_{Glu}$ and $\delta^{15}N_{Phe}$ between primary producers in aquatic ecosystems such as cyanobacteria, phytoplankton and algae and in terrestrial ecosystems such as vascular plants (Chikaraishi *et al.* 2007, 2010, 2014):

$$TP_{aqua} = [(\delta^{15}N_{Glu} - \delta^{15}N_{Phe} - 3.4)/7.6] + 1 \text{ for aquatic ecosystems}$$

$$TP_{ter} = [(\delta^{15}N_{Glu} - \delta^{15}N_{Phe} + 8.4)/7.6] + 1 \text{ for terrestrial ecosystem}$$

Chikaraishi *et al.* (2010) reported standard deviations in the difference between the $\delta^{15}N_{Glu}$ and $\delta^{15}N_{Phe}$ values for aquatic photoautotrophs (0.9‰) and C_3 plants (1.6‰); thus, each calculation included errors of 0.12 for aquatic ecosystems and 0.20 for terrestrial ecosystems (1σ; for details, see Chikaraishi *et al.* 2010). Although broad beans (legume) showed a TP_{ter} value (1.0) that was similar to the value for common C_3 plants, based on the amino acid analysis method in our study (Steffan *et al.* 2013, 2015; Chikaraishi *et al.* 2014; Itahashi *et al.* 2019), Styring *et al.* (2014) reported that legumes (broad beans and peas) had TP_{ter} values that differed from those of C_3 plants.

For a measurement of strontium isotope (^{87}Sr/^{86}Sr), a purification of strontium from teeth was conducted based on improvements of the methods used in previous research (Sillen 1986; Hoppe *et al.* 2003; Kusaka *et al.*

2011). At first, a dental drill equipped with a tungsten carbide burr is used to abrade the tooth enamel. Tooth enamels were washed by Milli-Q water followed by removing the supernatant. Sodium hypochlorite (2.5%) was used for over night to eliminate organic matters from the enamel and centrifuged, and then the supernatant was discarded. After washing by Milli-Q water, buffered acetic acid solution (0.1M, pH 4.4) was used to eliminate diagenetic contaminants from the enamel. The samples are immersed for 4 hours in the acetic acid solution, and then the supernatant is discarded. After washing, samples are dried during 1 night in an oven at 60°C. Then, 14M HNO_3 was added sample vials, and samples were dried on the hotplate at 200°C. The samples were dissolved to 2M HCl, and strontium (Sr) was separated chromatographically by using a cation exchange resin (DOWEX 50x8, 200-400 mesh).

Strontium isotope ratios were measured on a tungsten filament with thermal ionization mass spectrometer (TIMS) (a Thermo Fisher Scientific TRITON) at the Research Institute for Humanity and Nature (RIHN) in Japan. The analytical precision (1σ) was checked by ten replicate analyses of the NIST SRM 987. The ^{87}Sr/^{86}Sr of each sample was normalized by the standard reference material of the NIST SRM 987. As a local value of ^{87}Sr/^{86}Sr, a mean and 2 standard deviations by that of enamel of rodents such as mouse from Tell el-Kerkh were used.

4. Results

4-1. Stable Isotope Compositions of Charred Kernels

The δ^{13}C and δ^{15}N values for the 10 Emmer wheat grains from Tell el-Kerkh are presented in Table 10-1 (Itahashi *et al.* 2018). Isotope analyses of charred cereals from archaeological sites in Syria have shown that the δ^{15}N values for cereals prior to the commencement of cultivation are higher than those after cultivation was established (Araus *et al.* 2014). The mean δ^{15}N value for

Table 10-1. Isotopic results for wheat grains from Tell el-Kerkh (Itahashi *et al.* 2018). %C is the percentage of carbon in the charred samples. %N is the percentage of nitrogen in the charred samples.

Sample No.	δ^{13}C	δ^{15}N	%C	%N	Layer	Species	Period
STR840-01	−22.7‰	2.4‰	62.5%	3.8%	Layer 6	*T. turgidum* ssp. *dicoccum*	PN
STR840-02	−23.1‰	1.3‰	61.3%	3.9%	Layer 6	*T. turgidum* ssp. *dicoccum*	PN
STR840-03	−22.5‰	2.2‰	62.1%	4.6%	Layer 6	*T. turgidum* ssp. *dicoccum*	PN
STR840-04	−22.5‰	1.8‰	61.5%	4.8%	Layer 6	*T. turgidum* ssp. *dicoccum*	PN
STR840-05	−22.5‰	2.2‰	65.7%	3.7%	Layer 6	*T. turgidum* ssp. *dicoccum*	PN
STR840-06	−21.6‰	3.6‰	65.4%	3.4%	Layer 6	*T. turgidum* ssp. *dicoccum*	PN
STR840-07	−22.5‰	1.5‰	63.8%	4.5%	Layer 6	*T. turgidum* ssp. *dicoccum*	PN
STR840-08	−21.7‰	2.2‰	71.4%	4.5%	Layer 6	*T. turgidum* ssp. *dicoccum*	PN
STR840-09	−22.6‰	2.4‰	63.4%	3.9%	Layer 6	*T. turgidum* ssp. *dicoccum*	PN
STR840-10	−22.7‰	2.1‰	63.4%	3.9%	Layer 6	*T. turgidum* ssp. *dicoccum*	PN

the Emmer grains from Tell el-Kerkh (2.2 ± 0.6‰; mean ± 1σ) was lower than that for Einkorn wheat from Tell Qaramel, a PPNA site in the northern Levant (6.1‰), but similar to the value for Durum wheat (*Triticum durum*) from Tilbeshar, a Bronze Age site (1.7‰) (Araus *et al.* 2014).

4-2. Faunal Isotopic Compositions of Collagen

We attempted to extract collagen from 26 animal bones from PPNB layer, and 22 samples showed C/N ratios typical of biological materials (2.9–3.6) (Table 10-2). In addition, 16 mammal bones and 5 freshwater fish bones from PN layer were treated by gelatinization, and 15 mammal samples and only a fish specimen showed biological C/N ratios (Itahashi *et al.* 2018; Table 10-2). Some of samples with C/N ratios out of the biological range were excluded from the following discussion. The $\delta^{13}C_{col}$ and $\delta^{15}N_{col}$ values from faunal samples are plotted in Figure 10-1 and Figure 10-2.

At Tell el-Kerkh, *Bos* exhibited the highest $\delta^{15}N_{col}$ values (7.9 ± 0.5‰ for PPNB and 7.7 ± 0.6‰ for PN; mean ± 1s.d.) of all terrestrial herbivores. *Sus* exhibited

a wide range of $\delta^{15}N_{col}$ values (5.7 ± 1.1‰ for PN and mean, 6.5 ± 1.8‰ for PN). In *Ovis*, the mean $\delta^{15}N_{col}$ values were 7.2 ± 1.0‰ for PPNB and 6.1 ± 0.6‰ for PN. In *Capra*, the mean $\delta^{15}N_{col}$ value was 6.7 ± 2.5‰ for PPNB and 4.6 ± 1.1‰ for PN, which is lower than that of other ruminants. Among ruminant species, significant variability was observed in $\delta^{15}N_{col}$ values, which is similar to that observed at other Neolithic sites in Anatolia, including at Hasankeyf Höyük (Itahashi *et al.* 2017), Nevalı̇Çori (Lösch *et al.* 2006), Çayönü Tepesi (Pearson *et al.* 2007, 2013), Çatalhöyük (Richards *et al.* 2003; Pearson *et al.* 2013) and Hakemi Use (Itahashi *et al.* 2019). Two *Vulpes* showed $\delta^{15}N_{col}$ values of 9.2‰ and 9.6‰, which were higher than that of other herbivores, reflecting its habit as a carnivore. And these values were higher than a dog from PPNB (7.6‰). A cyprinid freshwater fish showed a $\delta^{15}N$ value of 11.0‰, which is higher than that of other terrestrial animals, suggesting that isotope values within each species maintain their ecological signatures with respect to collagen values.

In Çatalhöyük, because *Ovis* and *Bos* have higher $\delta^{13}C_{col}$ values than those of typical C_3 plant consumers

Table 10-2. Isotopic results for faunal skeletal remains from Tell el-Kerkh. C/N is the atomic ratio of carbon to nitrogen. %C is the percentage of carbon in the gelatin. %N is the percentage of nitrogen in the gelatin.

Period	Sample-No.	Genus	$\delta^{13}C_{col}$	$\delta^{15}N_{col}$	C/N	%C	%N	$\delta^{15}N_{Glu}$	$\delta^{15}N_{Phe}$	TP_{ter}
PPNB	KB02	*Bos*	−18.9	7.6	3.3	38.8	13.7			
	KB03	*Bos*	−20.1	7.1	3.5	44.1	14.7			
	KB04	*Bos*	−21.1	8.5	3.4	44.6	15.5			
	KB16	*Bos*	−19.0	8.0	3.2	42.7	15.7			
	KB17	*Bos*	−17.0	8.2	3.2	39.4	14.4			
	KB07	*Ovis*	−20.0	7.7	3.3	40.6	14.5			
	KB14	*Ovis*	−21.6	5.8	3.5	44.2	14.7			
	KB21	*Ovis*	−20.8	7.0	3.7	46.8	14.8			
	KB13	*Ovis*	−20.3	8.1	3.2	39.2	14.2			
	KB15	*Ovis*	−19.7	7.3	3.2	43.9	15.8			
	KB05	*Capra*	−18.2	9.6	3.2	35.2	12.7			
	KB06	*Capra*	−20.4	7.0	3.7	42.6	13.5			
	KB11	*Capra*	−20.7	5.1	3.2	39.9	14.5			
	KB12	*Capra*	−20.5	5.4	3.4	43.3	14.8			
	KB08	*Sus*	−20.1	5.4	3.2	43.1	15.9			
	KB09	*Sus*	−20.5	4.3	3.5	45.9	15.1			
	KB18	*Sus*	−20.5	6.5	3.8	42.0	12.8			
	KB19	*Sus*	−19.3	6.8	3.2	34.7	12.5			
	KB20	*Sus*	−19.8	6.1	3.3	33.2	11.8			
	KB01	*Gazella*	−17.4	6.8	3.3	39.0	13.9			
	KB22	*Gazella*	−21.2	6.5	3.2	34.3	12.3			
	KB23	*Lepus*	−21.2	5.7	3.2	41.9	15.1			
	KB27	*Lepus*	−19.6	6.8	2.5	12.1	5.7			
	KB28	*Lepus*	−21.3	5.8	3.1	40.7	15.2			
	KB24	*Canis*	−19.2	7.6	3.5	42.3	14.0			
	KB25	*Vulpes*	−19.2	9.2	3.3	37.3	13.3			

Table 10-2. Continued.

Period	Sample-No.	Genus	$\delta^{13}C_{col}$	$\delta^{15}N_{col}$	C/N	%C	%N	$\delta^{15}N_{Glu}$	$\delta^{15}N_{Phe}$	TP_{ter}
PN	KP17	*Bos*	−20.8	7.2	3.3	40.2	14.3	9.4	9.6	2.1
	KP19	*Bos*	−20.1	8.0	3.6	47.9	15.5			
	KP21	*Bos*	−20.9	7.1	3.5	41.4	14.0	9.5	9.2	2.1
	KP22	*Bos*	−21.3	8.3	3.4	41.4	14.0	9.5	9.7	2.1
	KP02	*Ovis*	−21.0	6.8	3.4	45.5	15.4	9.7	9.3	2.2
	KP04	*Ovis*	−20.9	5.7	3.3	42.4	15.1	7.6	8.7	2.0
	KP23	*Ovis*	−22.0	5.1	3.7	44.0	14.1			
	KP06	*Capra*	−21.2	3.4	3.6	45.2	14.6	7.4	8.9	1.9
	KP08	*Capra*	−20.9	5.6	3.2	40.9	14.8	9.3	9.6	2.1
	KP27	*Capra*	−21.8	3.9	3.4	45.6	15.4	8.6	10.1	1.9
	KP01	*Sus*	−20.0	5.1	3.3	44.8	15.7	9.7	8.5	2.3
	KP06	*Sus*	−20.9	5.7	3.3	41.5	14.7			
	KP12	*Sus*	−20.5	8.1	3.3	40.7	14.2			
	KP14	*Sus*	−20.0	6.8	3.3	39.1	14.0	10.6	10.5	2.1
	KP19	*Sus*	−19.9	8.8	3.4	46.5	16.1	14.2	12.4	2.3
	KP25	*Vulpes*	−18.7	9.6	3.3	40.6	14.3			
	KP38	*Cyprinidae*	−24.8	11.8	4.7	37.5	9.4			
	KP39	*Cyprinidae*	−21.4	9.9	3.8	32.3	10.0	21.4	3.0	4.5
	KP40	*Cyprinidae*	−21.1	15.2	3.8	42.0	12.8			
	KP41	*Cyprinidae*	−20.5	11.0	3.0	40.2	15.4	20.7	3.2	4.4
	KP81	*Cyprinidae*	−21.6	11.5	4.2	34.2	9.4			

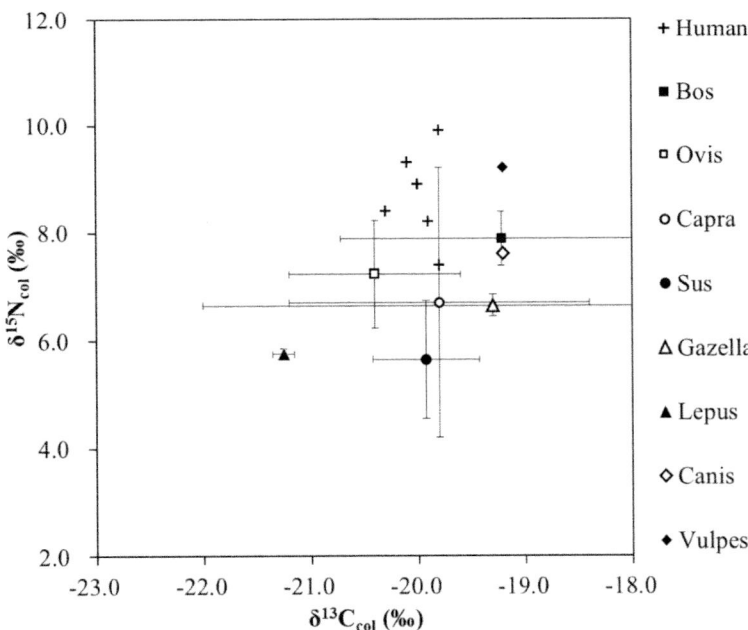

Figure 10-1. The $\delta^{13}C_{col}$ and $\delta^{15}N_{col}$ of human individuals from PPNB layer plotted with mean isotope values for fauna from PPNB layer (bars represent 1σ values) at Tell el-Kerkh.

the $\delta^{13}C$ values of herbivores were very similar to one another, around −21‰ although fox exhibited a $\delta^{13}C$ value of −18.7‰. The low $\delta^{13}C$ values of terrestrial herbivores from PN (approximately −20‰ or less) show that they consumed little or no C₄ plant material.

4-3. Human Isotopic Compositions of Collagen at Tell el-Kerkh

We determined the carbon and nitrogen stable isotopic compositions of six human bone samples from the PPNB layer at Tell el-Kerkh (Table 10-3). Of the 99 human bones in the PN layer at the same site, 89 were analyzed for carbon and nitrogen isotopic compositions (Table 10-4). None of the cremated skeletons contained sufficient collagen required for measurements.

(which is empirically defined by $\delta^{13}C_{col} \leq$ −18‰) it has been suggested that some livestock fed on C₄ plants (Richards *et al.* 2003; Pearson *et al.* 2015). As the remains of a *Bos* and a *Gazella* from PPNB layer, despite expected wild, showed $\delta^{13}C_{col}$ values ≥ −18‰, it is likely that they consumed C₄ plants. By contrast, in PN layer

The PPNB human bones were dated at 8800–9500 cal BP (Table 7-2), which is in close agreement with charcoal dates from the late PPNB (Chapter 7). Human remains from the PN cemetery were dated to 7600–8400 cal BP (Table 7-4).

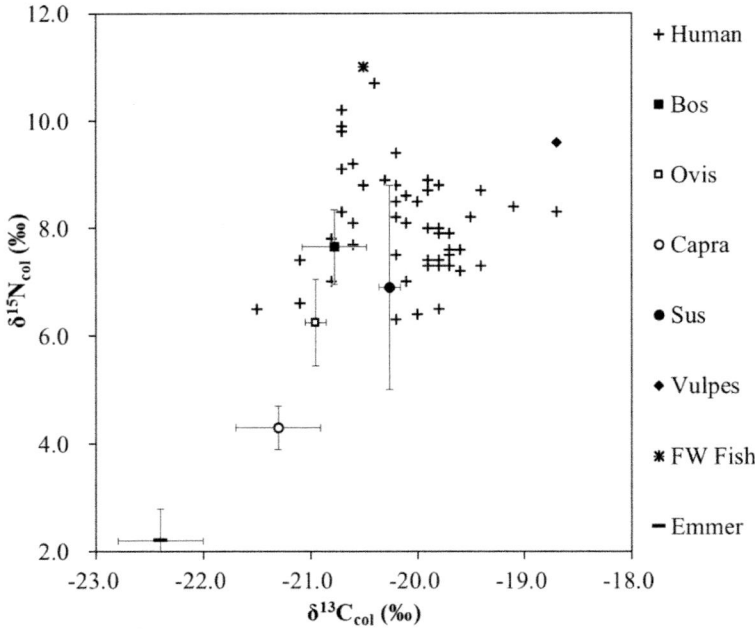

Figure 10-2. The $\delta^{13}C_{col}$ and $\delta^{15}N_{col}$ of human individuals from PN layer plotted with mean isotope values for fauna and cereals (emmer) from PN layer (bars represent 1σ values) at Tell el-Kerkh.

The $\delta^{13}C_{col}$ and $\delta^{15}N_{col}$ values of all humans are shown in Figures 10-1 and 10-2 and Tables 10-3 and 10-4. Because the stable isotopic compositions of breast-feeding infants are higher than those of the mothers (Fuller *et al.* 2006, Tsutaya *et al.* 2013, Reynard and Tuross 2015), we excluded infants under 4 years old from the study. By the result, the mean $\delta^{13}C_{col}$ value of PPNB samples at Tell el-Kerkh was –20.0 ± 0.2‰, and the mean $\delta^{15}N_{col}$ value was 8.7 ± 0.9‰. In addition, the mean $\delta^{13}C_{col}$ value of PN samples was –20.1 ± 0.5‰, and the mean $\delta^{15}N_{col}$ value was 8.1 ± 1.0‰.

Among the individuals of PN layer, mainly adult, there was a wide range of collagen carbon and nitrogen isotope values, which may be a result of the variety of species consumed and the scale of meat consumption. However the $\delta^{13}C_{col}$ and $\delta^{15}N_{col}$ values did not differ significantly between males (n = 19) and females (n

= 15) ($\delta^{13}C_{col}$: p = 0.25; $\delta^{15}N_{col}$: p = 0.50), as well as with (n = 19) and without (n = 28) the inclusion of burial goods ($\delta^{13}C_{col}$: p = 0.05; $\delta^{15}N_{col}$: p = 0.94). Differences in gender and burial goods among individuals at Tell el-Kerkh did not show any correlation with the isotope values of collagen.

4-4. Faunal Nitrogen Isotopic Compositions of Amino Acids by GC–C–IRMS

Freshwater fish and terrestrial herbivores from Tell el-Kerkh could be distinguished by the nitrogen isotope values of phenylalanine and glutamic acid (Itahashi *et al.* 2018; Figure 10-3). The $\delta^{15}N_{Phe}$ values for pigs at Tell el-Kerkh ranged from 8.5 to 12.4‰, and the $\delta^{15}N_{Glu}$ values ranged from 9.7 to 14.2‰. In contrast, the $\delta^{15}N_{Phe}$ values for other ruminants were similar and ranged from 8.9 to 9.7‰, while the $\delta^{15}N_{Glu}$ values ranged from 7.4 to 9.7‰. The trophic positions of ruminants were estimated based on the terrestrial equation, and were similar (*Bos*: 2.1; *Ovis*: 2.1; *Capra*: 2.0). Despite the variation in $\delta^{15}N$ values of bulk bone collagen among terrestrial animals, the pattern was consistent with the expected trophic positions of ruminants as primary consumers. The estimated trophic position of *Sus* was 2.2, which was higher than that for the ruminants. This trend of domestic pigs having TP_{ter} values slightly higher than those for domestic ruminants is similar to that for wild animals (wild ruminants: 2.0; wild boars: 2.1) at Hasankeyf Höyük and domestic animals (domestic ruminants: 2.0; domestic pigs: 2.2) at Hakemi Use (Itahashi *et al.* 2019) in southeastern Turkey (Itahashi *et al.* 2017). Interestingly, although

Table 10-3. Isotope compositions of collagen ($\delta^{13}C_{col}$ and $\delta^{15}N_{col}$), glutamic acid ($\delta^{15}N_{Glu}$) and phenylalanine ($\delta^{15}N_{Phe}$) for human skeletal remains from the PPNB layer at Tell el-Kerkh. C/N is the atomic ratio of carbon to nitrogen. %C is the percentage of carbon in the gelatin. %N is the percentage of nitrogen in the gelatin. ND is non determinant.

Sample-No.	$\delta^{13}C_{col}$	$\delta^{15}N_{col}$	C/N	%C	%N	$\delta^{15}N_{Glu}$	$\delta^{15}N_{Phe}$	TP_{ter}	Layer	Age
STR162	–19.8	7.4	3.2	41.7	15.0	10.1	11.0	1.99	3	6 years
STR179	–20.3	8.4	3.2	41.7	14.7	12.1	9.4	2.46	4	5 years
STR216	–20.0	8.9	3.4	40.8	13.6	12.8	10.2	2.45	5	Child
STR220	ND	ND	3.5	38.1	12.6				4	Child
STR232	–19.9	8.2	3.2	42.2	15.3	11.0	8.2	2.47	4	Child
STR242	–20.1	9.3	3.4	41.9	14.7				4	5 years
STR411	–19.8	9.9	3.6	39.6	12.0				5	Child

Table 10-4. Isotope compositions of collagen ($\delta^{13}C_{col}$ and $\delta^{15}N_{col}$), glutamic acid ($\delta^{15}N_{Glu}$) and phenylalanine ($\delta^{15}N_{Phe}$) for human skeletal remains from the PN layer of Tell el-Kerkh. Group indicates burial group which each individual belongs. C/N is the atomic ratio of carbon to nitrogen. %C is the percentage of carbon in the gelatin. %N is the percentage of nitrogen in the gelatin. ND is non determinant.

Sample-No.	Group	$\delta^{13}C_{col}$	$\delta^{15}N_{col}$	C/N	%C	%N	$\delta^{15}N_{Glu}$	$\delta^{15}N_{Phe}$	TP_{ter}	Layer	Age	Sex
STR19		−18.5	12.5	3.3	41.4	15.0				2	6 months	
STR29		−19.4	8.7	3.3	42.4	15.2				4a	Adult	Male
STR44		−19.9	8.7	3.4	40.8	14.1				4a	Adult	
STR45		−20.1	9.3	3.5	41.9	14.7				4a	2 years	
STR48		−18.8	9.8	3.3	41.3	14.4				3	Infant	
STR76		−19.2	9.5	3.4	41.4	14.9				5	Infant	
STR141		−19.3	8.1	3.2	42.1	14.9				5	Perinatal	
STR145		−19.0	9.7	3.4	41.7	15.1				5	Infant	
STR153		−19.7	9.6	3.4	40.0	14.1				6	Perinatal	
STR155		−19.3	9.6	3.3	41.3	15.1				6	Perinatal	
STR166		−20.0	7.5	3.3	41.0	14.5				6	Infant	
STR223		−18.9	9.8	3.2	41.8	15.1				1	Infant	
STR234		−19.8	9.1	3.5	40.4	13.9				4	Perinatal	
STR246		−20.3	8.9	3.3	41.9	14.5				3	Adult	Female
STR301		−19.7	7.5	3.2	42.2	15.4				4a	15 years	
STR307		−20.1	7.0	3.6	40.7	13.0				2	4 years	
STR309		−20.2	8.8	3.3	42.3	14.8				2	Juvenile	
STR331		−19.9	8.9	3.3	41.8	14.6				3	Infant	
STR339		−18.8	11.0	3.2	40.9	14.4				3	Infant	
STR402		−18.3	10.3	3.5	39.4	13.7				4a	Infant, 9-12 mths.	
STR426		−19.8	7.5	3.2	41.9	15.0				4a	Fetal	
STR433		−18.7	10.1	3.3	40.4	13.9				4a	Infant	
STR436		−18.2	10.9	3.3	39.6	14.1				4a	Infant	
STR502		−19.5	9.3	3.5	41.0	13.7				4	2-3 years	
STR504		−20.0	9.2	3.3	46.1	16.2				4	Perinatal	
STR507	1	−20.2	8.2	3.4	45.4	15.7	11.9	9.3	2.45	4	8-10 years	
STR513		−20.4	8.1	3.6	43.3	14.1	12.8	10.5	2.41	4	Perinatal	
STR519		−19.4	10.3	3.4	45.5	15.4				4	Fetal	
STR521	6	−19.4	7.3	3.3	44.5	15.7	12.6	10.1	2.43	4	12-15 years	
STR524		−19.6	7.6	3.4	43.4	14.9	12.6	9.9	2.46	4	Middle adult	Female
STR527		−19.3	7.7	3.3	41.6	14.7	11.7	10.8	2.22	4	Infant	
STR528		−19.3	10.1	3.5	42.4	14.2				4	1-3 years	
STR533	6	−20.0	8.5	3.5	43.5	14.4	12.3	9.0	2.54	4	40-50 years	Female
STR710	7	−20.1	8.1	3.2	40.5	14.6	13.4	12.4	2.24	4	Old adult	Male
STR711	4	−20.7	8.3	3.5	41.9	14.1				4	Subadult, 15-18yrs.	
STR712	7	−20.6	9.2	3.4	41.3	14.0	12.0	9.7	2.40	4	Middle adult	Female
STR713		ND	ND							4	10-12years	
STR714	4	−20.7	9.1	3.5	41.8	14.1	12.5	10.2	2.42	4	Adult	Male
STR715	7	−20.2	9.4	3.5	41.9	14.0	12.7	10.0	2.47	4	Young adult	Male
STR716	5	−20.4	10.7	3.4	41.6	14.2	14.1	11.5	2.45	4	Middle adult	Male
STR718	5	−20.7	9.8	3.5	41.7	14.1	13.3	10.3	2.50	4	Young adult	Female
STR719	5	−19.8	8.0	3.4	36.7	12.5				4	Adult	
STR720	5	−20.6	7.7	3.5	41.3	13.7				4	Adult	
STR725		−19.7	7.9	3.3	44.7	16.0				4	Young adult	Female
STR726		−19.1	11.7	3.2	41.2	14.9	17.1	14.3	2.47	4	Infant, 9-18mos.	
STR729	7	−20.7	10.2	3.2	42.2	14.8				4	Young adult	Female
STR730		−20.2	9.4	3.6	41.9	13.5				4	Juvenile, 2-3yrs.	
STR731		ND	ND							4	Young adult	Male
STR732		ND	ND							4	Subadult, 12-15yrs.	

Table 10-4. Continued.

Sample-No.	Group	δ¹³C_col	δ¹⁵N_col	C/N	%C	%N	δ¹⁵N_Glu	δ¹⁵N_Phe	TP_ter	Layer	Age	Sex
STR738		−18.9	11.0	3.3	41.7	14.7	16.6	14.2	2.42	4	Infant, Birth-3mos.	
STR739	2	−20.5	8.8	3.4	41.3	14.0	12.3	10.0	2.40	4	Middle adult	Male
STR743	5	−20.6	8.1	3.4	40.4	13.7				4	Middle adult	Male
STR746		ND	ND							4	Juvenile	
STR748	5	−20.7	9.9	3.4	41.2	14.0	13.0	10.7	2.42	5	Young adult	Male
STR750	10	−20.8	7.0	3.2	39.6	14.3				5	Juvenile, 5-6yrs.	
STR752	4	−20.2	7.5	3.3	41.1	14.7				4	Adult	Female
STR757	2	−20.8	7.8	3.2	41.1	14.5				4	Juvenile, 7-8yrs.	
STR803	2	−20.8	7.0	3.3	49.6	17.8				5	Young adult	Female
STR807	10	−20.0	6.4	3.3	46.3	16.2				5	Middle adult, 35-40yrs.	Male
STR823	2	−21.5	6.5	3.4	43.3	14.8				5	Subadult, 14-16yrs.	
STR825	5	−19.8	8.0	3.4	49.7	17.1				5	Juvenile, 10-12yrs.	
STR826	4	−21.1	6.6	3.5	47.6	16.0				5	Subadult, 14-15yrs.	
STR829		−19.2	10.1	3.3	50.5	18.0				5	Juvenile, 2-3yrs.	
STR830	9	−20.2	6.3	3.3	48.8	17.5				5	Middle adult	Male
STR834		−19.5	9.9	3.2	46.9	17.0				5	Juvenile, 2-3yrs.	
STR836	9	−21.1	7.4	3.2	43.3	15.7				5	Middle adult	Male
STR838		−19.8	8.5	3.4	47.4	16.3				5	Perinatal	
STR841		−19.7	10.5	3.4	47.4	16.3				5	Perinatal	
STR842		ND	ND							6	Middle adult	Male
STR851		−21.3	6.9	3.4	44.5	15.3				5	Infant, 10-12mos.	
STR852		ND	ND							5	Adult	Male
STR855		ND	ND							6	Young adult	Male
STR856		ND	ND							6	Adult	Female
STR857		ND	ND							6	Young adult	Male
STR858		ND	ND							6	Subadult	Female
STR902		−20.3	5.2	3.3	43.3	15.2				5	Juvenile, 1-2yrs.	
STR904		−19.8	7.9	3.2	41.8	15.1				5	Young adult	Male
STR908		−19.9	7.3	3.2	41.4	14.9				6	Subadult, 11-13yrs.	
STR909	9	−19.8	6.5	3.2	42.0	15.2				5	Young adult	Female
STR910	1	−20.2	8.5	3.6	39.5	12.8				6	Old adult	
STR913		−19.1	9.9	3.2	40.9	14.9				6	Juvenile, 1-2yrs.	
STR914		−19.5	7.8	3.3	40.8	14.6				6	Juvenile, 3-4yrs.	
STR920		−19.3	9.4	3.2	42.1	15.3				6	Juvenile, 3-4yrs.	
STR921	4	−19.6	7.2	3.4	41.0	14.3				6	Young adult	Male
STR924	9	−19.7	7.6	3.2	43.3	15.7				6	Young adult	Female
STR925		−20.0	8.1	3.2	37.8	13.8				6	Fetal	
STR926	3	−19.8	7.3	3.2	41.0	15.1	13.4	10.9	2.43	6	Adult	Female
STR927j	3	−19.1	8.4	3.3	40.1	14.3				6	Juvenile, 4-5yrs.	
STR927y	3	−18.7	8.3	3.2	42.1	15.4	12.9	9.8	2.51	6	Young adult	Female
STR930	3	−19.9	7.4	3.3	41.1	14.4	12.5	10.4	2.38	6	Adult	Female
STR941	10	−19.7	7.3	3.3	46.6	16.7				6	Middle adult	Female
STR943	4	−19.9	8.0	3.4	47.2	16.3				6	Young adult	Male
STR947	4	−19.8	7.4	3.2	47.3	17.1				6	Middle adult	Male
STR984	8	−19.9	8.9	3.5	47.6	16.1				6	Young adult	Male
STR988	8	−20.1	8.1	3.4	47.4	16.1				6	Middle adult	Female
STR1044	1	−20.1	8.6	3.4	47.5	16.4	12.3	9.2	2.51	4	Middle adult	Male
STR1047	1	−19.8	8.8	3.3	47.2	16.9	13.3	9.7	2.58	4	Young adult	Male
STR1050	1	−19.5	8.2	3.3	47.7	17.2	13.0	9.7	2.54	4	Young adult	Male

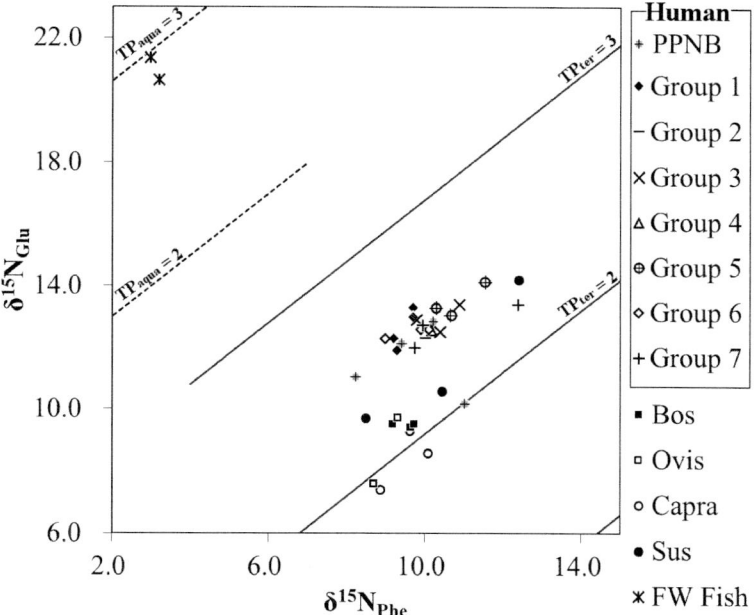

Figure 10-3. Comparisons of the nitrogen isotope compositions of glutamic acid and phenylalanine ($\delta^{15}N_{Glu}$ and $\delta^{15}N_{Phe}$) for human from PPNB layer, human and faunal remains from PN layer at Tell el-Kerkh. Solid lines represent expected $\delta^{15}N$ values for either TP_{ter} = 2 (primary consumer) or TP_{ter} = 3 (secondary consumer), and the dashed lines represent the expected $\delta^{15}N$ values for either TP_{aqua} = 2 (primary consumer) or TP_{aqua} = 3 (secondary consumer).

the pigs at Tell el-Kerkh and Hakemi Use are considered to have been domesticated, they seem to have consumed little animal protein, and few changed their diets compared with the wild boars at Hasankeyf Höyük.

4-4-1. Nitrogen isotopic compositions of amino acids from humans

The $\delta^{15}N_{Phe}$ values for individuals from PPNB layer of Tell el-Kerkh ranged from 8.2‰ to 11.0‰, and the $\delta^{15}N_{Glu}$ values ranged from 10.0‰ to 12.8‰ (Figure 10-3, Table 10-3). And the $\delta^{15}N_{Phe}$ values for individuals from PN layer of Tell el-Kerkh ranged from 9.0‰ to 12.4‰, and the $\delta^{15}N_{Glu}$ values ranged from 11.9‰ to 14.1‰ (Itahashi *et al.* 2018; Figure 10-3, Table 10-4). Based on the terrestrial ecosystem equation, the trophic position of PPNB humans ranged from 1.99 and 2.47, and also PN humans ranged from 2.24 to 2.58. Although one of PPNB human showed TP_{ter} as low as terrestrial herbivore, almost humans of PPNB and PN showed similar TP_{ter}, approximately 2.5. If humans mainly consume freshwater fish in addition to terrestrial food resources, their $\delta^{15}N_{Phe}$ values would be expected to diverge away from that of terrestrial animals toward that of freshwater fish. However, the $\delta^{15}N_{Phe}$ and TP_{ter} values associated with the human remains could be explained only by the use of terrestrial resources, including both C_3 plants and terrestrial animal protein. Notably, the

conventional isotope analysis of collagen revealed little about the contribution of freshwater fish to the Neolithic diet. However, the analysis of amino acids showed that the dietary contribution of freshwater resources was very limited for the inhabitants of Tell el-Kerkh between the PPNB to the PN periods. They seem to have depended largely on terrestrial food sources.

4-4-2. Strontium isotope values of tooth enamels of humans

As local range of $^{87}Sr/^{86}Sr$ around Tell el-Kerkh (0.707785 ± 0.000155), tooth enamels of rodents found from PN layer (mean ± 2s.d.) of Tell el-Kerkh were used (Table 10-4). If a human individual shows $^{87}Sr/^{86}Sr$ lying outside of the local range, the individual is considered as an immigrant from another region. By the result, the $^{87}Sr/^{86}Sr$ in tooth enamel of humans from PN layer was 0.707918 ± 0.000237, varying in the range of 0.707707–0.708654 (Figure 10-4, Table 10-4). Almost of individuals had the $^{87}Sr/^{86}Sr$ putting on the local range. By contrast, because three individuals, STR 521, 524 and 757, showed $^{87}Sr/^{86}Sr$ lying outside of the local range, they seem the immigrants. Although STR 521 is thought a subadult, 12–15 years old and STR 524 is a middle adult female, STR 757 is considered as juvenile, 7–8 years old. They were found from different place in the cemetery, and were not found a relationship to each other.

5. Discussion

5-1. Characterizing the Diet and Temporal Changes in the Diet of Neolithic Populations in the Northern Levant

Botanical studies have shown that wild varieties of wheat and barley were present in the PPNA layer at Tell Qaramel, and that domesticated wheat could be distinguished from wild wheat at Tell el-Kerkh (Tanno and Willcox 2006a, b). Isotope analyzes of charred cereals from archaeological sites in Syria have shown that $\delta^{15}N$ values of cereals before cultivation were higher than those after cultivation (Araus *et al.* 2014). The mean $\delta^{15}N$ value of emmer grains from the PN layer at Tell el-Kerkh (2.2 ± 0.6‰; Table 10-1) was lower than that for einkorn at Tell Qaramel (6.1‰), but similar to the value in durum (*Triticum durum*) from the Tilbeshar Bronze Age site (1.7‰; Araus *et al.* 2014). Thus, the differences in the

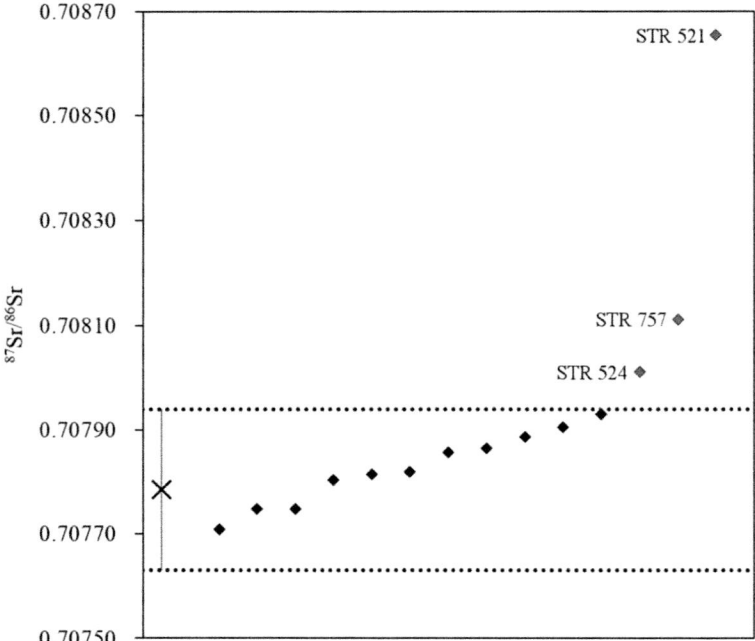

Figure 10-4. Strontium isotope ratios (^{87}Sr/^{86}Sr) in human tooth enamel. Dashed lines and a point (×) represent the local ^{87}Sr/^{86}Sr range based on the mean and the 2 standard deviations of rodents.

δ^{15}N values of consumed plants between sites might have affected human δ^{15}N$_{col}$ values.

The mean δ^{13}C value of emmer grains from Tell el-Kerkh was −22.4 ± 0.5‰ (Table 10-1), and the mean δ^{13}C value of einkorn grains from Tell Qaramel was −23.2‰ (Araus *et al.* 2014). The δ^{13}C$_{col}$ values of humans from both northern Levant sites seem mostly unchanged during the Neolithic period (approximately −20‰) (Figure 10-2). Because C$_4$ plant consumers generally show δ^{13}C$_{col}$ values (approximately −7‰), it would appear that humans did not consume a significant volume of C$_4$ plants in their daily diet. Similarly, marine and terrestrial sources in the food chain can be distinguished by δ^{13}C$_{col}$ values. The inhabitants of Tell el-Kerkh probably ate mainly C$_3$ plants and animals consuming C$_3$ plants.

The δ^{15}N$_{col}$ value of freshwater fish at Tell el-Kerkh was 11.0‰. At Pınarbaşı, an Epipalaeolithic site in central Anatolia, a δ^{15}N$_{col}$ value of inhabitants was approximately 15‰, and these inhabitants are considered to have consumed abundant fresh water foods (Baird *et al.* 2013). And although a part of hunter-gatherers of PPNA at Hasankeyf Höyük in upper Tigris was indicated as freshwater fish consumption based on the δ^{15}N$_{Glu}$ and δ^{15}N$_{Phe}$, they showed a δ^{15}N$_{col}$ value 8.8‰. The δ^{15}N$_{col}$ values of humans of PPNB and PN at Tell el-Kerkh were lower than those of humans at Pınarbaşı and similar to those of humans at Hasankeyf Höyük, despite the findings of fish, turtle and mollusc remains at Tell el-Kerkh. However, at least humans of PN at Tell el-Kerkh reflected few contributions

of freshwater fish based on the δ^{15}N$_{Glu}$ and δ^{15}N$_{Phe}$. In contrast to the Epipalaeolithic hunter–gatherers in central Anatolia and PPNA hunter–gatherers in upper Tigris, freshwater resources were not an important food source for Neolithic inhabitants in the Levant.

As another possibility, the variation of human nitrogen isotope values might be caused by a difference of animals consumed intensively. Faunal δ^{15}N$_{col}$ values at Tell el-Kerkh were highly variable among different herbivore species (Table 10-2, Figure 10-1 and Figure 10-2). Generally, a ~3.4‰ difference in δ^{15}N$_{col}$ values is observed between predators and prey on account of isotopic discrimination during assimilation/dissimilation processes (DeNiro and Epstein 1978; Minagawa and Wada 1984). However, the differences in the δ^{15}N$_{col}$ values of cattle and goats at Tell el-Kerkh are larger than typical ^{15}N-enrichment values

Table 10-5. Results of strontium isotope analysis of tooth enamel of humans and rodents from PN layer. Std Err indicates the 1 standard deviation of replicate analyses for each sample.

Species	Sample-No.	^{87}Sr/^{86}Sr	Std Err
Rodent	TKA36	0.707781	0.000005
Rodent	TKA37_1	0.707679	0.000005
Rodent	TKA37_2	0.707706	0.000006
Rodent	TKA51	0.707914	0.000005
Rodent	TKA55_1	0.707781	0.000005
Rodent	TKA55_2	0.707825	0.000007
Rodent	TKA79	0.707807	0.000049
Human	STR502	0.707930	0.000005
Human	STR521	0.708654	0.000005
Human	STR524	0.708011	0.000085
Human	STR533	0.707814	0.000014
Human	STR712	0.707819	0.000010
Human	STR718	0.707864	0.000007
Human	STR719	0.707746	0.000008
Human	STR720	0.707746	0.000005
Human	STR743	0.707886	0.000005
Human	STR748	0.707857	0.000005
Human	STR757	0.708111	0.000005
Human	STR1044	0.707803	0.000005
Human	STR1047	0.707707	0.000005
Human	STR1050	0.707905	0.000004

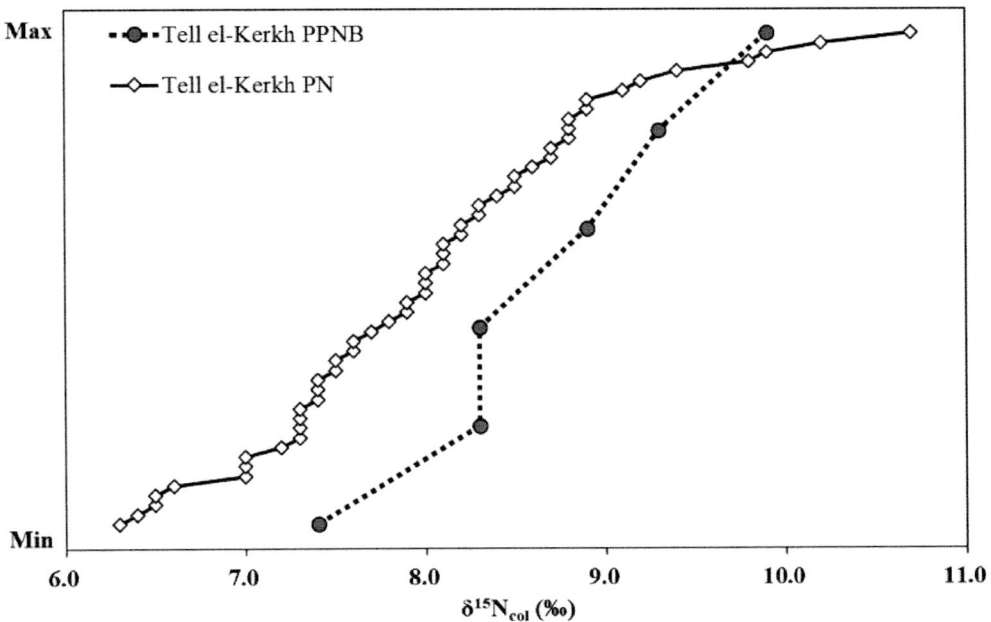

Figure 10-5. The $\delta^{15}N_{col}$ values of humans in the Tell el-Kerkh PPNB and PN layers
(plotted on the x-axis), with individual samples seriated from
minimum to maximum $\delta^{15}N_{col}$ on the y-axis.

distinguishing predators and prey. Similar variations in the $\delta^{15}N_{col}$ values of herbivores (~3.4‰) have been observed at other Neolithic sites in the Near East (e.g. Richards *et al.* 2003; Lösch *et al.* 2006; Itahashi *et al.* 2017; 2019); this probably reflects differences in the metabolic enrichment of ^{15}N among herbivores (Itahashi *et al.* 2014). Therefore, $\delta^{15}N_{col}$ differences among animal species could cause the variations in human $\delta^{15}N_{col}$ values observed at Neolithic sites. The higher $\delta^{15}N_{col}$ values of some individuals could be accounted for not only by increased meat consumption but also by more intensive consumption of cattle.

Interestingly, the $\delta^{15}N_{col}$ values of PPNB and PN individuals at Tell el-Kerkh showed no significant differences (U = 56, p = 0.13). However, the distribution of $\delta^{15}N_{col}$ values of PN individuals differs from that of PPNB individuals at Tell el-Kerkh, with values of PN individuals being slightly biased toward lower values (Figure 10-5). Despite variations in styles of subsistence, no significant differences were observed in the $\delta^{15}N_{col}$ values of human remains from the PPNB and PN layers at Tell el-Kerkh. Based on the isotopic compositions of bone collagen, the variations in diet associated with subsistence during the Neolithic period were perhaps smaller than the difference among PN inhabitants in the Tell el-Kerkh.

In Neolithic Anatolia, the $\delta^{15}N_{col}$ values of PPNB humans tended to be lower than those of late PN humans. For example, the southeastern Anatolia

PPNB sites at Çayönü Tepesi and Nevalı Çori showed lower $\delta^{15}N_{col}$ values than did other Neolithic sites such as Hakemi Use, the southeastern Anatolia PN site in the Near East (Lösch *et al.* 2006; Pearson *et al.* 2010, 2013; Itahashi *et al.* 2019). In addition, the PPNB humans at Aşıklı Höyük appeared to have lower $\delta^{15}N_{col}$ values than PN humans at Çatalhöyük in central Anatolia (Richards *et al.* 2003). Furthermore, late Neolithic and early Chalcolithic inhabitants at Aktopraklık, located in northwestern Anatolia, showed the highest reported $\delta^{15}N$ values (~9.0‰) of any humans in Neolithic Anatolia (Budd *et al.* 2013).

In addition, we compared the TP_{ter} by amino acid analysis between the Tell el-Kerkh site with the Anatolian Neolithic PN site at Çatalhöyük (String *et al.* 2015) and Hakemi Use (Itahashi *et al.* 2019). The mean TP_{ter} for inhabitants of PN layer of Tell el-Kerkh (2.44) was lower than that for the central Anatolian farmers of Çatalhöyük (2.53) and similar to that for the southeastern Anatolian farmer of Hakemi Use (2.45). Except an individual showing low TP_{ter}, PPNB humans showed TP_{ter} (2.46) similar to these PN sites. And the mean human $\delta^{15}N_{col}$ value for PPNB (8.7‰) and PN layer of Tell el-Kerkh (8.7‰) was lower than that for humans at Çatalhöyük (10.9‰) and higher than that for humans at Hakemi Use (7.2‰).

The differences in the $\delta^{15}N_{col}$ values of humans at PPNB sites in Anatolia can be explained by differences in the compositions of consumed plant and animal species (Pearson *et al.* 2010). In Tell el-Kerkh, the

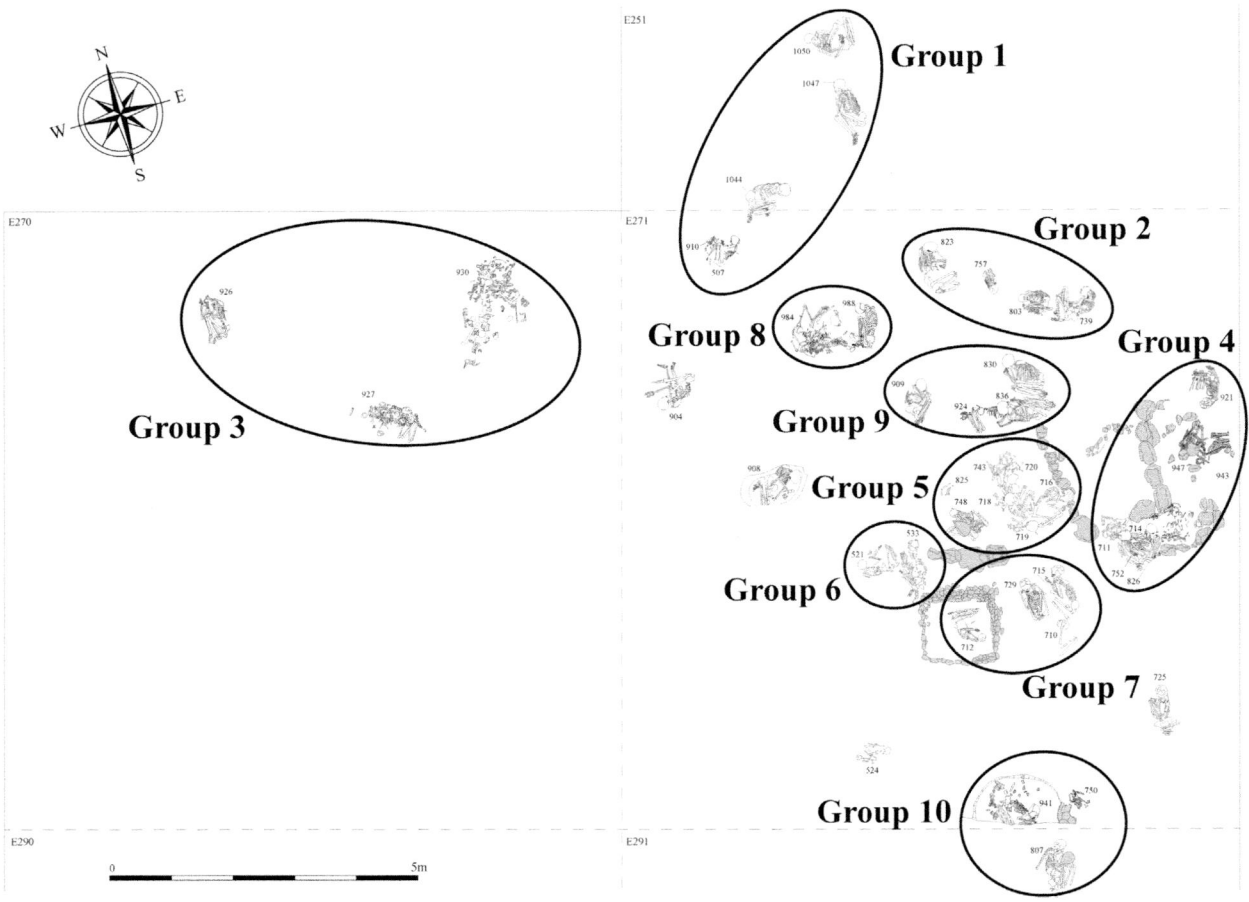

Figure 10-6. The location of burial groups (1–10) in PN layer.

cattle to animal remain ratios were 25% in the PPNB and 35% in the PN, and the pig to animal remain ratios were 25% in PPNB and 25% in the PN (Yano 2000). Furthermore, at Tell Aray, at a PN site located 12km from Tell el-Kerkh, *Bos* were considered the most important component of the animal fauna and *Sus* the second to most important (Hongo 1996). Also, in central Anatolia, *Bos* represented 9% of the mammal fauna at Aşıklı Höyük (Baird 2012), whereas in Çatalhöyük, *Bos* represented 20% of the mammal fauna (Russell *et al.* 2005). By contrast, *Ovis* and *Copra* formed the basis of the animal economy, while the proportion of *Bos* was less than 20% and following *Sus* at Hakemi Use (Omar 2013). Thus, the high $\delta^{15}N_{col}$ of humans at Tell el-Kerkh, and also Çatalhöyük, may have be caused by that *Bos* and *Sus* which showed $\delta^{15}N_{col}$ higher than other animals were important livestock since the beginning of herding at the sites. The higher $\delta^{15}N_{col}$ values observed at the Northern Levant sites indicate that *Bos* were important providers of meat, as were *Ovis*, *Copra* and *Sus* at these sites. If the Development of animal husbandry commonly included four livestock, i.e., *Bos*, *Sus*, *Ovis* and *Copra*, the regional differences in human diets in different food production communities of the PN might have

been smaller than differences involving hunting–gathering communities in each region.

5-2. Social Structure of PN Period

The PN cemetery consists of several layers containing the remains of more than 240 individuals (Chapters 4 and 5), and is one of the earliest examples of a nondomestic cemetery in the Near East (Tsuneki 2012). All age cohorts and sexes are represented in the cemetery, and were subject to similar burial practices. Among whole buried individuals, a part of individuals buried in Layers 4, 5 and 6 were divided into several main groups (Groups 1–10), based on the burial location within the cemetery. Not only were the groups spatially separated, but groups 4, 5, 6, and 7 were separated from each other by stone columns.

To interpret the contemporary distribution of isotope values among adults at Tell el-Kerkh we considered a number of discrete burial groups (Groups 1–10) within the cemetery (Figure 10-6). By strontium isotope analysis, almost of measured individuals of each group were considered as a local inhabitant. The results of analysis of isotopes of collagen and amino acids (Table 10-4) showed that the values varied with

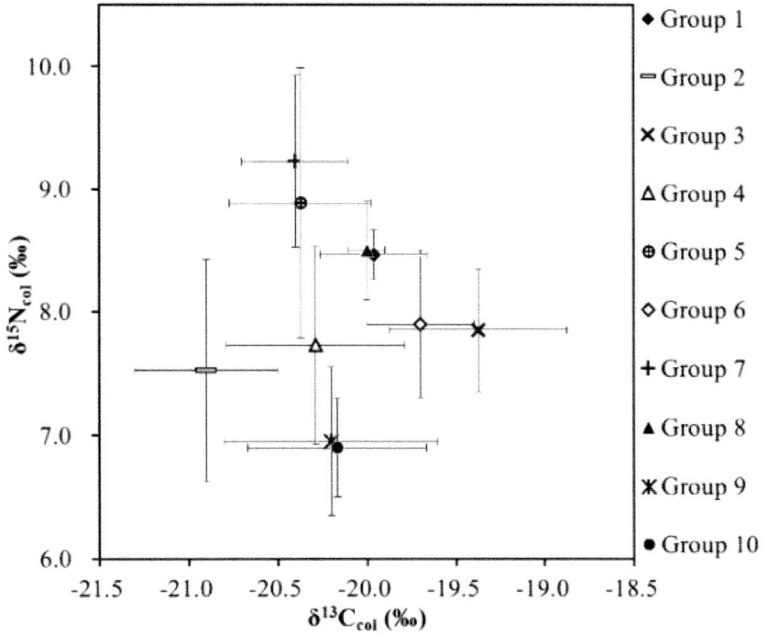

Figure 10-7. Plots of the mean $\delta^{13}C_{col}$ and $\delta^{15}N_{col}$ values for each burial group in the cemetery from PN layer with a standard deviation.

respect to burial location. To validate the uniformity of diets within each group, we plotted the mean and standard deviation of $\delta^{13}C_{col}$ and $\delta^{15}N_{col}$ values for each group with those for the entire site (Figure 10-7). The $\delta^{13}C_{col}$ and $\delta^{15}N_{col}$ values for human individuals within each group were more similar to each other than to most individuals in other groups, even though the ranges of values overlapped (Figure 10-3; Figure 10-7; Table 10-4). It indicates that individuals buried within a specific area consumed foods having similar isotope values, even within the limited isotope range for this inland environment. It also suggests that they lived in close relationships, and ate together regardless of sex, age and property.

In contrast, the estimated TP_{ter} values were inconsistent with the relative position estimated by the $\delta^{15}N_{col}$ among groups, and did not show obvious differences among groups (Figure 10-3). The individuals of Group 1 had the highest TP_{ter} (2.52 ± 0.1), although the $\delta^{15}N_{col}$ value for this group (8.5‰) was lower than for groups 2 (8.5‰), 4 (9.1‰), 5 (10.1‰), and 7 (8.9‰). The individuals of Group 5 had a TP_{ter} value (2.45 ± 0.0) intermediate among all groups, but had the highest $\delta^{15}N_{col}$ value (10.1‰), suggesting they may have consumed herbivores having high $\delta^{15}N_{col}$ ratios. While the collagen results imply some use of aquatic resources, the $\delta^{15}N_{phe}$ value (10.2‰) for Group 5 differed from that of freshwater fishes (3.1‰) (Figure 10-3), indicating that the diets of members of this group involved the consumption of terrestrial resources only. The differences in TP_{ter} values among the groups were smaller than the values expected

from $\delta^{15}N_{col}$, suggesting that the $\delta^{15}N_{col}$ values of individuals at Tell el-Kerkh may have been strongly influenced by differences in the main animals consumed, and less by differences in the quantity of animal protein in the diet.

This indicates that individuals at Tell el-Kerkh were buried among those with whom they shared common dietary sources, and were probably related and/ or household members. Henton (2013) interpreted evidence of a possible household-based herding system at Çatalhöyük, based on analysis of oxygen isotopes and the dental microwear of sheep. Thus, it is possible that the apparent intergroup differences in meat consumption at Tell el-Kerkh may be related to household-specific animal husbandry, with little sharing among households, although households did not necessarily consume only one species as animal protein.

Thus, Neolithic communities may have divided the burial space among households. The bias of distribution of resources among groups at Tell el-Kerkh might have derived from social behavior of individuals and/or sexual difference. Archaeological evidence suggests there was no hereditary social stratum established in the Pottery Neolithic period. However the division of subsistence among groups within the community had perhaps begun in the Neolithic period already, and it might have developed successional social stratum in the following periods.

6. Conclusions

Stable isotope analyzes of human and animal remains from Tell el-Kerkh have provided information on human diets in the Northern Levant during the middle–late Neolithic periods. Our results suggest that the inhabitants in the Northern Levant consumed terrestrial protein resources similar to those consumed in central and southeast Anatolia. Furthermore, the carbon and nitrogen isotope compositions and trophic position estimated by nitrogen isotope compositions of amino acids of humans did not dramatically change during the transition from the PPNB to PN periods in the Northern Levant; this shows that the populations in these different periods retained similar intake rates of animal proteins, and perhaps consumed similar proportions of animal species. In spite of the cultural changes that occurred during the transition from the PPN to PN periods, e.g. in burial behaviours and social organization, cattle may have remained an important protein resource for populations in the Northern Levant. These data provide new insights into the dietary shifts associated with Neolithisation, which showed substantial variations among different regions of the Near East. These regional differences were probably related to local adaptations of subsistence styles to regional environmental conditions prior to Neolithisation.

Chapter 11
Conclusion

Akira Tsuneki

Neolithic excavations in West Asia have often resulted in the discovery of buried human skeletons connected to building structures, such as building floors, building walls, and building courtyards. In the excavations of Tell el-Kerkh, which initiated a full-scale investigation in 1997, about 45 human skeletons were excavated from the LPPNB to the Pottery Neolithic period until 2002. Most of these were infant burials related to building structures. In the 2002 excavations, around ten human burials were discovered in Square E271a-c, which made me realize that burials were extraordinarily common in open spaces. However, 2003 and 2004 were study seasons and from 2005, we started new excavations in the East Trench. Thus, it was necessary to wait for the 2007 season to notice that Square E271 of the Central Area is part of the Pottery Neolithic cemetery. Moreover, in the Central Area's excavations from 2007 to 2010, there was an unexpected discovery of a large-scale outdoor Pottery Neolithic cemetery of approximately 200m^2 centrally located in Square E271.

Numerous human burials have been investigated in excavations of West Asian prehistoric sites. In addition to a few cases of Paleolithic burial excavations in West Asia, there has been a rapid increase in the number of discovered burials of the Natufian period of the Epipaleolithic (e.g., Belfer-Cohen 1995; Nadal 1995). Most of the burials in the late Epipaleolithic period were dispersed inside caves or under house floorings. Burials were commonly connected to the dwellings. Additionally, there are strong indications of primary burials in the Natufian period. Among Natufian burials, the most famous is 'Cemetery B,' discovered under three superimposed circular dwellings at Ain Mallaha (Valla 1988, 1991; Boyd 1995). About 12 primary burials, consisting of men and women of all ages, were discovered under the floor of a large circular-planned dwelling named Structure 131. We are not sure if these burials were built when the dwelling was still in use or after it was abandoned. However, these burials indicated family/relative-like relationships and close connections to the dwelling. At this point, I would like to call such burials 'house burials.' Secondary and collective burials were sometimes observed in addition to the primary burials. However, during the Natufian period, primary burials were predominantly 'house burials,' and sometimes cave burials. Although some scholars have asserted the existence of Natufian cemeteries (e.g., Goring-Morris and Belfer-Cohen 2010), land set aside as an outdoor cemetery had not yet appeared.

In the next Pre-pottery Neolithic period, a wide range of burials were recognized (e.g., Croucher 2012). Primary inhumation related to buildings, such as under the floor or near the walls of a dwelling, or in a courtyard, remained the main burial method for a long time. However, secondary treatments, such as skull removal, became popular after burials, and secondary burials, in which skulls and long bones were collected and cached, were also frequently performed. In addition to individual house burials, ossuaries have also been discovered. These contained a collection of human bones that had undergone secondary processing. The 'Skull Building' at Çayönü (Özdoğan 1999), 'the charnel room' in phase 8 at Tell Abu Hureyra (Moore *et al.* 2000), and 'maison des morts' at Dja'de al-Mughara (Coqueugniot 1999) are typical specimens of ossuaries. The skulls were often detached and re-deposited, while the other skeletons were gathered and replaced as collective interments in these houses. As the crania were sometimes decorated, they were displayed and used in rituals, especially in the sites of the southern Levant. In other words, Pre-pottery Neolithic people coexisted with the dead and the dead had to stay with the living for some time after they died. Individual burials were observed within these houses or often under the floor of ordinary dwellings. The seated burials at Tell Halula provide us with a unique funeral practice, which indicates how household members buried their dead (Guerrero, Molist, Kujit and Anfrunas 2009). The deceased were buried in one area of the building, individually and in a fully upright seated position. These are the ultimate house burials. In most cases, burials are discovered in connection with dwellings and ossuaries.

However, rather few burials have been excavated in the Pottery Neolithic period (e.g., Gopher and Orrelle 1995; Campbell 1995; Akkermans and Schwartz 2003: 145). Ossuaries had already disappeared, and most burials seemed to be individual and dispersed. Recent final report of Tell Shir near Hama provided us the traditional 'house burials' in the Pottery Neolithic society (Resch and Gresky 2018). We understand that the people continued to bury their deceased, especially infants and children, under the floors, walls and surroundings of their residential buildings in the early 7th millennium BC. Besides these 'house burials', the most notable graveyard is about 130 burials found at level 1 at the bottom of Tell es-Sawwan (Al-Wailly and Al-Soof 1965; Yasin 1970). It was detected under the floors of the dwellings of the Hassuna period, but identified as possibly belonging to the pre-Hassuna period, middle 7th millennium BC, based on the grave goods (Campbell 1995; Helwing 2016). If so, the majority of the burials are infants and not adults, however this could be one of the Pottery Neolithic cemeteries.

Many children's burials and very few adult burials were discovered in the Pottery Neolithic settlements. Therefore, most adults seemed to be buried elsewhere (Hole 1989). Some scholars maintain that the Pottery Neolithic people built communal cemeteries on or off the edge of the settlements, and these cemeteries have not yet been fully discovered. This is because from the end of the Pottery Neolithic period (Halaf and contemporary period) to the Chalcolithic period (Ubaid and contemporary period), many cemeteries were discovered outside or in the periphery of the settlement. For example, Yarim Tepe I, a Hassuna settlement, produced a Halafian cemetery consisting of approximately 20 shaft graves (Merpert and Munchaev 1993). These shaft graves dug from the surface of the tell are considered to be a part of a cemetery created by those who left the nearby Halafian settlement of Yarim Tepe II. Of the ten burials with identifiable human bones, nine were adult burials, and the rest belonged to infant's aged around four. This also indicates that these graves may have been a part of cemeteries located outside of the settlement, rather than being the burials connected to the dwellings within the settlement. Many cemeteries were built outside the settlements or on top of abandoned settlements during the Ubaid period, such as Tell Kashkashokh II (Matsutani 1991), Tell Mashnaqa (Monchambert 1987), Tell Arpachiyah (Marrowan and Rose 1935), and Tell Songor A (Kamada and Ohtsu 1981, 1991).

Many questions remain regarding the Pottery Neolithic burials. However, burials themselves during this period can be considered key for understanding how a full-fledged outdoor communal cemetery was formed, apart from individual dwelling houses. In this context, our discovery of the Kerkh Pottery Neolithic Cemetery provided a new perspective to this question. Although the cemetery was constructed within the settlement, it seemed to be a fledged outdoor communal cemetery. I would now like to summarize the processes in which the outdoor communal cemetery appeared in Squares E251–E270–E271 at Tell el-Kerkh.

Layer 7 (Figure 3-64 and Figure 4-15)

In Layer 7, the area of Squares E270–E271 was certainly a part of the habitation area. In this area, there are two rectangular-planned buildings: Strs. 827 and 916. Str. 827 was a pisé walled building, while Str. 916 was a pisé walled building with a stone foundation. These two buildings are lined up across a narrow street 0.7m wide, and undoubtedly, they coexisted at the same time in terms of the level and direction of the buildings. Both buildings were divided into small rooms. Based on the objects discovered in situ from Str. 827, this building was not an ordinary dwelling but a communal residence, common to several families' mills and/or kitchens. Str. 916 may have been an ordinary dwelling house. Many carbonized wooden timbers were discovered in the upper layers of objects along the central corridor of Str. 827, and the pisé walls were fully burnt. However, it remains unclear whether the building was burnt intentionally or accidentally.

Layer 6 (Figure 3-57 and Figure 4-16)

The area of Squares E270–E271 was used as a graveyard. After the abandonment of Strs. 827 and 916, Neolithic people did not level these buildings, nor did they build new ones in Squares E270–E271. Instead, they used the rooms of abandoned buildings to set up a graveyard and began burying the dead. At the ruin of Str. 827, a burial pit was dug into Room 5 on the northern side, and an 11-13-year-old subadult was buried in it. At the ruin of Str. 916, four adults were buried in the eastern room, and nine individuals (three adults, one subadult, four juveniles, and one fetus) were buried in the western room along the southern pisé wall/ stone foundation. It is assumed that these individuals were buried one after another, with a slight time gap, rather than being buried at the same time. Some were disturbed or reburied by the new inhumation. The eastern room of Str. 916 was severely destroyed by the construction of the C9 crematorium and the inhumation of four adults.

In addition to the above-mentioned burials, which were made using the previous two buildings, several types of burials were constructed in Squares E270–E271 of Layer 6 (For Square E251, excavation has not yet reached Layer 6). The main burials are C10 north and south, which are the collective burials built at the eastern end of Square E271; C6 is a crematorium pit built just south of C10 and C8 is a secondary burial consisting of cremated bones. Two other crematorium pits (C5 and C9) are also the main burials in this layer. The crematorium pits of C9 and C5 destroyed the eastern room and wall of Str. 916, respectively. In Square E270, Str. 930 was a bone accumulation consisting of three human adult skulls and many animal bones.

We found a total of 85 buried human bones in a relatively small area of approximately 100m² in Layer 6. Therefore, this area centered on Square E271 was exclusively used as a graveyard, and it can certainly be called a cemetery. The earliest burials were constructed in abandoned residential or communal buildings (Strs. 827 and 916). The burial pits were created by destroying some parts (walls or floors) of these abandoned buildings. However, the rooms, walls, or floors of the abandoned buildings were present when these burials were constructed. Although the nature of the relationship between these burials and abandoned buildings is unclear, there is no doubt that there is some link between them. This is because these burials were built in close connection with the houses, and they existed in the genealogy of 'house burials.'

The collective burial pits of C10 were surrounded by stone rows. However, these were not stone foundations for dwelling buildings. The pit of C10 North produced graves of at least 15 men and women of all ages, and it is believed to have been a collective burial of large families for a long time. In other words, it seems to be a symbolic act to enclose the family burial built outdoors with stone rows that were reminiscent of the stone foundations of the dwellings.

Notably, many of the burials in Layer 6 are collective rather than individual burials. They include crematorium pits discovered in the Kerkh Neolithic Cemetery. A very limited number of skull-removed skeletons were discovered in Layer 6. Secondary burials mixed with animal bones were also present. We suggest that the burials in the cemetery Layer 6 strongly retain some attributes of the burials from the previous period. One of the most conservative attributes of burial customs is the burial of the dead, which is deeply related to dwellings. When not buried in the wreckage of the building, the burial pits were purposely surrounded by stone rows, similar to the stone foundation of the dwellings.

Layer 5 (Figure 3-50 and Figure 4-20)

This is the middle phase of the cemetery, in which the Kerkh Cemetery evolves into a complete outdoor communal cemetery. We discovered 98 burials in the cemetery from the Layer 5 era, during which the land was leveled in the section of Squares E270–E271, and a new dwelling house (Str. 109) was constructed on its southern side, where the Str. 827 building was once built. This new dwelling house was inhabited and not used for burials, except for one perinatal burial (Str. 901). No other domestic structures were built in this area. Almost the entire area covering Squares E251–E271, on the north and east side of Building Str. 109, was used only as a cemetery. Many of the burials built in the cemetery were individual primary burials;

secondary burial pits, containing mainly skulls and long bones, are also visible, particularly in the eastern part of the cemetery.

The primary and secondary burials in this layer are basically pit graves and they are rarely separated or surrounded by stone rows. One of the burials, Str. 748, is surrounded by a stone row and is covered with lime plaster. However, burials with such stone rows are rare in this layer. Therefore, most burials in Layer 5 may appear to be independent of each other, but upon closer inspection, they can be classified into several burial groups that share the same burial location and the axial orientation of individuals. For example, a series of burials such as Strs. 1095, 1089, 1090, 1056, 1070, 1084, 1086, and 1096 are in the northern part of the Square E251. These burials have a body axis oriented toward the northwest-southeast direction. Therefore, they must have a strong relationship with each other.

If we focus on the burial locations, including the two secondary burial pits, we can divide them into groups of around ten, with a few to a dozen individuals for each group. We can also assume that each group had a strong resemblance to family ties.

Layer 4 (Figure 3-43 and Figure 4-23)

Layer 4 is the last phase of the Kerkh cemetery. Squares E251–E271, which had been the central space for the Kerkh cemetery, do not have a domestic building, and the entire area is used only as a cemetery. From this era, 61 burials were detected. Individual primary inhumation was the main burial type, followed by secondary burials. However, most of the secondary burials might be skeletons, especially the skull and long bones, which were excavated from the primary burials and replaced on the periphery of the new inhumation site. Therefore, even if human bones such as secondary burials are removed and seen, they are likely to have been treated as secondary burials simply to clean up former primary burials.

The burial locations of Layer 4 in the cemetery can be divided into two large groups: north and south. The northern group can be classified into three subgroups based on the burial location and axial orientation of individuals. The southern group can also be divided into four or five subgroups. Some subgroups, such as C2, were surrounded by stone rows similar to those in the Layer 6 burial groups. Therefore, it is possible that these two large burial groups differ not only in their burial locations, but also in their burial facilities.

In the southern group, Str. 712, a grave was found in the small square-planned stone enclosure, and a similar stone enclosure (Str. 153) was discovered under the floor of a residential building of Str. 74 in Square E290c in

Layer 5 (Figure 3-54). Of course, the latter example has been discovered in residential area outside Neolithic Cemetery, and a perinatal baby was discovered near the top level of the enclosed stone pit. The former example produced a middle adult female near the top level of an enclosed stone pit, too. In other words, the ages of the burials are completely different, and the burial locations are quite far apart. However, there is a commonality between these two burials, and flint points and blades have been discovered respectively along with each deceased. It is highly likely that they were buried with similar ritual practices.

Returning to Layer 4 cemetery, it is clear that the cemetery is divided into two large burial groups, northern and southern, as mentioned above, and it is likely that these burials of human groups had different attributions. Each group can be classified into three to five subgroups, with each subgroup producing a few to a dozen human skeletons of both sexes and all ages. Thus, it is reasonable to consider that each group represents an extended family and each subgroup represents its own family.

In the second half of the Layer 4 era, the area around Squares E251–E271 was no longer used as a graveyard. Thus, in the Layer 3 era, the area that was once a cemetery would be used again as a place for domestic activities, such as residential spaces and making bread with tannors.

Looking at the process of the formation, development, and abolition of the Kerkh Pottery Neolithic Cemetery, we find that the cemetery was initially used for traditional house burials in a corner of the settlement, eventually becoming a graveyard consisting only of graves, physically separated from the residential buildings. In other words, the burials that are deeply related to each house would develop into an outdoor communal cemetery of the settlement. Thus, it was a conversion from house burials to communal cemeteries. However, it should be noted that the interior of the communal cemetery was occupied by each family and clan, and each place in the communal cemetery has been buried in family units for decades. As discussed in Chapter 10, the results of stable isotope analyses of human bones excavated from the cemetery show that the eating habits were slightly different for each group divided by the difference in location in the cemetery. This also suggests that cemeteries might have been occupied by a number of different families and clans. The author has previously conducted an ethnoarchaeological survey of the relationship between the inhabitants and the cemetery at Ghanem al-ʿAli, a nomadic village that settled on the Euphrates River (Tsuneki 2010b). There were five small cemeteries for each clan and a large communal cemetery for the entire village. However, in the communal cemetery, there was a burial area for each clan and family. Burials outside the parcels were only allowed when the parcels were filled with burials. The cemetery, which seemed to be communal, was shared by each clan separately (ibid). Therefore, a deep commonality exists between the Kerkh Neolithic Cemetery and the modern Ghanem al-ʿAli village cemetery. In other words, in a society with strong tribal ties, it is highly possible that even though the entire village has a communal cemetery, it is divided into clan units forming a community.

This report describes the process by which the first large-scale outdoor communal cemetery in West Asia was established during the Kerkh Pottery Neolithic period. Following this, burials are overwhelmingly present in the communal cemeteries of the settlements despite being built in the courtyards or near each house. Thus, the Kerkh Cemetery was positioned as a precursor. To elucidate why the first large-scale outdoor communal cemetery was established in the Kerkh Pottery Neolithic settlement, it is essential to discuss the socio-economic background in depth, which is outside the scope of this report. Thus, I would like to be engaged with this greater detail in a future study.

Appendix
Neolithic Burials Outside of the Cemetery

Naoko Hironaga

The Neolithic burials outside the cemetery are summarized in a list in this appendix. Most of these burials were discovered during excavations between 1997 and 2001. Mark Hudson was mainly responsible for the bio-archaeological examination of these human bones (ex., Hudson 1999). Some human bones were later re-examined by Sean Dougherty. We listed 47 burials as burials outside the cemetery. These include 15 burials from the Rouj 2d period, 22 burials from the Rouj 2c period and 10 burials from the Rouj 1c period. As the list indicates, many of the burials are infants and juveniles; there are only four adult burials.

Table A-1. Burials from Rouj 2d period.

No.	Str. no.	Area / Square	Layer	Field season	Age and Sex	Burial type	Body position	Body axis	Head point	Face direction	Grave goods	Figure
1	21	Central Area	1	1997	—	Unknown	—	—	—	—	Pedestal bowl: 1 Cream bowl: 1 Cylindrical-necked jar: 1	Figures 3-31, 3-33 and 3-34
		E310c, d			A few burnt human bones were found in the bottom of a ritual pit (Str. 21). The structure was located in the open space of Square E310. All pottery was intentionally broken and placed on the human bones in the pit.							
2	22	Central Area	1	1997	Infant	Primary (disturbed)	—	—	—	—	DFBW bowl: 1 Hole mouthed jar: 1	Figures 3-31, 3-33 and 3-34
		E310b			A poorly preserved infant skeleton was found in a large, hole mouth jar with a cut bottom in a ritual pit (Str. 22). The location is similar to Str. 21. A DFBW shallow bowl was intentionally broken and combined with the jar in the pit.							
3	23	Central Area	1	1997	Infant, 9–12 mths.	Primary (disturbed)	L*	N–S	—	—	Stone vessel: 1 Stone bead: 1	Figures 3-31 and 3-35
		E310b			An infant burial was found in the eastern part of Square E310. The body position was not clear, but it seemed to be buried in a flexed position on its left side. One small stone vessel was placed near the skull. In addition, one blue stone bead was observed near the vertebrae.							
4	223	Central Area	1	1999	Infant, 9 mths.	Primary	R	SE–NW	SE	NE	—	Figures 3-31 and A-1
		E271c			A poorly preserved infant burial was found in the eastern part of Square E271c. The burial was located south of the large ash pit (Str. 222).							
5	1009	Central Area	1	2009	Young adult (male*)	Primary	R	N–S	N	W	—	Figures 3-31 and A-2
		E251c			An adult skeleton was found east of the stone foundations of Building Str. 1013 in Square E251c.							
6	19	Central Area	2	1997	Infant, 6 mths.	Primary	—	—	Upward	SW	—	Figures 3-36 and 3-38
		E270d			An urn burial was found south of the stone row (Str. 201) in the northern part of Square E270d. An infant skeleton was covered with a coarse pottery that was upside-down and cut off at the rim. The body was probably in a slightly sitting position because the skull was placed on the bones of the body.							

Table A-1. Continued.

No.	Str. no.	Area / Square	Layer	Field season	Age and Sex	Burial type	Body position	Body axis	Head point	Face direction	Grave goods	Figure
7	35	Central Area	2	1997	Infant, 9 mths.	Primary (disturbed)	—	NE–SW	NE	—	—	Figures 3-36 and 3-38
		E270a			An infant burial was found at the corner of stone foundations (Str. 24) in Square E270a. Although the building floor was completely removed, the burial was probably made under the floor.							
8	60	Central Area	2	1997	Subadult, 15–18 yrs.	Primary (disturbed)	—	E–W	—	—	—	Figures 3-36 and 3-38
		E270b			A subadult burial without a cranium was found in Square E270b. Almost all the bones were articulated, although the lower jaw was placed between the bones of the arms and legs. The location of the burial was surrounded by stone rows (Str. 24) and a *tannnor* (Str. 54).							
9	226	Central Area	2	1999	Infant	Unknown	—	—	—	—	Bone bead: 2	Figures 3-36 and A-3
		E271c			Partial infant ribs and long bones were found south of a stone row (Strs. 201 and 206) in Square E271c. Two bone beads were discovered near the tibia.							
10	307	Central Area	2	2000	Juvenile, 4 yrs.	Unknown	—	—	—	—	—	Figures 3-36 and 3-38
		E291c			Juvenile cranium fragments and a few ribs were found near an opening between the rooms of Building Str. 308 in Square E291c. The burial was probably placed below the floor of the residence.							
11	309	Central Area	2	2000	Juvenile	Primary	L	N–S	—	—	—	Figures 3-36 and 3-38
		E291c			A juvenile burial without skull or cervical spine was found north of Building Str. 308 in Square E291c.							
12	318	Central Area	2	2000	Juvenile, 10–11 yrs.	Unknown	—	—	—	—	—	Figure 3-36
		E291a			A few juvenile bone fragments were found in the northern part of the Str. 309 burials. The burial location is east of the *tannor* (Str. 330) in Square E291a.							
13	319	Central Area	2	2000	Infant	Unknown	—	—	—	—	—	Figure 3-36
		E311b			Infant bone fragments were found in a rectangular stone foundation (Str. 312) in the Square E311. The burial must have been located beneath the floor.							
14	320	Central Area	2	2000	Infant	Unknown	—	—	—	—	—	Figure 3-36
		E311a			Infant bone fragments were found between the stone foundations of Strs. 312 and 304 in Square E311. The head probably aligned to the north.							
15	339	Central Area	2	2000	Infant, 1.5–2 yrs.	Primary	R	NE–SW	NE	NW	—	Figures 3-36 and A-4
		E311b			An infant burial was found north of the Str. 320 burial. This burial was also located in the space between the stone foundations of Strs. 312 and 304.							

*: Probable

Body position L: Flexed position, lying on one's left side down;

R: Flexed position, lying on one's right side down;

S: Flexed and supine position;

P: Flexed and prone position

Figure A-1. Str. 223 Burial.

Figure A-2. Str. 1009 Burial.

Figure A-3. Str. 226 Burial.

Figure A-4. Str. 339 Burial.

Table A-2. Burials from Rouj 2c period.

No.	Str. no.	Area / Square	Layer	Field season	Age and sex	Burial type	Body position	Body axis	Head point	Face direction	Grave goods	Figure
1	48	Central Area	3	1997	Infant, 9 mths.	Primary	S	S–N	S	W	—	Figures 3-39 and A-5
		E290b			An infant burial was found within the stone foundation of Building Str. 17 in Square E290b. The burial mast was placed under the residence floor.							
2	246	Central Area	3	1999	Adult (female*)	Primary	L	NW–SE	NE	SE	—	Figures 3-39 and A-6
		E271c			An adult female burial was found across Squares E271c and E291a. Her legs were bent very tightly with her face very close to her knees. The burial was between a *tannor* (Str. 409) and a residential building (Str. 17).							
3	331	Central Area	3	2000	Infant, 0–6 mths.	Primary	S	NW–SE	NW	—	DFBW bowl: 1 Stone bead: many	Figures 3-39 and 3-41
		E311b			An infant burial was found under the floor of a residential building consisting of the stone rows of Strs. 315 and 311 in Square E311. The remains were covered with the fragments of a large DFBW jar. A small DFBW bowl was placed on the body. In addition, many beads were discovered near the shoulders and pelvis and under the ribs and vertebrae. Beads near the pelvis were chained for each color.							

Table A-2. Continued.

No.	Str. no.	Area / Square	Layer	Field season	Age and sex	Burial type	Body position	Body axis	Head point	Face direction	Grave goods	Figure
4	29	Central Area	4a	1997	Adult (male)	Primary	R	E–W	NE	Downward	—	Figures 3-42 and A-7
		E290d			An adult burial was found under the plastered floor and near the corner of Building Str. 55 in Square E290d. The upper body was twisted and slightly prone, and the face was turned toward the ground.							
5	44	Central Area	4a	1997	Adult	Primary (disturbed)	—	NW–SE	—	—	—	Figures 3-42 and A-8
		E290d			An adult skeleton was found under the floor of the same building (Str. 55), in Square E290d. The burial was located just east of the Str. 29 burial. The skull was not discovered, although part of the skeleton was articulated.							
6	45	Central Area	4a	1997	Infant, 1.5–2 yrs.	Primary (disturbed)	—	—	—	—	—	Figure 3-42
		E290d			A poorly preserved infant burial was found under the floor in the same building (Str. 55) where the Strs. 29 and 44 burials were identified.							
7	301	Central Area	4a	2000	Subadult, 15 yrs.	Primary (disturbed)	L	NW–SE	—	—	Bead: 2	Figures 3-42 and A-9
		E270c			A subadult burial was found in Square E270c. The burial was located north of the stone row (Sr. 46). The cranium and lower jaw were moved away from their original location. Two beads were observed near the skeleton.							
8	302	Central Area	4a	2000	Infant, 1–1.5 yrs.	Unknown	—	—	—	—	—	Figures 3-42 and A-10
		E270d			An infant burial was found east of the Str. 301 burial in Square E270d. These two burials may have been made at approximately the same time.							
9	402	Central Area	4a	2001	Infant, 9–12 mths.	Primary (disturbed)	—	S–N	S	—	—	Figures 3-42 and A-11
		E311b			A poorly preserved infant burial was found in the southern part of Square E311b. The burial was located north of a large fire installation / *tannor* (Str. 439).							
10	426	Central Area	4a	2001	Fetal	Primary* (disturbed)	—	—	—	—	—	Figures 3-42 and A-12
		E291c			Fetal skull, arm, and leg bones were found in the southern part of Square E291c. The burial was discovered above the plastered floor (Str. 428). Perhaps it was a secondary burial rather than a primary burial.							
11	431	Central Area	4a	2001	Infant, 6 mths.	Unknown	—	—	—	—	—	Figures 3-42 and A-13
		E291c			A few infant bones, animal bones, and small stones were found in a pit discovered northwest of Square E291c. It was not clear whether the pit was a grave.							
12	433	Central Area	4a	2001	Infant/ young juvenile	Primary	S	NE–SW	NE	—	—	Figures 3-42 and A-14
		E271c			An infant burial was found near the Str. 436 burial south of Square E271. The legs were bent, lifted, and spread. The arms were extended down and placed between the legs.							
13	436	Central Area	4a	2001	Infant/ young juvenile	Primary	L	S–N	S	W	Oyster shell: 1	Figures 3-42 and A-15
		E271c			An infant burial was found in the northwestern part of Square E271c. An oyster shell was observed near the feet.							
14	522	Central Area	4b	2002	Infant	Unknown	—	—	—	—	—	Figures 3-43 and A-16
		E291a			An infant cranium was found in the southeastern part of Square E291a. It was discovered near the large firing facility (Str. 512).							
15	76	Central Area	5	1997	1. Infant 2. Infant	1. Primary 2. Unknown	1. L 2. —	1. E–W 2. —	1. E 2. —	1. S 2. —	—	Figures 3-50 and A-17
		E290c			A grave found in burnt soil north of Building Str. 74 in Square E290c. Two infant skeletons were present in the grave.							

Table A-2. Continued.

No.	Str. no.	Area / Square	Layer	Field season	Age and sex	Burial type	Body position	Body axis	Head point	Face direction	Grave goods	Figure
16	141	Central Area	5	1998	1. Perinatal, 1 mth. 2. Perinatal, 2 mths.	1. Primary 2. Unknown	1. R 2. —	1. S–N 2. —	1. S 2. —	1. E 2. —	—	Figures 3-50 and A-18
		E290a			A grave was found on the floor near the wall of Building Str. 82 in Square E290c. Two perinatal bodies were in the grave, similar to the Str. 76 burial.							
17	145	Central Area	5	1998	Infant, 0–6 mths.	Primary (disturbed)	R	E–W	E	—	Tusk shell bead: 1	Figures 3-50 and A-19
		E290a			An infant burial was found under the eastern pisé wall of Building Str. 82 in Square E290a. A tusk shell bead was observed under the skull.							
18	153	Central Area	5	1998	Perinatal	Primary	L	W–E	W	NE	Flint point: 1 Bone pin: 1	Figures 3-50 and 3-54
		E290c			A perinatal burial was found just above the southwestern corner of the small, square-planned pit discovered under the floor of the residential building (Str. 74) in Square E290c. An Amuq-type flint point was observed near the chest.							
19	901	Central Area	5	2009	Perinatal	Primary	L	NE–SW	NE	Down-ward	—	Figures 3-50 and A-20
		E271c			A perinatal burial was found under the floor in the northwestern corner of a large room in Building Str. 109, in Squares E270 and E271. The upper body was in a slightly prone position, and the left humerus was located below the ribs.							
20	155	Central Area	6	1998	Perinatal	Primary	S	SE–NW	SE	NW	—	Figures 3-57 and 3-63
		E310d			A perinatal burial was found in the southern part of Square E310d. A hard surface found above the burial might indicate that the burial was made under the floor, although no structure was clearly detected. The neck was bent and the top of the head was facing up.							
21	166	Central Area	6	1998	Infant, 0–6 mths.	Primary (disturbed)	S	E–W	E	—	—	Figures 3-57 and 3-63
		E310d			An infant burial was found beside another burial in Str. 155, in the south of Square E310d. Together with the Str. 155 burial, this burial was probably made under a building's floor.							
22	810	Central Area	7	2008	Subadult, 14–16 yrs. (male*)	Unknown	—	—	W	—	—	Figures 3-64 and A-21
		E311b			An upside-down subadult skull was found in the residential building (Str. 811) in Square E311b. The burial was probably located under the plastered floor of Str. 811. The skull was discovered alongside the east wall of the excavation area, and the body parts extended outside the excavation area.							

*: Probable
Body position L: Flexed position, lying on one's left side down;
R: Flexed position, lying on one's right side down;
S: Flexed and supine position;
P: Flexed and prone position

Figure A-5. Str. 48 Burial.

Figure A-6. Str. 246 Burial.

Figure A-7. Str. 29 Burial.

Figure A-8. Str. 44 Burial.

Figure A-9. Str. 301 Burial.

Figure A-10. Str. 302 Burial.

Figure A-11. Str. 402 Burial.

Figure A-12. Str. 426 Burial.

Figure A-13. Str. 431 Burial.

Figure A-14. Str. 433 Burial.

Figure A-15. Str. 436 Burial.

Figure A-16. Str. 522 Burial.

Figure A-17. Str. 76 Burial.

Figure A-18. Str. 141 Burial.

Figure A-19. Str. 145 Burial.

Figure A-20. Str. 901 Burial.

Figure A-21. Str. 810 Burial.

Table A-3. Burials from Rouj 1c period.

No.	Str. no.	Area / Square	Layer	Field season	Age and sex	Burial type	Body position	Body axis	Head point	Face direction	Grave goods	Figure
1	162	North-west Area	3	1998	Juvenile, 6 yrs.	Primary	R	NE–SW	NE	N	—	Figures 3-6 and A-22
		D6b			A juvenile without leg bones was found at the center of Square D6. The burial was located near the stone clusters in Strs. 163 and 172. A few sheep bones were found with the body.								
2	179	North-west Area	4	1998	Juvenile, 5 yrs.	Primary	L	S–N	S	W	—	Figure A-23
		D6c			A juvenile found in the western part of Square D6c. The burial was probably located under the plastered floor.								
3	211	North-west Area	4	1999	Perinatal	Unknown	—	—	—	—	—	Figure 3-7
		D6b			Part of the perinatal cranium and finger bones were found in the ash-filled pit (Str.) in Square D6b. Many flint chips were collectively discovered in the pit.								
4	216	North-west Area	4	1999	Juvenile, 4 yrs.	Primary	L	NNE–SSW	NNE	SE	—	Figures 3-7 and 3-9
		D6b, d			A juvenile was found in the eastern part of Square D6. The arms seemed to embrace the knees.								
5	220	North-west Area	4	1999	Infant, 12–18 mths.	Primary (disturbed)	R	NE–SW	NE	NW	Flint flake: 14 Obsidian flake: 7 Flint tool: 1 Obsidian tool: 1	Figures 3-7 and 3-9
		D6d			An infant was found below a hearth or *tannor* (Str. 218) northwest of Square D6d. Many chipped stones were found in the abdomen and legs.								
6	232	North-west Area	4	1999	Juvenile, 4 yrs.	Primary	L	NE–SW	E	S	Flint flake: 2	Figures 3-7 and 3-9
		D6d			A juvenile was found at the western end of a pisé wall (Str. 231) south of Square D6d. The juvenile seemed to be buried below the wall.								
7	234	North-west Area	4	1999	Perinatal	Primary	L	NW–SE	NNW	NE	Point: 1	Figure 3-7
		D6d			A perinatal burial was found just below a pisé wall (Str. 231). The burial was discovered east of the Str. 232 burial in a similar situation below the wall. A flint point with a chipped tip was observed near the chest.								
8	242	North-west Area	5	1999	Juvenile, 4–5 yrs.	Primary	L	S–N	S	W	—	Figures 3-8a and 3-9
		D6d			A juvenile burial was found outside the southeastern corner of the Str. 244 stone foundation.								
9	411	North-west Area	5	2001	Infant	Primary	S	S–N	S	NW	—	Figures 3-8a and 3-9
		D6d			An infant burial was found east of the stone foundation of Str. 244. It was located c. 1.5 m north of Str. 242.								
10	656	East Trench	9'	2008	Juvenile, 10–12yrs.	Unknown	—	—	S	W	Flint blade: 1	Figure A-24
		E277b			A juvenile skull was found along the northern wall of the East Trench in Square E277b. The body was probably outside the excavation trench. A large flint blade was discovered near the back of the head.								

Body position L: Flexed position, lying on one's left side down;
R: Flexed position, lying on one's right side down;
S: Flexed and supine position;
P: Flexed and prone position

381

Figure A-22. Str. 162 Burial.

Figure A-23. Str. 179 Burial.

Figure A-24. Str. 656 Burial.

References

Adams, B.J. and Byrd, J.E. (eds) 2014. *Commingled Human Remains: Methods in Recovery, Analysis, and Identification.* Oxford: Academic Press.

Aghanabati, A. 1986. *Geological Map of the Middle East. Scale 1:5,000,000.* Tehran: Geological Society of Iran.

Akahane, S. 2003. Landforms and geology of the Rouj Basin. In Iwasaki, T. and Tsuneki, A. (eds), *Archaeology of the Rouj Basin: A Regional Study of the Transition from Village to City in Northwest Syria, Vol. I*: 11-27. Al-Shark 2, University of Tsukuba, Studies for West Asian Archaeology, Tsukuba: University of Tsukuba.

Akkermans, P.A., Boerma, J.A.K., Clason, A.T., Hill, S.G., Lohof, E., Meiklejohn, C., le Mière, M., Molgat, G.M.F., Roodenberg, J.J., Waterbolk-van Rooyen, W. and van Zeist, W. 1983. Bouqras revisited: Preliminary report on a project in eastern Syria. *Proceedings of the Prehistoric Society* 49: 335-372.

Akkermans, P.M.M.G. 1989. Halaf mortuary practices: A survey. In Haex, O.M.C., Curvers, H.H. and Akkermans, P.M.M.G. (eds), *To the Euphrates and Beyond: Archaeological Studies in Honour of Maurits N. van Loon*: 75-88. Rotterdam: A.A. Balkema Publisher.

Akkermans, P.M.M.G. 2008. Burying the dead in Late Neolithic Syria. In Córdoba, J.M., Molist, M., Pérez, C. Rubio, I. and Martínez, S. (eds), *Proceedings of the 5th International Congress on the Archaeology of the Ancient Near East*: 621-645. Madrid: Universidad Autónoma of Madrid.

Akkermans, P.M.M.G. 2013. Living space, temporality and community segmentation: Interpreting Late Neolithic settlement in northern Syria. In Nieuwenhuyse, O., Bernbeck, R., Akkermans P.M.M.G. and Rogasch, J. (eds), *Interpreting the Late Neolithic of Upper Mesopotamia*: 63-75. Turhout: Brepols.

Akkermans, P.M.M.G., Brüning, M.L., Hammers, N., Huigens, H., Kruijer, L., Meens, A., Nieuwenhuyse, O., Raat, A., Rogmans, E.F., Slappendel, C., Taipale, S., Tews, S. and Visser, E. 2012. Burning down the house: the burnt building V6 at Late Neolithic Tell Sabi Abyad, Syria. *Analecta Praehistorica Leidensia* 43/44: 307-324.

Akkermans, P.M.M.G., Brüning, M.L., Huigens, H.O. and Nieuwenhuyse, O.P. (eds) 2014. *Excavations at Late Neolithic Tell Sabi Abyad, Syria, The 1994-1999 Field Seasons.* Turnhout: Brepols Publishers.

Akkermans, P.M.M.G., Cappers, R., Cavallo, C., Nieuwenhuyse, O., Nilhamn, B. and Otte, I.N. 2006. Investigating the Early Pottery Neolithic of Northern Syria: New Evidence from Tell Sabi Abyad. *American Journal of Archaeology* 110 (1): 123-156.

Akkermans, P.M.M.G. and Schwartz, G.M. 2003. *The Archaeology of Syria: From Complex Hunter-Gatherers to Early Urban Societies (c. 16,000-300 BC).* Cambridge: Cambridge University Press.

Ambrose, S.H. 1991. Effects of diet, climate and physiology on nitrogen isotope abundances in terrestrial foodwebs. *Journal of Archaeolical Science* 18: 293-317.

Angel, J.L. 1946. Skeletal change in ancient Greece. *American Journal of Physical Anthropology* 4: 69-97.

Angel, J.L. 1966. Porotic hyperostosis, anemias, malarias, and marches in the prehistoric Eastern Mediterranean. *Science* 153: 760-763.

Arai, S. 1988. The obducted mantle – crustal slice to land; ophiolite. *Kagaku* 58: 685-695 (in Japanese).

Araus, J.L., Ferrio, J.P., Voltas, J., Aguilera, M. and Buxo, R. 2014. Agronomic conditions and crop evolution in ancient Near East agriculture. *Nature Communications* 5: 3953.

Arensburg, B. and Hershkovitz, I. 1988. Nahal Hemar cave. Neolithic human remains. *Atiqot English Series* 18: 50-58.

Arensburg, B. and Hershkovitz, I. 1989. Artificial skull 'treatment' in the PPNB period: Nahal Hemal. In Hershkovitz, I. (ed.), *People and Culture in Change: Proceedings of the Second Symposium on Upper Palaeolithic, Mesolithic and Neolithic Populations of Europe and the Mediterranean Basin*: 115-131. BAR International Series 508. Oxford: Archaeopress.

Arimura, M. 2019. Last PPNB blade maker in the Pottery Neolithic at Tell Ain el-Kerkh, northwest Syria: The demise of PPNB-type bidirectional blade technology. In Nakamura, S., Adachi, T. and Abe, M. (eds), *Decades in Deserts: Essays on Near Eastern Archaeology in honour of Sumio Fujii*: 191-204. Tokyo: Rokuichi Syobou.

Arimura, M. 2020. *The Neolithic Lithic Industry at Tell Ain El-Kerkh.* Al-Shark 4, University of Tsukuba, Studies for West Asian Archaeology, Oxrford: Archaeopress.

Arimura, M. and Suleiman, A. 2015. A cultural unity in northwestern Syria during the Neolithic. Tell Ain Dara III, a PPNB site in Afrin Valley. *Paléorient* 41 (2): 85-99.

Auerbach, B.M. and Ruff, C.B. 2004. Human body mass estimation: A comparison of 'morphometric' and 'mechanical' methods. *American Journal of Physical Anthropology* 125: 331-342.

Aufderheide, A.C. and Rodriguez-Martin, C. 1998. *The Cambridge Encyclopedia of Human Paleopathology.* Cambridge: Cambridge University Press.

Bacvarov, K. 2004. The birth-giving pot Neolithic jar burials in southeast Europe. In Nikolov, V., Bacvarov,

K. and Kalchev, P. (eds), *Prehistoric Thrace. Proceedings of the International Symposium in Stara Zagora*: 151-160. Sofia – Stara Zagora: Regional Museum of History -Stara Zagona.

Baird, D. 2012. The Late Epipaleolithic, Neolithic and Chalcolithic of the Anatolian Plateau, 13,000-4000 BC. In Potts, D.T. (ed.), *A Companion to the Archaeology of the Ancient Near East, Vol. I*: 431-465. Malden, Massachusetts: Wiley-Blackwell.

Baird, D., Asouti, E., Astruc, L., Baysal, A., Baysal, E., Carruthers, D., Fairbairn, A., Kabukcu, C., Jenkins, E., Lorentz, K., Middleton, C., Pearson, J. and Pirie, A. 2013. Juniper smoke, skulls and wolves' tails. The Epipaleolithic of the Anatolian plateau in its southwest Asian context; insights from Pınarbaşı. *Levant* 45: 175-209.

Bartl, K. (ed.) 2018. *The Late Neolithic Site of Shir / Syria, Volume 1 The Excavations at the South Area 2006-2009.* Damstadt: Philipp von Zabern.

Bar-Yosef, O. and Sillen, A. 1993. Implications of new accelerator date of the charred skeletons from Kebara Cave (Mt. Carmel). *Paléorient* 19 (1): 205-208.

Bass, W.M. 1987. *Human Osteology: A Laboratory and Field Manual,* 3rd (ed.). Columbia: Missouri Archaeological Society.

Belfer-Cohen, A. 1995. Rethinking social stratification in the Natufian culture: The evidence from burials. In Campbell, S. and Green, A. (eds), *The Archaeology of Death in the Ancient Near East*: 9-16. Oxford: Oxbow Monograph 51.

Benz, M. 2012. Little poor babies – Creation of history through death at the transition from foraging to farming. In Kienlin, L.T. and Zemmermann, A. (eds), *Beyond Elites Alternatives to Hierarchical Systems in Modelling Social Formations*: 169-172. Universitätsforschungen zur Prähistorischen Archäologie 215. Bonn: Habelt.

Benz, M., Gresky, J., Štefanisko, D., Alarashi, H., Knipper, C., Purschwitz, C., Bauer J. and Gebel, H.G.K. 2019. Burying power: New insights into incipient leadership in the Late Pre-Pottery Neolithic from an outstanding burial at Baʻja, southern Jordan. *PlosOne* 14 (8): e0221171. https://doi.org/10.1371/journal.pone.0221171

Bereczki, Z., Teschler-Nicola, M., Marcsik, A., Meinzer, N.J. and Baten, J. 2019. Growth disruption in children: Linear enamel hypoplasias. In Steckel, R.H., Larsen, C.S., Roberts, C.A. and Baten, J. (eds), *The Backbone of Europe: Health, Diet, Work, and Violence over Two Millennia*: 175-197. Cambridge: Cambridge University Press.

Bienert, H.D. 1991. Skull cult in the prehistoric Near East. *Journal of Prehistoric Religion* 5: 9-23.

Binford, L.R. 1971. Mortuary practices: Their study and potential. In *Approaches to the Social Dimensions of Mortuary Practices, Memoirs of the Society for American Archaeology* 25: 6-29.

Bocquet-Appel, J.P. 2002. Paleoanthropological traces of a Neolithic demographic transition. *Current Anthropology* 43: 637-650.

Bocquet-Appel, JP. and Masset, C. 1982. Farwell to paleodemography. *Journal of Human Evolution* 11: 321-333.

Bocquentin, F., Kodas, E. and Ortiz, A. 2016. Headless but still eloquent! Acephalous skeletons as witnesses of Pre-Pottery Neolithic north-south Levant connections and disconnections. *Paléorient* 42 (2): 33-52.

Bogin, B. 1999. *Patterns of Human Growth,* 2nd (ed.). Cambridge: Cambridge University Press.

Bonogofsky, M. 2005. A bioarchaeological study of plastered skulls from Anatolia: New discoveries and interpretations. *International Journal of Osteoarchaeology* 15: 124-135.

Bostanci, E.Y. 1959. Researches on the Mediterranean coast of Anatolia: A new Paleolithic site at Beldibi near Antalya. *Anatolia* 4 (9): 129-178.

Boyd, B. 1995. Houses and hearths, pits and burials: Natufian mortuary practices at Mallaha (Eynan), upper Jordan valley. In Campbell, S. and Green, A. (eds), *The Archaeology of Death in the Ancient Near East*: 17-23. Oxford: Oxbow Monograph 51.

Boz, B. and Hager, D.L. 2013. Living above the dead: Intramural burial practices at Çatalhöyük. In Hodder, I. (ed.), *Humans and Landscapes of Çatalhöyük: Reports from the 2000-2008 Seasons*: 413-440. London and Los Angeles: British Institute at Ankara and Cotsen Institute of Archaeology Press.

Boz, B. and Hager, D.L. 2014. Making sense of social behavior from disturbed and commingled skeletons: A case study from Çatalhöyük, Turkey. In Osterholtz, A.J. Baustian, K.M. and Martin, D.L. (eds), *Commingled and Disarticulated Human Remains: Working toward Improved Theory, Method and Data*: 17-33. New York: Springer.

Braidwood, R.J. and Braidwood, L.S. (eds) 1960. *Excavations in the Plain of Antioch.* University of Chicago. Oriental Institute Publication Vol. 61. University of Chicago.

Brickley, M.B. 2018. Cribra orbitalia and porotic hyperostosis: A biological approach to diagnosis. *American Journal of Physical Anthropology* 167: 896-902.

Bronk Ramsey, C. 1995. Radiocarbon calibration and analysis of stratigraphy: the OxCal Program. *Radiocarbon* 37: 425-430.

Bronk Ramsey, C. 2009. Bayesian analysis of radiocarbon dates. *Radiocarbon* 51: 337-360.

Bronk Ramsey, C. 2017. Methods for Summarizing Radiocarbon Datasets. *Radiocarbon* 59: 1809-1833.

Brothwell, D.R. 1963. *Digging Up Bones: The Excavation, Treatment and Study of Human Skeletal Remains.* London: The British Museum of Natural History.

Budd, C., Lillie, M., Alpaslan-Roodenberg, S., Karul, N. and Pinhasi, R. 2013. Stable isotope analysis of Neolithic and Chalcolithic populations from Aktopraklik, northern Anatolia. *Journal of Archaeological Science* 40: 860-867.

Buikstra, J.E. 1976. The Caribou Eskimo: General and specific disease. *American Journal of Physical Anthropology* 45: 351-368.

Buikstra, J.E., Konigsberg, L.W. and Bullington, J. 1986. Fertility and the development of agriculture in the prehistoric Midwest. *American Antiquity*: 51: 528-546.

Buikstra, J.E. and Ubelaker, D.H. 1994. *Standards for Data Collection from Human Skeletal Remains.* Arkansas Archaeological Survey Research Series No. 44.

Bustillo, M.A. and Ruiz-Ortiz, P.A. 1987. Chert occurrences in carbonate turbidites: Examples from the Upper Jurassic of the Betic Mountains (southern Spain). *Sedimentology* 34: 611-621.

Buzon, M.R. and Bombak, A. 2010. Dental disease in the Nile Valley during the New Kingdom. *International Journal of Osteoarchaeology* 20: 371-387.

Byrd, B.F. 2000. Households in transition. Neolithic social organization within Southwest Asia. In Kuijt, I. (ed.), *Life in Neolithic Farming Communities: Social Organization, Identity, and Differentiation*: 63-98. New York: Kluwer Academic.

Caffey, J. 1937. The skeletal changes in the chronic hemolytic anemias (erythroblastic anemia, sickle cell anemia, and chronic hemolytic icterus). *American Journal of Roentgenology and Radiation Therapy* 37: 293-324.

Campbell, S. 1995. Death for the living in the late Neolithic in north Mesopotamia. In Campbell, S. and Green, A. (eds), *The Archaeology of Death in the Ancient Near East*: 29-34. Oxford: Oxbow Monograph 51.

Cardoso, H.F.V. 2007. Environmental effects on skeletal versus dental development: sing a documented subadult skeletal sample to test a basic assumption in human osteological research. *American Journal of Physical Anthropology* 132: 223-233.

Cauvin, J. 1972. Nouvelles fouilles à Tell Mureybet (Syrie). *Annales Archéologiques Arabes Syriennes* 22: 105-115.

Cerezo-Román, J.I. 2014. Pathways to personhood: Cremation as a social practice among the Tucson Basin Hohokam. In Kuijt, I., Quinn, C. and Cooney, G. (eds), *Transformation by Fire: The Archaeology of Cremation in Cultural Context*: 148-167. Tucson: University of Arizona Press.

Chikaraishi, Y., Kashiyama, Y., Ogawa, N.O., Kitazato, H. and Ohkouchi, N. 2007. Metabolic control of nitrogen isotope composition of amino acids in macroalgae and gastropods: implications for aquatic food web studies. *Marine Ecology Progress Series* 342: 85-90.

Chikaraishi, Y., Ogawa, N.O., Kashiyama, Y., Takano, Y., Suga, H., Tomitani, A., Miyashita, H., Kitazato, H. and Ohkouchi, N. 2009. Determination of aquatic food-web structure based on compound-specific nitrogen isotopic composition of amino acids. *Limnology and Oceanography: Methods* 7: 740-750.

Chikaraishi, Y., Ogawa, N.O. and Ohkouchi, N. 2010. Further evaluation of the trophic level estimation based on nitrogen isotopic composition of amino acids. In Ohkouch, N., Tayasu, I., Koba, K. (eds), *Earth, Life, and Isotopes*: 37-51. Kyoto: Kyoto University Press.

Chikaraishi, Y., Steffan, S.A., Ogawa, N.O., Ishikawa, N.F., Sasaki, Y., Tsuchiya, M. and Ohkouchi, N. 2014. High-resolution food webs based on nitrogen isotopic composition of amino acids. *Ecology and Evolution* 4: 2423-2449.

Clarke, N.G., Carey, S.E., Srikandi, W., Hirsch, R.S. and Leppard, P.I. 1986. Periodontal disease in ancient populations. *American Journal of Physical Anthropology* 71: 173-183.

Cohen, M.N. and Armelagos, G.J., (eds) 2013. *Paleopathology at the Origins of Agriculture.* Gainsville: University of Florida Press.

Cohen, M.N. and Crane-Kramer, G.M.M. (eds) 2007. *Ancient Health: Skeletal Indicators of Agricultural and Economic Intensification.* Gainsville: University of Florida Press.

Cole, T.M. 1994. Size and shape of the femur and tibia in Northern Plains Indians. In Owsley, D.W. and Jantz, R.L. (eds), *Skeletal Biology in the Great Plains: A Multidisciplinary View*: 219-233. Washington: Smithsonian Institute Press.

Cooley, T.B., Witwer, E.R. and Lee, P. 1927. Anemia in children, with splenomegaly and peculiar changes in bones. *American Journal of Disease of Children* 34: 347-363.

Coqueugniot, E. 1999. Tell Dja'de el-Mughara. In Del Olno Lete, G. and Montero Fenollós J.L. (eds), *Archaeology of the Upper Syrian Euphrates Tishrin Dam Area*: 41-55. Barcelona: Institut del Pròxim Orient Antic, Universitat de Barcelona.

Courtois, J. 1973. Prospection archéologique dans la moyenne vallée de l'Oronte. (El Ghab et el Roudj-Syrie du nord-ouest). *Syria* 50: 53-99.

Croucher, K. 2012. *Death and Dying in the Neolithic Near East.* Oxford: Oxford University Press.

Dalhberg, A.A. 1960. The dentition of the first agriculturalists. *American Journal of Physical Anthropology* 18: 243-256.

DeNiro, M.J. 1985. Postmortem preservation and alteration of in vivo bone-collagen isotope ratios in relation to paleodietary reconstruction. *Nature* 317: 806-809.

DeNiro, M.J., Epstein, S. 1978. Influence of diet on the distribution of carbon isotopes in animals. *Geochimuca et Cosmochimica Acta* 42: 495-506.

Dewitte, S.N. and Bekvalac, J. 2011. The association between periodontal disease and periosteal lesions in the St. Mary Graces cemetery, London, England A.D. 1350-1538. *American Journal of Physical Anthropology* 146: 609-618.

Dougherty, S.P. 2011. Sickness and death: Evidence from human remains. In Tsuneki, A. and Hydar, J. (eds),

Life and Death in the Kerkh Neolithic Cemetery: 27-30. Tsukuba: Department of Archaeology, University of Tsukuba.

Dougherty, S.P. and Tsuneki, A. 2015. To snatch the baby from its mother's lap: Infant mortality and maternal health at Tell el-Kerkh, Syria. Poster Presented at *the 80th annual meeting of the Society for American Archaeology*, San Francisco, CA.

Eliason, E.L. 1921. Results of treatment of 115 cases of fracture of the shaft of the femur at the University of Pennsylvania Hospital. *Annals of Surgery 74:* 206-213.

El-Wailly, F. and Abu el-Soof, B. 1965. The excavations at Tell es-Sawwan. First preliminary report (1964). *Sumer* 21: 17-32.

Eng, L.L. 1958. Chronic iron deficiency anemia with bone changes resembling Cooley's anemia. *Acta Haematologica* 19: 263-268.

Erdal, Y.S. 2013. Life and death at Hakemi Use. In Nieuwenhuyse, O.P., Bernbeck, R., Akkermans, P.M.M.G. and Rogasch, J. (eds), *Interpreting the Late Neolithic of Upper Mesopotamia*: 213-223. Turnhout: Brepols Publishers.

Erdal, Y.S. 2015. Bone or flesh: Defleshing and post-depositional treatments at Körtik Tepe (Southeastern Anatolia, PPNA Period). *European Journal of Archaeology* 18 (1): 4-32.

Eshed, V., Gopher, A., Gage, T.B. and Hershkovitz, I. 2004a. Has the transition to agriculture reshaped the demographic structure of prehistoric populations? New evidence from the Levant. *American Journal of Physical Anthropology* 124: 315-329.

Eshed, V., Gopher, A., Gage, T.B. and Hershkovitz, I. 2004b. Musculoskeletal stress markers in Natufian hunter-gatherers and Neolithic farmers in the Levant: The upper limb. *American Journal of Physical Anthropology* 123: 303-315.

Eshed, V., Gopher, A. and Hershkovitz, I. 2006. Tooth wear and dental pathology at the advent of agriculture: New evidence from the Levant. *American Journal of Physical Anthropology* 130: 145-159.

Eshed, V., Gopher, A., Pinhasi, R. and Hershkovitz, I. 2010. Paleopathology and the origin of agriculture in the Levant. *American Journal of Physical Anthropology* 143: 121-133.

Eshed, V. and Nadel, D. 2015. Changes in burial customs from the Pre-Pottery to the Pottery Neolithic periods in the Levant: The case-study of Tel Roim West, orthern Israel. *Paléorient* 41 (2): 115-131.

Fazekas, I. and Kósa, F. 1978. *Forensic Fetal Osteology*. Budapest: Akadémiai Kiadó.

Fowler, K.D. 2004. *Neolithic Mortuary Practices in Greece*. BAR International Series 1314. Oxford: Archaeopress.

Frohlich, B., Ortner, D.J. and Froment, A. 2008. The osteology of the EBIA people. In Ortner, D.J. and Frohlich, B. (eds), *The Early Bronze Age I Tombs and Burials of Bâb edh-Dhrâ', Jordan*: 229-249. Lanham: Altamira Press.

Fuller, B.T., Fuller, J.L., Harris, D.A. and Hedges, R.E.M. 2006. Detection of breastfeeding and weaning in modern human infants with carbon and nitrogen stable isotope ratios. *American Journal of Physical Anthropology* 129: 279-293.

Gallis, K. 1982. *Kafseis Nekron apo tin Neolithiki Epochi sti Thessalia. Ekdosi Tameiou archaeologikon poron kai apallotrioseon.* Athens, Ekdosi Tameiou Archaeiologikon Poron kai Apallotrioseon. (in Greek)

Galloway, A. 1999. *Broken Bones: Anthropological Analyses of Blunt Force Trauma.* Springfield: Charles C. Thomas.

Garfunkel, Z. 1981. Internal structure of the Dead Sea leaky transform (Rift) in relation to plate kinematics. *Tectonophysics* 80: 81-108.

Garstang, J. 1953. *Prehistoric Mersin: Yümük Tepe in Southern Turkey.* Oxford, Clarendon Press.

Gebel, H.G.K. 1988. Late Epipalaeolithic-Aceramic Neolithic sites in the Petra area. In Garrard, A.N. and Gebel, H.G.K. (eds), *The Prehistory of Jordan, The State of Research in 1986*: 67-100. BAR International Series 396(1). Oxford: Archaeopress.

Gebel, H.G.K. and Hermansen, B.D. 2000. The 2000 Season at Late PPNB Ba'ja. *Neo-Lithics* 2-3: 20-22.

Gebel, H.G.K. and Hermansen, B.D. 2001. LPPNB Ba'ja 2001. A short note. *Neo-Lithics* 2: 15-20.

Geckeler, E.O. 1943. *Fractures and Dislocations for Practitioners.* Baltimore: Williams and Wilkins Company.

Gerritsen, F. and Sholts, S. 2004. Tell Kurdu excavations 2001. *Anatolica* 30: 37-75.

Ghirshman, R. 1939. *Fouilles de Sialk: près de Kashan, 1933, 1934, 1937.* Volume 1. Paris: Paul Geuthner.

Gibbs, K. and Banning, E.B. 2013. Late Neolithic society and village life: The view from the southern Levant. In Nieuwenhuyse, O., Akkermans, P., Bernbeck, R. and Rogasch, J. (eds), *Interpreting the Late Neolithic of Upper Mesopotamia*: 356-366. Turhout: Brepols Publishers.

Gilmore, C.C. and Grote, M.N. 2012. Estimating age from adult occlusal wear: A modification of the Miles method. *American Journal of Physical Anthropology* 149: 181-192.

Glass, G.B. 1991. Continuous eruption and periodontal status in pre-industrial dentitions. *International Journal of Osteoarchaeology* 1: 265-271.

Goodman, A.H. and Armelagos, G.J. 1985. Factors affecting the distribution of enamel hypoplasias within the human permanent dentition. *American Journal of Physical Anthropology* 68: 479-493.

Goodman, A.H., Armelagos, G.J. and Rose, J.C. 1980. Enamel hypoplasias as indicators of stress in three prehistoric populations from Illinois. *Human Biology* 52: 515-528.

Goodman, A.H. and Rose, J.C. 1990. Assessment of systemic physiological perturbations from dental enamel hypoplasias and associated histological structures. *Yearbook of Physical Anthropology* 33: 59-110.

Goodman, A.H., Martinez, C. and Chavez, C. 1991. Nutritional supplementation and the development of linear enamel hypoplasias in children from Tezonteopan, Mexico. *American Journal of Clinical Nutrition* 53: 773-781.

Gopher, A. and Orrelle, E. 1995. New data on burials from the Pottery Neolithic period (Sixth-fifth Millennium BC) in Israel. In Campbell, S. and Green, A. (eds), *The Archaeology of Death in the Ancient Near East*: 24-28. Oxford: Oxbow Monograph 51.

Goring-Morris, A.N.D. and Belfer-Cohen, A. 2010. Different ways of being, different ways of seeing... Changing world view in the Near East. In Finlayson, B. and Warren, G. (eds), *Landscapes in Transition*: 9-22. Oxford: Oxbow.

Gresky, J., Haelm, J. and Clare, L. 2017. Modified human crania from Göbekli Tepe provide evidence for a new form of Neolithic skull cult. *Science Advances* 3 (6): e1700564.

Guatelli-Steinberg, D. 2016. Dental stress indicators from micro- to macroscopic. In Irish, J.D. and Scott, G.R. (eds), *A Companion to Dental Anthropology*: 450-464. Oxford: John Wiley & Sons, Inc.

Guerrero, E., Molist, M., Kujit, I. and Anfruns, J. 2009. Seated memory: New insight into Near Eastern Neolithic mortuary variability from Tell Halula, Syria. *Current Anthropology* 50 (3): 379-391.

Gustafson, G. and Koch, G. 1974. Age estimation up to 16 years of age based on dental development. *Odontologisk Revy* 25: 297-306.

Haas, N. 1974. Les restes squelettiques découverts à Tel-Ely (Sheikh Aly). *Mitekufat Haeven: Journal of the Israel Prehistoric Society* 12: 36-46.

Haddow, S.D. and Knüsel, C.J. 2017. Skull retrieval and secondary burial practices in the Neolithic Near East: Recent insights from Çatalhöyük, Turkey. *Bioarchaeology International* 1: 52-71.

Hattori, I. 2008. *Chert and siliceous sediments- its sedimentation and diagenesis.* Nagoya: Kin-miraisha (in Japanese).

Hedges, R.E.M. and Reynard, L.M. 2007. Nitrogen isotopes and the trophic level of humans in archaeology. *Journal of Archaeological Science* 34: 1240-1251.

Helwing, B. 2016. Reconsidering the Neolithic graveyard at Tell es-Sawwan. *Paléorient* 42 (1): 129-142.

Hengen, O.P. 1971. Cribra orbitalia: Pathogenesis and probable etiology. *Homo* 22: 57-75.

Henton, E. 2013. Herding and settlement identity in the central Anatolian Neolithic: Herding decisions and organisation in Çatalhöyük, elucidated through oxygen isotopes and microwear in sheep teeth. In De Cupere, B., Linseele, V., Hamilton-Dyer, S. (eds), *Archaeozoology of the Near East X: Proceedings of the Tenth International Symposium on the Archaeozoology of South-western Asia and Adjacent Areas*: 69-100. Leuven: Peeters publishers.

Hershkovitz, I. and Galili, E. 1990. 8000 year-old human remains on the sea floor near Atlit, Israel. *Human Evolution* 5 (4): 319-358.

Hershkovitz, I. and Gopher, A. 1988. Human burials from Horvat Galili: A pre-pottery Neolithic site in Upper Galilee, Israel. *Paléorient* 14: 199-125.

Hertz, R. 1960. *Death and the Right Hand* (trans. R. Needham and C. Needham). Aberdeen: Cohen & West.

Hijara, I. 1978. Three New Graves at Arpachiyah. *World Archaeology* 10: 125-128.

Hillson, S.W. 1996. *Dental Anthropology.* Cambridge: Cambridge University Press.

Hillson, S.W., Larsen, C.S., Boz, B., Pilloud, M.A., Sadvari, J.W., Agarwal, S.C., Glencross, B., Beauchesne, P., Pearson, J., Ruff, C.B., Garofalo, E.M., Hager, L.D. and Haddow, S.D. 2013. The human remains I: Interpreting community structure, health and diet in Neolithic Çatalhöyük. In Hodder, I. (ed.), *Humans and Landscapes of Çatalhöyük: Reports from the 2000-2008 Seasons* (Çatalhöyük Research Project v.8): 339-396. London: British Institute at Ankara.

Hironaga, N. 2011. Cremation burials. In Tsuneki, A. and Hydar, J. (eds), *Life and Death in the Kerkh Neolithic Cemetery*: 13-17. Tsukuba, Department of Archaeology, University of Tsukuba.

Hisada, K. 2017. Geology based culture? In Tsuneki, A., Yamada, S. and Hisada, K. (eds), *Ancient West Asian Civilization: Geoenvironment and Society in the Pre-Islamic Middle East*: 15-38. New York: Springer.

Hisada, K. (ed.) 2018. *First miracle to mankind leaving Africa- Archaeogeology for Zagros in West Asia.* Tokyo: Aichi-shuppan (in Japanese).

Hodder, I. 2004. Introduction. In *Çatalhöyük 2004 Archive Report*.

Hodder, I. 2009. An archaeological response. *Paléorient* 35 (1): 105-36.

Hole, F. 1989. Patterns of burial in the fifth millennium. In Henrickson, E.F. and Thuesen, I. (eds), *Upon This Foundation -The 'Ubaid Reconsidered*: 149-180. Copenhagen: Museum Tusculanum Press.

Holland, T.D. 1995. Estimation of adult stature from the calcaneus and talus. *American Journal of Physical Anthropology* 96: 315-320.

Hongo, H. 1996. Faunal Remains from Tell Aray 2, Northwestern Syria. *Paléorient* 22: 125-144.

Hoppe, K.A., Koch, P.L. and Furutani, T.T. 2003. Assessing the preservation of biogenic strontium in fossil bones and tooth enamel. *International Journal of Osteoarchaeology* 13: 20-28.

Hudson, M. 1999. Human skeletal remains. In Tsuneki *et al*. Third Preliminary Report of the Excavations at Tell el-Kerkh (1999), Northwest Syria. *Bulletin of the Ancient Orient Museum* XX: 18-25.

Irish, J.D. and Turner, C.G. 1987. More lingual surface attrition of the maxillary anterior teeth in American Indians: Prehistoric Panamanians. *American Journal of Physical Anthropology* 73: 209-213.

Itahashi, Y., Chikaraishi, Y., Ohkouchi, N. and Yoneda, M. 2014. Refinement of reconstructed ancient food webs based on the nitrogen isotopic compositions of amino acids from bone collagen: A case study of archaeological herbivores from Tell Ain el-Kerkh, Syria. *Geochemical Journal* 48: E15-E19.

Itahashi, Y., Erdal, Y.S., Tekin, H., Omar, L., Miyake, Y., Chikaraishi, Y., Ohkouchi, N. and Yoneda, M. 2019. Amino acid ¹⁵N analysis reveals change in the importance of freshwater resources between the hunter-gatherer and farmer in the Neolithic upper Tigris. *American Journal of Physical Anthropology* 168: 676-686.

Itahashi, Y., Miyake, Y., Maeda, O., Kondo, O., Hongo, H., Van Neer, W., Chikaraishi, Y., Ohkouchi, N. and Yoneda, M. 2017. Preference for fish in a Neolithic hunter-gatherer community of the upper Tigris, elucidated by amino acid δ^{15}N analysis. *Journal of Archaeological Science* 82: 40-49.

Itahashi, Y., Tsuneki, A., Dougherty, S.P., Chikaraishi, Y., Ohkouchi, N. and Yoneda, M. 2018. Dining together: Reconstruction of Neolithic food consumption based on the δ^{15}N values for individual amino acids at Tell el-Kerkh, northern Levant. *Journal of Archaeological Science: Reports*, 17: 775-784.

Iwasaki, T. and Nishino, H. (eds) 1990. *An Archaeological Study on the Development of Civilization in Syria 1*. Report of University of Tsukuba Archaeological Mission to Syria 1. Tsukuba: University of Tsukuba (in Japanese with English summary).

Iwasaki, T. and Nishino, H. (eds) 1991. *An Archaeological Study on the Development of Civilization in Syria 2*. Report of University of Tsukuba Archaeological Mission to Syria 2. Tsukuba: University of Tsukuba (in Japanese with English summary).

Iwasaki, T. and Nishino, H. (eds) 1992. *An Archaeological Study on the Development of Civilization in Syria 3*. Report of University of Tsukuba Archaeological Mission to Syria 3. Tsukuba: University of Tsukuba (in Japanese with English summary).

Iwasaki, T., Nishino, H. and Tsuneki, A. 1995. The prehistory of the Rouj Basin, northwest Syria: A preliminary report. *Anatolica* 21: 143-187.

Iwasaki, T. and Tsuneki, A. (eds) 2003. *Archaeology of the Rouj Basin: A Regional Study of the Transition from Village to City in Northwest Syria*, Vol. I. Al-Shark 2: University of Tsukuba, Studies for West Asian Archaeology, Tsukuba: Department of Archaeology, Institute of History and Anthropology, University of Tsukuba.

James, V., Canerot, J., Meyer, A. and Biteau, J.-J. 2000. Growth and destruction of Bathonian silica nodules in the Western Pyrenees (France). *Sedimentary Geology* 132: 5-23.

Jammo, S. 2014. Skull removal practice in the ancient Near East Neolithic of Tell el-Kerkh, Syria. *Tsukuba Archaeological Studies* 25: 47-66.

Jammo, S. 2018. *Beyond Death: The Tale of a Neolithic Society and the Study of an Outdoor Communal Cemetery at Tell el-Kerkh, Northwest Syria*. A Dissertation Submitted to the University of Tsukuba in Partial Fulfillment of the Requirements for the Degree of Doctor of Philosophy in Literature.

Jammo, S. and Tsuneki, A. 2020. The outdoor communal Neolithic cemetery of Tell el-Kerkh, northwest Syria. In Otto, A., Herles, M., Kaniuth, K., Korn, L. and Heidenreich, A. (eds), *Proceedings of the 11th International Congress on the Archaeology of the Ancient Near East. Vol. 2*: 171-182. Wiesbaden: Harrassowitz Verlag.

Jammous, B. and Stordeur, D. 1996. Jerf el-Ahmar. In *Syrian-European Archaeology Exhibition: Working Together*: 27-29. Damascus: l'Institut Français d'Études Arabes de Damas.

Judd, M. 2006. Continuity of interpersonal violence between Nubian communities. *American Journal of Physical Anthropology* 131: 324-333.

Judd, M. 2008. The parry problem. *Journal of Archaeological Sciences* 35: 1658-1666.

Jurmain, R. 1999. *Stories from the Skeleton: Behavioral Reconstruction in Human Osteology*. Amsterdam: Gordon and Breach Publishers.

Jurmain, R., Cardosa, F.A., Henderson, C. and Villotte, S. 2012. Bioarchaeology's Holy Grail: The reconstruction of activity. In Grauer, A.L. (ed.), *A Companion to Paleopathology*: 531-552. Oxford: Blackwell Publishing, Ltd.

Kamada, H. and Ohtsu, T. 1981. Tell Songor A: *Al-Rāfidān* 2: 164-181.

Kamada, H. and Ohtsu, T. 1991. Second report on the excavations at Songor A: Ubaid graves. *Al-Rāfidān* 12: 221-248.

Kanjou, Y., Kuijt, I., Erdal, S.Y. and Kondo, O. 2015. Early human decapitation, 11,700–10, 700 cal BP, within the Pre-Pottery Neolithic village of Tell Qaramel, north Syria. *International Journal of Osteoarchaeology* 25: 743-752.

Kanstrup, M., Holst, M.K., Jensen, P.M., Thomsen, I.K. and Christensen, B.T. 2014. Searching for long-term trends in prehistoric manuring practice. δ^{15}N analyses of charred cereal grains from the 4th to the 1st millennium BC. *Journal of Archaeological Science* 51: 115-125.

Katayama, N., Morimoto, R., Kimura, T. and Takeuchi, H. (eds), 1970. *Geoscience dictionary (new version)- mineralogy, petrology, economic geology, geochemistry, and volcanology*. Tokyo: Kokon-shoin (in Japanese).

Katz, D. and Suchey, J.M. 1986. Age determination of the male os pubis. *American Journal of Physical Anthropology* 69: 427-435.

Keenleyside, A. 2008. Dental pathology and diet at Apollonia, a Greek colony on the Black Sea. *International Journal of Osteoarchaeology* 18: 262-279.

Kenyon, K.M. 1981. *Excavations at Jericho. Vol. 3. The Architecture and Stratigraphy of the Tell 3*. London: British School of Archaeology in Jerusalem.

Killick, R. and Roaf, M. 1983. Excavations in Iraq, 1981-82. *Iraq* 45 (2): 199-224.

King, S.E. and Ulijaszek, S.J. 1999. Invisible insults during growth and development: Contemporary theories and past populations. In Hoppa, R.D. and FitzGerald, C.M. (eds), *Human Growth in the Past: Studies from bones and teeth*: 161-182. Cambridge: Cambridge University Press.

Kitagawa, H., Masuzawa, T., Nakamura, T. and Matsumoto, E. 1993. A batch preparation method for graphite targets with low-background for AMS Area 34 measurements. *Radiocarbon* 35: 295-300.

Kızıltan, Z. and Polat, M.A. 2013. The Neolithic at Yenikapı: Marmaray-metro project rescue excavations. In Özdoğan, M., Başgelen, N. and Kuniholm, P. (eds), *The Neolithic in Turkey: New Excavations and New Research, Northwestern Turkey and Istanbul*: 113-165. Istanbul, Archaeology and Art Publication.

Klaus, H.D. and Tam, M.E. 2010. Oral health and the postcontact adaptive transition: A contextual reconstruction of diet at Mórrope, Peru. *American Journal of Physical Anthropology* 141: 594-609.

Knüsel, C.J. and Glencross, B. 2017. Çatalhöyük, archaeology, violence. *Contagion: Journal of Violence, Mimesis, and Culture* 24: 23-36.

Kobayashi, K., Niu, E., Itoh, S., Yamagata, H., Lotaidze, Z., Jorjliani, I., Nakamura, K. and Fujine, H. 2007. The compact ^{14}C AMS facility of Paleo Labo Co., Ltd., Japan. *Nuclear Instruments and Methods in Physics Research Section B* 259 (1): 31-35.

Koutsadelis, C. 2007. *Mortuary Practices in the Process of Levantine Neolithisation*. BAR International Series 1685. Oxford: John and Erica Hedges.

Kuijt, I. 1996. Negotiating equality through ritual: A consideration of Late Natufian and Pre-pottery Neolithic A period mortuary practices. *Journal of Anthropological Archaeology* 15 (4): 313-336.

Kuijt, I. (ed.) 2000. *Life in Neolithic Farming Communities, Social Organization, Identity, and Differentiation*. New York: Kluwer Academic/Plenum Publishers.

Kuijt, I. 2001. Place, death, and the transmission of social memory in early agricultural communities of the Near Eastern Pre-Pottery Neolithic. In Chesson, M.S. (ed.), *Social Memory, Identity, and Death: Intradisciplinary Perspective on Mortuary Rituals*: 80-99. Washington, DC, American Anthropological Association Archaeology Division (vol. 10).

Kuijt, I. 2008. The regeneration of life: Neolithic structures of symbolic remembering and forgetting. *Current Anthropology* 49 (2): 1-20.

Kuijt, I. and Goring-Morris, N. 2002. Foraging, farming, and social complexity in the Pre-Pottery Neolithic of the southern Levant: A review and synthesis. *Journal of World Prehistory* 16 (4): 361-440.

Kuijt, I., Quinn, C.P. and Cooney, G. (ed.) 2014. *Transformation by Fire. The Archaeology of Cremation in Cultural Context*. Tucson, The University of Arizona Press.

Kusaka, S. Nakano, T., Yumoto, T. and Nakatsukasa, M. 2011. Strontium isotope evidence of migration and diet in relation to ritual tooth ablation: a case study from the Inariyama Jomon site, Japan. *Journal of Archaeological Science* 38: 166-174.

Larsen, C.S. 1995. Biological changes in human populations with agriculture. *Annual Review of Anthropology* 24: 185-213.

Larsen, C.S. 1997. *Bioarchaeology: Interpreting Behavior from the Human Skeleton*. Cambridge: Cambridge University Press.

Larsen, C.S., Hillson, S.W., Ruff, C.B., Sadvari, J.W. and Garofalo, E.M. 2013. The human remains II: Interpreting lifestyle and activity in Neolithic Çatalhöyük. In Hodder, I. (ed.), *Humans and Landscapes of Çatalhöyük: Reports from the 2000-2008 seasons* (Çatalhöyük Research Project v.8): 397-412. London: British Institute at Ankara.

Larsen, C.S., Hillson, S.W., Boz, B., Pilloud, M.A., Sadvari, J.W., Agarwal, S.C., Glencross, B., Beauchesne, P., Pearson J., Ruff, C.B., Garofalo, E.M., Hager, L.D. Haddow, S.D. and Knüsel, C.J. 2015. Bioarchaeology of Neolithic Çatalhöyük: Lives and lifestyles of an early farming society in transition. *Journal of World Prehistory* 28: 27-68.

Larsen, C.S., Knüsel, C.J., Haddow, S.D., Pilloud, M.A, Milella, M., Sadvari, J.W., Pearson, J., Ruff, C.B., Garofalo, E.M., Bocaege, E., Betz, B.J., Dori, I., Glencross, B. 2019. Bioarchaeology of Neolithic Çatalhöyük reveals fundamental transitions in health, mobility, and lifestyle in early farmers. *Proceedings of the National Academy of Sciences* 116: 12615-12623.

Layrisse, M. and Roche, M. 1964. The relationship between anemia and hookworm infection: Results of surveys of rural Venezuelan population. *American Journal of Hygiene* 79: 279-301.

Le Mière, M. 2013. Neolithic pottery from the Khabur basin: A reassessment in the light of recent discoveries. In Nishiaki, Y., Kashima, K. and Verhoeven, M. (eds), *Neolithic Archaeology in the Khabur Valley, Upper Mesopotamia and Beyond*: 96-109. Berlin: ex oriente.

Le Mort, F., Erim-Özdoğan, A., Özbek, M. and Yilmaz, Y. 2000. Feu et archéoanthropologie au Proche-Orient (Épipaléolithique et Néolithique). Le lien avec les pratiques funéraires. Données nouvelles de Çayönü (Turquie). *Paléorient* 26 (2): 37-50.

Lewis, M.E. 2007. *The Bioarchaeology of Children*. Cambridge: Cambridge University Press.

Lewis, M.E. 2012. Thalassemia: Its diagnosis and interpretation in past skeletal populations. *International Journal of Osteoarchaeology* 22: 685-693.

Lichter, C. 2016. Burial customs of the Neolithic in Anatolia: An overview. In Yalçın, Ü. (ed.), *Anatolian Metal VII*, 71-83. Bochum: Deutsches Bergbau-Museum.

Lichter, C. 2017. The transition from the Mesolithic to the Neolithic between western Anatolia and the lower Danube: Evidence from burial customs. In Reingruber, A., Tsirtsoni, Z. and Nedelcheva, P. (eds), *Going West? The Dissemination of Neolithic Innovations between the Bosporus and the Carpathians*: 113-122. London and New York: Routledge.

Longin, R. 1971. New method of collagen extraction for radiocarbon dating. *Nature* 230: 241-242.

Lösch, S., Grupe, G. and Peters, J. 2006. Stable isotopes and dietary adaptations in humans and animals at Pre-Pottery Neolithic Nevall Çori, southeast Anatolia. *American Journal of Physical Anthropology* 131: 181-193.

Lovejoy, C.O. 1985. Dental wear in the Libben population: Its functional pattern and role in the determination of adult skeletal age at death. *American Journal of Physical Anthropology* 68: 47-56.

Lovejoy, C.O., Meindl, R.S., Pryzbeck, T.R. and Mensforth, R.P. 1985. Chronological metamorphosis of the auricular surface of the ilium: A new method for the determination of adult skeletal age at death. *American Journal of Physical Anthropology* 68: 15-28.

Lovell, N.C. 1997. Trauma analysis in paleopathology. *Yearbook of Physical Anthropology* 40: 139-170.

Lukacs, J.R. 2008. Fertility and agriculture accentuate sex differences in dental caries rates. *Current Anthropology* 49: 901-914.

Lukacs, J.R. 2017. Bioarchaeology of oral health: Sex and gender differences in dental disease. In Agarwal, S.C. and Wesp, J.K. (eds), *Exploring Sex and Gender in Bioarchaeology*: 263-290. Albuquerque: University of New Mexico Press.

Lukacs, J.R. and Pastor, R.F. 1988. Activity-induced patterns of dental abrasion in prehistoric Pakistan: Evidence from Mehrgarh and Harappa. *American Journal of Physical Anthropology* 76: 377-398.

Lukacs, J.R. and Largaespada, L.L. 2006. Explaining sex differences in dental caries prevalence: Saliva, hormones, and 'life-history' etiologies. *American Journal of Human Biology* 18: 540-555.

Maeda, O. 2010. Recent studies on the use of obsidian in the Neolithic Near East. *Journal of West Asian Archaeology* 11: 62-79.

Maeda, O. 2017. Development of exchange networks: The distribution of obsidian and marine shells in the Neolithic. *Archaeology Quarterly* 141: 41-44 (in Japanese).

Mallowan, M.E.L. 1936. The excavations at Tell Chagar Bazar, and an archaeological survey of the Habur Region, 1934-5. *Iraq* 3 (1): 1-59.

Mallowan, M.E.L. and Rose, J.C. 1935. Excavations at Tell Arpachiyah, 1933. *Iraq* 2: 1-178.

Mann, R.W. and Hunt, D.R. 2005. *Photographic Regional Atlas of Bone Disease*, 3rd (ed.). Springfield: Charles C. Thomas.

Manolis, S.K., Eliopoulos, C., Koilias, C.G. and Fox, S.C. 2009. Sex determination using metacarpal biometric data from the Athens collection. *Forensic Science International* 193: 130e.1-130e.6. https://doi.org/10.1016/j.forsciint.2009.09.015

Manspeizer, W. 1985. The Dead Sea Rift: Impact of climate and tectonism on Pleistocene and Holocene sedimentation. In K.T. Biddle and N. Christie-Blick (eds), *Strike-Slip Deformation, Basin Formation and Sedimentation*: 143-158. SEMP Special Publication No. 37. Oklahoma: SEPM Society for Sedimentary Geology.

Marques, C., Matos, V. and Meinzer, N.J. 2019. Proliferative periosteal reactions: Assessment of trends in Europe over the past two millennia. In Steckel, R.H., Larsen, C.S., Roberts, C.A. and Baten, J. (eds), *The Backbone of Europe: Health, diet, work, and violence over two millennia*: 137-174. Cambridge: Cambridge University Press.

Matsutani, T. (ed.) 1991. *Tell Kashkashok: The Excavations at Tell No. II*. Tokyo: Institute of Oriental Culture, University of Tokyo.

Matsuzaki, H., Nakano, C., Tsuchiya, Y.S., Kato, K., Maejima, Y., Miyairi, Y., Wakasa, S. and Aze, T. 2007. Multi-nuclide AMS performances at MALT. *Nuclear Instruments and Methods in Physics Research Section B* 259 (1): 36-40.

McCutchan, J.H. Jr., Lewis, W.M. Jr., Kendall, C. and McGrath, C.C. 2003. Variation in trophic shift for stable isotope ratios of carbon, nitrogen, and sulfur, *Oikos* 102-2: 378-390.

McFadden, C. and Oxenham, M.F. 2017. The D_{0-14}/D ratio: A new paleodemographic index and equation for estimating total fertility rates. *American Journal of Physical Anthropology* 165: 471-479.

McFadden, C. and Oxenham, M.F. 2019. The paleodemographic measure of maternal mortality and a multifaceted approach to maternal health. *Current Anthropology* 60: 141-146.

Meadows, L. and Jantz, R.L. 1992. Estimation of stature from metacarpal lengths. *Journal of Forensic Sciences* 37: 147-154.

Meindl, R.S. and Lovejoy, C.O. 1985. Ectocranial suture closure: A revised method for the determination of skeletal age at death based on the lateral-anterior sutures. *American Journal of Physical Anthropology* 68: 57-66.

Merbs, C.F. 1983. *Patterns of Activity-Induced Pathology in a Canadian Inuit Population*. Archaeological Survey of Canada, paper no. 119.

Merpert, N.Y. and Munchaev R.M. 1993. Burial practices of the Halaf Culture. In Yoffee, N. and Clark, J.J. (eds), *Early Stages in the Evolution of Mesopotamian Civilization: Soviet Excavations in Northern Iraq*: 207-224. Tucson: University of Arizona Press.

Merpert, N.Y., Munchaev, R.M. and Bader, N.O. 1976. The investigations of Soviet expedition in Iraq 1973. *Sumer* 32: 25-61.

Merpert, N.Y., Munchaev, R.M. and Bader, N.O. 1977. The investigations of Soviet expedition in Iraq 1974. *Sumer* 33 (1): 65-104.

390

Merpert, N.Y., Munchaev, R.M. and Bader, N.O. 1978. Soviet investigation of the Sinjar plain. *Sumer* 34: 27-71.

Merrett, D.C. and Meiklejohn, C. 2007. Is House 12 at Bouqras a charnel house? In Faerman, M., Kolska Horwitz, L., Kahana, T. and Zilberman U. (eds), *Faces from the Past. Skeletal Biology of Human Populations from the Eastern Mediterranean.* BAR International Series 1603: 127-139. Oxford: Archaeopress.

Metcalf, P. and Huntington, R. 1991. *Celebrations of Death: The Anthropology of Mortuary Ritual.* Second Edition. Cambridge: Cambridge University Press.

Migaszewwski, Z.M., Galuszka, A., Durakiewicz, T. and Starnawska, E. 2006. Middle Oxfordian – Lower Kimmeridgian chert nodules in the Holy Cross Mountains, south-central Poland. *Sedimentary Geology* 187: 11-28.

Minagawa, M. and Wada, E. 1984. Stepwise enrichment of ^{15}N along food chains: Further evidence and the relation between δ^{15}N and animal age, *Geochimica et Cosmochimica Acta* 48: 1135-1140.

Miyake, Y. 2003. Pottery. In Iwasaki, T. and Tsuneki, A. (eds), *Archaeology of the Rouj Basin: A Regional Study of the Transition from Village to City in Northwest Syria, Vol. I*: 119-141. Al-Shark 2: University of Tsukuba, Studies for West Asian Archaeology, Department of Archaeology, Institute of History and Anthropology, University of Tsukuba.

Miyake, Y. 2017. 'Neolithic revolution' revisited: Origins of agriculture and the Neolithic society. *Archaeology Quarterly* 141: 33-36 (in Japanese).

Miyake, Y., Maeda, O., Tao, M., Hongo, H., Tanno, K. and Yoshida, K. 2009. Preliminary report on the excavations at Slat Camii Yanı in southeast Anatolia: 2004-2008 season. *Tsukuba Archaeological Studies* 20: 75-112. (in Japanese).

Miyashita, S. 2018. World largest's ophiolite; Ocean crust – Upper mantle 100 million years ago. In Matsuo, M. (ed.), *55 chapters to know Oman.* Tokyo: Akashi-shoten (in Japanese).

Molleson, T.I. 2000. The people of Abu Hureyra. In Moore, A.M.T., Hillman, G.C. and Legge, A.J. (eds), *Village on the Euphrates: From foraging to farming at Abu Hureyra*: 301-324. Oxford: Oxford University Press.

Molleson, T.I. 2007. A method for the study of activity related skeletal morphologies. *Bioarchaeology of the Near East* 1: 5-33.

Molleson, T.I. Andrews, P. and Boz, B. 2005. Reconstruction of the Neolithic people of Çatalhöyük. In Hodder, I. (ed.), *Inhabiting Çatalhöyük: Reports from the 1995-99 seasons* (Çatalhöyük Research Project v. 4): 279-300. London: British Institute of Archaeology at Ankara.

Molnar, S. 1972. Tooth wear and culture: A survey of tooth functions among some prehistoric populations. *Current Anthropology* 13: 511-526.

Monchambert, J.Y. 1987. Tell Mashnaqa 1986: Rapport préliminnaire sur la deuxième campagne de fouilles. *Syria* 64: 47-78.

Moore, A.M.T., Hillman, G.C. and Legge, A.J. 2000. *Village on the Euphrates. From Foraging to Farming at Abu Hureyra.* New York: Oxford University Press.

Moore, A.M.T. and Molleson, T.I. 2000. Disposal of the dead. In Moore, A.M.T., Hillman, G.C. and Legge, A.J. (eds), *Village on the Euphrates from Foraging to Farming at Abu Hureyra*: 276-299. Oxford: Oxford University Press.

Moses, S. 2004. The children of Neolithic Çatalhöyük: Burial symbolism and social metaphor. *Çatalhöyük 2004 Archive Reports.* Çatalhöyük 2004 Archive Report (catalhoyuk.com).

Mouty, M. 2015. Campanian age of the Rudist Vautrinia Syriaca paleogeographic implications, Syria. *Damascus University Journal for Basic Sciences* 31: 83-97.

Nadal, D. 1995. The visibility of prehistoric burials in the southern Levant: How rare are the Upper Palaeolithic / Early Epipalaeolithic graves? In Campbell, S. and Green, A. (eds), *The Archaeology of Death in the Ancient Near East*: 1-8. Oxford: Oxbow Monograph 51.

Naito, Y.I., Chikaraishi, Y., Ohkouchi, N., Drucker, D.G. and Bocherens, H. 2013. Nitrogen isotopic composition of collagen amino acids as an indicator of aquatic resource consumption: insights from Mesolithic and Epipalaeolithic archaeological sites in France. *World Archaeology* 45: 338-359.

Naito, Y.I., Honch, N.V., Chikaraishi, Y., Ohkouchi, N. and Yoneda, M. 2010. Quantitative evaluation of marine protein contribution in ancient diets based on nitrogen isotope ratios of individual amino acids in bone collagen: An investigation at the Kitakogane Jomon site. *American Journal of Physical Anthropology* 143: 31-40.

Neiburger, E.J. 1990. Enamel hypoplasias: Poor indicators of dietary stress. *American Journal of Physical Anthropology* 82: 231-233.

Nelson, G.C. 2016. A host of other dental diseases and disorders. In Irish, J.D. and Scott, G.R. (eds), *A Companion to Dental Anthropology*: 465-483. Oxford: John Wiley and Sons, Inc.

Nieuwenhuyse, O. and Akkermans, P.M.M.G. 2019. Transforming the upper Mesopotamian landscape in the Late Neolithic. In Arkadiusz M. (ed.), *Concluding the Neolithic: The Near East in the Second Half of the Seventh Millennium BC.*: 103-137. Atlanta: Lockwood Press.

Nishiaki, Y. 2013. Introduction. In Nishiaki, Y., Kashima, K. and Verhoeven, M. (eds), *Neolithic Archaeology in the Khabur Valley, Upper Mesopotamia and Beyond*: 8-14. Berlin: ex oriente.

Nishiyama, S. and Sha'baan, H. 1998. A Roman-Byzantine tomb. In Tsuneki *et al.* Second Preliminary Report of the Excavations at Tell el-Kerkh (1998),

Northwestern Syria. *Bulletin of the Ancient Orient Museum* XIX: 29-35.

Odaka, T. 2013. Neolithic pottery in the northern Levant and its relations to the east. In Nishiaki, Y., Kashima, K. and Verhoeven, M. (eds), *Neolithic Archaeology in the Khabur Valley, Upper Mesopotamia and Beyond*: 205-217. Berlin: ex oriente.

Oestigaard, T. 1999. Cremations as transformations: When the dual cultural hypothesis was cremated and carried away in urns. *European Journal of Archaeology* 2: 345-364.

Omar, L. 2013. Assessing the pattern of subsistence strategies in Late Neolithic settlements in the northern Mesopotamian region. *Archaeological Review from Cambridge* 28: 14-31.

Orrelle, E. 2008. Infant jar burials – A ritual associated with early agriculture? In Bacvarov, K. (ed.), *Babies Reborn: Infant/Child Burials in Pre-and Protohistory*: 71-78. Oxford: BAR International Series 1832.

Orrelle, E. and Gopher, A. 2000. The Pottery Neolithic period questions about pottery decoration, symbolism, and meaning. In Kuijt, I. (ed.), *Life in Neolithic Farming Communities: Social Organization, Identity, and Differentiation*: 295-308. New York: Kluwer Academic.

Ortner, D.J. and Ericksen, M.F. 1997. Bone changes in the human skull probably resulting from scurvy in infancy and childhood. *International Journal of Osteoarchaeology* 7: 212-220.

Ortner, D.J. and Putschar, W.G.J. 1985. *Identification of Pathological Conditions in Human Skeletal Remains*. Washington: Smithsonian Institution Press.

Osterholtz, A.J. (ed.) 2016. *Theoretical Approaches to Analysis and Interpretation of Commingled Human Remains*. New York: Springer.

Osterholtz, A.J., Baustian, K.M. and Martin, D.L. (eds) 2014. *Commingled and Disarticulated Human Remains: Working toward Improved Theory, Method, and Data*. New York: Springer.

Oxenham, M.F. and Cavill, I. 2010. Porotic hyperostosis and cribra orbitalia: The erythropoietic response to iron-deficiency anemia. *Anthropological Science* 118: 199-200.

Özbal, R.D. 2006. *Households, Daily Practice, and Cultural Appropriation at Sixth Millennium Tell Kurdu*. Ph.D. dissertation. Northwestern University.

Özbal, R., Gerritsen, F., Diebold, B., Healey, E., Aydin, N., Loyet, M., Nardulli, F., Reese, D., Ekstrom, H., Sholts, S., Mekel-Bobrov, N. and Lahn, B. 2004. Tell Kurdu excavations 2001. *Anatolica* 30: 37-107.

Özbek, M. 1976. Étude anthropologique d'ossements humains néolithiques du VIIIe millénaire B.C. provenant de Mureybet, Syrie. *Annales Archéologiques Arabes Syriennes* 26: 161-180.

Özbek, M. 1998. Human skeletal remains from Aşikli: A Neolithic village near Aksaray, Turkey. In Arsebük, G., Mellink, J. and Schirmer, W. (eds), *Light on Top of*

the Black Hill: Studies Presented to Halet Çambel: 567-579. Istanbul: Eğe Yayınları.

Özbek, M. 2009. Remodeled human skulls in Köşk Höyük (Neolithic Age, Anatolia): A new appraisal in view of recent discoveries. *Journal of Archaeological Sciences* 36: 379-386.

Özdoğan, A. 1999. Çayönü. In Özdoğan, M. and Basgelen, N. (eds), *Neolithic in Turkey. The Cradle of Civilization*: 35-63. Istanbul: Arkeoloji ve Sanat Yayınları.

Özdoğan, A. 2013. Neolithic sites in the Marmara region Fikirtepe, Pendik, Yarımburgaz, Toptepe, Hoca Çeşme, and Asağı Pınar. In Özdoğan, M., Başgelen, N. and Kuniholm, P. (eds), *The Neolithic in Turkey. New Excavations and New Research. Vol. 5: Northwestern Turkey and Istanbul*: 167-269. Istanbul: Archaeology and Art Publications.

Öztan, A. 2011. Köşk Höyük, A Neolithic settlement in Niğde-Bor Plateau. In Özdoğan, M., Başgelen, N. and Kuniholm, P. (eds), *The Neolithic in Turkey, Vol. 3. New Excavations and New Research: Central Turkey*: 31-70. Istanbul: Archaeology and Art Publications.

Pearson, J.A., Buitenhuis, H., Hedges, R.E.M., Martin, I., Russell, N. and Twiss, K. 2007. New light on early caprine herding strategies from isotope analysis: a case study from Neolithic Anatolia. *Journal of Archaeological Science* 34: 2170-2179.

Pearson, J.A., Bogaard, A., Charles, M., Hillson, S.W., Larsen, C.S., Russell, N. and Twiss, K. 2015. Stable carbon and nitrogen isotope analysis at Neolithic Çatalhöyük: evidence for human and animal diet and their relationship to households. *Journal of Archaeological Science* 57: 69-79.

Pearson, J.A., Grove, M., Özbek, M. and Hongo, H. 2013. Food and social complexity at Çayönü Tepesi, southeastern Anatolia: Stable isotope evidence of differentiation in diet according to burial practice and sez in the early Neolithic. *Journal of Anthropological Archaeology* 32: 180-189.

Pearson, J.A., Hedges, R.E.M., Molleson, T.I. and Ozbek, M. 2010. Exploring the relationship between weaning and infant mortality: An isotope case study from Asikli Hoyuk and Çayönü Tepesi. *American Journal of Physical Anthropology* 143: 448-457.

Pearson, M.P. 2016. *The Archaeology of Death and Burial*. USA: Texas A&M University Press.

Phillips, S.M. 2003. Worked to the bone: The biomechanical consequences of 'labor therapy' at a nineteenth century asylum. In Herring DA, and Swedlund, A.C. (eds), *Human Biologists in the Archives*: 96-129. Cambridge: Cambridge University Press,

Pomeroy, E. and Zakrzewski, S.R. 2009. Sexual dimorphism in diaphyseal cross-sectional shape in the Medieval Muslim population of Écija, Spain, and Anglo-Saxon Great Chesterford, UK. *International Journal of Osteoarchaeology* 19: 50-65.

Ponikarov, V.P. (ed.) 1968. *The Geology of Syria: Explanatory Notes on the Geological Map of Syria. Scale 1:50,000.*

Damascus, Department of Geological and Mineral Research, Ministry of Petroleum, Electricity and Execution of Industrial Projects.

Plug, H. and Nieuwenhuyse, O. 2018. Ceramics from the cemeteries. In Nieuwenhuyse, O.P. (ed.), *Relentlessly Plain: Seventh Millennium Ceramic at Tell Sabi Abyad, Syria*: 335-352. Oxford: Oxbow Books.

Plug, H., Plicht, J.V.D. and Akkermans, P.M.M.G. 2014. Tell Sabi Abyad, Syria: Dating of Neolithic Cemeteries. *Radiocarbon* 56: 543-554.

Quinn, C.P., Goldstein, L., Cooney, G. and Kuijt, I. 2014. Perspectives: Complexities of terminologies and intellectual frameworks in cremation studies. In Kuijt, I., Quinn, C. and Cooney, G. (eds), *Transformation by Fire: The Archaeology of Cremation in Cultural Context*: 25-32. Tucson, University of Arizona Press.

Raxter, M.H., Ruff, C.B., Azab, A., Erfan, M., Soliman, M., El-Sawaf, A. 2008. Stature estimation in ancient Egyptians: A new technique based on anatomical reconstruction of stature. *American Journal of Physical Anthropology* 136: 147-155.

Reimer, P., Austin, W., Bard, E., Bayliss, A., Blackwell, P., Bronk Ramsey, C., Butzin, M., Cheng, H., Edwards, R., Friedrich, M., Grootes, P., Guilderson, T., Hajdas, I., Heaton, T., Hogg, A., Hughen, K., Kromer, B., Manning, S., Muscheler, R., Palmer, J., Pearson, C., van der Plicht, J., Reimer, R., Richards, D., Scott, E., Southon, J., Turney, C., Wacker, L., Adolphi, F., Büntgen, U., Capano, M., Fahrni, S., Fogtmann-Schulz, A., Friedrich, R., Köhler, P., Kudsk, S., Miyake, F., Olsen, J., Reinig, F., Sakamoto, M., Sookdeo, A. and Talamo, S. 2020. The IntCal20 Northern Hemisphere radiocarbon age calibration curve (0-55 cal kBP). *Radiocarbon* 62: 725-757.

Resch, D. and Gresky, J. 2018. IXa Burials and burial customs. In Bartl, K. (ed.), *The Late Neolithic Site of Shir / Syria, Volume 1 The Excavations at the South Area 2006-2009*: 603-632. Damstadt: Philipp von Zabern.

Reynard, L.M. and Tuross, N. 2015. The known, the unknown and the unknowable: weaning times from archaeological bones using nitrogen isotope ratios. *Journal of Archaeological Science* 53: 618-625.

Ribot, I. and Roberts, C. 1996. A study of non-specific stress indicators and skeletal growth in two mediaeval populations. *Journal of Archaeological Science* 23: 67-79.

Richards, M.P., Pearson, J.A., Molleson, T.I., Russell, N. and Martin, L. 2003. Stable isotope evidence of diet at Neolithic Çatalhöyük, Turkey. *Journal of Archaeological Science* 30: 67-76.

Roberts, C.A. and Buikstra, J.E. 2003. *The Bioarchaeology of Tuberculosis*. Gainsville: University of Florida Press.

Rohrer-Ertl, O., Frey, K.-W. and Newesly, H. 1988. Preliminary note on early Neolithic human remains from Basta and Sabra. In Garrard, A.N. and Gebel, H.G.K. (eds), *The Prehistory of Jordan, the State of Research in 1986*: 135-136. BAR International Series 396. Oxford: Archaeopress.

Rollefson, G.O. 1983. Ritual and ceremony at Neolithic 'Ain Ghazal (Jordan). *Paléorient* 9: 29-38.

Rollefson, G.O. 2000. Ritual and social structure at Neolithic 'Ain Ghazal. In Kuijt, I. (ed.), *Life in Neolithic Farming Communities: Social Organization, Identity, and Differentiation*: 163-188. New York: Kluwer Academic.

Rollefson, G.O. 2010. Blood loss: realignments in community social structures during the LPPNB of Highland Jordan. In Benz, M. (ed.), *The Principle of Sharing. Segregation and Construction of Social Identities at the Transition from Foraging to Farming. Studies in Early Near Eastern Production, Subsistence, and Environment 14*: 182–202. Berlin: ex oriente.

Rollefson, G.O. and Kafafi, Z.A. 2013. The town of 'Ain Ghazal. In Schmandt-Besserat, D. (ed.), *Symbols at 'Ain Ghazal. 'Ain Ghazal Excavation Reports 3*: 3-25. Bibliotheca Neolithica Asiae Meridionalis et Occidentalis & Yarmouk University, Monograph of the Faculty of Archaeology and Anthropology. Berlin: ex oriente.

Rollefson, G.O., Simmons, A.H. and Kafafi, Z.A. 1992. Neolithic cultures at 'Ain Ghazal, Jordan. *Journal of Field Archaeology* 19: 443-470.

Rothschild, B. 2002. Porotic hyperostosis as a marker of health and nutritional conditions. *American Journal of Human Biology* 14: 417-418.

Ruff, C.B. 1987. Sexual dimorphism in human lower limb bone structure: Relationship to subsistence strategy and sexual division of labor. *Journal of Human Evolution* 16: 391-416.

Ruff, C.B. 1994. Biomechanical analysis of Northern and Southern Plains femora: Behavioral implications. In Owsley, D.W. and Jantz, R.L. (eds), *Skeletal Biology in the Great Plains: A multidisciplinary view*: 235-245. Washington: Smithsonian Institute Press.

Ruff, C.B. 2000. Biomechanical analyses of archaeological human skeletons. In Katzenberg, M.A. and Saunders, S.R. (eds), *Bioanthropology Anthropology of the Human Skeleton*, 2nd (ed.): 71-102. New York: John Wiley and Sons, Inc.

Ruff, C.B. 2007. Body size prediction from juvenile skeletal remains. *American Journal of Physical Anthropology* 133: 698-716.

Ruff, C.B. 2019. Biomechanical analyses of archaeological human skeletons. In Katzenberg, M.A. and Grauer, A.L. (eds), *Biological Anthropology of the Human Skeleton*, 3rd (ed.): 189-224. Hoboken: John Wiley and Sons, Inc.

Ruff, C.B., Holt, B.M., Niskanen, M., Sladék, V., Berner, M., Garofalo, E., Garvin, H.M., Hora, M., Maijanen, H., Niinimaki, S., Salo, K., Schuplerová, E. and Tompkins, D. 2012. Stature and body mass estimation from skeletal remains in the European Holocene. *American Journal of Physical Anthropology* 148: 601-617.

Russell, N., Martin, L. and Buitenhuis, H. 2005. Cattle domestication at Çatalhöyük revisited. *Current Anthropology* 46 Suppl.: S101-S108.

Saito, K. 2010. Sheep metacarpi accompanying the dead at an underground tomb in Palmyra, Syria. In Bastl, B., Gassner, V. and Muss, U. (eds), *Zeitreisen, Syrien-Palmyra-Rom*: 201-208. Wein: Phoibos Verlag.

Santana, J., Velasco, J., Ibáñez, J.J. and Braemer, F. 2012. Crania with mutilated facial skeletons: A new ritual treatment in an early Pre-pottery Neolithic B cranial cache at Tell Qarassa North (South Syria). *American Journal of Physical Anthropology* 149: 205-216.

Sarnat, B.G. and Schour, I. 1941. Enamel hypoplasia (chronologic enamel aplasia) in relation to systemic disease: A chronologic, morphologic, and etiologic classification. *Journal of the American Dental Association* 28: 1989-2000.

Sattenspiel, L. and Harpending, H. 1983. Stable populations and skeletal age. *American Antiquity* 48: 489-498.

Saunders, S.R. and Barrans, L. 1999. What can be done about the infant category in skeletal samples? In Hoppa, R.D. and FitzGerald, C.M. (eds), *Human Growth in the Past: Studies from Bones and Teeth*: 183-209. Cambridge: Cambridge University Press.

Scheuer, L. and Black, S. 2000. *Developmental Juvenile Osteology.* New York, Academic Press.

Schoeninger, M.J. and Deniro, M.J. 1984. Nitrogen and carbon isotopic composition of bone-collagen from marine and terrestrial animals. *Geochimica et Cosmochimica Acta* 48: 625-639.

Scott, E.C. 1979. Dental wear scoring technique. *American Journal of Physical Anthropology* 51: 213-218.

Scott, J.C. 2017. *Against the Grain: A Deep History of the Earliest States.* New Haven: Yale University Press.

Sillen, A. 1986. Biogenic and diagenetic Sr/Ca in Plio-pleistocene fossils of the omo shungura formation. *Paleobiology* 12: 311-323.

Simmons, A.H. 2007. *The Neolithic Revolution in the Near East: Transforming the Human Landscape.* Tucson: The University of Arizona Press.

Smith, B.H. 1984. Patterns of molar wear in hunter-gathers and agriculturalists. *American Journal of Physical Anthropology* 63: 39-56.

Smith, P. 1972. Diet and attrition in Natufians. *American Journal of Physical Anthropology* 37: 233-238.

Smith, P. and Horwitz, L.K. 2007. Ancestors and inheritors: A bioanthropological perspective on the transition to agropastoralism in the southern Levant. In Cohen, M.N. and Crane-Kramer, G.M.M., (eds), *Ancient Health: Skeletal Indicators of Agricultural and Economic Intensification*: 207-222. Gainsville: University of Florida Press.

Snoddy, A.M.E., Buckley, H.R., Elliot, G.E., Standen, V.G., Arriaza, B.T. and Halcrow, S.E. 2018. Macroscopic features of scurvy in human skeletal remains: A literature synthesis and diagnostic guide. *American Journal of Physical Anthropology* 167: 876-895.

Sołtysiak, A. and Fazeli Nashli, H. 2016. Evidence of late Neolithic cremation at Tepe Sialk, Iran. *Iranica Antiqua* 51: 1-19.

Steadman, D.W. 2008. Warfare related trauma at Orendorf, a Middle Mississippian site in West-Central Illinois. *American Journal of Physical Anthropology* 136: 51-64.

Steffan, S.A., Chikaraishi, Y., Horton, D.R., Ohkouchi, N., Singleton, M.E., Miliczky, E., Hogg, D.B. and Jones, V.P. 2013. Trophic: Hierarchies Illuminated via Amino Acid Isotopic Analysis. *PLOS ONE* 8: e76152.

Steffan, S.A., Chikaraishi, Y., Currie, C.R., Horn, H., Gaines-Day, H.R., Pauli, J.N., Zalapa, J.E. and Ohkouchi, N. 2015. Microbes are trophic analogs of animals. *Proceedings of the National Academy of Sciences of the United States of America* 112: 15119-15124.

Steinbock, R.T. 1976. *Paleopathological Diagnosis and Interpretation.* Springfield: Charles C. Thomas.

Stewart, T.D. 1979. *Essentials of Forensic Anthropology.* Springfield: Thomas.

Stordeur, D. and Abbès, F. 2002. Du PPNA au PPNB: mise en lumière d'une phase de transition à Jerf el Ahmar (Syrie). *Bulletin de la Société Préhistorique Française* 99 (3): 563-595.

Stordeur, D., Brenet, M., Der Aprahamain, G. et Roux, J.-C. 2001. Les batiments communautaires de Jerf el Ahmar et Mureybet, horizon PPNA (Syrie). *Paléorient* 26: 29-44.

Stordeur, D., Helmer, D. and Willcox, G. 1997. Jerf el Ahmar: un nouveau site de l'horizon PPNA sur le moyen Euphrate syrien. *Bulletin de la Société Préhistorique Française* 94 (2): 282-285.

Stuart-Macadam, P. 1987. Porotic hyperostosis: New evidence to support the anemia theory. *American Journal of Physical Anthropology* 74: 521-526.

Stuart-Macadam, P. 1989. Porotic hyperostosis: Relationship between orbital and vault lesions. *American Journal of Physical Anthropology* 80: 187-193.

Stuart-Macadam, P. 1992. Anemia in past human populations. In Stuart-Macadam, P. and Kent, S., (eds), *Diet, Demography, and Disease: Changing Perspectives on Anemia*: 151-170. New York: Aldine de Gruyter.

Styring, A.K., Fraser, R.A., Arbogast, R.M., Halstead, P., Isaakidou, V., Pearson, J.A., Schafer, M., Triantaphyllou, S., Valamoti, S.M., Wallace, M., Bogaard, A. and Evershed, R.P. 2015. Refining human palaeodietary reconstruction using amino acid $\delta^{15}N$ values of plants, animals and humans. *Journal of Archaeological Science* 53: 504-515.

Styring, A.K., Fraser, R.A., Bogaard, A. and Evershed, R.P. 2014. Cereal grain, rachis and pulse seed amino acid $\delta^{15}N$ values as indicators of plant nitrogen metabolism. *Phytochemistry* 97: 20-29.

Styring, A.K., Sealy, J.C. and Evershed, R.P. 2010. Resolving the bulk $\delta^{15}N$ values of ancient human and animal bone collagen via compound-specific nitrogen isotope analysis of constituent amino acids. *Geochimica et Cosmochimica Acta* 74: 241-251.

Sullivan, A. 2005. Prevalence and etiology of acquired anemia in Medieval York, England. *American Journal of Physical Anthropology* 128: 252-272.

Şenyürek, M.S. 1954. A note on the skulls of Chalcolithic Age from Yümüktepe. *Belleten XVIII, Sayı* 69: 1-25.

Tanaka, A., Yoneda, M., Uchida, M., Uehiro, T., Shibata, Y. and Morita, M. 2000. Recent advances in ^{14}C measurement at NIES-TERRA. *Nuclear Instruments and Methods in Physics Research Section B* 172: 107-111.

Talalay, L.E. 2004. Heady business: Skulls, heads, and decapitation in Neolithic Anatolia and Greece. *Journal of Mediterranean Archaeology* 17: 139-163.

Taniguchi, Y., Hirao, Y., Shimadzu, Y. and Tsuneki, A. 2002. The first fake? Imitation turquoise beads recovered from a Syrian Neolithic site, Tell el-Kerkh. *Studies in Conservation* 47: 175-183.

Tanno, K. and Willcox, G. 2006a. How fast was wild wheat domesticated? *Science* 311: 1886-1886.

Tanno, K. and Willcox, G. 2006b. The origins of cultivation of Cicer arietinum L. and Vicia faba L.: early finds from Tell el-Kerkh, north-west Syria, late 10th millennium BP. *Vegetation Histtory and Archaeobotany* 15: 197-204.

Tarr, W.A. 1938. Terminology of the chemical siliceous sediments. In P.D. Trask (ed.), *Report of the Committee on Sedimentation for 1937-1938*: 8-27. Washington, DC: National Research Council.

Tekin, H. 2010. New discoveries on a Hassuna/Samarran site on the upper Tigris region: Hakemi Use. In Matthiae, P., Pinnock, F., Nigro, L. and Marchetti, N. (eds), *Proceeding of the 6th International Congress on the Archaeology of the Near East. May, 5th-10th 2008, Universita di Roma*: 685-696. Wiesbaden: Harrassowitz.

Tekin, H. 2011. Hakemi Use, a newly discovered Late Neolithic site in southeastern Anatolia. In Özdoğan, M., Başgelen, N. and Kuniholm, P. (eds), *The Neolithic in Turkey, Vol. 1. New Excavations and New Research: The Tigris Basin*: 151-172. Istanbul: Archaeology and Art Publications.

Temple, D.H. 2008. What can variation in stature reveal about environmental differences between prehistoric Jomon foragers? Understanding the impact of systemic stress on developmental stability. *American Journal of Human Biology* 20: 431-439.

Temple, D.H. 2016. Caries: The ancient scourge. In Irish, J.D. and Scott, G.R. (eds), *A Companion to Dental Anthropology*: 432-449. Oxford: John Wiley and Sons, Inc.

Thompson, T. 2015. Fire and body: Fire and people. In Thompson, T. (ed.), *The Archaeology of Cremation: Burned Human Remains in Funerary Studies*: 1-17. Oxford, Oxbow Books.

Todd, T.W. 1920. Age changes in the pubic bone I. The male white pubis. *American Journal of Physical Anthropology* 3: 285-334.

Trotter, M. and Gleser, G.C. 1952. Estimation of stature from long bones of American whites and Negroes.

American Journal of Physical Anthropology 16: 79-123.

Tsuneki, A. 2002. A Neolithic Foundation Deposit at Tell ʻAin el-Kerkh, In Gebel, H.G.K., Dahl Hermansen, B. and Hoffmann Jensen, C. (eds), *Magic Practices and Ritual in the Near Eastern Neolithic*: 133-148. Studies in Early Near Eastern Production, Subsistence, and Environment 8, Berlin: ex oriente.

Tsuneki, A. 2009. Chapter 2 Tell –type settlements around Tell Mastuma. In Iwasaki, T., Wakita, S., Ishida, K. and Wada, H. (eds), *Tell Mastuma: An Iron Age Settlement in Northwest Syria, Memoirs of Ancient Orient Museum Vol. III*: 11-54. Tokyo: Ancient Orient Museum.

Tsuneki, A. 2010a. A newly discovered Neolithic cemetery at Tell el-Kerkh, northwest Syria. In Matthiae, P., Pinnock, F., Nigro, L. and Marchetti, N. (eds), *Proceedings of the 6th International Congress on the Archaeology of the Ancient Near East, Volume 2*: 697-713. Wiesbaden: Harrasowitz Verlag.

Tsuneki, A. 2010b. Ethno-archaeological research on the modern cemeteries of Ghanem al-Ali village. In Onuma, K. (ed.), *Formation of Tribal Communities, Integrated Research in the Middle Euphrates, Syria. Al-Rāfidān Special Issue*: 79-90. Tokyo: Kokushikan University.

Tsuneki, A. 2011. A glimpse of human life from the Neolithic cemetery at Tell el-Kerkh, Northwest Syria. *Documenta Praehistorica* 38: 83-95.

Tsuneki, A. 2012. Tell el-Kerkh as a Neolithic mega site. *Orient* 47: 29-65.

Tsuneki, A. 2013. The archaeology of the death in the Late Neolithic: A view from Tell el-Kerkh. In Nieuwenhuyse, O.P., Bernbeck, R., Akkermans, P.M.M.G. and Rogasch, J. (eds), *Interpreting the Late Neolithic of Upper Mesopotamia*: 203-212. Turnhout: Brepols Publishers.

Tsuneki, A. 2017. The burial of Neolithic blade producer. *Al-Rāfidān* 38: 39-45.

Tsuneki, A., n.d., Ancient history of the Rouj Basin: Based on the study of settlement patterns. Paper for *Les annales archéologiques arabes syrienne*.

Tsuneki, A., Arimura, M., Maeda, O., Tanno, K. and Anezaki, T. 2006. The Early PPNB in the north Levant: A new perspective from Tell Ain El-Kerkh, northwest Syria. *Paléorient* 32 (1): 47-71.

Tsuneki, A. and Hydar, J. 2007. *A Decade of Excavations at Tell el-Kerkh, 1997-2006*. Tsukuba, University of Tsukuba.

Tsuneki, A. and Hydar, J. 2008. Tell el-Kerkh 2007, *Chronique Archéologique en Syrie, volume 3*: 75-85. Damascus: Direction Général des Antiquitiés et des Musées.

Tsuneki, A. and Hydar, J. 2009. Tell el-Kerkh 2008, *Chronique Archéologique en Syrie, volume 4*: 91-95. Damascus: The Directorate General of Antiquities and Museums.

Tsuneki, A. and Hydar, J. 2010. Tell el-Kerkh 2009. *Chronique Archéologique en Syrie, volume 5*: 69-78. Damascus: The Directorate General of Antiquities and Museums

Tsuneki, A., Hydar, J., Dougherty, S., Hasegawa, A., Hironaga, N., Masumori, K.D., Tatsumi, Y., Itahashi, Y., Iizuka, M., Matsushima, Y., Miyauchi, Y., Makino, M. and Sha'baan, H. 2011. *Life and Death in the Kerkh Neolithic Cemetery*. Tsukuba: Department of Archaeology, University of Tsukuba.

Tsuneki, A., Hydar, J., Miyake, Y., Akahane, S., Nakamura, T., Arimura, M. and Sekine, S. 1997. First Preliminary Report of the Excavations at Tell el-Kerkh (1997), Northwestern Syria. *Bulletin of the Ancient Orient Museum* XVIII: 1-40.

Tsuneki, A., Hydar, J., Miyake, Y., Akahane, S., Arimura, M., Nishiyama, S., Sha'baan, H., Anezaki, T. and Yano, S. 1998. Second Preliminary Report of the Excavations at Tell el-Kerkh (1998), Northwestern Syria. *Bulletin of the Ancient Orient Museum* XIX: 1-40.

Tsuneki, A., Hydar, J., Miyake, Y., Hudson, M., Arimura, M., Maeda, O., Odaka, T. and Yano, S. 1999. Third Preliminary Report of the Excavations at Tell el-Kerkh (1999), Northwest Syria. *Bulletin of the Ancient Orient Museum* XX: 1-32.

Tsuneki, A., Hydar, J., Miyake, Y., Maeda, O., Odaka, T. Tanno, K. and Hasegawa, A. 2000. Fourth Preliminary Report of the Excavations at Tell el-Kerkh (2000), Northwest Syria. *Bulletin of the Ancient Orient Museum* XXI: 1-30.

Tsuneki, A., Hydar, J., Odaka, T. and Hasegawa, A. 2007. *A Decade of Excavations at Tell el-Kerkh, 1997-2006*. Tsukuba: Department of Archaeology, University of Tsukuba.

Tsuneki, A. and Miyake, Y. 1996. The earliest pottery sequence of the Levant: New data from Tell el-Kerkh 2, northern Syria. *Paléorient* 22 (1): 109-123.

Tsutaya, T., Sawada, J., Dodo, Y., Mukai, H., Yoneda, M. 2013. Isotopic evidence of dietary variability in subadults at the Usu-moshiri site of the Epi-Jomon culture, Japan. *Journal of Archaeological Science* 40: 914–3925.

Tung, T.A. 2007. Trauma and violence in the Wari Empire of the Peruvian Andes: Warfare, raids, and ritual fights. *American Journal of Physical Anthropology* 133: 941-956.

Turner, C.G. and Machado, L.M.C. 1983. A new dental wear pattern and evidence for high carbohydrate consumption in a Brazilian archaic skeletal population. *American Journal of Physical Anthropology* 61: 125-130.

Turner, G. and Anderson, T. 2003. Marked occupational dental abrasion from Medieval Kent. *International Journal of Osteoarchaeology* 13: 168-172.

Turville-Petre, F. 1932. Excavations in the Mugharet el-Kebarah. *The Journal of the Royal Anthropological Institute of Great Britain and Ireland* 62: 271-276.

Ubelaker, D.H. 1987. *Human Skeletal Remains*, 3rd (ed.). Washington: Taraxacum.

Valla, F.R. 1988. Aspect du sol l'abri 131 de Mallaha (Eynan). *Paléorient* 14 (2): 283-296.

Valla, F.R. 1991. Les natoufiens de Mallaha et l'espace. In Bar-Yosef, O. and Valla, E.R. (eds), *The Natufian Culture in the Levant*: 111-122. Ann Arbor: International Monographs in Prehistory.

Urushibara, K. (ed.) 1996. *Karst-relationship between its environment and people*. Tokyo: Taimei-do (in Japanese).

van Gennep, A. 1960. *The Rites of Passage* (trans. M.B. Vizedom and G.L. Caffee). Chicago: The University of Chicago Press.

Verhoeven, M. 2000. Death, fire and abandonment. Ritual practice at Late Neolithic Tell Sabi Abyad, Syria. *Archaeological Dialogues* 7 (1): 46-83.

Verhoeven, M. 2002. Transformations of society: The changing role of ritual and symbolism in the PPNB and the PN in the Levant, Syria and south-east Anatolia. *Paléorient* 28 (1): 5-13.

Waldron, T. 2009. *Paleopathology*. Cambridge: Cambridge University Press.

Waldron, T. 2012. Joint disease. In Grauer, A.L. (ed.), *A Companion to Paleopathology*: 512-530. Oxford: Blackwell Publishing, Ltd.

Walker, P.L., Bathurst, R.R., Richman, R., Gjerdrum, T. and Andrushko, V.A. 2009. The cause of porotic hyperostosis and cribra orbitalia: A reappraisal of the iron-deficiency-anemia hypothesis. *American Journal of Physical Anthropology* 139: 109-125.

Watkins, T. 2015. Religion as practice in Neolithic societies. In Laneri, N. (ed.), *Defining the Sacred: Approaches to the Archaeology of Religion in the Near East*: 153-160. Oxford: Oxbow Books.

Webb, S.G. and Edwards, P.C. 2002. The Natufian human skeletal remains from Wadi Hammeh 27 (Jordan). *Paléorient* 28 (1): 103-124.

Weston, D.A. 2008. Investigating the specificity of periosteal reactions in pathology museum specimens. *American Journal of Physical Anthropology* 137: 48-59.

White, T.D., Black, M.T. and Folkens, P.A. 2012. *Human Osteology*, 3rd ed. New York: Academic Press.

Whittaker, D.K., Griffiths, S., Robson, A., Roger-Davies, P., Thomas, G. and Molleson, T. 1990. Continuing tooth eruption and alveolar crest height in an eighteenth-century population from Spitalfields, East London. *Archives of Oral Biology* 35: 81-85.

Wilbur, A.K. 1998. The utility of hand and foot bones for the determination of sex and the estimation of stature in a prehistoric population from West-Central Illinois. *International Journal of Osteoarchaeology* 8: 180-191.

Williams, K.D., Meinzer, N.J. and Larsen, C.S. 2019. History of degenerative joint disease in people across Europe: Bioarchaeological inferences about lifestyle and activity from osteoarthritis and vertebral osteophytosis. In Steckel, R.H., Larsen, C.S., Roberts, C.A. and Baten, J. (eds), *The Backbone of Europe: Health, Diet, Work, and Violence over Two Millennia*: 253-299. Cambridge: Cambridge University Press.

Wood, J.W., Milner, G.R., Harpending, H.C. and Weiss, K.M. 1992. The osteological paradox. *Current Anthropology* 33: 343-370.

Yano, S. 2000. Animal exploitation in Neolithic of northwestern Syria. *Tsukuba Archaeological Studies* 11: 83-102 (in Japanese).

Yasin, W. 1970. Excavation at Tell es-Sawwan 1969: Report on the sixth season of excavations. *Sumer* 26: 39-42.

Yener, K.A. 1999. Oriental Institute returns to the Amuq: 1998 excavation season at Tell Kurdu, Turkey. *The Oriental Institute News and Notes* 161: 1-3.

Yener, K.A., Edens, C., Harrison, T.P., Verstraete, J. and Wilkinson, T.J. 2000. The Amuq valley regional project, 1995-1998. *American Journal of Archeology* 104: 163-220.

Yoneda, M., Tanaka, A., Shibata, Y., Morita, M., Uzawa, K., Hirota, M. and Uchida, M. 2002. Radiocarbon marine reservoir effect in human remains from the Kitakogane Site, Hokkaido, Japan. *Journal of Archaeological Science* 29: 529-536.

من أركان المستوطنة السكنية، لتتحوّل في نهاية المطاف إلى مقبرة تتكوّن من القبور فقط ومنفصلة عن المباني السكنية. بعبارة أخرى، ستتطوّر المدافن التي كانت ترتبط ارتباطاً وثيقاً بكل منزل إلى مقبرة جماعية في الهواء الطلق داخل حدود المستوطنة السكنية. وهكذا كان التحوّل التدريجي من القبور المنزلية إلى المقابر الجماعية. تجدر الإشارة إلى أن عدداً من الأسر أو الجماعات استثمروا المقبرة ودفنوا موتاها فيها ضمن قبور عائلية، واستمروا في استخدام هذه القبور لعقود. وكما نوقش في الفصل العاشر، أظهرت نتائج تحليلات النظائر المستقرّة للعظام البشرية التي أُخذتْ من عدد من مجموعات الدفن في المقبرة، أنّ النظام الغذائي لكل مجموعة كان مختلف قليلاً بحسب الاختلاف في موقع الدفن في المقبرة. مما يدّل أيضاً إلى أن عدداً من الأسر والجماعات المختلفة ربما شغلوا المقبرة واستخدموها لدفن موتاهم.

أجرى المؤلَّف الأول في الماضي بحثاً إثنوغرافياً لدراسة العلاقة بين السكّان والمقبرة في غانم العلي، وهي قرية بدوية استقرّت على ضفاف نهر الفرات (انظر Tsuneki 2010b). أظهرت الدراسة وجود خمس مقابر صغيرة لكل عشيرة، ومقبرة جماعية كبيرة للقرية بأكملها. وكان في المقبرة الجماعية منطقة محدّدة لدفن موتى كل أسرة وعشيرة. ولم يكن يُسمح بالدفن خارج المنطقة المخصّصة لكل عشيرة إلا في حال كانت مليئة بالقبور. كانت المقبرة، التي بدت مشتركة، تتقاسمها كل عشيرة على حِدَة (المرجع السابق نفسه). بناء على ذلك، يمكن الإشارة إلى وجود قواسم مشتركة واضحة بين مقبرة العصر الحجري الحديث في تل الكرخ ومقبرة قرية غانم العلي الحديثة. بعبارة أخرى، حتى في المجتمع القائم على الروابط القَبَلِيّة القويّة، ورغم وجود مقبرة جماعية للقرية، من الممكن جداً أن تنقسم إلى وحدات عشائرية وتُشكّل مجتمعاً متماسكاً.

يعرض هـذا التقرير تسلسل ظهـور أول مقبرة جماعيّة في الهواء الطلق في الشرق الأدنى خلال فترة العصر الحجري الحديث الفخّاري في تل الكرخ. ظهرت القبور بشكل لافت في المقبرة الجماعيّة داخل المستوطنة السكنية في فناءات المباني أو بالقرب منها. وبالتالي، يُعتبر اِكتشاف مقبرة تل الكرخ سابقاً لظهور المقابر الجماعيّة. ولمعرفة العوامل والأسباب وراء إنشاء أول مقبرة جماعيّة في الهواء الطلق في مستوطنة العصر الحجري الحديث الفخّاري في تل الكرخ، لابدّ من دراسة ومناقشة الخلفية الاجتماعية والعوامل الاقتصادية بتمعّن، إلّا أنّ هذه المواضيع خارج إطار هذا التقرير. وبالتالي، سنركّز على هذه المواضيع في دراساتنا المُستقبلية.

- ٦ -

أفراد. الملُفت للنظر بأن الموتى في هذه القبور دُفنوا وفق محور جسد موحّد باتجاه الشمال الغربي أو الجنوب الشرقي. يبدو أن هذه المجموعة من الموتى تربطهم علاقة متينة مع بعضهم البعض، ربما علاقة أُسرية، وقد اتّبعت هذه الأسرة نمط دفن موحّد يُشير إلى عادة محدّدة لأفرادها المتوفين تُميّزهم عن بقية المجموعات الأخرى في المجتمع.

إذا ما نظرنا إلى أماكن توزّع القبور، بما في ذلك حفرتي الدفن الثانويتين، فيمكننا تقسيمها إلى عدّة مجموعات من القبور المؤلّفة من عدد من الأفراد التي تتراوح أعدادهم ما بين ٣ - ٢١ فرد. ويمكننا أيضاً أن نفترض أنَّ التشابه في الدفن في كلّ مجموعة من القبور يُشير إلى وجود روابط أُسرية.

الطبقة الرابعة (الشكلين ٤٣-٣ و ٢٣-٤)

الطبقـة الرابعـة هـي الطبقـة الأخيرة فـي مقبرة تـل الكرخ. استخدمت المنطقة المركزية في المربعين E251, E271 بأكملها كمقبرة فـي الهـواء الطلـق تحـوي قبـور عـلى وجه الخصـوص ولم يُبنى فيها أي مبنى. اكتشف ٦١ فرد متوفى خلال فترة استيطان الطبقة الرابعة. كان الدفن الأوّلي الفردي هو السائد ثم يليه الدفن الثانوي. ربما تكون معظم الهياكل العظمية في الدفن الثانوي، وخاصة الجماجم والعظام الطويلة، قد استخرجت مـن الدفن الأوّلي وأُعيد دفنها في موضعها الجديد.

يمكن تقسـيم مواقـع قبور الطبقـة الرابعة فـي المقبرة إلى مجموعتين كبيرتين: مجموعـة في الشمال وأُخـرى فـي الجنوب. ويمكن تقسيم المجموعة الشمالية إلى ثلاث مجموعات دفن فرعية بناء على موقع الدفن واتّجاه محور جسد الموتى. كما يمكن تقسيم المجموعة الجنوبية أيضاً إلى أربع أو خمس مجموعات دفـن فرعية. كانت بعض المجموعـات الفرعية، مثل C2، مُحاطة بصفوف مـن الحجارة مُشابهة لتلك التي اكتشفت فـي الطبقة السادسة. لذلك، مـن الممكن أن تختلف مجموعتا الدفن الكبيرتان ليس فقط في مواقع الدفن الخاص بهـما، بـل أيضاً في طريقة تحضير القبر.

عُثر في مجموعـة الدفـن الجنوبية عـلى قبر .Str 712 مُحاط بإطار صغير مـن الحجارة عـلى شكل مربّع، واكتشف أيضاً قـبر مُماثل .Str 153 تحـت أرضيـة مبنى سكني .Str 74 في المربّع E290c في الطبقة الخامسة (الشكل ٥٤-٣). وبطبيعة الحـال، وُجِدَ المثـال الأخير في منطقة سكنية خارج حدود مقبرة العصر الحجري الحديث، وعُثر عـلى متوفى صغير في الفترة المحيطـة بالـولادة بالقـرب مـن المستوى العُلوي مـن حفرة القبر المُحاطـة بالحجارة. في حين وُجدت أنثى بالغة في القبر الآخـر بالقرب مـن أعـلى مستوى حفرة القبر المُحاطـة بالحجارة أيضاً، وكان أعمار الموتى في كِلا القبرين مختلفة تماماً، ومواقـع الدفن متباعدة أيضاً. ومع ذلك، هناك قواسم مشتركة بينهما، حيث اكتشفت نصـال صوّانيـة وشفرات عـلى التـوالي جنباً إلى جنب مـع كل متوفى. وبالتـالي، مـن المرجّح أن يكون كِلا المتوفيين قد دُفنا وفق طقوس جنائزية مُماثلة.

بالعـودة إلى الطبقـة الرابعـة مـن المقبرة وكما ذكـر أعـلاه، تنقسـم مواقـع القبور إلى مجموعتي دفـن كبيرتين، في الشمال والجنوب، ومـن المرجّح أن هـذه المجموعات كان لهـا سمات مختلفة. ويمكن تصنيف كل مجموعـة دفـن مـن ثـلاث إلى خمس مجموعات فرعية، حيـث وُجِدَ في كل مجموعة فرعية عـدد مـن المـوتى يتراوح عددهـم بـين ٤ - ١٣ فرد مـن كِلا الجنسين وجميع الأعمار. وبالتـالي، مـن المعقول اعتبار أن كلّ مجموعة دفن كبيرة تُمثّل أسرة ممتدّة، وأن كـل مجموعة فرعية تُمثّل أسرة خاصّة.

لم تعد المنطقـة المحيطـة بالمربعات E251, E271 تُستخدم كمقبرة في النصف الثاني مـن مرحلة السكن في الطبقة الرابعة. وهكذا، في المرحلـة التاليـة في الطبقـة الثالثـة، سيتم استخدام المنطقة التي كانت مقبرة في السابق كمكان لأداء الأنشطة اليومية وصنع الخبز في التنّور والسكن.

بالنظر إلى تسلسل ظهور وتطوّر ونهاية استخدام مقبرة العصر الحجري الحديث الفخّاري في تـل الكرخ، نجد أنَّ المقبرة كانت تُستخدم في البدايـة للدفن المنزلي التقليدي وتَركّز ذلك في ركن

الطبقة. أدّى إنشاء حفر حرق الجثث C5 و C9 في المبنى Str. 916 إلى تدمير الغرفة الشرقية للمبنى والجدار الشرقي على التوالي. عُثر في المربّع E270 على القبر Str. 930 وهو عبارة عن تراكم من العظام يحتوي بشكل أساسي على ثلاث جماجم بشرية لإناث بالغات والعديد من عظام الحيوانات المختلطة مع بعضها.

إكتشفنا في الطبقة السادسة ما مجموعه ٨٥ فرد متوفى دُفنوا في منطقة صغيرة نسبياً تبلغ حوالي ١٠٠م². استخدمت هذه المنطقة المتمركزة في المربّع E271 كمكان مخصّص لدفن الموتى، وعليه يمكن تسميتها دون أدنى شك بالمقبرة. وقد عُثر على أقدم القبور في المقبرة في المباني السكنية أو الجماعية المهجورة Str. 916 و Str. 827. أُنشأت حفر القبور عن طريق تدمير بعض أجزاء جدران أو أرضيات المباني المهجورة. إلّا أنّ غرف وجدران وأرضيات هذه المباني كانت موجودة عند إنشاء المدافن. على الرغم من أن طبيعة العلاقة بين هذه القبور والمباني المهجورة غير واضحة، فلا شكّ في أن هناك صلة ما بينهما، وذلك لأن هذه القبور مرتبطة بشكل وثيق مع المنازل، أو أنّها "قبور عائلية" قائمة على النسب.

كانت حفرة القبر الجماعي C10 مُحاطة بصفوف من الحجارة، إلّا أنّها لم تكن أساسات لمبنى سكني. اكتشف في القسم الشمالي من القبر بقايا عظمية لـ ١٥ فرد على الأقّل من كافّة الأعمار، ويُعتقد أنّه كان قبراً جماعياً لعائلة كبيرة استخدمته لدفن موتاها لفترة طويلة. وبعبارة أُخرى، يبدو أن إحاطة القبر العائلي في الهواء الطلق بصفوف من الحجارة يحمل دلالة رمزية تذكّر بالأساسات الحجرية للمساكن.

تجدر الإشارة إلى أن أغلب الموتى في الطبقة السادسة دفنوا بشكل جماعي ونسبة قليلة بشكل فردي. وتشمل هذه القبور الجماعية حفر محارق الجثث المكتشفة في المقبرة. اكتشف عدد محدود جداً من الهياكل العظمية مفصولة الرأس في الطبقة السادسة، بالإضافة إلى قبور دفن ثانوي تحتوي عظام بشرية وحيوانية معاً. وقد لُوحظ أنّ أسلوب

الدفن في الطبقة السادسة من المقبرة يحافظ على بعض سمات الدفن التي كانت سائدة في الفترة السابقة. من أكثر السّمات التقليدية المتعلّقة بالقبور هي دفن الموتى وارتباطهم ارتباطاً وثيقاً بالمساكن. وعندما لا يُدفن الموتى في حطام المباني، كان يتم احاطة حفرة القبر عمداً بصفّ من الحجارة على غرار الأساسات الحجرية للمباني السكنية.

الطبقة الخامسة (الشكلين ٥٠-٣ و ٢٠-٤)
تُعتبر الطبقة الخامسة هي الطبقة الوسطى من المقبرة، حيث تتطوّر مقبرة الكرخ لتصبح مقبرة جماعية كاملة في الهواء الطلق. اكتشفنا ٩٨ فرد متوفى خلال فترة استيطان الطبقة الخامسة، حيث تم تسوية الأرض في المربّعان E270, E271، وبُني منزل سكني جديد Str. 109 في القسم الجنوبي في نفس المكان الذي شُيِّد به المبنى Str. 827 في الماضي. وكان هذا المسكن الجديد مأهولاً ولم يُستخدم لأغراض الدفن، باستثناء العثور على قبر واحد يحتوي متوفى صغير في الفترة المحيطة بالولادة Str. 901. لم تُبنى أية مبانٍ أخرى في هذه المنطقة واستخدمتْ تقريباً كامل المساحة التي يُغطّيها المربّعان E251, E271 إلى الشمال والشرق من المبنى Str. 901 كمقبرة على وجه الخصوص. وكانت العديد من القبور في هذه الطبقة تحتوي دفن أوّلي فردي، كما تظهر قبور الدفن الثانوي التي تحتوي بشكل أساسي على جماجم وعظام طويلة، ولا سيما في الجزء الشرقي من المقبرة.

الدفن الأوّلي والثانوي في هذه الطبقة هما في الأساس حفر قبور، ونادراً ما فُصلت عن بعضها أو أُحيطتْ بصفوف من الحجارة. كان أحد القبور Str. 748 مُحاطاً بصفّ من الحجارة ومُغطى بطبقة من الجص الجيري، إلّا أنّ هذا النوع من القبور كان نادراً في هذه الطبقة. لذلك، قد تبدو معظم عمليات الدفن في الطبقة الخامسة مستقلّة عن بعضها البعض. ولكن التحقيقات الدقيقة بيّنت لنا بأنه يمكن تصنيفها إلى عدّة قبور جماعيّة تشارك نفس مكان الدفن، والموتى دُفنوا بنفس اتّجاه محور الجسم. على سبيل المثال، إكتشفنا في الجزء الشمالي من المربّع E251 مجموعة من القبور تضم ثمانية

أرضيـات وجـدران المبانـي وفـي المناطـق المُحيطـة بالمبانـي السـكنية في أوائـل الألفيـة السـابعة قبـل الميـلاد.

لا تـزال هنـاك العديـد مـن الأسـئلة المتعلّقـة بالدفـن وأسـاليبه في فتـرة العصـر الحجـري الحديـث الفخـاري. ويمكـن اعتبـار المدافـن بحـدّ ذاتهـا خـلال هـذه الفتـرة مفتاحـاً لفهـم كيفيـة ظهـور المقبـرة الجماعيـة فـي الهـواء الطلـق بعيـداً عـن المنـازل السـكنية الفرديـة. في هـذا السـياق، قـدّم إكتشـافنا لمقبـرة تـل الكـرخ منظـوراً جديـداً لفهـم هـذه المسـألة. علـى الرغـم مـن أن المقبـرة أُنشـأت داخـل حـدود المسـتوطنة السـكنية، ولكنّهـا بـدّت كأنّهـا مقبـرة جماعيـة فـي الهـواء الطلـق. ومـن هنـا، سـنلخّص مراحـل ظهـور المقبـرة الجماعيّـة الخارجيّـة التـي اكتشـفت فـي مربعـات التنقيـب رقـم E251, E270, E271 فـي موقـع تـل الكـرخ.

الطبقـة السـابعة (الشـكلين ٣-٦٤ و ٤-١٥)
كانـت المسـاحة التـي تغطِّيهـا المربعـات رقـم E251, E270, E271 فـي الطبقـة السـابعة جـزءاً مـن المنطقـة السـكنية. اسـفرت التنقيبـات فـي هـذه المنطقـة عـن إكتشـاف مبنيـين ذو مخطـط مسـتطيل وهمـا Str. 916 و Str. 827. كان المبنـى Str. 827 مبنيّ مـن التربـة المدكوكـة، في حيـن كان المبنـى Str. 916 مبنيّ مـن التربـة المدكوكـة فـوق أسـاس حجـري. يصطَـف المبنيـان علـى طـول ممـرّ ضيّـق يفصـل بينهمـا عرضـه ٧٠ سـم، ولا شـكّ أنّهمـا كانـا معاصـران لبعضهمـا وذلـك اسـتناداً إلى الطبقـة التـي اكتشـفا فيهـا واتجـاه محوريهمـا المـوحّد. كان كِلا المبنيـين مُقسّـم إلى غـرف صغيـرة. وتَبَيّـن لنـا اسـتناداً إلى اللُقـى الأثريـة المُكتشـفة في موضعهـا الأصلـي في المبنـى Str. 827 بأنّـه لـم يكـن مجـرّد مسـكن عـادي، بـل كان مبنـى جماعـي مشـترك تسـتخدمه عـدد مـن الأسـر لجـرش الحبـوب أو كمطبـخ جماعـي. في حيـن أن المبنـى Str. 916 قـد يكـون مسـكن عـادي. عُثِـر علـى الكثيـر مـن البقايـا الخشـبيّة المحترقـة والمتفحّمـة فـوق اللُقـى الأثريـة علـى طـول الممـر المحـوري المركـزي للمبنـى Str. 827، وكانـت جـدران التربـة المدكوكـة محترقـة بالكامـل. يبـدو أن البقايـا الخشـبية المتفحّمـة كانـت جـزءاً مـن السـقف، وقـد تسـاقطتْ إلى الأرض فـوق اللُقـى إثـر حريـق لحـق بالمبنـى. ولكـن لا يـزال مـن غيـر الواضـح فيمـا

إذا كان المبنـى قـد أُحـرق عمـداً، أو أنّـه أُحتـرق بسـبب حريـق عَـرَضيّ.

الطبقـة السادسـة (الشـكلين ٣-٧٥ و ٤-١٦)
اسـتغلّت المسـاحة التـي يغطيهـا المربعـان E270, E271 واسـتخدمت كمقبـرة. لـم يُقـدم سـكان العصـر الحجـري الحديـث في تـل الكـرخ بعـد هجـرة المبنيـين Str. 916 و Str. 827 والتخلّي عـن وظيفتيهمـا الأصليـة علـى تسـويتهما بالأرض، كمـا لـم يبنـوا مبـانٍ جديـدة فـي المربعـين E270, E271. عوضـاً عـن ذلـك، اسـتخدموا غـرف المبانـي المهجـورة لإنشـاء المقبـرة وبـدأوا في دفـن موتاهـم فيهـا. في أنقـاض المبنـى Str. 827، حُفـر قبـر في الغرفـة رقـم ٥ في الجانـب الشـمالي للمبنـى ودُفـن في داخلـه شـخص بالـغ يبلـغ مـن العمـر ١١ - ١٣عـام. أمّـا في أنقـاض المبنـى Str. 916، دُفـن أربعـة بالغـين في الغرفـة الشـرقية، وتسـعة أفـراد (ثلاثـة بالغـين، وشـخص شـبه بالـغ، وأربعـة أحـداث، وجنـين واحـد) في الغرفـة الغربيـة علـى طـول الجـدار الجنوبـي المبنـي مـن التربـة المدكوكـة فـوق أسـاس حجـري. ويُفتـرض أن هـؤلاء الأفـراد دُفنـوا واحـداً تلـو الآخـر بعـد فتـرة وجيـزة مـن موتهـم ولـم يُدفنـوا جميعـاً في نفـس الوقـت. كانـت بعـض الهياكـل العظميـة مضطربـة أو أعيـد دفنهـا عنـد إدخـال فـرد جديـد في القبـر. وقـد دُمّـرت الغرفـة الشـرقية للمبنـى Str. 916 تدميـراً شـديداً بسـبب إنشـاء مَحرقـة الجثـث C9 ودفـن الأشـخاص البالغـة الأربعـة فيهـا.

إضافـة إلى القبـور التـي ذُكـرت أعـلاه والتـي أُنشـأت علـى أنقـاض المبنيـين السـابقين، اكتشـفت أنـواع عديـدة مـن القبـور في المربعـين E270, E271 في الطبقـة السادسـة (لـم تكتمـل التنقيبـات بعـد لتصـل إلى الطبقـة السادسـة في المربـع E251). مـن القبـور الرئيسـية التـي عُثـر عليهـا في هـذه الطبقـة هـو C10 (شـمال، جنـوب)، وهـو قبـر جماعـي أُنشـأ في الطـرف الشـرقي للمربـع E271. بالإضافـة إلى C6، وهـو عبـارة عـن مَحرقـة للجثـث علـى شـكل حفـرة أُنشـأت جنـوب القبـر C10. وأيضـاً C8، وهـو عبـارة عـن قبـر ثانـوي يحتـوي بالكامـل علـى عظـام محترقـة. كمـا تُعتَـبر محرقتـي الجثـث C5 و C9 أيضـاً مـن القبـور الرئيسـة في هـذه

كشفت التنقيبات التي استمرت في المقبرة حتى عـام ٢٠١٠ عـن عـدد كبـير مـن القبـور التـي تضـمُّ هياكـل عظميـة تعـود لأكثر مـن ٢٤٠ فرد متوفى. تُشير دراسـاتنا بوضـوح إلى أنّ هـذه المقبرة هـي واحـدة مـن أقـدم المقابـر الجماعيـة في الهـواء الطلـق المُكتشـفة ليس فقـط في غـرب آسـيا، بـل في العـالم. وقـد أدّى اكتشاف هـذه المقبرة إلى زيـادة أهمّيّتهـا في فهـم تاريـخ البشرية. استمرّت التنقيبـات في المقبرة حتى عـام ٢٠١٠، ولكـن لم يتسـنَّ لنـا الكشـف عـن كامـل المسـاحة التـي تُغطّيهـا. ومـع ذلـك، كان مـن الـضروري نـشر الجوانـب المعروفـة لهـذه المقبرة الغنيّـة مـن العـصر الحجـري الحديـث في أسرع وقـت ممكـن. لذلـك، اتّخذنـا القـرار بنـشر التقريـر النهـائي لمقبرة العـصر الحجـري الحديـث في تـل الكـرخ باعتبـاره المجلـد الثـاني مـن التقاريـر النهائيـة للتنقيبـات في الموقـع.

أُجريـت الأبحـاث والدراسـات عـلى العديـد مـن القبـور التـي تحـوي هياكـل عظميّـة والتـي اكتشـفت أثنـاء الحفريـات في مواقـع عصور مـا قبـل التاريـخ في غـرب آسـيا. بالنظـر إلى العـدد القليـل مـن المدافـن التـي ظهـرت في مواقـع التنقيـب في العـصر الحجـري القديـم (Paleolithic) في غـرب آسـيا، كانـت هنـاك زيـادة سريعة في عـدد القبـور المُكتشـفة في الفـترة النطوفيـة مـن العـصر الحجـري القديـم (انظـر Belfer-Cohen 1995؛ 1995 Nadal). عُـثر عـلى مُعظـم القبـور التـي تعـود إلى أواخـر العـصر الحجـري القديـم داخـل الكهـوف حيـث دُفِنَ الموتى تحـت أرضيـات المنـازل، أي أنّهـا كانـت مرتبطـة بشـكل عـام بالمسـاكن. أشـارت الدراسـات حـول هـذه القبـور إلى وجـود علاقـات عائليـة أو علاقـات قائمـة عـلى القرابـة وارتباطهـا ارتباطـاً وثيقـاً بالمسـاكن. نُطلـق عـلى هـذه القبـور في هـذه المرحلـة اسـم "قبـور عائليـة".

في الفـترة التاليـة في العـصر الحجـري الحديـث مـا قبـل الفخـاري (Pre-Pottery Neolithic) PPN، اكتشـفت مجموعـة كبـيرة مـن القبـور (انظـر Croucher 2012). كان الدفـن الأوّلي المرتبـط بالمبـاني سـائداً في تلـك الفـترة، ووُجـدت أغلـب القبـور تحـت أرضيـات أو بالقـرب مـن جـدران المسـاكن أو في الفنـاء الخارجـي، وقـد اسـتمرَّ أسـلوب الدفـن هـذا لفـترات طويلـة، إلّا أنّ الطقـوس

الجنائزيـة الثانويـة، مثـل إزالـة الجمجمـة بعـد الدفـن، والدفـن الـذي يضـمّ عـدداً مـن الجماجـم والعظـام الطويلـة التـي تـم جمعهـا وتخزينهـا في مخبـأ، أصبحـت شـائعة في هـذه الفـترة. بالإضافـة إلى المدافـن الفرديـة المنزليـة، عُـثر عـلى مبـاني لحفـظ رُفـات الموتى. وكانـت هـذه المبـاني تحتـوي عـلى عظـام بشريـة خضعـت لطقـوس ومعالجـات جنائزيـة ثانويـة. ويُعتـبر "مبنى الجماجـم" "Skull building" في موقـع شـايونو Çayönü (Özdoğan 1999)، و"حجـرة الجثـث" "the charnel room" في الطبقـة الثامنـة في تـل أبـو هريـرة (Moore et al. 2000)، و"بيـت الأمـوات" "maison des morts" في موقـع جعـدة المغـارة (Coqueugniot 1999)، مـن المواقـع النموذجيـة التـي عُـثر فيهـا عـلى مبـاني لحفـظ البقايـا العظميـة للموتى.

غالبـاً مـا كان يتـم فصـل الجماجـم عـن الأجسـاد وإزالتهـا مـن القبـر الأصـلي وإعـادة إيداعهـا في مكـان آخـر، في حـين كانـت تُنقـل الهيـاكل العظميـة الأخـرى وتُجمَـع ضمـن مدافـن جماعيـة في هـذه المنـازل. كانـت الجماجـم المفصولـة تُزيَّـن في بعـض الأحيـان بعـد قولبتهـا بالجـصّ ليتـم عرضهـا واسـتخدامها في الطقـوس الجنائزيـة، وقـد سـادت هـذه الطقـوس بشـكل خـاص في مواقـع جنـوب بـلاد الشـام. بعبـارة أُخـرى، كان الإنسـان في العـصر الحجـري الحديـث مـا قبـل الفخـاري يتعايـش مـع الموتى، وكان عـلى الموتى البقـاء مـع الأحيـاء لبعـض الوقـت بعـد وفاتهـم. اكتشـفت القبـور الفرديـة داخـل هـذه المنـازل أو في كثـير مـن الأحيـان تحـت أرضيـات المسـاكن العاديـة. إلا أنّ عـدد القبـور المكتشـفة في الفـترة التاليـة في العـصر الحجـري الحديـث الفخـاري كانـت قليلـة نسـبياً (انظـر Gopher and Orrelle 1995؛ Campbell 1995؛ Akkermans and Schwartz 2003:145). بالإضافـة إلى ذلـك، اختفـت مبـاني حفـظ رُفـات الموتى، ويبـدو أنّ الموتى كانـوا يُدفنـون بأسـلوب فـردي ومتفـرق. يُشـير تقريـر التنقيـب النهـائي الأخـير في تـل الشـير بالقـرب مـن مدينـة حمـاه إلى اِكتشـاف "مدافـن منزليـة" تقليديـة في مجتمـع العـصر الحجـري الحديـث الفخـاري (Resch and Gresky 2018 انظـر). نفهـم مـن خـلال هـذه المكتشـفات في هـذه الفـترة بأنّ الإنسـان القديـم اسـتمرَّ في دفـن موتـاه، وخاصّـة الرُّضّـع والأطفـال، تحـت

- ٢ -

ملخّص البحث

مقبرة العصر الحجري الحديث
في تل الكرخ

مازالـت التسـاؤلات تُطـرح عـلى الـدوام حـول متـى وأيـن بـدأ التغـيّر في أسـلوب حيـاة الإنسـان والتحـوّل مـن الاعتـماد في قوتـه عـلى الصيـد والالتقـاط إلى الزراعـة والرعـي؟ ولمـاذا أصبحـت المجتمعـات البشـرية ذات بُنيـة اجتماعيـة معقّـدة؟ والأسـباب وراء بـدء الإنسـان تأسـيس مسـتوطنات بشـرية ضخمـة ومـن ثـم بنـاء المـدن الكبـيرة؟ ويبـدو أن هـذه الأسـئلة مازالـت الأكـثر تحديّـاً وإثـارةً في دراسـة تاريـخ البشـرية. وقـد ظهـرتْ جميـع هـذه التحـوّلات الكُـبرى في تاريـخ البشـرية في الشـرق الأدنى (غـرب آسـيا) في وقـت أبكـر مـن أي منطقـة أُخـرى في العـالم. لذلـك، فـإن علـم الآثـار في غـرب آسـيا يُغرينـا ويجـذب انتباهنـا. وعليـه، تُوفّـر الأبحـاث والتحقيقـات الأثريـة في تلـك المنطقـة الأُسُـس للإجابـة عـن بعـض هـذه التسـاؤلات.

بـدأت جامعـة تسـوكوبا اليابانيـة أولى الأبحـاث الأثريـة في حـوض الـروج في محافظـة إدلـب شـمال غـرب سـورية في الفتـرة مـا بـين عـام ١٩٩٠ حتـى عـام ١٩٩٢. وقـع الاختيـار عـلى حـوض الـروج للقيـام بالأبحـاث وذلـك لصغـر مسـاحته، حيـث يبلـغ طولـه ٣٧ كـم مـن الشـمال إلى الجنـوب و٢-٧ كـم مـن الـشرق إلى الغـرب، وتميّـزه بالتربـة الخصبـة والميـاه الوفيـرة المناسـبة للزراعـة. وقـد بَيَّنـت التحقيقـات الأثريـة التـي أُجريـت لثلاثـة مواسـم غنـى حـوض الـروج بالآثـار التـي تعـود إلى عصـور مـا قبـل التاريـخ والعصـور التاريخيـة. قـادتْ التحقيقـات التـي أجريناهـا إلى اِكتشـاف ثمانيـة وثلاثـين مسـتوطنة سـكنية عـلى شـكل تـلال أثريـة داخـل الحـوض الصغـير نسـبياً. وسـعياً لتحقيـق هدفنـا البحثـي في دراسـة ظهـور المجتمعـات الزراعيـة وتطوّرهـا، قمنـا بإجـراء مُسـوحات أثريـة في المسـتوطنات المنتشـرة في الحـوض، وأظهـرت الأدلّـة وجـود بقايـا أثريـة تعـود إلى العصـر الحجـري الحديـث (Neolithic) في اثنتـان وعشـرون مسـتوطنة أثريـة مـن أصـل ثمـاني وثلاثـين. لذلـك، لـم يكـن لدينـا أدنى شـكّ في أن حـوض

الـروج كان منطقـة غنيّـة جـداً للتركيـز عليـه وإجـراء أبحاثنـا فيـه.

يقـع تـل الكـرخ في جنـوب حـوض الـروج، وهـو تجمّـع تـلال ضخـم يعـود الى العصـر الحجـري الحديـث. إن حجـم التـل الضخـم كمسـتوطنة مـن العصـر الحجـري الحديـث، كان شـيء يفـوق تخيّلاتنـا. وباعتقادنـا، أن إجـراء المزيـد مـن التحقيقـات مـن شـأنه أن يكشـف لنـا كيـف بـدأ الإنسـان القديـم بإنشـاء مسـتوطنات سـكنية كبـيرة اعتمـاداً عـلى أسـلوب الحيـاة الجديـد القائـم عـلى الزراعـة. كـما يبـدو أيضـاً أن التنقيبـات في الموقـع سـتقدّم لنـا لمحـة لفهـم خلفيـة تكويـن المجتمعـات ذات البُنيـة الاجتماعيـة المُعقّـدة وبالتـالي فهمنـا لظهـور المجتمعـات الحضريـة.

حصلنـا عـلى الموافقـة مـن المديريـة العامـة للآثـار والمتاحـف في سـورية لبـدء التنقيـب في موقـع تـل الكـرخ. وفي نهايـة المطـاف، قـرّرت المديريـة العامـة للآثـار والمتاحـف البـدء ببعثـة أثريـة مشـتركة بالتعـاون مـع جامعـة تسـوكوبا للتنقيـب في تـل الكـرخ. بنـاء عـلى طيـب نواياهـم، بـدأت التنقيبـات الجديـدة في الموقـع عـام ١٩٩٧، واسـتمرت حتـى عـام ٢٠١٠.

أسـفرت سـنوات مـن التنقيبـات التـي اسـتمرّت اثنـي عـشر عامـاً عـن العديـد مـن النتائـج الأثريـة الغـير متوقّعـة. كشـفت التنقيبـات عـن وجـود سلسـلة مـن المجتمعـات الكبـيرة ذات البُنيـة الاجتماعيـة المُعقّـدة في أواخـر العصـر الحجـري الحديـث مـا قبـل الفخـاري - ب - PPNB (Pre-Pottery Neolithic B) وأوائـل العصـر الحجـري الحديـث الفخـاري PN (-Pottery Neo lithic) (حـوالي ٧٦٠٠ - ٦٠٠٠ عـام قبـل الميـلاد). بالإضافـة إلى مكتشـفات العصـر الحجـري الحديـث، كان الموقـع غنيـاً أيضـاً بعـدّة مميّـزات ثقافيـة تاريخيـة. مـن أبـرز نتائـج التنقيبـات في تـل الكـرخ اكتشـاف مقبـرة تعـود للعصـر الحجـري الحديـث.

الشرق (٥)

جامعة تسوكوبا: دراسات في علم آثار غرب آسيا

تقارير التنقيب في تل الكرخ شمال غرب سورية
المجلّد ٢
تحرير سلسلة التقارير: أكيرا تسونيكي وجمال حيدر

مقبرة العصر الحجري الحديث في تل الكرخ

تحرير

أكيرا تسونيكي

ناوكو هيروناغا

ساري جمو

بالاشتراك مع

شون دورتي، كين إيتشيرو هيسادا، يوكو مياوتشي،
يوكي تاتسومي، مينورو يونيدا، يو إيتاهاشي